KOR

A History of the
Workers' Defense Committee in Poland
1976–1981

11289639

STUDIES IN SOCIETY AND CULTURE IN EAST-CENTRAL EUROPE

General Editors
Jan T. Gross
Irena Grudzinska-Gross

Jan Józef Lipski, KOR: A History of the Workers' Defense Committee
in Poland, 1976–1981

KOR

A History of the Workers' Defense Committee in Poland, 1976–1981

JAN JÓZEF LIPSKI

Translated by
Olga Amsterdamska
and
Gene M. Moore

UNIVERSITY OF CALIFORNIA PRESS

Berkeley • Los Angeles • London

The Publisher wishes to thank the Alfred Jurzykowski Foundation, Inc., New York, N.Y. and the Polish American Congress, Chicago, Ill., for their generous contributions toward the publication of this important work.

University of California Press
Berkeley and Los Angeles, California

University of California Press, Ltd.
London, England

Library of Congress Cataloging in Publication Data

Lipski, Jan Józef.
    KOR: a history of the Workers' Defense Committee in Poland, 1976–1981.

    Translation of: KOR
    Includes index.
    1. Komitet Obrony Robotników—History.   2. Labor and laboring classes—Poland—Political activity—History.
3. Trade-unions—Poland—Political activity—History.
4. Poland—Politics and government—1945–1980.
5. Poland—Politics and government—1980–   .   I. Title.
II. Title: K.O.R.
HD8537.K563L5713   1984   322'.2'09438   84-16353
ISBN 0-520-05243-9

Printed in the United States of America
1 2 3 4 5 6 7 8 9

for Marysia and Łukasz Hirszowicz

Contents

Introduction

Although this book is based mainly on documents, it is not exactly a scholarly work. This is so not only because some gaps have been filled from memory (there are not many such places, and they are not particularly significant); nor is it because a critical reader will uncover the subjective judgments and perspectives of the author (something that would be difficult to avoid in a work devoted to a recent historical period). Rather, it is not scholarly because it is too much of a chronicle and does not sufficiently attempt a synthesis that would order the sequences of facts within a theoretical framework that—as I firmly believe—no work with scholarly ambitions can do without.

If this is the case, there are several reasons for it, perhaps not the least important being my lack of the necessary abilities and talents. But this is not all. Given a situation in which information about the Workers' Defense Committee will have to be one-sided for a long time to come, so long as the political and police archives concerning the issues addressed here remain inaccessible, and so long as participants in the movement have to exercise discretion concerning not only such information as the addresses of print shops (the owners of flats where they were set up would not like to be named even now, in the days of "Solidarity") but also such historically more important information as the sources of specific news items published in the KOR press or the identities of persons using pen names—it seems that in such a situation, to attempt a more ambitious approach to the subject would be deceptive and naive.

Works about the seventies and about KOR are needed for many reasons, and one can reasonably hope that they will one day be written. Such articles might also prove useful for scholarship. In the humanities, intelligent, incisive, and intellectually inventive journalism has frequently achieved results necessary for the formulation of scholarly problems, and sometimes its cognitive value can be compared favorably with more strictly scholarly attempts devoid of intellectual pathos. Though not without my own bias based on a critical self-evaluation, I prefer to leave such judgments to others.

It goes without saying that in acknowledging the need for a historical journalism that would examine the events and processes of the latter half of the seventies, I do not have in mind a particular journalistic genre, namely the police scribbling that appears in *Żołnierz Wolności** (*Soldier of Freedom*), *Trybuna Ludu*** (*People's Tribune*), and many other newspapers and periodicals, which fulfills the functions of propaganda, disinformation, and even provocation, but never those of providing information or knowledge.

Today, topics of contemporary history need to be treated in works that, without being overly ambitious, attempt nevertheless to introduce some order into specific problems. Anyone who has ever been concerned with scholarly research, even superficially and with a minimum of methodological awareness, knows that information rarely has an absolute and unassailable cognitive value. Important facts and trivial facts constitute elements of wider contexts, and these are always cognitive constructs. Despite all this, work on the foundations of future syntheses, work that organizes the available information, has generally not been proven useless, but rather the opposite, even when this work is still theoretically naive.

So much about the theoretical credo that, as I believe, needed to be made explicit.

Why did I decide that a history of the Workers' Defense Committee was worth undertaking?

The simplest answer, and one that requires no deeper justification, one that—who knows?—may be entirely sufficient, is that as a participant in the creation of this fragment of history, I felt it necessary and was competent to present the events described in this book; with similar justification, an author of memoirs can publish his work and by the same token render a service to historians and to all other readers interested in the subject.

But there is another reason. As a participant and even coauthor of the events described in the book, I have my own theoretical (or perhaps hypothetical) point of view from which the history of KOR is particularly meaningful. It is my conviction (probably determined by my participation and therefore largely subjective, which does not mean that it is false)

*The official Polish army daily.
**The official daily of the Central Committee of the Polish United Workers' Party PUWP).

that during at least the first four of the five years of the committee's existence, the voluntaristic factor in the great socio-politico-economic mechanism of Polish history was represented almost exclusively by KOR.

How is one to understand this not entirely modest, and moreover, none too clear sentence?

After the bloody revolt of the workers on the Baltic coast in 1970, Edward Gierek's team, which replaced Władysław Gomułka's rule, had a chance to influence the course of development in the country through its decisions. Yet the influence of those in power is often more apparent than real. If they alter nothing in the structure and programming of the system, they become objects more than subjects, and their decisions can be understood more as an element of a situationally determined mechanical process than as creative acts. Gierek's team not only had a chance but even used it to a certain extent.

The decisions made at that time were in part conservative, changing little, and in part new, modifying the mechanism a little bit. The words, "a little bit," are important. The economic circumstances (the fatal ease with which this ruling group was able for several years to receive credits) meant that the *memento mori* hanging over the country in 1970 was only postponed. Only the blind and the stupid failed to notice that this was merely a respite. The mechanism, modified a little bit, began to work according to the iron laws of sociology and economy. In spite of what has occasionally been written about the voluntarism of Gierek's team, a pure determinism of causes and effects was at work. Among these causes and effects were decisions that followed both from the distribution of social and economic forces after December 1970 and from the initial assumptions that programmed this system in a spirit of party conservatism, that is, as a mechanism that works logically when examined from the point of view of the laws governing the social and economic life of a communist country, but which appears surrealistic when observed in terms of the goals to which such mechanisms should be dedicated.

The unjustified imputation of voluntarism to Gierek's team is due precisely to this surrealism, and can be justified, if barely, by only one circumstance: the decisions made by this team, forced upon them by the situation, were marked also by a total ignorance of the functioning of the economy, of social and cultural life, and the like.

The decisions made during Gierek's rule were of no benefit to society (since they pushed the country toward catastrophe while robbing its citizens first of their rights and then, a short time later, of their very modest possessions, economic as well as social and cultural); nor did they benefit the ruling class, that is, the party-government bureaucracy (although they assured the domination of this class, they hastened threats to its domination); nor did they benefit even the empire of which Poland is a part (something about which both the majority of Poles and I care little), since they weakened it rather than strengthening it. But at least, from the point of view of the empire, these decisions allowed, even if only in the short run, for the maintenance of Polish dependence. This probably seemed sufficient, since as a last resort, as always in the past twenty-five or thirty years, there remained the appeal to the military power of the USSR and the Warsaw Pact. The only chance for this nightmarish mechanism relentlessly nearing catastrophe was the appearance of a voluntaristic factor that would be able to change at least some of the elements programming the whole.

My understanding of social life is neither deterministic nor voluntaristic. I believe simply that human will and the intellect directing it (or the emotions, but not—God forbid—the emotions alone) are also a part of reality and cannot be disregarded. As a result, all mechanisms that are basically determined are subject to conscious modifications of structure and program, and this means that the future can only rarely be seen as a unique and unavoidable consequence of the present. In other words, there exist both a theoretical and a practical possibility of social engineering and of politics.

In my opinion, it was precisely the Workers' Defense Committee that functioned as such a voluntaristic factor and that—thanks in part to the intelligence, inventiveness, stubbornness, determination, and hard work of its leaders and participants, and in part to circumstances—was able to modify considerably the course of events that could have been anticipated from the perspective of mid-1975 (the issue of the Constitution). KOR modified the course of events *considerably,* but only within the bounds of its own possibilities, which were limited not simply by the numerical strength of the movement but also by the tremendous inertia of the system. Even so, this was possible only because the government limited its response to the activities of KOR to restraints and repressions that represented a negation of the need for reforms.

This negation was both actual and verbal, although this second aspect is perhaps less visible in the theoretical haze of the propaganda. For the ruling group, any plan to revise the existing situation inevitably became "revisionism," while projects to reform social, economic, or political mechanisms became "reformism." Magic incantations of these two terms reflected more than anything else the inertia of the system.

No one today can tell what would have happened had the authorities attempted to introduce reforms after the workers' revolts in 1976, especially because no one knows what kinds of reforms would have been involved or how much they would have changed. Perhaps they would have changed little or nothing at all in the long run, and would only have postponed new tensions. But in that case KOR (or any other similar attempt) would not have gone down in the history of Poland as the only, and then for several years the main factor, in the reprogramming of social life.

A reform movement in the power elites and structures, even when the system is essentially unreformable, controls possibilities and perspectives to such an extent that oppositional centers have a difficult time trying to compete. Such a reform movement is attractive simply because it provides an opportunity to avoid dangerous conflicts with the authorities and also because it offers direct access both to the things that are to be reformed and to the means necessary for reforming them; while an opposition working within a totalitarian system can create its own institutions but cannot have even the slightest influence on official institutions. And this is why KOR would not have come through had there been attempts to introduce reforms.

What I have said about KOR as the unique factor reprogramming social life and about its lack of competition should not be understood as disregard or disrespect toward other oppositional groups. Their achievements are certainly not inconsiderable, and on the whole positive, and occasionally they strengthened the activities of KOR substantially (although sometimes, luckily only marginally, one could observe a rivalry that weakened the effectiveness of the Committee). But KOR created not only an original model of opposition but above all it was unrivaled in its actions, which extended from help for the workers in 1976, through the periodical *Robotnik* (*The Worker*) and the Initiating Committees of Free Trade Unions (KZ WZZ), and eventually to Solidarity.[1]

I appreciate fully the achievements of others, especially of the Young Poland Movement, which made authentic and manifold contributions in Gdańsk, the birthplace of the new social force that changed the face of the country. These contributions date both from the period preceding the great strike movement of the summer of 1980 (for example, helping organize anniversary commemorations of December 1970*) and from the period of July and August 1980. Their cooperation was concrete

*See chapter 2.

and fruitful, characterized by an unassuming attitude toward the emerging movement.

Also useful was the awakening of patriotism achieved through the demonstrations organized by the Movement in Defense of Human and Civil Rights (ROPCiO). Much was accomplished by the large-scale gathering of signatures on the petition to broadcast the Mass on radio and television, and by the Committees of Religious Believers (partially connected with KOR). The Lublin group of the periodical *Spotkania* (*Meetings*) exerted a positive influence on the awareness of Catholic youth, while the quarterly *Res Publica* worked to deepen political consciousness. Important contributions to the independent peasant movement were made by *Gospodarz* (*Farmer*), a ROPCiO periodical, and by those peasant activists who were closer to ROPCiO than to KOR (though in the peasant movement the conflicts between ROPCiO and KOR were, fortunately, not particularly bothersome). Finally, institutions close to KOR, such as the worthy Society for Scientific Courses (TKN) or *Zapis*,* did much good work that cannot be attributed simply to KOR, despite the numerous connections between KOR and these institutions. If they are discussed in this work, it is not in an attempt to convey such an impression.

All this does not invalidate my thesis that KOR was initially the only, and then the main, active voluntaristic force reprogramming social life in Poland. After August 31, 1980, KOR found itself relegated to the sidelines of history. Although KOR and its people played an important role in the building of Solidarity, this was a service role that, even when it was conceptually and ideologically creative, was being accomplished within the framework of the new and powerful movement.

I also have my own opinion about the role of KOR not so much within the sociopolitical structure of the Polish People's Republic but as an ideologically creative milieu and as a group dedicated to social action beyond the scope of its own successive actions and declarations. These problems are addressed to some extent in the chapter on the ethos of KOR and its methods of action. I considered it essential to include this chapter early in the book; without it, too much in the book would appear incomprehensible and exotic.

Mention has already been made of the fact that to a considerable extent this book is a chronicle. This is not only a result of my conviction that a knowledge of the facts is necessary for the understanding of any historical or social phenomenon but also that any other sort of history,

---

*Independent literary periodical that began publication in January 1977.

if perhaps more valuable intellectually, would misrepresent what KOR really was. That this movement was very original, while at the same time having so many aspects and such a differentiated and broad reach, was determined largely by its starting point—help for individuals. Given the entire sociopolitical system of beliefs, it was this starting point that determined the particularly personal orientation of KOR. Problems are problems, and strategy is strategy; but for everyone in KOR—from Jacek Kurón, a very typical representative of *homo politicus,* to Rev. Jan Zieja— everything was put aside whenever it appeared that Chomicki in Radom or Majewski in Ursus needed help.

One cannot hold it against the people of KOR that their comrades-in-arms were the most important thing, and that to defend them, they were prepared to make large sacrifices. Thus, entire chapters of KOR's history are marked with the names of specific people who were being defended. There were cases in which those who had been defended did not reciprocate with friendship. I am convinced, however, that not one person from KOR is sorry for what he did in their behalf (moreover, he did it not just for this one person but for everyone else as well).

I do not wish to succumb to moralistic and idealizing exaggeration and will not pursue this line of thought. In any event, it has important repercussions for the structure of this book. The story of Jerzy Geresz, who was sadistically beaten while under arrest and repeatedly went on lonely hunger strikes, and for whom KOR searched unsuccessfully for over a month before finally locating him, constitutes something more than an example of the methods used by the police and the Security Service in their struggle against the opposition. This small chapter in the history of KOR has an astronomical value in comparison with all possible generalizations and tactical situations. Whoever fails to understand this fact will never understand what KOR was and what it had to be in order to fulfill its mission.

This was a struggle with totalitarianism in its Bolshevik version, for which any individual life counted for nothing and could be sacrificed at any time to the Moloch of a so-called socialism, to the interests of the ruling class, party, or clique. KOR had no choice but to be different; here one could offer a sacrifice only of oneself, when one believed that it was necessary and right, but never of anyone else, although this was never discussed in KOR and any discussion would have been considered inappropriate.

The reader will have no difficulty locating data that will allow him to distinguish KOR and its agencies from other groups close to the committee, or even distant from it, who were engaged in their own struggle against totalitarianism alongside KOR. A certain breadth in the presentation of oppositional movements in Poland was both necessary and justified by the subject matter, and therefore this book deals not only with KOR.

The reader will probably note that I do not equally like all the groups and all the activists. Probably it should not be this way; but even if this were a book about the turn of the century, or about the January 1863 uprising, I would have been unable to summon as much sympathy (or indifference) for Stefan Bobrowski as for Gustaw Awejde.*

This is a book about the efforts of a group of people who were very different one from another, who decided to stand up in defense of beaten and imprisoned workers, to oppose totalitarianism, and to create a movement that would build an independent and democratic Poland of the future from the very foundations, showing by their example that it is possible to be defiant. This is a book about people who were united by common moral standards, but who were only human—who were often wrong, made mistakes, fought among themselves, and yet could work together as a team, as a Workers' Defense Committee.

---

*Leaders of competing (moderate and radical) factions in the January Uprising (1863) against tsarist rule in partitioned Poland.

1

The Prehistory of KOR

The Workers' Defense Committee, like any other institution, has not only a history but also a prehistory. This prehistory has nothing in common with the revelations of journalists who seek their inspiration in the Ministry of Internal Affairs on Rakowiecka Street, and who publish a new fabrication every few months in such periodicals as *Żolnierz Wolności*. They are not concerned if their successive versions are contradictory. For example, at one point one could read in the newspapers that KOR was formed in Geneva in 1975. This claim seems to have been forgotten today. Were one to evaluate the efficiency of the Polish Security Service—which surely are eager to know everything about KOR—on the basis of these articles, one might begin to wonder whether the large sums of money allocated for this purpose were not in fact being wasted so that a bunch of amateurs could make a comfortable living. These newspaper articles contribute nothing of substance, neither as information nor as denunciation or propaganda.

The prehistory of KOR consists above all in the histories of the various social circles without which the committee would probably never have been created and could not have functioned. There are several such groups. As one would expect, they overlap, intersecting through friendships and contacts, by the presence of the same people in various places at different times.

These circles will be discussed here not according to their relative importance but rather chronologically.

The Club of the Crooked Circle

The oldest precursor of KOR was a group of activists connected with the Club of the Crooked Circle between 1956 and 1962. This club functioned for several years as a discussion forum for independent thought in Warsaw, and occasionally it undertook other kinds of initiatives as well, such as, for example, approaching worker-activists of the workers' council movement that emerged in 1956, and was suppressed a short time later. Even before Gomułka came to power, there was a joint meeting of the club with activists from the Automobile Factory in Żerań, led by Lechosław Goździk. Together with the editors of the periodical *Po prostu** (*Simply Speaking*), the club also initiated what proved to be an unsuccessful attempt to form an October Front, a representative body of workers' councils and social associations that would attempt to press for the election of its own candidates to the Diet. During the first political trials of the Gomułka period, the club organized legal defense for its members (in the case of Hanna Szarzyńska-Rewska, a participant in the Kutschera assassination, and again in the case of Anna Rudzińska, both of whom were accused of collaboration with the Paris journal *Kultura*).**

The Club of the Crooked Circle (CCC) was organized (probably in early 1956) in a private apartment; it was dominated by a group of academics, former members of a scientific-discussion club that had been disbanded by the Security Office in 1953.[1] The CCC played an important role in the formation of attitudes and ideologies, and in the exchange of ideas among the large and influential milieu of Warsaw intellectuals, and an even greater role in the integration of this milieu. New acquaintances and friendships were made. Every participant in the discussions widened the circle of people with whom it was possible to find a common language, and this would prove useful more than a decade later. Among the members and sympathizers of the club were initiators of various kinds of protest actions during the Gomułka and Gierek eras. Active in the club were Ludwik Cohn, Edward Lipiński, Jan Józef Lipski, Aniela Steinsbergowa, and Wojciech Ziembiński, all of whom were later among the founding members of KOR. Jan Olszewski, one of the attorneys defending the workers after June 1976, was also a club member.

Many other members of the club could later be found among the associates of KOR. Were it not for the passage of time and the deaths that ravaged the ranks of the former club, one would also have expected to find among the founders of KOR the last chairman of the club, the

---

*A sociopolitical weekly publication which championed democratization and liberalization of the communist regime in Poland during the period of de-Stalinization (1955–1957).

**A literary-political monthly published by the émigré Institut Littéraire, under the editorship of Jerzy Giedroyć. Among its eminent regular contributors are Czesław Miłosz, Witold Gombrowicz, Gustaw Herling Grudziński, Leszek Kołakowski, and many others.

excellent essayist Paweł Jasienica (L. L. Beynar); professors Stanisław Ossowski and Maria Ossowska, distinguished sociologists who gathered together a wide group that set the general tone of the club (that of a leftist and liberal milieu, consciously and consistently antitotalitarian); Jan Wolski, the nestor of the Polish cooperative movement and a follower of the anarcho-cooperativist social theories of Edward Abramowski; Jan Zbrożyna, a socialist supporter of local self-governments during the interwar period in Poland; and the great writer Antoni Słonimski, who, however, was less closely associated with the club than the others. Unfortunately, none of these members lived to see the period of KOR.

Dissident Writers and Scholars

Next we must mention a group that could be described as "revisionist" were it not for the fact that by 1976, when KOR was created, this term had already become inapplicable, since by then these intellectuals had gone beyond revising Marxism and had distanced themselves both from Marxist thought and from the Communist party. In KOR, this was true of Jerzy Andrzejewski, Leszek Kołakowski, and Edward Lipiński.[2] Many of the associates of KOR of the older and middle generations had followed a similar path; they were especially numerous in the literary quarterly *Zapis* and in the Society for Scientific Courses (TKN, the Flying University).*

As these people distanced themselves more and more from Marxist revisionism, they became closer to other dissident writers and scientists, which meant that in *Zapis* one could find former revisionists (Wiktor Woroszylski, Jacek Bocheński, Kazimierz Brandys) along with writers who had never been "revisionist" (for example KOR member Jerzy Ficowski). TKN, however, was always less socially homogeneous. There were artists and writers as well as scholars; in addition to former revisionists who were influential in TKN (led by Bronisław Geremek, Jerzy Jedlicki, and Adam Kersten, all historians of the middle generation, and by philosopher of science Stefan Amsterdamski), there were also publicists and scholars associated with the Catholic group "Znak" (Władysław Bartoszewski, Bohdan Cywiński, Tadeusz Mazowiecki, Adam Stanowski). Not all the activists of TKN could be considered associates of KOR, although many of them were.

*See chapter 7.

The prehistory of KOR also includes the "Letter of 34" written in 1964 by thirty-four writers and scholars, members of the intellectual elite who, on the initiative of Antoni Słonimski, wrote to the authorities to protest against the censorship and the cultural policies of the government. The repressions that followed consisted mainly of bans against publication, prohibitions against television appearances, public readings, and the like.[3] For over ten years, the "Letter of 34" served as a model for other similar protests, and it played an important role in the realization that some forms of resistance were possible despite everything.

The tradition leading to KOR also includes another important episode from the history of the literary milieu, namely, the role of writers in the 1968 protest against the closing of Mickiewicz's play *Forefathers' Eve*, as a result of censorship.* Two future members of KOR (Jerzy Ficowski and Jan Józef Lipski) and two future associates (Tomasz Burek and Wanda Leopold) were active in the ad hoc committee that gathered signatures on a petition calling for an extraordinary meeting of the Warsaw Section of the Union of Polish Writers (ZLP).

Finally, among the later members or associates of KOR were the lawyers who had played an important role in the composition of a now-forgotten document, *The State of the Law in Poland*, a letter addressed to Gierek by professors Maria Ossowska, Edward Lipiński (its initiator), Leon Manteuffel, Włodzimierz Zonn, Stanisław Herbst, and Andrzej Grzegorczyk.

"Commandos": The Club of the Seekers of Contradictions

The "commandos" played a very important part in the formation and in the activities of KOR. The name was forged in the cell of the Polish United Workers party (PUWP) at Warsaw University; it was given to a group of politically obstreperous young people who had begun before 1968 to set the tone of student life politically and intellectually.

Some of these young people came from the Club of the Seekers of Contradictions, and others from the "Walterites," pupils of Jacek Kuroń.

Adam Michnik was the leading spirit of the Club of the Seekers of Contradictions. In the fall of 1961, Michnik and his friend Jan Gross

---

*Adam Mickiewicz, 1798–1855, the greatest Polish poet; champion of Polish national freedom.

were introduced to a meeting of the Club of the Crooked Circle by Aniela Steinsbergowa, a friend of Gross' mother. At the time, Michnik and Gross were fifteen-year-old high school students. Before the authorities closed the Club of the Crooked Circle in February 1962, these boys not only attended the discussion meetings regularly but also introduced their own friends to the club. Their presence was striking: they distinguished themselves sharply by their still childish appearance, which was especially noticeable because only a few university students came to the club. The authorities immediately informed the Club that it was no fit place for high school youth, and demanded that the students not be allowed into the meetings. The club was dissolved shortly thereafter, so the board of the Club of the Crooked Circle never had time to address this issue.

These young people were extremely upset at the liquidation of the club; they had enjoyed its atmosphere of open discussion. At that point, Lipski suggested that the young people form their own club for discussions and self-education. After various perturbations and difficulties a new club was created, whose members were students from several Warsaw high schools. At Lipski's suggestion a delegation of the organizing group visited Adam Schaff, then professor of philosophy at Warsaw University and a member of the Central Committee. The idea was that such an inter-school club should have adequate protection that would prevent interference from the school administration, while at the same time the protection should be nominal, allowing for full self-government. Schaff, delighted to discover that young, intelligent students were seeking his patronage and that they knew his work, quickly agreed to give them a place to meet at the university.[4] And, as was anticipated, Schaff had no intention of wasting his time trying to control the new club. Although he delegated this task to one of his assistants, the assistant also treated it as a formality and did not even bother to attend the meetings. During the 1968 witch-hunt for Zionists and revisionists, Schaff—who in this case was totally innocent—was attacked, among other things, as the patron of the Club of the Seekers of Contradiction.

This club was dissolved in typical fashion after a year of activity. Stanisław Manturzewski, an activist of the then-defunct Club of the Crooked Circle, often attended the meetings of the new club.[5] At the time, in 1962, Manturzewski was producing an interesting series of television reports entitled "Pedagogical Experiments." Manturzewski had the idea of presenting the Club of the Seekers of Contradiction on television. What was worse, he showed the club together with a group

of young workers from the town of Mińsk Mazowiecki who met in the
Cactus Club of their local cultural center. It was a good documentary,
but it was seen by some party dignitary who ordered the liquidation of
both clubs, and not without reason. Mixing young intelligentsia with
young workers manifesting social and intellectual ambitions might be
explosive. In the Polish People's Republic, nothing was feared quite so
much as the removal of barriers separating the young intelligentsia from
the workers.

"Commandos": Walterites

The case of the Walterites is not only less familiar to me
but it is also more controversial; it arouses strong emotions to this day,
especially among the older cadres of scout instructors and young people.
Whenever Jacek Kuroń is under attack—regardless from which side the
attack is coming—the issue of the Walterite scout troop returns. This
topic demands a separate, and as far as possible a dispassionate, historical
investigation based on primary sources.

The Walterites chose for their name the *nom de guerre* of General
Karol Świerczewski, the "General Walter" of the Spanish Civil War, and
thus they identified themselves ideologically with the communist tradition. Jacek Kuroń was the founder of the Walterite scout troops. The
pedagogical ideas of the Walterites were formed in clear opposition to
the Baden-Powell traditions of Polish scouting. The Walterites promoted
unequivocal and uncompromising political involvement, so that the Walterite scout troops were more clearly and more consistently Marxist-
communist than the rest of Polish scouting (which is also directed by the
party). The Walterite upbringing promoted an awakening of social interests and encouraged the participation of young people in authentic
social life; it also supported the idea that work should be voluntary and
based on trust.

The moral atmosphere evoked by Kuroń was anticonformist and saturated with a striving for truth and a faith that the more genuine life
was in the scout troops, the more obvious the victory of the communist
idea. At the same time, this ideological involvement often took on shades
of fanaticism, and the Walterites were often accused of being fanatics.
The result was easy to foresee: an unavoidable ideological conflict between the nonconformist youth on the one hand, and on the other, the
authorities, the system, and finally the official ideology. The authorities

saw the Walterites as a serious threat, and they liquidated the movement by means of bureaucratic prohibitions. They dissolved the troops and expelled the instructor cadres from the Polish Scouting Union. From their official perspective, there was certainly a point in doing this: witness the role of the Walterites in 1968 and later in the KOR movement. One could point to Seweryn Blumsztajn and Adam Michnik as persons representative of this milieu, in addition to Jacek Kuroń. Not for nothing has it been said: ye shall know them by their fruits. Yet to this very day, a severe phobia exists toward the Walterites on the part of the activists of traditional scouting. Later conflicts within KOR also had their roots here.

Before March 1968, these young people—both the Seekers of Contradiction and the Walterites—considered Jacek Kuroń and Karol Modzelewski, two young scholars working at Warsaw University, as their models and leaders. At the university they were active in the Discussion Club sponsored by the Union of Socialist Youth, which functioned as an open forum before being dissolved by the authorities in 1964. They also invented the tactic of organizing student opposition around discussion clubs. The authority of Kuroń and Modzelewski increased even more after their trial in 1965 and their imprisonment for the "Open Letter to the Members of the Basic Party Organizations of PUWP and to Members of the University Cell of the Union of Socialist Youth at Warsaw University." After their release from prison at the end of 1967, both men emerged as the natural leaders of the student movement at the university.

Kołakowski's Lecture—
1966 and the March Events—1968

Even before Kuroń and Modzelewski were released from jail, the commandos had arranged for the Union of Socialist Youth (or ZMS, among whom they also had sympathizers) to invite Professor Leszek Kołakowski to speak on the occasion of the tenth anniversary of the events of October 1956 in Poland. In his lecture Kołakowski spoke about squandered hopes, and made explicit the need to restore them. A number of students participating in the discussion expressed similar thoughts in a very outspoken manner. As a result, Kołakowski was expelled from the party and disciplinary actions were initiated against the most active discussants (among them Adam Michnik). A number of writers and

scientists reacted to Kołakowski's expulsion by handing in their own party
cards in protest. Many academics from Warsaw University signed a letter
of protest against the disciplinary proceedings, which ended in temporary suspensions and reprimands.

The commandos were also the main instigators of the 1968 student
protests. Following the decision by the censors to ban Mickiewicz's *Forefathers' Eve* from the stage of the National Theatre, they called for a
demonstration, first inside the theater and then in front of Mickiewicz's
monument. This resulted in action by the police and Security Service,
and a number of demonstrators were put on trial before Sentencing
Boards for Misdemeanors and before the Disciplinary Commission at
the university. The commandos responded with a mass action, gathering
signatures on petitions protesting the interference of the censor in the
staging of a literary masterpiece. When the minister of Higher Education
(then Henryk Jablonski, who is now chairman of the Council of State),
exceeding his authority, expelled two students from the university (Adam
Michnik and Henryk Szlajfer), the commandos responded by calling for
a demonstration to be held on the university campus on March 8, 1968.
The police and its reserve forces (ORMO) broke up the demonstration
with a brutality that had not been seen in Warsaw for many years. Mass
arrests and a campaign of slander in the mass media followed. At the
same time, the anti-Semitic tendencies of the ruling group, which had
been gaining strength for several years, came to the fore with an intensity
and with methods that shocked Polish and world opinion. In spite of all
this, disturbances and strikes occurred in all Polish cities with institutions
of higher learning and were also accompanied by mature and interesting
attempts to formulate political programs.

The movement was brutally suppressed in the course of several weeks.
Thousands of young people were detained, and an even larger number
were expelled from the universities. The commandos were among those
imprisoned (their leadership already had been arrested on the morning
of March 8).

March 1968 brought about an enormous change in consciousness,
especially among the young people studying at the universities. The
commando movement had developed within the sphere of influence of
revisionist ideology; that is, it was governed by a desire for renewal, for
the humanization and democratization of Marxism, and it was grounded
in the belief that the political system created by Bolshevism could be
reformed. This was not a typical attitude of the young people of the
time, but it was an attitude one often encountered. In 1968 the clubs of

the "forces of order" and the anti-Semitic propaganda dashed these illusions permanently. A large number of young people abandoned the Bolshevik ideology once and for all.

Protests Against the Intervention in Czechoslovakia

The few protests that followed the invasion of Czechoslovakia constituted the last act of the March movement. Their small scale can be explained by the lingering sense of defeat and the general disarray. There was a letter from Jerzy Andrzejewski to the chairman of the Writers' Union, and a letter from Zygmunt Mycielski to the chairman of the Composers' Union in Czechoslovakia. A group of students distributed leaflets, among them Bogusława Blajfer, Eugeniusz Smolar, and Andrzej Seweryn.[6] Eight years later, in 1976, all these young people—many of them still under 30—constituted the foundation of the KOR movement: commandos and noncommandos, participants in the 1968 strikes and demonstrations, often former political prisoners, experienced and aware of the mistakes made during the 1968 student protests.

Scouts from "Black Troop No. 1"

Next we must mention the milieu of the scouts of Black Troop No. 1 and the Band of Vagabonds, who were contemporaneous with the commandos. One of the best high schools in Warsaw, named after Tadeusz Rejtan,[7] housed first one, and later several troops of scouts with the oldest traditions in Warsaw, dating back to the period before World War I, when scouting was carried on secretly under the Russian partition. The first Warsaw Scout Troop was known as Black Troop No. 1 because of the color of their neckerchiefs. The scoutmasters and troop leaders of Black Troop No. 1, together with former scouts who had graduated from high school, created a circle of "old boys" that was also known as the Band of Vagabonds. They met several times a year, mainly to discuss current issues in social and national life. It is obvious why the Security Service soon began to take an interest in the band. In the early 1970s this interest found expression in a huge police action: under cover of darkness, a police detachment surrounded the suburban Warsaw villa of Mr. and Mrs. Doroszewski, first to check the identities of those who had gathered there and then to disperse them. To their credit, the scouting authorities defended the Band of Vagabonds, recognizing the legality of their meetings.

This group of young people was very committed ideologically and very integrated socially; their older associates had participated in the March events, and had often been subjected to interrogations and imprisonment. They owed much to the traditions of Polish scouting, to Baden-Powellism, and to the Gray Ranks, a scouting organization connected with the Home Army during the German occupation.* As many as four members of KOR, and later of KSS KOR, had their roots in the Band of Vagabonds: Antoni Macierewicz, Piotr Naimski, Wojciech Onyszkiewicz, and Andrzej Celiński. Two editors of *Głos* (*The Voice*), Urszula Doroszewska and Ludwik Dorn, also came from the band, as did Marian Barański, who played an important role in TKN, Dariusz Kupiecki, and others. The Band of Vagabonds also put together the original team that organized help for the workers from Ursus in 1976. One might also add that KOR member Mirosław Chojecki, who was for a while the head of the Radom team and later the founder of the Independent Publishing House (NOWa), had also been a scouting activist, though not a member of the band.

Young People from the Warsaw Club
of Catholic Intelligentsia

Students and young university graduates associated with the Warsaw Club of Catholic Intelligentsia (KIK) also played an important part in the history of KOR. To a lesser degree, this was also true of some of the older activists of KIK. Combining their activities in KOR with the activities of the officially recognized Club of Catholic Intelligentsia was a difficult problem for them. It was important that this club, an institution useful in promoting intellectual and social life in Warsaw, not become subject to reprisals. For this reason, some members of KIK who were indeed very involved in the work of KOR chose to decline formal membership in KOR despite their actual role in the committee. As a result, the only person from this group who became a member of KOR was Henryk Wujec.[8] Maria Wosiek, although also a Catholic activist, was less involved in the club. In May 1977, following demonstrations in Cracow supported by KOR in response to the murder of the student

*Polish anti-Nazi underground conspiracy active during World War II.

Stanisław Pyjas, the members and collaborators of KOR were arrested according to the degree of their supposed effectiveness as KOR activists and organizers; among those locked up in Mokotów Prison were two associates of KOR from the circle of KIK youth: Wojciech Arkuszewski and Wojciech Ostrowski.

Academic Ministry Circles in Gdańsk and Lublin

Academic ministries exist in every Polish city in which there is an institution of higher learning. Occasionally they develop extensive educational programs. Between 1976 and 1980, two such centers in Gdańsk and Lublin were especially active. The role of Dominican Father Ludwik Wiśniewski offers a classic example of the influence that can be exerted by an outstanding personality with exceptional educational talent. He directed the academic ministry first in Gdańsk and then in Lublin. Many of his students were supporters of the KOR movement; later, a majority joined either the Movement in Defense of Civil and Human Rights created in 1977 (after the divisions within ROPCiO, they created the Young Poland Movement) or they were associated with the publication of the Lublin quarterly *Spotkania*. A few people from this milieu remained in KOR, among them one exceptionally active KOR member, Bogdan Borusewicz, a young historian from Gdańsk.

We must add that relations between KOR and this milieu were generally good. Very friendly relations were maintained with the *Spotkania* group, whose perspective, close to that of *Więź* (*The Link*), excluded the insinuation of politically and socially obscurantist views under the label of Catholicism. (I must add quickly that *Spotkania* was not the only group that gave cause for optimism in this regard.) Relations were also loyal and comradely with the Young Poland Movement, the group from Gdańsk, assembled around the uncensored periodical *Bratniak*, directed by Aleksander Hall.

Not without reason have the relations between KOR and the circles of the academic ministries, especially in Gdańsk and Lublin, been characterized only as "generally good"; and there was also a reason for my reference to the smuggling in of obscurantist notions under the label of Catholicism. The young people connected with the academic ministry in Gdańsk also formed a relatively small but rather noisy Independent Political Group which from the very beginning acted aggressively (including physical aggression) against their colleagues, while sounding off with chauvinistic and anti-Semitic slogans. For their favorite ideologist they chose Jędrzej Giertych, an émigré politician from the extreme nationalist right wing of the National party. In their bulletin they published, uncritically, such things as the *Protocols of the Elders of Zion*. They fought against all the democratic opposition, not only against KOR but also against ROPCiO.

Scarcely better was a group active under the name of the Committee in Defense of Life, Family, and the Nation. Ostentatiously Catholic, they were unmistakably close to fascism. Their main topic—the fight against abortion—was "strengthened" by anti-Semitism and other such favorite themes. Otherwise, their approach to their basic ideological issue was also original: they furiously attacked other Catholic activists who were no less involved in the fight against abortion (Rev. Stanisław Małkowski, Father Ludwik Wiśniewski, Adam Stanowski), and these attacks were motivated simply by the fact that the other activists stressed their democratic views and distanced themselves from the methods used by their opponents.

The Milieu of "Ruch"

A sizable number of KOR activists came from the former Ruch (Movement). This was a secret oppositional organization active in several cities, formed in the last years of Gomułka's reign. Ruch was broken up by the security forces in the last months of 1970, and its leaders were imprisoned. Most of the activists of Ruch, led by Andrzej Czuma, found themselves in the Movement in Defense of Civil and Human Rights. However, a large part of the Ruch organization in Łódź associated with KOR (Jacek Bierezin, Ewa Sułkowska-Bierezinowa, Witold Sułkowski, Joanna Szczęsna). Also connected with Ruch was KOR member Wiesław Kęcik and his wife Marzena, and Emil Morgiewicz, a KOR member who moved to ROPCiO in September 1977.

The "Tatra Mountaineers"

Among the groups and events that later influenced the formation of KOR, one can also mention the trial of the so-called Tatra Mountaineers. In 1969 several young people were arrested for having organized, in collaboration with some Czechs, the smuggling of copies of Paris *Kultura* into Poland by way of Czechoslovakia and across the Tatra Mountains. Two well-known activists of the KOR movement were in this group: the sociologists Jakub Karpiński (one of the better-known publicists of KOR, who signed his works Marek Tarniewski), and Jan Kelus (a social worker in the Intervention Bureau of KOR, as well as an author and performer of popular songs).

Protests Against the Unification of Student Organizations

In 1973, the Polish United Workers' Party (PUWP) decided to "simplify" the organizational life of students. The Union of Socialist Youth (ZMS), which was also active in the universities, was neither a popular nor an energetic organization; it could not recover from the losses it suffered in 1968. Student interest in political life, already minimal, seemed to be declining. Paradoxically, ZMS was losing the competition to the Union of Polish Students (ZSP).

The Union of Polish Students was neither an independent nor a dissenting organization. Like almost everything else in Poland, it was subordinated to the leadership of the Communist party. However, since membership in ZSP did not entail such an unequivocal political and ideological self-definition as did membership in ZMS, and since ZSP functioned more or less like a student trade union and was in charge of student life (financial and material issues, the organization of cultural life, sports, tourism, etc.), a large part of the student body felt no need to belong to yet another organization.

A decision was made to change this state of affairs and to merge the Union of Polish Students with the Union of Socialist Youth into a new organization, which, like ZMS, would be politically affiliated with PUWP, but which would also inherit from ZSP a monopoly over the organization of all social life in institutions of higher learning.

The students were understandably displeased. There was, of course, no question of resistance on the part of ZSP, an organization whose leadership was in practice nominated by the party all the way down to the lowest organizational ranks. Nevertheless, there was visible ferment, which led to an antiunification movement that was especially strong at Warsaw University. A programmatic thesis written by Konrad Bieliński and Stanisław Krajewski appeared on bulletin boards. Informal action groups began to organize protests in individual departments and university institutes. Taking part in these activities were most of the future associates of KOR in Warsaw, who in 1976 were still finishing their studies or had graduated only recently.

The protest against the unification of student organizations does not as yet appear to have been discussed in detail in any publication. This is a pity, since this protest formed an important link between the student revolt of 1968 and the future KOR student movement in the years 1976–1980. Given this situation, I do not have much to contribute on this subject. It is known that, in addition to the two activists mentioned already, Kazimierz Wóycicki and Irena Holakówna (later Wóycicka) were among the leaders of this movement. Their success was not insignificant: anyone who knows the mechanisms of official organizational life in Poland will understand the importance of the fact that as many as five delegates who protested openly against the unification were elected to participate in the convention that was called to form the new, united youth organization.

Minigroups

Characteristic of KOR was the fact that almost every member was surrounded by a kind of minigroup made up of sympathizers and associates of the committee whose own contact with the committee led precisely through these personal channels. In this manner, for example, did Janusz Przewłocki, a future member of the editorial board of the *Information Bulletin,* come to KOR from the group of people working in PAX who initially maintained contact with KOR through its member Anka Kowalska. Similarly, the KOR membership of Prof. Jan Kielanowski followed an active association that had grown naturally from his friendship with Edward Lipiński.

There were some associates whose names were never made known—their apartments were not searched, they were never detained, they did not sign their names on the periodical publications of KOR, and so on. I believe that their names should not be made public without their permission (which I have no means to acquire at this time).

Intelligentsia, Workers, and Peasants

The KOR milieu had many branches, and of course not everyone knew everyone else; even when people did know one another, they did not necessarily know that they were working together in the committee (because they were in different cities, or because of the necessity for secrecy in certain tasks, such as printing, etc.). In the beginning the KOR circle was composed exclusively of members from the intelligentsia, but workers began to appear as early as 1976. Increasing numbers of workers were involved following the creation of *Robotnik* (*The Worker*). Later, farmers began to number among the activists associated with KOR. Nevertheless, the intelligentsia dominated the committee, whereas strong worker and farmer groups had a tendency to constitute themselves into Initiating Committees of Free Trade Unions or Peasant Self-Defense Committees, which acted independently of KOR although they maintained contact. These committees provided a common ground for cooperation among worker and peasant activists associated with KOR and with ROPCiO.

The Defense of Persecuted Students

Of particular importance in the history of KOR were two cases that integrated the dissident milieu during the period preceding the formation of the committee. Without this integration, the action of the Workers' Defense Committee could not have begun as efficiently as it actually did in 1976. The first of these cases involved students organizing the defense of Kruszewski and Smykała. The second case had a broader scope and louder reverberations and involved protests against changes in the Constitution of the Polish People's Republic.

Jacek Smykała was a student at the Pomeranian Medical Academy in Szczecin. He was expelled from school for "provoking doubts" with remarks he made after attending a lecture on the foundations of social science. The final decision in this matter was signed by the deputy director of the Department of Education and Science in the Ministry of Health and Social Welfare, L. Dawidziuk. Immediately afterward, Smykała was conscripted into the army. Stanisław Kruszewski, a student at the Catholic University in Lublin, was given a ten-month prison term for "false information" transmitted in private letters to his wife, his brother, and a friend. The decision to speak up in their defense—in a letter addressed to the authorities—was initiated by students connected with the academic ministry in Lublin. Their actions were supported by students in Warsaw.

The Protest Against Amending the Constitution

The protest against introducing changes in the Constitution of the Polish People's Republic (PRL) had farther-reaching effects. The issue was somewhat paradoxical. In 1952, the Polish Diet had adopted a new Constitution. Those were the days of the Stalinist terror: people were tortured and murdered, and they were condemned to death or to long prison terms on the basis of ridiculous and implausible documents or slanders; every aspect of life was under the control of the Security Service and of PUWP. The Constitution adopted at that time was simply a Stalinist document, which does not mean, however, that it sanctioned all these practices. One of the fundamental differences between communist and fascist totalitarianisms is that the latter is less steeped in hypocrisy, and based on a narrower gap between the law—a cruel law that often rejects without shame principles elaborated through centuries of Christianity and later of liberalism in Europe—and an even crueler practice. Communist legislation, and especially documents such as the constitution, which are not linked directly to actual legal regulations, are stylized in a manner so as not to offend the world and to offer support for mendacious domestic propaganda. Thus, these documents contain guarantees of freedom of conscience, assurances of freedom of association and assembly, declarations about freedom of speech, and the like. Obviously, no one operating within the Stalinist system ever expected that citizens would protest against the discrepancies between the Constitution and reality. As a result, the Constitutions adopted at that time functioned as rather elegant false fronts.

But times have changed. Even in the USSR, the terror of Brezhnev's era—frightening in itself—did not compare even approximately with the terror of the Stalinist period. Moreover, the Stalinist terror in Poland never reached the proportions it attained in the Soviet Union (in 1936–1937). After 1956, its character changed fundamentally; political trials became rare, and sentences were still shocking, but only when measured against the legal standards of Western Europe rather than the practices of the Soviet Union. The general atmosphere was also incomparably more liberal. As a result, people became more audacious and began appealing to the Constitution, which promised much better than the actual practice, even though the practice itself had improved.

In addition, the conclusion of the Helsinki Conference on Security and Cooperation had come, and the Final Act had also been signed, though only after much stalling, by the Polish People's Republic. The opposition in Poland feared Helsinki at first: they expected that the conference would result mainly, or even exclusively, in formal recognition of the division of Europe into two spheres of influence. However, they soon noticed—not just in Poland, but also in the USSR and in Czechoslovakia—that there existed an opportunity to appeal to the Final Act. In many instances, freedoms that, through the Helsinki agreements, were to be guaranteed by international accords had already long been "accorded" to the citizens of the Polish People's Republic by their own Constitution; and this fact intensified and facilitated their appeals to the Constitution. In this manner, the Constitution achieved the peculiar authority of a document which, while it was not honored by the state authorities, at least gave dissenting individuals a sense that the law was on their side. The appeal to abide by the Constitution became a subversive, antigovernment slogan. This was probably how the idea of "improving" the Constitution originated.

Late in 1975, politicians began to make references in their speeches to the need to amend the Constitution. Information was rationed out in small doses, but gradually, the public found out that these changes would concern three issues.

First, it was announced that the Constitution would contain an article stating that a citizen would be entitled to exercise his rights only if he fulfilled his obligations toward the state. This provision was to create a starting point for the exclusion from the law of entire categories of citizens, and for the implementation of the favorite idea of most totalitarian elements within PUWP: the introduction of forced labor.

Second, it was announced that an article would be introduced into the Constitution recognizing Poland's faithful alliance with the USSR; that is, there would be a constitutional limitation of Polish sovereignty.

Third, it was announced that the leading role of the party in the state and in society would be recognized in the Constitution.

These proposals stirred much discontent. It was clear that constitutional changes of this nature, even if they did not alter the actual state of affairs, were unfavorable for the society. The proposal to introduce the alliance with the USSR into the Constitution was regarded as a particularly grievous insult. A significant part of Polish society accepted the existing state of affairs in this area, and there was a rather common feeling that any questioning of Polish participation in the Warsaw Pact would invite mortal danger. Under these conditions, the proposed constitutional amendment had a purely moral significance: it was only another humiliating slap in the face, while for those who lied to themselves by believing that they lived in a sovereign state, it was simply an acknowledgment of the existing state of affairs. In a word, it was a manifestation of political stupidity. But the statement about the leading role of the party—which explicitly reminded everyone that the citizens of the Polish People's Republic could be divided into those who were leading and those who were being led—also had the character of an equally gratuitous insult, which aroused frustration and aggression.

It was the first issue, however, that posed the most serious danger. As against the other proposals, this one could be expected to find a much deeper social resonance. Totalitarianism, which for years had been deforming the social psyche, had not generally succeeded in promoting love for the Soviet Union, the Bolshevik system, the Communist party, but was more successful in generating attitudes that testified to deep frustration and the belief that the best remedy for social ills was the use of repression and compulsion. Thinking in terms of repression may be considered an inseparable aspect of totalitarianism, and this type of thought was characteristic also of those elements of society that were hostile to communist totalitarianism. Often large segments of society approved of the brutal force used by the communists against long-haired or eccentrically-dressed young people, or believed that the only way to counteract increases in juvenile delinquency involved the application of Draconian measures. This ideology was formulated and spread in a particularly systematic and consistent manner by television and by *Prawo i Życie* (*Law and Life*), a weekly publication of communist lawyers with an especially totalitarian orientation. In this one respect, the communists had a chance to gain some public support, and therefore also a chance to isolate the liberal opposition.

Luckily, the Church decided to use its authority in addressing this issue. In his third Holy Cross Sermon (i.e., in a series of sermons delivered in the Church of the Holy Cross in Warsaw), Primate Stefan Cardinal Wyszyński stated explicitly that even the drunkard lying against the fence, who seems at that moment to be devoid of all human features and who contributes nothing to social life, must have his full civil and human rights, if only because he is human. This was a decisive voice even for those who did not really understand what it all meant, or why the primate was saying such strange things.

The idea of a protest action against changes in the Constitution was formulated during a gathering of four people in the apartment of attorney Aniela Steinsbergowa. It had been suggested initially by a well-known Warsaw lawyer, and was taken up enthusiastically by Jacek Kuroń. Based on the experience of previous protests, it was apparent that the degree of social resonance would depend both on the number of signatories and on their prestige and popularity. Therefore, it was important to find adherents and representatives among the intellectuals, so that signatures could be gathered through various channels among scholars, writers, artists, and the like. The idea was "bought"—as Warsaw slang would put it—by a group of Warsaw writers who quickly began to coordinate the action, so that this group controlled not only the organizational aspects, but also the strategy of gathering signatures on the letter known later as the "Letter of 101." The various strands of the action were held together by Jerzy Andrzejewski; the staffing and implementation were directed by Wiktor Woroszylski, Jacek Bocheński, Andrzej Drawicz, Marek Nowakowski, Witold Dąbrowski, Irena Lewandowska, and others. In a word, this was exactly the same group that would later create and edit the uncensored literary periodical *Zapis*.

The first to appear, however, was the "Letter of 59," important not only because it was first but also because it contained a positive program of fundamental civil liberties. It contained no ideological revelations, but was important for another reason: it boldly appealed for that which has long seemed obvious in many countries in the world. We must also pause here to explain an issue that was to have serious repercussions in the future. The "Letter of 59" should pass into the history of opposition in Poland as the "Letter of 66." When the names were being listed and copied, as many as seven signatures disappeared due to technical disarray. Among these signatures was the name of Wojciech Ziembiński. The victim attributed this omission to intrigues by some of his colleagues, placing the responsibility mainly on Jacek Kuroń, despite the fact that someone else was in control of the successive stages of implementation that produced the mistake. I have tried very hard to investigate the circumstances of this unfortunate occurrence, and I am convinced that the error was accidental, especially since it involved others as well as Ziembiński. Nevertheless, the passed-over signatory, who was doubtless morally short-changed even though no one meant him any harm, remained convinced that he was a victim of someone's hostility. This regrettable and not inconsequential oversight was compounded by yet another error: on January 21, 1976, Lipiński sent a supplement to the "Letter of 59" to the marshal of the Diet, one that contained the missing seven names, but he in turn made a mistake in the name of Wojciech Ziembiński, who this time appeared as Ludwik.

Worse yet, there was a third, more serious mistake. After a speech by Edward Babiuch* which contained more information about the planned changes in the Constitution, a circle of social activists that included Władysław Bartoszewski, the attorneys Jan Olszewski and Stanisław Szczuka, and again Wojciech Ziembiński, drafted a new letter against the consti-

---

*At the time secretary of the Central Commitee and member of the Politbureau of the Polish United Workers' party.

tutional amendment limiting Polish sovereignty. This letter was signed—separately, and without consulting the initiating group—by a large number of the signatories of the "Letter of 66," who regarded it as an expression of their support for a worthwhile cause. This supporting letter was treated in the West as if it were the original letter—perhaps because it reached the West first—while the original letter was treated as a supplement.

There were many more letters about the Constitution, and a full list of all the signatories would convey a sense of the formation of open opposition among intellectuals and artists. Here we have mentioned only those letters that, because of their initiators and signatories, can be considered in connection with the prehistory of KOR. The "constitutional action" played an extremely important role in the crystallization of political opposition and social resistance in Poland. Voices were raised over this issue not only by groups of well-known people who formulated their demands openly and broadly in a manner that had not been seen in Poland for many years but also by the Church, an institution that enjoys even greater prestige and is of tremendous significance in Poland; and for this reason these protests must be considered of historical importance. It is true that the Communist party did not retreat before this wave of protest, which was also a serious warning to them. Still, the amendments were slightly rephrased, so that their stylistic fangs and claws were somewhat dulled. All this gave the initiators of the protest a sense of success.

The Main Council of the Episcopate defended the initiators of the protest against the persecutions to be expected in a totalitarian system (and which had already begun) in a "Clarification" of March 1976, which included the following passage:

> We all expect that those citizens who answered the appeal of the Extraordinary Constitutional Commission, and who legally expressed their views in letters to this Commission, will be treated with respect. They have availed themselves of the rights of free citizens, to which they are entitled, and they have fulfilled moral and political responsibilities, which testifies to their civil maturity. A respect for inalienable human rights, for the rights of human beings, is a basic task of a just social and state system. This respect goes hand in hand with a recognition of the rights of the Polish Nation, which has earned a sovereign existence in its own State through long historical experience and labor.

The Episcopate's expectation was not fulfilled. Repressions followed, although it is difficult to determine the principles underlying their application. People were fired from their jobs, expelled from the universities, prevented from exercising their professions by illegal prohibitions, denied the right to travel abroad, conscripted into the army, and subjected to other discriminations.

Despite social protests, the Diet of the Polish People's Republic passed the constitutional amendments of February 10, 1976. Only one deputy abstained from voting: Stanisław Stomma from the "Znak" circle. The other deputies from "Znak" voted in favor of the ignoble amendments; just as, four months later, they would again vote with shameless unanimity for government proposals, participating first in a farcical support for price increases, then voting for their repeal.*

Lipiński's Letter to Gierek

The final act of opposition by intellectuals before the creation of KOR was a letter from Edward Lipiński to Edward Gierek.[9] This document, which contained a many-sided critique of the system of governing and warned of a catastrophe, became an important factor influencing the formation of a new social consciousness among the intelligentsia, and many of the ideas it contained were to enter into the standard repertoire of later attempts to formulate a program.

*See chapter 2.

2
The "June Events" of 1976

Price Increases

In Poland the problem of price structure for basic food-stuffs has been insoluble for many years. During the Gomułka period, the leadership, fearful of an explosion of dissatisfaction among workers, generally did not tamper with prices, even though many individual items (both food and industrial goods) were becoming more expensive. An entire book could be written about how surreptitious price increases were introduced. One must remember that prices in Poland are not regulated by a market mechanism, but arbitrarily fixed by decisions of the state administration. But human nature being what it is, even under such a system one can observe that individual enterprises still want to maximize their profits. Although these profits are transferred in large part from the enterprise to the state treasury, they are not without influence on the evaluation of the director of a firm by his superiors. Various absurd tricks were used to circumvent the obstacles posed by the central institutions responsible for controlling prices. "New, improved" quality was obtained through minimal changes in ingredients. The name of the product would be changed, and by pretending that the product itself had changed, its price could be changed as well. New packaging would be introduced, and the price of the product increased by a sum many times greater than the cost of the new packaging. There were many such methods, all equally unethical. Incidentally, this also produced nonsensical effects in other areas besides the economy. Since a supposedly new product needed a new name, traders, who are not always very adept in creating neologisms, coined freak words that became a constant topic of satires. The infamous "male hang" (a necktie) dates from this era.

All these methods were only half-measures and did not deal with the problem in its entirety. The relative freeze on prices—especially of basic foodstuffs—resulted in absurd disproportions between the price of food and the price of industrial articles, between the price of production and the price to the consumer. The central planners became increasingly helpless in the face of these processes. Disproportionate prices warped and retarded the growth of the economy. Every quarter brought a new worsening of the situation.

Thus the price-hike operation of December 1970 was not in itself inappropriate. But because it was introduced after a long delay, and all at once, it created a shock by its arbitrary character and scope and by resulting in a sudden lowering of the standard of living. Moreover, with typical bureaucratic savoir faire, it was not noticed that the effect of introducing price hikes right before the Christmas holidays would be particularly strong. Workers on the Baltic coast answered with strikes and demonstrations, and of course they attacked what the workers in Poland hate most of all: the centers of power. The buildings of the party committees went up in flames. The party responded with a massacre of the workers, the exact dimensions of which cannot be determined to this day. Literally on the eve of disturbances nationwide, a few personnel changes were made in the positions of highest authority. Gomułka was replaced by Gierek. During a meeting with Gierek, the shipyard workers shouted their famous "We shall help!"* and it appeared that the price operation would be successful. The price increases had to be withdrawn, however, following strikes in February in Łódź. There was nobody to talk to in Łódź. The workforce in the textile mills, the industry with the lowest wages in Poland, was composed largely of women; they did not choose strike committees nor did they occupy their factories; their protest was shapeless and therefore impossible to control.

The problem of disproportionate prices remained and grew deeper during the later years of the pseudo-prosperity achieved in the first half of Gierek's reign. The economic revival had been achieved at the price of a steadily increasing foreign debt. Anyone with ears to listen, or who had a passing acquaintance with economists or engineers, knew that corruption was reaching frightening proportions; that nonsensical licenses were being bought; that low-quality goods, bordering on trash, were being imported at ridiculous prices; that billions were being wasted; that changes in investment were introduced chaotically into various sec-

---

*Barely one month after December 1970 strikes on the Baltic coast, another strike broke out in the Szczecin Shipyards. Edward Gierek, by then first secretary of the PUWP, with a whole retinue of highest government and party officials went to the shipyards and confronted the striking workers in some ten hours' long session. He won their confidence in the end, and to his final question "Will you help us?" they answered "We shall help." The meeting was secretly taped and its transcript later published in the West.

tors of the economy without regard for the actual needs of the economy, but rather according to the distribution of power among communist palatinates struggling for authority and influence; and that enormous investments, largest among them the Katowice Steel Mill, were economic monstrosities, were badly located, and required miracles of accounting. It was becoming increasingly evident to everyone except those who did not want to know that the censorship and the lack of democracy were serving above all to protect stupidity and theft.

The entire period of Gierek's reign before June 1976 was dominated by an atmosphere of fear of the workers. The intelligentsia was disregarded: it had proven in December 1970 that it was not dangerous. But the fear of the working class worsened and hardened the price disproportions (while salaries continued to increase). At every step, these disproportions were smothering the economy a little more.

On June 24, 1976, the prime minister proposed to the Diet a general increase in food prices. The Diet readily adopted the increases. Something was said about "consultations with society," but no one knew what consultations were meant, nor could they have known. One thing only was clear to people from the opposition: tomorrow there would be strikes and unrest among the workers.

Regardless of the economic justifications for the increases—which even specialists have difficulty in ascertaining because much of the data is kept secret and censorship is extensive—the average Pole could understand immediately how his pocket would be hit by increases of 69 percent in the prices of meat and fish (including processed meats and fish); of 30 percent in the price of poultry; of over 50 percent in the prices of butter and cheese; of 100 percent in the price of sugar; and of 30 percent in the prices of flour, beans, peas, and processed vegetables. Even those with little economic imagination could immediately evaluate such price increases critically. On average, food prices increased by 46 percent and the prices of fresh vegetables, potatoes, and fruit were expected to rise shortly. Food figures very prominently in the budget of every Polish family; earnings are relatively low and the population is generally poor. In addition, this was already a period of sharp inflation and of hidden price increases that were eating up increases in wages. The average Pole felt despair and hopelessness. On June 25, there were strikes and street demonstrations in three workers' centers: in Radom, Ursus, and Płock. Płock did not become as famous as Radom and Ursus because the disturbances there were suppressed less brutally, but also because the Workers' Defense Committee got to Płock later than to

Radom and Ursus, and complete documentation could not be assembled successfully. In addition, a wave of strikes of various magnitudes swept throughout Poland and was met with various degrees of repression.

I shall attempt to describe the course of events.

Strikes and Demonstrations in Radom

The largest demonstrations and corresponding police actions took place in Radom, if only because Radom is a sizable industrial city and provincial capital, while Ursus is barely a town (it lies formally within the city limits of Warsaw).

The workers at the General Walter Metal Works initiated the strike in Radom. When the workers did not start work in the morning, someone from management tried unsuccessfully to talk to them. The strike was declared in the factory courtyard, but no strike committee was chosen. First, it was decided that other industrial enterprises had to be informed. To accomplish this, groups of workers drove across Radom, some borrowing for this purpose the electric carts used for internal factory transport. At 10:00 A.M. the workers left Walter and began to march toward the building of the Provincial Committee of PUWP. This is a typical phenomenon under such circumstances: whenever the workers' anger boils over, the party committees alone, and not the organs of state government, are treated as the centers of power. Several thousand workers gathered in front of the committee building. One of the secretaries from the committee promised that around 2:00 P.M. there would be an answer concerning wage increases. However, when at noon it became obvious that only civilian police functionaries and several lower-level officials remained inside the building, while the higher functionaries had escaped (probably through a rear exit), the crowd forced its way into the building, ramming in the doors and breaking windows with stones. When they reached the canteen, they began throwing cans of ham out into the street, along with other products that had been unavailable in the stores for a long time. Systematic destruction began around 1:00 P.M. Television sets, desks, and armchairs were thrown out of the windows, and at around 3:00 P.M. the building was set on fire. Firemen were not allowed to approach the building, and to prevent this, people set up a barricade of cars, trucks, tractors, and trailers across First of May Street. One of the fire engines was also set on fire. A tragic accident occurred at that time: two workers were crushed to death by a tractor trailer.

The Police Action in Radom

While these events were occurring in front of and inside the committee building, the rest of the city was quiet. During this time, several men armed with clubs appeared on Żeromski Street (the main shopping street in Radom); walking from one store window to the next, they systematically smashed the glass. The police did not react; they looked on and took pictures. All the plate glass store windows on a relatively long street were broken by only a few people.[1] At around 5:00 P.M. some people began looting these stores, throwing their contents out into the street and destroying their interiors. There is no doubt that later the police used unacceptable means in an attempt to force people who had been detained only for participating in the demonstration to plead guilty to theft as well. The police even staged situations which they photographed and then presented as evidence of looting. The entire course of events in Radom was to a large extent stage-managed in such a way as to support the future direction of the propaganda already being planned.

Around noon, Motorized Detachments of the Citizens' Militia (ZOMO) landed at Radom Airport. These are professional units, housed in barracks and schooled exclusively in methods of combatting street demonstrations and breaking strikes. These units were put into action only around 5:00 P.M. Approximately two hours later, the city was under the control of the police. Most of the arrests were made during this time, that is, between 5:00 and 7:00 P.M.; about 2,000 people were detained.

The action was conducted with extreme brutality. ZOMO uses rubber clubs about two and a half feet long, reinforced with wire. These clubs were used to attack people regardless of age and gender or whether they were resisting or not. Such incidents do occur occasionally when demonstrations are being dispersed, but there is no doubt that on this occasion exceptional brutality was used. Even worse things happened inside police headquarters to defenseless people who had already been beaten and arrested. These were not individual abuses. The chief method of torture inside police headquarters involved the so-called path of health, in which the detainee was forced to run the gauntlet, passing through a long row of policemen, each of whom would strike the victim.[2] This was a collective action, conducted probably on the orders, and certainly with the knowledge, of superiors.

Józef Szczepanik: "hit in the temple, I lost consciousness. Friends told me later that after I fainted, one of the policemen grabbed me by the throat and carried me in this way to the other end of the cell, while another one walked alongside and was beating me on the legs and chest."

Zbigniew Cibor: "I was beaten and kicked by police functionaries and by the prison guards so that I was bleeding from the nose and ears."

Piotr Wójcik: "five of them threw themselves on me and tied me to a heater; they were beating me all together, so that I quickly lost consciousness . . . they used clubs, using the handle, which had lead inside it; they kicked me over my whole body. . . . Most of them were under the influence of alcohol. This lasted for five days."

Stanisław Adamski: "I was told that I was going through the 'path of health' and that this would help me. After being beaten for about two hours, I was thrown unconscious into a cell."

Kazimierz Rybski: "when I regained consciousness, one of them asked me, 'Didn't you get enough?' and ordered another: 'Give him some more.' They began to beat me with clubs and to kick me as I lay on the floor."

Ferdynand Ufniarz: "I was taken to a room at the city headquarters of the police and there they began to beat me until I passed out. I came to in another room. My nose was broken. . . . In the recreation room some corporal began beating and kicking me again. First I fell down, and then I lost consciousness again. I woke up without teeth."

Grzegorz Jaroszek: "Then they began beating me on the feet with clubs. At first I felt pain in my feet; later I felt as if someone was hammering nails into my head."

Waldemar Michalski: "On the first day I walked the 'path of health' on the way from a truck to the police van, about 50 meters. They ordered me to walk slowly so that each one could hit me. They beat me with fists, clubs, boots. At the very end, I fell down. I couldn't get up again under the hail of clubs. The nearest ones dragged me. . . . We were taken to Police Head-quarters. A 'path of health' from the van to the second floor . . . when they took us to get haircuts—another 'path of health' some 40 meters long, from the door of the room all the way to the car. . . . Yet another 10 meters in the corridor leading to the table. . . . Then, a 'path of health' (10 meters) to cell number nine—we had to walk slowly, since if one of them didn't manage to strike, he ordered us to go back. In the cell . . . after 15 minutes the police came in . . . and took us to the court in a prison truck; of course another 'path of health' led all the way to the stairs. But there were too many 'clients,' so they turned us back through the same 'path' and into the truck, then again a 'path' from prison to prison. I survived another 'path of health' in the morning when they took me to Kielce, where there was no path and they finally gave us some food."

BOGDAN GOLIAT: "I also watched as the police were dragging a woman who was screaming 'Don't beat me, I'm pregnant.' 'Then miscarry, you whore' answered the functionary dragging her and began to beat her."

These methods were also used as torture to extort confessions. In this respect Ursus was no different from Radom at all.

The Deaths of Jan Brożyna and Rev. Roman Kotlarz

The so-called June events did not end as night fell over Radom on June 25. For a long time afterward, police patrols spread fear through the city, behaving like an occupying army in a conquered town. It was just such a patrol that killed Jan Brożyna (the circumstances of his death, together with the trial of his supposed assassins, will be discussed in chapter 5). In view of such brutality, it might appear surprising that KOR discovered so few cases of death or permanent injury. Obviously, fear might have played a role in this, by preventing people from informing KOR about particularly drastic cases. For example, KOR knew of a man who lost an eye as a result of the beatings, despite a year-long treatment by the best ophthalmologists in Radom and Warsaw, but who did not want his name to be made public in a KOR communiqué. In any event, apart from the casualties that occurred when a tractor trailer crushed two people during the construction of a barricade, and apart from Jan Brożyna who also lost his life following June 25, KOR publications named only one other person who died as a result of the June events: Rev. Roman Kotlarz.

Reverend Kotlarz was interrogated by the Security Service on several occasions as a result of denunciations claiming that he had given his blessing to the demonstrators. He himself explained to his Church superiors that, realizing the seriousness of the situation and the brutality of the police and fearing fatalities, he had given absolutions *in articulo mortis*. The condition of Kotlarz after his interrogation suggested that he had been beaten, but he told no one. On the critical day, a cleaning woman found him beaten to unconsciousness in his own apartment. The assault did not involve a robbery. The cleaning woman informed the psychiatric hospital in Krychnowice near Radom, since she knew that Kotlarz, who was a priest there, was friendly with the doctors. Kotlarz was pronounced dead on arrival at the hospital. The conduct of a public investigation of the matter was made more difficult by the fact that at Kotlarz's funeral, a high church official stated publicly that his was a natural death. On the basis of the information gathered, KOR suspected that this opinion was precipitous and irresponsible.

How Many Died in Radom on June 25, 1976?

Were there really no fatalities in Radom resulting directly or indirectly from the June events? It is difficult to answer this question with absolute certainty. The communiqués of KOR initially mentioned rumors that eleven people had died. Attempts to confirm this were unsuccessful. Stories were repeated about bodies buried secretly in plastic bags. One way in which the truth could be established would be to investigate all death certificates dated late June and early July 1976. In the course of its investigations, for example, KOR found one case where the deceased was probably a prisoner in one of the police precincts in Radom (at least this was the claim made by people who knew him and who had also been detained). It was impossible, however, to establish this person's identity with full certainty. Someone also drew KOR's attention to the fact that an unusually high number of suicides was reported in Radom during this period. As a rule, it is the other way around: when something intense is happening in social life, the number of suicides decreases. Unfortunately, the appropriate investigations of this circumstantial evidence were not successful.

When Solidarity planned commemorations of the events in Radom of June 1976, it was expected that unexplained disappearances from that period would be brought to its attention. Nothing of the sort happened. Under these circumstances, the police can be charged with beatings, which often endangered health and life, and connected with injuries incurred during tortures used both to extract depositions and as a means of intimidation; but so far as the action of June 25, 1976 is concerned, the charges cannot include murder. The political and police authorities decided that this time they would not use firearms. Thanks to this decision, a repetition of the massacre on the coast in 1970 was avoided, as were the political consequences of such a massacre.

An enormous propaganda campaign followed the quelling of demonstrations and strikes. The press and television reported a flood of telegrams and letters condemning "troublemakers" and "brawlers." Resolutions against them were adopted during rallies organized in the larger cities. In Warsaw, one such rally took place in the Tenth Anniversary Stadium on June 29. It was composed of bureaucrats. The only workers present were the few PUWP activists from large industrial enterprises. Attendance was checked before the trip to the stadium. Another such rally occurred in Radom on June 30; its participants were transported to Radom by bus from other locations. The mayor of the city spoke about the high wages earned in one department of the Walter factory.

In keeping with a custom often observed in wartime, the final act of the police "conquest" of Radom took the form of a parade of the victorious occupying forces through the conquered city. This occurred in October, on the day honoring the Citizens' Militia and the Security Service.

Ursus, June 25, 1976

The events in Ursus were similar to those in Radom; the differences resulted from the fact that Radom is a large city and a provincial center of political authority, a trading center, and so on, while Ursus is a small factory settlement. But the police "pacification" followed basically the same course, was equally brutal, and involved the use of the same methods, though in Ursus a larger number of those detained apparently managed to avoid being beaten. The Ursus events also displayed a certain originality in that they involved the interruption of traffic on two of the most important railway lines in the country.

The workers at Ursus were aware that a strike—even one in a factory as large as Ursus, with several thousand workers—could pass unnoticed because of the government's monopoly of information; hence their idea of blocking traffic on two railroad lines that also service international trains. Ursus is situated between the rail line leading from Warsaw to Poznań, Berlin, and Paris, and the line leading from Warsaw to Łódź, Katowice, and Vienna. Both lines were blocked: the tracks were cut with acetylene torches, and a locomotive was then derailed into the gap. Two trucks carrying eggs and sugar were also stopped, and their contents were distributed among bystanders. All these activities were filmed by the Security Service from a helicopter.

The police action in Ursus began only as people began to disperse to return home after listening to another speech by Prime Minister Jaroszewicz, who this time revoked the price increases. A mass roundup in the streets was accompanied by beatings. It was an act of pure revenge.

Generally, the KOR documentations contain no indications that would speak either well or ill of the role of the official trade unions during the June events and afterward. This was not the case in Ursus, where the trade unions were in evidence: union activists took part in helping to identify the photographs taken by the Security Service on June 25.

Demonstrations and the Strike Movement in June 1976 Outside of Radom and Ursus

The events that occurred in Płock are less familiar than those in Radom and Ursus. At 6:00 A.M. on June 25, the workers at Petrochemia, one of the largest refineries in Poland (which is supplied from the USSR by pipeline) went on strike. A rally took place around 10:00 A.M., and street demonstrations followed that lasted until evening. With the exception of a few broken windows at the Provincial Committee of PUWP, there were at first no incidents. Only at 8:00 P.M. did police detachments brought in from outside attack the demonstrators and also a number of people who were just leaving the cinema. The reports from Płock—less numerous and less exact, in any case—contained no details that would testify to the same degree of brutality as occurred in Radom and Ursus.

The decision to revoke the price increases was probably influenced more by the strikes, which did not involve street demonstrations, than by the demonstrations themselves. According to the available information, roughly 75 percent of the largest industrial enterprises in Poland went on strike. The percentage was less among the smaller factories. The first alarm came to the Central Committee of PUWP not from the police and the Security Service but from the central distributor of electrical power, where the drop in energy consumption, as compared with the normal morning hours of a regular work day, was so large as to indicate a general strike. The data gathered by KOR on this subject is inadequate and fragmentary.

In Łódź, the strikes of June 25 were not accompanied by street demonstrations. Their course varied from factory to factory. Sometimes work stopped and a rally was organized, occasionally with the participation of the management, which tried to pacify the workforce. In other factories there were no rallies, but departments chose representatives or made up lists of demands that were signed by the workers. A strike committee was elected in the M. Fornalska Textile Mills. Between July 1 and July 7, strikers in Łódź were dismissed from their jobs. It appears that the number of those fired was close to three hundred. *KOR Communiqué* No. 5, of December 21, 1976, lists twelve factories where strikes were followed by such repressions. KOR could find no evidence of arrests.

Also in Łódź, a large percentage of those fired later availed themselves of their right to sue the factory for illegal dismissal from work, first in the grievance commissions (these appeals were never successful) and then in the Labor Court, which did return some people to work. In the fall, those who had not been reinstated appealed to the Central Trade Union Council, asking for an extraordinary review of the decisions of the Labor Court confirming dismissals in connection with the June strikes. In late March, 1977, the Central Trade Union Council answered that the acts of the workers (participation in a strike) came under Article 52 of the Labor Code, and that therefore the claims of the workers were groundless. In this manner, the Central Trade Union Council confirmed the interpretation of this article as an antistrike law.

Despite the fact that KOR was created in Warsaw and that most of its earliest associations originated in Warsaw, the evidence about strikes in Warsaw is indirect and weak. The available evidence is based on information about factories where people had been dismissed from their jobs. It is paradoxical that it was precisely in Warsaw that KOR failed to develop a wider relief action (apart from a certain number of employees of Warsaw factories who lived in Ursus, which itself belongs administratively to Warsaw). Repressions were greatest in the precision instruments factory named after Karol Świerczewski, from which approximately two hundred persons were fired. There was also some information about repressions in, among others, Kasprzak Enterprises, the Polish Optical Factory, and "Zelmet" Enterprises.

During this initial period, KOR's presence was also weak in Gdańsk, where approximately three hundred people were dismissed from their jobs in the Lenin Shipyards. Workers were also fired from ZREMB (construction machinery) and BUDIMER (construction industry), from Dairy Industry Machinery Enterprises, and probably also from other factories.

In Gdańsk, two people were also sentenced to prison terms (suspended) for turning off electricity on a welding line.

KOR had precise information about Grudziądz, since the workers dismissed from the Pomeranian Foundry and Enamel Shop had become organized and when they appealed to KOR for help, they were already a group with certain achievements in the area of self-help based on their former workplaces. From this factory forty-three people had been fired.

In Starachowice, between one hundred and three hundred people were thrown out of work following a strike in the Truck Factory.

One of the most original strikes took place in the Nowy Targ Leather Industry Enterprises. Nothing happened on June 25. Then the local chapter of PUWP sent a letter to the authorities condemning strikes in the name of the entire work crew. As a result, the workers struck on June 29, simply to protest against this abuse. Here again, the number of those fired is difficult to establish today; between one hundred and three hundred people were involved. In the great majority of cases, even such rough estimates as these exceeded the abilities of KOR, which was then only in its organizational stage. Those who announced their willingness to work with KOR were immediately swamped with more work than they could easily handle.

In addition, attempts to gather information met with many difficulties, mainly from the police and the Security Service, but not only from this quarter. For example, the following incident was probably not the only one of its kind: hearing of a strike and repressions in a brewery in Suwałki, one KOR associate went to visit the place. The workers' suspicions were aroused by his attempts to establish contacts and to gather information, and they regarded him as a police informer; luckily he was not beaten up, but he had to return to Warsaw rather quickly. Thus, the mistrust and fear felt by the victims of repression also served as an obstacle to the gathering of information.

Approximate Data About the Extent of Repressions

KOR did not attempt, after the fact, to reconstruct the strike movement of 1976 in full detail. Nor was this done during the period of Solidarity, since people were then too busy with current issues, while KOR was itself an institution dedicated to action and not a historical institute. As a result, the data concerning the repressions that followed in the wake of June 1976 are imprecise. Probably somewhere between ten and twenty thousand workers were dismissed from their jobs. The number of those detained is also difficult to establish, but here the estimate is a little more precise: about 2,500 people were involved, of whom

approximately 373 were sentenced to prison terms or fines as a result
of summary proceedings by Sentencing Boards for Misdemeanors.[3]
Criminal court proceedings were initiated against approximately another
500 persons.

The results of the court trials were frightening. They will be described
in the chapter dealing with the first period of KOR activity; but it is
necessary to realize that sentences as severe as ten years' imprisonment
were handed out to people against whom little had been proven.

KOR as a Result of Repressions
Against the Workers

The group of people who created the Workers' Defense
Committee decided to stand up against terror and lawlessness, to give
help to the persecuted, and to present the truth to society, countering
the lies of propaganda. This was both a moral imperative and an imperative of rational thought in social and national categories. A small
group of people could not accomplish these tasks alone; it was necessary
to appeal to the consciences of others, to invoke human and civil solidarity, and to call upon others to cooperate and gather financial support
for the relief actions.

It was as if a group of madmen had undertaken impossible tasks. It
soon became clear, however, that those who regarded the creators of
KOR as lunatics were wrong. A general determination and an acceptance
of the risk of long imprisonment and perhaps even death at the hands
of "unknown perpetrators" (this is no pathetic exaggeration: such was
the fate of Stanisław Pyjas) were accompanied by rational calculation,
political discrimination, and organizational talent of at least some of the
people who began this work.

In this way the Workers' Defense Committee—KOR—came into being.

3
The Founding of the Workers' Defense Committee

The Crystallization of the Idea of KOR

Ideas that appear suddenly within social groups that are already more or less conscious of their aims can be said to be collective creations, even if a specific individual gave these ideas their final form. The idea of a committee that would institutionalize the support of the intelligentsia for workers came about in just such a communal manner, but it had two fathers who gave it a definite form: these were Jacek Kuroń and Antoni Macierewicz. In future memoirs, should such be written, the authors' point of view will determine which of these two activists will be regarded as the more important. Any attempt to establish priority, however, or to decide which elements of the idea of KOR were created by whom, seems doomed to failure (the broader the understanding of the problematics of KOR, the greater the number of putative inventors of ideas). Rivalry on this score is hopeless as far as the chances of establishing historical truth are concerned (this is so not only because of the methodological difficulties but also because of the nature of these ideas themselves); and rivalry is also politically harmful, since it can become a source of unnecessary conflict. From my point of view, the role of Kuroń was more visible, but trustworthy accounts by others suggest that occasionally Macierewicz appeared in the foreground.

In any case, the idea of the committee crystallized in July 1976. Nothing had yet been said about the committee when, immediately after the June events, a group of people who were ready to do something in connection with the workers' protest met together in Laski (where Adam Michnik was living in the House Above the Meadows, which had often been occupied in the past by Jerzy Zawieyski, and was writing his book *The Church and the Left: A Dialogue*). But by the time of the first Ursus trial on July 17, the idea of a committee was fully formed.

What was the basic idea of KOR? To answer this question, several issues must be considered side by side, since different issues will be regarded as basic depending on one's point of view.

First, there was the idea of an action that would appeal above all to ethical values, to general moral standards rather than political attitudes. Obviously, whoever takes a stand against totalitarian power in any area of life is committing a political act. In this sense, an artist who painted an abstract or surrealistic picture in the quiet of his own private studio during the period of Zhdanov's cultural policy was committing a political act classified as hostile to the system and its ideology.* Totalitarianism is defined precisely by the fact that, since the authorities aim to extend their control over every aspect of life, everything ultimately becomes political. Above all, the authorities want to control the consciousness of the people as it relates to social issues, in order to make them behave in accordance with their own successive decrees and decisions. Thus, anyone who appeals to an apolitical attitude in order to renounce solidarity with those persecuted under a totalitarian system is expressing the view that the highest absolute principle is to refrain from opposing the authorities, regardless of whether they are upholding moral norms and values. Such an apolitical attitude would seem to be absurd for all those who do not subscribe to totalitarian beliefs. But in practice, this principle constitutes a justification for people (and organizations) who, out of fear or opportunism, propagate and practice "neutrality" toward evil when it has been stamped with an official seal of approval. Anyone who has ever fought against communist totalitarianism knows that it is just as important to break down such opportunistic attitudes as it is to break down barriers of fear and inertia. Thus, from the very beginning, KOR acted consciously on the assumption that it would unite people in the struggle against totalitarianism, and in an area that left no doubt that what was at stake was the defense of ethical values: above all, by bringing organized help to people persecuted by the totalitarian authorities.

Second, there was the notion that the committee's activities should be overt. Neither the existence of the committee nor its membership were to be kept secret. This included a rather ostentatious public announcement of the addresses and telephone numbers of KOR members. The idea of openness was derived from previous forms of protest, since the signatories of letters, declarations, and petitions had had to make their

---

*Andrei Zhdanov, 1896–1948. Soviet Communist party official responsible for the imposition of highly restrictive cultural policies after World War II.

identity public by revealing their first and last names. This was always accompanied by fear of reprisals, but it also made the document more trustworthy. The founders of KOR knew that overcoming the barrier of fear would constitute a condition necessary for the success of KOR, but this struggle against fear was also one of the committee's basic goals, which had not only a political and social but also a moral significance. It was obvious that those involved in the creation of the committee would also have to serve as examples.

Third, there was the idea that activity should not only be overt but also legal. Opportunities for legal action were provided by the international agreements ratified by the People's Republic of Poland, including the Final Act of the Helsinki Conference and the Polish Constitution, as well as other laws. Even the very existence of KOR—the legality of which was questioned by the Security Service, since KOR never applied for official registration and thus for official permission to act—was not without legal justification. There was an old but still valid law from the 1930s which allowed for the formation of committees devoted to relief actions (aid to flood or fire victims, for example), and such committees did not have to be registered.[1] In addition, KOR had only one characteristic of an organization: members. It had no bylaws or statutes, no chairmen, no membership fees. There was also a legal loophole: any group attempting to register becomes illegal if it is denied registration, and any further activity by such an organization is then subject to criminal sanctions. This is not the case for organizations that simply neglect to register, and which are then subject only to administrative sanctions. In this, and in all similar cases, KOR knew very well that repression (or the lack of it) would depend solely on the degree of self-confidence felt by the authorities, and not on the law; but KOR wanted to have the law on its side as far as possible.

The First Protest Documents After June 25, 1976

The first document proclaiming the solidarity of a group from the dissident intelligentsia with the persecuted workers was drafted during the meeting in Laski mentioned above.[2] For a variety of reasons, several participants in that meeting did not sign the letter, while a number of others who were not present signed it later. Other protests included a letter from Jerzy Andrzejewski to the persecuted workers, the "Statement of the Eleven," and the "Letter of the Thirteen to Western Intellectuals." Andrzejewski's letter was better known than the group letters, and made a profound impression. This was not surprising, since it was written by a distinguished writer whose name was remembered by young workers from their school assignments. Another noteworthy group protest appealed for an amnesty for the arrested and convicted workers; this "Letter of Nine to the Chairman of the Council of State," dated August 20, 1976, was signed by a group of activists from the Club of Catholic Intelligentsia.

July 17—The Beginning of Real KOR Activity

There seems to be no controversy about the date of KOR's birth, that is, the day on which the first real KOR activity began, even though KOR did not yet exist as an organization: the first Ursus trial took place on July 17, 1976 in the Leszno Courts (Świerczewski Street), and this was the day of KOR's first contacts with the families of persecuted workers.

An important threshold had been crossed. A tremendous effort is made by the entire political system of communist countries, and especially by the political police (although the problem is not limited to the police), to prevent communication among different social strata. In prewar Poland there were a number of institutions, such as the Society of Workers' Universities (TUR) or the People's (i.e., Peasant) Universities, and so on—not to mention political parties—which allowed for easy contacts between the intelligentsia and the workers and peasants, especially between their young elites with intellectual and educational ambitions. In postwar Poland, such institutions either did not exist at all or were fictitious: stripped of self-management and subjected to the party-state bureaucracy, they were no longer able to fulfill their multiple social functions. A wall, difficult to penetrate, separated the intellectuals from the workers. It was rare for members of the intelligentsia to meet privately with workers. The first problem to be faced by the emerging movement was the establishment of contacts with the terrorized workers of Radom and Ursus.

On July 17, the corridors of the Provincial Court in Leszno offered an unusual sight: the police had cordoned off the section of the corridor closest to the courtroom in which the Ursus trials were scheduled to take place. It was impossible even to read the court calendar hanging on the door. This provoked indignation and irritation among the foreign correspondents. In the crowd that began gathering in the building early in the morning, it was easy to spot the few workers and the families of those in the defendant's dock. More numerous than the workers and their families were the plainclothes agents of the Security Service, including some old and familiar faces which also left no doubt about their identity. In addition, there were about a dozen dissidents, among them Jacek Kuroń (who had been called to serve in the army during the first days of July, but who was still fighting the order and presenting various medical certificates), Antoni Macierewicz with a group of his scouting friends, Jan Józef Lipski (who, thanks to his cooperation with church-sponsored organizations after 1968, had in his possession on this day a sum of money that, although insignificant as far as more general needs were concerned, would nevertheless prove important during these early days), and others.

It was clear from the beginning that establishing contact would not be easy. The families of the accused were understandably suspicious of the large audience. The plainclothes policemen did not let the known dissident activists out of their sight and were constantly—and none too discreetly—taking their pictures and attempting to listen in on their conversations. Not everyone is capable of approaching suspicious strangers and striking up a conversation, and this psychological difficulty was exacerbated by police surveillance. The success of the action depended on overcoming these obstacles. During one of the recesses in the trial, Małgorzata Łukasiewiczówna and her friend Ewa approached one of the crying women. A brief, heartfelt expression of sympathy broke the ice. The families of the accused were unhappy with the court-appointed defense attorneys (and did not know how to find others; in this respect the situation was better for those defendants, mostly in Radom, who had had some previous experience of the "judicial system" and knew what had to be done); so one of the first steps was to recommend attorneys who could be trusted fully, and to assure the families that the expenses for these attorneys would not be a burden.

The first letters granting power of attorney were signed on the very same day, following a conference between Jan Olszewski and the family of one of the accused. The first financial help was also passed along. When one of the women expressed the worry that she would not be able to attend her husband's trial because the neighbor who was minding her children would not be available on that particular day, deputy scoutmaster Piotr Naimski suggested that uniformed scouts would come early that morning to take care of the children. He assured the woman that they could do this "professionally," since they had already served as counselors for preschool children at a summer camp. This form of help was immediately accepted and appreciated. From then on, it was obvious that given a little time, it would be possible to set up contacts in Ursus.

The Work of the Ursus Team Begins

Work began immediately in Ursus thanks to an enterprising and resourceful group of scouts from the Band of Vagabonds connected with the Tadeusz Rejtan High School in Warsaw. They were assisted by Henryk Wujec, a young activist from the Club of Catholic Intelligentsia in Warsaw, and soon they were joined by a whole group of his friends from KIK. It is difficult to overestimate the amount of work that was accomplished at that time. Boys and girls quickly won the confidence and sympathy of the workers' families, and could count on their help in collecting information about the persecuted workers, or about the fate of those in prison or dismissed from their work. They also distributed the first financial help, established contacts with lawyers, and sought out doctors for the sick (who were often sick from having been beaten, but who, because they had been subject to disciplinary dismissal from their jobs, were also deprived of medical help). KOR began to assemble its documentation and files. Publishing began on July 25, 1976, with "A Description of Repressive Actions Taken Against the Workers of 'Ursus' and Other Enterprises," based on the testimonies of numerous witnesses, which was distributed in dozens of copies. This was the germ of the future *KOR Communiqué*.

The first problems appeared: Where could one get the money needed for relief? How should this money be distributed? How should expenses be documented? How should one account for the money, and to whom? Work continued in the meantime. The appeal for funds that was voiced in the dissident circles went quickly beyond those who had already been active in the opposition, and became popular first in Warsaw only, then in other cities, and finally even in the villages, to which access was of course much more difficult. Money began pouring in. Other problems that had been anticipated also began at about the same time: the surveillance of dissident activists (in part only an intensification of surveillance that had been conducted since December 1975 or even earlier); house searches; and the first forty-eight-hour detentions. The first attempts to intimidate the workers also appeared. Police and security functionaries visited the workers at home and held conversations to "warn" them against agents of foreign intelligence networks, or against Radio Free Europe, or the Jews. The impact of this was insignificant.

Work on the Formation of the Committee

Shortly after the Ursus trial, Jacek Kuroń was conscripted into the army despite having produced statements from doctors certifying that his EKG showed that he had suffered a coronary infarct. Before entering the army, Kuroń wrote his celebrated "Open Letter to Berlinguer."[3] This turned out to have been an excellent tactical maneuver, although it was later used as an argument for labeling Kuroń a "Eurocommunist," which was a misunderstanding. By this time it was known that a Committee would be formed; that it would assume responsibility for the money donated by the public to help the workers; that it would appeal to the public for cooperation and help; and that it would bring together people willing to work, organize aid for the persecuted activists, and gather information about the course of the June events, their effects, relief actions, and new repressions.

The issue of membership in such a committee was influenced by experience gained from the writing of protest letters, which demonstrated that while the authorities can easily arrest young people whose names are unknown, they are much more restrained toward those who are highly respected in society, enjoy great authority, and are well known at least among the elite. Thus, it was felt that the committee should be composed both of well-known individuals, often advanced in age, who had "names" and reputations, and also of relatively unknown young people who in fact were already working for KOR.

Jan Józef Lipski was given the task of undertaking actions directed toward the formation of the committee, since it happened that among those who could have been assigned this task, he appeared to be the most qualified (for example, one of the necessary prerequisites was a broad circle of acquaintances among intellectuals of oppositional inclinations).[4]

This decision had serious shortcomings. In the first place, the preparatory stages demanded organizational talents rather greater than those of Lipski; second, they required what might be called "penetrating force," the ability to impress a more or less unified attitude upon a large group of people with distinct and forceful personalities. As a result, a meeting of potential members of the future committee took place on September 4, and produced no decisive results. The meeting was held in the apartment of Edward Lipiński. There were approximately twenty participants, mainly writers and scholars and activists of the older and middle generations. The younger people were represented by Antoni Macierewicz, Piotr Naimski, and Mirosław Chojecki. Lipski opened the meeting with a discussion of the situation resulting from the June events, describing the extent of the reprisals, the conditions and needs of the relief action, and the reasons for the formation of a committee. At that time the proposed name was the "Committee in Defense of Human and Civil Rights," thus referring simultaneously to the United Nations Charter, the Final Act of Helsinki, the appeals of U.S. President Jimmy Carter, and to an even older tradition: the League for the Defense of Human and Civil Rights that had been active in Poland during the 1930s, and in which Edward Lipiński had held office.

Many of those present at the meeting were shocked at the idea of forming such a committee. This was not surprising: the idea was new and unusual, and it was difficult to predict whether conditions for effective work could be created in this manner. Few people had any desire to engage in a mere demonstration that would lead straight to jail. Those present at the meeting were sensible and mature individuals, well aware of the responsibility they would be taking upon themselves. And so they preferred to think the idea through, although as it happened, there was hardly any time for this. If Kuroń, with his "penetrating force" and stubbornness, had been present at the meeting, the committee might have been formed on September 4. Meanwhile, it was decided that a preliminary commission should be formed, and the entire issue was postponed (if I remember correctly, this preliminary commission was composed of Ludwik Cohn, Józef Rybicki, and Aniela Steinsbergowa, and possibly others as well).

New circumstances developed in September. The movement was growing like an avalanche. Early in the month the relief action was extended to Radom, where needs were greater than in Ursus, and where new and previously unknown problems arose. (For example, as a result of a deliberate and cynical policy on the part of the Security Service, those prosecuted in Radom included a large number of people from the fringe of society. Since the general public was unaware of this manipulation by the authorities, the situation required that some responsible social group explain what was happening.) Above all, the surveillance and the immediate reprisals against those attempting to help the workers had intensified. For the first time, young activists in the relief action were being beaten up. On September 16, Ludwik Dorn was beaten in the Provincial Headquarters of the MO in Radom. Detentions were becoming increasingly common. The existence of a committee could help to lessen the probability of dangerous reprisals simply by conferring social authority on the young people who, from then on, would be acting in its name.

Moreover, it became clear that the relief action could count on the moral support of the Church. The September 9 Communiqué of the Plenary Conference of the Polish Episcopate, which was partially confiscated by the police but published in *Information Bulletin* No. 2 (a KOR publication), stated:

> The Plenary Conference of the Episcopate asks that the highest state authorities cease all repressive acts against workers who partipated in protests against the excessive increases in food prices that were announced by the government in June. The rights of the workers who took part in these protests should be restored, along with their social and professional status; the wrongs done to them should be rectified appropriately; and those who have already been sentenced should be amnestied.

As a result of the communiqué, something occurred which had the makings of a coup d'etat: the young people involved in the relief action demanded that a committee be created immediately, and they warned that otherwise they would form one by themselves. Jacek Kuroń gave them total and enthusiastic support from his garrison in Białystck, and using couriers to maintain contact, he constantly urged Lipski to expedite matters. As a result, the "Appeal to Society and to the Authorities of PRL" (see Appendix) was composed "in circulation."[5] The name "Workers' Defense Committee," suggested apparently by someone from Black Troop No. 1, possibly by Macierewicz himself, was adopted, and signatures were collected.

The Founders of the Committee

The KOR "Appeal" was not signed by all those who had gathered on September 4 in Lipiński's apartment. Some had various reservations and doubts concerning both the merits of the case and the formal procedures. Nonetheless, all these people took an active part in the later work of KOR and the institutions related to KOR. Among those signing the KOR "Appeal" were others who had not been present at the meeting on September 4. The first fourteen signers were:

Jerzy Andrzejewski, Stanisław Barańczak, Ludwik Cohn, Jacek Kuroń, Edward Lipiński, Jan Józef Lipski, Antoni Macierewicz, Piotr Naimski, Antoni Pajdak, Józef Rybicki, Aniela Steinsbergowa, Adam Szczypiorski, Rev. Jan Zieja, and Wojciech Ziembiński.

All these names are familiar today, if not to the entire public, at least to the part of it that takes an active interest in public life. In September 1976, some of these names were known only to a few. Let us review this list to see who was who, and to examine what kinds of biographies would prove capable of inspiring public trust.

Jerzy Andrzejewski. The name of one of the most outstanding contemporary writers in Poland requires no introduction. One might note, however, that before KOR came into existence, Andrzejewski had already established his place in public memory not only by his strictly literary works but also by such acts as his letter to the chairman of the Czechoslovak Writers' Union, Edward Goldstücker, written after the 1968 invasion of Czechoslovakia by Warsaw Pact troops, and by his letter to the Polish workers written after the June events. Throughout the time of KOR's existence, Andrzejewski was also an editor of the uncensored literary periodical *Zapis*.

Stanisław Barańczak is one of the truly outstanding younger poets, historians, and theoreticians of literature in Poland. Like Andrzejewski, Barańczak was also on the editorial board of *Zapis*. Since he lived permanently in Poznań, he became, as it were, the representative of KOR to Wielkopolska. He left Poland after August 1980 to assume a professorship at Harvard University. This was the result of a case that blatantly reveals the attitude of the Polish government to culture. Following the retirement of Professor Wiktor Weintraub, there was a vacancy in the Slavic Department at Harvard. Slavic departments in American universities generally pay little attention to Polish studies; but the department at Harvard was different, since a distinguished Polish scholar had lectured there for many years. The university decided to continue this tradition and offered the position to Barańczak. Retaining a Polish chair in the department and staffing it with a Polish scholar was very important for Polish culture and its propagation in the United States among ethnic Poles and others. This made no difference to the Polish authorities; for them it was far more important to take revenge against Barańczak as one of the founders of KOR. He was refused a passport. The department waited for several years. At one point it appeared that the case was lost: Harvard offered the position to Viegut, a German scholar and the author of many works on Polish literature. Fortunately, Viegut refused on the grounds that he did not wish to benefit from the effects of police discrimination against his Polish colleague. August 1980 saved the position for Polish culture. Barańczak was a member of PUWP for several years.

Ludwik Cohn is an attorney who acted as counsel for the defense in many political trials, and later served as legal counsel to Warsaw publishing houses. He was a distinguished socialist activist before the war, and was a member of the Union of Independent Socialist Youth, the Youth Organization of the Society of Workers' Universities (OMTUR), as well as of the Polish Socialist party, where he was active in the left-wing faction led by Stanisław Dubois. After the war he was a member of the underground Polish Socialist party "Freedom, Equality, Independence" (PPS-WRN); this eventually led him to share the defendant's box in the trial of Kazimierz Pużak (he was found guilty). He took part in the battle for Warsaw in 1920 and in the defense of the city in September 1939. He was held in a German POW camp for officers, and was thrice decorated with the Cross of Valor. From 1956 to 1962, he was an activist of the Club of the Crooked Circle.

Jacek Kuroń was educated as a historian, but his interests and vocation lie rather in pedagogy. As mentioned in the first chapter, he was a scouting activist. He was twice expelled from PUWP: first in 1955, and, then, permanently in 1965. He played a particularly important role in KOR as an exceptionally dynamic and inventive activist, a talented strategist and tactician who naturally attracted groups of co-workers. By the time he participated in the formation of KOR, he had already survived two political trials and almost six years of imprisonment. His wife Grażyna, who loyally accompanied him through all his difficulties, also played a vital role in KOR in 1977, when responsibility for its fate rested on those members and associates who remained free after the May 1977 arrests.* Their son Maciej was also an associate of KOR.

Edward Lipiński is a great scholar and economist, and a historian of economic thought; he has been a socialist since 1906. He is a member of the Polish Academy of Sciences and of many foreign scientific societies. Lipiński made extraordinary contributions to higher education which

*See chapter 6.

was conducted in secret during the German occupation, when he directed the underground work of the Central Trade School. In 1948, together with many members of the overt Polish Socialist party, he found himself a member of PUWP. When KOR was founded, he was the only member of the committee who still carried a party card (which was taken away from him several years later). Despite his advanced age—he was born in 1888—he took a lively part in KOR activities. As a member of the Funds Council and the Editorial Board, he joined in discussions and decision-making during the plenary meetings, and he also granted interviews. He impresses everyone with his tremendous clarity of mind, his iron logic, and the boldness of his thinking and its manner of expression. From 1956 to 1962 he was also an activist in the Club of the Crooked Circle.

Jan Józef Lipski is a literary critic and historian. He was a soldier in the Home Army and participated in the Warsaw Uprising (wounded, he was decorated with the Cross of Valor). From 1957 to 1962 he was chairman and a board member of the Club of the Crooked Circle. He was also on the editorial board of *Po prostu* (1957), and in 1964 he helped to organize the "Letter of the 34." On several occasions he was punished for his activity with a ban against publication. His children, Jan Tomasz and Agnieszka, also participated in the KOR movement.

Antoni Macierewicz is a historian and a scouting activist. In 1968 he participated in the student movement and spent several months in jail. He gathered around him a dynamic group of students and alumni involved in the scouting movement through the Band of Vagabonds.

Piotr Naimski is a biochemist (he received his Ph.D. during the period of KOR activity). He is a friend of Macierewicz through their common scouting activities, and is a deputy scoutmaster.

Antoni Pajdak is an attorney and a doctor of laws. He was one of Piłsudski's Legionnaires, and between the wars was an outstanding activist in the Polish Socialist party and in the trade unions. He was a member of the civilian government of the Polish underground state during World War II. Arrested by Soviet authorities in 1945, he subsequently was tried and imprisoned in Moscow. He returned to Poland in 1956.

Józef Rybicki holds a doctorate in classical philology. Before the war, he directed institutions of secondary education. He was a soldier in 1920 and 1939; during World War II he was an officer in the Home Army, and in 1944 he led the Diversionary Command (Kedyw) for the Warsaw District. He was a member of the command of Freedom and Independence (WiN),* and was in prison in the PRL for many years. He was decorated with the Silver Cross Virtuti Militari. He was also active in the antialcoholism movement, and has cooperated with the Episcopal commission for the fight against alcoholism. He is also a well-known bibliophile.

Rybicki is highly respected in veteran circles apart from the official Union of Fighters for Freedom and Democracy (ZBOWiD). In 1968 he became well-known in Warsaw for his outspoken stand against official propagandists who were looking for people willing to make public statements about Polish aid to the Jews during World War II. Rybicki believed that this topic should have been addressed either before 1968 or later, but not during a rampant anti-Semitic campaign.

Aniela Steinsbergowa is an attorney; she has served as defense counsel in many political trials. Before the war she defended, among others, the workers involved in the events following a strike in Semperit in Cracow. After 1956 she played an important part in organizing public pressure on the authorities to initiate trials that would rehabilitate soldiers of the Home Army and activists of the underground Polish state.[6] Later she served as an attorney in those trials (which are described in her documentary memoir, *The View from the Defender's Bench,* published by the Institut Littéraire in Paris). She was an activist in the Polish Socialist party, and she also took part in the work of the Club of the Crooked Circle.

Adam Szczypiorski is a historian and professor in the Institute for the History of Material Culture in the Polish Academy of Sciences, where he specializes in historical demography. He was an activist in the Polish Socialist party. He distinguished himself as an organizer of Polish education in the West after the war.

Rev. Jan Zieja, before the war, was a social activist connected with the Laski milieu and the educational activity of Wici. Under the occupation, he was head chaplain of the Gray Ranks, and then of the Baszta regiment during the Warsaw Uprising. He was decorated with the Silver Cross Virtuti Militari. Zieja earned special respect from opposition circles for a sermon he delivered in Warsaw Cathedral on September 17, 1974, on the occasion of the thirty-fifth anniversary of the Soviet invasion of Poland. Zieja said then: "Let us pray for the freedom of our brother Lithuanians, our brother Bielorussians, our brother Ukrainians, and for the freedom of all those who pray and the freedom of those who seek."

---

*WiN—Freedom and Independence—an underground anti-Communist organization established in Poland after World War II.

Wojciech Ziembiński is a technical editor and the author of many works about decorative printed graphics. He was imprisoned in Nazi labor camps during World War II following his capture in France while attempting to get through to the Polish Armed Forces in Great Britain. He was also an activist in the Club of the Crooked Circle.

Later Members of KOR

On September 26, several days after its initial appeal, KOR was joined by *Halina Mikołajska*. A great actress and twice the recipient of state prizes, Mikołajska was among those members, like Józef Rybicki and Rev. Jan Zieja, who represented no specific political orientation apart from a general antitotalitarian attitude in favor of democracy and national independence.

Only an accident prevented Mikołajska from being one of the founders of KOR. She had already long decided to sign the "Appeal" and made arrangements for this, but in the hurry and—why conceal it?— the general disarray that accompanied the creation of KOR, she was not contacted until several days later.

KOR Communiqué No. 3, dated October 30, 1976, included information about three new members of KOR: Mirosław Chojecki, Emil Morgiewicz, and Wacław Zawadzki.

Mirosław Chojecki was involved in KOR activity even before the committee was organized. A man of tremendous organizational talents, hardworking, and dedicated, he became the head of the team working to provide aid for Radom, and as a result soon became an object of particular interest to the Security Service. His membership in KOR followed naturally from the role he had played in the work of the committee, and it gave him some protection.[7] Chojecki was a chemist by profession and worked in the Institute of Nuclear Research. He was also a scouting activist, though not from Black Troop No. 1.

Emil Morgiewicz, a journalist, was a member of the secret organization Ruch that was active during the final years of Gomułka's regime but later crushed by the police. Following his release from prison in 1972, he sent a report to Amnesty International, which he subsequently joined, on conditions in the Polish prison system. Accordingly, he was welcomed into KOR as a specialist in an area which was from the very beginning of particular interest to the committee, and also as a representative of a milieu which KOR members saw as being dedicated to similar goals, though thus far it had not been involved in the work leading to the creation of the committee.

Wacław Zawadzki began his association with KOR before he became a member. A former activist of the Polish Socialist party, he was expelled in 1948 after the unification of PPS with the Communist party. Believing in the possibility of renewal, he joined PUWP after October 1956. In 1967, after Prof. Leszek Kołakowski was expelled from PUWP, Zawadzki returned his party card. An outstanding expert in the field of publishing, he was for many years the director of the large publishing house Wiedza, associated with PPS, and for a short time after 1956 he was deputy editor-in-chief in the State Publishing Institute (PIW). Zawadzki was the editor of many Polish memoirs, a bibliophile, and a member of the Union of Polish Writers and the Polish PEN-Club.

KOR Communiqué No. 4 of December 13, 1976, carried information about two additional members of KOR: Bogdan Borusewicz and Józef Śreniowski.

Bogdan Borusewicz is a historian from Gdańsk. He is associated ideologically with the academic ministry milieu in Gdańsk, the group gathered around the uncensored periodical *Bratniak*, directed by Aleksander Hall. Hall's group, however, attached itself to ROPCiO, and then formed the separate Young Poland Movement. Borusewicz chose KOR.

Józef Śreniowski is a sociologist and ethnographer. A participant in the 1968 student movement, he was designated by KOR to represent the committee in Łódź, where he played an important role as an organizer.

KOR Communiqué No. 6 of January 15, 1977, carried information about three new members of KOR: Anka Kowalska, Stefan Kaczorowski, and Wojciech Onyszkiewicz.

Anka Kowalska is a poet and writer. An editor in the publishing house PAX and recipient of the Pietrzak literary prize, she left the PAX association in March 1968 but kept her job in the publishing house. Upon joining KOR, she immediately began intensive work.

Stefan Kaczorowski is an attorney and former secretary-general of the Christian Democratic party. As chairman of the board of the capital's Labor party during the occupation, he took part in the Warsaw Uprising, and was a publicist and activist of Odrodzenie. He was the only committee member whose membership—initiated at the request of KOR associates of Christian-Democratic persuasion—was not preceded by a period of cooperation. Although KOR made no effort to try to represent a variety of political tendencies, such an enrichment appeared appropriate. Immediately upon receiving membership, Counselor Kaczorowski came from Łódź in order to make a formal motion for the exclusion of Jacek Kuroń from the committee on the grounds that Kuroń was a crypto-communist and a traitor, as evidenced by two ideas set forth in Kuroń's interviews and political writings: (a) the "finlandization" of Poland as a real and positive goal, and (b) an eventual understanding between society and Moscow, over the heads of the authorities of the PRL, guaranteeing that Poland did not wish, and would not seek, to harm the USSR. (At a later time Stefan Kisielewski advanced similar proposals.) The motion was not taken seriously. In March, Kaczorowski was among the first signatories of the document that created ROPCiO, and in September he left KOR.

Wojciech Onyszkiewicz is a historian and scouting activist connected with Black Troop No. 1 and with the Band of Vagabonds. He was among the organizers of KOR's team in Ursus, and later worked with the group editing *Robotnik.*

On May 1, 1977, immediately before his return to Poland, *Adam Michnik,* one of the founders of the committee, became a member of KOR. Michnik, a historian by training, was a worker in the Rosa Luxemburg Enterprises in Warsaw following his release from prison in 1969. For many years he initiated a variety of dissident actions. During his stay in the West in 1976–1977, he helped the committee with his tremendous propaganda work, and also published his well-known book, *The Church and the Left: A Dialogue,* which has been translated into several foreign languages.

Membership and Association with KOR

In order to understand the way KOR worked, it is necessary to know what membership in it entailed.

In the milieu from which KOR originated it was obvious that those who took public responsibility for activity conducted in the name of KOR could not remain simply the signatories on the statements issued but must also serve as the actual governing board of a broad social movement. As a result, membership was the only formalized aspect of KOR. The public had to know exactly who was signing declarations and appeals, who was collectively responsible for the funds, and so on. At the same time, KOR respected the principle that there should be no hierarchy among the members. This principle was taken so seriously that KOR had neither a chairman nor a secretary nor press spokesmen.[8] The fact that various foreign correspondents met most often with Jacek Kuroń and, on their own initiative, referred to him as a "KOR spokesman" (and could not be dissuaded from doing so) was a source of numerous misunderstandings and generated some dissatisfaction within KOR because of the principle of equality.

KOR's decisions and statements were arrived at through "circulation" or were adopted at meetings. In time, an editorial board was created, whose task was not only the preparation of statements and resolutions for the general meetings but also the drafting of those statements that had the character of interventions and referred to specific individual cases, without the political or ideological involvement of KOR. It was known, however, that the work of KOR was being done by hundreds and thousands of its associates from almost all social groups, who maintained and developed contacts, gathered information, distributed funds, organized self-education and discussion groups, edited the KOR press, printed on duplicating machines, collated and bound the publications, and distributed them. One special group of KOR associates was composed of lawyers who had the courage to risk such reprisals as a disciplinary suspension from the right to practice their profession to take the cases of workers from various parts of Poland—which often involved arduous travel as well—and who conducted the defense of KOR members and associates. In addition, there were associates who made their apartments available for meetings, for printing and bookbinding, for points of distribution, paper storage, and so on. There were those who copied KOR statements and communiqués, or made available their cars to transport lawyers and observers to trials, or to transport and distribute periodicals. It is impossible to list all the myriad forms of help, and even less possible to list all the people involved, especially since in addition to regular associates there were also occasional co-workers. The entire KOR milieu was aware that it was all these people who in fact did the work, while what was officially called KOR was the committee of an enormous social movement.

Since the ideology of this movement was a program of democratic change in Poland, the problem frequently arose of whether KOR should become a body of elected representatives, or an organization consisting of thousands of members who would choose their own committee of leaders. There were many obstacles, however, of which the most formidable was the difficulty of defining who was a member of the movement. A far-reaching formalization in this regard appeared undesirable, while total freedom to join would be dangerous. Another obstacle was the limited communication within KOR which, despite its overt character, nevertheless had to conceal certain aspects of its activities and the people engaged in them from the curiosity of the police. Moreover, one other fact—technical, but crucial—played an important role: any organizational reform, however it was designed, would have resulted in an increase in the number of members of KOR's governing committee, but this number was limited in fact simply by the size of the rooms available.[9]

The problem of the representative nature of KOR, or at least the problem of maintaining the flow of opinions and suggestions between KOR members and KOR associates, recurred constantly, and there was a general awareness that it was never really solved. One of the results of this state of affairs was that one could easily name as KOR associates as many persons as there were official members of KOR, and the role and influence of these associates in the work of the committee were so great that their absence from the list of members seemed surprising.

Informing Polish Society and the World

The establishment of the *KOR Communiqué* was one of the indispensable acts that assured KOR of the conditions necessary to its ability to function efficiently. *Communiqué* No. 1 is dated September 29, 1976. It carries no information about the creation of KOR, but starts instead *in medias res* with information about the extent of the aid given to the workers of Ursus and Radom, about the reprisals against those who had attended the open court proceedings, and news about the appeal to the Supreme Court in Warsaw by those workers sentenced in Ursus in July. Beginning with this first issue, the names of KOR members were listed together with their addresses and telephone numbers, and this became a permanent feature of the *Communiqué*.

The second necessity, no less important than the *Communiqué*, was to inform the outside world. Here it was necessary to overcome barriers of fear and prejudice, and this occurred gradually. While the publication of the *Communiqué* aroused fears of arrest (especially after duplicating machines were put into service), the passing of information abroad was taboo, and trying to inform the outside world about our problems was even more difficult. The official propaganda succeeded in convincing a large number of citizens that there was something suspicious and improper, like the proverbial washing of dirty laundry in public, about giving out such information. No one in KOR held this opinion, but the fact that it was shared by others acted as a constraint. The view that Poles abroad had the same right to hear about Poland and Polish affairs as we here at home came to be shared quite early, and from this came the practice of passing statements and more important information through all available channels, including monitored telephones, to the circle of friends from Aneks. Some time later, Jacek Kuroń broke through another barrier not only by talking with Western journalists accredited in Poland but also by calling press conferences (not to mention the many interviews he granted on his own, in which he also spoke of KOR).

With the publication of *KOR Communiqué* No. 1 and the transfer of the first documents and information about KOR to our friends abroad, the initiating actions drew to a close, and five long years of hard work amid constantly changing conditions and social moods had begun.

4
The Ethos of the Workers' Defense Committee

Within the realm of its effectiveness, the Workers' Defense Commmittee represented not only a specific idea of social action but also a certain style of action, which was refined gradually over the course of several years, although some of its characteristics were apparent from the very beginning.

Above all, KOR meant social and not political activity; this was a consequence of its initial assumptions, although they need not have been reflected in reality. Obviously, some members of KOR (such as Jacek Kuroń, Adam Michnik, and Antoni Macierewicz) were political activists above all, both in their temperament and interests. As a result it became necessary for them to distinguish their activities in KOR from their own political writings, for which they alone were responsible. Among the members and associates of KOR there were some who held well-defined political opinions, and others who were not particularly interested in politics, and whose entire political program could be reduced to the desire for sovereignty and democracy in Poland, with no attempt to specify the means of achieving these goals. Moreover, those KOR activists who did hold political opinions represented a variety of orientations and viewpoints. It was obvious that under these circumstances KOR could never have become a political party, but its conscious antitotalitarian attitude, together with its program in defense of moral and humanitarian values, created a broad base of understanding and an opportunity to gain public support.

KOR's dominant role was in the area of social work. What did this mean? Above all, it meant that KOR's primary interest was in real people who needed help: money, advice, legal or medical aid, a job, or sometimes simply moral support. It was necessary to find the time and the means to provide such help, even if this interfered with other activities. KOR activists were aware that the committee's work in this area was sometimes better and sometimes worse, but even among KOR members the rep-utation of the committee was determined by its performance in this area. At the same time, the work involved broader social interests that went beyond a readiness to offer help to individuals. As one example we might cite one issue of the *Information Bulletin* which could be described as a social monograph on Radom. The Radom team not only rendered actual help to specific individuals but also observed their lives, tried to under-stand them, and to draw conclusions about the living conditions and the needs of the people of Radom. The members of this team had been trained in a variety of professions; they were not only activists but also had a sociological calling. It is only when an individual attitude toward a specific person is combined with a broader sociological perspective that one can achieve a fully mature style of social work. In some dissident circles—in the Confederation of Independent Poland, for example—KOR members were sneered at as "social workers." Within KOR, such a designation by one's colleagues was regarded as an honor.

The special position of the KOR Intervention Bureau, which had dozens of associates, as well as of the earlier Radom and Ursus teams, bears witness to the dominance of this social work style in the committee. All of KOR regarded the results of the work of the Intervention Bureau as a legitimation for the entire committee. The situation was similar in other areas of KOR activity, where hard work and concrete results were always regarded with high esteem. Without them it was difficult to gain recognition in the committee. For example, in spite of his innovative ideas and his organizational drive, Jacek Kuroń would not have enjoyed such great respect among most of the committee's members and asso-ciates had it not been known that he also bore primary responsibility for the communications of KOR (externally and in part also internally), which was terribly hard work and meant the conversion of his apartment into a twenty-four-hour communications and information office, and occasionally even into a hotel. His wife Grażyna, one of the greatest and most heroic individuals in KOR, paid a heavy price for this commitment.[1]

The same criteria were used to evaluate other activists. But good intentions were also appreciated, and those who were sick or lacked the talent for social work were treated with indulgence. There was respect for the past contributions of older people who could not work so inten-sively because of their age.

At the same time, KOR imposed no work discipline as such. There was no question of ordering someone by command of the organization to do something he did not want to do. Since not all activities are equally attractive, there were occasions when volunteers had to be sought, while there were too many volunteers for other kinds of work, or when it became necessary to appeal to a sense of responsibility. As a rule, when people came to the committee to offer their help, they were able to work within the committee and the movement on those things which they particularly enjoyed doing, even when these were seemingly minor matters. Often the new people came with their own notions of what should be done. There was a principle that if what they wanted to do was not contrary to the principles of KOR, they should be allowed to pursue their own ideas. And this is why everything that was done was by people motivated by their own initiative and enthusiasm, and this produced the best results.

This principle, which could be called the principle of genuine autonomy of action, influenced the formation of the ethos of KOR and was also directly connected with one of KOR's most important strategic ideas: namely, that the long-range goal of KOR was to stimulate new centers of autonomous activity in a variety of areas and among a variety of social groups independent of KOR. Not only did KOR agree to their independence but also wanted them to be independent. Thus, the formation of such entirely independent institutions as the publishing house NOWa, the Student Solidarity Committees, and the others, were not in conflict with one another.

Also important for the atmosphere in the committee was its attitude toward the possibility that KOR might be infiltrated by the Security Service. Accordingly, it was more difficult to gain access to some kinds of work than to others. The rule of overtness could not be extended to the addresses of print shops and storage places, or to the files of those receiving help. Thus a certain degree of selection was necessary for those granted access to this kind of work. But basically KOR had a different recruitment policy. Anyone could present himself as ready to work. If one came with references from some trustworthy people, so much the better, but references were not required. KOR's doctrine was to trust everyone within the bounds of common sense. Apart from those instances of house searches and arrests in which the hand of an agent could clearly be discerned, any consideration of possible links between a KOR associate and the Security Service was inadmissible. These problems and approaches were formulated with particular clarity by Jacek Kuroń, who gained full approval for his position. There was agreement that in a movement such as KOR, an atmosphere in which everyone suspected everyone else would ultimately be more dangerous than the possibility of overlooking a few agents.

This approach passed the test. The milieu was infiltrated only to an insignificant degree, as became apparent especially at moments of crisis, for example during the Cracow demonstrations following the death of Stanisław Pyjas. There were episodes that can be attributed only to the activity of agents, such as the police forcing entry into a house near Otwock where a duplicator was in operation, or the discovery of a hiding place in the Romaszewskis' apartment. But such events were rare. In the first of these instances, KOR broke off all cooperation with the person involved; and in the second, since suspicions did not point clearly to any one person, investigations were concluded with a resolve to be more discreet.

In general, both the experiences of KOR and those groups prior to its formation have demonstrated that if certain basic principles of discretion are observed (something which is not always easy among a group of people who form a close-knit milieu), then despite modern means of surveillance, the Security Service will end up knowing only as much as someone will let slip, either directly or indirectly, through sheer stupidity. For this reason, every new associate of KOR underwent a brief training session in the *Code of Criminal Procedure,* which could be reduced to a single precept: one does not talk to the Security Service and one refuses to participate in interrogations. The *Code of Criminal Procedure* provides a rather detailed description of the various procedures prescribed in connection with forty-eight-hour detentions, interrogations, personal body searches, house searches, and the like. Because the Security Service has always had a tendency to disregard these rules, young people who were defending the workers were expertly informed of the regulations to be followed by the police and the SB. They also knew to demand that the regulations be followed, and to answer disregard of the rules with a refusal to give evidence.

At the same time, everyone knew—and later every KOR associate was required—not to answer questions about KOR apart from providing one's own personal data. In order to do this, one relied either on the informality of the interrogation (such as the lack of information concerning whether one were being interrogated as a witness or as a suspect, or the fact that no official record was being taken at the time, etc.). One could also refuse to answer by stating that the circumstances of detention made it appear doubtful that one were being interrogated as a witness, and that to the contrary, the person under interrogation felt, despite assurances by the interrogator, that he was being treated as a suspect, and as a suspect he had the right to refuse to give testimony. Finally, one could refuse to answer questions by citing Article 166, which provides for the right to refuse giving evidence if the person being interrogated fears criminal responsibility for his answers. This last method, though very effective, was used very rarely, and only by old hands, because to use it required breaking down the difficult psychological barrier involved in telling the interrogator that one had something to hide. In practice, nothing unfavorable would follow; nevertheless, the person under interrogation would feel strange when the investigating officer shouted in triumph: "And so you admit to being guilty!"

What had to be fought especially hard was the conceited idea that there was nothing to fear because an intelligent dissident would always be able to lead a stupid "cop" around by the nose. The reality was rather that the dissident was not always so intelligent, and the interrogator was usually not an idiot. The technique of not participating in any conversation at all during interrogations was not always easy to accept psychologically, especially for a novice, so that associates were constantly being drilled in its use. Usually this approach was successful, and it became something more than a rule in an unwritten code: loyalty toward the committee and toward one's colleagues was a matter of honor and good form.

This refusal to testify was one of the differences between KOR and many earlier movements (I am referring to the post-Stalinist period; before that, highly refined tortures had been used, so that the situations cannot be compared, although the history of KOR also notes cases in which beatings were used to extort testimony). Earlier, people inexperienced and untrained had given evidence under interrogation, bringing harm to themselves and others, even when they did not break down and were able to maintain a dignified posture, which involved above all the principle of not implicating one's colleagues. But whoever starts giving evidence will always say a few words too many, and very often does not know which information is important or new to the person conducting the interrogation. One must add that KOR was against giving false testimony, both on ethical grounds and because of the harsh criminal sanctions that could then be invoked. From the practice described above came the formula used in the *KOR Communiqués:* "attempted interrogation." This meant that the interrogated person had refused to answer questions.

The principles of discretion mentioned above also involved the directive: "don't wag your tongue," do not tell stories about actual KOR work, even among people you trust. Why should you? These principles of discretion, developed in the Home Army, were taught above all by Józef Rybicki, who explained that it was not a matter of mistrust or even of rationally applied caution, but of something more: one had to instill in oneself and in one's closest associates a feeling of responsibility for everything and everybody.

Discretion was the hardest thing to achieve, both because of the natural tendency against it shared by many, especially among the young (but not only among the young) associates, and also because KOR associates were supposed to spread the word about KOR and its activities to others, so that it was often difficult to draw a line between promoting the work of KOR and indiscretion. It was easier to subject oneself to the often bothersome rigors of silence about the specifics of KOR work in apartments suspected of being bugged (and basically all the apartments of known KOR associates were suspected), or of writing on a piece of paper that would be destroyed immediately, or discussing delicate matters during walks, far from possible listeners. After only a few weeks, not to mention several years, such behavior would become automatic, but it was always annoying, and—what was worse—it reaffirmed the sense that one was living under abnormal, crazy conditions.

A separate area important for the description of KOR was the issue of public money and of the committee's attitude toward it. The problems and principles of financing KOR are discussed elsewhere; here we are only concerned with the ethos. It is obvious that the money at KOR's disposal was considered a sacred trust that could be used only for its designated purpose. Conflicts first arose when it became necessary to ask whether this meant only for aiding those who had been wronged, or for the press as well. This seems to have been a manifestation of an excess of scruple. It was impossible to give aid, and gain support for it, without informing people and suggesting a course of action. It is, however, symptomatic that even here there were doubts. These doubts decreased with time, as people began giving money "for KOR," "for the free word," and so on, increasing KOR's freedom of action.

Financial accounting was based on statements by the payers of allowances, or persons who did the shopping, distributed papers, or accepted donations. It soon became clear that for the sake of effective work it would be necessary to reimburse people for their travel expenses. For many young people this was a difficult experience: they began to doubt their own disinterestedness. However, without reimbursement they would have had to limit their travels. After a while, KOR observed a disquieting tendency in the ease with which some people decided to take a taxi when a cheaper but more tiring means of transportation would have sufficed.

Just as KOR managed to avoid serious or deep penetration by the Security Service, so there were very few instances of—not so much embezzlement (there were only two instances of misappropriation of funds) as, let us say—reprehensible thoughtlessness in this area. Obviously, in these cases cooperation had to be broken off.

Certain difficulties emerged when NOWa and the periodicals connected with the KOR circle began paying for some basic work to assure that deadlines would be met and that work would proceed regularly. At the same time, this was a form of aid to those who had been proscribed by the authorities or thrown out of work. The question was raised as to why certain professionals were to be employed in publishing, while others traveling for the Intervention Bureau were reimbursed only for their travel expenses, and not always even for this. But things stayed this way until the end.

What about the issue that was picked up so eagerly by the police press: How was it that some of the members and associates of KOR were unemployed, yet still had money to live on? This stubbornly repeated question eventually began to worry people. In order for the question even to be asked, the person under scrutiny had to have been first thrown out of work. The answers varied: some lived from what they published, others painted walls, and still others relied on help from family or friends. All worked hard enough not to be considered parasites. The members of KOR received no allowances, loans, or salaries from KOR funds. The one exception occurred when KOR asked a member to stop earning his living by painting apartments, since he was indispensable to the work of the committee. This person received a modest salary from KOR for approximately half a year.

One important ethical principle adopted by KOR was that KOR did not lie. This principle also had a pragmatic basis and justification, to a greater extent even than the principle of renouncing violence and hatred: in a struggle with authorities who had especially compromised themselves when it came to telling the truth, it was better to renounce falsehood completely and gain confidence in this manner than to lay oneself open to the possibility that every departure from the truth could be blown up by the mass media. The charges by the official press and television that KOR was telling lies would remain without effect for only so long as the reader of KOR statements and communiqués could not himself detect any lies or misrepresentations on the part of KOR.

Two examples may serve as illustrations:

In one of its statements, KOR made public the name of a functionary of the Security Service whose description was thought to match that of the person escorting Pyjas when he was last seen alive. This functionary sued the editors of the *Information Bulletin* for libel. A verdict of guilty was pronounced, and KOR was required among other things to publish a correction in the press. At the same time, KOR decided that its publications would also print an apology, since the descriptions indeed failed to coincide in one important point. It was necessary to do this if the struggle for human dignity was not to become a hollow phrase.

The second example involves an automobile accident that took place as several KOR associates were returning from Cracow to Warsaw after the demonstrations following Pyjas's death. There were suspicions, based on the initial information, that the accident may actually have been an assassination attempt. The *Information Bulletin* quoted the statement of a witness who expressed the hypothesis that the car carrying the KOR people had been pushed off the road by a truck it had tried to pass. No further assertions were made, since later information reduced the probability of this interpretation. And yet *Perspektywy* seized on the topic and published an extensive report about the accident, quoting the testimony of the witness as proof that KOR was lying.

This principle of sticking to the truth without compromise was of great benefit to KOR; it preserved the movement from the distortions resulting from bluffing or mythomania. The same cannot be said for all dissident groups.

There were times when KOR and its press had to face the question of whether passing something over in silence did not violate the principle of truthfulness. This occurred during the periods of conflict with ROPCiO, and then with the Confederation of Independent Poland (KPN). KOR often used the tactic of silence in these instances, and with a serious justification: it was not just a question of imposing an "information blockade," but to a much greater extent of avoiding open conflict, which, by a mechanism well known in history, would have the effect of excluding more important issues from the dissident press. An open struggle could not have been avoided at this time if KOR had stated its position and vented its grievances in public, and this would definitely have happened were it not for the decision to remain silent about the conflict with ROPCiO and then with KPN. Nevertheless, this decision met with great resistance within KOR, especially among the young people. Their reproach was based on the idea that the tactic of silence amounted to a kind of lie, and that this made KOR's information comparable to official communist information. These arguments cannot be refuted completely. It is still difficult to say what choices should have been made at the time.

It is interesting to note that the principle of sticking only to the truth, suggesting nothing beyond what was actually being asserted directly, and refusing to color the facts or fill in gaps in information with empty phrases had a tremendous influence on the style of KOR communiqués. As a result of striving for precision without ambiguity, KOR developed a monotonous language that reminded one of a police report: a description of facts (details that pedantically placed the event in time and space, plus a selection of expressions adequate to indicate, when such information was available at all, that, for example, a blow had been struck with the palm of the hand, with a fist, the side of the hand, etc.), followed possibly by a brief account of the present state of affairs, ending with a conclusion usually accompanied by a demand or an appeal. Certain formulas and expressions were reiterated stubbornly and monotonously because they had taken on the meaning of technical terms, so that it became undesirable to replace them with synonyms. Perhaps a great writer, using these principles, might be able to produce a great work of Polish literature; unfortunately, the communiqués were always collective creations (and even if one person wrote them, the style was that of a collective), and thus they had to satisfy everyone, or perhaps in the end no one. Still, certain expressions were stylistically offensive (e.g., "x number of cases were included in information," which was supposed to mean that "x number of cases had been registered"). In this manner, a praiseworthy ethical intention gave birth to an unattractive language that the KOR young people jokingly referred to as "KORk-pistol" (*korkowiec*).

Renunciation of the use of force was a steadfast ideological principle of KOR. Thus, an agent who was uncovered risked nothing more than social ostracism. A spy was safe in a dark alley where a trap could have been awaiting him; a provocateur knew that his blow would not be returned. Only once, as Jacek Kuroń's apartment was being invaded by a goon squad of karate experts and other thugs from the Academy of Physical Education and the Union of Polish Students, one of those present was unable to restrain himself and returned a blow. This detail was singled out in the official media for repetition ad nauseam, while the invasion as a whole yielded two concussions, one heart attack, and several severe beatings. The general opinion was that the principle of nonviolence was not just a tactical rule, not just an expression of concern for the safety of KOR itself or an attempt to prevent further retaliation but the deliberate reflection of a conscious attitude.

This opinion was connected with the belief that if KOR had responded with hatred to beatings, arrests, provocations, and slanders, then it would have been doomed to failure, since hatred is self-destructive. Perhaps on no other issue did KOR exhibit so deeply the influence of Christian ethics.

KOR's sensitivity to this issue can be illustrated by a discussion within its milieu about reports published in the *Information Bulletin* concerning the trial of the chief administrator of the Office of the Prosecutor General, Witold Rozwens. During a period of intensive repressions against KOR, Rozwens had lied publicly about the committee. Some time later, while on a hunting trip, Rozwens, probably drunk, was shooting near some buildings at dusk and killed a peasant child. The reports in the *Information Bulletin* were nasty and aggressive, though they were very well written and did not distort the truth. It turned out, however, that a large number of KOR activists had doubts about whether the boundaries of the acceptable were not being violated through a demonstration of something like *Schadenfreude,* in an attempt to show the true nature of one who persecuted KOR. People asked whether this was not an expression of revenge and hatred against a man who found himself in a situation in which, despite everything, he deserved compassion—before the court. The principle of rejecting hatred, however, was not accepted without resistance. It was easier for the older people to accept than for the younger, and easier for the intelligentsia than for the workers (of course this is a very superficial statistic), although it seems that there were no differences in this regard between the attitudes of believers and nonbelievers.

In KOR and among its young associates one would almost never hear threats against the security men or the police, or meet with "speculation" about their fate when the communist system would collapse. On the contrary, one found an awareness that there might yet come a time of great testing, when one would have to take great risks in order to save a man, to protect him from revenge or even from lynching. This was a topic of many conversations, and I never encountered a single case in which a KOR associate expressed the belief that his place should be among those doing the lynching. At most, some believed that in such a situation they could allow themselves to remain passive from fear and to refrain from defending the person actively. There was no doubt that among the members of such a lynch mob there would be not one of those who today have the courage to fight for others who have been beaten.

In our social life, both the problem of attitudes of trust or suspicion, and the enormous complex of questions about the limits of forgiveness and about the right to judge others, are implicated in questions frequently raised about the proper attitude toward those who bear a common responsibility for Stalinism, who participated in the enslavement of the nation and society, or who were themselves, for a period of their lives, on the side of those doing the enslaving. KOR was criticized for the fact that among its members and associates were people who at some time in their lives had collaborated to various degrees with the Communist party, that is, with a totalitarian party. Conflicts and disagreements over this issue also occurred within KOR. Issues of ethical and political judgments were mixed here with disagreements about the interpretation of historical events, and with fundamental questions about the ability to alter one's views, or even one's mentality, about the limits of responsibility, about the subjectivity and objectivity of guilt. This is too broad and basic a problem to be addressed here extensively, and we must limit ourselves to a superficial characterization of the views on this matter.

At least theoretically, KOR adopted a general principle that not only mistakes but even evil done to another man should be forgiven. But by whom? Generally, the evil in question has been done to society, so that every member of society should have his part in the process of forgiveness. Obviously, people often added: forgiveness can be offered only under certain conditions. The condition of compensation for one's past is clear, but a person engaged in a struggle with evil is meeting this condition. The conscious recognition of someone's honest decision to reform is a matter of trust; and this varied. It seems, however, that the very fact of cooperation with KOR regulated this issue at least in part. Penance was not difficult to find in KOR, although it is likely that neither those involved nor their colleagues would be willing to accept this term and this presentation of the problem. When two comrades-in-arms are being beaten, it is difficult to say that for one it is a penance, the payment of a debt, and at the same time a credit or merit to another.

The most complicated problem was that of an honest admission of guilt. First: to whom should this guilt be confessed? To everyone? Then why does the Catholic Church, wise in these matters, believe that this is an issue to be taken up between the individual and God, although with the mediation of God's representative? Then again, public admissions of guilt are frequently demanded, and these demands are easy to understand. Conversely, resistance to such demands is also easy to understand: contrite repentance (if not before God) is generally not viewed with favor, and a moral compulsion to repent is difficult to accept, especially since the evil done to society by the Stalinists often seemed to be the result of a certain kind of madness, an illness that did not exclude good intentions. This was a complicated tangle of good intentions and self-deception, of knowledge and ignorance, of moral and intellectual madness and of a certain self-control over this madness. The evaluation of one's own guilt is often accompanied by the conviction, ex post facto but honest and justified, that the whole truth could be discovered only by revealing all the motives in all their ramifications, and that any other truth would be unfair to the person who is doing the accounting. This, however, makes understanding more difficult, since the plaintiffs are themselves among those who were treated unfairly, often pitilessly.

The author believes that it was a good thing that KOR did not try to resolve these issues in a general fashion or to pass judgments; although there did occur several clashes that were in some sense unavoidable and reflected problems pervasive in the society (and known to all societies that have endured a true totalitarianism, that is, one in which an ideology is truly alive). If the milieu was indeed fundamentally conditioned by Christian ethics, then there was probably some shared memory of the joy of finding one's lost sheep; or that Peter denied Christ three times out of fear; or that Saul, the oppressor of Christians, was rightly forgiven when he came to join them; or that only those who are themselves without sin have the right to cast the first stone.

A different but related problem was the attitude of KOR activists toward people from outside the movement—not to those who persecuted KOR or who were clearly sympathetic but to the rather large group of those in between, who did not want to get into trouble with the authorities (for a variety of reasons, not always out of opportunism), and who, in their search for an explanation to justify their attitudes, occasionally constructed intricate and twisted justifications compounded of a mixture of criticisms of KOR and of the opposition in general (sometimes valid, but often blatantly unfair), dubious attempts to excuse the authorities, and apologetics for their own contributions to the general good. The same modes of thinking would recur: (a) everything done by the opposition is grist for the mills of the hardliners in their struggle with the liberals; (b) because of this, one can find a hidden provocation behind every move of the opposition; and (c) the greatest good and the only strategy is to save (obviously for a price) various influential positions for enlightened and basically honest people. This problem was illustrated by one satirical cartoon that showed an executioner holding an ax and whispering to the condemned man: "You're lucky you got me—deep down I also cry 'Down with the King!'"

The heavy burden of self-delusion, opportunism, and often perfidy which accompanied these attitudes was unmasked by Piotr Wierzbicki, a gifted feuilletonist and satirist connected with the KOR movement, in his "Treatise on Ticks" and other writings. In a critique, Adam Michnik drew attention to the fact that it is too easy to label as "ticks" many people who should be attracted rather than rejected, and who in their jobs often played an indispensable role in society by defending actual cultural and scientific values, so that their presence in official life might be beneficial rather than harmful to society. Michnik also noted the dangers of what might be called "dissidents' conceit": "Whoever is not with us is against us," since only we are good and noble.

This discussion was a classic example of a necessary polemic in which both sides were right, but neither fully understood the arguments of the other. The phenomena that had angered Wierzbicki really did exist, but as Michnik noted, there were also real dangers in Wierzbicki's attitude.

This dispute was never resolved—in a sense it is an "eternal" question—but it was important to the formation of the ethos of KOR. It exemplified the possibility of two differing parties both being "right" in their expression of two actually existing attitudes (I should stress again that the actual differences were not as great as they might appear if one were to take literally the rhetorical exaggerations of both parties).

Not all the aspects and consequences of this dilemma can be described here. But one of these problems—strategic rather than ethical—needs to be mentioned. A movement like KOR could take one of two paths: it could either clearly separate the opposition from everything that was not distinctly oppositional and critical, in order to maintain the purity and consistency of the movement; or it could adopt a view of social life in Poland according to which there existed, between the poles of official authority and the opposition, a great number of intermediate positions forming almost a continuum and allowing for the constant expansion of the opposition toward groups and strata that were vacillating. This second approach made it more difficult for the authorities to destroy an opposition that was broadly extending its influence, even if only to a limited degree, throughout various areas of social life.

It seems that KOR never made a final choice between these two options.

The ethos of KOR was influenced by a variety of sources and traditions. First, it was a Christian ethos, which a decisive majority of the nonreligious members of KOR also adopted as their own. Years ago, before the creation of KOR, this attitude was described by Jacek Kuroń in an essay entitled "A Christian Without God," published in *Znak* (under the pen name Elżbieta Borucka). His far-reaching acceptance of the principles of Christian ethics, his rejection of ethical relativism and view of ethical values as if they were transcendent, and his refusal to make a distinction between the ethics of public life and the ethics of private life—all this made Kuroń into one of the most "Christian" of those who do not accept the Christian faith, and yet he was representative of his ideological milieu.

One must remember, however, that the entire sphere of macrosocial life—that is, the sphere that goes beyond the attitude of man toward his neighbors—is considered but little in the Gospels and the Acts of the Apostles; so that those who wish to apply Christian ethics to social life must make an effort of interpretation and adaptation. It is not surprising, for example, that Christianity was unable to state clearly that slavery is a sin.

Among today's ethical concepts there are many that refer to the sphere of public life, but we do not owe them to Christianity. I am referring mainly to the problem of enslavement, broadly understood as depriving another of his subjectivity in some aspect or area of life. In our culture, this tradition can be said to have developed alongside Christianity, only in the sense that it did not contradict Christian ethics. But it was created apart from Christianity, and even often against it, if Christianity is understood as the conservative institutions claiming Christian faith as their foundation, though *today* these problematics are deeply rooted in the Christian tradition.

Is the idea of democracy Christian? Yes and no. If democracy is understood as a concept of social life that minimizes the enslavement of the individual and maximizes his social subjectivity, then the idea of democracy should be considered Christian. But it was not always so.

Briefly stated, different ideas of a cultural milieu have enriched the Christian ethos for centuries; they have joined with it, creating a richer whole. Only those enrichments that did not contradict the foundations of Christian ethics turned out to be important.

One particular ethical tradition was developed by the Polish secular intelligentsia during the late nineteenth and early twentieth centuries. This tradition was consciously invoked by a large segment of the KOR milieu. It also became the source of vehement attacks against KOR, which was seen as an ideologically unified entity. This was a conscious abuse (and not the only such case) on the part of certain antagonists. Another such abuse, clearly addressed, was the misuse of the term "secular left" (from Adam Michnik's book *The Church and the Left: A Dialogue*) to refer not to a certain sociocultural formation but to a putative political group. This is as if one were to speak about a "Catholic right," uniting the fascist Bolesław Piasecki, the liberal Stefan Kisielewski, the democratic neo-nationalist Aleksander Hall and several other similarly chosen people into a group and then claiming they were engaged in a common conspiracy.

For a long time there has been a need to find a common ideological language for the Catholic and the secular parts of the same oppositional milieu or of related groups, in order to discover what they shared and to enable them to defend themselves more effectively together. This tendency was evident even during the Stalinist days, and became distinct in (for example) the Club of the Crooked Circle.

To a large extent, this need was met and the new union or alliance was given historical and ideological expression in Bohdan Cywiński's book *Genealogies of the Unsubmissive*. This work enjoyed tremendous authority and was very influential in the circles from which KOR originated. It also influenced their ethical consciousness by showing the harmony between Catholic and "secular" ethicosocial traditions in related currents of social work for the good of others and of the nation in a spirit of more than mere tolerance.

Patriotism and its world of values, together with the recent memory of World War II, the Home Army, and the Underground State, also played a large role in the formation of the ethos of the KOR milieu. The young people who came to KOR from scouting brought with them a specific experience of the patriotic tradition connected with the scouting organization.

Several times in the course of its activity KOR stated clearly that among its goals was the recovery of Polish independence. This topic was not discussed or written about daily. Even when KPN seized the opportunity to speak about this subject louder or more frequently, KOR behaved with a restraint that did not allow for intoxication with patriotic declarations. Reticence was not the only reason for this; there were other more substantive motives. I think that no one in KOR believed that the possibility of regaining full independence was near. Even at the price of lesser popularity, KOR left to the swindlers and the cranks all promises that if the nation would only lend its support, independence could be arranged right away, by the first of the month. What was important was to preserve in the nation—and especially among its young people—a will to "break through to independence," and yet at the same time not to encourage hopes and moods that would threaten the security of the country.

Nonetheless, KOR believed firmly that among the necessary conditions for any future independence were national reintegration and solidarity; a renewal of social ties both on a micro- and a macro-scale; and enormous educational work in all social strata, designed to deepen the knowledge of national, European, and world history, together with an understanding of the contemporary world; as well as work to assure ability to function in the future with democratic institutions. KOR knew that this was the real work for independence and democracy, that it was the most effective, and that it would not fail.

At the same time, KOR did not like patriotic pronouncements, or the overuse of the words "motherland" and "nation." It disliked patriotic props and the overuse of symbols: Polish crowned eagles, signs of Fighting Poland, or calendars of oppositional work which went from one glorious anniversary to the next, and so on. Perhaps because of this, KOR sometimes lost credit in the eyes of those who like this style of patriotic exhibitionism. Any characterization of the ethos of KOR must make very clear that patriotism in various forms, which was a general attitude, has nothing to do with nationalism and xenophobia, against which there existed a decisively and consciously negative attitude in KOR.

I would not be very astonished if the reader were to treat what has been said above with a dose of skepticism, or even express his surprise at this self-apologetic attitude on behalf of KOR. Among the readers there will also be some for whom KOR was a creation of the devil, so that by definition it did no good but only evil, and was guided not by ethical values but only by conceit and greed for power, or that (at best) it only served various factions within PUWP rather than serving society, the nation, justice, and so on. These readers are likely to be infuriated by this chapter; they may tear their hair, and suggest that—at the very least—its author should be stoned.

I would like to remind these readers that the title of this chapter contains the word "ethos," and that this word has been used fully consciously; that this was not a description of the moral state of individual

KOR members who, probably in contradistinction to their noble antagonists, on many occasions overstepped some of the provisions of the Ten Commandments—and not only of the Ten Commandments—because they are humans and not epitomes of moral nobility.

This has been an attempt to describe the general principles of action accepted within KOR, together with its moral atmosphere, which meant that we were not worse than we actually were and—what is more—we had the ambition and the good intention of becoming better. Thanks to this, what we accomplished as a group, despite all the faults and imperfections in our deeds, was better than most of us individually.

5

From the Founding of KOR to the Death of Pyjas
(June 1976–May 1977)

The Actions in Ursus and Radom

The Workers' Defense Committee started its actual work on July 17, 1976, when intensive activity began for the group that was later to be called the Ursus team. The fact that KOR was not established formally until September 23, 1976, made little difference. The Radom team also began working in September, but in this case the exact date is more difficult to determine.

While the work in Ursus was done primarily by "Black Troop No. 1" and the young people from KIK, the composition of the Radom team was more heterogeneous; the central roles were played by Zofia and Zbigniew Romaszewski, Krystyna and Stefan Starczewski, and Mirosław Chojecki. Chojecki was the informal head of the team at first, but following his move into publishing he was replaced by Zofia and Zbigniew Romaszewski.[1] Altogether there were dozens of KOR associates who took part in the Radom action at various times. Accidents sometimes played a part. Even before contacts were established in the corridors of the courtroom (on the model of Ursus), KOR had succeeded in contacting one of the persecuted Radom workers because a worker from Ursus had met him in jail and remembered his address. Coordinating the work of the various people and groups arriving in Radom was made possible because of chance social acquaintances of the Romaszewskis and because someone who was working in Radom "bumped into" Bogdan Borusewicz from the circle of the Gdańsk Academic Ministry.

It was necessary to gather as much information as possible from the people with whom contact had already been established. What course were the strikes and demonstrations taking? how had they started? had there been any attempts to form a strike organization? what was the actual sequence of events? how did the technicians behave? the party organization? the management? (there was little point in asking about the trade unions). When did the police intervene, and what course of action did they take? Who had suffered which injuries? What other reprisals were being used against the workers?

Did these new acquaintances know of others who had been beaten, detained, arrested, or dismissed from work? If they did, could they provide their addresses, or even better, go there together with one of the KOR members or associates, since this made contact easier and reduced the initial suspicions? Thus began the registration of people and the collection of testimonies concerning the course of the June events. It was often a thankless task: someone—whose identity is not exactly known to the interlocutor—proceeds to ask questions and take notes in the manner usually associated with policemen or functionaries or agents of the Security Service. The registration had to be detailed, since it would serve as the basis for the organization of aid, and also for the dissemination of precise, and if necessary, extensive information. It was not a matter of indifference when help was needed by a family with five small children whose father was in jail and whose mother had just left the hospital and had no job, and at the same time by a bachelor without responsibilities who had just gotten a new job.

Actual assistance began in just this manner. The Ursus team started with an ambitious program of unemployment compensation designed to match former salaries; this proved unrealistic almost immediately. The means were limited, after all; and differences in earnings were sometimes so blatantly unfair that even though the KOR action was not egalitarian (nor could it have been), these disparities would have been difficult to ignore. In addition, another issue quickly came to the fore: the average standard of living and the cultural level in Ursus were higher than in Radom, and this immediately raised new difficulties with the distribution of aid, since the two situations were incomparable from the start, even before the June events. This led to hectic attempts to establish some fairly objective criteria, or at least some general guidelines for the distribution of aid. As a result, several directives were adopted that can be reduced to a single rule: the basic criterion was the economic situation of the family, and this could usually, though not exclusively, be related to the number of children or other dependents and to the state of health of the family members. However, KOR also recognized that if there were two families in similar situations, but that in one of them the children's shoes were falling apart, then new shoes had to be provided even if this constituted a certain kind of "premium" for the family that was less adept at managing its finances. KOR was concerned with the immediate countering of the effects of police and economic terror, and not with long-term economic education or absolute justice. Who should presume to teach this economic lesson anyway? Twenty-year-olds from the families of the intelligentsia, who were usually not too well acquainted with the hard realities of life? Their task should rather be made easier, and they should not be required to make decisions that were beyond their strength and experience.

Those who received help were naturally reluctant to sign any receipts, and this became a serious problem right at the beginning. The organizers of the relief action faced a dilemma: should they refuse help where it was needed simply because of difficulties in control and documentation, or should they expose the action to the charge that it lacked supervision, which might also result in demoralization? Neither of these choices was acceptable. A solution was adopted in which the principle of trust would prevail over the principle of control. A file was created for those receiving help: it contained all the necessary data, and individual or family cards noted what aid had been given. The information provided by the KOR associates who delivered the funds had to be accepted as correct. In the course of the action it would often happen that one courier would have to be replaced by another (although it was wise to avoid this for security reasons), and there were other circumstances which at times made possible only an incomplete, random, or unplanned control. But not once was even the slightest suspicion raised that something had gone wrong.

Then there was another, moral problem: Was it an abuse to keep a file on people of whom a majority would probably not wish for such a file to be kept, especially since by its very nature this documentation constituted material for which the police were searching with particular interest? Despite such doubts it was impossible to forego the use of this technical tool, without which not only control but also any effective relief would have been impossible. Still, it was decided that the file should be protected with special care. In spite of hundreds of house searches and continuous surveillance, only once did several cards from the file fall into the hands of the police when they discovered a hiding place that had on many former occasions been overlooked.

Legal and Medical Aid

The equitable distribution of financial aid was a significant problem, but KOR adopted without hesitation the principle that not only all fines but also all legal costs associated with the court cases would be paid by the committee. These were not insignificant sums: in many cases these costs rose as high as 50,000 zlotys or even more.

In the case of legal costs, KOR, as far as was possible, tried to see to it that workers would have attorneys who, for ideological or humanitarian reasons, were unafraid to undertake their defense.[2] This was the origin of an informal group composed of a few brave lawyers, men of principle who accepted these cases without prior conditions in the full awareness that they would be defending clients not only against criminal sanctions but also against attempts to deprive them of their human dignity and honor. This small group was composed of Andrzej Grabiński, Witold Lis-Olszewski, Jan Olszewski, Władysław Siła-Nowicki, Stanisław Szczuka, and later Jacek Taylor from Gdańsk. When necessary, individual defenses were also conducted by other attorneys, mostly from Radom, who fulfilled their responsibilities conscientiously.[3]

One curiosity remaining from this period is a resolution adopted on January 22, 1977, by members of the Legal Council in Katowice, and by a number of directors and vice-directors, inspectors, and political activists as well: "The Bar of the province of Katowice, the daughter of the great industrial working class . . . wishes to separate itself from troublesome activity." This "troublesome activity" was the defense of the Radom and Ursus workers.

Even though the motives of the KOR attorneys were not financial but based on principle, the defense they provided still cost money. In Poland honorariums are paid not to individual attorneys but to their law firms. Every attorney is obliged to belong to such a cooperative and receives his salary according to a method of calculation that does not require analysis here. An attorney is not allowed to conduct a defense if payment has not been received by the cooperative, and any attorney who did so might become subject to disciplinary proceedings. Obtaining an exemption from such payments required a number of worrisome and basically ineffective procedures. And so, despite the disinterested idealism of the individual lawyers, these costs of defense still had to be paid. One should perhaps add that the acceptance of an honorarium in no way invalidates the disinterested nature of the defense: otherwise—if he were to work for free—an attorney who regularly represented defendants in political trials would himself be automatically condemned to death by starvation.

Attorneys were needed after the June events for more than defenses. Whenever a persecuted worker (or any other employee) loses his job, he is entitled to two appeals of the decision. KOR tried to encourage workers to avail themselves of this right and also paid the costs. Despite pressure from the police, there were instances, rather numerous if one considers the omnipotence of the police, when the labor court reversed its decisions ordering dismissals from work.

Medical aid was also organized. In Poland, an employee who has been punitively dismissed from work is deprived of medical coverage, together with his family. There were no instances when doctors refused their help, even when hospitalization was needed (these doctors were not always associated with KOR, although help was generally asked of doctors who were). In cases involving beatings it was especially important that the victim be examined by a doctor and receive a certificate that could later be introduced as evidence against the police, or as a basis for claims of compensation. It was very rare for a doctor to refuse to provide such a certificate out of fear of the Security Service (although such cases did occur).

KOR provided information to the then Minister of Health and Social Services, Marian Śliwiński, about the fact that workers dismissed from their jobs after June were deprived of medical care, and KOR asked him to remedy this situation in a spirit of social justice and humanitarianism. The letter written on behalf of KOR was sent by Edward Lipiński, the Nestor of Polish science; but in keeping with current tradition in the Polish People's Republic, Lipiński never received an answer. Similarly, the chairman of the Polish Red Cross, the Polish Committee on Social Welfare, and the Society of Friends of the Child also ignored all appeals for help. Worse yet, neither the Minister of Health and Social Services nor the other officials ever did anything in this matter.[4] The Society of Friends of the Child did provide some aid in Ursus, but since KOR was not aware of such help in other locations, it was probably the initiative of the local activists.

The Achievements of KOR Before the Actual Formation of the Committee

When *Communiqué* No. 1 appeared on September 29, 1976, fairly large teams of volunteers had already been working for some time to provide help to the persecuted workers. KOR cited the following statistics in the first *Communiqué:*

In Ursus, 126 persons subjected to reprisals have been registered by name. Of these 19 were convicted by courts; 13 were under investigative arrest; 59 were convicted by sentencing boards for misdemeanors; 32

were "merely" dismissed from their jobs;[5] and 3 had been released. Aid was also being given to 67 families (or individuals). Approximately 139,200 zlotys had been spent. In Radom the assistance started only around the tenth of September, but already 70 persons subjected to reprisals have been registered by name. Of these, 44 were convicted by courts; 7 were under investigative arrests; 13 were convicted by sentencing boards for misdemeanors; 6 were "merely" dismissed from their jobs. Aid was being given to 30 families (or individuals). The numerical ratio between Ursus and Radom was soon reversed.

These data were proof to the public that the circle of people who had taken the initiative of coming to the aid of the workers and had appealed to society for the means to make this action possible, was capable not only of a courageous protest but also of real action. The position of a group asking for assistance becomes different when it is clear that the group has begun doing something specific.

The Struggle with the Security Service for Openness of Court Proceedings

It is difficult today to say just when the teams of young people who went to Ursus to bring aid to the persecuted workers were first noticed by the Security Service. It is conceivable that this may not have happened immediately. The idea was a new one, so police vigilance in this area may have been nonexistent. Among the persecuted to whom KOR activists were directed by friends and neighbors, there were probably no agents or informers. And so, in the beginning, the action developed without meeting any special obstacles.

The first reprisals were directed against the observers of the trials taking place in Radom. On September 16, after one of the trials for participation in the June demonstrations, the police stopped six people in the court building: Ludwik Dorn, Zofia Krajewska, Jan Tomasz Lipski, Antoni Macierewicz, Stanisław Puzyna, and Zofia Winawer. The men were handcuffed and all six were taken to the provincial headquarters of the police. According to *Communiqué* No. 1, "they were subjected there to attempts at informal interrogation."

It was obvious that the interrogation was in contravention of the Code of Criminal Procedure in almost every respect (for example, it took place at night), including the most important one—one of the detainees, Ludwik Dorn, was beaten and choked. It was evidently no accident that he had been singled out for the beatings: the *Communiqué* adds that

"L. Dorn was reviled with anti-Semitic invectives." Thus, alongside one of the motifs of the history of KOR—beatings—we find another in anti-Semitism, which for five years was constantly invoked in the war against the committee.

Thus the first battle between KOR and the Security Service was a battle for the right of observers from the committee to take part as members of the audience in the trials of the workers of Radom.

During KOR's second trip to Radom (Ludwik Dorn, Grażyna Jaglarska, Antoni Macierewicz, and Marek Tomczyk), there was another detention and two beatings this time: Dorn and Tomczyk were beaten in the provincial headquarters of the police.

Ludwik Dorn was beaten in a particularly refined manner, with a rubber truncheon on the heels, which is extremely painful and may injure spinal reflexes. KOR, which existed officially by this time, decided not to allow Dorn to travel to Radom, at least in the near future, because of concern for his health and even his life. This was one of the rare cases in which the committee forbade someone to participate.

On October 1, during the third trip to Radom (Jan Józef Lipski, Jan Tomasz Lipski, and Antoni Macierewicz), there were again detentions and threats of interrogation, body searches were conducted which involved stripping off all one's clothes, and those detained were menaced with clubs by the policemen present. During the fourth trip, however (Antoni Macierewicz, Antoni Pajdak, and Wacław Zawadzki—these last two distinguished activists advanced in years), the group returned from Radom without problems.

"Unknown Perpetrators": Radom, Fall and Winter 1976

The campaign for the right to observe the trials had basically been won, but it happened just a short time later that this was not to be the end of the story. While sporadic detentions were still occurring and the court had forbidden observers to make notes during the trials, the main effort of combatting KOR observers was transferred to "unknown perpetrators."

The trips to Radom were made in a variety of ways: by train or bus, or occasionally by private car. Several times Halina Mikołajska not only served as an observer but also transported the entire team in her car. The automobiles used for this purpose were repeatedly damaged by "unknown perpetrators": the air would be let out of the tires, or the tires slashed or punctured, or there were break-ins, or worse, the cars were tampered with in a way that could cause an accident. The Radom police were indifferent to all these exploits, which were usually performed in broad daylight in front of the court building in the midst of heavy traffic. But occasionally there were also moral rewards: the first time Mikołajska's car was towed to the repair shop in Radom, the famous actress, who had appeared only recently on television, was immediately recognized. Her car was taken out of turn and repaired, and payment was refused with the explanation that, after all, everyone knew why she had come to Radom, and in the future the repair shop would be at her service and that of her friends.

Unknown perpetrators were set against Mirosław Chojecki, who was twice beaten in addition to many detentions. The first beating was basically a symbolic warning, although painful: late one evening Chojecki was pushed into a passageway and received several hard blows and jabs, that was all. But on December 30 in the court building in Radom he was surrounded by a large group of unknown perpetrators, and beaten and kicked; a professional butt in the face resulted in a subcutaneous hemorrhage over half of his face.[6] Finally an attempt was made to throw Chojecki down a flight of steep and high stairs. Although stunned, he managed to save himself with a daring jump and escaped. The incident lasted a good while. The police, however, though always present during this period in the corridors of the Radom court building, turned out to be unavailable despite the fact that witnesses to the event were screaming for help, and the attorney, Andrzej Grabiński, was banging on the door of the policemen on duty, demanding intervention. On the same day, two Radom workers who tried to defend Chojecki, KOR associates Józef Szczepanik and Ryszard Figura, were also beaten.

A larger action against KOR was organized on January 10 in the court corridors. Ten KOR observers were present on that day. During a court recess, a large group of unknown perpetrators began shouting insults at the observers and the attorney Władysław Siła-Nowicki, and then began throwing eggs. (Let us note parenthetically that at that time eggs were unavailable in Radom.) This circumstance provoked additional hostility among the bystanders ("There are no eggs for the children, and these guys here are breaking them!")—but this was expressed only in shouts of indignation. There was a large quantity of eggs—luckily the initiator of this action probably had trouble finding rotten ones—and both the KOR observers and the attorney were dripping with them. But the aggressors did not stop with eggs: Jacek Kuroń was struck in the face and received several hard kicks. Attorney Siła-Nowicki attempted to fetch the police but to no avail, since the policemen from the local precinct had locked themselves in their office and did not respond to knocks on their door. At this moment Siła-Nowicki decided to lead the group under attack into a courtroom in which a case having nothing to do with the June events was in progress. And so, eggs began flying across the courtroom and landing in front of the judge's bench.

This was too much for the Radom judges. The outraged chairman of the Provincial Court demanded by telephone that the police intervene, and ordered the postponement of all cases scheduled for that day. The unknown perpetrators disappeared without a trace, without being stopped by anyone, and two hours later two policemen appeared. Gradually it became possible to establish the indentities of several members of this goon squad, who had been recruited from among activists of the party and the Voluntary Reserves of the police (ORMO). As we learned later, the aggressors had been rewarded with gift certificates of from 500 to 1500 zlotys.

These events had an unexpected ending. The attorneys Andrzej Grabiński, Ewa Milewska (from Radom), and Władysław Siła-Nowicki filed formal complaints with the prosecutor about the assaults against them in the Radom court building. On May 17, they were informed that the proceedings had been dropped "in view of the minimal social harmfulness of these acts."

From then on, it seemed things had quieted down in the Radom court buildings, and the fight for the presence of observers at the trials had been won. But during the last period of trials, in April 1977, problems again appeared. On April 22, Mirosław Chojecki and Bogusława Blajfer were detained at the bus station in Radom for what eventually amounted to forty-eight hours. On April 28, Halina Mikołajska (who was driving), Anka Kowalska, and Wacław Heinrich were stopped on the road to Radom near Białobrzegi and had to spend seven hours at the local police headquarters there, which obviously made it impossible for them to attend the trial. These were the first signs of a new storm.

In the Courts

A large number of the participants in the June demonstrations detained by the police or the Security Service were tried in the courts. The word *court* is used here in the colloquial sense of the term, since many of the workers were sent to jail by Sentencing Boards of Misdemeanors. There may be a few Polish citizens who are convinced of the independence of the courts, but these sentencing boards are commonly treated as a farce, a mockery of justice.

But even the regular courts bear only a distant resemblance to similar institutions in law-abiding countries. The manner in which the courts are treated in Poland is exemplified by the fact that on February 3, 1977, during a meeting with party activists of Ursus broadcast by radio and television, Edward Gierek spoke explicitly about his instructions to the courts (which were never made public, and thus were secret), despite the fact that Article 62 of the Polish Constitution asserts that "Judges shall be independent and subject only to the law." In reality, judges are nominated and it is always possible to remove them from office. A judge who is insubordinate to the party and the administration quickly ceases to be a judge. Judges known for their submissiveness are specially chosen for political trials. The normal practice is that whenever an unexpected situation arises, the court orders a recess, not in order to deliberate but to ask for instructions by phone. Investigations are conducted either by the police or by the Security Service, under the formal supervision of the prosecutor's office, which prepares the indictment. The position of investigating magistrate is unknown in Poland. Attorneys who meet their responsibilities independently are subjected to disciplinary proceedings under any pretext. This method had been used on many occasions against defense attorneys in political trials, and against other attorneys when the Security Service was involved. The profitability of the courts constitutes another curiosity of the Polish system of justice: high fines and arbitrary determinations of court costs influence the evaluation of judges, which is conducted by their superiors from the point of view of financial effectiveness.

Apart from rough estimates, little can be said about the role of the sentencing boards in connection with the events of June 1976, since they sentenced the workers before KOR began its activity. It is known that they complied with their instructions and were uninterested in the visible signs that the accused had been beaten. But the courts, and more generally the "justice system" and the battles waged in the courts at that time, all constitute an important chapter in the history of KOR.

First, it was obvious that it would be utterly impossible to prove that a large percentage of those tried and sentenced had ever had anything to do with the demonstrations on June 26. How was this possible? Well, it turned out that it was possible. This was an idea that probably originated in the Security Service, but perhaps even higher in the apparatus of power.

Whenever workers protested in Poland, the version of the events provided by the party-government propaganda was always the same: the demonstrations did not have a working-class character, but amounted rather to hooligans' brawls (a terrifying vision of tens and even hundreds of thousands of hooligans) incited by criminal elements and people from the fringes of society, including derelicts, alcoholics, and parasites who did not work anywhere. If any workers were present, these were the bad workers who, in addition, had been duped by Radio Free Europe. Obviously such riots had to be accompanied by burglaries and acts of vandalism. However, this line of propaganda was never very effective. After the massacre on the coast in 1970, the television and all the press in Poland showed a picture of a young man who was supposed to have looted something from a demolished store, and to have escaped, it seems, to Puławy, where he was caught. Given the scale of the events, this is indeed a meager harvest (not to mention the fact that we still do not know whether it actually occurred).

One must add that certain practices well known in the PRL are immediately employed on such occasions: once a person has been convicted of something, he is regarded by the police as their property, and on various future occasions he will be accused of new crimes regardless of whether any material proof exists. In this manner the police improve their statistical record of detecting criminals, and it also happens that such false accusations are frequently brought about by a refusal to function as a police informer, or by some other act of insubordination. As a rule, the courts convict the accused as a recidivist without going deeper into the matter. This was the propaganda trick that would be used in Radom and a number of trials were prepared systematically with this tactic in mind. The selection of the accused was designed to compromise the underlying social causes of the protests of June 25.

First, even during the arrests, those who were caught were forced to pick up from the street (or sometimes even in police headquarters) objects taken from the demolished stores, and this was done solely for the purpose of making photographs. There were so many independent reports about this practice that it is impossible to treat them all as a coincidence.

Second, a new wave of arrests occurred in Radom three weeks after the events. The key to these arrests was the police records of people convicted in the past for minor misdemeanors, or even more serious crimes. On this occasion those newly arrested were charged by the police with certain criminal acts committed on June 25. If these lovely methods of applying the law are to work, it is also necessary to extort evidence from defendants by means of interrogations. The accused from Radom and Ursus complained to the court on many occasions about being beaten and tortured, while at the same time retracting their depositions. At these moments the court became deaf. But not always.

From July 17 to July 19 one Ursus worker, Mirosław Chmielewski, who was being tried with others for blocking a railroad line, testified extensively in court about beatings he had received during the investigation. The Provincial Court in Warsaw paid no attention, and sentenced Chmielewski to five years of imprisonment. On September 27, however, the Supreme Court announced that the prosecutor's office would launch an investigation into the beatings, and Chmielewski's prison term was reduced to a suspended sentence of one year with three years probation. It would be naive, however, to believe that this investigation was ever conducted. In Poland, the Supreme Court is a weak institution, too weak to be taken seriously by the prosecutor's office, not to mention the Security Service.[7]

Complaints about beatings during pretrial investigations were raised during another Ursus trial that was held in the Provincial Court in Warsaw on December 29, 1976. Two of the three accused Ursus workers, Marek Majewski and Adam Żukowski, gave testimony about having been beaten during the investigation. This influenced the sentences they received—three years—whereas their colleague, accused of the same act and on the basis of the same material evidence, was given a suspended sentence of one year with three years probation. This was the first trial in this case, and it had been long delayed. The reason for the delay was that Majewski spent three months in the prison hospital because his jaw had been broken in two places (it was intact at the moment of his arrest). Neither the court nor the prosecutor was interested in this circumstance. The Supreme Court upheld these differentiated sentences.

One especially important fact also needs to be emphasized here: the principle of collective responsibility was applied against the accused. Every indictment from the Radom trials contained the following phrase: "on June 25 in Radom the accused, acting in a hooliganish manner, took part in a public gathering whose participants jointly committed violent assaults against public functionaries and installations of the socialized economy, causing, as a consequence of this assault, bodily harm to seventy-five functionaries of the MO and losses of public property in the amount of more than 28 million zlotys." In order to gain a conviction it was enough to prove (and this usually was "proven") that the accused had taken part in a gathering (that is, to find a witness who would testify that he had seen the accused in the crowd, regardless of what he might have been doing there). Mirosław Chojecki, who observed many Radom trials, stated in his report that the presentation of evidence usually amounted only to proofs of this kind.[8]

The effects of the "violent assaults" in Radom constituted another problem. The indictments listed the names of seventy-five victimized functionaries of the police together with a description of the injuries they had suffered. Eight of these cases were described as serious. It is, however, difficult to attribute direct responsibility for the burns to both hands of policeman Antoni Adamowicz to any particular person, although these burns were probably connected with the fire in the Provincial Committee or on one of the street barricades. The traumatic injury to the right knee of Officer Józef Mózg might have been a direct result of the disturbances, and the same could be said even more surely about the concussion suffered by Dariusz Krajewski; but the rest of the list is composed of such injuries as indigestion, or a susceptibility to neurosis, or a blue mark on the wrist.

Another list in the indictments names the institutions that suffered damage. It is strange that the building housing the Provincial Committee of PUWP which had been set on fire is not named on this list, and figures there only as "one of the buildings."

The testimony of a single witness-policeman, whether uniformed or in plainclothes, was enough for the court to decide on the guilt of a defendant. Such testimonies were regarded by the court as unassailable, even then they contradicted one another. This must be understood as one of the mysteries of Marxist dialectics. The trustworthiness of a policeman's testimony was not impugned by the fact that during one of the previous trials he had testified about events taking place at the same time, but in a different part of Radom, when he had observed happenings at two distant places at the same moment in time; or when, in the same case, his testimony during the investigations differed from that during the trial; or when he testified in different trials that a number of different defendants had each been attempting separately to strangle him at precisely the same time; or when successive witnesses testified in a series of trials that the very same glass case had been thrown to the ground by a series of different defendants; or when several different defendants had forced their way through the same door, and every one of them was the first to emerge. The battle cry: "Give me some fire, I will burn these communists," supposedly shouted by a leader of the crowd storming the party headquarters, turned out to be a request mumbled by a drunkard to his neighbor, a policeman, as they stood before the building where they both lived: "Give me a light! I hate you communists!" Such revelations made no difference during the trials. In the courtroom, the leader of the hooligans storming a building turned out to be a retarded man barely able to mumble answers to questions, probably the only resident of Radom who did not know what was happening in the city on June 25, since from early morning onward he lay completely drunk on a lawn in the middle of a busy street. In the courtroom it was clear that he understood only that some injustice was being done to him.

None of this mattered to the judges. In order not to complicate its work, and so as not to raise questions about the testimony of the policemen-witnesses, the court did not allow the testimony of witnesses for the defense. In the best of cases, the police were unable to locate the witnesses. The prestige of the police was at stake. So it is not surprising that there were such curiosities as a nine-year prison sentence given to Ryszard Grudzień, who, as the result of an accident suffered at work ten days before June 25, had a broken right arm (in a cast from his shoulder to the middle of his fingers), two broken ribs, and a sprained left shoulder joint. Yet, according to witnesses, none of this prevented him from throwing stones, destroying property, and brutally attacking policemen. The cast was not taken off until July 5.

It must be said that matters looked rather better in Ursus from the point of view of legal procedures and evidence. There, some material evidence was sometimes available: for example, pictures taken from a helicopter played some part in the trials of those accused of cutting the tracks and derailing a locomotive, although the identification of individuals might raise many doubts.

One further characteristic of these trials was the almost general rule that the court attributed "hooliganish motives" to all the accused. In Polish law this refers to criminal acts or misdemeanors committed for *no reason* or for *trivial* reasons, and moreover this in itself might constitute grounds for increasing a sentence by half. In this manner the workers' demonstration was evaluated entirely as a mammoth act of hooliganism, committed for no reason, "just for the hell of it." It is also worth noting what kinds of sentences were handed down to participants (or supposed participants) in the demonstration whose specific actions were punished in a manner that was particularly severe.

Zygmunt Zaborowski was allegedly the first to enter the building of the Provincial Committee of PUWP (in other trials, Kobyłko, Skrzypek, and Chomicki shared the honor of being "first"). Zaborowski was supposed to have broken windows and destroyed the interior (one of the witness-policemen stubbornly maintained that Zaborowski had not broken any windows, but the testimonies of policemen were decisive only when they went against the accused). He was also supposed to have torn down the flag. No attempt was made to establish when, or under what circumstances, he had committed the acts with which he was charged. Sentence—10 years.

The *Mitak* brothers—*Tadeusz* (age 20) and *Wojciech* (18) were, according to the testimony of policemen, supposed to have destroyed the car of the first secretary of the Provincial Committee. Sentences: 8 years and 6 years, later reduced by the Supreme Court to 6 and 4½ years in consideration of the ages of the accused.

Tomasz Mitak (age 19), who suffered from a nervous condition and, judging by various circumstances in the case, did not leave his house at all on June 25, was convicted on the basis of testimony by policemen who spoke in the plural about "the Mitaks."

Henryk Bednarczyk (21) was arrested, if one is to believe the records of his case, for offenses in three different places in Radom, although it is not clear that these occurred in Radom. The records of his case contain a medical statement describing injuries to the head and other signs of beatings. During the investigation Bednarczyk admitted everything, but he retracted his testimony during the trial. The court decided that it was not worthwhile to examine the witness he called. He was sentenced in Radom to 4 years in prison; the Supreme Court ordered a retrial.

Wiesław Kobyłko (27) was not only another "first" to storm the committee building but was also accused of demolishing a kiosk inside the building in spite of the fact that someone else (Gniadek) had already been convicted of this act. Sentence: 8 years.

Stanisław Kowalski was convicted for entering the committee building and there throwing a bottle of Coca-Cola against a wall. In the first trial he received a sentence of 3 years; the Supreme Court gave him a 2-year suspended sentence.

Bohdan Borkowicz (22) was given 6 years in prison for throwing stones at the committee building and for using vulgar language. Police officer Majak, who was supposed to have seen him outside the building, testified in a different trial to being inside the building observing another defendant (Zaborowski) at exactly the same time. Another policeman, Opolski, also saw Borkowicz, but in a different case this policeman claimed to have witnessed events that were taking place at the same time in front of the Provincial Headquarters of the police. The court did not allow the testimony of witnesses called to confirm an alibi for Borkowicz by testifying that at this time he had been somewhere else entirely. The Supreme Court upheld his 6-year sentence.

Wacław Skrzypek (49), suffering from tuberculosis, was another "first" person to storm the committee building. Once inside, he was supposed to have broken a window with the leg of a chair, broken a telephone, and sat drunk on a rug (!). This cost him a 9-year prison sentence.

Czesław Chomicki (21) received a 9-year sentence in a situation in which he claimed that not only did he not take part in the destruction but helped to extinguish a fire together with a friend who was neither arrested nor accused (his story was confirmed by the testimony of policemen). The court claimed that it would not hear the testimony of his friend, since he was probably in hiding.

Wiesław Długosz (21) was given a 9-year prison term, reduced to 4 years by the Supreme Court, for participating in the demonstration, shouting, stopping traffic, and lying down in the street. His mother took him away from the scene before the demolition of the committee building had begun.

Waldemar Gutowski (21) was charged and sentenced to 4 years (the Supreme Court reduced the sentence to 2 years) for beating Police Major Palka during the (unsuccessful) storming of the Provincial Headquarters at 5:00 P.M. The fact that police records of detention and body search indicate that he was already under arrest by 3:00 P.M. made no difference.

Marian Janicki (28), suffering from tuberculosis, was supposed to have been breaking windows, using vulgar language, and shouting "Red bourgeoisie!" Sentence in Radom: 5 years; in the Supreme Court: 3 years.

And so on and so on. It would be possible to compose an entire book out of such materials. Today, years later, this would be easier to do about those convicted for demonstrations in Radom than in Ursus, not because the Ursus trials were different from those in Radom (with the exception of the trials of those accused of destroying or blocking railroad lines), but rather because KOR assembled a richer and more exact collective record for Radom than for Ursus, and the author does not have access to court archives.

A future historian of the June events, especially in Radom, will have to solve a number of puzzles. There are many indications that police informers were among those convicted in Radom. Their convictions, and the occasionally high sentences they received, can be attributed either to the fact that at a crucial moment they went over to the side of the crowd, or perhaps to some settling of internal accounts within the police force. But since we have only circumstantial evidence in this case, this topic must be left to future investigators, and we can only note that the problem does exist.

The Trial for the Murder of Jan Brożyna

The murder of Jan Brożyna (twenty-eight years old) occupies a special place in the history of the Radom trials.

The exact number of those who lost their lives in connection with the June events in Radom is still an open question. By "June events" we must understand not only June 25, the day the demonstration occurred and was quelled by the police and the Security Service, but also the following days, during which the police in the streets of Radom behaved as if they were patrolling a conquered and occupied city; or perhaps even the three following weeks, which ended with a great manhunt ordered for the purpose of enriching the lists of those under arrest with others who already had criminal records.

Jan Brożyna died during the night of June 29. That night, two police functionaries brought him to the Radom drunk tank after he had been severely beaten. The doctor who registered him recorded only an "alcoholic intoxication and a black eye," a lie, as revealed by the death certificate. Jan Brożyna died a couple of hours later as a result of the injuries he had suffered. Dr. Fundowicz, who conducted the autopsy, stated that "The character of the traumatic injuries indicates that they could have arisen from the use, most probably by another person, of a blunt and smooth object, narrow and elongated. . . . There is no basis for supposing that the injuries evident in the corpse could have been the result of a fall from a high place. . . . The rupture of the spleen was not the cause of death; this rupture resulted most probably from a blow with the described object, or from a kick."

Who injured Brożyna this way?

From the very beginning it was obvious that the authorities officially charged with investigating crimes, of which murder is the most serious, were interested in only one thing: preventing the truth from being discovered. It is very likely that Brożyna was indeed drunk that evening or night. However, the general state of his health was not such that this alone would explain his death, nor did anyone propose such a hypothesis.

The issue of the injuries described in the death certificate remained. One could accept—giving credence to the statement by the doctor who admitted Brożyna to the drunk tank—that he suffered his injuries while he was in this institution. Anyone who knows life in the PRL knows that this is probable. But there were witnesses who claimed something else.

From the very beginning, Janina Brożyna, the wife of the murdered man, refused to believe the official version. When she discovered that the police had brought her husband in from Koszarowa Street, she conducted her own investigation. She located the address from which her husband had been taken to the drunk tank, and she talked with the people who lived there. She found some who had seen during the night a police patrol beating and kicking with great vehemence a man who was lying down. What was more, these people were prepared to testify to what they had seen. After a consultation with KOR, Janina Brożyna filed an official complaint about the murder committed against her husband.

What followed next happens as a rule in Poland. It can be formulated as follows: "Whoever files a complaint in the Prosecutor's Office asserting that he has been beaten by a policeman (or policemen) will be in turn accused of assaulting a policeman; a similar fate awaits the witnesses of a police beating who are willing to testify to the innocence of the person thus condemned by the police." If there are such things as laws that effectively regulate social life, the above formulation is a good example of one such law.

On March 25, 1977, Wiesława Skórkiewicz was arrested together with two men, Roman Piasecki and Stanisław Nowakowski. A short time later, Stanisław Ejmowski was also arrested, though he was accused only of giving false testimony. These persons, of their own free will, had announced their willingness to testify and had provided internally consistent testimony about the circumstances of Brożyna's death. This was the only evidence capable of explaining the findings of the autopsy. It was not the police who had expressed interest in these people; rather they were located by Janina Brożyna, and they suffered misfortune as a result. Their arrests were an unequivocal act of self-defense on the part of a powerful institution that identifies its own interests with the impunity of its employees.

The treatment of Janina Brożyna during the investigation was typical. The main subject of interest to the police during her interrogation was her contacts with KOR and with the relief action. During one of the interrogations she was warned that if she continued to be concerned with the case of her husband's murder, she would never see her children again. For several months she lived under constant and overt surveillance, which led her to the brink of a nervous breakdown. On June 16, 1977, the police conducted a search of her apartment, "looking for stolen goods," which was obviously unsuccessful. On the same day, similar searches were conducted in two apartments of her relatives. It was clear that no one in the prosecutor's office or the police was interested in establishing the true cause of Brożyna's death. Their task was rather to bring about the ruin of his wife and to get rid of the witnesses.

This was accomplished in classic style: the witnesses to the act were accused of having committed it. Nowakowski and Piasecki, together with Wiesława Skórkiewicz, had supposedly thrown Brożyna out of a window (although it was unclear why they should have done such a thing), thus causing his death. It did not matter that someone thrown from a window could not possibly have suffered injuries such as those inflicted on Brożyna. The obliging expert in the field of forensic medicine, Prof. Zdzisław Marek from Cracow, existed for just such cases.[9] But even he did not understand what was needed at first. He stated on December 7, 1976, in agreement with Dr. Fundowicz, that he doubted that a fall from a window could have caused Brożyna's death, and he only expressed the suspicion that Brożyna might have suffered his injuries in a place distant from where he allegedly fell (thus shifting responsibility from the police to "unknown perpetrators"). By July 27, 1977, he had changed his mind and acknowledged that the cause of death was indeed a fall from a second-story window.

During the main trial in Radom on December 7, 1977, there appeared not three, but only two defendants. In the course of the investigation, Nowakowski had given extensive evidence and accused Skórkiewicz and Piasecki. As a result, the investigation against him was dropped and he became the chief witness for the prosecution. Nonetheless, he was not released from jail. He was accused in turn of refusing to help Brożyna, but since this was covered by the amnesty of July 1977, he was accused in addition of a robbery in 1971. This case had been tried several years earlier and the perpetrators had not only been convicted but had already served their sentences. Nowakowski was not among the suspects. It is strange that criminal proceedings were initiated against Nowakowski at the very time when he agreed to serve as a witness in the case of Brożyna's murder. Obviously a pretext was needed to isolate him. But it did not work; once he found himself facing the court instead of functionaries of the Security Service, he retracted his testimony. He must have been aware of the danger he was incurring with this move. After all, a criminal trial in which he was to be the defendant was awaiting him and, moreover, for the entire time he would be in the hands of his oppressors. In any case, he did not face the court again. The date of his trial for robbery was postponed, since he was in the prison hospital, from which he was discharged as healthy in April. His mother saw him during a visit on April 28, 1978. The trial on appeal in the case of Brożyna's murder was scheduled for May 23, 1978. On May 17, Nowakowski died in jail. This was the second instance within a relatively short period of time of the death of a witness who was to testify in a case involving functionaries of the police or the Security Service who were suspected of murder.[10]

Nowakowski's death cast an even grimmer light on the circumstances of Brożyna's murder. In this case, as in many others, there existed, on the one hand, the internally inconsistent instructions of the Security Service, and on the other, the internally consistent testimony of witnesses who were themselves later to become the accused. KOR members who were of necessity acquainted with all the details of this case were deeply convinced that neither Wiesława Skórkiewicz nor Roman Piasecki was guilty of the death of Brożyna. Unfortunately, despite numerous actions and protests by KOR, which extended into the period of Solidarity, those convicted were neither released nor rehabilitated (Piasecki was sentenced to 8 years of imprisonment; Skórkiewicz to 6 years).

The Fall and Winter Counteractions of KOR Following the June Events

Organizing help for the persecuted, collecting money for this purpose, mobilizing Polish and international opinion on behalf of the workers of Radom and Ursus, and struggling to be present during their trials—all these were exclusively defensive actions. Quite soon, however, KOR became convinced that this was not enough, and that it would be necessary for KOR and the other interested parties to respond with a counterattack, and to accuse the police, the Security Service, the prosecutor's office, and the courts, and by the same token the highest political authorities, who had conspired in breaking the law, or at the very least had condoned lawbreaking.

This counterattack took several forms.

1. KOR began organizing workers who were still employed in the tractor factory in Ursus to make a collective demand for the reinstatement of those who had been persecuted.

2. In both Radom and Ursus KOR attempted to make the victimized workers and their families aware of the necessity of accusing the police and the Security Service of beatings and tortures.

3. KOR urged various groups of people throughout Poland to demand that a special Diet commission be called to investigate the events in Radom and Ursus.

4. KOR adopted the tactic of immediate rectification of official lies about Radom, Ursus, and the entire strike movement in June 1976, and this rectification was connected with accusations against those who were really guilty.

The Letter from Ursus Workers to Gierek

For several reasons it was not easy to organize a collective letter from the Ursus workers. The shock following the terrorist police action was still being felt, and in a less spectacular form the terror was still going on. Despite the expectations of KOR activists, the contacts established with the workers provided KOR with only a few associates relative to the number of acquaintances and people who were given relief. But not every one who takes part in a mass movement at the time of an explosion has the temperament and the qualifications to become an activist in a period as difficult as that coinciding with the beginning of KOR. In addition, the Ursus and Radom teams adopted an iron rule: the providing of aid cannot be accompanied by recruitment. This may have been unwise from a pragmatic point of view, but morally it was correct. The only help that was rigorously demanded by KOR activists— and never refused by the workers—was that those who were being helped should point to others who were in similar situations, and that they should act as intermediaries to facilitate making contact. Nothing more was suggested, although offers of cooperation were gladly accepted. Those workers who did become associates of KOR were as valuable as the members of the intelligentsia, not only for moral and ideological reasons, but also for practical reasons: on their own turf they were invisible to agents of the Security Service and the police. But again, there were relatively few of them.

The idea of a collective letter to the highest authorities in Poland in defense of those who were suffering persecution became increasingly popular, and many Ursus workers were involved in it who otherwise were not especially active. The text began circulating secretly in the production halls, passed from hand to hand; the document itself bore the traces of this. A production worker, knowing what he was about to sign, would usually go and wash his hands, and treated the pages with respect. But the circumstances were specific: someone would want to take another look at the text before making his decision; someone else would put the sheets down on a workbench that was not very clean. The same text circulated in the factory in many identical copies which were signed separately. In addition, the circulating letters had to be hidden from agents and never—God forbid—given to people who were not trustworthy.

It must be clearly emphasized that despite KOR's initiative in this matter and the important role of the coordinator of the whole action, Wojciech Onyszkiewicz, the entire action had a working-class character. The idea was taken up enthusiastically, and the text was carefully discussed with the workers and corrected according to their wishes. The execution of the action was in the hands of the workers and expressed their own convictions and acceptance almost 100 percent.

It seems that the Security Service did not realize what was happening until quite late. Still, it was necessary to expedite the completion of the action. In November 1976, 889 employees of the Ursus Mechanical Enterprises sent off their collective letter.[11] More than two hundred additional workers signed the letter in the course of the following few weeks. KOR issued a statement in connection with this letter expressing solidarity with the signers and proposing the idea of Workers' Commissions (unfortunately, the workers of Ursus did not begin to realize this idea until the spring of 1980).

The second sentence in the KOR statement indicated a general strategy and the goals which the Committee was suggesting to the workers:

> The events of June 25 have reaffirmed once again the inability of the trade unions to fulfill their function of representing the workers. They were unable to offer even the weakest protest against reprisals, and they allowed themselves to be drawn into active collaboration with the repression. Therefore, the workers themselves must take the defense of their interests into their own hands. The solidary action of the workers of Ursus is an example to all work crews touched by reprisals. The spontaneous emergence of the forms of collective defense is a first step on the road to the formation of authentic representations of the working people.

The sending of the letter and its publication by KOR did not end the matter; signatures were still being collected, though less intensively.

It was an ambition of the worker activists organizing the action to "break down the barrier of fear," as KOR used to describe it. Thus, the signatures had to be, and were, legible. This was a challenge. It was followed by a revolving door of interrogations, reprisals, pressures to retract the signature, to deny that one had signed the letter, to declare that one had been misled, or even bribed. Conversations, or rather interrogations, were conducted by three-person teams composed of representatives of the management, the party organization, and the Security Service or the police. The attitude of the workers was excellent; no dismissals from work occurred.

A sense of success remained. The workers of Ursus had shaken off, at least to some extent, their fear and sense of defeat. This was an indication to KOR that the party authorities were afraid of a further worsening of conflicts with the working class.

The Workers of Radom and Ursus Complain to the Prosecutor's Office

While the letter from the Ursus workers to Gierek on behalf of those who had been fired was regarded by KOR as a form of pressure that might bring immediate practical results (hastening a resolution of the problem, even if not in the most optimal manner), the complaints to the prosecutor's office were to constitute one element in the mobilization of public opinion toward a future victory in the struggle for the rule of law. This task was not easy: the workers did not have much understanding of what was at stake, and since the police in Poland commonly resort to beatings during detentions and interrogations, such measures are regarded as something obvious and natural. In this action KOR took special care not to arouse in the workers any false hopes of immediate results, and to warn them of the risks. Without exception, declarations of war on the Security Service and the police have always met with long-lasting consequences in the Polish People's Republic (PRL). Making the workers aware of this risk was not only a matter of ethics (one cannot encourage someone to commit a dangerous act and conceal the fact that he is exposing himself to danger) but also a pragmatic issue: every complaint that would later be withdrawn—and withdrawn on conditions dictated by the Security Service—would constitute a failure for KOR. And it was known from the start that this would be the direction of the efforts of the police and Security Service. Therefore, it was important for the workers who filed complaints to know what was in store for them, and that they should rather refuse KOR's suggestions than withdraw their complaints later. Also, those inside the Committee predicted from the start that there was only a small chance in a hundred of perseverance among people against whom every method of pressure would be applied.

This entire action took place in close collaboration between KOR and the people writing the complaints. Among undereducated workers the ability to compose a complicated letter is rare, so that advice was needed, and even help in writing. Moreover, it was necessary to make sure that the complaints contained no punishable insults or threats, that they stuck to the topic and to events that the author knew at first hand, and did not include rumors. This was an enormous effort for the already over-worked Ursus and Radom teams to undertake.

There were over a hundred individual complaints to the Office of the Prosecutor General. They were written and sent during the fall of 1976 and the spring of 1977. They constitute an ample and many-sided mono-graph on the subject of the lawlessness and cruelty encountered by the workers in June 1976. Although never published in a collection, these letters were frequently cited in KOR publications. The reader has already found a sample of them in chapter 2. The relevant portions of KOR's *Madrid Report* were also based on these materials.[12]

In addition to the individual complaints there were two collective letters of complaint. On November 30, sixty-five Radom workers sent a letter to the Office of the Prosecutor General containing a general de-scription of the behavior of the police on June 25, 1976; and on Decem-ber 1 there was a letter written on the same topic by seventeen relatives of imprisoned workers.

Both collective letters were written in response to the lies of the Pros-ecutor General, Lucjan Czubiński, published in "Information from the Prosecutor General of the PRL," that appeared in the newspapers on October 30, 1976. In this "disinformation" Czubiński stated:

> All these cases were considered carefully, and both the act and the person-ality of the accused were taken into consideration. This refers equally to the preparatory proceedings on the part of the police and the prosecutors and to the court trials.

Earlier, in its statement of November 4, 1976, KOR had also re-sponded to Czubiński's claims:

> The Workers' Defense Committee declares that almost all of those arrested on June 25 and the following days were beaten brutally. A large number of the workers detained at the time affirm that during the preparatory proce-

dures testimony was forced out of them by means of torture. We know of many cases in which the defendants' complaints about the physical coercion used against them were voiced during court proceedings and were ignored by the judges.

Czubiński's "Information" also contained a reference to seventy-eight persons who were then in prison in connection with the events in Radom and Ursus: "all of them bear responsibility for participation in criminal activities, above all in the looting of stores."

In the statement quoted above, KOR decisively countered this statement, demonstrating that on the contrary, a large number of those named were accused only of having participated in a political demonstration, which also included the burning of the building of the party committee. The collective letters brought about a vehement campaign by the Security Service and the police against the workers who either wrote or signed these letters. People were detained and investigated, and threatened with arrest, imprisonment, trials, even with "accidental" death. The signatories and their families were visited at home and offered bribes. Workers were threatened with trials for treason and espionage, and with fifteen-year prison sentences. At the same time, KOR was being described as an espionage organization composed of traitors and Jews, paid for by Israeli and West German intelligence.

In the daily papers on January 6, 1977, there appeared another statement by Prosecutor General Czubiński describing as groundless allegations that the police and the Security Service had used impermissible methods in Radom and Ursus. He added that among the several dozens of persons who had signed these complaints, some twenty had categorically declared that they had not really signed them, while about a dozen others asserted that they had only consented to sign because they were urged to do so and were given financial help. Almost half of those who had signed were supposed to be people with prior criminal records.

The number of those authors of complaints who broke down and made statements extorted by the Security Service is arguable, but in any case the number is not greater than twenty.

The drama of the workers' struggle to set forth their complaints, and their trustworthiness, are best illustrated by the story of Stanisław Wijata. A worker in Department P-3 in the "General Walter" Enterprises in Radom, Wijata sent his complaint to the prosecutor's office on October 27. On June 25, the day of the demonstration, he was stopped by the police early in the morning in front of the factory. From that time on, he was beaten on numerous occasions both individually and in "paths of health" through which he was made to run the gauntlet with others, as described in detail in his complaint. His letter was answered with several "visits" by the Security Service to his home and workplace. These were polite talks, and no threats were made. Around November 23, Wijata was summoned by telephone (i.e., informally) to come to the Provincial Headquarters of the police. There he was ordered to undress, which he understood to be a preparation for beatings. He was threatened with arrest. He was asked about the help he had received while he was unemployed. Finally Wijata agreed to withdraw his complaint and made a statement that he had been paid 2000 zlotys to write it. For this he twice received a thousand zlotys from the police (half of this amount was to pay the costs of the sentencing board). On November 30, Wijata, tormented by a guilty conscience, went to see one of the Warsaw attorneys who had come to Radom in connection with the workers' trials that were then in progress. On the very same day, Wijata was interrogated once again. Wijata was threatened that he would "be done away with," that he need not appeal to Warsaw since they, the police and the Security Service, were right there. After this, Wijata made up his mind: on December 3, 1976, he retracted his retraction, enclosing a detailed description of the circumstances under which he had made it. He also signed the collective complaint on December 1.

Several other workers in addition to Wijata did the same thing. Today it is difficult to establish exactly how many there were, but there were at least five, or rather at least five of them informed KOR about their actions.

The Letters to Form a Diet Commission

On November 29, 1976, KOR issued a public appeal calling on citizens to write letters to the Diet demanding the formation of a special Diet Commission to investigate and make known to the public instances of lawbreaking committed by the organs of public "order" in connection with the events of June 25, 1976. KOR decided to issue this appeal because of the lack of any response to the workers' complaints other than new reprisals and threats.

KOR did not expect that the Diet would form such a commission, at least not at that time. This institution—staffed basically by nomination, though masked by a primitive farce of an "election"—had compromised itself sufficiently on June 24 and 25, when it voted unanimously for the price increases, and then on the following day, with equal unanimity, changed its mind without expressing any reaction to the news that workers were being beaten and tortured, and fired from their jobs en masse. While the party was hated and feared—although occasionally people did count on the fact that the Central Committee might do something positive, at least in its own interest—the Diet was simply held in contempt. Letters were written to the Diet only for the purpose of mobilizing society, to draw new groups into the protest on behalf of the victimized workers, and to extend the influence of KOR in an effort to further organize the struggle against official lawlessness. If such a commission were to be called, KOR was convinced that it could act to prevent the commission from being a complete fraud like the Diet.

Public response to the appeal was broad, and it must be regarded as a success despite the fact that KOR had expected an even greater response. KOR attached great importance to the collective letter signed by thirty-four professors in institutions of higher learning and research institutes, primarily in Warsaw and Wrocław. "Priestly" collective letters were also very important. In the single diocese of Przemyśl, one such letter was signed by 293 Catholic priests.[13] A letter bearing 296 signatures from cultural and scholarly circles—along with other letters like that of the professors—demonstrated that since December 1975, support for the opposition had also grown among these groups. From the point of view of mass influence, it was significant that this letter had been signed by well-known figures from motion pictures and television (among them Daniel Olbrychski, Zdzisław Mrożewski, and Piotr Fronczewski). A letter signed by twelve workers from the Lenin Shipyards and from ZREMB in Gdańsk was particularly valuable. It was another link in the chain that led from the events of 1970–1971 to the Initiating Committees of Free Trade Unions on the coast and then to the strike in August 1980 and to Solidarity. The organizers were very pleased with the letter signed by five engineers from the Lenin Steel Mills in Nowa Huta, because on previous occasions members of the technical intelligentsia had rarely participated in oppositional actions.

Young people dominated the letters: there were 321 signatures on a letter from Gdańsk, 730 signatures from Warsaw University, 517 signatures from Cracow, and 176 from Łódź. These letters were signed by students and recent alumni, and rarely included the signatures of older people. A similar letter was signed by 285 students and faculty both of the Catholic University and other institutions of higher learning in Lublin who were connected with the academic ministry there. And so on, and so on. Sometimes letters were sent by small groups, or by individuals. Obviously KOR could count only those letters of which copies were also forwarded to the committee. Certainly there were more letters than KOR knew about. The number of signatories registered by the committee was approximately 3,000.

In order to judge whether or not this number is significant, one needs to witness at least one gathering of signatures under conditions of police blockade and counteraction (at this time there could no longer be any question of surprise). It is enough to say modestly that such actions were difficult. And unfortunately, it is rare for such letters to be composed even under more favorable conditions, even in a sympathetic milieu, when there is no clear initiative from a center capable of organizing the entire action. At the time, KOR was not yet strong enough to reach out directly beyond the several industrial and university cities. This is why the potential possibilities accruing from the public respect which KOR enjoyed already by this time were not exploited to the fullest extent. Nevertheless the action fulfilled its goals: it opened up new channels of social communication, integrated new groups, and broadened the front of social resistance.

The Act of "Clemency" and the Intensification of Reprisals

The word *clemency* appears in quotation marks in the subhead because it is difficult to regard as merciful an act that was forced upon the authorities. They could have resisted further, but every day they lost more ground to KOR. KOR's position in its accusations against the authorities was obviously moral and humanitarian; therefore the belief that KOR's demands were just reached out to ever greater numbers of people, strengthening the opposition. The authorities had a choice between two possibilities: they could arrest people from KOR (soon this variant was also tried), or they could retreat one step, and call it an act of clemency for the sake of their prestige, counting on the fact that in this manner the motive that had been a decisive factor in the success of the opposition would be removed. Had this maneuver been executed with consistency, it might have given the authorities a great advantage.

On February 3, the Council of State, on the initiative—as it was announced—of the first secretary of the Central Committee of PUWP

"recommended that the Commission for Acts of Clemency, the Prosecutor's Office, and the organs of the justice system prepare petitions for
the remission, reduction, temporary suspension, or interruption of the
sentences of those convicted in connection with the events of June 25
who have shown repentance and given hope that they will not again
enter upon the path of crime." On February 5, 1977, the Workers' Defense Committee addressed itself to this "act of clemency" and once again
presented its arguments against the official version of the events of June
25, and against the behavior of the prosecutors and judges during the
trials.

KOR welcomed the decision of the Council of State, but at the same
time emphasized that it could be considered only a first step, and not as
the end of the matter. The condition of repentance was severely criticized, as demeaning in every case, since it excluded the conscious defenders of the workers' interests from the benefits of the act, and it was
equally unfair to those who either would not admit guilt or admitted it
only as a result of torture. They were rather the ones who had the right
to expect repentance from those who had done them wrong. KOR protested strongly against the positive appraisal of the investigative organs
and the justice system in connection with the June events, which was
also contained in the resolution of the Council of State. Once again,
KOR's accusations against them were presented in a short synthesis. The
sentence that one of the defense attorneys had uttered in the courtroom
was reiterated: "A court sentence must be different from the vengeance
of an owner who is scared of losing his property."

In early May 1977 only five of the participants in the June events
were still in prison: three from Radom convicted for taking part in the
demonstration, and two from Ursus sentenced to three years for blocking
the railroad tracks. Also, however slowly and with great difficulty, an
increasing number of those who had been dismissed from their jobs
were finding some new—and usually worse—employment.

The act of clemency caused some confusion among KOR supporters
and in the circles of the political opposition (these two groups were not
completely identical). For a time one would hear questions about whether
KOR would now dissolve itself. It was understood quite soon, however,
that this would make no sense in view of the situation existing at the
time. Nevertheless, the release of almost all (and in the course of several
months, indeed all) the workers, and the fact that the remainder had
found jobs, became an argument for those dissident groups that were
not friendly toward KOR, who felt that KOR had done what it had to

do and was no longer necessary. In the committee itself, the act of clemency hastened the decision to broaden the tasks of the committee and thus to make some organizational changes.

It is interesting, however, that the decision of the Council of State did not diminish the activity of the police and the Security Service in harassing those who had been persecuted before. On the contrary, one could observe a new wave of reprisals against these people. It is difficult for me today to say why this was so. Two explanations are possible: the first is that the central authorities, having decided to deprive KOR of the arguments it had been using, which were finding great public sympathy, was at the same time fearful that the act of clemency would embolden both the workers and the opposition, and decided to let both groups know that there was no cause for joy. The second explanation is that the hard-line faction was countering the more liberal elements in the party by deliberately attempting to aggravate the situation.

In any case, on March 19, KOR was forced to issue another statement describing the widespread use of psychological terror against workers who had also been persecuted in June. This involved their being stopped constantly in the streets to have their identity papers checked, summonses by telephone (usually made to the workplace), visits at work and at home, interrogations (also of family members), and attempts to convince people to turn informer, in which a combination of threats and bribery was used. At the same time, KOR noted that according to the act of clemency the workers had been released from prison only temporarily, thanks to a conditional suspension of sentence that left them at the mercy of the police. It was precisely during this counteroffensive by the Security Service and the police following the amnesty that the sudden turn of events occurred in the Brożyna trial, and the witnesses were arrested.

The action against KOR also did not subside but, on the contrary, entered a new phase. On April 27, 1977, Prosecutor Wiesława Bardonowa presented Jacek Kuroń and Jan Józef Lipski with an indictment based on Article 132 of the Criminal Code (and on Art. 58) charging that together with Adam Michnik (who was still in the West) they were working to the detriment of the Polish People's Republic in collaboration with hostile organizations, among them the Paris *Kultura* and Radio Free Europe. Both of the accused, of course, refused categorically to offer any explanations. The interrogation and the presentation of the indictment occurred in the presence of Inspector Karpacz of the Security Service. In this manner we discovered that a trial involving at least three members of KOR was being prepared, though it was clear that regardless of the formal accusations, this would be a trial against KOR in its entirety. When he learned about the indictments against Kuroń and Lipski, Adam Michnik interrupted his stay in the West, acting on the conviction that he had to answer these mendacious and illegal slanders in person.

At the same time, the police actions against KOR intensified: there were more detentions, more intrusions into small gatherings (sometimes these get-togethers were indeed exclusively social in nature), more summonses to interrogations—the entire rich repertory of repression.

The atmosphere was thickening.

The Uncensored Press

This section was almost headed "The Secret Press." But that would have been an error. This press was secret in the sense that only a few initiates knew the details: where it was being printed, where the distribution points were and how it got there, which cars were used to transport bundles of printed issues, where the paper was stored. But at the same time it was overt: every KOR periodical named at least one person (and usually more) who was on the editorial board. At the same time, there were efforts to protect the secrecy of pennames. Thus it was both secret and overt. The word *secret* is often associated with the word *illegal.* In this respect, KOR held a clear opinion based on principle: the Constitution of the PRL, together with international agreements signed and ratified by Poland such as the Final Act of the Helsinki Conference on Security and Cooperation in Europe, all guarantee freedom of the word and of speech; therefore what was illegal was not the press, which the authorities did not like, but the police reprisals against it. The KOR press began at the same time as the committee.

There is some question whether the official organ of KOR, the *Communiqué,* can really be called a periodical. But why not? It was not entirely regular, but it did appear approximately once a month; it contained information for which KOR accepted responsibility, and (although not from the very beginning) the full texts of KOR statements. Every issue published details and statistics about the reprisals against workers, and provided information about the extent of aid (which constituted a public accounting of funds to the society that had donated them), about reprisals against KOR and its associates, and about all other independent social initiatives. It also published lists, unfortunately incomplete, of the names of all those who had beaten, tortured, denounced, or otherwise persecuted the workers of June 25 or later, as well as KOR members and associates.

The *Communiqué* was edited at first by Antoni Macierewicz, then by Anka Kowalska, and was presented to KOR for approval. When it became possible to duplicate the *Information Bulletin*, it became the basic, and later practically the only form of publication of the *Communiqué*. However, this state of affairs caused displeasure among some KOR members. We will return later to the nature, background, and causes of this development. For now it is enough to say that for a time the *Communiqué* appeared separately, only to be reinserted in the *Bulletin* toward the end of the committee's existence.

In the beginning, typographic techniques were rather poor. The *Communiqué* was edited collectively—which means with a great deal of trouble—and was copied on a typewriter with the maximum number of copies technically possible, generally on tissue-thin paper. From this first stack, single copies were given to those who were willing to copy them, with the request that they return the copies to the committee. Apart from multiplying in this manner the number of copies of the *Communiqué*, this also provided a discreet means assuring that the issue was actually being copied. The copyist knew that if he were not to lose the trust of the committee, he would not be allowed to change anything, to add or subtract. Indeed, the *Communiqué* was treated with such great (sometimes even excessive) respect that even accidental typing errors were recopied, a situation KOR preferred to license. It was also possible to copy the individual statements of KOR separately, though without using the title of *KOR Communiqué*.

The *Communiqués* put into circulation in this manner multiplied like rabbits, quickly reaching places remote both geographically and socially from the point of origin. Nevertheless, there were still more places into which the *Communiqués* did not reach, or reached only sporadically.

With time, the transfer to duplicator technique made the *Communiqué* more popular, but it also had its negative aspects. It turned out quickly that there were fewer and fewer people willing to retype the text from a duplicated copy, which was also understandable psychologically. If copying was still being done, it was only by workers and peasants, and sometimes by young students who made copies by hand using carbon paper. But it did not occur on the same scale as before, and this had a negative effect on the social nature of the distribution: if the text travels from typewriter to typewriter, it will travel farther from the distribution center than a single duplicated copy. After a while the question was even raised of whether this technical innovation was indeed worthwhile, both for the reasons already mentioned and for ideological and psychological reasons. Retyping was a form of active participation, and linked people to the movement more closely than reading a single copy and then passing this copy on to a friend. Duplication introduced one more factor that impeded circulation: only at that point did copies truly become collectors' items. Initially, a collector who wanted to have a complete set of issues had to be prepared to copy them himself or give them to others to be copied. Later, collectors were often more interested in the *Communiqué* as an artifact produced in an underground print shop, so they withdrew issues from circulation. Nonetheless, duplication increased the prestige of KOR significantly, especially once production teams had overcome the initial technical difficulties and achieved a professional standard. Moreover, only then could the size of the periodicals really increase.

Basically, everything that applies to the technical side of the production of the *Communiqué* and its psychosocial effects also applies to the *Information Bulletin*. For four years, that is, throughout the entire time of its existence, its initiator and editor-in-chief was Seweryn Blumsztajn, a former Walterite and participant in the March student movement. From the beginning to the end, Joanna Szczęsna was also a coeditor of the *Bulletin;* she had become a friend of the editor-in-chief when they were students at the Catholic University in Lublin, which both of them had entered, along with other friends, straight from jail. Jan Lityński (his background was almost identical with that of Blumsztajn, though he did not attend the Catholic University) also assisted at the birth of the *Bulletin,* later leaving it to work on *Robotnik,* of which he was the principal founder. As members of the editorial board one can name (this is not a rhetorical phrase; some of them never made their names known publicly): Anka Kowalska; Eugeniusz Kloc, a participant in the March movement, an associate of KOR from its very beginning, and one of those most often beaten; Jan Walc, also an early participant in the KOR movement and a literary critic who during the time of KOR wrote his dissertation on Tadeusz Konwicki; Janusz Przewłocki, like Anka Kowalska an employee of the PAX publishing house; and Przemysław Cieślak.

The *Information Bulletin* was in the strict sense of the term the first periodical of the KOR movement. In the beginning it had a purely informational character, but it evolved into a periodical carrying essays and information with a clear social-democratic slant, although this description neither exhausts its content nor describes the orientation of all the members of the editoral board and its associates. The title of the *Bulletin* was no accident; it referred to the title of the main Home Army periodical. Similarly, *Głos* (*The Voice*), *Krytyka,* and *Robotnik* recalled the traditions of the Polish press, while *Placówka* (*The Outpost*) referred to the literary tradition. The creators of the KOR press felt strongly that they were the heirs of a historical tradition dating back not only to their predecessors during World War II but also to the more distant past. The publication by NOWa of Józef Piłsudski's *Bibuła* (*Underground Publications*) was understood as an expression of homage.

One more example played a role. When KOR and its press were just getting started, the golden period of the "samizdat" in the USSR had unfortunately ended, destroyed by the secret police. But more than one member of KOR recalled asking of himself: "They can do it, so why can't we?"—especially since the price that people there had to pay for this sort of work was known. The word *samizdat* is still alive in Poland, though now it is used less frequently. In particular, it is easy to note the influence of the idea and the style of the Russian *Chronicle of Current Events* when one reads the *KOR Communiqués.* This was a language of maximally concise, dry, unambiguous, and precise information, designed to convey as much, but only as much, as was known by the person providing the information, with no evaluations, rhetoric, or decoration. In all such cases, the facts speak for themselves.

The *Information Bulletin* was certainly the first on the list of opposition periodicals appearing after 1976. The second, it seems, was *U Progu* (*On the Threshold*), a journal that began appearing in October 1976 with a small circulation, published by the group that would create the Movement in Defense of Human and Civil Rights some six months later.

The first issue of the literary quarterly *Zapis* appeared in January 1977. This periodical was not really a KOR publication, since institutionally it was completely independent. Nevertheless, an overwhelming majority of its editors and of the authors who published in it were members and associates of KOR, or at least sympathizers. The second issue came out in April, and subsequent issues appeared regularly every quarter. It represented a new and a very important step on the road to liberation in a totalitarian country, this time in the field of literature. The KOR milieu valued very highly all independent activity in the field of culture and education, and such activity also had the full support of the circles of workers associated with KOR.

It must also be noted that the first pamphlet publication of KOR, *In the Name of the Polish People's Republic,* appeared in April 1977. This was a documentary publication concerning four Radom trials, or rather their appeals to the Supreme Court (including a précis of the speeches of the defense attorneys and excerpts from the judgments and sentences). In May 1977 a second pamphlet, *The June Events and the Activities of the Workers' Defense Committee*, was published in a large edition.[14] Shortly afterward, in August 1977, the Independent Publishing House (NOWa) began its activities.

Funds

Questions about the origin of the funds at the disposition of KOR arose frequently, raised sometimes in good faith, sometimes not. The answer is both easy and difficult: easy because there is nothing mysterious about these funds, and difficult because someone might be omitted.

KOR began with funds gathered through collections, first among circles of friends and acquaintances and then, soon afterward, among a much larger group of people. Immediately after the appeal by KOR, money began flowing in. As already mentioned, the money received from the Ministry of Charity played a significant role early on; although the amount was not large, it made possible the start of the action. At the beginning, money gathered on collection plates in several churches was among the funds coming in for aid to the Radom and Ursus workers. The pioneer in this area was without doubt Rev. Leon Kantorski from Podkowa Leśna near Warsaw.

The impossibility of collecting money by mail caused some difficulty: all money sent to KOR members through the mail was seized by a bailiff and later confiscated as the result of a decision by the Sentencing Board for Misdemeanors, which made no attempt to present evidence that the collection was connected with any criminal activity. Moreover, a sentencing board would levy a fine of 5,000 zlotys. This was the reason underlying KOR's constant appeals not to send money through the mail, which certainly lowered the number of contributors, especially among those living in distant provinces.

Shortly after the creation of KOR, various bank accounts and relief funds were established in the West. The two main ones were: the Citizens' Committee under the direction of Ambassador Edward Raczyński, located in London, and the international committee, the Appeal for Polish Workers. "Raczyński's Committee," as the first of these was commonly called, involved a large group of known political emigrés from Poland, and money came from people of Polish descent living abroad. For a long time this fund was designated for KOR's use only, and was at its disposal. The "Appeal for Polish Workers" was signed by a large group of people well known in the Western cultural and scholarly world.[15] Two persons were particularly important both because of their initiative and because of the authorizations they received from the other members of the committee: Prof. Leszek Kołakowski, whose well-known name has been connected with all democratic movements in Poland for the last quarter of a century; and Prof. Włodzimierz Brus, an economist with a worldwide reputation and who was devoted to the cause of relief. The worldwide scope and effectiveness of the "Appeal" were also assured by members of the *Aneks* team. Many Western writers and scholars supported the committee, and several of them donated their honorariums earned in Polish zlotys to KOR (Saul Bellow, Heinrich Böll, Günter Grass, and Max Frisch). As ill luck would have it, 50,000 zlotys from Böll were confiscated during a house search in Naimski's apartment on December 31, 1976. At the time, the Security Service probably did not know the source of this money.

A short while later, donations addressed to Paris *Kultura* also began playing an important role, becoming during the later period of KOR's activity more substantial than those derived from other sources. *Kultura* publicly noted the amounts and the names of the donors, and it did not limit its collections to the committee. Funds for KOR were also collected by the Polish-American Congress; the Union of Poles in Canada; the editors of *Nowy Dziennik* in New York; by Polish unionists and socialists in Belgium, Great Britain, and Germany; and by the Society of Friends of *Kultura* in Sweden. This surely is only a partial list.

While the use of funds from collections in Poland caused no difficulties (other than technical difficulties connected with violating the prohibition against taking collections without the consent of the police), the issue of money from abroad was rather more complicated.

Anyone acquainted with conditions in the Soviet empire knows that any connection between social activity that is not under the control of the Communist party (which in itself constitutes a horrendous transgression against public order) and any centers abroad is simply a crime. Under Stalin one paid for it with charges of spying, that is, with one's life or with years of imprisonment (in the USSR, in a labor camp). The fear of such charges was a remnant of those times, though even in more recent years this fear was by no means groundless. It seized both those who were active and those who were watching from the sidelines. As a result of reflexes conditioned over many years by the propaganda and the political police, a significant number of newspaper readers and television spectators react with horror to revelations that someone politically undesirable has connections, not to mention financial connections, with the West. Occasionally this causes indignation. Here also, things began to change in recent years.

KOR faced the issue squarely: it accepted aid from abroad and spoke about it loudly. Poles, regardless of where they now lived (and many of them had fought for Polish freedom and paid for it with their blood) had a right to participate in the fate of their country, as did all people of goodwill throughout the world who wanted to express their human solidarity with the oppressed. No one could take this away from them, and especially not KOR. On the contrary, KOR was always grateful for this help. During the first year of KOR's activity the West European Trade Unions were an important source of support, both material and moral: union federations in Sweden, Norway, Brussels, and the (communist!) Italian Federation of Metal Workers gave their support on international forum to the cause of the Polish workers, especially when asked to do so by KOR.

Quite early, significant sums were spent on actions designed to uncover police murders and beatings. Almost every such investigation involved repeated trips to the scene of the crime, often for extended periods of time and under conditions requiring some pretext for being there, so as to establish contacts with many people, usually not connected with the opposition, while not becoming conspicuous to the police. A partial result of these investigations was included in the *Documents of Lawlessness,* a grim record of the murders committed by the police that were discovered by KOR. Even before KOR transformed itself into the Social Self-Defense Committee, its help began to extend not only to the workers persecuted after June 25 but also to others who had been wronged.

At first, the *Communiqué* and the *Information Bulletin* needed no additional funding. However, when these periodicals and the subsequent periodicals of KOR and of related groups began to be duplicated, which increased the number of copies and made distribution less accidental, donations for the press began to occupy an important place in KOR's budget.

Many social initiatives close to KOR, but independent from it, used gifts or loans from KOR (which were usually later reimbursed). This was the case with the Society for Scientific Courses (TKN), *Zapis*, and other press initiatives. Various independent social initiatives began appealing to KOR for support quite early on. This was the case, for example, with the later campaign of the Self-Defense Committees of Believers in favor of broadcasts of the Holy Masses on radio and television, which was conducted by groups that were also in contact with ROPCiO, and was scantily funded by KOR (scantily because the organizers were able to conduct this action at little expense). Later KOR also gave loans to ROPCiO (Czuma's group), *Bratniak*, *Spotkania* (*Meetings*, the periodical of a group of young Catholics from Lublin), the Father Kolbe Publishing House, "Sacrosong," and others.

The Movement in Defense of Human and Civil Rights

That the struggle for KOR's basic goals might be won in the foreseeable future (probably with the exception of the demand that the guilty be punished) began to seem a realistic possibility as early as December 1976, though at the time there was still very little evidence to support this expectation. In any event, it was apparent that the authorities somehow were beginning to resign themselves to the existence of the opposition, and therefore that they would have to do something to take away from it the weapon that had proven so effective. At the same time, KOR was being informed about an ever greater number of cases that were unrelated to the events of June 1976 and their aftermath, and it was becoming clear that the KOR movement would be compromised if it were to ignore them. Therefore, the first ideas about how to transform KOR so that it could fulfill wider functions originated at this time. One element of these notions was to make KOR more representative by launching an appeal to groups that could help intensify the activity of KOR, which suffered from a chronic lack of people to work on newer and broader tasks. Jacek Kuroń suggested this issue be discussed with Andrzej Czuma, the leader of the Ruch group that had been destroyed by the police in 1970. Sporadic contacts with Czuma began when he and his friends were released from jail following the intervention of Professor Lipiński with Gierek. The presence in KOR of Emil Morgiewicz, who was also from Ruch, had not led to a greater participation of this milieu in the work of KOR.

Contacts were established not only with Czuma, but also with Leszek Moczulski, who moved closer to Ruch just at that time. Some members of KOR were already acquainted with Moczulski as a result of chance social contacts. The necessity of talking with Leszek Moczulski did not make KOR happy. For many years Moczulski was one of the people determining the profile of *Stolica* (*The Capital*), an illustrated weekly of a regional character. During the events of 1968, this periodical was connected with the faction of General Moczar, and Moczulski, together with Krzysztof Naumienko, wrote articles attacking the student and intellectual movement at that time. Not much had changed since Moczar's position had been weakened by a Gomułka-Gierek coalition, nor under the reign of Gierek.

Stolica, like the weekly *Ekran* (*The Screen*), eagerly took up campaigns against "scoffers." In the circle of journalists sympathetic to Moczar (which was later transformed into the Patriotic Association Grunwald), this was the name for all artists, writers, and journalists who were in any way critical or revisionist, or who—and this was regarded as most reprehensible—treated the stereotypes of national history with any sense of humor. One of the episodes in this holy war was a demonstration organized in a theater by Moczulski and Wysznacka against the play *The Death of the Colonel*, by Stanisław Mrożek. In addition, Moczulski himself later admitted that he was the author of the speech delivered by Józef Kępa, the first secretary of the Warsaw party committee, at the inauguration of the social Committee to Rebuild the Royal Castle in Warsaw. All this was not conducive to a proper atmosphere for talks, especially since Moczulski himself, probably unwittingly, was making it even more difficult by telling KOR members strange stories about propositions he had received from the Central Committee of PUWP—which he of course rejected—about forming an organization that would be parallel to KOR and in competition with it.

Nevertheless, talks continued in ever larger groups. By general agreement, the committee to be formed jointly would not be simply a transformation of KOR (for the participants in these discussions, this was a matter of prestige), and it would obviously have broader tasks than KOR. It was to be called the Committee in Defense of Human and Civil Rights. An impasse occurred in the progress of the preparations, which was especially unnerving to Andrzej Czuma. He began to accuse KOR of stalling the talks and the preparations. These charges were not totally unjustified: within KOR there was great concern that the public would fail to understand the nature of the change, while the name of the committee, which had achieved great authority, would disappear, and as a result—despite the fact that the names of KOR members would reappear in the new committee—the vital continuity of the movement would be lost. This state of affairs influenced some activists who conducted talks with KOR, foremost among them Andrzej Czuma. Nonetheless, it appeared that the question of the composition of the new committee would not cause any particular problems.

Work on a common declaration was entrusted to Aniela Steinsbergowa and Jan Olszewski. The text was prepared with little difficulty, and it was accepted as a working text by KOR. Relatively minor amendments were then suggested by Czuma and Moczulski. They seemed acceptable to KOR. Everything seemed to be going well. On Thursday, March 24, 1977, there was a working session attended by Jan Józef Lipski, Józef Rybicki, and Leszek Moczulski, who agreed that on the following Tuesday a joint declaration would be signed establishing the new committee. This would be a complicated operation both because of the Security Service and, given the circumstances, because of the large number of signatories.

On the morning of Saturday, March 26, some foreign correspondents, who did not understand the situation, transmitted to KOR a strange piece of information. They had been informed that a press conference of a new oppositional organization called the Movement in Defense of Human and Civil Rights would be held that afternoon. The journalists were told that two spokesmen would be present: Andrzej Czuma and Leszek Moczulski. The conference was to be held in the apartment of Antoni Pajdak. Since Pajdak was not home in the morning and noon hours, it was impossible to clarify anything. Aniela Steinsbergowa asked Jacek Kuroń what was going on, since she had been approached to sign the declaration which she knew so well. She had not signed it because she was unable to find out why this was being arranged in such an unorthodox manner. At that time KOR members began contacting one another, and it transpired that some other members of KOR had also been asked to sign the declaration, and that Reverend Zieja was certainly among them, for he had signed the document with which he was familiar. He became worried about the unclear situation, however, and immediately asked his younger colleagues from KOR to find Moczulski or Czuma and inform them that temporarily he would not grant them permission to make his signature public. Józef Rybicki was contacted by telephone at home in Milanówek near Warsaw and informed about the situation. At that time it turned out that Moczulski was just then at Rybicki's house, and he was immediately told of Zieja's wishes.

It must be noted that at that time the relations between Rybicki and Moczulski were very good, and that Moczulski probably thought that he could count on a common front with Rybicki against the majority of KOR. But Rybicki, astonished at the sudden change in the timing of the creation of the new committee, began asking increasingly inquisitive questions, the last of which was whether the main authors of the declaration were aware of the new situation. When Rybicki was told that the text did not have an author, he asked Moczulski to leave his apartment. Anyone who knows Józef Rybicki would have known that this result was unavoidable, regardless of the good relations between the discussants until that moment.[16]

KOR decided to send the editor-in-chief of the *Information Bulletin* to the press conference. Both of the announced spokesmen were present and they acquainted the journalists there with the declaration of the Movement in Defense of Human and Civil Rights and with the list of its signatories. This list contained the following names: Mieczysław Boruta-Spiechowicz, Andrzej Czuma, Karol Głogowski, Kazimierz Janusz, Stefan Kaczorowski, Leszek Moczulski, Marek Myszkiewicz-Niesiołowski, Antoni Pajdak, Rev. Bolesław Papiernik, Zbigniew Sekulski, Zbigniew Siemiński, Bogusław Studziński, Piotr Typiak, Rev. Ludwik Wiśniewski, Adam Wojciechowski, Andrzej Woźnicki, Jan Zieja (!), Wojciech Ziembiński.

This was no doubt an important list, composed both of names long known and respected in Poland and of the names of young social activists who had already made themselves known by their various collective and individual actions. Most of them had until then cooperated with KOR either occasionally or systematically. The presence on the list of as many as four members of KOR was noteworthy. As we know, the announcement of the name of Jan Zieja was a serious abuse that was difficult to understand, and this is how Zieja himself regarded it, and he so informed the spokesman of ROPCiO (it was hard to understand, since its effects could only be short-lived and were sure to bring troublesome consequences). The presence of Pajdak's name was the result of a misunderstanding. (On one or two occasions Pajdak had signed ROPCiO statements on specific topics that were not of an organizational character.) After a while, the name of Father Ludwik Wiśniewski also ceased to appear on ROPCiO documents, since Wiśniewski, disappointed by internal quarrels within the opposition, returned to his activities in the circle of young people connected with the academic ministry, mainly in Lublin. The signatures of Stefan Kaczorowski and Wojciech Ziembiński were a sign of future factional struggles within KOR.

Under these circumstances it was difficult to expect harmonious cooperation between the two oppositional groups. KOR adopted the tactics of reticence toward ROPCiO; in any case it refrained from attacks. Extensive materials about the creation of ROPCiO appeared in the *Bulletin* of May 10, 1977, under the rubric "Protests Among the Intelligentsia," along with information about the first reprisals directed against the movement: the dismissals of Kazimierz Janusz and Leszek Moczulski from their jobs. The *KOR Communiqué* tried to register repressions against ROPCiO, although this was made more difficult by the fact that ROPCiO activists generally saw no reason to inform KOR about detentions, searches, and the like. Nevertheless, KOR was blamed for these gaps in information.

For a time, the Movement in Defense of Human and Civil Rights followed the tenet that whatever in Poland was not contrary to the declaration and goals of ROPCiO was part of this movement. Quite soon, however, it became clear that this was a fiction that could not be continued: for example, it was impossible to treat KOR as a part of ROPCiO, and it was a fact that the creation of ROPCiO meant that there was a second dissident organization that was parallel to KOR and in competition with the committee.

While in KOR it was clear who the members were, that is, who participated in statements that were collectively drafted and jointly adopted (in contradistinction to KOR associates, who had no formal status), ROPCiO adopted the principle of "participation in the Movement" and did not introduce a differentiation of rights. This decision would result in many future difficulties for ROPCiO, which it tried to avoid by creating various occasional bodies, which will not be discussed here because they are not a part of the history of KOR, not even indirectly. In the meantime, ROPCiO was represented by its spokesmen, and these spokesmen (Andrzej Czuma and Leszek Moczulski) were at the same time the actual leaders of the movement.

Thus, in the course of the first half year following the creation of KOR, the situation in the dissident movement had changed radically. KOR ceased to be the only group of its kind. Of course, throughout this time, the Polish League for Independence (PPN) had also existed and acted alongside KOR; however, it worked by very different methods, and since it was secret, it offered no alternative to those who were eager to become active, simply because no one knew where to look for it.

The new situation no doubt had both its pluses and its minuses. The major negative factor was that the split within the opposition, coming as it did at this moment, could result in much energy being wasted because of the lack of coordination, and it could also create the danger (which turned out to be real to some extent) that effort would be expended on conflicts and frictions. But competition and even mutual control are positive phenomena in themselves, representing a realization of the postulate of pluralism. If this last aspect was not fully appreciated by those who were worried about the break up of the opposition movement, this was mainly because it was not clear what divided ROPCiO from KOR, nor were the ideological and programmatic differences between them clear. This state of affairs always arouses the concern that these differences result from personal ambitions, which are rarely fruitful. Were there then any substantive differences between these two groups? The answer is not an easy one.

Broadly speaking, a typical associate of KOR would be farther to the left than a participant in ROPCiO. Of course the Polish people have been subject to confusion for a long time, and not only on the issue of right and left. If being on the left is understood as an attitude that emphasizes the possibility and the necessity of reconciling human liberty with human equality, while being on the right is understood as an attitude that may mean sacrificing the postulate of human freedom in favor of various kinds of social collectives and structures, or foregoing the postulate of equality in the name of laissez-faire, then the above statement about the difference between an average KOR associate and an average ROPCiO participant will be understandable. To put it differently, one was more likely to encounter ethnocentric and traditionalist attitudes among participants in ROPCiO than among the associates of KOR. But this is a generalization. One sometimes encountered rightists among KOR associates, and conversely, in ROPCiO there were also people of leftist views, while these differences were rarely present in extreme forms and intermediate positions were more common.

Thus, it was hard to find a nationalist in KOR, but not in ROPCiO, which does not mean that they were the dominant force there. In KOR one could never meet an anti-Semite, while in ROPCiO there were some, although the occasional charge that anti-Semitism was a dominant attitude of ROPCiO is unfair. From the milieu of ROPCiO or of those close to ROPCiO came accusations that KOR was not patriotic, or at least that a large number of its activists were not, and that KOR was indifferent to the issue of regaining Polish sovereignty. These accusations, undoubtedly unfair, made KOR associates furious and were taken as an intentional insult which made the conflicts worse.

ROPCiO willingly proclaimed its Catholicism. It seems indeed (although probably not without exception) that the majority in ROPCiO were religious, while KOR was in this respect a coalition or conglomeration of people with a variety of philosophies. It seems also that there was some difference between the Catholics in KOR and those in ROPCiO: the KOR group was convinced that in the struggle with evil, a person with the same ethical principles is a natural ally even if he is not religious. But it needs to be stressed once again that these are only general differences. Everyone who worked in KOR knows that in a variety of contacts, and sometimes even in cooperation, a common language could be found without great difficulty.

ROPCiO quickly became a competitor with KOR as far as the press was concerned. The first issue of *Opinia*, which was well edited, though rather in the style of a political evening paper, appeared on April 30, 1977, reproduced on a duplicator and edited by Kazimierz Janusz, Leszek Moczulski, and Wojciech Ziembiński. We should also list among ROPCiO publications the factual and well-edited periodical for peasants, *Gospodarz* (*The Farmer*), and the periodical of young people from Gdańsk, *Bratniak*, which was very interesting and upheld high standards. Despite all its efforts, ROPCiO could not compete with the KOR press neither in terms of numbers of issues nor in the extent of its distribution nor in the range of its interests and views.

KOR never felt threatened by ROPCiO's competition in the area of social work. While the committee regarded this aspect of its own work as fundamental, in ROPCiO it was marginal, and influenced neither ROPCiO's style of work nor its strategy and tactics, nor did it consume a large share of the finances, nor was social aid of particular interest to the majority of its participants. The few social problems with which ROPCiO dealt were almost exclusively in the hands of Bogusław Studziński, a KIK activist and a talented social worker, with whom KOR was always able to cooperate, not only because he found in KOR the means to meet a significant part of his needs, but also because it was easy for the people of KOR to speak a common language with him.

ROPCiO did not long exist in the form in which it was conceived. Within a period of eighteen months there occurred a series of ruptures caused by Leszek Moczulski, who tried to impose his leadership on his colleagues. As a result of a series of battles, the following components emerged: ROPCiO proper, that is, Czuma's group; the Confederation of Independent Poland (KPN), Moczulski's group; the Young Poland Movement (*Bratniak*'s group, headed by Aleksander Hall); the Movement of Independent Democrats in Łódź (Karol Głogowski, Andrzej Mazur, Andrzej Ostoja-Owsiany, Adam Wojciechowski, and Andrzej Woźnicki); and the Committee for National Self-Determination (Wojciech Ziembiński).

Following the splits within ROPCiO, KOR maintained correct relations with some of these groups. This was the case with the Young Poland Movement, which had a neo-endecja orientation,[17] and which was respected by KOR not only because of the intellectual ability of its leaders but also because of their loyalty in situations of conflict (this applies above all to Aleksander Hall), which made possible an atmosphere of moral trust. Cooperation with Czuma's group was correct, and in some instances even friendly (this included, among others, Bogusław Studziński, Kazimierz Janusz, Jerzy Brykczyński, and Piotr Typiak, a well-known peasant activist). Both of these groups occasionally relied on loans from KOR.

Relations with the Movement of Independent Democrats were worse, but correct at least to the extent that there were no disgraceful quarrels. With the Committee for National Self-Determination KOR had neither contacts (apart from social contacts) nor conflicts. This was a small group composed basically of three persons who could nevertheless always count on the signatures of at least a dozen generally respected people from the circles of veterans, led by General Boruta Spiechowicz. They published a periodical called *Rzeczypospolita* (*Commonwealth*). Worst of all were relations with Moczulski's KPN, which vehemently attacked KOR both in Poland and abroad. KPN's propaganda portrayed KOR as a group connected with some faction within PUWP (without indicating which faction), crypto-communist and opposed to Polish independence. This stance obviously made cooperation impossible.

Both the Committee for National Self-Determination and KPN laid strong claim to the cult of Józef Piłsudski. Moczulski even described himself as a "Piłsudski-man," and claimed that KPN was the only organization in Poland that sought independence, a ridiculous usurpation. KPN as a group was neither larger nor more powerful than Czuma's group, and it was certainly less influential than the Young Poland Movement. If some had a different impression, it was only because the Young Poland Movement avoided bluffing. But following the arrest of the KPN leaders and during their trial, the popularity and actual influence of this group were clearly on the increase.

The Price of Activism

Various "counterfeits"[18] and slanders printed in the official press frequently suggested, or even stated directly that KOR's work was a source of profit to its members and associates. I do not exclude the possibility that in some instances such claims may have been written in good faith, although not on the basis of any evidence, not even circumstantial, but rather because of the mentality of the authors. There are people who find it difficult to imagine that someone who has public funds at his disposal, and who is necessarily less controlled than a bank teller, would not embezzle the money, or that the reward for the hardships endured by the people of KOR could be anything other than salaries and payments drawn from some wealthy source. In fact, there is the problem of the price paid by KOR members and associates for what they were doing.

First, let us ask what KOR managed to accomplish from the time of the committee's creation until the shock of Pyjas' death.

Ursus: 202 persecuted workers from the Ursus Mechanical Enterprises were registered, together with 64 people working in several other Warsaw factories, but living in Ursus; 169 families received help; cost, 715,470 zlotys.

Radom: 511 persecuted workers were registered; 274 families received financial help; 92 persons received legal help; and 274 people received medical help; cost, 1,663,560 zlotys.

Gdańsk: 93 persecuted persons were registered; 34 families were given financial help; cost, 80,810 zlotys.

Łódź: 68 persecuted workers (or families) were registered and received financial help; cost, 182,550 zlotys.

Płock: 44 persecuted workers were registered; 32 families received help, cost, 400,000 zlotys.

Grudziądz: 43 persecuted workers were registered; 25 families received help; cost, 180,800 zlotys.

As anyone can see, there were more places in Poland that KOR did not reach with its help than those with which it had contact. One can also observe evident disproportions in aid, resulting from a variety of causes: whether KOR arrived with its help earlier or later, or whether in a given city the problem of getting back on one's job was more or less serious (for example, the situation was not too bad in Płock, somewhat worse in Radom, and very bad in Ursus).

Some people might reproach KOR bitterly for the fact that the committee did not reach whole areas of Poland, that it was too late in reaching other places, and that even in Radom and Ursus it was able to provide aid only to some of those who had been wronged. Of course, not everyone can be accorded the moral right to offer such criticisms, only those who announced their willingness to work and did so, however little. After all, in addition to other obstacles and limitations in KOR's work, such as interference from the police and the Security Service, limited financial means, and difficulty of access (distance, lack of contacts, etc.), there was one more difficulty that needs to be remembered: the limited physical energy of what was in truth too small a group of people for such a large country of some thirty million people. Some people were indifferent or afraid, others probably really could not help, because of their health, or their large families, or sometimes because of other truly important social or scientific or other obligations that would have been jeopardized by their participation in KOR, although this last argument, used to appease one's conscience, was notoriously abused. Mostly, it was the barrier of fear and the problem of inertia or indifference that limited participation. Most of these people never attacked KOR, and many of them looked up to those who were active in KOR with admiration or even gratitude. But there were also others who searched for an ideology to excuse their own cowardice or indifference or impotence. These people gladly heeded the propaganda (and not only party propaganda) according to which KOR was composed of traitors who had sold themselves (either to the communists or to the Jews, or the Germans, or the CIA, or maybe to all of them a little bit) or at best careerists who were ingeniously investing in their future positions as dignitaries.

But were there reasons to be afraid? What was the actual price to be paid for working in KOR? This price varied; it ranged from the necessity of giving up every minute of one's free time all the way to the price of life itself. This was the price paid by Stanisław Pyjas. The types and examples of repressions that were used, which are described below, all exclusively from the first period of KOR activity, which ended with the death of Pyjas. In this respect, every period had its own specific character, and this is why they must be discussed separately.

Loss of Work or Expulsion from the University

Dismissal from work has always been one of the basic forms of repression used against politically undesirable activists in the Polish People's Republic; this time was no exception.

On October 14, 1976, by order of Zygmunt Rybicki, the rector of Warsaw University, Antoni Macierewicz was dismissed from his job in the Department of Iberian Languages.

On October 21, Mirosław Chojecki, an associate and later a member of KOR, was summarily dismissed from his job in the Institute of Nuclear Research.

On February 14, 1977, the Regional Appeals Commission for Warsaw-Center not only dismissed the complaint filed by Andrzej Celiński, an associate and later a member of KOR, against Warsaw University for illegal dismissal from work, but it also declared that political views constituted a valid reason for such dismissal.

On April 15, 1977, Ryszard Babicz, an associate of KOR, was fired from his job in the Spare Parts Trading Enterprise in Poznań. Also dismissed from work during the same period were: Seweryn Blumsztajn, Jan Lityński, Joanna Szczęsna, and Wojciech Ziembiński (although the Labor Court later reversed the dismissal of Ziembiński).

An even greater wave of dismissals came in May 1977.

KOR also encountered one case of a worker dismissed from work in Gdańsk because he arranged a meeting and collected signatures in defense of a colleague persecuted after June 25. This initiative was apparently the only one of its kind, not connected with KOR but completely individual. The person dismissed was Henryk Kicha from the Gdańsk Shipyard, the chairman of the Socialist Union of Polish Youth.

Unfavorable transfers to different jobs, for example, as applied to KOR member Józef Śreniowski, constituted a less painful form of repression.

Such reprisals in the Reytan High School caused great consternation in Warsaw.[19] Toward the end of January, six teachers from this school, three of them retired, had signed one of the letters demanding the formation of a special Diet commission to investigate the events of June 1976 (Anna Modrzejewska, Anna Sosin, Ireneusz Gugulski, Maria Kilkoska, Ewa Ostrowska, and Stefania Światłowska). In late February, the first three, who were not retired, were officially transferred to other Warsaw schools (without agreement, but also without protest, from the Union of Polish Teachers). This action caused an immediate protest on the part of the students. Letters against these measures were signed by 159 students and 252 alumni. One of the transfers was annulled.

Expulsion from an institution of higher learning is comparable to dismissal from work. It seems that from fear of the consequences, this weapon was used rather sparingly, and some pretext, usually false, was considered necessary. During the period in question, Jacek Bierezin, an associate of KOR and later the editor of the literary periodical *Puls*, was expelled from Łódź University.

Obviously, dismissals or unfavorable transfers are not the only ways in which employees can be harassed. Some methods are all but imperceptible, such as, for example, the blocking of promotions. Additional methods were used for scholars: in the case of Łukasz Czuma, who was connected with the opposition through his brothers Andrzej and Benedykt, the Qualifying Commission of the Council of Ministers[20] refused to confirm the habilitation he had completed at the Catholic University in Lublin. The same thing happened to Jan Józef Lipski's habilitation in the Institute of Literary Studies of the Polish Academy of Sciences. Another method of repression in the area of professional work is the so-called notation of the censorship, that is, the prohibition against publishing the works of a given author or even of publishing any mention of him. Virtually all the writers connected with the opposition had received such notations in the course of their careers, often extending over a period of many years.

Yet another form of repression, and one less severe in its consequences than dismissal from work or other work-related repressions, was the elimination of KOR members and associates from various areas of social life. The expulsion of two active scouting instructors, Piotr Naimski and Wojciech Onyszkiewicz, from the Union of Polish Scouts can serve as an example.[21] Similarly, Karol Głogowski, who was connected with ROPCiO, was expelled from the Association of Polish Lawyers.

Surveillance, Interrogations, Detentions, and Searches

Every member of KOR who was able to look around a little knew at first hand what it meant to be under surveillance. Surveillance could assume a variety of forms: from the discreet and relatively imperceptible shadowing used by the political police when they really wanted to learn where a given person was going, to the very ostentatious and even impudent spying used when the suspected person or his circle was to be frightened; sometimes the latter was also done in order to paralyze the activities of a suspect. Every police agent was equipped with a radiotelephone, and several usually worked together in a team using one or two automobiles also equipped with radiotelephones. Even with more discreet forms of surveillance it was very easy to recognize the "quiet ones," as the agents were called by those being followed. Still, approximately an hour and a half of hard work was required in order to make sure that one was not under surveillance. Helpful for this purpose were empty streets or little-known passageways through courtyards or buildings, or tactics such as running, doubling back suddenly, or momentarily attempting to hide. These methods are not available to everyone, since everyone is not sufficiently in shape. Cases in which the guards became aggressive were rare, but not unheard of. A person being followed might be taught that he could be run over by a car approaching at great speed and passing as close as possible just when the "victim" was trying to cross the street on a green light: one KOR member managed to identify an elderly couple as agents; while on another occasion a woman with a child in a carriage took part in surveillance!

Usually surveillance had a practical motive: it was supposed to supply information or paralyze activity. But on less resistant persons long weeks of surveillance can have harmful psychological effects, and it is not very pleasant to find oneself alone with the "quiet ones" in an empty street late at night or in a dark stairway, especially sometimes when contact was almost physical. When surveillance was ostentatious and the agent did not leave the person he was watching for a moment, and walked with him shoulder to shoulder, it would sometimes happen that friends or acquaintances saying hello in the street would try to shake hands with the plainclothesman. One then had to tell them as quickly as possible that this was a mistake, and explain why. It was especially difficult when one was neither young nor healthy to escape surveillance if, let us say, there were six plainclothesmen using two cars and who were always able to summon additional police cars for help (although the drivers cannot be counted: they were not supposed to leave their cars except in exceptional instances).

Once a discreet surveillance had been identified, should one then let the followers know that they had been recognized? The question to ask is: "for what purpose?" It happened, though rarely, that such a team that had been recognized would be taken off, or replaced with another team after an hour or so. But the frustration of the "quiet ones" had also to be taken into account—their bosses would not praise them if they let themselves be recognized too often.

Electronic surveillance was a completely different matter. This was a possibility from the very beginning, and was considered as a certainty a short while later. If, half an hour before departure, I would tell my wife at home that I was going to travel by train to a different city, and this brought about surveillance that started at the railroad station, then the existence of bugging devices in the apartment had to be considered seriously. The result was that KOR people communicated in apartments with a piece of paper on the table and a pen in their hands. Anything that could be considered useful to the Security Service was written down, not spoken aloud, and the pieces of paper were destroyed as soon as possible.

Was this an excessive precaution? Probably not. KOR not only had circumstantial evidence that bugging was taking place but on three occasions a bugging device was actually found in an apartment, and in every instance the discovery was accidental. This happened in the Warsaw apartment of Sergiusz Kowalski, a young mathematician; in the apartment of Jacek Bierezin, a young poet and the editor-in-chief of *Puls;* and also in the apartment of one of the Radom associates of KOR. In the first of these cases, an expert participated in the discovery of the device, although the idea of the search was the result of an accident. The listening device was extracted in the presence of several excited foreign correspondents in Warsaw. (The letters "UK" found on the microphone meant that the device came from the United Kingdom.) Bierezin discovered a listening device in a ventilator. He invited some friends to look it over, and then the police and the Security Service entered the apartment under the pretext of an alleged burglary at a nearby newspaper stand by unknown perpetrators. In the midst of a crowded studio, the device was not confiscated but made to disappear so skillfully that one might suspect that in the Security Service team there was a high-class professional thief.

Obviously, electronic surveillance can assume a variety of forms, although generally it was done by means of devices similar to those that were discovered, which were rather primitive, although they did their job, and by telephone wiretapping, which is so widespread it hardly needs mentioning.

Most normal people certainly would not find it easy to live with the knowledge that everything one does can be overheard by others, even in the privacy of one's bedroom. But given time, it is possible to adjust to anything, and gradually one ceased to think of those who were eaves-dropping as human beings (which obviously was a kind of moral aberration).

The people of KOR were also harassed by detentions. In the Polish People's Republic the police have the right to detain any citizen, that is, to deprive him of his freedom, for up to forty-eight hours. The prosecutor need not be informed nor does the detention require his agreement or approval *ex post facto*. In fact, the police and the Security Service regard the possibility of detaining a citizen as their unconditional privilege—and no one has ever heard of a case in which the police were required to explain why they were detaining someone. This is an area of total discretion, because, among other things, detention has no legal consequences. It is at the same time an excellent method of harassing a person, since nothing stops the police from detaining someone three times in a single week, each time for forty-eight hours. One instruction from Prosecutor General Czubiński published by Solidarity in 1980 made reference to *de facto* arrests for several days as a result of transporting the detained person from one police precinct to another after forty-eight hours, and then again after another forty-eight hours, and so on, so that the person subjected to this treatment was never out of the hands of the police even for a moment. The instruction recommended this practice, which made a mockery of the law. The institution of such completely unwarranted detentions has been impressed on the legal mentality of Polish citizens to such an extent that on many occasions even dissidents, upon hearing of someone's detention or telling stories about their own, would say: "but they have a right to do this," even though not one of the conditions provided for in the Code of Criminal Procedure had been observed.

One unpleasant aspect of detentions, among others, was that the police are not required to inform the family about the event. If the detention occurs on the street with no witnesses who know the address or the telephone number of the detainee, the family may spend two days searching for their relative in hospitals, emergency rooms, and other such places, since police headquarters or precincts do not give out such information. There are a number of other burdens: for example, the detainee receives neither a mattress nor a blanket.

One of the few responsibilities of all KOR associates was related to detentions: people were required to let others know as soon as possible about their release. There was also a requirement of giving information about the detention of others. The "Information Bank" was managed by Grażyna Kuroń together with her entire family: the famous "logbooks" contained all the information that came in, except for news that had to be kept totally secret. These successive logbooks were usually confiscated during searches of Kuroń's apartment. There were never enough people working in KOR to be able to prepare current copies of these logbooks and keep them well hidden.

The exact registration of detentions was regarded as one of the basic responsibilities of KOR, since it was connected with the ability to monitor the security of KOR members and associates. Whoever disappeared, when it was not certain that he was detained, could have been a victim of an accident or an attack. He could also have been detained—and this was the most likely possibility—in such a manner that there was no one who could have informed KOR. The detainee could then have been exposed to the danger of being sentenced to pay a fine by a sentencing board for misdemeanors, and if he were unable to pay it immediately he could have been put in prison without anyone being informed of this.

Foreign correspondents were also informed about detentions. This was not "news" for them, but they also knew—although they did not hide their boredom—that they had to register this data if they wanted to receive other information from KOR. In addition, the Smolar brothers, foreign associates of KOR in the West, were always informed about detentions by telephone.

When detention lasted longer than forty-eight hours, it meant either that the person had received a prosecutor's sanction and was under arrest, or that the police had seriously violated the Code of Criminal Procedure. Thus, any associate of KOR who did not inform KOR immediately about his release was exposing the committee to the danger of raising a false alarm, which would have endangered the trustworthiness and the authority of the committee.

On numerous occasions, the police and the Security Service detained members and associates of KOR on absurd accusations having something to do with investigations of criminal cases. Thus, for example, the great actress and KOR member Halina Mikołajska was detained in Cracow under the pretext that a sheepskin coat had been lost in one of the Cracow coffeehouses, and that its description was similar to the one the actress was wearing. A search was conducted in the house of KOR associate Hanna Ostrowska in Radom in connection with a bootlegging operation. But the police were more interested in typewritten manuscripts than in pots and pipes, and soon the pretext changed into a prosecutor's sanction charging that Ostrowska was collaborating with hostile centers and was accordingly preparing false information. Józef Śreniowski was informed that the police were looking for a child-murderer; the Barańczaks frequently resembled a pair of notorious criminals; Hanna Turczyn looked to the police like a purse-snatcher; while Mariusz Muskat resembled a foreign currency tradesman, and so on. One could extend this list illustrating the various types of repressions that were not terribly dangerous, but galling and bothersome in daily life.

The goal of this activity was not only to generate pretexts, but also to create an atmosphere of fear, in a sense to push people closer to crime, to induce a condition of neurotic dread by demonstrating the ease with which such demeaning accusations can be directed against honest citizens. The more absurd the pretexts, the stronger was the neurotic reaction (since people became convinced that "they can do anything"). These harassments were a premeditated manifestation of disregard for truth and law, designed to paralyze, at least to some degree, the activity of the persecuted.[22]

But detention was not always accompanied by explanations. Most often, no one took the trouble to justify why a person was being held. Detentions took place under a variety of circumstances. For example, in Radom most detentions occurred after the trials, and not before. Why? God knows, but in any case this was a little more decent toward the KOR associates and members whose mission, after all, was to observe the trials. It was almost a rule that after a house search a person would be taken to police headquarters. Participants in gatherings, even of only five people, were detained after the police would invade the apartment. As a result, for a long time, attempts to hold a meeting of all the members of KOR were unsuccessful. During detention attempts were sometimes made to interrogate, but not always; sometimes people would be released the same day, sometimes only after forty-eight hours.

Detention required a stay in one of the police headquarters. The sanitary conditions were not the best; sometimes they were scandalous, and there were only boards to sleep on. The company was that of criminals, which had both its faults and its advantages. If the politicals behaved with tact, or unless he had been promised something in return, the average criminal in Poland was not aggressive toward the politicals but, to the contrary, generally showed sympathy. Such a common stay "under the cell"[23] was usually educational to both parties: the criminals widened their political and intellectual horizons, while the politicals not only learned about the criminal milieu, but also about prisoners, and about how they were being treated in disregard of the law. These meetings in shared cells were to some degree responsible for the fact that Solidarity later fought with understanding, and with some success, for the humanization of conditions in prisons and during arrests. During the period in question, approximately one hundred members and associates of KOR were deprived of their freedom. Some were detained repeatedly.

A house search, a "domicilary visit" in the official jargon, should in principle take place on the basis of a decision by the prosecutor's office. Sometimes the team that came to perform the search showed such a warrant; sometimes the person searched received it *ex post facto*, after he demanded to see it. The searches took place either under some frivolous or imaginary pretext, or for no known reason at all. They had their own ritual, but their thoroughness and severity varied, according to the different social classes. In the apartment of a member of the intelligentsia, especially in a large city, a search left no traces. Every book that was examined (and basically, in a search of average thoroughness conducted for political reasons, all books were examined) was afterward returned to its place; every piece of clothing remained where it had been; even papers in and on the desk were arranged just as they had been before. A degree of courtesy was generally shown unless the person who was being searched chose to observe a different convention.

In the houses of the intelligentsia, books and periodicals published in Poland without censorship, or abroad by the émigrés, were especially prized during the searches. In particular, all books published by the hated Literary Institute in Paris, including volumes of poetry, by Miłosz, among others, were confiscated without explanation (the legal basis for this is not known). But it also happened that books would be taken because they were printed in Hebrew,[24] or in some other foreign language, or in the area of, for example, history of art, because something in the title seemed worrisome. In these cases, the report would contain the formula: "a foreign-language work." This was a universal description. It designated everything written, whether by hand or typed or printed, in any foreign language.

The searches in workers' apartments were different. Here both the vocabulary and the behavior were different, and after a search the apartment would look like it had been hit by a tornado, or as it used to look after searches in the days of Hitler or Stalin. The contents of drawers, closets, chests, and shelves lay all mixed up and trampled in the middle of the room. On many occasions in Radom the police requested that they remain alone in the apartment with the person being searched, while his wife and children were asked out onto the staircase, which was often not heated. Usually they were taken in by the neighbors, and we can note parenthetically that this had a positive influence on solidarity among the workers.

A search of the house of a peasant would resemble that of a worker's apartment, with the addition that in the peasant's house the police gladly broke something: a piece of machinery, or some equipment in the pigsty, or the tops of beehives would be removed in the winter and somehow the police would "forget" to put them back on, so that all the bees would freeze, and so on. One particularly wonderful "game" was for the police to destroy something and then offer this as a proof of the neglected state of the farm, which could even lead to dispossession. This was the favorite method used, for example, against Janusz Rożek, a peasant activist from the Lublin area.

In the KOR circle, searches usually meant the loss of a typewriter. It was taken ostensibly for the purpose of checking the cut of the letters, but it would never be returned, even if it had not been used for oppositional work. In the course of four years approximately forty typewriters were lost in this manner. Sometimes, out of sheer exuberance, photographic equipment, tape recorders, and on two occasions radios were also confiscated.

Foreign currency was taken as a rule and was never returned (the possession of foreign currency is legal; it is only illegal to trade in it). Some losses were incurred in this manner during the initial period of KOR's activity. Altogether a sum of roughly $1,000 in various denominations was confiscated. Later, the methods used for hiding foreign currency were improved, and it was no longer a problem. Still, even larger sums in zlotys could meet the same fate. The confiscation of cans of food from Chojecki's apartment topped everything else. The cans were indeed earmarked for unemployed workers in Radom, but this was not written on them! True, a *KOR Communiqué* had reported that KOR had received some cans, so the idea of confiscating them must have come from this.

There were approximately thirty house searches during this period, and the police interrupted meetings in private apartments on about ten different occasions. One of these intrusions, into the apartment of KOR associate Antoni Buchner, took place before a concert which the famous violinist Irena Dubińska was to give before a mixed audience of workers and intellectuals. The workers were from Radom. They were successfully evacuated from the apartment before the police entered.

There were also violations of personal liberty which bear a stronger resemblance to kidnappings or abductions than to police arrests. Andrzej Zdziarski, a student, was kidnapped from a Warsaw street late on the night of October 8, 1976. He was taken some thirty miles north of the city (past Radzymin, near Beniaminów). During the trip he was threatened with death. The kidnappers identified themselves only by metal police badges. When he got out of the car he was prepared for the worst. Zdziarski was left in a forest in the middle of the night.

On October 9, Grażyna Kowalczyk was dragged into a car right in front of her building. The kidnappers, who introduced themselves as agents of counterintelligence, took the young woman to a motel in Świdry Małe. She was urged to collaborate with the Security Service and in return was promised help in gaining admission to the university.

On November 10, KOR member Piotr Naimski was kidnapped to Zalesie Górne, where attempts were made to interrogate him.

The Concentration of Fire on Halina Mikołajska

The Security Service launched a particularly massive attack against Halina Mikołajska. According to the predictions of Security Service experts, she was not expected to withstand it, and indeed, a momentary but severe breakdown did take place and she attempted to commit suicide. The great actress was saved after having swallowed a large quantity of sleeping pills. The rescue was successful because her body was accustomed to this particular medication, and the attempt to save her came in time. The repertory of the Security Service was varied. There were constant telephone calls at all hours of the day or night. All the members and some associates of KOR were subjected to this. The telephone calls also varied. Most often they began with vulgar insults, or insults would follow unexpectedly after two sentences spoken in a different tone. Threats were made, both by telephone and in letters ("it is very easy to kill a man"). Sometimes there were attempts to arrange a meeting in a matter "not suitable for the telephone." It would then turn out that deserted locations were suggested for this meeting, and proposals to meet in a less isolated place were answered by hanging up. Mikołajska and other members of KOR received as many as five letters a day. They followed different standards, from outright vulgarity all the way to persuasions that could have been penned, let us say, by an intelligent teacher from the provinces. Some KOR members would naively answer in writing to the address of the sender. As a rule, these letters would be returned with a note from the post office that the addressee was unknown, that there was no such house number or even that the street did not exist. These letters would start arriving en masse one day, and then, as if on order, they would as suddenly stop.

The Security Service poured paint all over Mikołajska's car, stinking gas or fluid was put inside the gas tank, so that the stench disappeared only after several weeks, and the starter was broken, causing the danger of an explosion. In Radom the tires were punctured or cut on her car. On one occasion, the locks on Mikołajska's apartment door were destroyed; on another a burglary was simulated; and early one morning a dozen or so men entered her apartment claiming that they were workers, and for several hours they refused to leave. They screamed, shouted insults, waved their hands in front of her face, and predicted she would be beaten up, or that rotten eggs would be thrown at her during her next theater performance. It is highly unlikely that these were really people from Ursus, as they claimed, not even from the party organization there, since it is usually impossible to form such a goon squad in total secrecy, and it is always possible to find out some of their names. But all attempts to establish the identity of this group were completely unsuccessful, despite the fact that many workers of Ursus tried to investigate this matter. The atmosphere of these days, and especially the terror used against Halina, found literary expression in a beautiful memoir written by her husband, Marian Brandys, entitled "From One Ring to the Next," in the volume, *My Adventures with History* (1981).[25]

Slanders, Lies, and "Counterfeits"

Another affliction resulting from affiliation with KOR involved being constantly under fire from slanders, libels, and lies.[26] The repertory was diverse. For example, Antoni Macierewicz, who was waiting for a cooperative apartment, had to wander with his family from one apartment to another: someone would leave for several months, or someone else would then take them in, but he was constantly hounded by the Security Service, who would terrorize his hosts. Once, during a short stay in one such temporary "encampment," it turned out that "unknown perpetrators" had stuck a leaflet in the doors of all the neighbors in a high-rise apartment building warning them against the "so-and-so" (first and last name included) living in such-and-such an apartment, who was well known to the police as a sexual pervert. Accordingly, the parents of girls were warned to take good care of their daughters. It is true that as one result of this, two neighbors visited the "pervert" and offered him donations for KOR, but there is no way of knowing how many others were indeed scared.

The "counterfeits" mentioned previously were another method of slander. These pamphlets were printed better than the publications of KOR at the time. One could learn from them that donations given to help the workers went instead into private pockets, or were spent simply on vodka, and that in any case, they were simply supplements to funds from the CIA or the West German revanchists, Hupka and Czaja, who generously rewarded the saboteurs of KOR. These last two names became such a common refrain that they usually provoked laughter.

The many counterfeits originating inside Poland in the Security Service were also aided not by counterfeits but by authentic letters coming from abroad, from the Polish emigration. The famous letter of Jędrzej Giertych was the first such "genuine counterfeit." The letter reached Poland in July 1976, when KOR's work was just beginning but KOR itself did not yet exist. This compilation of drivel, according to which all dissident activities in Poland were inspired jointly by the intelligence services of the United States, West Germany, Israel, and China in order to answer Soviet successes in Angola and elsewhere by a diversion in Poland, was treated by the addressees as a "counterfeit" from Rakowiecka Street. To everyone's surprise it turned out that it was nothing of the sort. This was an authentic expression of the political thought of Jędrzej Giertych. More interesting than the contents of the letter were the technical details connected with it.

It is difficult to say how many of these letters were sent (it was a nice printing job done in a London printshop). In any case, there were more than one hundred, probably many more. Every addressee received it more or less on the same day (there were minimal differences): an unusual small cream-colored envelope. The date of the London postmark was identical on all of them, as was the format of the addresses and other details. The usually so inquisitive and active Security Service had no trouble at all letting an entire bag of letters conspicuous by their atypical and standardized appearance go through. Well, the secrecy of correspondence is, after all, honored in the Polish People's Republic.

It is not easy to establish a hundred (or more) Polish addresses from London. This is a tremendous job. Those active in Poland who had once in a while composed mailing lists even in their own city know something about this. For example, the telephone book lists the address, that is, the street and the house number, but not the apartment number. Jędrzej Giertych had compiled all these numbers precisely. Sometimes he also addressed his letter to the workplace, and he knew, as it turned out, the place of employment of the wife of a known opposition activist. He had up-to-date knowledge of the most recent changes in workplace or address. He made no mistakes in details. One has to admire the organizational talent and the hard work of Jędrzej Giertych, and especially of his collaborators.

Antoni Gronowicz, a writer living in the United States, also accused KOR of embezzling funds, and at the same time he reproached the Jurzykowski Foundation, charging that under the pretext of awarding a prize to Jan Józef Lipski it had sent money to KOR. This also was not a counterfeit; it was a denunciation with a clear intent. It was to constitute the basis for confiscating this money, had it been sent to Poland, while at the same time it threatened the foundation's worthy practice of granting awards also to Poles living in Poland.

A faked interview with Leszek Kołakowski and Adam Michnik that appeared in the *Deutsche Nazionale Zeitung* (March 25, 1977) was something else again. Only by means of a lawsuit were the two dissidents able to force the newspaper to publish a retraction stating that the interview was a forgery. In the meantime, journalists in Poland, of the ilk of W. Wysocki, Masłowski (M. A. Styks), and J. Kossak, took up this issue and of course they never retracted their claims later. This is an interesting example of the collaboration between the centers directing the struggle against KOR and the West German nationalists.

In October 1976 a number of cultural institutions received an appeal supposedly from Jerzy Andrzejewski in support of equality for sexual minorities. His signature had been forged.

In October and November, unknown perpetrators put into circulation *KOR Communiqués* (numbered 3 and 4) which were forgeries, as was an unnumbered "Clarifying Communiqué." A forged statement by Brus, Kołakowski, and Michnik was also distributed.

In December, Edward Lipiński and at least a dozen others received a letter from Paris, sent supposedly from the Revolutionary Communist League (the French Section of the Fourth Internationale) charging that KOR had embezzled money it had received from this organization. The idea was clever: it accommodated both the favorite notion of the Security Service, that KOR was acting out of Trotskyist inspiration, and even with Trotskyist money, while at the same time it was supposed to arouse doubts about the personal honesty of KOR members. The leadership of the league declared that this letter was a forgery.

Surely this list is not complete. The most interesting aspect is that despite the effort put into this action, today, from the perspective of time, it can be evaluated not only as futile but what is more, it augmented sympathy for KOR. Every lie and forgery that KOR unmasked generated new feelings of moral solidarity with KOR.

Equally futile were the anti-KOR publications in the press, since public reaction to them was similar. KOR registered these articles under the rubric of its "blacklist," but in truth it owed thanks (but not respect) to their authors. Let us pause to recall here again the names of those who aided the police and the Security Service at that time: Barbara Dróżdż, Irena Dryl, Kira Gałczyńska, Wojciech Giełżyński (pen name Alfred Łoś), Anna Kłodzińska, Michał Misiorny, Edmund Osmańczyk, Bohdan Roliński, Marian Wojciechowski. This is certainly not a full list, though it is copied from the *KOR Communiqués* of this period. But who in those days really had the time to follow these things?

Soon, in May and June 1977, new names would be added.

Anti-Semitism as a Weapon Against KOR

The CIA, not to mention Hupka and Czaja, was nothing compared to the Zionists and Trotskyists. These appeared not only in "counterfeits" but was a common motif of party propaganda, and even of some publications of the Polish political emigration in the West. While earlier, in 1968, the password had been "Zionist," which veiled the anti-Semitic campaign somewhat, this word was now being replaced by the synonym "Trotskyist," used also totally nonsensically, and also used instead of the word "Jew." This is obviously no insult, even if used with this intention, but it conceals the slanderous accusation of camouflage and attempts to mislead the public.

Anti-Semitism could fill a whole chapter in the history of combatting KOR, from conversations warning the workers of Ursus and Radom not to take money from the Jews in KOR, to anti-Semitic vituperations against Ludwik Dorn as he was being beaten in the headquarters of the Radom police, all the way to huge graffiti beautifully painted on walls and fences with the green oil paint that was at that time completely unavailable in the stores—"KOR IS JEWS"—slogans that were painted over only after many protests by residents of the neighborhood, whereas all others were painted over immediately. In Castle Square in Warsaw, a particularly public place visited by crowds of tourists, one such sign could be seen for over a year. Standing at a bus stop, one could hear a plainclothesman sigh, "Mr. X, why do you get involved with these Jews?" if the person being followed was considered "Aryan." It was after the sentencing board had passed sentence on the leaders of a patriotic demonstration on November 11, which had been organized by participants in ROPCiO, that the famous shout of a policeman frustrated by the prohibitions against beating was heard: "Let's get the hell out of here, it stinks of garlic and matzoh," to which a surprised Jacek Kuroń (who also likes garlic) answered: "But matzoh doesn't stink!"[27]

A classic example of the methods used to combat KOR was the statement made by Dr. Andrzej W. Sobociński from Gdańsk University, who expressed his opinion about the fast in the Church of Saint Martin (see chapter 6) by stating that since it was mostly Semites who were participating in it, a synagogue would have been a more appropriate place for this protest than a church. Of course he added the sacramental: "I am not an anti-Semite."

(Let me note parenthetically that many traditional anti-Semitic insults such as, for example, that Jews smell of garlic and onion, mean nothing to the young people of today. Thus, when early in KOR's activity a poem beginning the same way as the children's poem "Locomotive," by Julian Tuwim—but full of indiscriminate insults and ideas aimed at members of KOR—was being widely circulated, my daughter did not understand why the poem referred to her father as: "Faithful friend of the Elders of Zion / Would plant onion in many fields"; and she asked, "Do they think that we have a vegetable grower in the family?" Thus, this propaganda, in this case written perhaps by a professional versifier and a member of the Union of Polish Writers, who remembered prewar times, often struck in a vacuum.)

The Intensification of Terror and Its Culmination

As was mentioned at the beginning of this chapter, the observers at the open court trials in Radom were often subjected to beatings. Toward the end of the period in question, beatings again returned as a form of struggle against the opposition, as reported in the *KOR Communiqués*. On February 20, unknown perpetrators beat up two students at Poznań University, Piotr Liszek and Lech Krzywda-Pogorzelski, after which both were detained. KOR publications were taken away from them and they were interrogated until 2:00 A.M.

Great anxiety was felt in KOR over the beating of Władysław Sulecki, a miner from the Gliwice mine. He was a very energetic and brave associate of the committee who was active in an extremely difficult area, since Upper Silesia was known as an area the authorities controlled with an iron hand, and the police were extremely brutal. On May 4, 1977, Sulecki was dragged out of his apartment by the hair and beaten until he passed out, while no attention was paid to the presence of numerous witnesses, including his neighbors. A serious injury to the right side of his chest resulted from the beating. This was clearly a terrorist action.

After a while the perpetrators must have begun to worry about the effects of their "work," for Sulecki was driven to doctors who were collaborators of the Security Service and who presented the perpetrators with documents stating that nothing had happened to Sulecki. It was at that time that a well-known incident occurred: a female doctor, neurologist Hatossy, attempted to combine a medical exam with an interrogation (asking Sulecki about his trips to Warsaw, about his contacts there, etc.). Then Sulecki, a miner with only an elementary school education, asked her whether she had not perhaps forgotten the Hippocratic Oath, and then recited it to her. The doctor-policewoman was visibly shaken and stopped playing the interrogator.

Beatings and other manifestations of increased activity on the part of the Security Service were connected with renewed detentions of the KOR observers of court cases in Radom, and in general with a clear intensification of police actions against the committee.

On May 7, 1977, the body of KOR associate Stanisław Pyjas was discovered in Cracow. The circumstances allowed for no doubt about what had happened. At that moment began one of the most dramatic chapters in the history of the Workers' Defense Committee.

6

From the Death of Pyjas to the Transformation of KOR into KSS "KOR"
(May 1977–September 1977)

The Death of Staszek Pyjas

On May 7, 1977, in Cracow, the corpse of KOR associate Stansław (Staszek) Pyjas was discovered.

Stanisław Pyjas was among the earliest associates of KOR in Cracow. He was known as a particularly active young man who had, among other things, participated in the discussion and training meeting of dissident groups of young people, mainly from Cracow and Warsaw, that was held in Gorce during the winter. Thanks to this, he was known not only among the circle of students at the Jagiellonian University, where he was a fifth-year student of Polish literature, but he also lived in the dormitory "Żaczek." He came from a peasant background.

On May 7, two waitresses from a coffeehouse located in the courtyard of the house at 7, Szewska Street in Cracow arrived at work early in the morning. They arrived before 7:00 A.M. In the passageway connecting the street with the courtyard, they found a young man lying on his stomach, his head toward the courtyard. Near his head there was a puddle of blood, probably from the wound in the back of his head. The waitresses quickly realized that the man was dead and informed the police.

The case was immediately taken up by the homicide division of the Cracow police, but after only ten hours the investigation was taken out of their hands by the Security Service, although the policemen were not happy about this. One of the first things established by the police was that death had occurred at approximately 3:00 A.M. as a result of head injuries.

The news that a corpse had been discovered in the heart of old downtown Cracow spread through the city with lightning speed, and soon reached Pyjas's friends.

In order to better understand the case, we need to recall the letter written on April 21 by six students at the Jagiellonian University who belonged to a group cooperating with KOR. The letter was addressed to the District Prosecutor's Office in the Podgórze Quarter of Cracow. I cite this document in full because of the gravity of the case.

Appellants:

1. *Lesław Maleszka, Cracow, 6a Bławatkowa Street, Apt. 2*
2. *Bronisław Wildstein, Cracow, 5 Chocimska Street, Apt. 3*
3. *Mieczysław Godyń, Cracow, 7 Daszyński Street, Apt. 24*
4. *Andrzej Balcerak, Cracow, 13 Kwiaty Polskie Street*
5. *Bogusław Bek, Cracow, 5 Third of May Avenue, Room 688*
    (Student House "Żaczek")
6. *Stanisław Pyjas, Cracow, 5 Third of May Avenue, Room 444*
    (Student House "Żaczek")

Notification about the Commission of a Crime Under Article 166 and Others of the Criminal Code

On April 19–20, 1977, anonymous letters were sent by mail to Lesław Maleszka, Bronisław Wildstein, Mieczysław Godyń, and Andrzej Balcerak, while a letter to Bogusław Bek was planted in his room by an unknown perpetrator.

In addition to unusually vulgar insults and false libels concerning especially our friend Stanisław Pyjas (as well as other addressees), these letters also contained statements in which the unknown author demanded a brutal settling of accounts with the student Stanisław Pyjas (e.g., "the extermination of his kind . . . is the most important task at the present moment"—a quotation from a letter to Lesław Maleszka). Incitement to crime in this manner and the making of threats against a person constitute criminal activity according to Article 166 of the Criminal Code.

In addition, it is noteworthy that the author of these anonymous letters uses a particular form of blackmail toward all the addressees. Thus, he states that the Cracow Security Service relies in its activities on the work of informers of dubious moral reputation, who profit from monetary rewards and enjoy a variety of special privileges, for example, in relation to their studies. The Security Service is also supposed—according to the sender of these letters— to direct its activities against students who took part in gathering signatures on a petition to the Diet after the events of June 25, 1976. We do not wish here to analyze the methods of the Security Service; but we must state, however, that the right of citizens to petition is guaranteed to everyone by Article 82 of the Polish Constitution and in related decisions of the authorities, so that no one can be blackmailed by threats of reprisals from the justice system for making use of this right.

Since threats of this nature constitute a form of repression against us, and because we are worried about the potential for their realization, we hereby inform the Prosecutor's Office about the above and ask that appropriate steps be taken in this case.

LESŁAW MALESZKA
BOGUSŁAW BEK
STANISŁAW PYJAS
BRONISŁAW WILDSTEIN
ANDRZEJ BALCERAK
MIECZYSŁAW GODYŃ

enclosures: 5 copies of anonymous letters

In view of these circumstances, the question immediately arose of whether the death threat made by the Security Service on many occasions had not at least been realized. One should remember that Mirosław Chojecki, Eugeniusz Kloc, and Andrzej Zdziarski had all been threatened with death during interrogations, and there were also threats made by "unknown perpetrators" against all the members of KOR either by telephone or by anonymous letter.

Knowing that this question was being asked, on the very next day the prosecutor's office presented its version of Pyjas's death in the local press. Their version was simple: Pyjas was drunk and fell down the stairs, injuring himself so severely that he died by drowning in his own blood. As it turned out later, the forensic certificate was the work of Zdzisław Marek, the same doctor who had given expert testimony about the circumstances of the death of Jan Brożyna.

It is difficult to understand why the prosecutor's office made this statement without even the most rudimentary visit to the scene of the crime. This was done by the young activists of KOR, who assembled the initial documentation and questioned the residents of the building and the waitresses who found the body. As early as May 9, KOR member Lipski received trustworthy materials from the hands of the person participating in this attempt to get at the truth.

First, in the entryway of the building at 7 Szewska Street there are no stairs from which Pyjas could have fallen. The house is old and historical, and has no staircases at all, but rather galleries surrounding the courtyard, which are reached by wooden stairs. A fall from these stairs so tragic in its consequences would have made a tremendous amount of noise. No residents of the house had heard anything. Only one person who suffered from chronic insomnia had heard something, but it was definitely not a fall from the stairs, and occurred at a later hour.

Even if Pyjas had suffered a mortal fall down the stairs, why was he found in the entryway? If he had walked this distance, or crawled it, there would have been traces of blood in the courtyard. There was nothing of the sort. Blood was found only near Pyjas's head (and not much of it), and nowhere else. Furthermore, a person crawling toward the exit would certainly have done so with his head facing toward the street, and not backward, meaning that as he collapsed he would not have been lying in Pyjas's position. Had he choked on his own blood, there surely would have been traces of a struggle resulting from reflexes; there were none. Moreover, Pyjas was not found lying on his back, while cases of choking in one's own blood can occur only in this position. What had caused Pyjas's head wound? A silent impact against wooden steps?

And there was one more question: what strange fate had overtaken the bag with Pyjas's things? It was found near the stairs at 7 Szewska Street, as if to make the version of the fall down the stairs more plausible. In the bag there had been a report from Cracow for KOR (this was certainly not the cause of his misfortune, since the report did not contain revelations worth killing a man for). However, when the bag was found, the report was gone. All of this taken together, including the public statement by the prosecutor's office, was very strange.

Who had seen Pyjas last? A friend of Pyjas, Stanisław Pietraszko, visited the attorney Andrzej Rozmarynowicz, who agreed to represent Pyjas's family in connection with Staszek's death. The two young men had known each other since early childhood as schoolmates from neighboring villages; they attended the same elementary and high schools, and finally the Jagiellonian University, where they lived in the same student dormitory. But they were not united by common activities: Pietraszko was an activist of the Socialist Union of Polish Students. Rozmarynowicz took down Pietraszko's statement, and suggested he go to the prosecutor's office. This he did, and the files of the investigation contain Pietraszko's testimony. Pietraszko was the last person known to have seen Pyjas on the day of his death. According to him, as he was returning to the dormitory around 5:00 P.M., he passed Pyjas, who was accompanied by someone. In the words of Pietraszko, it looked as if Pyjas was being escorted. This seemed so strange to him that he turned around and observed the two men on the street for some time. Pietraszko gave a description of this man, and he was the only person who would have been able to recognize him during a chance meeting in the street or in a confrontation.

The witness Pietraszko is dead. On August 1, his corpse was found in the Soliński Reservoir. The investigation of the circumstances and causes of Pyjas's death was still in progress. An investigation conducted by the Intervention Bureau into the circumstances surrounding Pietraszko's was directed by one of the most intelligent and responsible associates of KOR, and produced the following results.

Pietraszko had received an unexpected organizational order from the Socialist Union of Polish Students to go to Bieszczady to one of the student summer camps. On July 30, he stopped at a camping site on the shores of Soliński Reservoir. Toward dusk he went to the lake to wash himself. His body was discovered floating in the weeds on August 1. According to forensic specialists consulted by KOR, if Pietraszko had drowned his body would not have floated up until somewhat later, as a result of decomposition. That it was floating on the surface suggests that there was air, not water, in the lungs. This could indicate that the body had been thrown into the water after suffering death from a cause other than drowning. From Krosno, where the autopsy was performed, KOR received information that the doctor who performed the autopsy had said that there was no water in the lungs. But when questioned directly, he denied this. KOR never saw the results of the autopsy.

The argument that drowning was the cause of death was problematic for another reason: Pietraszko's friends claimed that he was afraid of water and he would not have left the bank at dusk. Moreover, the lake bottom is shallow and sloped gently downward in this area. A careful investigation of the area did, however, discover an underwater ditch (a remnant of a gully) several hundred meters away. But it is doubtful that Pietraszko would have taken such a walk in the dark.

The family of Stanisław Pietraszko was called to Krosno. His brothers arrived. His body was transported back to his village in a car provided by the authorities, under police escort, which was rather unusual. The escort did not agree to drive through Cracow, despite the fact that for some reason Pietraszko's brothers wanted this done. By order of the authorities, the burial formalities were conducted very rapidly and the funeral was held at the cemetery in his village.

In spite of all these considerations, after a careful analysis of all the circumstances, KOR did not present publicly the thesis that Pietraszko had been murdered. The strange behavior of the police in this case might have been a result of their fear of public disturbances and their consequences. The autopsy report could explain and settle quite a lot. KOR, together with the Pyjas family's attorney Rozmarynowicz, drew attention to the need for a more precise examination of the circumstances surrounding Pietraszko's death, but without success, especially since Pietraszko's family did not have the courage to involve themselves in this matter in the way that Pyjas's family had done.

Those in KOR who knew the results of the investigations conducted by the Intervention Bureau were convinced that Pietraszko had been murdered. On the basis of information in KOR's possession, it was suspected that the murder had been committed by a person or persons who feared that Pietraszko would recognize the man escorting Pyjas on the day of his death. But even if KOR had publicly claimed that Pietraszko was murdered, it would not have been able to go beyond the formula of "unknown perpetrators."

The Death of Pyjas: An Accident or a Provocation?

The full truth about Pyjas's death is still not known, although it is difficult to doubt that he was murdered. One cannot exclude, however, the possibility that an accident may have played a role. According to this interpretation, which was widely held in KOR, Pyjas was supposed to be beaten up in the same way as, for example, Sulecki, though not as brutally. This would have been an act of terrorism that would have been understood unequivocally by the opposition, but murder was not intended. However, when the beating is severe enough, an accident can always occur, and perhaps that is what happened this time.

The visible lack of professionalism in planting the body speaks in favor of such an interpretation. It was done sloppily, perhaps in a panic that could be explained if those who were doing the beating suddenly realized that their victim was dead.

But there could be another explanation.

The tenth issue of the *Information Bulletin* for May 1977 carried on the front page an editorial about the tougher line being taken against KOR; and on the last page it reported the information about Pyjas's death. Although it was no rubric for "late notices," the text of the editorial makes it clear that the information about Pyjas's death had come in after the issue was already completed. The editorial says in part:

> On April 14, 1977, during the Plenary Meeting of the Central Committee of PUWP, Edward Gierek said: "We cannot . . . agree to violations of the law, to abuses of socialist democracy and of civil liberties, to activities resulting from alien class positions and directed against our socialist country. . . . We must and we will counteract this activity using all necessary means." This formulation marked a new accent in the statements of the First Secretary of the Central Committee of PUWP. Usually he emphasized political methods of struggling against the opposition movement in Poland.

The article went on to cite facts testifying to the intensification of terror against the opposition. Most important politically was the fate of the mysterious case "II DS 201/76," or rather of the investigations against "unknown perpetrators," "distributing false information that can cause serious harm to the interest of the Polish People's Republic" (Article 271 of the Criminal Code). Searches, detentions, and summonses to interrogations had often been marked with this code number. Among others, Kuroń and Lipski were called as witnesses, as was Michnik after his return from the West. And now, suddenly, the situation ripened. All three were indicted, but on the basis of a different article, number 132. It is easy to figure out why the article had been changed: to avoid a discussion of whether the information was true or false. The charge of collaboration with hostile centers (Radio Free Europe and the Paris *Kultura*) sounds dangerous, almost like spying, and can scare many away.

The *Information Bulletin* asks at this point: "Are all these facts to be interpreted as a decision on the part of the authorities to go for a full confrontation with the KOR movement by means of police methods?" and goes on to state: "The answer to this is by no means clear," listing the arguments in favor of a different interpretation. On the last page, however, the reader can find the news about Pyjas's death.

Thus, perhaps the political leadership had given the police a free hand. It is also possible that arrests were to be preceded by a provocation, justifying the intensification of repressions. For this purpose the beatings were not enough. It should be noted that the possibility cannot be excluded, judging by the anonymous letters to Pyjas's friends, that accusing the opposition of his murder had also been considered. In this case, only a decisive and sharp reaction prevented it.

Finally, there exists the possibility of a different scenario, namely that it was an "unfortunate accident in the workplace," used later by the Security Service to gain political domination. But if such an interpretation is considered, one might also ask whether the unfortunate accident was perhaps not an unintentional murder, but a premeditated crime? Perhaps the seemingly unprofessional abandonment of the body was really the very professional behavior of provocateurs who wanted the murder to be regarded as a murder, causing anger and a strong reaction. If the police apparatus was waiting for a chance to make its move (more against the central party apparatus than against KOR), then it could have imagined that even twenty severe beatings would not cause the reaction that would result from a single murder in the middle of the city, in an easily inflammable milieu that was just beginning to bring forth its own leaders.

One interesting contribution to these and future reflections concerning the mechanism and the political significance of the sequence of events (Pyjas's death—the demonstrations—the arrests in KOR—the amnesty) is contained in *Information Bulletin* No. 12 in an article signed with the initials J. N. entitled "The Political Breeze and a Police Faction." J. N. noted that in *Życie Warszawy** of June 4/5, 1977, in one of the many (surely forged) letters "to the Editor," all of which are basically installments of a single text supposed to portray the state of "public opinion," there occurs a passage directed against "those of our comrades who gladly hang the label of a communist around their necks," but who are afraid of "even the slightest political breeze." J. N. interpreted this letter as addressed, among others, to the authorities attempting to control "the police zeal of the editors of this newspaper [*Życie Warszawy*]." The passage "Onward, comrades from *Życie Warszawy*" which appears in the letter bears an uncanny resemblance to the cry of "Onward, Wieslaw [Gomulka]" from 1968. J. N. recalled some of the most important articles appearing in *Życie Warszawy* in 1976 and 1977 that would justify the characterization of *Życie Warszawy* as a *Polizeizeitung*, and finally he drew attention to the fact that the editorial board clearly wanted to provoke the party authorities to intensify their struggle against the opposition, and perhaps also against the Church.[1] According to J. N., the letter was intended not as an offense, but as an act of self-defense, given a situation in which the newspaper was not allowed free rein to indulge in police propaganda. At the same time, according to J. N., "this was an attempt to create a political platform for struggles within PUWP."

Without archives, indiscretion, historical witnesses, memoirs, and so on, it is impossible to answer all the questions arising in connection with the events between April and July 1977. It is known that this was not

*Warsaw daily newspaper.

only a period of intense struggle against the opposition on the part of the Security Service and PUWP but also of struggle within the power elite, including struggles between various branches of the apparatus of power.

The author is well aware that simply by posing these questions he is laying himself open to charges, and sometimes rather offensive insinuations, concerning the alleged connections between KOR and some factions within the party, or at least the desires of some factions in KOR to push the committee in this direction. Nevertheless, avoiding questions does not make problems go away, and the struggle for power within PUWP conducted at that time, as well as before and afterward, does not appear to be an illusion. Avoiding discussion of the problems connected with this struggle for power is not rational behavior for a historian, and this is true all the more for someone involved in politics.

I tend to agree with the version of events generally accepted by KOR, according to which Pyjas's death was an "accident at the workplace," as a result of which an immediate decision was made in the Ministry of Interior on Rakowiecka Street to use this accident as a weapon in the struggle for power. The lack of consistency in the further conduct of this case argues against the claim that Gierek gave the "green light" to the Security Service. It would be easier to believe that the provocation was staged from beginning to end by the Security Service, but in this case, one would have expected that it would be carried through to the end. However, the detention of Michnik and Kuroń in Warsaw, which prevented them from going to Cracow, does not appear to serve this purpose. Moreover, the riots could have been encouraged—they could even have been arranged. It seems that no one was prepared either in Cracow or in Warsaw for such eventualities.

All of this amounts only to speculation in an attempt to make order among possible variants. No one can be absolutely certain to this day. One thing was clear to KOR: Pyjas was killed by the same people who had beaten Sulecki and other activists of KOR and ROPCiO—the functionaries or agents of the secret political police.

The Demonstrations Following the Death of Pyjas

On May 12, a group of Pyjas's friends, who were also associates of KOR, decided to declare May 15 a day of public mourning for their friend who had been tragically murdered. It was to be both an homage and a protest. KOR was informed at once.

A large group of young people, members and associates of KOR, immediately left Warsaw for Cracow. They were to play a double role. First, some knew how to construct primitive but functional duplicating machines quickly and from whatever material happened to be at hand, and it was known that the Cracow action would require leaflets and posters. Second, the Warsaw teams were already experienced activists, which made it easier to overcome all sorts of psychological barriers in moments of tension. At the same time, it was known that the Cracow group was not large and that it would need help. Since the decision to hold street demonstrations had already been made, and the danger of provocation is always present in such situations, success would depend on whether or not a sizable group of people would be able to direct the crowd. This group would have to be composed of those who knew what they wanted and were familiar with the agenda, who would issue compatible directives, and above all, who would possess the proper psychological attitude—a will to action, a sense of orientation, decisiveness, quick reflexes, and the ability to maintain discipline in a group.

It must be noted that both the Cracow organizers and their helpers from Warsaw passed this test with flying colors, also in terms of their organizational efficiency.

Who were these young people composing the Cracow contingent of KOR? Just as in Warsaw, it was a varied group, although people connected with various Catholic institutions (like the Cracow Club of Catholic Intelligentsia and the academic ministry) were more numerous than in Warsaw.

How did it happen that KOR, which was usually cautious and disinclined toward street demonstrations throughout the period of its existence, accepted the tactic in this case? There were two reasons. First, the initiative and the decision came from the Cracow group. KOR could not permit or prohibit anything, since the KOR movement was not an army and KOR was not a general staff. The committee could either support the action with all its authority and all its organizational capabilities, or it could refuse. Second, after Pyjas's death there was a fear that from then on, the corpses of young KOR associates would be found more and more often in various places. The committee had to respond to this danger very forcefully, in order to make the authorities aware of the risks attached to this method of combatting the opposition.

The first team from Warsaw reached Cracow without difficulty; it was hidden on arrival, mostly in student dormitories, and began to organize the necessary typographic facilities. At the same time, mourning flags and armbands were quickly being sewn. The plan was simple: an appeal would be made to students to boycott, as a sign of mourning, the Juvenalia* that were just then taking place under the auspices of official organizations; obituary notices would be posted; leaflets would be distributed; there would be a Mass, a march through the streets of Cracow, and a public announcement of the creation of a Student Solidarity Committee.

The first conflict occurred on May 11 and immediately compromised the Socialist Union of Polish Students (SZSP), the main sponsor of the Juvenalia. The so-called Juvenalia Guard, that is, those SZSP activists responsible for keeping order during the festival, first placed Macierewicz, Malicki, and Ostrowski under arrest, as well as Piłka (a ROPCiO activist from the Catholic University in Lublin), then delivered them into the hands of the Security Service.

On the morning of May 15, before the funeral Mass for Staszek Pyjas, the Security Service detained students who were hanging black flags around the Dominican Church. The Mass was celebrated at 9:00 A.M. in the presence of approximately 5,000 people inside the church and in front of it. A group of workers from Nowa Huta also took part. After the Mass, marchers carrying black flags walked to 7 Szewska Street, where Pyjas's body had been found on May 7.[2] There, KOR's statement of May 9 was read aloud, and Pyjas was honored with a minute of silence. A communiqué was read about the detention of people—including Jacek Kuroń—attempting to come to the ceremonies from Warsaw, Lublin, and other cities. Finally everyone was invited to take part in a mourning march to Wawel at 9:00 P.M.

Minor incidents took place in the city throughout the day. There were attempts to tear down obituary notices, but they stopped when honor guards appeared near the notices posted in the most public places. There were no more significant problems with the Juvenalia. Few were willing to continue the festivities in this atmosphere.

At 9:00 P.M. a demonstration of many thousands of people carrying black flags or lighted candles and torches moved from Szewska Street along Grodska Street toward Wawel. At this time a provocation occurred that could have had serious consequences were it not for the presence of mind of the people directing the march. A group of civilians cut through the demonstration, dividing it in half. A confrontation, with all its consequences, could easily have occurred. The crowd, very disciplined and efficiently led, changed its path and went around the obstacle, and

*Annual student's carnival.

rejoined the head of the demonstration near Wawel. At the foot of Wawel, the declaration announcing the formation of a Student Solidary Committee (SKS) in Cracow was read.

After a minute of silence in honor of the murder victim, the national anthem was sung and the crowd dispersed peacefully, without being attacked.

Students in other cities also gave vent to their anger upon learning of Pyjas's death, but nowhere was the protest so intense as in Cracow. Łódź in particular reacted quickly and forcefully. As early as May 10, the first obituary notices for Pyjas appeared on the walls. They were being torn down by the police and the SB. A meeting of students of Polish literature at Łódź University was held on May 12, and Pyjas's memory was honored with a minute of silence. On May 16 in Łódź a Mass was held for Pyjas in which about 500 people participated. After the Mass, the KOR statement of May 9 was read, as was the declaration of the Cracow Student Solidarity Committee. Also read was a letter signed by 150 students in Łódź expressing their solidarity with the students in Cracow.

Between May 16 and 19, the Security Service in Łódź conducted searches and detained KOR activists. Śreniowski was detained twice. Some detentions exceeded forty-eight hours (Piotr Amsterdamski, fifty-two hours; Elżbieta Lewińska, fifty hours). A record in the length of nonstop interrogation was also established that remained unbroken throughout the existence of KOR. Anna Bazel was interrogated without pause for seventeen hours. There was also a search of the apartment of a ROPCiO participant, Andrzej Woźnicki, who was detained afterward.

On May 19, an open meeting was held in the District Council of the Socialist Union of Polish Students in which about 2,000 people took part. SZSP gave students a guarantee of unlimited duration that they would be neither searched nor interrogated (!).

Masses were held for Pyjas in Lublin and Poznań (eight people from Lublin were detained on their way to Cracow to participate in the memorial services). There was a relatively stronger, though delayed, reaction by the students of Wrocław. During the Mass on May 25, the cathedral and the square in front of it were filled with people. After the Mass, about 1,000 students marched to the monument to Pope John XXIII, where the declaration of the Cracow SKS was read. There were no incidents.

In Gdańsk, a mass for Pyjas was celebrated on May 24. There were no incidents. Obituary notices were posted in student dormitories. On

May 23, at the demand of the students, a discussion meeting about KOR was held in the dormitory for students of the Electronics Department of Gdańsk Polytechnic. On June 15, three students of Gdańsk Polytechnic began a fast in protest against the arrest of KOR activists, but they abandoned their fast at the request of the Polytechnic authorities, who appealed to them in the name of the good of the school.

In Warsaw, the Mass for Pyjas was held on May 20. The crowd inside and in front of the church observed a memorial silence. Eugeniusz Kloc was detained in the city and beaten.

Nothing more could really have been done in Warsaw if one considers that a large group of especially active young people had left Warsaw for Cracow; that many who attempted to travel to Cracow a little later had been detained (Mikołajska, Pajdak, Jacek Kuroń, Maciej Kuroń, Naimski, and Gronowicz); that during the return from Cracow to Warsaw an automobile accident had occurred that temporarily disabled several persons, including KOR member Wojciech Onyszkiewicz, who was seriously injured and remained incapacitated for much longer; and that after May 16 there had been numerous detentions, house searches, and police traps in the city.[3]

The students of Poznań reacted to Pyjas's death and to the memorial ceremonies in a letter expressing support for the Cracow SKS that had been signed by 133 students and three Dominican fathers.

Detentions and Arrests in Warsaw and the Campaign of Slanders

Detentions and arrests in Warsaw began on the evening of May 14 and continued until May 21. The "big roundup" involved forty-eight detentions and eleven arrests. The prosecutor's office brought indictments against eleven KOR members and associates: Wojciech Arkuszewski and Seweryn Blumsztajn (Articles 271 and 273 of the Criminal Code), Mirosław Chojecki (132 and 58), Jacek Kuroń (132 and 58), Jan Józef Lipski (132 and 58), Jan Lityński (271 and 273), Antoni Macierewicz (132 and 58), Adam Michnik (132 and 58), Piotr Naimski (132 and 58), Hanna Ostrowska from Radom and Wojciech Ostrowski (no relation; 11 and 271); on May 14, ROPCiO participant Marian Piłka was also arrested (271), but he was released on May 23.[4]

The arrests were accompanied by a campaign of slanders. *Życie Warszawy* was worse than the rest, but the others did not lag far behind.

Quoting from *KOR Communiqué* No. 11 of June 30, I cite here the names of those journalists who took advantage of a profitable impunity: Michał Czarniecki (*Żołnierz Wolności*), Edward Dylawerski (*Życie Warszawy*), Jerzy Grzymek (*Trybuna Ludu*), Dominik Horodyński (*Trybuna Ludu*), Marek Jaworski (*Trybuna Ludu*), Anna Kłodzińska (*Życie Warszawy*), Adam Kramarz (*Trybuna Ludu*), Władysław Machejek (*Życie Literackie*), Michał Misiorny (*Trybuna Ludu*), Zdzisław Morawski (*Życie Warszawy*), Andrzej Rayzacher (*Życie Warszawy*), Bohdan Roliński (*Życie Warszawy*), Ryszard Świerkowski (*Perspektywy*), and Adam Wysocki (*Życie Warszawy*). One special performance, and that in front of a Western audience, was given by Bohdan Roliński. In an interview for *Svenska Dagbladet* (June 11), he described the ideology of KOR as a mixture of utopian, Trotskyist, social-democratic, Christian-democratic, and Zionist ideas ("There is Zionism there, but well hidden"). Roliński said that the Zionists had collaborated with Hitler and had made known their activities in Poland in 1968. He also said that KOR had contacts with people who emigrated from Poland out of hatred.

From this moment on, everything depended on whether society, scared by the attack, would play dead and let itself be terrorized, abandoning an isolated KOR to its own fate, or whether the arrests would be answered by an avalanche of protests, which did not necessarily need to be immediate and massive, but would have to be persistent. Much also depended on the membership of KOR. Would it cease its activity as a result of intimidation, or the loss of eleven very active members as well as the simultaneous paralysis of its activity because of increased surveillance and searches? Or on the contrary, would it mobilize all its forces, energy, and reserves in order to survive, and not just to survive but to maintain at least the level of visibility that had already been won? Also, given the worsening economic situation, the voices of world opinion began to have an importance much greater than previously.

Society in Defense of KOR

The most immediate reaction to the arrests occurred among the Warsaw intellectuals. The arrests were not yet over when on May 18, the day before the greatest wave of detentions in the history of KOR, seventeen signatories—among them thirteen writers, a violinist, a mathematician, and a producer of documentary films—requested the authorities of the PRL to reverse the arrests, and called on public opinion in Poland and abroad to defend political prisoners in Poland and to demand their release.[5] It is true that this was the voice of a milieu friendly to KOR: several KOR associates and even one future member of KSS "KOR" were among the signatories. Nevertheless, this almost instinctive reaction bore witness to the distance traveled from the days when even the best had looked to others for initiative. Equally immediate was the reaction of ROPCiO contained in a statement signed on May 18 by Andrzej Czuma and Leszek Moczulski.

Four faculty members of the Catholic University in Lublin wrote a letter to "Znak" deputy Prof. Ryszard Bender. This letter was particularly noteworthy because those who signed it were known to be close to the archbishop of Cracow, Karol Cardinal Wojtyła.[6]

Another small group of only five people[7] addressed a letter in defense of KOR activists to Gierek and Jaroszewicz,* which contained the sentence: "The crisis of confidence between the rulers and the ruled demands fundamental changes in political life, which constitute a necessary condition for the socialist future of the country."

On May 28, 18 persons who belonged to the Warsaw intelligentsia wrote to the Diet Commission for Internal Affairs and for the Administration of Justice demanding that the Diet intervene in the cases of the death of Stanisław Pyjas and of the arrests of KOR members and associates. This letter was to have included approximately 140 names, but Marian Piłka was arrested on the day he was to mail it, and the Security Service confiscated from him the sheets with the other signatures.

Four hundred twenty-five people from various circles presented Prof. Jan Kielanowski with a letter in which they demanded the release of those arrested and an end to the campaign of lies and slanders. Since this letter was also sent to several other addressees (including the first secretary of the Central Committee of PUWP, the chairman of the Council of State, the marshal of the Diet, and the prosecutor general) and became the basis for reprisals against its signatories, Kielanowski made it public.

A letter protesting against the arrests was also sent by 45 scientists from Wrocław, including many professors; 629 students from Cracow sent a letter in defense of all the arrested and of KOR to Cracow deputy Tadeusz Hołuj. A similar letter was sent by 99 students from Łódź to the Marshal of the Diet. However, it was probably two collective letters

---

*Edward Gierek was at the time first secretary of the Central Committee of the PUWP. Piótr Jaroszewicz was prime minister at the time.

from different social groups which gave the authorities most to think about. The first of these was a letter from 97 miners at the Gliwice mine, which contained only expressions of their solidarity with KOR and the Cracow SKS.* The second was a letter from 349 residents of the village of Zbrosza Duża and its surrounding area (near Grójec, south of Warsaw) demanding the immediate release of the workers arrested after the June events, together with their defenders.

These were signals that this time the authorities would have to deal not only with protests of the intelligentsia but also the workers and peasants. One might suspect that these two collective letters played an especially significant role, testifying as they did to the fact that the arrests of activists from KOR were not a matter of indifference to workers and peasants. They were the harbingers of the approaching storm.

Interventions on behalf of single individuals had a different character. A large number of scientists from the Institute of Biochemistry and Biophysics of the Polish Academy of Sciences (PAN) sent a letter to the authorities in defense of their colleague, Piotr Naimski. The same was done for Jan Józef Lipski by many of his colleagues in the Institute of Literary Studies of PAN. These voices of solidarity against the repressions, which could also have been turned at any moment against the signatories of the letters, apparently played an important role beyond the immediate struggle for the release of those arrested. Naimski and Lipski, after their release from jail, turned out to be the only ones among those arrested who had not been dismissed from their jobs as well. Apparently the authorities were afraid of further protests in these two institutes.

The interventions of the boards of the Polish PEN Club and the Union of Polish Writers also had an individual character, appealing for the release of their member Jan Józef Lipski. The PEN Club appealed not only to the minister of Culture and Art and to the prosecutor general but also contacted the International PEN Club in London and asked for support. The chairman of the Union of Polish Writers, Jarosław Iwaszkiewicz, intervened on behalf of Jan Józef Lipski in the name of the Central Board of the Union of Polish Writers.

The board of the Club of Catholic Intelligentsia intervened on behalf of two arrested KOR associates, Arkuszewski and Ostrowski, who had acted in defense of persecuted workers in conjunction with their activities in the club. The attitude of the Church toward the arrests requires a

---

*SKS—Students' Solidarity Committee formed after Pyjas's death.

separate discussion. After his release from prison, Lipski was invited for a conversation by Bishop Bronisław Dąbrowski, the secretary of the Polish Episcopate. At the wish of Primate Stefan Wyszyński, Bishop Dąbrowski presented Lipski with interventions the Church had made on behalf of all the arrested KOR activists, and especially of Lipski himself (because of the state of his health), and assured him that these interventions would be continued.[8]

Also characteristic were the public statements of the two greatest authorities in the Polish Church, Primate Stefan Wyszyński and the Archbishop of Cracow, Karol Wojtyła. Although neither of these statements directly intervened on behalf of those imprisoned, they nevertheless addressed the problems that had been confronted by those arrested, and in this sense the Church stood by them.

In a sermon in the Church of Saint Anne in Warsaw, the Primate said:

> As a result . . . of the primacy of things over persons, a situation can come about in which the individual becomes the least important thing in social, civic, and national issues, and even seems to be an irritant when he speaks of his fundamental rights as a person, and when he asks for them, maybe sometimes in an impatient or drastic manner, but maybe because he feels a noose tightening around his throat and screams: "Help, help, a man is perishing!" . . . Here we must revise the entire system of ruling over man, retreating from many positions and from methods used against the individual. One must not overestimate the system, one must not overestimate various repressions against people, because these will be the first to strike against this entire system of social life, which would like to feed itself only on police repressions.

Archbishop Wojtyła said:

> The press must not falsify the image of society, if the society is to take it seriously. . . . The people who write must be careful not to abuse others in their publications, not to marshal an opinion against an individual or group who cannot defend themselves. . . . Surely it is in the interest of all the authorities in the world, as also in Poland and in Cracow, to understand the need for respecting human rights, civil rights, and the rights of the individual. A man who feels deprived in this area is a man ready for anything; he is prepared for any number of sacrifices.

The social context, both in the press and in the country at large, made these words fully understandable.

Public Opinion Abroad in Defense of KOR

The arrests in Poland were echoed fairly loudly in the Western mass media, which almost without exception expressed disappointment in the course of Gierek's politics, seen until then as fairly liberal. In a difficult economic situation, and given Polish dependence on credits from abroad, this reaction was probably not without influence on later government decisions in this matter.

The list of various Western pronouncements in defense of KOR is quite long. I will cite only those that were most important from various points of view.

The reaction of the Italian Federation of Metal Workers was indicative of the deepening split between the Eurocommunists and Moscow. From the beginning of KOR's existence, this federation was especially sensitive to KOR's appeals in defense of the workers, and gave them international support. On this occasion, the chairman of the Federation, Bruno Frenlin, a communist, published a statement protesting against repression in Poland, and he appealed to the Central Council of Trade Unions in Poland to defend the workers who still remained in prison, as well as the members and associates of KOR. This kind of appeal might even seem funny, like an appeal to a fox to protect a chicken, but it had to be taken into account as yet another element of the political situation.

The Italian Confederation of Christian Trade Unions passed a resolution demanding the immediate release of political prisoners in Poland and an amnesty for the workers. Representatives of the Italian Committee for Security in Europe expressed their concern about the arrests during their visit to Poland. Amnesty was demanded also by young Swedish liberals and by representatives of the Belgian left.

A telegram from JUSO, a youth organization associated with the SDP in West Germany, was probably also important to the authorities. This organization, on the left wing of the Social-Democratic party, had offered hope to communist political centers in the East, on various occasions. For example, the Polish press often stressed the political radicalism of JUSO, which had been a source of friction between JUSO members and the leaders of the West German Social Democrats.

Interventions on behalf of the imprisoned KOR activists were made by Amnesty International, and especially by its Swedish section, which not only cabled the Polish authorities with a demand that those who had been arrested be released but also appealed to the Swedish public, giving the addresses of Gierek and Justice Minister Berutowicz, to which protest telegrams should be sent.

An appeal by intellectuals from the United States, who also demanded the immediate release of KOR members, was surely significant for world opinion. It was signed by 136 persons, among them three Nobel Prize laureates (Kenneth J. Arrow, William Lipscomb, and George Wald); a group of writers known throughout the world (Edward Albee; the Russian poet, Joseph Brodsky; Jerzy Kosinski, the chairman of the American PEN Club and a Pole; as well as Bernard Malamud, Mary McCarthy, Arthur Miller, Czesław Miłosz, Kurt Vonnegut, Jr., and Robert Penn Warren); and a number of distinguished scholars (linguists Roman Jakobson and Noam Chomsky; philosophers Robert Cohen and Leszek Kołakowski; sociologists Seymour M. Lipset and Robert K. Merton; Slavicist Gleb Struve; economist Paul M. Sweezy; and mathematician Alfred Tarski), as well as the actress Liv Ullmann.

Twenty-two West German intellectuals, including the writers Böll and Grass, answered a letter from Michnik that had been smuggled out of prison, and assured him that they would not cease demanding his freedom and that of his friends.

The release of KOR members was also demanded by thirty-five Italian Slavicists, eighty-one professors of Swiss universities, and seven distinguished public and intellectual figures in Holland.

In France, a group of editors-in-chief of the most respected French periodicals (including Jean-Paul Sartre of *Les Temps modernes,* Jean Daniel from *Le Nouvel Observateur,* and Paul K. Thibaud from *Esprit*) appealed to the French trade unions and parties of the left to intervene. Their appeal contained the words: "It is our trial that is being prepared in Poland. It is also yours." In response, the board of Force Ouvrière appealed to the French president to intervene on behalf of the arrested KOR activists.

Jean-Marie Domenach, the great Catholic essayist and activist and a former editor of *Esprit,* issued a personal appeal on behalf of the KOR members.

It is surprising that sixty-seven intellectuals, emigrants from Eastern Europe, including many Russians, also raised their voices in protest.

On June 4, French radio broadcast an hour-long program on the situation in Poland, in the course of which Jean Daniel appealed to the French left to support the opposition in Poland.

Another voice not without interest to the Polish government came from the United States: the Polish-American Congress asked President

Carter to intervene publicly on behalf of the prisoners. The president issued a statement to the Senate Commission on Monitoring the Realization of the Helsinki Agreements, in which he raised the issue of the arrests of the KOR activists.

No less important politically was the appeal to the British government made by ninety-seven members of Parliament from the Labor party and two Conservatives protesting against the arrest of KOR activists as a violation of the Helsinki agreements.

There were demonstrations in Stockholm, during the visit of the Polish minister of foreign affairs, Emil Wojtaszek, and in Paris and London as well. In Geneva a group occupied the offices of Lot, the Polish airlines, in protest against the arrests.

The Polish authorities made a clumsy attempt to persuade Western public opinion that there was no repression in Poland, and that those arrested were common criminals. This was the none too logical position taken by the Polish ambassador to London, Artur Starewicz, during his press conference; by Mieczysław Rakowski in an interview with the West German press; by Edward Gierek in an interview for *The New York Times,* and by the press attaché of the Polish embassy in Paris, Orłowski, in a letter published in *Le Monde.* It seems that from the point of view of the Polish authorities, the results of these attempts could not have been worse.

The Fast in the Church of St. Martin

One of the best-known elements of the struggle for the release of the imprisoned was the collective fast in the Church of St. Martin on Piwna Street in the Old Town of Warsaw.

The decision to fast had been made much earlier, even before Pyjas's death and the arrests in KOR. After the act of clemency for the convicted workers, it transpired that five workers were still imprisoned. KOR was determined to fight for their release as stubbornly as it had fought when dozens of workers were still imprisoned. KOR believed that the five still in prison were being detained as unjustly as those who had been released, and the fact that there were only five of them made no difference. Still, there remained the question of what methods should be used to mobilize society to demand that these five workers be freed.

I am unable to determine who first had the idea of a fast. This method of struggle was little known in Poland. Political prisoners had used it on

occasion, as did common criminals in situations of exceptional lawlessness, or when they felt subjected to particular injustice. This time, however, it was to be a fast for freedom. In order for it to be credible and
to reach the public consciousness, it had to be a public fast. A church
seemed to be the best location, because only there could one expect
(without, however, being sure) that the police and the Security Service
would not enter. In order to begin, it was necessary to find a parish
priest or a church rector willing to discuss this issue, who would agree
to do everything necessary to obtain at least the silent approval of his
superiors.

So many conditions had to be met at the same time that only a few
churches were appropriate (e.g., the rooms had to be arranged in such
a way that physiological needs could be accommodated outside of the
sacred part of the church, but without it being necessary to leave the
church, which would make provocations or police detentions possible.)

The fast took place in the Church of St. Martin. It was an excellent
choice, and the circumstances were very propitious. The Church of St.
Martin is a convent church of the order of the Franciscan Sisters Servants
of the Cross, one of the most beautiful pages in the history of the Church
in Poland. Founded as one of the branches of the Franciscans during
the early years of independent Poland in the 1920s, the order has as its
main work caring for the blind; the center in Laski near Warsaw was
established for this purpose (because of this, the order is commonly
known as the "sisters from Laski"). This center gained recognition not
only because of its exemplary humanitarian work but also because it
attracted people from groups of radical, secular intelligentsia primarily
from Warsaw which, during the interwar period and even earlier, did
not maintain the best relations with the Church. It was the birthplace
of mutual understanding, in an atmosphere characterized by principles
and attitudes that became popular only after Vatican II. The editorial
board of the periodical *Verbum* was also connected with Laski. Laski
represented everything that was most enlightened, open, and imbued
with the spirit of *caritas* and *humanitas* in the Polish Church. This atmosphere has not changed to this day, but now it is a less exotic phenomenon. The KOR activists fasting in protest, whether religious or not,
could not have felt more at home in this church than anywhere else.

Dr. Bronisław Dembowski is the rector of the Church of St. Martin.
He was chosen for a reason: the church has special ecumenical tasks.
Among the various functions of Reverend Dembowski is also the pastoral
responsibility for the Warsaw Club of Catholic Intelligentsia, and because

of this he already knew some of the younger activists of KOR. That this protest by KOR was to be of a moral, rather than a political nature was a sufficient argument for Bronisław Dembowski.

Before the fast even began, there appeared an additional cause for protest, resulting in a second purpose for those about to participate, and introducing additional drama. A large number of those fasting had various emotional ties with the arrested KOR activists. At the same time, the unity of the group deepened: the family members of imprisoned workers were fasting not only for their close relatives but also for members of KOR, while the friends of the KOR activists were fasting for the imprisoned workers, most of whom they had never even seen.

For people undertaking a protest such as a fast, the atmosphere of the surroundings is of tremendous importance (this is why hunger strikes are so difficult and often so heroic in prison, in a hostile environment). Here there was full understanding and sympathy. A fast of definite duration, which is a sacrifice and a mortification but has nothing in common with suicide, is for those who are deeply religious, and thus also for the nuns, something understandable and morally pure, so that they surrounded those who were fasting with their prayers and goodwill.

The physical conditions in the convent church buildings were ideal. They offered the possibility of walks in a beautiful garden without the danger of encountering any agents of the Security Service or any provocations.

On May 25, eight people began the fast: Bogusława Blajfer, a Warsaw philosophy student; Danuta Chomicka from Radom, wife of imprisoned worker Czesław Chomicki; Lucyna Chomicka from Radom, Czesław's sister; Bohdan Cywiński from Cracow, editor-in-chief of the Catholic periodical *Znak;* Jerzy Geresz from Warsaw, a student of mathematics; Aleksander Hauke-Ligowski from Poznań, a Dominican priest; Barbara Toruńczyk from Warsaw, a sociologist; and Henryk Wujec from Warsaw, a physicist and an activist of the Club of Catholic Intelligentsia. In the evening of the same day, they were joined by Eugeniusz Kloc from Warsaw, a student of Polish literature, and by Ozjasz Szechter from Warsaw, Adam Michnik's father, an editor in a publishing house and former communist activist. On May 26, Joanna Szczęsna, a Warsaw journalist, also joined the fast; and on May 27, the literary scholar Stanisław Baranczak arrived from Poznań, and two other previously unknown persons also asked to be allowed to take part: Zenon Pałka, a technician from Wrocław, and Kazimierz Świtoń, a radio technician from Katowice.

In the Mokotów jail, Jan Józef Lipski joined the fast for four days—

so as to end it together with the others. He learned that the planned protest was actually taking place from a mention in a newspaper that the prison censor had overlooked.

At the request of those taking part in the fast, Tadeusz Mazowiecki, the editor-in-chief of the Catholic monthly *Więź*, became their spokesman, and through him they maintained contact with the outside world. In a statement declaring the fast and describing its purpose, the participants wrote in part:

> For the faithful, it will be a form of prayer; for all of us, an appeal to society and to the authorities.
>
> We are consciously choosing a fast as a form of struggle for law and justice, for human dignity, and against coercion, and yet without recourse to force and coercion. We have many predecessors in such a struggle, ranging from Mahatma Gandhi and pastor Martin Luther King all the way to fighters who by fasting in Spanish churches for freedom and democracy were struggling against the dictatorship in their country.

The collective fast—a form of protest unknown until then in Warsaw—made a tremendous impression. The Church of St. Martin, surrounded by entire gangs of agents, literally became a place of pilgrimage and collective prayer in support of those taking part in the fast, and of their goals. Flowers were laid at the foot of the grille separating the chapel in which the fast was occurring from the rest of the church, and flowers were also intertwined into the grillwork, just as several years later they would be placed at the gate of the Gdańsk Shipyard.

The official press rained invectives upon the participants in the fast, including anti-Semitic slurs; Ozjasz Szechter answered them with dignity in his letter to *Trybuna Ludu*.[9]

There was concern over whether ending the fast after a week would not be met with a provocation. The spokesman of the participants conducted negotiations to avoid this possibility. There were no incidents.

The fast has been accorded much attention in Poland not because of its propaganda and political significance, which was indeed considerable, but because it played a more serious and profound role in the history of KOR. The KOR milieu still remembers the fast as a great moment, as a time in which a great fund of moral energy was accumulated, from which KOR would draw, not always consciously, in the years to come. This was the result above all of an atmosphere of seriousness and deep concentration, which was achieved not at the price of isolation, but in relation to others, to the human ties and feelings among friends. In addition, the fast united both believers and nonbelievers around common values and the goals ensuing from them, and therefore it became a great event of what might be called ethical-ecumenical significance.

I know of the fast in the Church of St. Martin from stories, but I know its profound effects at firsthand—from observing people. It seems that never again, in subsequent fasts, would so much be achieved in the spiritual realm.

I am not competent to decide who was responsible for this. One might suspect that everyone was, but the choice of the spokesman, Tadeusz Mazowiecki, on whom so much depends in such situations, was certainly an excellent one.

The Work of KOR after the Many Arrests

For those who adhered to the notion that KOR was composed of a small group of intellectuals, among whom the really active role was played by only a few stubborn participants in protests that had been taking place for years, and who therefore were all well known to the Security Service, it was obvious that eleven arrests accompanied by dozens of detentions and searches would be sufficient to paralyze the activities of the committee.

This was probable. KOR was only ten months old (if one counts from its beginnings in July and not September); it was not yet as deeply rooted as it would shortly become. If this blow were to prove effective, and the work of KOR were to cease, it would be an important argument for the hard-liners not to retreat, and thus an argument in favor of political trials. A great deal would depend on whether the people in KOR would show perseverance and discipline at this moment, and on whether they would be able to increase their efforts.

It must be said that KOR passed this test both as a group composed of members who remained free and as a milieu. Although distasteful incidents did occur twice, they took place on the borderline between ROPCiO and KOR. One activist chose this moment to withdraw from all activity, gave an account of all the funds at his disposition, and declared that he should no longer be counted on; while another chose this time to accuse Jacek Kuroń of misusing KOR funds in order to divert them toward Eurocommunist political activity. This slander was nonsensical in substance, not only because Kuroń at that time had no connection with any communist orientation, but also because he had no control over any KOR funds. He simply was not involved in this aspect of the committee's work, and had no access to any KOR money. But when the accusation was made, he was under investigative arrest in Mokotów jail and could not even answer these charges.

It was clear that when the situation returned to normal, all cooperation with these two individuals would be impossible. But with these exceptions, all the rest of KOR in the broadest sense met the challenge superbly. The work was not interrupted; on the contrary, it had to be intensified in a struggle to obtain the release of imprisoned colleagues.

On May 16, 20, and 23, members of KOR who remained free made collective visits to the Prosecutor General's Office and demanded an interview with the prosecutor general, without success. The atmosphere of crudity in the prosecutor's office and the general level of behavior there are best exemplified by a remark made to the venerable Professor Lipiński, who was told by one of the prosecutors on duty that no one had ever heard of such a professor.

On the same day, those KOR members who were not under arrest issued a brief statement demanding the release of the members of the committee and warning of the negative consequences of these arrests on public peace. On May 23, following a third unsuccessful visit to the Prosecutor General's Office, Lipiński addressed a letter to the prosecutor general in the name of the entire committee, which concluded: "As members of KOR we consider ourselves to be fully as responsible for the entire activity of KOR as our arrested colleagues."

Also on that day, KOR made available to foreign correspondents a somewhat longer text of similar content.

On June 5, KOR issued a statement in connection with the Belgrade Conference of the States Signatories to the Final Act of the Helsinki Conference on Security and Cooperation in Europe, which was scheduled to begin on June 15. This statement declared that the agreements contained in the Covenant on Civil and Political Rights were not being respected in Poland, and cited the arrests of KOR activists as one example.

On June 8, Lipiński sent an open letter to the general secretaries of the Communist parties of France, Spain, and Italy—Georges Marchais, Santiago Carillo, and Enrico Berlinguer—containing an appeal to join the campaign for the release of the imprisoned KOR activists.

On June 14, Lipiński and Antoni Pajdak sent a cable in the name of KOR to the Congress of Trade Unions in Italy, which was just then getting under way, thanking them for their support and appealing for new interventions.

On June 25, KOR made public a statement in which it expressed its opinion about the television news interview granted on June 1 by the chief administrator of the Office of the Prosecutor General, W. Rozwens.

On the same day, the first anniversary of the June events, leaflets circulating in Ursus reminded people about the workers who were still in prison and about the arrested KOR activists.

On July 5, KOR issued another statement in connection with the Belgrade Conference. It described the work of KOR and argued against the thesis that the activities of the committee threatened international understanding:

> Security and peace on the European continent will be safer when détente and the agreements will refer to nations and societies in which authentic social life is not suppressed. When there are no independent centers of social activity, and when the possibility of communication among citizens is virtually non-existent, society is likely to react unpredictably and uncontrollably. Such reactions are dangerous to peace and security within a given country, but under contemporary conditions, they might also prove dangerous in the international arena.

On July 12, Lipski, who had already been released, addressed a letter in the name of KOR to the General Secretary of the United Nations, Kurt Waldheim, asking him to intervene on behalf of the still imprisoned Radom and Ursus workers persecuted for the June 1976 demonstrations and also the arrested members and associates of KOR. This letter was delivered to Waldheim during ceremonies at Warsaw University on the occasion of his receiving an honorary doctorate. The first associate of KOR who attempted to deliver the letter, Jan Ajzner, was detained under the eyes of the General Secretary of the UN, but Bogusława Blajfer succeeded in handing him the letter. Blajfer was detained immediately afterward. An officer of the Security Service, Zalewski (a.k.a. Zakrzewski), twisted her arms and thus forced her to hand him the keys to her apartment, which was then searched.

Statements and letters can be produced even by a single individual, and although they were needed and even indispensable, something more was necessary to demonstrate that KOR still existed and was active. Three successive *KOR Communiqués* (Nos. 10, 11, and 12) appeared during the period between Pyjas's death and the amnesty. *Communiqué* No. 10 is devoted entirely to Pyjas's death and its consequences, including the defense of those arrested. But already *Communiqués* No. 11 and 12 returned to the practice of providing information about the daily work of

KOR, and changed only the customary organization of the material. Previously, information about relief actions was presented separately from information about reprisals against KOR activists, while in these two issues, both were combined under the common rubric: "Repressions by the Authorities and the Extent of the Aid Provided by KOR." The *Communiqués* carried information that trials were still taking place and workers continued to be persecuted.[10] In spite of the arrests, KOR was able to register all this information, and keep it up-to-date and make it public, as well as distributing financial aid, and the like. By no means were these *Communiqués* less rich in information than previous issues.

As already mentioned, almost every member and associate of KOR who remained free played a part in these activities. Still, there was a need for a cell that would be able to coordinate everything, manage the information bank, gain an overview of KOR activity in its entirety, and serve as a connection between senior members of the committee, who were now in the majority, and the young people working in the "front lines." This working cell, which had no formal authority, was created by three women: Anka Kowalska, who was mainly in charge of the *Communiqués* and information; Grażyna Kuroń (who was not even formally a member of KOR), who handled the complicated internal communications within the committee; and Halina Mikołajska, who became at that time a press spokesperson for KOR. Their jobs were made significantly easier by the fact that the blows inflicted by the Security Service had only a slight effect on the basic area of KOR's work, providing aid to the persecuted, which was directed by Zofia and Zbigniew Romaszewski.

But KOR's press was not crushed either. The *Information Bulletin* found itself in a difficult situation following the arrests of two members of the editorial board, Seweryn Blumsztajn and Jan Lityński. How this was overcome is apparent if one reads a letter which Blumsztajn and Lityński, who were freed along with other KOR members and associates after the amnesty, published in the introduction to No. 13/14 of the *Bulletin*. Blumsztajn and Lityński wrote: "We wish to thank Barbara Toruńczyk and Stanisław Barańczak, who replaced us as editors of the *Bulletin;* we also wish to thank all those who joined in the editorial work during our imprisonment—thanks to them, successive issues of our periodical were able to appear."[11]

The situation was similar in all aspects of KOR's work. It turned out that KOR was so strong that this type of attack could not destroy it. The authorities faced a choice between two alternative methods for dealing with the situation: they could intensify the terror, changing its quality, that is, they could arrest not only all the members of KOR but also its associates, in a situation of growing social tension and displeasure with the arrests, which would result in protests and condemnations by ever wider circles of public opinion in the West from which new credits and debt rescheduling were expected; or, the authorities could retreat in whatever manner would be least painful to their prestige.

The Amnesty

An amnesty was the simplest path of retreat. July 22 is a state holiday in the Polish People's Republic, celebrating the anniversary of the Chełm announcement of the PKWN Manifesto;* it is a traditional day for amnesties. Before the amnesty was announced, the number of KOR activists held in jail was reduced to nine. On June 8, several days after he had suffered a heart attack, Jan Józef Lipski was released because of the state of his health.[12] Hanna Ostrowska was released early in July, also for reasons of health.

The release of Lipski was accompanied by a provocation designed to compromise KOR. On the morning of June 8, during a meeting of the editorial board of *Polityka*, the editor-in-chief of this weekly, Mieczysław Rakowski, told those assembled that he had just learned that Lipski had died in prison, and that he was concerned that this might lead to a dangerous situation, at least in the university. The information quickly spread throughout the city. Luckily it did not reach the wife of the "deceased," who was isolated from any information by her colleagues at work. Lipski's son, Jan Tomasz Lipski, went to the prison in which his father was being held and demanded from the warden either to see his father or to be shown his body, which astounded the warden and made him furious. He stated that Lipski would leave the prison at 4:00 P.M.

This entire affair had only one goal. At noon, a press conference was to be held in Halina Mikołajska's apartment. If, during the press conference, the foreign correspondents had been told about the death of one of the founders of KOR, the news would immediately have been spread throughout the world, and the reliability of KOR's information

*PKWN (Polish Committee of National Liberation,) established on July 20, 1944 to administer those parts of Poland being liberated by the Red Army. On July 22 it issued a manifesto laying out principles of government of postwar Poland. Communist authorities celebrate this date as a national holiday commemorating the establishment of the Polish People's Republic.

would have been undermined. However, Mikolajska, with iron determination, despite her nervousness, followed the KOR criteria according to which information could not be considered reliable until it had been confirmed. As a result, the provocation did not work. Later, Rakowski claimed that he was given the false alarm by Jerzy Łukaszewicz, a secretary of the Central Committee of PUWP. Whatever the actual truth of the matter, it is amazing that there are people willing to undermine their own trustworthiness to such a degree for such dubious ends, which, given the certainty that the truth would out, are not only minor but also short-term.

On July 21, the Provincial Prosecutor's Office in Warsaw levied additional indictments against KOR members Jacek Kuroń and Adam Michnik, who were still in Mokotów jail, and against Jan Józef Lipski, which were based on Articles 271 and 273 of the Criminal Code, sharply increasing the possible criminal penalties. On July 23, the chief administrator in the Prosecutor General's Office, Rozwens, told Lipiński, who was invited especially for this purpose, that all the workers who were still in jail as a result of the events of June 1976 would be released, and that the investigations against the members and associates of KOR were being dropped. This was a crazy turn of events, involving: (a) the intensification of the accusations; (b) the invitation to Lipiński, which amounted to something like a de facto recognition of KOR; and (c) the release of workers and KOR members and associates from prisons. This can only be explained by assuming that up until the last moments, a sharp political struggle over how to solve this issue was taking place in the highest echelons of power.

The amnesty decree (in 1977 this was not a Diet resolution) was different from all other amnesty acts in Poland. This is not surprising, since it had to deal with several different issues at the same time: it had to assure the release of people, some of whom were serving long sentences (of up to ten years!), and it had to do this without infringing upon the principles of Polish amnesties, which generally do not apply to those serving such lengthy sentences; and moreover, it had to discontinue the investigation against the activists of KOR.

All this was taken care of. On July 23, KOR activists received notifications that the investigations against them had been discontinued, and those who were under arrest were released. The last of the workers of Ursus and Radom also regained their freedom. The amnesty had another echo: on September 25, 1977, a group of Radom workers and representatives of KOR who were participating in the annual pilgrimage from Warsaw to Jasna Góra placed a votive offering in the Marian Sanctuary on Jasna Góra. This was a cross that had been cast especially for this purpose in the Walter Enterprises in Radom. The cross was inscribed with a quote from the Thirty-first Psalm:

> Let the lying lips be put to silence;
> Which speak grievous things proudly and contemptuously
> Against the righteous.

An amnesty of this kind was certainly a wise step. It brought to an end an issue that as long as it remained open could only continue to harm the authorities. The amnesty broke the chain of protests that was integrating the opposition in Poland. It also increased the international credit of trust in Gierek's team as a moderate and liberal group. However, all this came much too late. For example, an amnesty in September 1976 would have prevented the formation of KOR; in December 1976 it would have taken away from KOR its *raison d'être*, at least in the eyes of significant sections of society. And had the clemency act been as far-reaching as the amnesty, its effects would already have been smaller, but still similar. After May 1977, it was obvious that the authorities made concessions only when they were forced to do so, and this lessened the benefits that accrued to them and strengthened their opposition. As late as in April, things might have been different. Moreover, the blows inflicted against the opposition in April and May had pushed it toward a broader concept of social action. By the end of July, much of the work connected with this broader approach was in its advanced stages.

New KOR Institutions

KOR met on May 9, that is, as soon as possible after the news of Pyjas's death, although still before the police action against the committee. During this meeting, the committee finalized its decision to create new internal institutions within KOR designed to make its activities more efficient, and to introduce order into them. KOR was becoming increasingly aware of the enormity of the lawlessness, and even of the crimes committed by the police, the prosecutor's offices, the courts, the sentencing boards, the administration, and so on and so forth. Even at the cost of personal risk, new applicants were constantly coming to KOR in search of help or justice. The immensity of the tasks was becoming apparent; without some deep structural changes, these horrendous Augean stables could not be cleaned by a still narrow circle of activists, while the sincere and sensitive social workers could in no way acquiesce in this state of affairs. This was the source of the idea of a specialized Intervention Bureau to organize the struggle against the injustices committed by the authorities. This struggle would no longer be conducted on an ad hoc basis, but would be systematic and organized inclusively. This meant the coordination of help case by case, a full legal understanding of the situation, the elaboration of a strategy and tactics for combatting evil, the training of competent activists, and working to inform the public about the possibilities for resistance.

The financial management of KOR also needed systematization. There was a need for a conscious, long-range plan for the division of funds to satisfy a variety of goals: for the Intervention Bureau, KOR publications, and for new social initiatives that would need support by donations or loans so that what were, after all, limited amounts would be divided in the manner that would be socially the most effective. In any case, it was becoming apparent that KOR would have to aid independent cultural, publishing, and educational initiatives. In order to accomplish this goal KOR decided to create a fund for Social Self-Defense, which would be managed by a Funds Council elected by KOR.

Finally a decision was made to create an Editorial Board that would have two responsibilities: it would prepare drafts of KOR statements and other documents; and during the intervals between the plenary meetings, it would publish documents in the name of the entire committee, when these documents referred only to specific interventions, which KOR had to publicize without becoming involved ideologically or politically.

Zofia and Zbigniew Romaszewski, who assumed the direction of the Radom team after Chojecki's departure, were to head the Intervention Bureau. Dozens of activists throughout the entire country, though mainly in Warsaw, worked for the bureau. Many of them were devoted exclusively to social work and alien to politics, and they became quiet and anonymous associates of KOR, even if they were well known in their professional lives. A number of future outstanding and well-known Solidarity activists were also connected with the Intervention Bureau (for example, Andrzej Gwiazda, the Bureau's representative in Gdańsk).

The *KOR Communiqués* published information about the work of the bureau. Both the especially important and the very typical cases were described in a section of the *Information Bulletin* that was edited separately by the Intervention Bureau. KOR's Intervention Bureau also left behind it two publications of enormous importance, which will be described later: the *Documents of Lawlessness,* a description of the murders, assaults, and severe beatings committed and then covered up by the police and the Security Service (which involved rigged trials in several instances); and the *Madrid Report* on all issues connected with the Final Act of Helsinki, an enormous documentary study of inestimable social and historical importance.

The running of the Intervention Bureau involved a tremendous amount of work. People who appealed to it included not only those who had been wronged by the authorities but also a number of crooks, swindlers, and the mentally ill. Every case had to be examined, and sometimes this involved a trip and the launching of an investigation only to discover that the case was not for KOR. Moreover, KOR could not deal with every injustice. The avalanche of cases would have been uncontrollable. Sometimes out of necessity only advice could be offered. Facing the necessity of selection, without a sufficient number of people and adequate means to undertake all the cases, the Intervention Bureau chose those that seemed to offer hope that if they were won, they would constitute a precedent for similar pending or future cases. The work was conducted under the very difficult conditions typical for KOR (surveillance, searches, detentions). Discipline was greater here than in any other part of KOR. In the event of police intervention, what was at stake here was not only a duplicating machine but a human being seeking help. Here every departure and every return had to be reported to the bureau, so that an associate could not disappear without a trace. And it was here that much money was spent. And every investigation and every client contain the materials for a story or a novel.

Swamped with work, the bureau had to forgo many problems and issues which were worth taking up. Here is one example.

The mentally ill, usually suffering from persecution mania, were the nightmare of the Intervention Bureau. It was quickly observed in the bureau that ours are no longer the times of would-be Napoleons, but rather of poor frightened people who are being irradiated with mysterious rays, slowly poisoned by terrible concoctions, or whose thoughts are being read. This was being done, according to them, by the Security Service which, in the majority of these cases, if not as pure as the driven snow, was at least overestimated in its real abilities. But the mass nature of these phenomena, the monotonous repetitiveness of these fears, do, after all, come from somewhere (for example, the mentally ill are generally not afraid of creatures from outer space, but rather look to them for help and hope).

There is nothing strange in the fact that the first impulse of an associate of the bureau when he encountered a client with such symptoms was to try to get rid of him. And suddenly, a pattern was discovered: in Poland, whenever a lonely person with some property falls mentally ill, he also falls victim to a gang of some local power elite who seek to rob by crude legal means. Even if the victim of such a robbery encounters an honest prosecutor or a journalist, they quickly become discouraged once they hear his stories, in which radiation, the police, and creatures from outer space are all thoroughly mixed up, and so they get rid of him quickly. If there had been more available young people, and a psychiatrist, perhaps KOR would have been able to wage a fight against such gangs as well.

In any case, how is one to distinguish those who are suffering from persecution mania from those who are not? For example, some old people from around Wrocław, exhibiting paranoid symptoms, were complaining that they were being poisoned by the police (and can a young person, let us say a mathematician arriving from a distant area, possess the knowledge necessary to deal with these kinds of cases and the time necessary to investigate the problem in depth?). Their apartment does indeed stink. And suddenly, a revelation occurs while getting back into Mikołajska's car: it is the same smell! After a break-in committed by "unknown perpetrators," and the spraying of something in her car, the stench had remained for many weeks. And so, who is mentally ill and who is not? The associates of the KOR Intervention Bureau should write a collective memoir about their work. It would be the most staggering and the most surrealistic book of this quarter of a century.

The May 9 KOR statement announced the decision to create a Social Self-Defense Fund in the near future, following an audit of the accounts. A Funds Council was delegated to draft the principles under which the fund would be managed and operated. It was composed of Jan Kielanowski,[13] Edward Lipiński, Jan Józef Lipski, Halina Mikołajska, Józef Rybicki, Wacław Zawadzki, and Jan Zieja. These were still temporary arrangements.

The *KOR Communiqué* did not publish information about the nomination of the Editorial Board, since it was agreed that the internal structure of KOR and the manner in which its work was organized did not need to be known publicly, especially since this would facilitate moves by the Security Service designed to paralyze the activities of the committee. But since the composition of the Editorial Board was not made public at the time, it is presently difficult to establish the history of its changing membership with precision. It seems that originally it was composed of Ludwik Cohn, Edward Lipiński, Jan Józef Lipski, Antoni Macierewicz, Adam Michnik, Piotr Naimski, Józef Rybicki, Aniela Steinsbergowa, and Adam Szczypiorski. KOR adopted the principle that every member of KOR had the right to be present and to voice his opinions during meetings of the Editorial Board.

Changes in KOR Membership

As of July 23, Wojciech Ziembiński resigned from participation in the work of KOR, justifying his decision on the basis of his activities in ROPCiO, mostly involved with editing the periodical *Opinia*. At the same time, he declared that he accepted his full share of responsibility for the activities of KOR until that time. This temporary resignation turned out to be permanent, which came as no surprise. KOR stated that Ziembiński would participate in the outstanding work connected with the preparation of reports and audits. Ziembiński's departure was, apart from the stated reasons, also a result of conflicts within KOR, mainly with Kuroń, and—for other reasons—with Rybicki and other members of the committee, as well as the disagreements existing between KOR and ROPCiO.

The Workers' Defense Committee gained two new members:

Rev. Zbigniew Kamiński was for a long time the priest of an academic ministry, and during the war he was a chaplain in the Home Army in the Diversionary Command (Kedyw) of the Warsaw District.

Prof. Jan Kielanowski is a zoologist and a member of the Polish Academy of Sciences and the German Academy of Agricultural Sciences; he received honorary doctorates from Humboldt University in Berlin and Edinburgh University, among others, and was formerly the director of the Institute of Animal Feeding of the Polish Academy of Sciences in Jabłonna. During the war he served as a soldier in the Home Army.

The Student Solidarity Committees

As mentioned previously, the creation in Cracow of the Student Solidarity Committee was one direct consequence of the death of Staszek Pyjas. Its formation was announced during the evening demonstration near Wawel Castle on May 15, 1977. The SKS was created by a tightly-knit and energetic group of Cracow students associated with KOR. The names of some will be repeated often in the history of the opposition movement in Poland before 1980, and then in Solidarity.[14] Let us note parenthetically that the name Student Solidarity Committee was the result of a conscious ideological decision. To the question, "Solidarity with whom?" the answer was, "Solidarity is an idea uniting everyone with everyone else into a community, a moral and social bond." This is why in Gdańsk, during the strikes of August 1980, when KOR member Konrad Bieliński organized the strike print shop and then began editing the daily bulletin for the strike, he suggested that it be known as "Solidarity."

Apart from references to Pyjas's death and appeals for mourning, the first statement of the Cracow SKS contained only two programmatic elements: that the SKS was being formed "in order to initiate work aimed at the creation of an authentic and independent representation of students" (after a statement that the Socialist Union of Polish Students had "lost completely its moral right to represent the students"), and also a declaration: "We assert that we will organize in self-defense against reprisals." On May 17, a *Declaration* of the Cracow SKS expressed solidarity with KOR.

This is probably not much for the beginning of a movement whose founders intended to clear a path for essential changes in the life of the institutions of higher learning. But the statement was composed at a very hectic time, and in a hurry. It is worth noting that one of the key words of the KOR movement, self-defense, gave the movement much dynamism. Simply speaking, the history of KOR was a proof of the richness of this word or password, so comprehensible and mobilizing. The reading of the SKS statement from Cracow is a constant element in the information from other academic centers throughout Poland about their response to Pyjas's death and to the demonstrations in Cracow. It was a matter of time before the interested parties decided whether, as a result of these events, cells of a national SKS should be created in various academic centers, or whether each local milieu should form its own committee. The second course was adopted.

As has been mentioned, the Cracow SKS was created by a group of KOR associates. The situation was similar in most other cities. It does not follow that KOR activists were the only persons active in these committees, but rather that the initiative was taken by people connected with KOR, and that these people played a dominant role in the committees. This was not true of Gdańsk, where the SKS was closer to ROPCiO and became better known in the history of the opposition as the *Bratniak* group. It needs to be stated explicitly that the connections between most of the SKSs and KOR were of a historical and personal character, but there were no institutional dependencies. According to the KOR principle of self-government and autonomy, such dependency was out of the question. It can be said that the KOR associates who joined SKSs did not cease to be activists of KOR. This is true, but even as associates of KOR they were not bound by any discipline.

The Cracow SKS began with a meager introductory announcement, but by May 25 it made public *The Assumptions and Goals of the Independent Student Movement*. This document contains mainly a critique of the Socialist Union of Polish Students based on the arguments used by the student "anti-unification movement" that had protested in 1973 against the liquidation of the Union of Polish Students and its organizational incorporation, together with the academic Union of Socialist Youth, into the Socialist Union of Polish Students (see chapter 1). At the same time, the SKS emphasized that "the student movement cannot be limited exclusively to the problems of the student milieu. We are affected by the conditions prevailing throughout society, which we can influence only if we reject institutional and organizational dependence. For this reason, we should pay the closest attention to the observance of individual rights as guaranteed by the Polish Constitution and the Covenant on Civil and Political Rights."

During the summer, the student groups were preparing to enlarge the movement. The Cracow SKS organized a number of discussion camps, with the participation of students from various cities. Two texts were written to serve as a basis for the discussions: Lesław Maleszka, from the Cracow SKS, wrote *Some Reflections on Involvement;* while Ludwik Dorn, Sergiusz Kowalski, and Piotr Łukasiewicz from Warsaw prepared a *Thesis for the Discussion of the Independent Student Movement*. The Warsaw thesis, postulating the creation of an SKS in Warsaw, read in part:

> The primary goal of an SKS would be the creation of a state of affairs in which students would themselves determine the goals and the methods of their activities. The SKS, which would not be an organization, would not have any right toward the student body, but would have the role of informing and intervening. . . . The student movement should not limit itself to the problems of the student milieu, since social solidarity is a broader concept than the solidarity of students. The important problems facing the country should also be reflected at the institutions of higher learning.

The creation and development of the new Student Solidarity Committees constitute the next chapter in the history of the KOR movement.

The Independent Publishing House and the Publishing Movement

The first publication of the Independent Publishing House (NOWa) was Marek Tarniewski's *The Origins of the System,* which appeared in August 1977, after the amnesty.[15]

From the very beginning, KOR was convinced that journalistic publications alone were not sufficient. There was a need to exploit the possibilities offered by the very fact of independent organizing, not only to serve persecuted individuals, but also to serve a constantly persecuted Polish culture. The goals were to make available to Poles living in Poland the great achievements of émigré literature: Gombrowicz, Miłosz, Wierzyński, and others; to bring back forbidden literary works of the past and present; to offer Polish writers of all generations the possibility of reaching readers inside the country; to make possible the debuts of those who would never pass through the eye of the censor's needle; to bring in forbidden works by foreign writers; to enrich the spiritual culture of the intelligentsia, the workers, and the peasants by offering them works that help them to understand social processes, history, and a complicated reality; to give to young people and to all of society books that are not mendacious; and above all, to free writers from the internal censorship that was strangling them. All these tasks certainly exceeded the existing possibilities, but those who began this work knew that it was better to do a little than to do nothing.

The appearance of *Zapis,* a serious literary quarterly of high quality edited by a group of writers from various generations who cooperated or sympathized with KOR, was greeted with joy. But *Zapis* made it particularly evident that there was a need for an independent publishing house, operating with its own printing equipment. The few, necessarily expensive typescripts, which by their very nature could reach only a very limited audience, were not yet enough.

Mirek Chojecki was the initiator, the creator, and then the excellent director of NOWa. He transferred the efficient Radom team (the seed of the Intervention Bureau) to others to run, and began to organize printing. He had great organizational talent and an ability to learn new things. He gathered around himself a team of people able to manage a publishing house: it had to include printers (both professionals and amateurs), supply managers, others who would organize distribution, and still others able to develop a list of books worthy of being published. Among the participants who made the greatest contributions, one should mention two of Chojecki's successive assistants: first Konrad Bieliński and then Grzegorz Boguta, along with the professional printer Bogdan Grzesiak, and Adam Michnik, who was chiefly responsible for editorial recommendations.

KOR decided to support this idea. The starting capital of NOWa, rather modest in itself, came from KOR. It consisted of duplicating machines and some money in the form of a donation. Shortly afterward, NOWa had its own accounts, although on many occasions it availed itself of loans given without interest by the Social Self-Defense Fund. In the later period of KOR, NOWa became self-sufficient, and even made some loans to the fund. KOR was given a guarantee that leaflets and other KOR publications would be printed by NOWa, without having to wait in turn, and at cost. It should be added that basically every press initiative of KOR created its own independent printing operation. The *Information Bulletin, Głos,* and *Robotnik* were not dependent on NOWa equipment.

The achievement of the Independent Publishing House during these years was truly impressive. There were well over a hundred publications, from small pamphlets to books in several volumes (Andrzejewski's *Miazga* in three volumes; two volumes of Grass's *The Tin Drum*). There were works by new writers (Zdzisław Jaskuła, Jan Polkowski) as well as classics (Witold Gombrowicz, Kazimierz Wierzyński, Stefan Żeromski). Current political and economic works (Zbigniew Brzeziński, Marek Tarniewski, Władysław Bieńkowski, Jacek Kuroń, Waldemar Kuczyński) were published alongside previously unavailable works indispensable to an understanding of intellectual and political culture (Tomasz Masaryk). There were works essential to the developing self-education movement (Władysław Bartoszewski, *The Polish Underground State 1939–1945;* Bohdan Cywiński, *A History of the Catholic Church in Independent Poland;* Igor Gołomsztok, *Artistic Language Under Totalitarian Conditions;* Tomasz Burek) and there were also songbooks. Polish readers were presented with unknown works by Western writers (Grass and Orwell), as well as Russian works (Mandelstam, Brodsky, Yerofeev) and works from neighboring countries (Hrabal). Piłsudski's *Underground Publications* were brought out in homage to NOWa's predecessors, as was Michnik's *Shadows of Forgotten Ancestors.* Polish contemporary lyric poetry was richly represented by Stanisław Barańczak, Jacek Bierezin, Jerzy Ficowski, Zdzisław Jaskuła, Jan Polkowski, Wiktor Woroszylski, and volumes of Miłosz, so that it could not be said that for over thirty years no one in Poland had published the works of the Polish Nobel laureate who followed Sienkiewicz and Reymont. The NOWa catalog listed satire (Janusz Szpotański) and prose (Jerzy Andrzejewski, Kazimierz Brandys, Marek Hłasko, Tadeusz Konwicki, Julian Stryjkowski, Piotr Wierzbicki) as well as literary, philosophical, and historical essays (Paweł Jasienica, Andrzej Kijowski, Jan Józef Lipski, and Adam Michnik), memoirs (Józef Czapski, Jan Nowak, Zygmont Żuławski), and documentary publications (among others, such sensational titles as *Two Conversations—Moscow 1960;* transcripts from the Polish-Chinese talks; or *Pravda,* a selection of articles from the Moscow newspaper of September 1939; or *From the Book of Prohibitions of the Main Office for the Control of the Press, Publications, and Performances,* that is, the secret documents of the censorship) and handbooks (*The Citizen and the Security Service*). The issues of *Zapis, Puls,* and *Krytyka* published by NOWa alone account for some thirty volumes!

It is interesting that the only voices expressing doubts about "whether we could afford" Miłosz, Gombrowicz, or Grass, while there was a lack of political pamphlets and handbooks, came from the intelligentsia. These doubts were never raised by the workers, even though they felt the shortage of popular political literature in their own activity. One could easily observe that the workers fully understood the task of promoting culture. Their attitude was not marked by snobbism nor by shame of betraying indifference toward cultural values, nor by shyness in expressing their own opinions. Theirs was an authentic pride that somehow they were helping out, that they were participating in the great task of enriching the national culture. This experience also increased the workers' interest in what the opposition published. More and more often one came across workers who read, who educated themselves, and tried to understand everything—and themselves propagated literature. I do not wish to be accused of developing a blind cult of the idealized worker, but those workers who were active in KOR either represented a high intellectual and cultural level, or at least understood that these were important values for the life of the nation, values worth preserving even if they did not feel drawn to them personally. Moreover—and Solidarity was similar in this respect—these workers had great respect for education, knowledge, and artistic talent, without a trace of an inferiority complex.

NOWa showed the way. New publishing houses were being created. It is not possible to list all of them, to say nothing of their publications.

The Library of *Głos,* and later also of "Krąg" (Circle), was connected with the KOR milieu. "Klin" (Wedge) gained great popularity by publishing Gombrowicz's *Diaries;* this publishing house also used other names, and in general was very conspiratorial (though not to the extent of hiding from KOR) as far as its personnel and even the location of its activity were concerned. KOS (the Cracow Student Publishing House) was close to the circle of activists who founded the first SKS in Poland. The Showcase of Critics and Writers was a publishing house in Poznań.

The Father Kolbe Publishing House was more involved in printing leaflets (connected with anti-abortion propaganda) than in actual publishing activity, but its personnel was also close to KOR.

The Lublin Catholic milieu around the periodical *Spotkania* also published several valuable books.

The Third of May Publishing House was originally close to ROPCiO, though in time it ventured away from its base and became more willing and eager to cooperate with KOR. They also issued a number of important publications.

There was no lack of ephemeral publishing ventures, of firms that appeared and then after one or two publications disappeared without a trace. It is not clear whether one can include here as "publishing activity" the activities of the secret student library in Warsaw, which in its first period was aided financially by KOR. When the library wanted to have a book, they photocopied it in a quantity greater than they needed, so that the surplus generated by sales of the extra copies covered their expenses. In this manner a dozen or so copies of Aniela Steinsbergowa's memoir, *The View from the Defender's Bench,* were put into circulation, and several other books as well.

Now a few words about the technical infrastructure of the publishing houses.

Of necessity, this was the most secret area of oppositional work. Perhaps memoirs will be written some day by the managers or the workers, although in this milieu their roles were not clearly separated: the photograph of Mirek Chojecki that showed his hands dripping with printer's ink was not staged. There already exists one such memoir entitled "We, the Free-Rollers," written by Jan Walc, who described the printing of one of the *Information Bulletins.*[16]

The first printing attempts were made with homemade "frames" and clotheswringers, just as in 1968. Outmoded duplicators using alcohol and terrible stencils produced pathetic results. Much water flowed under the bridge before the KOR printers began to produce decent, meaning merely readable, copies. Then the first duplicating machines began arriving from the West. The equipment became better and the KOR workers more effective, especially so after some professional printers appeared. There were never enough machines. They kept breaking down, and the work could not wait for repairs. The machines had to be distributed in the provinces, and they also fell into the hands of the police during searches and other accidents. There were not too many people who really mastered the printing techniques. After a while this situation resulted in the problem of payment, since one could not expect the unemployed to stop painting apartments for a week, or for a professional printer to take a week of unpaid vacation in order to finish a book quickly, or to print a large edition of a periodical. This was the only KOR work that was remunerated.

NOWa had its own, regular financial accounting, though foreign purchases were made with the money collected in the West for KOR. This was not an abuse since at that time collections were already being made "for KOR" and not exclusively for aid to the persecuted. NOWa also had some money of its own in the West, resulting from its relations with Western publishers with whom it acted as a middleman for copyright. Deciding which money belonged to KOR and which to NOWa presented a difficult problem of accounting.

Certain publications were printed on government installations. This was consistent with the Constitution, which guarantees that printing facilities will serve the working people of towns and villages, but it also meant risking a criminal trial for the use of someone else's—state-owned—equipment and materials. Nevertheless, during this period most offset publications were printed in this manner.

Not only the duplicating machines but also stencils, printer's ink, binding gadgets, and other equipment traveled secretly across the border, making the work in supply extremely bothersome and difficult. But paper was never imported; often it was even bought retail. All this material, including the reserves, had to be stored somewhere. New locations for print shops had to be sought out constantly, and they had to meet at least certain minimum requirements. Even housing was not a simple task for the printing services. The paper, the equipment, and the printed editions had to be transported from place to place. Sometimes bags and knapsacks were sufficient; usually cars were needed. Thus, there emerged a circle of specialized associates of KOR, NOWa, and the individual periodicals, whose job was precisely to take care of all this.

Distribution started from storage places, and then the transports were gradually broken down into smaller and smaller parcels, until they reached rank-and-file carriers. Even the best known KOR members and associates took part. It was rare for entire editions to be confiscated by the police, but losses "on the lines," in the last or near the last stage of distribution were not uncommon, and were the most severe.

Money for the purchased issues, together with donations "for the free word," would travel back through the same channels in which books and periodicals went out to apartments, factories, schools and institutions, to villages and towns.

The First Signs of the Birth of a New Peasant Movement

During the police repressions against KOR following Pyjas's death there occurred two acts testifying to the fact that the peasant movement was emerging from a deep sleep. The first of these events has already been discussed: the letter of peasants from the village and neighborhood of Zbrosza Duża in defense of the arrested KOR members. A short time later, Zbrosza Duża was to emerge as a true bastion of the peasant movement.

The second event had no direct connection with KOR. Twenty-two senior activists of the peasant movement wrote a letter to the Central Committee of the United Peasant Party (ZSL) severely criticizing the assumptions contained in a proposed law about retirement coverage for individual farmers. Predictably a witchhunt was initiated against the activists immediately afterward. It was led by Jan Kaźmierczak, the chairman of the Capital Seniors' Club of the ZSL. There were insinuations about collaboration with Radio Free Europe, and a meeting condemning the letter was held in the seniors' club. The result was that the number of signatures increased to thirty-three. The board of the club removed five signatories of the letter from the list of its members. A year later, in the summer of 1978, the first Peasants' Self-Defense Committee was created precisely on the basis of resistance to the law on pensions for farmers.

The Front of the Struggle for Freedom of Religion

In the summer of 1977, the police and administrative authorities made a very unwise decision to strike at the Oases of the Living Church (also known as Oases of the Altar Service and Recollection Oases). The dispersal of the Oases camps had begun in June 1976, under the high patronage of the voivode of Nowy Sącz, Lech Bafia. On July 11, the Episcopate intervened strongly, and on July 24, Cardinal Wojtyła addressed the faithful of those parishes where the Oases recollections were taking place:

> I would like to state that all . . . these difficulties are illegal, and that the abuses of the administrative authorities have the goal of religious discrimination. . . . Should these difficulties continue, I assure you that the Cracow Ministry of Liturgic Services, which organizes the Oases of Recollection on behalf of the Polish Episcopate, will offer material and legal help if unjust fines and taxes are assessed.

The Oases movement (they were also known as the "Light-Life Movement") developed dynamically, and expressed an increasing interest in general social concerns.

During this period KOR also became involved in the defense of Stanisław Karpik from the village of Opole Stare, near Siedlce. In 1973, Karpik built a chapel on his farm. It was destroyed, and Karpik was sentenced to fifty days in jail by a sentencing board for misdemeanors. At that time, Karpik designed one of the rooms in his building to serve as a chapel. On April 8, 1977, while the owner was absent, eight police functionaries broke into the building and destroyed the interior, including the chapel. The paneling was torn down from the walls; the host was scattered about and the sacramental wine had been drunk. Books had disappeared, as had some 11,000 zlotys. Later there were attempts to confine Karpik in a hospital for the mentally ill. KOR published this information and remained in touch with Karpik. He shortly became a participant in the independent peasant movement. The Security Service battled with him until the spring of 1980. This hard-won chapel became an important center of social self-defense. By 1980 it was a center of social and religious life for the peasants living nearby, while at the same time it was a base for the Oases.

The Repressions from May to September 1977

The May arrests were followed by a difficult period for KOR. The torn network of internal communications, based mostly on personal contacts, was in need of repair. Those who were arrested, and who were after all very active before their arrests, had to be replaced in such a way that no area of KOR's activity would be hurt. The barrier of fear rose again during this period of almost two and a half months. The Security Service and the police were very sure of themselves. Basically, however, neither the methods nor the scale of the struggle against KOR had changed. Above all, there was no second general attack against KOR, although the list of detentions continued to be long.

Beatings were still used as a method of fighting KOR. Around noon on May 29, Andrzej Zdziarski was stopped and beaten in public. Since a crowd had gathered (this took place in front of the Palace of Culture and Art during a folk arts and crafts fair), the police explained that he had raped a woman who had already been taken away in another police car. (It would be interesting to know how many people believed this nonsense.) On June 30, at 3:30 P.M., two university students, Jakub Bułat and Michał Worwąg, were detained on the street and beaten inside a police car. On August 29, Roman Wojciechowski was kidnapped in the evening from the center of Warsaw and taken out of town to Łomianki. He was beaten to unconsciousness, and then abandoned. On September 3, "unknown perpetrators" attacked Władysław Sulecki; Bogusława Blajfer's arm was sprained; Józef Szczepanik, a worker from Radom was threatened with death.

Dismissals from work became more common, both of KOR associates and of participants in public protests. In less than five months, fifteen activists lost their jobs. Most of them were scholars, while others worked in a variety of professions (an editor in a publishing house, a theater director, a film director, a teacher, a librarian, a metallurgical engineer). Franciszek Grabczyk, an engineer at the Lenin Steel Mills in Nowa Huta, was told by the director of a department in the Ministry of Heavy Industry that he would never be allowed to work again in the metallurgical industry. The following are the names of the others who were dismissed: Stanisław Barańczak, Władysław Bartosiewicz, Grzegorz Boguta, Wojciech Fałkowski, Helena Z. Gromiec, Włodzimierz Gromiec, Bohdan Kosiński (who returned to work after several months following a court decision), Ewa Ligocka, Wojciech Malicki, Jerzy Markuszewski, Małgorzata Naimska, Wojciech Ostrowski, Eugeniusz Porada, and Ludmiła Wujec.

A reprisal less painful than the loss of a job was aimed at the same time against two professors of mathematics, Roman Duda and Stanisław Hartman, who were deprived of their right to serve as scientific advisors. Doctors Tadeusz Jakubowski, Eugeniusz Porada, Ludwik Rudolf, and Jan Waszkiewicz (all of them faculty members in institutions of higher learning) were not permitted to work part time in the Mickiewicz High School in Wrocław, which specialized in mathematics.

A new form of repression, which luckily did not become more common, involved the eviction of Dr. Witold Niedźwiedzki of Łódź University from his apartment.[17] A reader from outside Poland, from the West, who does not know conditions in Poland, might not understand the horror of such a reprisal. This is a sentence which condemns a person and his family to at least a dozen or so years (or even longer, who can say?) of homelessness, with all its consequences. A typical Pole, who understands what this means, would probably prefer several years of imprisonment.

Several workers from the ZREMB Enterprises in Radom were subjected to unusual treatment. They were told to come to work on the morning of June 25, 1977, the first anniversary of the June events. They were taken by car to a recreational center in Nieporęt, near Warsaw, where they were told to paint a fence. Since they were not prepared for the trip, they did not have, nor did they receive any money for return travel.

Another form of repression used on many occasions involved the imposition of a fine of up to 5,000 zlotys by a sentencing board for misdemeanors, for such things as using an apartment for a meeting, refusing to identify oneself, and so on. Among other things, KOR members and associates who were held in investigative prisons were thus sentenced *in absentia* without even knowing (except for the number of the article in the Code of Misdemeanors) what they were being punished for, and they were not allowed to entrust their cases to an attorney.

The Workers after the Amnesty

As the preceding section has demonstrated, the situation of KOR activists was the same after the July amnesty as it had been before the arrests in May. The activists were beaten, threatened with death, dismissed from work, and persecuted in various other ways. Obviously, this was true both for the workers and for the intellectuals. The workers who were sentenced for participating in the June strikes and demonstrations, but who did not cooperate with KOR after they were pardoned or given amnesty, constitute a separate category. They remained in touch with the committee for as long as they continued to feel that they were objects of interest to the Security Service; gradually, however, they disappeared from KOR's field of vision.

June 1976 did not produce many working class dissident activists: there were a few from Radom, a small group in Ursus which merely maintained contact, and several people in Grudziądz and in Łódź; there were one or two active sympathizers in different areas rather than activists.

Why was this the case? There were evidently many reasons. The events of June 1976 did not promote the creation of elites. Strike committees were rarely chosen, and collective actions developed quickly and then rapidly died down, before groups could form and leaders emerge. The arrests and other repressions were not very selective. If they really did have a greater effect on those who were noticeable, this happened primarily to those who were impulsive or aggressive, and these were not always traits characteristic of activists. In addition, at least in Radom, the police selection was clearly directed toward socially marginal people.

KOR entered this environment at first as a guardian and a rescuer, not as an organizer. It is possible that the fact that KOR did not try from the very beginning to create some semiformal structures was a mistake. In any case, actions such as the letter of 1,100 workers from Ursus asking for the rehiring of their colleagues, or the collective letters from Radom about beatings and tortures, had an ad hoc character, and once they ended, those involved ceased to be active. Only the formation of *Robotnik*, which was conceived as a newspaper/organizer, changed this state of affairs. On the whole, during the first months following the amnesty, the workers of Radom, Ursus, and other centers could still be seen mostly as victims, who were offered help and who expected help, but who were not yet ready to act for themselves.

The situation after the amnesty was described in *KOR Communiqués* No. 13 of August 13 and No. 14 of September 29. In all locations where workers had been dismissed from work after June 25, 1976, and about which KOR had information—that is, in Radom, Ursus, Płock, Łódź, Gdańsk, and Grudziądz—the fired workers received new employment which did not correspond with their qualifications and which was by the same token less remunerative. These wage differences were drastic and meant losses of up to two-thirds of their previous salaries. Exceptions were very rare. New employment was not easy to find. For example, in Łódź, factories stubbornly refused to rehire even those workers whose cases had been decided in their favor by the Labor Court. Even at the end of September there were still some who had not yet found new jobs, and not because they did not want to find them. For example, Jan Sadowski from Radom was refused employment seven times. Finally in September he got work as a bus cleaner, which paid him starvation wages of less than 2,000 zlotys per month; on this he had to support three children and a wife unable to work because of a serious illness. Sadowski had a high school education and had completed occupational training courses in his factory.

The participants in the June strikes and demonstrations lost the largest part of their means of support, as well as the so-called continuity of work, together with supplements for their length of service. During their many months of forced unemployment, they were deprived of regular earnings (KOR relief could not fully compensate them for this, and the courts sentenced them to pay high fines and court costs). Most of these families found themselves in poverty. Their daily lives were plagued by visits at home and at work by the police and the Security Service; by surveillance; by provocations in the street (a functionary waiting outside a person's home would ask, for example, where the person had been and why he had not returned home straight from work); and by summonses by the police in order to be interrogated on unspecified subjects. KOR also noted attempts at provocations in the workplaces directed against former participants in the June demonstrations.[18]

On August 15, three workers from Grudziądz—that is, from the center where the workers punitively dismissed from work had organized themselves and turned to KOR as an already active group—sent a letter to Gierek in which they demanded to be rehabilitated, returned to work under their former conditions, and compensated for wages lost as a result of forced and repressive unemployment. They demanded this not only for themselves but for all forty-three of the workers fired from the Pomeranian Foundry and Enamel Shop in Grudziądz. They noted in their letter that the work stoppage (they did not use the word "strike") had been peaceful, and that the discipline necessary to avoid destruction and unnecessary waste had been maintained. They mentioned the attitudes of the Regional Appeals Commission in Grudziądz and of the Labor Court in Toruń, according to which participation in a work stoppage itself constituted a reason sufficient to warrant being fired disciplinarily from work. They stressed that workers with twenty-four years of experience, who had been awarded badges as Leaders of Socialist Labor and who were delegates to the trade unions, had also been treated in this manner. The letter was signed by Mirosława Kocińska, Maksymilian Moździński (who, several months before the strike, had received, as the best worker, a banner for the results of the factory's work), and Renata Nagel. Of course the letter was never answered. But one must admit that the signatories were neither beaten nor arrested.

A Summary of the First Year of KOR's Work

A summary of the year's work of KOR is contained in a report of the Citizens' Commission that was established at the request of the committee. This commission was composed of Władysław Bieńkowski, Andrzej Kijowski, and Stefan Kisielewski.[19] The creation of such a commission was not easy, even for formal purposes. It was clear that KOR should be audited from the outside, at least on this occasion.

For the future, a different solution was provided for by the formation of a Funds Council that would supervise the treasurer (later this office was held by two people, a treasurer and his deputy, who shared executive and reporting functions), in addition to defining the direction and the principles of administering the fund, the manner of distributing the funds among the various agencies and cells of KOR, including the responsibility for making decisions about expenses exceeding 10,000 zlotys (this responsibility extended also to loans given by KOR to other independent institutions). Finally, the results of the financial audits and the reports prepared by the council were to be submitted to KOR for approval. It could be said that the Funds Council would become an audit commission within KOR, one that would also be authorized to develop the general financial policy of the committee.

But who was to conduct the audit this time, and how were they to be selected? It certainly could not be done by the Highest Control Chamber or some other similar state institution, hence the idea of forming a Citizens' Commission. The trouble was that KOR, which wanted to be audited, was itself responsible for naming the auditors. But who else could do so? A discreet sounding in the Church made clear what had been expected: it was not convenient for the Church to delegate someone officially for this function, since this would tie the Church to the opposition. No one else could be considered. Thus, everything depended on whether the persons chosen by KOR would enjoy sufficient public trust for their authority not to be questioned, and, should they declare the accounts in order, for them not to be accused of protecting the good name of KOR contrary to their own consciences.

The people approached by KOR warranted such trust. They were in general highly respected and they were not otherwise involved in KOR activities, while at the same time they were known for their involvement in social affairs and had an understanding of the realities of social activities, which was also a necessary condition for a fair audit.

What materials were presented to the commission? Above all, the commission was given access to KOR files, which gave it an opportunity to make spot comparisons of notations in the files against the statements of people who had received help. They also were given all the materials and notes concerning contributions and expenditures. Something resembling hearings were also held, so that the commission would be able to clarify otherwise unclear circumstances. The text of the commission's report read:

Warsaw, September 29, 1977

The Workers' Defense Committee requested the undersigned—Władysław Bieńkowski, Andrzej Kijowski, and Stefan Kisielewski—to accept the role of a public audit commission to examine the entirety of KOR's activities. Having acted on this request, the signers of this report, who familiarized themselves with reports and with all the existing documentation, hereby declare:

1. The Workers' Defense Committee was formed on September 23, 1976, in Warsaw. The reason for the creation of KOR was the widespread reprisals and clear violations of the rule of law following the events of June 1976; in response to these repressions, a spontaneous relief action to provide help to the persecuted existed in the country even earlier. KOR immediately informed the Diet of the Polish People's Republic, in the person of its Marshal, Stanisław Gucwa, about the formation of the Committee.

2. Until the day it closed its books, KOR transmitted a total sum of 3,251,300 zlotys to those affected by repressions and to the families of workers who needed help. This sum was composed of voluntary contributions both from Poland and abroad.

3. The financial help offered by the Committee was based on information collected by its numerous and generous associates. Altogether, 943 families from Ursus, Radom, Łódź, Płock, Grudziądz, and Gdańsk were included in the evidence.

4. The materials that were gathered illustrate the extent of repressions, and their moral and social effects; they also expose the willful lawlessness of the police apparatus, blatant irregularities in the functioning of the justice system, and loopholes in the law. The research done by KOR also produced valuable information about the material situation of the workers' families, especially the poorest ones.

5. Members of the Committee and its associates attended the court trials of workers who were accused of participation in the strikes and demonstrations of June 25, 1976. In this manner KOR offered moral support to the defendants. KOR helped the families of the accused to receive legal and medical aid and covered the necessary expenses. KOR members and associates also informed the accused and their families of their rights.

6. In regularly published *Communiqués* KOR informed the general public of its activities, providing information about the course of the trials and of sentences, and about all other forms of repression used against the participants in the June events and against members and associates of the Committee; moreover, it rectified false information propagated by the mass media, and made public the names of those individuals who were particularly well known for violating the law and misrepresenting the truth.

7. KOR addressed the highest state authorities, including the Diet, appealing for an end to lawlessness and violence, for a cessation of the repres-

sions against workers and their families, and for a full and unconditional amnesty for all participants in the events of June 25, 1976 and for their return to work under the original conditions. It also appealed to charitable institutions, that is, to the Main Board of the Polish Red Cross and to the Main Board of the Society of Friends of the Child, as well as to the Ministry of Health and Social Welfare, for aid to families whose material situation had worsened dramatically as a result of the imprisonment or dismissal from work of the main breadwinner. In most instances these appeals were not answered.

8. In connection with complaints and requests directed to the Committee in cases not directly related to the events of June 25, the Committee organized the Intervention Bureau and designated appropriate means for its activities.

9. The members of the Workers' Defense Committee and its associates performed all work connected with the Committee's activities gratis. Many of them were subject to discrimination, repression, and attempts at intimidation; there were cases of severe beatings, either by unknown persons or by functionaries of the police apparatus. On many occasions, large sums of money gathered through contributions were confiscated, along with typewriters which were their private property. The apartments of KOR members and associates were searched on numerous occasions. Six members of the Committee and five associates were held under investigative arrest, in most cases for a period of two months, with the exception of two persons released earlier because of the state of their health. Many members of the Committee were required to pay large fines.

The signers of this document declare that the WORKERS' DEFENSE COMMITTEE has acted according to the goals and principles it set for itself. It has brought immediate relief to the needy and has moved public opinion. Without violating the laws of the Polish People's Republic, it has created new forms of collective action, of social self-help, and of gathering and disseminating information. It has contributed to the spiritual unification of Polish society around deeply-rooted traditions based on ideals of personal freedom and dignity, social solidarity, the rule of law, and openness in public life. It has broken down the barriers dividing various social groups, separating people holding various worldviews or belonging to different generations.

Following their examination of the state of the funds remaining under the disposition of the Workers' Defense Committee, the undersigned consider it legitimate that these funds be transferred to the Social Self-Defense Fund for the purposes specified in the resolution of the Committee calling for the creation of the Intervention Bureau.

WŁADYSŁAW BIEŃKOWSKI   ANDRZEJ KIJOWSKI   STEFAN KISIELEWSKI

This text requires certain additions. Above all, there is the issue of the number of people who were given help. The report speaks about families "included in the evidence," which corresponds with the rather clumsy phrase used in the *KOR Communiqués,* referring to people "included in the information." The number cited is 943. *KOR Communiqué* No. 13 of August 31, 1977 provides the following data about people included in the evidence: Radom, 511; Ursus, 202 plus 64 (the second figure refers to workers from Warsaw factories who were cared for by the Ursus team, though not all of them lived in Ursus); Gdańsk, 93; Łódź, 68; Grudziądz, 43; Płock, 44. This adds up to 1,025. What is the source of the discrepancy?

On the basis of my knowledge of these matters, the discrepancy can be explained by the following facts: the Citizens' Commission was not presented with the list of persons from Radom who were given legal and medical aid (this file was kept separately only for Radom) because in the case of doctors the help was free, while the legal aid, which did cost something, was also noted in the general file, and its presentation in a special file would lead to duplication. Although the special file also contained the cases of those for whom various payments connected with the trials had not been made before the end of August, under the rubric of "legal help" the amounts were zero. In other words, the number of cases included in evidence was larger than the number cited in the report.

The number of those given financial aid was in fact lower than the number of persons registered. Why does the report not specify the number of people (or families) who were given relief, instead of citing only the number of those who were registered? This can be explained by the phrase occasionally used in the *Communiqués:* "In Ursus . . . continuous contact is being maintained with 169 families." This figure represents, unfortunately none too precisely, the number of people who were receiving regular stipends. It does not include families (or persons) who received money on only one occasion, or who received it sporadically. These last cases were noted in the files and were reflected in the general amount of help distributed by KOR. It was very difficult to decide when people given sporadic aid should be included (sometimes help involved ridiculously small sums, for example, the costs of transportation). At the same time, their inclusion would sharply increase the number of people who were being helped. Considering all this, and attempting to avoid undue complications, the general number of registered persons was the only one cited in the report.

Let me cite the number of persons (or families) that for a time received regular help according to *KOR Communiqué* No. 13: Radom, 274; Ursus, 169; Gdańsk, 34; Łódź, 68; Grudziądz, 25; Płock, 32. The total was 602 families (or persons), plus a number of people who received unique or sporadic grants, which cannot be specified precisely. Is this an impressive result? On the scale of the entire country, it certainly is not. One can, however, venture to say that more was done than would have seemed possible for such a small group of people to provide under the conditions existing in Poland.

Why does the account show no sums spent for printing and publications? In order to organize the financial situation of KOR by the Funds Council, expenditures for publications, which were rather small during the first year, were taken not from the contributions made to help the workers, but from separate gifts, both from Poland and abroad. These were sums on the order of several tens of thousands of zlotys; unfortunately, the bookkeeping was not precise.

7

From the Transformation of KOR to the Founding of the Initiating Committees of Free Trade Unions

(September 1977 to March/April 1978)

The Reasons for the Transformation of KOR

An awareness among its members that KOR might indeed survive until its basic goals were met began to develop some time in late November or early December 1976. KOR believed that these basic goals would be fulfilled when the workers were released from jail and returned to their jobs. At the same time, everyone expected that punishing the guilty would be more difficult than obtaining the release of those in prison. KOR even declared publicly that it would lose its *raison d'être* when its goals were achieved (one must add, however, that these goals included both punishing the guilty and returning the persecuted workers to employment for earnings compatible with their qualifications). It would be nonsensical, however, if punishing the guilty were to remain the only goal for which KOR would continue to fight. Simply speaking, the social conscience of the KOR activists revolted against this.

Above all, through its appeals and its basically open style of action, KOR brought about a definite social situation: there was a mobilization of public consciousness, perhaps not yet on a mass scale but fairly broadly based, and it took place in full view of the police and the security apparatus, which responded not only with immediate reprisals but also registered events and names. KOR developed a certain system of self-defense, perhaps not too efficient, but nevertheless assuring a minimum of relative security, because KOR answered every terrorist and repressive act of the authorities by making it known to Polish and world public opinion. After the dissolution of KOR, every discovered activist or small group of activists would suddenly be left face to face with the Security Service, which was only waiting for such a moment. It can be said that something like a vicious circle was created: activity brought on revenge and persecution, but these would probably become even harsher and more general if all organized activity were to cease.

There was, however, another reason to resist the dissolution of KOR. Even during the early stages of the committee's activities, people who had been mistreated in various ways by the power apparatus or who knew of such cases of lawlessness began approaching the committee. They appealed for help, and frequently offered their cooperation, which sometimes went beyond their own personal concerns. In the more drastic cases, it was simply impossible to tell these people (and oneself) that their problems lay beyond the goals and the sphere of activities of KOR. There were different kinds of cases: instances in which beatings and tortures were used against those who had been arrested were discovered throughout Poland. Sometimes these methods were used to extort testimony or admissions of guilt, and sometimes they were used for personal reasons, out of revenge or sadism. They resulted in permanent injuries and even in deaths. The standard practice of the so-called investigative apparatus was to prevent any trials of the perpetrators, and this encouraged feelings of impunity and contempt for the law within the police and the Security Service.

KOR was presented with cases that illustrated the impotence of a citizen before the labor court system that defended the interests of the employer, that is, of the state, of which the justice system was also an organ.[1] The power of provincial gangs composed of local power elites, and the corruption of this apparatus, were being revealed, as were the obvious mechanisms of economic failure in certain areas, for example in agriculture, where the feudalization of relations between the farmer and the administration proved to be an essential obstacle to production, and so on. The majority of the problems that were becoming apparent were never even taken up by KOR because it lacked the ability to do so. There were always too few people to do the work, and those who were active were notoriously overworked. But one could not accept this with indifference. The cases were far too serious, and there was too much human misery involved. And the fate of Poland depended too much on whether a war would be waged against these indignities and whether it would be won. This was the source of the idea of social self-defense as a task involving independent and self-governing social initiatives.

The Apolitical and Political Character
of KOR and of KSS "KOR"

It was obvious that the transformation of KOR would change
its character significantly and above all that it would make its activities
more political. The problem of the political or apolitical nature of KOR
is so complex and unclear that in this respect the very documents of the
history of the committee appear contradictory. On the one hand, there
is no lack of statements emphasizing the fact that KOR had no political
goals, while on the other, even the early appearance of the term *domestic
opposition,* which was readily used by the KOR press, testifies to something
else. But the problem is not that of a simple lack of consistency or of a
camouflage. KOR was created out of moral indignation and because of
the need to bring help to the persecuted (this does not mean that this
was the only motivation of every activist of KOR). But the persecutor
was the state, and its persecutions were not incidental, but committed
in full awareness of their nature.

When one wants to describe the motives for the creation of KOR, one
can adopt either of two different attitudes. According to the first, certain
moral values are accepted, and thus one believes that a certain moral
code is binding (however this code is understood). What is more, the
priority of moral values and of the moral code is respected. If this posture
is adopted, then it does not matter whether the criminal committed the
crime for reasons of personal revenge, or because he wanted to appropriate the property of his victim, or because he was told to do so by a
ministerial instruction. In all these instances, the reasons for opposition
are ethical, not political. According to the other—totalitarian—attitude,
resistance against the state is always sacrilegious and a matter of politics.

KOR brought together people who were antitotalitarian. They shared
a moral motivation for their opposition, although individually, they emphasized different aspects of it. Certainly, the antitotalitarianism of Reverend Zieja emphasized its moral character, while the antitotalitarianism
of Jacek Kuroń was to a large extent also political. But the fundamental
unifying bond of the committee was this shared moral motivation of
antitotalitarianism, plus a certain minimum political commitment accepted also by even the apolitical members of KOR: that is, the striving
for a sovereign and democratic Poland.

In this respect one should not be surprised by the fact that even those
KOR activists who were not without political interests also stressed the
apolitical nature of the committee. It was clear to them— as it was to all
the other members that KOR would never create a full and detailed

political program; that it could not transform itself into a political party (if only because of the differences among its members); and that it would not become an instrument in the struggle for power. But a transformed KOR, directing its activities toward social self-defense, had by the same token to broaden the sphere of its conflicts with the authorities, and move closer to political matters; frequently it had to raise its voice and intervene on issues that are usually of interest to political groups (for example, the general state of the legal system, the educational and cultural policies of the state, assumptions concerning agricultural policy, and so on). It was known in advance that this would create new problems for KOR. How was the committee to maintain the domination of the moral over the political attitude as the glue holding KOR together, or how to protect the committee from internal polarization and factionalism for as long as an institution like KOR would be needed by society? This situation was becoming more and more difficult as time passed, and not only the social but also the more strictly political conflicts became sharper.

Organizational Preparations for the Transformation of KOR

The dramatic moments in the history of the committee— the murder of Pyjas and the arrests of the KOR activists—were preceded not only by an awareness that the time to transform KOR was approaching but also by specific preparations for this transformation. Thus, during the several days between Pyjas's death and the attack on KOR by the Security Service, the main institutions that were to define the mode of action of the committee for several years were created inside KOR. Then suddenly everything had to be halted: the fight to free those who had been imprisoned and the effort to maintain something like the same level of activity as before became the main goals. Only after the amnesty and a short respite was the issue taken up again.

Basically, four things had to be done: financial accounts had to be prepared, an independent body that would serve as an audit commission had to be nominated, a consensus about the transformation of KOR had to be achieved, and the necessary documents had to be prepared. In addition, a general meeting of the committee had to be called (which could have proven difficult).

The financial accounting was to be conducted by the Social Self-Defense Funds Council (of course, they could not be held responsible for the funds, since this body had just been created), and by others who, practically speaking, handled all the money flowing through KOR. KOR also nominated a three-person Citizens' Commission to audit the past year's work of KOR, in terms both of finances and of substantive achievements (see Chapter 6). Nonetheless, a consensus about the transformation of KOR was never fully achieved.

The Transformation of the Workers' Defense Committee into the Social Self-Defense Committee "KOR"

On September 29, 1977, the Workers' Defense Committee held a meeting, chaired by Adam Szczypiorski in the apartment of Professor Lipiński. Basically, three issues were on the agenda: the presentation of the financial accounts (expenditures and the current state of the funds) including the report of the Citizens' Commission called to audit the funds and activities of KOR, the transfer of funds from the hands of KOR to the Social Self-Defense Funds Council, and the transformation of KOR into the Social Self-Defense Committee.

The idea of transforming KOR—and thus broadening its sphere of action and accordingly changing its name—met with the disapproval of three members of the committee: Stefan Kaczorowski, Emil Morgiewicz, and Wojciech Ziembiński. Such opposition was to be expected in the cases of Kaczorowski and Ziembiński, both of whom had signed the declaration creating ROPCiO; but Morgiewicz's stand was somewhat surprising, since the fact that he had not signed the ROPCiO declaration was taken as a sign that he wished to distance himself from that movement. All three argued that since KOR had accomplished its goals, it should dissolve itself. According to them, ROPCiO was created in order to fight for human and civil rights in Poland, and it could successfully undertake the task of social self-defense. In their view, KOR's funds should be transferred to ROPCiO.

The meeting was taking place in an atmosphere of very sharp polemics. To the majority of members it was clear that ROPCiO, which represented a three-person faction within KOR, would like to become the only center of opposition in Poland, and that it wanted to eliminate KOR, allowing at most for the possibility that some of the dissolved committee's members and associates might become involved in the work of ROPCiO. This was an unrealistic conception and it was unacceptable to the other members of KOR. As an argument in the discussion, Wojciech Ziembiński cited the principle of a veto which, according to him, KOR had accepted. It is true that the committee developed a custom such that, even if only one person objected to something, the final decision in this matter was, if possible, postponed until some compromise formula could be found. But the principle of a veto was never formally adopted by KOR, and one could now foresee the danger that the ROPCiO participants within the committee might be able to paralyze KOR by means of a *liberum veto*.*

Among the questions facing the majority of KOR who planned the transformation of the committee—certainly not the most important question, but one that demanded a precise answer—was what to call the new committee. As we already know, the name Committee for the Defense of Human and Civil Rights has already appeared twice before in the history of the committee. In September 1976 this name lost out to the name Workers' Defense Committee; and in March 1977, with a slight change the unused name was appropriated by ROPCiO. The popularity of the name, which would define the committee by mentioning its goals of defending human and civil rights, can be explained both by its link with tradition and by its anticipated worldwide spread connected with Helsinki. But it was out of the question for two inevitably competing groups within the democratic opposition to be called "ROPCiO" and "KOPCiO," even if they had been very friendly with each other. Something else had to be devised.

Thus, it was decided to turn to one of the favorite key words in KOR: Self-Defense. If Self-Government was not chosen instead, it was because this seemed less adequate to the existing situation, while the name Social Solidarity Committee seemed too optimistic in view of the conflicts dividing society, however unevenly. The capital letters "KOR" in quotation marks were kept to indicate the continuity of the committee. Kaczorowski, Morgiewicz, and Ziembiński also opposed this last idea. The motion to transform the committee passed on the votes of the remaining members of KOR, with the same three people still in opposition. These three asserted that they were lodging a dissenting opinion. At that time it was decided by the vote of the majority that the next part of the meeting, now a meeting of KSS "KOR," would take place following a recess of an hour and a half, so that those who by voicing their separate

*The legal right of each member of the Polish Diet to defeat by his vote alone any measure under consideration, or to dissolve the Diet and nullify all acts passed during its session. This led to paralysis of the Polish Commonwealth in the seventeenth and eighteenth centuries. It was abolished by the Constitution of May 3, 1791.

vote had declared their intention not to participate in the work of KSS "KOR" could leave the meeting. In this manner, the three members left the committee.

As planned, the first meeting of KSS "KOR" took place on the same day, and adopted a resolution stating the goals of the transformed committee:

The Goals of the Social Self-Defense Committee "KOR" are:

1. To struggle against repressions used for reasons of conscience, politics, religion, or race, and to give aid to those persecuted for these reasons.

2. To struggle against violations of the rule of law, and to help those who have been wronged.

3. To fight for the institutional protection of civil rights and freedoms.

4. To support and defend all social initiatives aiming to realize Human and Civil Rights.

New Members of KSS "KOR"

KOR Communiqué No. 15 of October 31 carried information about eight new members of the committee.

KONRAD BIELIŃSKI, a mathematician, was one of the leaders of the Warsaw University movement against the liquidation of the Union of Polish students in 1973. He was an associate of KOR from the beginning of its existence, and a deputy of Chojecki in NOWa.

SEWERYN BLUMSZTAJN, a sociologist, was one of the main defendants in the March 1968 trials, and was a political prisoner. The creator and editor-in-chief of the *Information Bulletin*, he was an associate of KOR from the beginning of its existence.

ANDRZEJ CELIŃSKI, a sociologist, also participated in the 1968 student movement. He was the organizer of self-educational work among students of Warsaw University, which led to the "Flying University," and he was a co-founder of the Society for Scientific Courses. He was also an associate of KOR from the beginning.

LESZEK KOŁAKOWSKI, a philosopher and writer, was an associate of KOR abroad from the beginning of its existence, and a co-organizer of the international action to help KOR.

JAN LITYŃSKI, a computer scientist, was one of the main defendants in the March 1968 trials, and was a political prisoner. He was one of the organizers and participants in the Radom action, a member of the editorial board of the *Information Bulletin*, and later a co-founder and editor of *Robotnik*.

ZBIGNIEW ROMASZEWSKI, a physicist, was a co-organizer and participant in the Radom action, later its chief, and the co-founder and director of the Intervention Bureau of KOR.

MARIA WOSIEK, a theater scholar and Catholic activist, was an associate of KOR from the beginning.

HENRYK WUJEC, a physicist, was an activist in the Club of the Catholic Intelligentsia; he was also a co-organizer and participant in the Ursus action, and a member of the editorial board of *Robotnik*.

The Declaration of the Democratic Movement and the Founding of *Głos*

Following the transformation of KOR into KSS "KOR" and the broadening of its sphere of activities, a good many KOR activists began to feel the need for a more precise self-definition and for a sketch of the perspectives for a movement that was encompassing increasingly larger social circles. This was the source of the *Declaration of the Democratic Movement*. This text was not written by KOR, but it is one of the basic documents showing the ideological development of the milieu participating in KOR. The phrase *ideological development* needs to be emphasized. In the intention of its creators, the *Declaration of the Democratic Movement* was meant to be much more: it was to serve as a basis for the formation of a broad new platform that should result in the creation of institutional structures; in other words, it was a step in the direction of initiating a genuine political life. At the same time, the *Declaration* would also be a starting point for further, more specific programmatic works.

All these far-reaching plans failed for regrettable reasons. The group that wrote the *Declaration* decided to found a new periodical that would serve as an organ for gathering and organizing its adherents, and at the same time as a workshop for further programmatic work. The periodical was entitled *Głos*.[2] Antoni Macierewicz was to be its editor-in-chief. But immediately after the founding of the periodical, its editorial board split; luckily this did not cause a split within KOR, but as the split widened it led later to very sharp conflicts and to polarization within the committee.

The direct cause of the split was an article by Michnik (who was a member of the editorial board) that was rejected by Macierewicz, who saw in the article a tendency to "reach an agreement" with the authorities. The old (sacramental) accusation that Kuroń and Michnik wanted to appeal to one of the party factions was invoked once again. It needs to be said that neither side showed a desire to work out a compromise.

This was not the first confrontation, but it was decisive. Kuroń and Michnik were unwilling to accept an argument "from the sidelines" for the sake of creating some chance of patching up the split; that is, they did not accept the argument that everything printed in the first issue of a new periodical is of special importance, so that the suggestion that only one of the possible variants be taken into account might be read as a political manifesto of strategic significance. As a result, Kuroń and Michnik left *Głos;* and the "antkowcy"—as the followers of Antek Macierewicz were known by the KOR young people—remained on the editorial board of *Głos.*

Głos remained a serious periodical of the KOR milieu. But it was known that certain names would not be found there (such as Blumsztajn, Lityński, Michnik, and Kuroń), just as the *Information Bulletin, Robotnik,* and later *Krytyka* could not count on the collaboration of Dorn, Doroszewska, Macierewicz, or Naimski. Fortunately the atmosphere was not such that the publication in one or another of these journals was considered a betrayal, a declaration of war, a final self-definition, and so on. This was so, among other reasons, because some who did not identify themselves with the *Głos* group remained nominally on its editorial board, hoping that their continued presence would create a bridge between the factions and blunt their mutual attacks. Nevertheless, all this resulted in the formation not only of an editorial board for *Głos,* but also of a *Głos* group or faction within KOR. Certain conflicts between this group and the circle around Kuroń and Michnik belong to the history of KOR, and we will return to them later.

Who were the members of the *Głos* group? Basically this group included two members of KOR, Macierewicz and Naimski; Ludwik Dorn, an intelligent young sociologist with a tendency to exaggerate his judgments and attitudes; Urszula Doroszewska, a sociologist with journalistic talent; and others. Jakub Karpiński, an outstanding mind and individualist, also played an important role in *Głos;* he came from the milieu of the Club of the Crooked Circle and of the sociologists Maria and Stanisław Ossowski. There were also a number of young activists who did not declare themselves unequivocally, did not burn their bridges, yet leaned toward Macierewicz and toward *Głos.* Among these were Stefan Kawalec and Sergiusz Kowalski, both mathematicians who for a while played an important role in the creation of an opposition movement at Warsaw University.

Another interesting phenomenon was the significant evolution of this milieu toward the right. During the early days of KOR, Macierewicz liked to point to the work of Abramowski as to an ideological tradition that was especially dear to him. Toward the end of the committee's existence, he used the words "the left" and "leftist" exclusively as insults. He did not like to answer questions about ideological self-definition; thus there remained always something unclear and unspoken about it, so that it is also difficult to characterize his attitude.

During the Solidarity convention in Gdańsk, people from *Głos* signed the declaration of the Club in the Service of Independence. It is moderate in tone and content, but the membership of the club indicated that its direction would be clearly to the right. Despite everything, even after several years had passed, it seems that *Głos* did not fully fit there.

The Student Movement

After the May student movement in response to the murder of Pyjas, student groups in various academic centers throughout the country were ready to create their own independent organizations. The first signs of this in the new academic year of 1977 were the periodicals *Bratniak* and *Indeks*.

Bratniak, a periodical whose title invokes the tradition of self-governing student mutual aid organizations, appeared in Gdańsk on October 1, 1977. The first issue listed the names of Aleksander Hall and Marian Piłka from Lublin as representatives of the editorial board. The *Bratniak* group was the source of the future Young Poland Movement, which the KOR milieu respected and regarded with much sympathy, knowing that in every situation one could count on fair play on their part. The members of the Young Poland Movement gained additional respect in August 1980 when they supported the strikes with evident humility and disinterestedness, which does not mean that they did not, by the same token, attempt to develop their own political influence, but that this was not their major goal.

The national periodical *Indeks*, published first in Warsaw and later in Cracow, was also close to KOR. The membership of the editorial board listed in the first issue, which appeared in mid-October 1977, showed that three academic communities were involved: Cracow (Lesław Maleszka, Tomasz Schoen, and Bronisław Wildstein); Warsaw (Jan Ajzner, Ludwik Dorn, Urszula Doroszewska, and Sergiusz Kowalski); and Łódź (Paweł Spodenkiewicz). Unfortunately, *Indeks* appeared irregularly after its transfer to Cracow.

Five new Student Solidarity Committees were formed during the 1977–1978 academic year: in Warsaw on October 20, in Gdańsk on November 5, in Poznań on November 15, in Wrocław on December 14, and in Szczecin on May 10. The Warsaw SKS was organized by a group of student associates of KOR. The first issue they took up, on October 27, concerned the expulsion of Maciej Grzywaczewski from the Catholic Theological Academy. He was a second-year philosophy student and participant in ROPCiO.

In addition to the SKS, student groups in Warsaw undertook a new initiative with the well-defined and limited goal of organizing libraries of *librorum prohibitorum*, that is, of forbidden books. The first such library, the Student Library (which was organized not exactly by students but rather by one of the activists from the 1968 movement) had great energy and a broad range, and it worked efficiently for at least two years. It made available a number of books to which young people otherwise had no access. As mentioned before, it was even involved in some small-scale publishing activity of its own. Remarkably few of its books fell into the hands of the police, probably owing to a very cleverly developed technique of lending books through couriers. This technique made theft easier, but police infiltration more difficult. The Sociological Library was different, since it worked together with the Scientific Circle of Sociology Students, gathering research materials and works that had not been published, often because of censorship, or other works that were "hard to get"; they were distributed in a manner similar to that used by the Student Library.

The *SKS Bulletin* was the organ of the Warsaw Student Solidarity Committee. Its first issue appeared on November 12, 1977. It is difficult to say exactly how many issues were published, but we know that there were at least three.

The Gdańsk SKS had a mixed composition as far as the divisions within the opposition were concerned: its members adhered either to ROPCiO or to KOR. But since *Bratniak* was very integrated, the tendency represented by the periodical dominated the Gdańsk student milieu. We should add that the various oppositional groups in Gdańsk cooperated with one another very well. Following the divisions within ROPCiO, when the Gdańsk circle formed its own ideological and political group, the Young Poland Movement, the Gdańsk SKS ceased to exist.

One important impulse for the creation of the SKS in Poznań was the case of Stanisław Barańczak, a young faculty member at Poznań University who was very popular with students. Barańczak was one of the first opposition activists to be indicted in a trumped-up case involving an alleged attempt to bribe an official. On July 14, during university vacations, Barańczak was deprived of the right to teach by the university disciplinary commission. But the university authorities did not manage to avoid student protests: on October 26, 290 students and alumni of Poznań University appealed to the minister of higher education, science, and technology for Barańczak's reinstatement. This appeal led to a counterattack on the part of the university authorities: they held "conversations" during which they slandered Barańczak and pressured students to withdraw their signatures. (Six students did so.) A short time after, the Poznań SKS was formed by associates of KOR. In its first statement, the SKS explained patiently and logically to the university authorities why their treatment of Barańczak had been improper.

The Wrocław SKS was also closely connected with KOR, and played an important role in the history of the opposition movement in Wrocław. In one respect it worked under more favorable conditions than other student committees: for some time, at least since 1975, a group of professors in Wrocław had been participating in various protest actions. By the nature of the case, there were close ties between the student and the faculty groups, and this gave the young people important moral support.

In the spring of 1978 the Wrocław SKS came out with the interesting idea of creating a student self-government that would be independent of the Socialist Union of Polish Students. In the first days of May, such self-governments were elected by first- and second-year classes in the Department of Philosophy, and by second-year classes in the Department of Mathematics. This initiative was disregarded by the university authorities, but unfortunately it did not develop any further.

The SKS in Szczecin was the last to be created. The rectors of the colleges in that city openly warned student activists that they would resort to any pretext to expel these students from their schools. It was not easy to gather information about the Szczecin SKS, and for this reason it is impossible to define the political orientation of its members more precisely. It is also difficult to understand why an SKS was not created in Łódź. As we know, the immediate reaction to Pyjas's death was strongest in Łódź, and it seems that there were student activists able to play a leading, or at least an initiating role.

The first SKS, from Cracow, began the new academic year with a struggle against drastic limitations of student access to entire sections of the Jagiellonian Library. On July 15, the rector of the Jagiellonian University, Mieczysław Hess (whose name should pass into the annals of infamy of Polish culture), issued a prohibition against lending any books published in or before 1968. After a sharp protest by the SKS, which argued that such a prohibition would lower the level of university studies, the order was rescinded on October 8.

The next issue was a battle over library prohibitions that were discreetly marked in the catalog with the letters "res," standing for "réservé."[3] On November 21 the SKS issued a statement and began disseminating information about these library prohibitions, which involved works in all areas of the humanities, including the works of the greatest Polish writers of the mid-twentieth century, Witold Gombrowicz and Czesław Miłosz, without whose work the serious study of Polish literature is impossible. A poster showing a book closed with a padlock was printed and posted. These actions against the "res" books were answered with apartment searches by the Security Service.

In all of Poland, the general response to the creation and the actions of these Student Solidarity Committees involved police repressions, often carried out by the rectors of the colleges themselves. In Cracow, Ziemowit Pochitonow, a fourth-year student in the Agriculture Academy and a spokesman for the SKS, was expelled for his "improper attitude." The dean of the Agricultural Department and the rector of this school played the role of policemen. The Cracow SKS appealed to academic circles throughout the country to defend Pochitonow. The Student Solidarity Committees in Gdańsk, Poznań, Warsaw, and Wrocław appealed to the minister and to the rector for Pochitonow's readmission. On April 20, 1978, a delegation of thirty persons went to the rector, Professor Tadeusz Wojtaszek, to present him with a petition signed by 402 students from Cracow, and with resolutions about this matter passed during various departmental meetings in the Jagiellonian University. A letter of solidarity from the students of Cologne was also transmitted. Someone representing Wojtaszek received the delegation and read a statement by the rector, which later had to be reconstructed from memory by the students, because their request for a copy of the text was refused:

> This case has been settled definitively. Go talk to your friends in West Germany, who make appeals for Pochitonow "in the name of humanity." No rector in Poland, and especially not a rector of an Agricultural Academy, will accept advice about humanity from the Germans, whom for years yet to come we will not forgive for our experiences during the war.

Among the people intervening on behalf of Pochitonow was Prof. Jan Kielanowski. Rector Wojtaszek expressed his surprise that Kielanowski

was defending a student whose transcript showed that he was an igno-
ramus. After the conversation, Kielanowski was shown Pochitonow's
transcript: how strange, his grades were excellent. For a long time afterward, Kielanowski looked for opportunities to state publicly and in
Wojtaszek's presence that Wojtaszek was a liar.

As already mentioned, the SKS in Warsaw began its activities by defending Maciej Grzywaczewski, a student at the Catholic Theological
Academy. He was expelled from the Academy in July 1977 under the
pretext of not fulfilling his responsibilities as a student. The rector of
the Academy, Rev. Jan Stępień, was evidently prepared to go a long way
to accommodate the security authorities in persecuting students (and,
as it turned out shortly afterward, faculty members as well). In this he
was in competition with the rector of Warsaw University, a famous policeman with a professorial title, Zygmunt Rybicki. Even a December
1977 letter from the esteemed chancellor of the Catholic Theological
Academy, who was at the same time the primate of Poland, was unable
to change the decision of the rector of the academy, not to mention the
request (not a protest) by 118 students of the academy asking that the
rights of a student be restored to Maciej Grzywaczewski. Moreover, when
Hanna Grabińska, a lecturer in English, defended the expelled student,
she was simply given notice of dismissal. Two SKS activists, Roland Kruk
and Agnieszka Lipska, were expelled from Warsaw University on the
basis of an interpretation of university regulations that had never been
used before and was entirely arbitrary.

A different weapon was used against the group of SKS activists who
lived in the dormitory on Kicka Street and were involved with the information and distribution center of the committee located there. Toward the end of May, four students (M. Książczak, J. Naumowicz,
R. Romaniuk, and J. Siewierski) were evicted from the dormitory on the
basis of a letter from the pro-rector of Warsaw University, Stanisław
Orłowski. Nonetheless, after a protest by the SKS, the information and
distribution center was reopened in the dormitory on Kicka Street on
May 30. Two student meetings were held, and as a result, the official
Dormitory Council, whose opinion had been invoked falsely by Orłowski,
protested against the evictions. But the attempt to have them rescinded
was unsuccessful.

The repressions in Poznań were directed above all against the circle
of the student "Theatre of the Eighth Day," whose members were at the
same time active in the Poznań SKS.

In Wrocław, the disciplinary spokesman of the university, Dr. Zabielski,
threatened four SKS activists with expulsion if they did not forego their

activities, and he initiated proceedings against them. During the night of May 12, 1977, Marek Adamkiewicz, a spokesman of the SKS in Wrocław, was beaten four times by the police, while unknown perpetrators beat up Roman Kołakowski, the chairman of the student self-government for the first-year class of the Department of Polish Philology.

In Szczecin, SKS activist Ewa Rynasiewicz was expelled from school for "lack of progress" during a time when she was in the hospital.

Obviously, we have not included in this account any of the house searches, detentions, and similar methods of harassment—these were everyday events in the lives of activists. One must say, however, that while the student movement connected with these committees showed a relatively high level of activity during the first year of its existence, and while it constituted an important chapter in the history of the opposition, it later lost much of its significance as student activists moved on to social action outside of their colleges.

The "Flying University" and the Society for Scientific Courses

    The November issue of the *Information Bulletin* contained a piece of information that opened a new chapter in the history of independent movements in Poland:

> For the freedom to learn. In November of this year a group of scholars took the initiative of organizing a series of lecture courses to be held outside official scholarly organizations. These lectures . . . will address problems that are falsified or disregarded in university studies. Meetings are to take place in private apartments in Warsaw and in other university cities. The planned courses will include: "On the History of People's Poland"—Adam Michnik; "On Economic History and the History of Economic Thought in Contemporary Poland"—Tadeusz Kowalik; "Contemporary Political Ideologies"— Jerzy Jedlicki; "An Overview of Great Discussions of the Postwar Period"— Jan Strzelecki; "The Polish Issue in Political Thought and Social Mentality During the Period of Partitions"—Bohdan Cywiński; "Literature as an Expression of Social Consciousness"—Tomasz Burek; "Tradition and the Realization of Socialist Culture"—Jan Tyszka. Information about the exact program of lectures, as well as about locations and dates, can be obtained from members of the Warsaw SKS.

This was the birth of the "Flying University." The name was not new; on the contrary, it referred to traditions dating from the turn of the century, and to the history of the Warsaw leftist intelligentsia, which at that time had created an institution without parallel anywhere else in the world: this Flying University functioned in Warsaw for a number of years. Its name reflected the fact that the University did not have a permanent location and had to move from place to place in order to hide from the Russian secret police, the "Okhrana." Andrzej Celiński, a sociologist who had been dismissed from work at the Institute of Social Prophylactics and Resocialization at Warsaw University, played a central role in organizing this new institution.[4] He was able to bring together a group of persons willing to share their knowledge by holding "illegal" lectures.

To its credit, KOR agreed immediately that the Flying University was one of the most important social initiatives, and that it had to be supported because of its importance for the national culture. We must also give credit to the intelligence of those in charge of the Security Service that they decided quickly (after several months) that in a totalitarian system such an undertaking constituted a particularly dangerous threat. In order to liquidate this institution, the secret political police, acting on the correct assumption that the stifling of national culture and higher education was crucial to its future good, resorted to particularly brutal methods.

Can the circle of people connected with the Flying University (and later with the Society for Scientific Courses) be considered the same group as KOR, and can its history be seen as a part of the history of KOR? Not really. It is true that among the organizers and lecturers of the Flying University and activists of TKN there were many members and associates of KOR; and it is also true that KOR sympathizers were in the majority, while other oppositional groups had no influence whatsoever in this group. But it is also true that the majority within the group (and therefore also the various sympathizers) did not consider it appropriate to become personally engaged in KOR activities, and that the Society for Scientific Courses, which was created a short time later, was careful to maintain complete independence from KOR, and tried to insure that this would be the case not only in fact but also in the eyes of public opinion. This policy even led to conflicts between the KOR members in TKN and some of the other members, as when, for example, some of the latter expressed doubts about whether Kuroń (in addition to Michnik) could teach a course in TKN without doing harm to the public perception of TKN's independence from KOR. When they were first raised, Kuroń and the activists of KOR regarded these doubts as implying approval for social discrimination against members of the committee. Still, the histories of these two institutions were so dramatically intertwined that it is impossible to exclude the Flying University and the Society for Scientific Courses from our account of the history of KOR.

The police did not begin their fierce attack against the Flying University immediately. In the beginning they were satisfied with stopping listeners in the street after a lecture to ask them for their identity papers, and with issuing threats in the schools.

The great interest in the lectures of the Flying University, the large number of participants, and the eagerness of young people not only to participate but also to become active in self-education (which required organizational help), all led to the need to create the Society for Scientific Courses, which became a patron of this action and guaranteed appropriate standards of scholarship and authority.[5]

Despite the fact that the preparations had been completed, and the documents initiating the activity of TKN had been prepared and signed, there were still a number of doubts that caused delays in the formation of TKN. This was finally accomplished on January 22, 1978, but not announced publicly right away. It is difficult to understand why this was the case. Just as on so many previous occasions in the history of the opposition in Poland, the police finally decided this issue as well.

In hindsight it is obvious that the work of the Flying University infuriated the police, and that the topic of Michnik's lectures, together with the name of the lecturer, aroused particular fury. This young historian already had a broad knowledge of the political history of the Polish People's Republic, and as this fact was acknowledged by competent scholars, there was nothing strange about the organizers' agreeing to allow him to lecture on this important subject. Nevertheless, to those who did not know any better, and who still thought of Michnik as the student leader of 1968, this new role was surprising. The idea of focusing the attack on Michnik's series of lectures was probably connected with the notion that public opinion would regard it as a new police action against KOR, that is, as something to which it was already somewhat accustomed, rather than an attack against the dissemination of knowledge.

The unexpected and brutal attack of the Security Service took place on February 10, 11, and 12 in Cracow. Michnik had just begun to travel with his lectures throughout Poland, since students in cities outside of Warsaw also wanted to take part in the classes of the Flying University. On February 10, Adam Michnik and Stanisław Barańczak were detained at the railroad station in Cracow. On February 11, the police and the

Security Service invaded the apartment in which Michnik was giving his lecture. Approximately 120 listeners were present. Since the lecturer did not stop speaking despite the police intrusion, the police used tear gas and violence. On February 12, functionaries of the police attacked Michnik in the street, together with three activists of the Cracow SKS, Liliana Batko, Elżbieta Krawczy, and Lesław Maleszka, and beat them. This decided the matter, and all hesitations ended. The Society for Scientific Courses announced its formation.

The declaration establishing TKN was signed by fifty-eight persons. Of these, seventeen were full professors; there were nine persons with habilitations, and eleven held doctoral degrees. These circumstances must be noted (though in themselves they are not too important), since the composition of TKN, even formally, guaranteed conditions that were not met by many other Polish institutions of higher learning. TKN announced its program of courses for the second semester. In addition to the previous lectures that were to be continued, there were new ones: "Social Problems of Education"—Adam Stanowski; "The Centralized Structure of Power and Social Life"—Irena Nowakowa; "Social Problems of Science"—Stefan Amsterdamski; "Ideological Features of the Polish Cinema"—Andrzej Werner; "Society and Education"—Jacek Kuroń; "Selected Phenomena and Problems in Recent Russian Literature"— Wiktor Woroszylski; "The Political History of Poland, 1918–1945"— Władysław Bartoszewski. In addition to Warsaw, lectures were held in Cracow, Łódź, Poznań, and Wrocław. Lectures—or sometimes only a single lecture—were also delivered by Czesław Bobrowski, Stefan Kurowski, Edward Lipiński, Edward Łukawer, Zdzisław Szpakowski, Karol Tarnowski, and Jan Walc.

TKN's great battle had begun. The *Information Bulletin* described it: "Students and intellectuals, the entire democratic opposition has no choice in this matter, since this is a question of an elementary right: the right to truth." The first engagement was an attack against Michnik. In order to prevent him from lecturing in other cities, the police detained him five times in the course of two weeks. When he did not make it to his lecture in Warsaw, the students listened to a tape that had been prepared for just such an eventuality.

Scenes similar to those in Cracow took place in Sopot. On February 22 the police invaded a self-education seminar in history being conducted by eleven people in the apartment of Bogdan Borusewicz. According to the official warrant, the search was to be conducted in connection with a robbery. Tear gas and physical force were used. After detentions of forty-eight hours, Borusewicz was sentenced to fourteen days of arrest under summary proceedings for hooliganism; in the same manner, Stanisław Śmigło received a seven-day sentence, and Andrzej Stefaniak a fine of 3,000 zlotys.

The Sentencing Boards for Misdemeanors played a major role in the war against the dissemination of humanistic knowledge. As a rule, they imposed fines of 5,000 zlotys for allowing an apartment to be used for a lecture (at that time this amounted to an average monthly salary). There were also fines for attending the lectures; these, however, were used selectively and were usually smaller.

Important support for TKN came from the March 1978 communiqué of the Polish Episcopate, which expressed "disapproval of all actions that restrain the human spirit from freely creating cultural values." It also stated that "the Church will support initiatives that aim to present culture, the creations of the human spirit, and the history of the Nation in an authentic form, since the Nation has a right to the objective truth about itself." This found a particularly concrete expression in Cracow, where, thanks mainly to Karol Cardinal Wojtyła, the Society for Scientific Courses was able on many occasions to use quarters belonging to the Church.

As TKN ended the first year of its activities in May 1978, it could already claim important accomplishments: 120 lectures had been delivered, including 13 courses. Between one and two thousand listeners had participated. Despite the reprisals, which were by now serious, TKN had yet to face its most difficult moments.

The Black Book of Censorship

Like NOWa, the KOR press, *Zapis,* and other publishing and press ventures not connected with KOR, the Society for Scientific Courses also fought against the widespread censorship of public life in Poland, including scientific life. At that time KOR also managed to strike a blow against censorship in the strict sense, that is, against the Main Office for Control of the Press, Publications, and Performances (GUKPPiW).

On March 10, 1977, Tomasz Strzyżewski, who had been a censor in Cracow since August 1975, arrived in Sweden and asked for political asylum. He had smuggled out with him a portion of the secret documentation of GUKPPiW. Western public opinion could learn about this indirectly, thanks to a two-part article written by Leo Łabędz and published in the London *Times* of September 26 and 27, 1977. When KOR transformed itself into KSS "KOR," Strzyżewski gave the materials he had taken out of Poland to the committee. On November 2, 1977, copies of these materials (approximately 700 pages) reached KOR in Warsaw. On November 18, KOR issued a long statement informing the Polish public about these documents. The material was published in its entirety by the Aneks publishing house in London (Vol. I in 1977, Vol. II in 1978) under the title, *The Black Book of Censorship in the Polish People's Republic.** An extensive selection of these materials was published by NOWa under the same title in December 1977. It is not surprising that it proved to be a stick in the anthill.

The materials in the *Black Book* included:

1. General guidelines for the censors, including prohibitions as well as the so-called notations referring to specific persons, facts, numbers, and events.

2. A register of specific interventions by the censors, prepared every two weeks.

3. Instruction materials of the Secondary Controlling Agency, pointing out things that had been overlooked and instances of excessive eagerness. An analysis of the overlooked items is provided for purposes of instruction.

The first section includes the infamous *Book of Notations and Directives of GUKPPiW*, which is divided into chapters. Here are some examples:

From the chapter on "The Central Authority and Institutions, Proposed Resolutions and Regulations": "No materials about proposals for changes in the administrative division of the country or in the structure of state administration should be allowed in print."

From the chapter on "The Political Relations of the Polish People's Republic with Other Countries": "Only the following terms may be used to describe the western frontier of Poland: the Oder-Neisse border; the border between Poland and the German Democratic Republic; the Polish-German Democratic Republic frontier; one should not use the designation: Polish-German border. [!] . . . One must not permit the publication of any information suggesting the existence of any contacts . . . between Poland and the regimes of South Korea, Taiwan, South

---

*Extensive selections of these documents also came out under the same title, edited and translated by Jane Leftwich Curry (New York: Vintage Books, Random House, 1984).

Africa, or Rhodesia, which are not recognized by our country, or any contacts with firms or citizens of those territories. . . . This notation is intended only for the information of the censors."

From the chapter on the "Council of Mutual Economic Assistance": "One should not reveal the existence within Comecon of the Commission on the Arms Industry, nor of the connections between Comecon and the Warsaw Pact. . . . It is forbidden to publish exchange rates or coefficients between the national currencies in the countries of Comecon . . . or in Yugoslavia, and the common currency, that is, the transfer ruble."

From the chapter on "Economic Relations Between Poland and Other Countries": "Information about licenses bought by Poland from capitalist countries is to be eliminated from the mass media. . . . This notation is dictated by the need to avoid an overflow of material about the purchase of licenses in capitalist countries. The accumulation of such information could lead an average reader to believe that our attempt to modernize the country is based on the purchase of licenses in the developed capitalist countries. . . . One should not permit the publication of any information about the sale of meat to the USSR by Poland. This notation is intended only for the information of the censors. . . . One should not publish any information or data about the purchase of meat or meat products from the German Democratic Republic."

From the chapter on "Industry, Raw Materials, Marine Economy, and Agriculture": "In works, notes, etc., about the electronics industry in Poland, one should not allow the printing of materials critical of our program of developing electronics, or which suggest that this program should be based not on cooperation with the USSR but on cooperation with capitalist countries. . . . All publications containing generalizations or combined numerical data for departments, branches, or areas of the economy, either in individual enterprises or for the country as a whole, or concerning the state of safety and hygiene in the workplace, or occupational diseases, should be stopped. They are not to be published in the press, nor on radio or television, nor in any other publishing institutions. . . . The mass media are not allowed to publish demands that tractors (either new or used) be sold to individual private farmers. It is also necessary to eliminate materials which illustrate the farmers' need (market) for tractors."

From the chapter on "Wages, Prices, Pensions, Health Services, Social Welfare": "All comments, discussions, lectures, etc., about the increase of average wages thoughout the entire socialized economy, including retirement pay, pensions, and other social services that have already been introduced or have been announced in the materials for the Seventh Party Congress should not go beyond the statements contained in these materials. . . . All information about mass poisonings and illnesses (regardless of the cause) . . . can be published in the mass media only if it has received the prior approval of the Ministry of Health and Social Welfare or the Main Sanitary Inspection Board. . . . It is necessary to eliminate from works about environmental protection or about threats to the natural environment in Poland all information concerning immediate dangers to human life and health posed by industry or by chemical substances used in agriculture. This prohibition includes actual cases of pollution of the atmosphere, water, earth, or food which are dangerous to life and health. This prohibition applies in addition to all information about the threat to the health of workers employed in the production of polyvinyl chloride (PCV) and about the dangers of using these products of the chemical industry in, for example, construction, or introducing them into the market. . . . It is absolutely necessary to eliminate (from the Polish Press Agency, from the press, the radio, and TV) all collected data about the number of traffic accidents, fires, and drownings, and to tone down overly drastic forms of publication on these topics. This notation does not concern descriptions or reports about individual accidents, or materials supporting preventive actions (without detailed numerical data)."

From the chapter on "Emigration": "Because certain circles of Poles living abroad are sensitive to contacts with official representatives of our country, when publishing the name of comrade Wiesław Adamski one should mention only his social function as general secretary of the 'Polonia' Society, and eliminate, in every instance, his title of deputy premier. This notation should be held in total secrecy."

From the chapter on "Culture": here personal notations are an especially common form, such as, for example: "One should not allow the publication of any work by Kazimierz Orłoś." Notations concerning émigré writers (ninety-nine names) divide them into three categories: (a) partial elimination, with a prohibition against favorable evaluations; (b) elimination except for scholarly works; and (c) unconditional elimination.

"One should not allow the publication of any polemics with the material published in *Trybuna Ludu* or *Nowe Drogi*. The text of this notation cannot be passed on to the editorial boards." The extensive notation about Katyń reveals the nuances of censorship in detail, all of which makes one thing clear: "Any attempt to burden the Soviet Union with responsibility for the deaths of Polish officers in Katyń Forest is forbidden." This was the purpose of the notation against giving the date of a death in Katyń as prior to July 1941. One of the notations lists most of the names from the "Letter of 59" from the period of the campaign against changes in the Constitution of the PRL.

From the chapter on "Religious Issues": "It is necessary to eliminate from religious publications all criticisms of Marxism. Only in the specialist periodicals mentioned below [here there is a list of six periodicals, headed by *Colledarea Theologica*] and in specialized philosophical-theological books can one permit theoretical elaborations which include polemical accents against the Marxist concepts of religion, communism, or the individual and the collectivity." The notations in this chapter have a particularly systematic character.

Separately, in the chapter entitled "Miscellaneous," one can find a particularly shocking notation: "Numerical data about the extent and growth of alcoholism in Poland as a whole should not be published in the mass media. Such data can be allowed only in serious specialized publications." Another notation orders the elimination of descriptions of the forms and methods of organizing strikes. Still another says: "It is necessary to eliminate from the mass media all suggestions for the creation of a separate administrative court system or of an Administrative Tribunal."

The chapter on "Recommendations" contains an interesting detail about the cooperation between the censorship and the United Peasant party: "In the case of attempts to print the obituaries of activists from the interwar and the immediate postwar period, it is necessary to consult with the Central Committee of the United Peasant party, or with the Provincial Committee of this party."

The notation that "It is forbidden to publish any information about the accident in the Katowice mine that killed four miners" has a particularly grim tone, but it is not the only notation concerning mining accidents.

It is interesting to observe yet another notation: "One should not permit the publication of any information about state decorations presented in the Main Council of the Polish-Soviet Friendship Society. Information about these decorations will be published only in the weekly *Przyjaźń* [*Friendship*].[6] This notation is intended only for the eyes of the censors."

"One cannot permit the publication of obituaries, inserts, or other forms of publication in the press, radio, and TV, as well as posters announcing various meetings at cemeteries, monuments, places of battles, etc. [on the occasion of the anniversaries of the beginning of the Warsaw Uprising and its various episodes] by former groups and divisions of the Home Army and other right-wing organizations which participated in the Warsaw Uprising. However, one can allow the publication of obituaries and other information about services held in churches."

The materials swarm with prohibitions against reviewing various books and movies, and against publishing positive comments on various topics. The censorship book is so interesting that were it not for its size, one would be tempted to cite it in its entirety.

Other chapters of the *Black Book* are equally interesting.

Despite the fact that a Polish journalist, a writer, or a scholar, especially in one of the humanistic disciplines, had almost daily contact with the activities of censorship and was familiar with its problematics, the *Black Book* caused a shock in these groups. It was compared—despite the fact that it concerned a different sphere of life and did not contain horrors of the same magnitude—with the revelations of Józef Światło* about the Stalinist security police in Poland.

Letters to the authorities sent by the Main Council of the Polish PEN Club, and by the councils of the Polish Sociological Association and the Polish Philosophical Association reveal the extent of public agitation on this issue. Especially important was a statement of the Polish Episcopate issued in the communiqué from its 162d Conference:

> The Conference expresses its disapproval of all actions which restrain the human spirit in its free creation of cultural values. Thus, the fact that scientific, research, artistic, and religious work is limited by state censorship is highly regrettable. The existence of a censorship with such a broad sphere of intervention is a harmful misunderstanding.

KOR attempted to reach out to various circles with information about the activities of censorship. It devoted much attention to this topic in its press and in the distribution of the Polish edition of the *Black Book of Censorship* according to a conscious strategy aimed at specific social groups. All this probably played a role in creating the understanding with which workers and peasants in 1980 and later greeted the idea of, if not eliminating, at least limiting censorship.

---

*A colonel in the Security Service who defected to the West in December 1953 and then broadcast to Poland a series of talks about the workings of the Security Service over Radio Free Europe.

The Documents of Lawlessness

The *Documents of Lawlessness* announced in a KSS "KOR" statement of April 7, 1978, must be counted among the fundamental achievements of KOR and of KSS "KOR." Work on the *Documents of Lawlessness* began early, long before the transformation of the committee, since from its very beginnings KOR had had to deal with the bestiality of the police, who beat people first in the streets while detaining them, then again in police precincts and headquarters, in order to extort confessions or with no particular goal in mind, but always under the protection of their superiors in the police and the Security Service as well as the prosecutor's office, which acted in such cases only to cover up the problem. This, in turn, strengthened the feeling of impunity among those who did the beating, which was an important factor in encouraging the crime.

As the reader already knows, a KOR activist or an activist of another dissident group could at any moment be assaulted in the street by "unknown perpetrators" or by uniformed policemen in their headquarters (and could even be killed, as in the case of Pyjas). The beatings could be either discreet or ostentatious, as a form of intimidation (Sulecki's case). Nonetheless, there were a number of restraints that operated specifically in the case of dissidents: it was known that dissidents would not ignore reprisals, that they would spread the news and begin investigating. Although the sense of impunity was great, there was some fear of countermeasures in information and propaganda. Thus, the practice of beating dissidents (especially after detention) was used sporadically, while it was used regularly against the socially marginal and against those suspected of criminal transgressions, or even against those detained by accident and other anonymous people.

From the beginning, KOR was aware of the fact that one could not remain indifferent to this phenomenon. As a result, the registration of such facts began very early. As it happened, the very attempt to address this issue was neither simple nor easy. Without doubt, a normal, typical Pole would react with indignation if confronted with the fact that someone has been murdered at a police precinct. But it is not certain that his reaction would be the same if he were told that a criminal had been beaten up. It is difficult to move the average reader to respond to the problem of beatings perpetrated against imprisoned criminals, even though the very same reader probably does not like the police, or may even hate them. The police in Poland not only beat prisoners in police precincts and headquarters but they also kill them, and this action could no longer count on public support in any area.

The *Documents of Lawlessness* describe twenty-five cases of murders and serious beatings. The files of KOR contained more such cases, but two conditions had to be met before the cases could be publicized: (1) the documentation had to be sufficiently complete and certain so that KOR would not risk a trial for slander by publishing it; and (2) KOR had to have not only the agreement of the interested party (or in the case of murder, of his family) but, in addition, it required trustworthy assurances of cooperation in possible further developments in the case (such as, for example, a power of attorney granted to one of the lawyers associated with KOR). In the majority of cases these conditions were impossible to satisfy.

KOR investigations constitute a separate topic. This was "normal" detective work conducted under dangerous conditions in which, for the good of the case and for one's own good, one had to act carefully and very discreetly, with the very limited means at one's disposal. As an example, let me offer a short summary of one of the cases. Before midnight on October 26, 1978, two functionaries of the police woke up Piotr Łukasiewicz (twenty-two years old) and took him from his apartment, on the grounds that he was thought to have witnessed something. Since he did not feel like going, and complained about feeling bad, he was dragged out of his apartment in his underwear. He was heaved into a waiting car, swung by his arms and legs (two eyewitnesses to the event were not believed by the prosecutor's office). Five days later, his mother found him dying in the Barlicki hospital in Łódź. Three times she was not allowed to see her son. He died a short time later. The cause of death was given as traumatic brain injury. The autopsy also showed other injuries. Łukasiewicz was taken to the hospital from the drunk tank. The doctor on duty there stated that Łukasiewicz had been brought in around 1:20 A.M. (what had happened to him during the previous hour and a half was never established). He was carried in by a policeman. The doctor noted symptoms of paralysis of the left half of the body and a failure of the right eye to respond to light, as well as the absence of any smell of alcohol on his breath.

The prosecutor's office in Łódź discontinued the investigation because of the absence of any signs that a crime had been committed. One side effect of this case was that Zenobia Łukaszewicz, the mother of the dead boy, became one of the most devoted and effective activists working in the Intervention Bureau of KSS "KOR." Her name is listed among those associates of the bureau mentioned on the first page of the *Madrid Report* of October 1980, in which the *Documents of Lawlessness* were partially reprinted and supplemented with later cases.

The *Documents of Lawlessness* also include the following notes in connection with the death of Zbigniew Gidelski, which again illustrate well the practices of the police:

> Three cases of deaths connected with the Bałuty District Headquarters of the police in Łódź occupy a special place in this work. They constitute an accusation against the Provincial Prosecutor's Office in Łódź and against all those who have covered up the many crimes committed in these headquarters, including among others the murder of Zbigniew Gidelski. In Gidelski's case we again encounter the name of the suspect, policeman Zdzisław Pająk, yet this was not taken as a warning sign. Not only was he not arrested but he was not even suspended from his official duties. Thus, there is nothing surprising in the fact that even during the period of investigation of Gidelski's case, this policeman, convinced of his impunity, was involved in two further cases of death, those of Jan Kowalczyk and Piotr Łukasiewicz. Zdzisław Pająk is still a functionary of the Citizens' Militia [i.e., police].

It happened only once that a prosecutor, disregarding the fact that he was inviting the disapproval of his superiors, decided to pursue a case of police murder. This was a deputy prosecutor in the Regional Prosecutor's Office in Kalisz. He collected material evidence that showed that the death of Ryszard Mikołajczyk (twenty-one years old), whose body was found on the tracks of a narrow-gauge railway in Dzierzbin on the night of March 16, 1977, was not the result of a suicide, but of a murder, and that the policeman Wiesław Paszkowski was suspected, together with his brothers Henryk and Kazimierz. As a result, prosecutor Bogusław Śliwa was prevented from having any further influence on the conduct of the investigation. Śliwa appealed to the Office of the Prosecutor General, but received no answer. He was, moreover, subjected to constant pressure to declare the death of Mikołajczyk a suicide. Finally, the Provincial Prosecutor's Office discontinued the investigation. Śliwa described the case in a letter to the Council of State dated March 3, 1978, in which he made specific accusations that demonstrated the biased manner in which the investigation had been conducted, and its disregard of the evidence. Śliwa sent copies of his letter to twenty other addressees (to institutions officially responsible for taking an interest in such cases, to several deputies of the Diet, and to eight editors of periodicals and newspapers). He asserted that he was doing so "in order to assure his own personal safety." Bogusław Śliwa was suspended and then dismissed from his job in the prosecutor's office. For a long time afterward he remained unemployed. When Śliwa received no answer from any of the twenty addressees of his letter, he came to KOR with his case. He became an expert associate of the committee.

We must mention here an aspect of this issue which is not always adequately noticed. The practice of beatings and murders committed by policemen is possible only while they enjoy impunity. The majority of citizens have nothing to say about this, just as they have nothing to say about other problems inconvenient to the authorities (or considered inconvenient by them); at most these citizens can only expose themselves to reprisals. But there are those who, because of their position and influence, could do something about this, even if they also would get into trouble with the police or with highly-placed political authorities protecting the police. There were also deputies to the Diet among the addressees of prosecutor Śliwa's letters. Few people in Poland treat Diet deputies seriously. Nevertheless, formally speaking, they do take upon themselves certain responsibilities. And this is why it can be said that certain deputies, for example, the actor Mariusz Dmochowski and Prof. Jan Józef Szczepański, as recipients of this letter, share responsibility not only for the personal fate of the prosecutor but also for the impunity of the murderers of Ryszard Mikołajczyk. What is more, they themselves have entered the circle of those who by negligence have made future murders possible. They cannot say that they did not know.

Basically, KOR was unable to break down the customary impunity of murderers in police uniforms. Nevertheless, there were some successes.

In the trial for the murder of Kazimierz Kwiek (on November 17, 1976, Kwiek was severely beaten and then shot as he was lying down or kneeling), the Provincial Court sentenced Corporal Stanisław Kwaśny to three years imprisonment for involuntary manslaughter. Kwaśny spent three months in jail and was then released. Rearrest of the sentenced policeman was never ordered by the Provincial Court that had sentenced him or by the Supreme Court that had upheld the sentence. Nevertheless, it did turn out that a policeman might be tried and even sentenced, and that was a step forward.

On October 13, 1978, the Regional Court in the town of Police (located in Szczecin) found the Dobosz family not guilty of charges that they had assaulted a policeman, and the Provincial Court upheld this verdict. The Doboszes had been severely beaten by police functionaries, and when the family lodged a complaint, the police trumped up a case in which

they claimed themselves to be the injured party. In this area, too, although it was not a great victory, it turned out that it was possible to
break the general practice of automatically convicting those who dared
to lodge complaints in the prosecutor's office because they had been
beaten by the police.

On September 27, 1978, the Provincial Court in Łódź sentenced a
policeman to four years of imprisonment for involuntary manslaughter.
According to the court, the policeman had simulated the suicide of an
arrested man by hanging him. He did so thinking that the man was dead,
in order to avoid responsibility for not having fulfilled his official duties.
He failed to notice the fact that the arrested man was dying because of
a fractured skull and a cerebral hemorrhage. Neither the prosecutor
nor the court was interested in the question of who had beaten this man
while he was still alive. This was the strangest case, and the strangest
sentence, encountered by the Intervention Bureau.

Still, KOR hoped that gradually, by acting stubbornly and with determination, it could put an end to the impunity that shielded such
practices, and by the same token, end them. This area of KOR's work
has been described here in such detail because it illustrates so precisely
the state of lawlessness prevailing in the Polish People's Republic, where
the final argument over the Constitution, the code of law, or political
and ideological phraseology is always a policeman's club.

From the Work of the Intervention Bureau

The *Documents of Lawlessness* describe only one of the areas
of work of the Intervention Bureau of KSS "KOR." The bureau dealt
daily with infringements of the labor law or conflicts with the administrative apparatus and the police resulting from a variety of causes: from
a "bad" political record, often attributed to individual self-styled "world
improvers," who were generally apolitical but sensitive to the problems
of the rule of law and to injustices committed either against them or
against others; from the personal motives of representatives of the authorities (revenge, defense against the unmasking of a theft, of abuses,
etc., or aggression committed for personal profit); often simply from
accidents that occurred when the representatives of the authorities considered themselves lords ruling over the rabble, sure of their own impunity. A normal day also included spotting and turning away the mentally

ill, people suffering from delusions, pettifoggers, and sometimes con men and frauds. But such cases were not common, although inevitably KOR was sometimes taken for a ride, or someone who really needed help was turned away.

This last occurrence was more likely, since everyone soon realized that the influx of cases exceeded the capacity of the Intervention Bureau, both because the number of activists working for the bureau was too small (although in peak moments there were several dozen working associates); and also because the Funds Council had limited means at its disposal, and even the leadership of the Intervention Bureau understood that it should not allow for the paralysis of other areas of KOR's work by making excessive demands. As a result, the Intervention Bureau concentrated its attention either on especially blatant cases or on precedents, attacking general social problems in this manner. In other cases it limited itself only to advising, or to providing a single, limited donation. It was impossible to do otherwise. With its funds and associates, KOR could not replace the work of the state, the trade unions, or the dormant or nonexistent social organizations.

The associates of the Intervention Bureau gained experience quickly. They became practiced spokesmen for social interests, which created new situations. It was discovered early on that sometimes a discreet warning that KOR was ready to take up a given issue was itself sufficient to induce a local lordling to hide his claws and quietly retreat. At times something in the nature of an agreement was worked out. KOR activists knew that any agreement between a bandit and the victim of an attack always benefits the bandit and has little to do with justice; but they also knew (and this was important to KOR) that they were not representing any doctrine, or Justice with a capital "J," but rather real people and their interests. It was not permissible to suggest to an individual that he forgo his dignity and demean himself in order to get out from under the oppression or to recoup his losses. But it was permissible to advise him to accept even a compromise, if otherwise he might expect only defeat. However, whenever the wronged person, having been well informed about the consequences, told KOR that he wanted to fight the injustice to the end, if this was his conscious choice, KOR would involve itself in his struggle to the extent that it could, and thanks to this, KOR gained devoted associates for the committee.

What was the Intervention Bureau dealing with apart from cases such as those described in the *Documents of Lawlessness*, and apart from daily battles over infringements of the labor law? Here are some examples that have more to say than a long theoretical essay about the political or apolitical nature of social self-defense in a totalitarian police state.

The case of Jerzy Grzebieluch. In June 1971, while crossing the street in a crosswalk in the center of Katowice, Jerzy Grzebieluch was hit by a car driven by a captain of the police, Kazimierz Skrzyński. Skrzyński, together with a passenger not in uniform whose name was Kunisz and who was also a police functionary, beat and kicked the wounded Grzebieluch as he lay in the street. There were many witnesses who did not remain passive, but defended the victim. The car was damaged by the crowd, but Grzebieluch (suffering from a torn biceps muscle of the thigh and other knee and neck injuries) was arrested on suspicion of taking part in a public gathering whose participants violently assaulted people and property. The arrested man was not placed in the prison hospital. Released only after he was kept for seven weeks, he then underwent surgery, but as a result of this long delay in medical treatment he remained 30 percent disabled. From then on, Grzebieluch tried to seek compensation through legal proceedings. That is how he came to KOR. He did not accomplish much in his battles for compensation, but he became an associate of the committee.

The case of Paweł Świstak. Świstak was a mountaineering guide who during the war had been a soldier of the Home Army in the Stanisławów District. On July 15, 1973, in his garden in Zakopane, Świstak erected a little monument in memory of General Władysław Sikorski.* He was arrested on July 17, and his monument was removed after midnight on July 18. He was in a prison hospital until his trial. On June 21, 1974, he was sentenced to one year in prison for having insulted the head of the financial department in Zakopane, and was fined 40,000 zlotys for having built the monument. After his release from prison, Świstak began demanding the return of his monument. In answer to this, his house, which was the legal property of his wife, was forcibly expropriated, supposedly for the purpose of creating a medical center on the basis of a decision by the Ministry of Health and Social Welfare. It did not help that the ministry claimed officially that it knew nothing about the case, or that the house was unfit for such a purpose. By a decision of the city's mayor, Lech Bafia, the expropriation was approved; and when Świstak appealed to the voivode, the same Lech Bafia, who had just been promoted to voivode of Nowy Sącz, confirmed his own previous decision. The ex-

---

*The prime minister of the Polish wartime government-in-exile in London.

propriation was accomplished by breaking into the house and taking out all the personal belongings, which Świstak was later unable to get back. Świstak's struggle lasted several years. In the last period, when Solidarity was already active, he stopped coming to KOR, so the author is unable to say whether his losses were ever compensated. An additional twist to the case was an attack against Świstak in the press by a journalist who was publicly known as a notorious collaborator of the Security Service. Świstak was presented as a Gestapo agent, and at the same time as a Jew who had escaped from the ghetto and pretended to be a Ukrainian, as could be "proven" by a nameplate on his door that read, in Ukrainian: "Pawło Swystak—Gestapo associate." None of this made any sense. Świstak sued the journalist for slander, but the trial bogged down a short time later.

The case of Bolesław Cygan. Cygan, an employee of the District Mining Rescue Station (a supervisor of mining equipment) and a master locksmith, came into conflict with the mangement since he had not received the salary he had been promised when he was hired. Cygan discovered the existence of a false account book containing the forged signatures of 876 fictitious mechanics who were supposed to have commuted from elsewhere in order to repair some equipment. A commission called especially for this purpose confirmed Cygan's findings. As a result, in accordance with the logic of events in the PRL, the persecution of Cygan began. He was fired, and his position was taken by one of the people involved in the affair. A higher-ranking embezzler remained unscathed. In answer to Cygan's complaint, the Ministry of Mining and Energy informed him that everything was in order, the guilty had been punished, and the case was closed. Bolesław Cygan became an associate of KOR and later was among the founders of the Initiating Committees of Free Trade Unions in Katowice.

The case of Józef Lewszyk. Following a decision by the Provincial Court, Lewszyk, a resident of Wrocław, was forcibly interned in a psychiatric hospital. The Intervention Bureau found that the decision, and the manner in which the internment had been accomplished, severely violated the rule of law.[7] On December 20, 1945, Lewszyk had been sentenced to death by a military tribunal in Grodno. On appeal, the sentence was reduced to twenty years of imprisonment, with the justification that Lewszyk had "belonged to the anti-Soviet Polish-German organization called the Home Army." Lewszyk spent fourteen years in prisons and camps. He did not hide his past, and his troubles stemmed from that fact.

This is just a small sample of the diverse problems dealt with by the Intervention Bureau. What does "dealt with" mean in this context? What did the Intervention Bureau do? After learning about a case, an investigation was conducted, to assure that KOR's information would not be one-sided, and to prevent KOR from getting involved in dubious cases. Documentation would then be prepared so that the attorney would not need to start from scratch. The attorney who took the case from the bureau would use its services throughout the entire course of the case (to supplement the documentation, find witnesses, etc.). The Intervention Bureau financed the case (payments to the attorneys and all court costs). The strategy of litigation or administrative action was worked out among the interested party, the attorney recommended by KOR, and the Intervention Bureau. Throughout the entire duration of the case, the Intervention Bureau remained in touch with its client, especially because this was the time when the person was particularly exposed to acts of revenge and to reprisals. Often the victims also needed financial help, which the Intervention Bureau provided. The publication of data about the case in the *KOR Communiqués* or in the KOR press occurred only with the consent of the client, except for accounts of court trials open to everyone regardless of the wishes of the interested parties. I do not think that this account exhausts all the ways in which KOR and the Intervention Bureau participated in these cases.

The KOR Press and NOWa (continued)

It seems proper to say something about how KOR waged war against censorship by actively ignoring it. In this respect there were no significant changes from the previous period. The uncensored press can be divided into three categories:

1. The *KSS "KOR" Communiqué* was a continuation of the *KOR Communiqué* and remained the only official organ of the committee. During this period, it ceased to appear as a separate publication. The March issue of the *Information Bulletin* (No. 18) carried an announcement signed jointly by KSS "KOR" and by the editorial board of the *Information Bulletin*:

> Beginning with this issue, the *Communiqué* of the Social Self-Defense Committee "KOR" and the *Information Bulletin* will be published jointly. This merger is of a purely technical character; it will allow us to avoid the repetition of

information, and facilitates the distribution of both publications. The *Communiqué* continues to be edited and signed by the members of the Social Self-Defense Committee "KOR," while the *Bulletin* is edited by a separate, independent editorial board. The editorial board bears sole responsibility for the texts published in the *Information Bulletin.*

This announcement was reprinted in several successive issues of the *Bulletin,* and then was omitted. It is important to note this last detail as, in the future, this state of affairs would become the cause or the pretext for a sharp conflict within KOR and between *Głos* and the *Information Bulletin.*

2. The press of the KOR milieu in general. KOR did not interfere in the editorial policy of these periodicals, since their publication was the responsibility of their own editorial boards. In any case, this was the situation with the *Information Bulletin,* which at about that time became in fact an informational-opinion monthly, and also with *Głos,* whose editorial format was growing increasingly similar to that of the *Bulletin.* The case of *Robotnik* was somewhat different, and will be discussed in the next section. But in this case as well, editorial work was not subject to interference, although it was expected that a periodical that played such an important role for KOR, not only by informing and influencing the consciousness of workers but also as an organizer of workers' groups and cells, would reflect the strategy and tactics of KOR. It must be said that although one cannot speak of the full autonomy of *Robotnik,* there were no conflicts. Perhaps this was the case because the group involved in this periodical was precisely the same group as that which had formed KOR's attitude toward the workers.

3. The press of circles so friendly with KOR that one can refer to them as collective associates of the committee. Above all one has to mention *Zapis,* which continued to appear. The first issue of *Puls,* a Łódź magazine of young writers, appeared in October 1977. This periodical was even closer to KOR than *Zapis,* because the entire editorial board of *Puls* was involved in the daily work of the committee. There were also the periodicals of the Student Solidarity Committees, which were discussed in connection with the student movement. In addition to what was said about NOWa in the preceding chapter, one might add that it did not cease its work despite being hounded by swarms of agents. It published works necessary to the development of Polish culture, and its activity should become the subject of a separate monograph.

Robotnik

The first issue of the biweekly *Robotnik* appeared in September 1977 (though it was not always able to stick to its fortnightly schedule). In the overall history of KOR, the publication of *Robotnik* was no less important than the transformation of KOR into KSS "KOR."

Robotnik was meant to be read by workers. It had been decided that only a minimal number of copies would be distributed other than those that went directly to large industrial enterprises. From the very beginning it was known that it would be not only a periodical designed to transmit information, thoughts, and ideas, but that it would also serve to organize the workers. The idea was to ensure that wherever *Robotnik* reached, cells of distributors would also become a network of the periodical's correspondents. Eventually these functions were to be connected with self-education, civil education, and training designed to prepare people for the specific role of future activists in trade unions.

Thus, the contents of the periodical were largely directed to the specific interests of the workers, resulting from their social and economic situation; at the same time, it was remembered that these interests were, and should be, broader than just factory, wages, prices, work safety and health conditions, and that the worker was also a citizen who wanted to know about issues of concern to the nation, society, and the state, and in the future to influence these matters, to be a participant.

The name of the periodical carried on a tradition: between 1884 and 1906 under the Russian partition, an irregular and illegal organ of the Polish Socialist party (PPS) bore the same title and, like the party, promoted a program of social revolution, political democracy, and Polish independence among the working classes. This periodical was edited for a long time by Józef Piłsudski, who was then connected with the socialist movement; and the most outstanding PPS activists were on its editorial board. During the interwar period, *Robotnik* was the main daily organ of the PPS, and continued to appear until September 23, 1939 (that is, until the occupation of Warsaw).

The second number of *Robotnik* was signed, for the editorial board, by Bogdan Borusewicz (a KOR member who had conducted intensive organizing among the workers on the coast); Leopold Gierek (one of the tried and convicted Radom workers who joined the KOR movement); Jan Lityński (in fact the editor-in-chief of *Robotnik* for the four years of the periodical's existence, who had just become a member of KSS "KOR"; he also signed the first issue); Wojciech Onyszkiewicz (from the Ursus team, a KOR member who also signed the first issue); Józef Ruszar (a Catholic activist connected with the Cracow SKS); Władysław Sulecki (an associate of KOR, a miner from Gliwice who as a young boy served as a soldier in the Home Army, as a courier and member of the Gray Ranks in northern Masuria, which during the war was incorporated into the Reich); and Józef Śreniowski (a KOR member and a representative of the Łódź milieu, active mainly among the workers of Łódź and its surrounding region; he also signed the first issue). The editorial board named among the founders of *Robotnik:* Stefan Kawalec, Dariusz Kupiecki, Helena and Witold Łuczywo, Irena Wóycicka, and Ludwika and Henryk Wujec. Along with Lityński, Wujec played a central role in *Robotnik.*

During the several years of the periodical's existence, there were of course some changes in its editorial board. The most dramatic of these was the departure of Władysław Sulecki, not only from *Robotnik* but from Poland (see chapter 8, the section on the Initiating Committees of Free Trade Unions). In April 1978, Józef Ruszar also left the editorial board of *Robotnik.*

In time, the editorial board of *Robotnik* was joined by workers who were KOR activists. One of the first was Edmund Zadrożyński from Grudziądz, who was arrested on July 1, 1978, on false criminal charges, and was freed only as a result of the Gdańsk Agreements of August 31, 1980 (thus for over a year his presence on the list of members of the editorial board was symbolic). Other worker activists on the editorial board at various times included Franciszek Grabczyk, an engineer from Nowa Huta (from October 1978 until September 1980), Jan Witkowski from Gryfino on the Szczecin coast, Stefan Kozłowski from Szczecin, Jacek Pilchowski from Wałbrzych, and Andrzej Spyra from Gliwice. All were connected with *Robotnik* until the end. It must be said, however, that throughout the entire period, the members of the editorial board from outside Warsaw functioned, for technical and communication reasons, more as correspondents and members of an editorial council than as editors in the strict sense of the term.

The first issue was four pages long and printed on a primitive duplicating machine in an edition of only some 400 copies. Little more than a year later, *Robotnik* was printed every two weeks using a technique developed by Witold Łuczywo (screen printing with the photographic reduction of the text according to printing needs) with approximately 20,000 copies, which meant that a sheet would contain twelve readable pages of typescript. Distribution began with contacts dating back to the relief action of 1976. Gradually it widened to include a significant part of the industrial centers in the country. Often the distribution in places that had been blank areas on the map of KOR would begin with the handing out of copies in the streets.

Robotnik also indicated methods and possibilities in connection with the struggle for independent workers' trade unions, including the election of authentic workers' representatives to the trade union councils, or the creation of workers' councils like those in Spain under Franco. Various texts containing specific instructions were also printed ("How to Strike?" "What to Demand?").

Robotnik carried extensive information about infringements of workers' rights, dangers to life and health, accidents, the practice of lengthening the working day, wage-system injustices, and strikes. It unmasked the introduction of such methods of enslavement as those used in Radoskór in December 1978, where, after the factory gates were closed, workers were forced to work nonstop for sixteen hours in order to save the factory's plan of production. *Robotnik* also commented on an order by the president of the city of Cracow, Barszcz, which prohibited the hiring of any workers who had left their jobs in the Lenin Steel Mills in Nowa Huta. Such materials published in *Robotnik* constitute an unusual chronicle of the everyday lives of workers in a "socialist country." More and more often, the information gathered for the periodical became a basis for analyses and articles that were then printed in it.

Minor local successes were not unknown: in order to deprive *Robotnik* of a topic after the publication of some information, the authorities would, for example, install a new bathroom in the Gliwice Mine, or heating in the October Revolution Print Shop, or they would open a medical clinic in the Strzemięcin district of Grudziądz.

Robotnik and the cells of its distributors were the germs of a future organization. In issue No. 35 of August 1979, *Robotnik* published the *Charter of Workers' Rights*, the first program signed by over a hundred activists. It reads in part:

> Wherever there are strong organized groups of workers able to defend their representatives should they be dismissed from work or arrested, committees of free trade unions should be formed. . . . Only independent trade unions that are supported by the workers they represent have any chance of resisting the authorities; only they can constitute a force with which the authorities will have to reckon, and with which they will negotiate on a basis of equality.

Another important chapter in the history of *Robotnik* and of KOR involves cooperation with a group of activists on the coast, who at first distributed *Robotnik* and then edited their own *Robotnik Wybrzeża* (*The Coastal Worker*), as well as promoting self-education work and organizing demonstrations on the anniversaries of December 1970. This group included, among others: KOR members Bogdan Borusewicz, Joanna Duda-Gwiazda, Andrzej Gwiazda, Bogdan Lis, Maryla Płońska, Alina Pieńkowska, Anna Walentynowicz, Lech Wałęsa, and the brothers Błażej and Krzysztof Wyszkowski. In August 1980 they galvanized the coast, organizing the strike that began the history of Solidarity. But the Initiating Committees of Trade Unions, although closely connected to *Robotnik*, constitute a separate chapter in the history of the opposition movement in Poland before Solidarity.

The Anniversary of the Massacre on the Coast

The first demonstration on the anniversary of the December events organized by activists of the KOR and ROPCiO movements and of the Student Solidarity Committee in the tri-city area (Gdańsk-Gdynia-Sopot) took place in 1977. On December 14 and 15, the organizers posted information around Gdańsk, including the Lenin Shipyards, that a wreath would be laid on the seventh anniversary of the massacre, December 16 at 2:00 P.M. near Shipyard Gate No. 2, where the first of the wounded and slain workers had fallen in 1970. One of the persons putting up the posters, Bożena Rybicka, was detained and fined 5,000 zlotys by a sentencing board. On the morning of the demonstration, at the railroad station in Gdańsk, Józef Śreniowski, a KOR member on the editorial board of *Robotnik*, and KOR associate Anna Bazel were stopped and detained for twelve hours, in order to prevent them from taking part.

Approximately a thousand people, mostly workers, gathered around the gate. Since the gate itself was blocked by buses, the wreath was laid at the foot of the shipyard wall. After a minute of silence to honor those who had fallen, followed by the singing of the national anthem, the crowd dispersed peacefully. The police detained four persons with cameras and confiscated three films. "Unknown perpetrators" assaulted KSS "KOR" member Bogdan Borusewicz. They managed to grab his bag, which contained a camera, and to run away with it. The camera was later found in the provincial headquarters of the police, where Boru-sewicz went together with witnesses in order to inform the police about the robbery. The officer on duty at the headquarters refused a telephone request that he conduct a personal search of the person who was lodging the complaint and his witnesses. But they were searched anyway by a captain of the Security Service, Zygmunt Wasilewski, who came to the headquarters specifically for this purpose. This was the end of the first demonstration in front of Gate No. 2 of the shipyards. From then on, demonstrations were held there every year, and in 1980 a monument in the form of three giant crosses was erected nearby.

Initiatives Accompanying KOR

In addition to the great campaigns and battles, there were smaller skirmishes fought by KOR and its circle, and these also were significant.

KOR was not successful in organizing movements in the defense of the consumer, the environment, or cooperative ventures (especially in housing), and the like, although there were some first attempts and plans. It was still too weak. But occasionally there were small-scale initiatives such as, for example, the attempt of KOR associate Maciej Rayzacher to organize, completely independently of KOR, a day-care center for chil-dren from his neighborhood. This project was based in part on scouting methods, and in part represented an attempt to introduce educational methods known from experiments in the West and East involving the creation of a micro-society of children designed to prepare them for future life in civil society. The police and the Security Service responded by interrogating the children! For their own good it became necessary to close down this very promising educational experiment.

Another such initiative was the "salon" of Mr. and Mrs. Walendowski. Obviously the word "salon" must be put in quotation marks, since the mass of mostly young people who came to listen to a lecture, to meet with an editorial board of one of the opposition periodicals, or to listen to the songs of a dissident singer did not recall at all such things as, for example, the Benni salon of the second half of the nineteenth century in Warsaw, in which, after the tsarist rulers had liquidated almost all forms of Polish public life, the intellectual elite and social activists met regularly in a roomy, huge, private apartment. Here the majority was young, there midde-aged or older persons; here the dominant style was that of contemporary youth, there the elegance of the nineteenth-century establishment. But both here and there, something similar was going on: an attempt to forge a strategy and tactics in the struggle to realize national aspirations. From this point of view, the youthful character of Walendowski's salon did not diminish its seriousness: these were precisely the people who were originating (and immediately implementing) new ideas, new institutions, new forms of resistance and attack.

The Walendowskis were associates of KOR, especially Tadeusz, a theater director without an assignment, who, after attempts to create an oppositional cultural and informational agency, joined the Łódź group of *Puls* and participated in many other actions. Despite this KOR orientation, the Walendowskis steered their "salon" (I do not want to use the word "club," which for me is a collective and a group and not just a place for events that are managed by one or two persons) in a very open manner, which made events there both sensible and tasteful. What was especially important was the fact that they created a place where one could, for example, meet and discuss things with the editorial board of *Bratniak* or engage in an argument over principles with Prof. Adam Bromke, or in general, a place where one could go beyond one's circle and meet people who thought differently. And it should also be mentioned that the presentation of works by writers and singers outside the censorship, which was dominant in this "salon," created a different and a very important way of encountering the living word and the live presence of the artists.

The Security Service did not enter Walendowski's salon. Ania Walendowska, a young doctor and the granddaughter of Melchior Wankowicz, was born in the United States and had been living as an American citizen in Poland for several years. The authorities regarded the mass gatherings in Walendowski's apartment with unconcealed anger, but they tolerated them, probably because they wanted to avoid interventions from the American consul. The immunity of this apartment ended when, after the Walendowskis moved back to America, the Naimskis moved in and tried to organize TKN lectures there.

One should also mention the exhibition of the Polish democratic opposition movement. The exhibition was organized by a group of KOR associates, who smuggled the exhibits to the West in order to show them during the Venice Biennale, which was devoted to the dissidents of Eastern and Central Europe. The exhibit included a set of independent periodicals, some publications of NOWa, and documentation of the religious movement in Poland (documents and photographs of pilgrimages to Częstochowa and Piekary, of Corpus Christi processions, sacrosongs, etc.); materials concerning the activities of KSS "KOR," the Student Solidarity Committees, and ROPCiO; documentation of the Pyjas case, together with a photographic report on the funeral demonstrations and an original obituary poster; a description of the fast in the Church of St. Martin; pictures of the members of KSS "KOR" and of the *Zapis* writers; and some of the graphic works of W. Wołyński and M. Bogucki.

Repressions from September 1977 to April 1978

Just as in the previous chapters, we will not list such "trifles" as detentions, house searches, or fines imposed by the sentencing boards. There were simply too many of these, and their register would look too much like a telephone directory.

It is curious to notice the geography of the detentions and house searches: they indicated the widening of the movement. At first they took place only in the largest Polish cities, with the overwhelming preponderance in Warsaw. Gradually, however, the disproportion ceased to be so striking, and one could see that Cracow, Wrocław, Łódź, Gdańsk, Poznań, and Lublin were also becoming important centers of opposition. Later, the list of names of cities and towns, and villages too, became longer and longer.

In Katowice, during one of the house searches, the police confiscated materials concerning environmental protection from KOR associate Wojciech Rzucidło. Despite the fact that no "green" movement was ever organized alongside KOR, the committee attempted to provide at least current information about the more scandalous violations of regulations concerning the protection of the natural environment. Rzucidło was gathering such materials about Silesia.

Radom also had its share of repressions, and was apparently the only center where the group cooperating with *Robotnik* made its existence known publicly.

In Wałbrzych, simultaneous searches in the houses of eight people speak for themselves.

One of the most active groups cooperating with KOR was formed in Gryfino in the province of Szczecin, and ten issues of *Robotnik* were fished out during searches of workers' lockers conducted in department R-E of the Lower Oder Electrical Plant.

Among those detained in this period was a large and distinct group of ROPCiO activists who were conducting a campaign to gather signatures on an appeal from Amnesty International for an amnesty for political prisoners in all the countries of the world. For this they were hunted down by the police and the Security Service and punished with fines by sentencing boards. This episode is connected with KOR only because all the members of the committee collectively became signatories of this appeal.

This period was characterized by a concentration of the police on the publications and printing activities of KOR. Four duplicating machines were discovered in December 1977 alone, which under the conditions of KOR's work was a serious blow. On many occasions, large portions of the printings of periodicals were confiscated. Despite this, the police were unable to paralyze the publications and the press.

The decrease in the number of beatings during this period might seem surprising. On Christmas Eve, Zenon Pałka was beaten up (though not for his activity, but because after an accidental detention he ascertained that he was missing several thousand zlotys). On March 22, 1978, Tadeusz Stachnik was beaten in Świder near Warsaw. In addition, for the first time in the history of KOR, after Stachnik filed a complaint in the Provincial Prosecutor's Office, the Regional Prosecutor's Office prepared a crime report (though without further effects).

The practice of repressive dismissal from work continued. During this period, jobs were lost by Lech Dymarski from Poznań, Mieczysław Grudziński from Warsaw, Bohdan Kosiński from Warsaw, Piotr Starzyński from Wrocław, and Henryk Wujec from Warsaw. KSS "KOR" member Henryk Wujec was fired from his job on the excuse that "his tenure in his present position was too short." Wujec, a physicist, had worked for nine years in the TEWA Semiconductor Research and Production Center. After the May fast (for which Wujec, like the majority of the participants, had used vacation time he was due), he was demoted from his position as director of a laboratory to that of a rank-and-file employee; almost a year later he received his final dismissal slip. Dismissals from Warsaw University will not be discussed here because they will be taken up in the next chapter.

Similar repressions were widespread, ranging from such drastic measures as cutting off all bonuses and allowances, which play a large role in the salaries of such (for Poland) relatively well-paying occupations as mining, where the cuts made it difficult to support a family (Władysław

Sulecki), to dismissing members from scientific commissions in the Polish Academy of Sciences (e.g., Prof. Adam Szczypiorski from the Demographic Commission).

The attempt to prevent Władysław Siła-Nowicki, an attorney who had done much to defend the workers, from practicing his profession was treated by KOR as a particularly serious matter. On the basis of a complaint lodged by the Regional Court in Radom, Siła-Nowicki was charged with abusing freedom of speech by giving his arguments in the trial of Zofia Sadowska an antistate character. This was a reference to his critique of the methods used by the functionaries of the police in Radom in 1976, and to his presentation of the background of the events. As it turned out, the entire case against Siła-Nowicki was instigated by the Provincial Police Headquarters in Radom. Judge Elżbieta Dobrowolska from Radom, who testified as a witness in Siła-Nowicki's trial, presented to the Disciplinary Commission her understanding of the rights of defenders, according to which the attorney for the defense had the right to discuss the background of a case only in certain instances, and that in this particular case the defense should not have contained a general evaluation of the situation.

Nevertheless, the Disciplinary Commissions of the Attorneys' Councils (the Warsaw and the National Commissions) found Siła-Nowicki not guilty in both trials. The Higher Disciplinary Commission declared that "the principle of the attorney's immunity must be interpreted as broadly as possible, since freedom of speech in the practice of the legal profession is the most effective guarantee that the law will be upheld in the adversary process," and that "the right to subjective evaluations and to the possibility of a mistake encompasses also the right to express political opinions in connection with a particular case, and allows for the criticism of individual representatives of the authorities."

Given the political conditions of the Polish People's Republic, these formulations were almost revolutionary; in any case they were revelations, despite the fact that they were supplemented by a certain caveat: "with the provision that any criticism of the basic principles of the socialist system would be unacceptable." KOR was aware of the importance of Siła-Nowicki's acquittal and of the general statements made in this case. The *Information Bulletin* carried extensive information several pages long about the case and the verdict.

The practice of *Berufsverbot* was an effective element of action against KOR and the democratic opposition, but only when it did not meet with collective resistance. The case of Jerzy Markuszewski is an example of this. Since February 1976, Markuszewski, a director, had not been hired to work in theater, radio, or television, which deprived him of the right to practice his profession. His blacklisting was connected with his role in organizing the protest against the changes in the Constitution. Markuszewski was also a signatory of the first protest letter on this issue. Later, the "trespasses" of 1975 were augmented by his cooperation with KOR. In mid-1977, a group of well-known and highly respected people from the theater, altogether over sixty actors, directors, and translators, wrote a letter to the Minister of Culture and Art, Józef Tejchma, demanding that Markuszewski's right to work be restored. They also asked for the intervention of the chairman of the Association of Polish Theatre and Cinema Artists (SPATiF), Gustaw Holoubek.

After a meeting between the Main Council of SPATiF and a secretary of the Central Committee of PUWP, Jerzy Łukaszewicz, it seemed that nothing stood in the way of removing Markuszewski from the blacklist. In December 1977 he was offered employment in the Old Theatre in Cracow. In recognition of this offer, the signatories of the letter to Minister Tejchma decided not to mail their letter. In March 1978, Markuszewski was told that the City Office in Cracow had prohibited his being hired. Only at that time did Irena and Tadeusz Byrski and Maciej Rayzacher send the collective letter, which was originally intended for Tejchma, to the premier, supplementing its contents with a description of the further course of the case.

As a result of the attitude within theater circles, Markuszewski was hired by the Variety Theatre in Warsaw in May 1978. The Department of Culture of the Warsaw City Office did not yet know that the prohibition against hiring him had been rescinded, and for a while did not want to allow his employment.

The case of Markuszewski reveals the mechanics of the Polish *Berufsverbot*, and at the same time shows how it can be broken. If there were people in Poland who could not get work for years because of repressions (for example, Dr. Łukawer, an economist from Cracow), they could blame it not only on the persecuting communist authorities but also on the indifference or cowardice of their own milieu.

The police attack on the Poznań "Theatre of the Eighth Day" occupies a special place among the acts of repression used against the opposition activists. This group was organized in 1962 as a student theater with high artistic and ideological ambitions. It was especially respected for three shows: *In One Breath*, based on texts by Stanisław Barańczak and connected with the December 1970 events on the coast; *Visit to the Scene of the Crime,* an attempt to portray the cultural, social, and political sources of the nazification of the consciousness of a common man; and *Sale for Everybody,* a synthesis of the artistic and intellectual experiences of the actors. With the passage of time the theater did not fall apart, but continued its activities. Though obviously losing its purely student character, it maintained close contact with the academic milieu.

From the beginning of KOR, the people involved in the "Theatre of the Eighth Day" were clearly supportive of the committee. As a result, all were exposed to surveillance, searches, detentions, and other repressions. In March typewriters were illegally confiscated from the theater. In 1977 an investigation about supposed embezzlement was started suddenly and dropped with equal suddenness (the case made no sense whatsoever). The activities of the theater were systematically limited. The group was not allowed to travel abroad or to give performances at festivals outside of Poznań. The city authorities in Poznań expropriated the theater's quarters, which had just been remodeled into a performance hall.

In April 1978 five of its actors who were en route from Poznań to Lublin did not manage in their haste to buy tickets for a bus that was taking them from one station to another in Warsaw. An inspector appeared, who was strangely also a functionary of the Security Service. By an equally "strange" turn of events, the driver of the car following the bus also turned out to be a plainclothes policeman who came to help his colleague the inspector. Even some of the chance witnesses of the scene that followed demonstrated an amazing clairvoyance, and accompanied the action with shouts of "Artists! Drug Addicts!" although it was not clear how they knew that the "hooligans" were also artists. The actors expressed their readiness to pay their fare for the ride on the spot, as well as the fine for traveling without a ticket, but the inspector refused to accept their offer and called the police, which immediately beat up two of the actors, and then a third during the ride to the district police precinct. In the precinct on Wilcza Street, all five were beaten, and their glasses, watches, and other personal items were destroyed in the process. According to the customs of the police, the victims of these beatings were themselves charged with a hooligan assault and with insulting a functionary of the police. The maximum penalty for this according to the relevant articles of the Criminal Code is twelve years of imprisonment.[8]

In its statement of May 29, 1978, KSS "KOR" appealed to artistic unions and circles to defend the "Theatre of the Eighth Day," and Halina Mikołajska issued an open letter in this matter to the artistic and cultural milieu. The Cracow SKS also defended the actors, and 497 Cracow students sent a letter to the Diet. The sentences ranged from six months to one year in prison, but they were made probationary for three or four years.

A rather original form, not so much of repression as of prevention, was used in Łódź, where the functionaries of the Security Service conducted "warning conversations" with the parents of young, but nevertheless legally adult associates of KOR. One characteristic feature of these conversations was the use of anti-Semitic motifs, which constantly accompanied the attacks of the Security Service against KOR, and which were unfortunately also picked up at times by other persons hostile to KOR, but who doubtless had nothing in common with the Security Service except for anti-Semitism.

The repressions used during this six-month period were more or less the same as those used previously, but they were concentrated on the student movement and on the Society for Scientific Courses. This was also the period in which a new factor began to appear on the scene: the Initiating Committees of Free Trade Unions. They were to change the quality and direction of the activities of KOR and of the entire democratic opposition. A straight though difficult road led from these committees to Solidarity.

8

From the Founding of the Initiating Committees of Free Trade Unions to the Polish Pilgrimage of Pope John Paul II
(April 1978–June 1979)

The Independent Workers' Movement

The Initiating Committee of Free Trade Unions (KZ WZZ) in Katowice was formed in mid-March 1978. Its founders were Bolesław Cygan, Roman Kściuczek, Kazimierz Świtoń, and Władysław Sulecki. This committee was of a mixed character, composed of adherents of ROPCiO as well as KOR. With the exception of Kściuczek, the other names are already familiar to the reader. Sulecki, a miner from the Gliwice mine, was popular and had strong support among his co-workers. He could be beaten up in his neighborhood, or his salary could be cut, but they did not dare to fire him; he was responsible for circulating the letter from ninety-seven workers of this mine who expressed their solidarity with KOR after the arrests of May 1977. Świtoń, who first appeared on the horizon of the democratic opposition during the fast in the Church of St. Martin, later chose to follow ROPCiO rather than KOR. He was a radio mechanic and the owner of a small radio and television repair shop. Like Świtoń, Kściuczek also aligned himself with ROPCiO, though later there was a parting of the ways. As we know, Cygan was an associate of KOR. In a somewhat later period, which still falls within this chapter, the KZ WZZ was also joined by Jan Bal, Zdzisław Mnich, Andrzej Spyra, and Jan Świtoń.

Immediately after the formation of the KZ WZZ in Katowice, there occurred a conflict between Kuroń on the one hand, and Świtoń and

Kścuiczek on the other, who had just come to Warsaw with information about the founding of the new KZ WZZ. The argument left Świtoń with such a dislike of Kuroń that he later attacked him and KOR in the official government press during the period of Solidarity.

After talking with the co-founders of the new KZ WZZ, Kuroń, who knew the realities of such situations, expressed the opinion that they had committed a mistake by making a premature collective statement when they still did not have sufficiently organized support in the area of their activity. Now they would be watched closely and would not be able to make further progress. His prognosis proved to be correct. From then on, the apartments of the founders of the Katowice KZ WZZ resembled outposts under siege. The surveillance became very painful, and the distribution of publications along this route was almost completely paralyzed. In general, the province of Katowice was a difficult terrain, held tightly in the grip of the police and the Security Service, and this is why the actual role of the members of the Katowice KZ WZZ during the strikes of August 1980 was minimal, in contradistinction to the fundamental importance of the KZ WZZ of the coastal region during this period.

Therefore, despite the good will and the personal courage of the members of the Initiating Committee in Katowice, not much was achieved in practical terms. Nevertheless, the publicity undertaken by KOR, especially during the action in defense of Świtoń, was surely of some moral and informational significance. In the summer of 1980, the striking Katowice Steel Mill freed Kazimierz Świtoń from house arrest and named him a secretary of the Strike Committee, which meant that the workers of Silesia knew and remembered the heroic fight for the free trade unions in Katowice.

One especially tragic chapter in the history of the KZ WZZ in Katowice was Sulecki's decision to emigrate with his family from Poland. By leaving Poland, Sulecki was saving his family from destruction, since his Silesian wife, who was in a state of nervous breakdown because of the persecutions, accepted the opportunity to emigrate to West Germany regardless of the cost of this departure. The open letter written by Sulecki on the eve of his emigration is a shattering document.[1]

The Initiating Committee of Free Trade Unions on the coast was formed on April 29, 1978. Its origins, however, go back farther. The group that founded this committee was quite well integrated during the period of their joint work for KOR, which involved the distribution of publications, especially of *Robotnik;* cooperation with the Intervention

Bureau (mainly the Gwiazdas); gathering information for KOR about the social problems of the tri-city and coastal areas; and making some first attempts at self-education, which later, during the period of the KZ WZZ, were developed further with some help from the Society for Scientific Courses.[2] The group was created around the Gwiazdas. Both Andrzej and his wife, Joanna Duda-Gwiazda, are ship construction engineers. They established contact with Bogdan Borusewicz, a KOR member on the coast. The Wyszkowski brothers, especially Krzysztof, also played an important role. During the early stages, Anna Walentynowicz and Lech Wałęsa, two worker activists with very different personalities, were also very important in the formation of the profile of the committee. It might be said that Alina Pieńkowska came out of nowhere. She found the address of Borusewicz in a *KOR Communiqué*, came to visit him, and stayed in the KOR movement. It is difficult for the author to say just how Andrzej Bulc found himself in the committee. Jan Zapolnik was the only member of ROPCiO in this group; he joined the editorial board of *Ruth Związkowy* (*The Union Movement*). This periodical had the ambition of unifying all trade union initiatives. Three issues were published.

There were also black sheep. A certain A. S. could not withstand the threats and succumbed to the enticements of bribery. Edwin Myszk, a charming Cashubian in love with the traditions and ethnic distinctiveness of his people (this pose was probably genuine) turned out simply to have been an agent of the Security Service. Later, the coastal KZ WZZ was joined by two other members of the future leadership of the August strikes: Bogdan Lis (the only member of PUWP in this group), and Andrzej Kołodziej.

The very painful case of A. S., who was a co-founder of the coastal KZ WZZ, is worth retelling, for it illustrates the methods of the Security Service, and shows human weakness in a saddening way, since the worst possible thing happened—a man debased himself. For this reason, he is designated here only by his initials. A. S. was a welder who lost his job in June 1976, then sued the Lenin Shipyards demanding compensation for two occupational diseases (anthracosis and a vibration disease), and for eight months of unemployment pay. On May 5, following the announcement of the formation of the KZ WZZ, the director of the Internal Affairs Department of the provincial administration, Gromadzki, offered A. S., who was a co-founder of the committee, a payment of 54,000 zlotys as the first installment of a settlement. A. S. not only accepted the money but also signed a statement to the effect that he had never joined the KZ WZZ. On June 3, *Życie Warszawy* published a letter allegedly written by A. S. in which he expressed his indignation at Radio Free Europe for using his name. The commentary to the letter noted that A. S. claimed never even to have heard about the committee whose declaration he was alleged to have signed. On June 5, A. S. reacted to this in a letter to *Życie Warszawy*, a copy of which he gave to his colleagues in the KZ WZZ. The letter begins:

> I, A. S., did not send the letter to the editors of *Życie Warszawy* that appeared in the article entitled "The Next Mishap." I protest against and do not agree with the lies written by the editor. I am asking that the truth be told describing the injustices done to me and my six-member family by those scoundrels in high positions. I worked in the Gdańsk shipyards for twenty-three years, my four children studied, my wife did not work for nineteen years, and I had only my house and piecework as a welder. Two occupational diseases—from the age of seventeen I worked in such a heavy industry. I was fired from my job on July 8, 1976, through Article 56 of the [Labor] Code.

This is the frightening voice of a man caught in a terrible trap, who still wants to be honest and to stand beside his friends.

It is not surprising that this genuine letter from A. S. was never printed in *Życie Warszawy*. On June 6, A. S. was again detained. A dramatic conversation ensued. He was threatened with revenge and blackmailed by being told that his signature was proof of extortion. Gramadzki was now offering him 106,000 zlotys. A. S. refused, but on the following day he accepted 150,000. On June 10, *Życie Warszawy* published a photocopy of his letter, an authentic one this time (which, by the way, showed that the first letter had indeed been a forgery). A. S., by now morally shattered, made no secret of the amount he received. In his admission there is both despair and cynical boasting; not one of his former friends will speak to him. Who were the members of the coastal KZ WZZ?

Their names figure in the history of the strike movement of 1980 and of Solidarity. The whole world knows the name of Lech Wałęsa, an activist endowed with great stubbornness, iron character, and intuition, who strives steadily toward his goal of free trade unions. The names of others are known almost as well: Andrzej Gwiazda, Wałęsa's future antagonist, a noble man with the mind of an intellectual; Anna Walentynowicz, a moral authority in the shipyard and during the strike of 1980; and Bogdan Lis, the deputy chairman of Solidarity and a man of outstanding intelligence. Joanna Duda-Gwiazda, Andrzej's wife, an engineer with artistic inclinations, is a person with a very rich internal and emotional life; her opinions counted no less than those of her husband. Alina

Pieńkowska, very girlish, a nurse by profession, proved in August to be an efficient commander of the strike guard, although at moments of extreme tension she would burst into tears, without expecting to be consoled. Andrzej Bulc, a young electronics technician who received his training in a technical high school, later became an able and competent educational activist in Solidarity for the Mazowsze Region. Krzysztof Wyszkowski deserves a chapter to himself: a worker-intellectual, a qualified carpenter, and a fan of literature and the arts, in August 1980, during the negotiations with Vice-Premier Jagielski, he interrupted the vice-premier's long-winded ramblings on the issue of censorship by shouting out: "Isn't it a disgrace that Gombrowicz has never been published?" His brother Błażej co-founded the SKS in Gdańsk as a student, and then as a beginning engineer became involved in the free trade union movement. He was an outstanding sailor and an Olympic athlete. Jan Zapolnik was respected for his character and integrity.

The coastal KZ WZZ was able quickly to establish its own periodical, *Robotnik Wybrzeża,* a local journal whose editorial board cooperated closely with the Warsaw *Robotnik.* The first issue appeared in August 1978. It was distinguished by its high quality, but it was also fully accessible to a poorly educated reader.

Just as in Upper Silesia, repressions soon followed. Gwiazda stood before the court on charges of beating up a child.[3] He was given a suspended sentence of two years of imprisonment and a fine of 12,000 zlotys. Sentence was pronounced by Judge Sułkowski, and the witness for the prosecution was Security Service agent Piotr Widelski, who had been assigned to follow Gwiazda.

Krzysztof Wyszkowski and Jan Zapolnik were beaten up. An attempt was made to trump up criminal charges against Wałęsa (who, following a period of unemployment, had been given work in the ZREMB Enterprises), but this attempt was dropped in view of the threatening attitude of his co-workers. It was also necessary to retract his dismissal from work at ZREMB—but not for long; he was finally fired in December.

Andrzej Bulc lost his job at ZELMOR in Gdańsk.

Błażej Wyszkowski was arrested, and his defense also played a major role in the history of this group. On May 28, the police invaded the apartment of Krzysztof Wyszkowski to prevent a meeting of representatives of the coastal KZ WZZ, of KSS "KOR," and of the Gdańsk SKS. Forty police functionaries, both uniformed and in plain clothes, took part in the operation. Ten people were detained. Krzysztof Wyszkowski was beaten up in a police car. Błażej Wyszkowski was arrested and charged with "causing a gathering on May 28, and disturbing the peace with noise and screams in the courtyard of the building at 14 Pomorska Street." The real issue was that Błażej Wyszkowski had defended a student, Anna Młynik, as she was being led out of the apartment, and had pulled her from a police car. On May 30 a sentencing board condemned him to two months imprisonment; this sentence was upheld by the Regional Court on September 29. It was typical that the court allowed no witnesses for the defense, claiming that the testimony of the police would be sufficient. Wyszkowski began a hunger strike on the day of his detention and abandoned it only after thirty-three days (incidentally, he was begged to do so by KOR); during this time he was force-fed. On his account an eight-day protest fast was undertaken by Bogdan Borusewicz, Piotr Dyk, and Krzysztof Wyszkowski; Józef Śreniowski fasted for nine days. Following a telegram sent by KOR to Amnesty International, this organization adopted Błażej Wyszkowski as a prisoner of conscience.

Beginning on June 3, public prayers were held daily in the Marian Church in Gdańsk for Błażej Wyszkowski and the participants in the fast. KOR in Warsaw and the Student Solidarity Committees in Warsaw, Łódź, and Gdańsk distributed leaflets in behalf of Wyszkowski. Ten thousand leaflets were handed out in front of a dozen churches in Warsaw on two Sundays, June 18 and 25. Leaflets were also distributed in front of the gates to the shipyards in Gdańsk and Gdynia. This action in defense of Wyszkowski served to unite the opposition on the Gdańsk coast.

The coastal KZ WZZ became the main initiator and host of the annual wreath-laying at Gate No. 2 of the Gdańsk Shipyard on the anniversary of the December events. Since its inception in 1977, this ceremony had always been a joint commemoration on the part of the KZ WZZ, KOR, ROPCiO, the SKS, and later the Young Poland Movement—the entire opposition from the tri-city area. These ceremonies had attained a significant dimension by 1978. Above all, a considerable amount of attention was provided by the police and the Security Service. The *KOR Communiqué* noted that from December 17 to 20 there were twenty-eight detentions, and remarked that this number included only members of the democratic opposition. Moreover, many passersby walking with flowers and bouquets were also detained, though they later told no one about this. There were also twenty-five house searches. Lech Wałęsa was sentenced to a fine of 5,000 zlotys for disturbing the peace (he was stopped on the street while carrying a wreath from the coastal KZ WZZ). The prosecuting attorney had demanded three months of imprisonment.

Four thousand people gathered in front of Shipyard Gate No. 2 on December 18. Borusewicz achieved the improbable by managing to lay a wreath from KSS "KOR," the only wreath to survive the police round-ups. Borusewicz also made a speech, as did Kazimierz Szołach, a member of the Shipyard Strike Committee of 1970 and an associate of the coastal KZ WZZ. Three songs were sung: the national anthem, the hymn "God Save Poland," and the "Internationale." A minute of silence was observed in memory of the fallen.

Other workers' groups considered themselves too weak to form new KZ WZZ organizations, and they were probably right. There was never a conflict in Gdańsk between KOR and ROPCiO (thanks to both sides, and especially to Borusewicz); while the coastal KZ WZZ, because of its close cooperation with the entire opposition on the coast, commanded a large number of activists for the realization of its projects, so that it could not easily be eliminated by means of police surveillance and house arrests. The distributing and self-educational groups of *Robotnik* scattered throughout the country were in a worse situation, so they limited themselves to their basic tasks and were in no hurry to proclaim their existence publicly.

Only the group in Grudziądz undertook public initiatives involving the gathering of signatures for collective letters on a variety of issues. On May 19, 1978, three workers were detained and searched: Maksymilian Moździński, Zdzisław Wojanowski, and Edmund Zadrożyński. Found in their possession and confiscated was a letter to the Council of State demanding the restoration of the rights lost by workers fired from the Pomeranian Foundry and Enamel Works in June 1976 (i.e., credit for continuous work and seniority). The letter had been signed by 148 citizens of Grudziądz. On May 27, five workers, including the three named above, complained to the Council of State about this illegal step on the part of the police authorities.

In December 1978 and January 1979, the same group sent as many as six collectively signed letters to various authorities in the PRL. The subjects of these letters included police repressions, the unavailability of goods, and other social matters in Grudziądz, as well as the situation in the factories. They protested against the practice of not allowing visits to the factory by Edmund Zadrożyński, an invalid who had been a worker in the Pomeranian Foundry and Enamel Works until he was pensioned off following an accident there in 1974. They attacked the deputy to the Diet from Grudziądz, Kazimierz Roszkowski, a worker in the same factory, and pointed out the compromising participation of the official trade unions in police repressions. In December 1978, a letter signed by 291 citizens of Grudziądz was sent to the Council of State that demanded an end to persecutions against activists of the democratic opposition.

In April approximately 500 residents of Grudziądz wrote to the Diet about the situation in the markets, about the waste involved in a decision to suspend the construction of a dormitory for occupational schools, and about the lack of stores in suburban settlements. But even this milieu did not yet feel itself strong enough to form a KZ WZZ. There is a difference between a large center such as the tri-city area and a medium-sized town such as Grudziądz.

The creation of the Initiating Committees of Free Trade Unions did not free KOR from the responsibility of making statements on those issues that would normally be subjects of concern and pressure from the trade unions. As an example we might cite the statement of KSS "KOR" of August 7, 1978, which was issued at the request of miners from Upper Silesia, who asked that the committee make a statement on the lengthening of their work day. The statement condemned the compulsory employment of miners on so-called "draft Sundays," which were supposedly voluntary; the elimination of twelve free Saturdays which the miners were supposed to receive yearly; making all bonuses (up to 50 percent of a salary) dependent on working without fail during all required days, so that neither serious illness nor the death of a close family member was a sufficient excuse; and pressures on the health services to limit sick leaves. The statement points out that such practices increase the number of work-related accidents, worsen the state of the miners' health, and deprive the miners of family and cultural life.

Strikes and Work Stoppages

Periods in which there have been no strikes in Poland are rare. This area of the social history of Poland cannot be properly investigated as long as the archives of the police and the Ministry of Internal Affairs remain closed, and they are not likely to be opened soon. Except for the police, no one registered these events, and they were rarely noticed outside of the factory being struck. They did not last long, and very rarely did they have an organized character or produce a strike committee. The press never wrote about this situation. The authorities almost always allowed the factory management to find a compromise with the workers. The demands expressed during these strikes most often concerned wages (usually changes in production norms and bonuses); more rarely they involved matters of work safety and hygiene. Usually these demands were at least partially met. The authorities tended to avoid breaking strikes by force. After a strike, however, its leaders were usually fired, and since they were registered by the Security Service, they became subject from then on to discreet surveillance and discrimination. It was precisely such people who constituted a dominant group among those conscripted into the army in June 1976, before the announcement of price increases.

After the wave of strikes that was brutally suppressed in June 1976, the authorities enjoyed relative peace for a while. Although there is very little information, it is known that Malmor (an enterprise that launches ships in cooperation with the shipyard) and the Tube Works Department of the Gdańsk Shipyard both struck in 1977. However, these strikes were not only local but also not very decisive and rather short-lived. In accordance with the general rule, they resulted in short-term concessions on the part of the management.

In the summer of 1978, however, it was already possible to notice a wave of strikes testifying to increasing social tensions. The list of striking mines, surely incomplete, includes the Rydułtowy, First of May, Boryn, Thirtieth Anniversary, and Jastrzębie. In Łódź there were strikes in the Marchlewski textile factory and in the Defenders of the Peace factory. The miners struck to protest the lengthening of their working day and the shortages of meat. These shortages also induced textile workers to strike, who also demanded wage increases (their wages were among the lowest in Poland). These strikes were really, according to the official terminology, short-term work stoppages, which ended after the workers listened to promises. Generally, the supply situation in the stores improved for several days afterward.

The next wave of strikes occurred in the fourth quarter of 1978. From October 9 to October 11, there was a strike in the Pabianice Bandages Factory (PASO). Workers of the Pabianice Pharmaceutical Enterprises "Polfa" struck from October 10 to October 14. On October 26 there was a strike in the Łódź Candy Factory Optima, on November 18 a strike in the Pabianice Light Bulb Factory POLAM; and on December 1 in the Pabianice Technical Textiles Factory. These strikes resulted from the lowering of wages.

On December 29, KSS "KOR" issued a statement about the new wave of strikes. It pointed out that the strikes were motivated by self-defense, or the restoration of lost benefits, and that the official trade unions were not fulfilling their responsibility to represent the interests of the workers, making strikes inevitable. KSS "KOR" argued that it was necessary to create permanent bodies to represent the workers, and gave notice that it would offer help to the victims of repressions following strikes.

Robotnik usually reacted immediately to the moods among the workers of big industrial enterprises. Thus, the issue of June 17, 1978, printed an instructive article by Józef Śreniowski entitled "Strikes in the PRL: Security, Effectiveness, and Representation," which dealt with strikes concerning limited economic objectives. The article placed great emphasis on the principle of solidarity with persecuted workers.

Yet another problem at this time and in the following years involved work stoppages in factories caused by shortages of raw materials, the lack of spare parts for machines, or energy shortages. This was an economic and organizational problem, but at the same time it encouraged strikes. The management often tried to compensate for losses incurred during such stoppages by increasing their pressure on the productivity of workers, often by lengthening the work day, while at the same time they tended to avoid the payment of additional costs, which led the workers to resist. However, workers who witness stoppages brought about by the malfunction of the industrial and economic system become immune to arguments that strikes result in economic losses. The *Information Bulletin* of June/July 1978 presented alarming information about such interruptions in industrial production. At the same time, the official press was filled with self-congratulatory statements about the economic situation in Poland.

The Defense of Świtoń

From the moment the Initiating Committee of Free Trade Unions was formed in Katowice, the names of its founders constantly appeared in the independent press. Three of the founders were severely beaten: Sulecki, Cygan, and finally Świtoń. All kinds of pretexts were used against them.

Take, for example, Świtoń: his house was searched on April 6; he was detained for forty-eight hours on April 7; leaflets presenting him as a Nazi war criminal who had tortured Poles appeared on April 8 (Świtoń was born in 1931); on April 21, there was another forty-eight-hour detention; on April 24, a sentencing board for misdemeanors sentenced him to five weeks of imprisonment for failing to renew a permit for his air rifle.

The story of the rifle is typical. Świtoń did indeed own an air gun. It was broken and had been sent to a repair shop. Świtoń decided to donate it to a school, so he did not renew his permit.[4] He carried the repaired gun to the school, and precisely at the moment he was giving it up, the police entered triumphantly, confiscated this potential tool of revolt (social revolution or national uprising?), and arrested him. On April 27, Świtoń was again detained for forty-eight hours, and so on and on. From January until October 1978, Świtoń was detained a total of twelve times.

Something new happened on October 14, 1978. This was a Sunday, and Świtoń was leaving church together with his wife. While still on the grounds of the church, inside the fence, he was attacked by four individuals and dragged outside. There he grabbed a fence post, and at this moment uniformed policemen appeared and began beating Świtoń and pulling him away from the fence in front of many witnesses. This was taking place near a bus stop, so that a police car (supposedly there by chance, according to police witnesses) stopped a little farther on. Świtoń was dragged to it, so that the difficult operation of pushing him into the car would not have to be conducted so publicly. By then Świtoń was unconscious, and the car drove to police headquarters with its door partially open because his legs were sticking out. For reasons difficult to understand, his persecutors decided initially that a sentencing board would be sufficient to try him for disturbing the peace.

As we know, a Polish citizen who has been beaten by the police has two options: he can pretend that nothing happened, in which case the matter ends with, at most, a sentencing board for misdemeanors and a sentence for disturbing the peace, or with a hospital, or if one is unlucky, with both of these; or he can sue the police for assault, and then (but only then, for the police, with admirable forbearance, are rarely prompt to charge that they have themselves been assaulted) one faces a prosecutor and a court that trusts only those who did the beating and pronounces an appropriate sentence. These are situations in which one can feel quite free to chose one's own fate.

Świtoń faced the sentencing board on October 16. According to the police rules of the game, no one was as yet accusing him of assault; no such accusation appeared in the official notes or in the testimony given by policemen before the board. None of the uniformed or plainclothes policemen had as yet noticed that Świtoń had hurt him. What is more, even during the hearing on appeal, on November 4, those who had been beaten still failed to notice it. And then it turned out that Świtoń was simply being disloyal, for he claimed that he had been beaten. In this case, the situation changes entirely.

It now appeared that Świtoń, who is not particularly tall and is rather slim, managed to beat up four functionaries of the police, causing a "derangement of their health," and what is more, he also damaged a car. In the initial trial Świtoń was sentenced to one year of imprisonment and a fine. But even before his sentencing, immediately after the beating took place and Świtoń was arrested, KOR made some energetic moves. They were of two kinds: first, the committee tried to alert world and national opinion by presenting Świtoń's case in statements and telegrams, and appealing for participation in his defense; and second, KOR began a large leaflet action in Upper Silesia to make sure that the appeals reached those they needed to reach most—Świtoń's neighbors.

In connection with Świtoń's case, KOR adopted and published the following documents:

1. On October 21, 1978, a telegram to Amnesty International and to the central offices of trade unions throughout the world, which included a description of the repressions used against Świtoń up to October 14, a description of Świtoń's beating and arrest, and a request for intervention.

2. An appeal to the Upper Silesian community, transmitted to His Excellency Bishop Herbert Bednorz on October 30, 1978, which, after a description of the repressions used against Świtoń since the time of his participation in the fast in the Church of St. Martin in May 1977, contained the following appeal:

> We appeal with great urgency to the entire Upper Silesian community, to the Church in Silesia and its hierarchy, and to the parishioners in Świtoń's church, who know him as an active and honest man, not to allow Kazimierz Świtoń and his family to suffer alone, but to defend him publicly and to offer protection to his family.

3. A "Report Concerning the Case of Kazimierz Świtoń," prepared for Amnesty International and dated November 28, 1978.

4. A statement of December 18, 1978.

5. A letter to Joe Gormley, the chairman of the National Union of Miners in Great Britain.

6. *The White Book of Kazimierz Świtoń*, with a January 8, 1979, Statement by KSS "KOR" as an introduction. This was a chronology of the reprisals used against Świtoń, and of his defense

7. A letter to the International Meeting and Conference Against Repression of January 25, 1979, which appealed for the protection of Jarosłav Sabata (Charter 77) and Kazimierz Świtoń.

8. A statement of January 26, 1979, concerning the renewal of investigative arrest for Świtoń, action in his defense, and a description of the beatings which were perpetrated in the police headquarters in Katowice against three participants in the leaflet action in defense of Świtoń.

The traditional method of protest, a letter to the authorities, was also used. On this occasion five intellectuals, among them two members of KSS "KOR," addressed their demand that Świtoń be released to the chairman of the Council of State. This letter was signed by Bohdan Cywiński, Reverend Aleksander Hauke-Ligowski, Edward Lipiński, Tadeusz Mazowiecki, and Adam Szczypiorski. This letter, together with others in defense of Świtoń, was then signed by a further 2,700 citizens. Janusz Groszkowski, a former chairman of the Polish Academy of Sciences and former vice-chairman of the Council of State, was so embittered by his futile struggle to punish a certain pseudo-scientist and gangster that when he was asked by one of the members of KSS "KOR" to sign this letter, he refused his signature, claiming that he would never again appeal to those who wield power in Poland. Instead, he gave a letter to Dorota Świtoń in which he expressed his admiration and solidarity for her husband, at the same time agreeing to the publication of this letter.

In addition, KSS "KOR" organized a large leaflet campaign, involving mass distribution in cities or regions where brutal actions of the police or the Security Service had been observed. The leaflets distributed in the streets not only carried information but also called for specific actions. This was intended as a step to discourage provincial lordlings from undertaking or tolerating brutal terror in their regions, if they wanted to avoid an extra offensive by the opposition. In the period of Świtoń's case, the materials distributed by KOR included not only the statements of KOR and the *White Book* but also *Robotnik*, the "Appeal to Society" of October 10, 1978, "On the Sixtieth Anniversary" (of Polish independence) of November 10, 1978, and other documents. This distribution had an immediate effect, not counting its long-range influence, which is difficult to estimate. Toward the end of the action, groups of local workers and students were participating in the defense of Świtoń alongside distributors commuting from Warsaw, Cracow, and Wrocław (KOR associates and students of SKS). Only about a dozen persons were involved, but it was a victory, if only because they had contacted KSS "KOR" on their own initiative.

The *KSS "KOR" Communiqué* notes that 7,000 copies of the "Appeal to Society" (together with materials about Świtoń) had been distributed in Upper Silesia by January 21, 1979. Obviously, the police of the entire Upper Silesian region were occupied during this period mainly with catching the distributors. A KSS "KOR" statement of January 26 records that three of them were beaten by the police with clubs after being taken to police headquarters. Of the three distributors mentioned above, two decided not to inform the prosecutor's office in writing, but one of them (Jan Tomasz Lipski) did so, including a report from his doctor's examination, and he also informed the prosecutor's office about the beatings of others.[5]

Świtoń's trial took place in a predictable atmosphere, which was well described in a report by Anka Kowalska published in the *Information Bulletin*. The lack of consistency and decisiveness on the part of the police was characteristic: they could not decide whether those who wanted to attend the trial should be arrested or not. As a result, some were arrested, and others were not. About ten persons did not make it to the trial. There was an attempt to detain and check the identity of Władysław Siła-Nowicki, Świtoń's attorney, despite the fact that he was wearing a lawyer's toga. "I did not permit any of these things to happen," Siła-Nowicki said to the court, not without pride.[6]

As usual, policemen served as witnesses for the prosecution. Despite help from the court, they were unable to explain cogently how they had been beaten up. Lieutenant Forma, answering the questions of the defense on this matter, said that such hooligan attacks are too common, that this was "just one more such report" (for the record, the judge dictated this statement as: "In the official report, I wrote what I thought appropriate"). According to Lieutenant Forma, Świtoń had started running away as soon as he saw the police (although obviously he did not run far, and it was really rather difficult to understand why, leaving the church "clean," as it were, without a single uncensored leaflet on his person, Świtoń, who was leading his wife by the arm, should suddenly start running away). When Forma was asked whether he perhaps had "visited" Świtoń previously during the searches of Świtoń's apartment, he answered grudgingly, "This cannot be excluded." (Kowalska summarized this rather nicely: "I really like this answer: it has multiple meanings and is laconic, like a good line in a poem.")

There were some difficulties with the witnesses for the defense. On the day before the trial, during a house search in Świtoń's apartment, the police confiscated a list of those persons who had told Mrs. Świtoń that they had witnessed the events and would be willing to testify. The police were rounding up those who had thus announced themselves. Nevertheless, several persons were still left, and their testimony corroborated Świtoń's version.

The sentence was pronounced: one year in prison and a fine of 12,000 zlotys. Sentencing was suspended pending appeal, and Świtoń was released from jail. And so the case died.

Świtoń was not only an activist of the Initiating Committees of Free Trade Unions but also of ROPCiO (this word "initiating" was suggested by Kuroń, who convinced the interested parties that this humbler version would make a more serious impression on people who did not like exaggerations and fantasy). Despite the action of KOR in the leaflet campaign, which was prepared with great energy, Świtoń did not join the organization.

The Appeal to Society

In connection with Świtoń's defense, the young KOR people from Cracow, Warsaw, and Wrocław had persistently distributed the "Appeal to Society" (of October 10, 1978). What sort of document was it? We will not cite it here in its entirety. The "Appeal" was designed to play a specific current role, to constitute a program for a single step, without which any broader programs would have to remain forever in the sphere of wishful thinking. It was composed of three chapters: the first described the situation in a manner that allowed each reader to compare this description with his own everyday experience; the second chapter formulated the most general principles of social strategy and summarized the successes that had been achieved already; the third chapter offered suggestions for action on the part of every citizen.

Chapter One: (1) Prices are going up continually, while at the same time, the lack of supplies is constantly becoming worse; increases in the cost of living are particularly difficult for the poorest strata to bear. (2) Hospital care is in a dismal state; there is a shortage of necessary drugs in pharmacies and hospitals, while at the same time, a luxurious hospital is being built in Międzylesie for dignitaries. (3) The housing situation is worsening. (4) The exploitation of workers at their workplaces is increasing; in many industries the working day has been extended to ten or twelve hours. (5) Further social polarization is taking place; the growing poverty of the working masses is accompanied by an increase in privileges for the ruling strata. (6) The crisis in agriculture is deepening, to a large extent because of the discrimination against private family farming. (7) The violation of the rule of law by the police, the sentencing boards, the prosecutor's offices, and the courts is a common practice. (8) Uncontrolled and willful party decisions pose a threat to Polish culture and science; the activities of the censorship and other similar mechanisms have as a side effect the spreading of disinformation among the authorities themselves, which in turn is reflected in social and economic life. Changes that are dangerous and difficult to reverse have thus been introduced into the mentality of the citizens.

Chapter Two: The primary condition for the liberation of the still existing social reserves of initiative and activity is the creation of authentic bodies representative of all social groups. The improvement of the economic and social situation is possible only through cooperation between the authorities and society in general. Constant, general, and organized public pressure is necessary in order to force concessions from the authorities. It is necessary to create social ties that are independent of the official organizational structures (at this point, the already existing independent initiatives are listed).

Chapter Three: (1) Every citizen should demand truth from the authorities and strive to break the state monopoly on information by supporting an independent press and by informing it about the problems in his own milieu. Citizens should also initiate and participate in discussions about the improvements in the state of the Republic. (2) People should organize for the defense of their rights, by electing authentic representatives to existing institutions and by creating new, independent institutions. (3) All collective actions should have an organized character. Participants in the struggle must be defended: "without organization and solidarity we shall achieve nothing." (4) The International Covenant on Civil and Political Rights supplies a legal basis for such activities.

> When Polish society will be able to organize itself to defend its rights, this very fact will mark the beginning of the process of overcoming the social, economic, and political crises. The deepest cause of the crises in our country is the expropriation of rights from the citizens and of sovereignty from the state.

Peasant Committees

Naturally, KOR's work among the peasants began somewhat later than its work among the workers, and it is difficult today to establish the details of this process with precision. As we have already mentioned, peasants from Zbrosza Duża, near Grójec, made a collective appeal in May 1977 in defense of eleven members and associates of KOR. Obviously, KOR did not forgo this opportunity to establish closer contact. It is possible, however, that contacts with two other peasant activists, Janusz Rożek and Jan Kozłowski, had occurred earlier. Stanisław Karpik, the builder of the chapel, was another peasant activist who has already been mentioned. Thus, by late spring or early summer 1977, KOR did have some contacts among peasants, though in the case of Zbrosza Duża they involved mainly the delivery of uncensored publications.

Signs of serious unrest among peasant activists appeared for the first time in connection with a public announcement by the authorities of a proposed system of pension insurance for farmers. On May 16, 1977, twenty-two elder activists of the peasant movement sent a memorandum sharply critical on this issue to the Central Committee of the United Peasant party. They criticized the government project: (1) because it dealt only with retirement pensions and ignored insurance in cases such as illness, maternity allowances, and the like; (2) because it provided for retirement pensions only for the owners of those farms that annually sold at least 15,000 zlotys worth of farm produce to the state; (3) because it discriminated against farmers as compared with other working people, something that should be eliminated at least as far as the lowest level pensions are concerned; and (4) because it proposed that pensions be paid to farmers starting only in 1980, three years after retirement dues would begin to be collected (a measure that would also delay the transfer of farms to younger workers).

The authors of the memorandum noted that the financial means for the realization of their demands could be obtained by halting the enlargement of the State Farms (PGR) sector. In 1976 state expenditures for such farms amounted to 13,740 zlotys per hectare of farm land, or a total of 44 billion zlotys (in addition to another such sum from unpaid loans), while the productivity of land in private farms was 25 percent higher than in state farms. Without exception, the signatories of the memorandum were well-known and distinguished activists from the prewar, wartime, and postwar periods.

As one would expect, the authorities of the United Peasant party answered the memorandum only with repressions. The council of the Elders' Club in the United Peasant party eliminated five of the signatories from its membership list, suspended four signatories for a year, and expelled Tadeusz Nawrocki from the party altogether. The activists who were thus persecuted protested publicly against the repressions. In addition, two of the signers of the memorandum, Michał Jagiełło and Tadeusz Nawrocki, wrote their own analyses of the situation.

A majority of the private farmers in Poland were hostile to the retirement pension proposal. New arguments were added to those used by the elders of the peasant movement. As it happened, this particular issue became a catalyst for the creation of a new social movement.

On July 30, 1978, some two hundred peasants from eighteen villages of the Milejów commune in the province of Lublin held a rally in Ostrówek (actually in a forest clearing near Ostrówek) and formed the first Temporary Peasant Self-Defense Committee. This move resulted from a conflict with the authorities. The peasants, convinced of the unfairness of the retirement law, had refused to pay their dues, and the authorities had responded by sending in bailiffs and Security Service agents. The peasants responded with a one-day warning strike during which they halted deliveries of milk. The committee elected at the founding meeting was authorized to negotiate with the authorities.

The same meeting provided an occasion for raising many of the issues that, taken together, could serve as a sketch of a program for the committee. These issues concerned: (1) village self-government, (2) the need for authentic representation of the political interests of the peasants, (3) the demand for tax reform, (4) the need to revise prices for materials used in agricultural production, which included a huge hidden tax, and (5) the demand to change the retirement pension law. One important part of the resolution was a protest against the introduction to the retirement pension law, which stated in part that the goal of the law was to introduce socialist relations in agriculture.[7] In conclusion, the committee appealed for solidarity from all Polish peasants.

Janusz Rożek became the chairman of the committee. He was a former soldier of the Peasant Battalions from the World War II underground. The statement was also signed by Kazimierz Danieluk, Michał Niessen (a paratrooper in the Red Army during World War II), Edward Paczkowski, and Jan Skoczylas.

Although these activists were closer to ROPCiO than to KOR, they asked those members of KOR who were present at the founding rally to help in editing their founding resolution (one sign of this is evident in the name of the committee).[8] Of course, the police and the Security Service immediately began to attack. They concentrated above all on worker-peasants, threatening to have them fired if they did not pay their dues to the retirement fund. On August 10, the Peasant Self-Defense

Committee threatened to suspend deliveries of farm products if the repressions did not stop, and called on workers to get their food supplies directly from the striking peasants, ignoring the state stores.

The region of the villages involved in the activities of the committee began to resemble a camp under siege. Patrols with dogs appeared on the roads. ZOMO was posted at most road crossings. Members of the committee were subjected to constant surveillance, Security Service visits, detentions (among other things, they were maliciously kept from work during periods of increased need for labor in the fields), and interrogations that also involved threats. The peasants in Emilianów (approximately fifty people) and Marynów (also some fifty people) were interrogated en masse. Local agricultural circles refused to meet their statutory obligations toward those farmers who were committee members. Despite a contract to deliver wheat, Rożek did not get the use of a harvester until his wheat had spoiled, while a promised delivery of building materials was not made to Skoczylas. Finally, two peasants unable to withstand the pressure left the committee. In conformity with long-observed principles, this first crack in the solidarity within the group under attack only intensified the pressure from authorities.

Rożek paid the highest price for his activity. He was beaten up three times, especially on October 31, when he went to Milejów to withdraw money from the Cooperative Bank. He was dragged out of the building by the police and beaten on the head with fists, which led to a partial loss of hearing. A certain Rafalczuk, a commander at a local police precinct, shouted during the beating: "You . . . [vulgarity], you will take your hat off your head when you see me even from far away, and when you see me alone you will kneel and hold your hat to the ground." During the searches in Rożek's house in the village of Górne, his floorboards were torn out and the kitchen stove destroyed. Finally, the Lublin newspaper *Sztandar Ludu* published a report about his farm in which he was slanderously portrayed as a bad farmer, and indirectly threatened with forced expropriation. KOR reacted sharply to these attacks.

The breakdown and resignation of several activists of the Peasant Self-Defense Committee in Lublin Province caused a serious crisis. Conflicts within ROPCiO only intensified it: Janusz Rożek stayed with Czuma's group, while Niessen went with Moczulski. The committee never recovered from this rift, and lost its former significance. We must add, however, that Rożek never laid down his arms, and that his resistance lasted until the critical summer of 1980.

The second Peasant Self-Defense Committee was created on September 9, 1978, in the village of Zbrosza Duża, south of Warsaw. Its founding resolution begins in an unusual manner with a quotation from Piotr Skarga, a renaissance classic of Polish literature and a great Polish preacher: "Nothing more infectious can come to a kingdom than corrupt and unjust laws: for God's revenge will not forgive such kingdoms, and human wrongs do plague them." The committee was formed by representatives from fifteen villages. The resolution is concise:

1. Our region suffered enormous wrongs and repressions during the struggle to build the church in Zbrosza. These wrongs have not been righted to this day. We do not want new wrongs to be added to the old ones.
2. The retirement pension law is unfair and must be changed.
3. The decisions about villages are made without peasant participation, while nothing that concerns us should happen without us.
4. The supply to the villages of food and materials used in farming is in a state of crisis, and harvesters have never been as hungry as they are today.
5. The social situation of the peasant in Poland is getting worse every year. If this continues, a social catastrophe will follow.

During the meeting, it was decided that in the coming period:

1. We will not pay contributions to the retirement fund in its present form, and we will oppose attempts to withhold these dues by administrative means.
2. We will call for better supply to the villages. This representative group has adopted the name of the Peasant Self-Defense Committee of the Grójec Region.

The document carried the signatures of 188 people, and the founding resolution was deposited with Rev. Czesław Sadłowski, the local priest and spiritual leader of the villages participating in the founding of the committee.

KOR maintained especially close and warm relations with this committee. The KOR members and associates always remembered the protest by many peasants from Zbrosza when KOR activists were in jail, and KOR appreciated the importance of this. In Zbrosza, people trusted in KOR's good faith, although efforts to undermine and negate this trust were not lacking.

One might speculate about why the fates of the two Peasant Self-Defense Committees in the Lublin and Grójec regions were so different.

There were probably many reasons for this, but it seems that the most important was that Zbrosza and its environs had been toughened by the difficult struggles for the church, which had taken place only a few years earlier, and which had even cost a human life. In contrast, the peasants from the Milejów area were like draftees who were not yet accustomed to repressions or united into a closely integrated group. It is also significant that the authority of Rev. Sadłowski in Zbrosza was more difficult to question than the authority of Janusz Rożek in Milejów, despite the great merits of this activist.

In September and October 1978, Zbrosza Duża also looked like an encampment under siege. Yet after a month of this repression, when the Peasant Solidarity Committee threatened an agricultural strike, the police and Security Service posts were dismantled. This was followed by a period of successes for the committee, which seemed to indicate that the local authorities might accept the new state of affairs after all, and allow the Peasant Self-Defense Committee to take on the functions of self-government. Thus, the committee won the battle to stop the dairy "cooperative" from deducting retirement pension contributions from the money that it owed peasants for milk. The committee demanded that the construction of a paved road be completed, and work on the road started again (with peasant help and participation). It demanded that the number of stores be increased, and stores were opened in Zbrosza Duża and Kozie Głowy. The peasants criticized the inadequate equipment of the fire department, and fire trucks replaced horse-drawn fire carriages in Zbrosza. This is not a full list of accomplishments. It seemed that relations with the authorities in this region could be arranged reasonably. But when the committee decided to fight against waste and theft by, for example, sending materials to the central authorities about embezzlements in the agricultural circles in Promno and Jasienice, or informing the Highest Chamber of Control about the cement that was going to waste, their hopes turned out to have been unjustified.

A sharp conflict developed when the villages began to be visited by bailiffs attempting to collect pension dues. In answer to an appeal by the Peasant Self-Defense Committee, thirty-three villages in the region refused to deliver milk between December 18 and 20.

The attempt to reconstruct the Peasant Universities is also connected with Zbrosza Duża. Institutions carrying this name played a large role in the history of the Polish countryside. They raised the ideological, cultural, and education level in the villages, and educated an excellent cadre of activists in various areas of the social, professional, and economic life of the peasants. The Peasant Self-Defense Committees, the Committee of the Independent Trade Union of Farmers, and the Podlesie Committee for the Self-Defense of Believers all decided to join in an effort to recreate the Peasant University. The first lectures, for approximately thirty peasant activists from throughout Poland, took place in Warsaw. Lectures were delivered by Anna Godzalanka-Bojarowa,[9] Michał Jagła, Wiesław Kęcik, Adam Michnik, Zbigniew Romaszewski, Czesław Szczerba, and Piotr Typiak. It was decided, however, that Zbrosza Duża would be the permanent location of the Peasant University. Zbrosza Duża again became a village under siege. Patrols were waiting on all roads and even on field paths in order to prevent the lectures from being held. Between March 2 and March 4, seven people were detained and five were turned back to Warsaw. Despite this, the lecture series took place.

The Peasant Self-Defense Committee of the Grójec region paid much attention to the economic issues in its immediate environment. Grójec is an area of orchards. The committee made an analysis of the economic situation of the fruit growers. It turned out that while apples were unavailable in the cities, they lay rotting in peasant storage rooms because the purchasing center would not buy them. A bribe was required for even the best varieties to be accepted by the purchasing center, while the retail trade was selling fruit for twice the purchase price. The analysis ended with an appeal to workplaces and to individual citizens: "Come to us and take the fruit before it rots. You can buy apples from us for the price established by the purchasing center." Since the situation with purchasing did not improve, the committee decided to stage a spectacular demonstration. On May 20, 1979, farmers from the Zbrosza area blocked traffic on the Cracow and Katowice roads for several hours by dumping out tons of apples, most already rotten.

The Committee of the Independent Trade Union of Farmers was founded on September 10. Its center was in the village of Lisów, near Białobrzegi, and its associates included Henryk Bąk, a peasant activist and editor of the periodical *Postęp* (*Progress*), Jan Kozłowski, Edward Koleja, and others.

The Peasant Self-Defense Committee of the Rzeszów region was formed on November 12 in the village of Łowisko. Here the immediate impulse was to resist an attempt to expropriate farms in order to create grazing land for a state calf farm. The peasants who opposed expropriation were ruthlessly persecuted. The committee immediately began to work to convert the empty Rural Teachers' House into a medical clinic (the nearest doctor was eight kilometers away), and to build a church. One of the repressions used against the committee was the malicious idea of Józef Czubaty, administrative head of the Kamień commune, where Łowisko was located. Pretending that it was lying fallow, Czubaty ordered that twenty acres of an osier plantation belonging to one of the members of the committee be plowed under. The losses approximated 150,000 zlotys, not counting the cost of plowing. Despite complaints, Czubata was not punished in any way for this act.

On March 15 peasants from the Wola Żarczycka village near Leżajsko announced an extensive eight-point "Statement" in which they addressed the most important problems in their village; without founding their own committee, they expressed their solidarity with the committee of the Rzeszów region.

On November 26 the residents of six villages near Siedlce formed the peasant Committee for the Self-Defense of Believers in Opole Stare. The direct reason for this was the order to destroy the newly-built chapel in the courtyard of Stanisław Karpik's farm. Through its *Communiqués*, the new committee concentrated its attention on the struggle for the right to maintain places of collective prayer (for example in Terespol, Dębowa Kłoda, and Dziewule), but it did not ignore other social issues important to the region. Karpik was no longer alone in his struggle. A short time later, his house and the chapel became an important center for the activities of the Oases and of students from the academic ministry in Podlesie.

A separate committee was not formed in Bieszczady, but KOR was asked to help there. The basic problem for peasants from the Arłamowo area was being in the neighborhood of a large government hunting grounds. A huge triangle bordering the Polish-Soviet frontier, it was surrounded by a fence 120 kilometers long. The area measured thousands of hectares. The fence was not adequately maintained, and herds of animals, including boars, bears, deer, and bison, trampled the crops. Hordes of police, no less numerous, watched to make sure that no one harmed the animals. The payment of compensation for lost harvests—in any event disproportionately low compared with the losses—took years to obtain. The peasants were not allowed to chase the animals or to use dogs to protect their crops. This situation brought to mind historical descriptions of relations in prerevolutionary, feudal France.

The peasants who had settled in Bieszczady in the late sixties, who had cleared the land and built their houses, often taking out large loans, began thinking about leaving this area. In 1978 the harvest was almost entirely destroyed, so that the peasants decided to leave part of the land fallow. In the spring of 1978, 180 peasants wrote to Gierek asking him to intervene. The Ministry of Forestry and of the Timber Industry answered that there were increasing numbers of animals in the country and that nothing could be done about this. So the peasants asked KOR for help. Wiesław Kęcik went to Bieszczady on November 5. During the next visit, on December 3, Kęcik and Rayzacher were detained for forty-eight hours and sentenced to pay fines of 4,000 zlotys. From then on, until it was replaced by Solidarity, KOR stubbornly returned to the case of Arłamowo.

Late in the spring of 1978, the residents of the village of Jodłowo in the province of Cracow won a battle to elect the village administrator they wanted, counting the votes publicly. They insisted on true pre-electoral meetings, with authentic speeches in which the local administration offices were criticized, a program for village development was formulated, and so on. Uncensored leaflets constituted another element of this electoral struggle.

In Kluszkowce village near Czorsztyn, organized peasants selected a representative body to negotiate the payment of compensations which they said were due in connection with preparatory work for the construction of a dam on the Dunajec River. They made further construction work impossible unless the compensation were paid.

Each of these successes was very valuable from the point of view of social education. The news about each of them would carry far, repeated by *Placówka, Gospodarz,* the *KOR Communiqués,* the *Information Bulletin,* and other independent periodicals. A new model of social struggle for the interests of the countryside was being created in this manner.

Other initiatives of peasant activists were also multiplying. One might mention here above all the statement of thirty-two activists on the fiftieth anniversary of the creation of the peasant youth organization Wici. The signatories of this document emphasized the fact that the liquidation of Wici in 1948 had taken place against the will of its members, and that the single existing youth organization could not pretend to represent the entire young generation. This statement was signed by Prof. Andrzej Burda, Franciszek Kamiński (who was commander-in-chief of the Peasant Battalions during the war), Wiktor Kulerski, and Maria Maniakówna (a member of the General Staff of the Peasant Battalions), among others. The statement of sixty-four peasant activists from the provinces of Warsaw and Rzeszow demanding changes in the retirement pension law for individual farmers also had a one-time-only character. The statement of the Peasant Self-Defense Committee of the Lublin region, dated September 4, 1978, contains a description of how the police used force to remove Gadzalanka-Bojarowa from Rożek's house, to which she had come in connection with this statement.

Periodicals of the independent peasant movement also began appearing. By October 1978, the periodical *Independent Peasant Movement* was being published in Zbrosza Duża. The first issue of *Placówka* in March 1979 resembled the *Information Bulletin* in its format. The editorial board was composed both of activists of the peasant committees (Jerzy Górski and Zdzisław Ostatek from the Grójec Region Committee,[10] and Jan Kozłowski from the Temporary Committee of the Independent Trade Unions of Farmers) and of KOR activists who chose the villages as their area of work (Józef Baran, Wiesław Kęcik, and Edward Koleja). The title of this periodical was of course taken from the novel by Bolesław Prus, and according to its creators and friends, this title was perfectly suited to the idea around which the peasant movement was organized: the defense of family farming.

The strength of *Placówka* came from the fact that among the peasant-editors there were a number of people with genuine journalistic talent. Jan Kozłowski had been for years a regional correspondent of *Gromada Rolnika Polskiego* (*The Commune of the Polish Farmer*). During the period of his collaboration with *Placówka*, Kozłowski sent the editors of *Gromada* a letter-article about the need to reconstruct a peasant self-government. *Gromada* published this very well-written text together with a positive commentary from the editors. And a fracas began. What *Gromada* had not noticed was noticed by the Central Committee: that the author of the article about peasant self-government was also a co-editor of *Placówka*. Someone in *Gromada* was demoted; someone else received a reprimand. The second issue of *Placówka* carried two very interesting articles written by Jerzy Górski and Stanisław Karpik, in which they described the histories of their committees.

In view of these new facts testifying to the formation of an independent peasant movement, it would have seemed that the formation of the Center for Peasant Thought on June 2, 1979, would be an event of very basic significance.[11] KSS "KOR" was informed about the beginning of the work of this center in a letter from Gadzalanka-Bojarowa and Jagła. The *Statement* of the center is without doubt a serious programmatic document. It was signed by twenty-two peasant activists from various generations. No doubt Michał Jagła played the most important role in the center. A former editor of *Społem* and *Wici*, deputy chairman of Wici after the war and a deputy to the National Council (KRN), Jagła was an experienced activist with large political ambition. Seven members of the editorial board of *Placówka* constituted a numerous group within the center. Two ROPCiO participants and editors of *Gospodarz*, Studziński and Typiak, also joined the center. Rożek's name also appears among the signatories.

Despite great expectations, the center did not live up to its promise. Although it brought together serious and accomplished activists, they never formed any programmatic working groups or became involved in any broader actions. A short time later, the center ceased to exist.

Thugs Against Education

The Flying University, sponsored by the Society for Scientific Courses, began the second year of its activities in October 1978. There was much hope that the position of the Church, as expressed by Primate Wyszyński, who regarded the educational activity as socially valuable, would prevent further Security Service repressions. And indeed, thanks to the good will of Cardinal Wojtyła, the Church made available some lecture halls for the use of the university in Cracow. This meant more than providing a place to meet; it also guaranteed security for teachers and students.

The authorities of the Church of St. Martin in Warsaw warmly welcomed a plan to hold the main TKN lecture series, devoted to the subject of tradition, in the church. As a lecture hall, the church guaranteed seriousness and peace, not to mention better conditions than the usual cramped apartments. Above all, however, this was an offer of asylum for the persecuted.

The reader is already familiar with the role that Laski and the Franciscan Sisters, Servants of the Cross, and their Warsaw branch (the convent on Piwna Street and the Church of St. Martin) have played in the Polish Church, in Polish culture, and in expressing a particular form of ecumenism which has united both believers and nonbelievers in common work for others, first in the interwar period, and then during and after the war. Symbolically, there was no more appropriate place for the TKN lectures. After all, TKN itself was an expression of a special kind of ecumenism: it was a meeting-place for intellectuals of various worldviews who shared a common concern about the future of Polish culture, national self-awareness, and independent thought. These intentions were expressed clearly and forcefully in the official programmatic declaration of TKN, which was published at the beginning of the academic year and widely distributed under the title, "Why Tradition?" The basic series of lectures (to be delivered by a number of lecturers) was also entitled "Tradition."

The members of TKN were convinced that an understanding and conscious use of tradition were necessary for the rebuilding of social life in Poland. This was especially true in a situation where even the Communist party did not respect its own history and legacy, a disrespect expressed in various ways, ranging from changes in the traditional names of institutions to changes in school and university curricula.[12] As a result, entire generations have grown up in the Polish People's Republic without knowing the history of their own country. Not only left-wing but right-wing and centrist political and social currents also had difficulties drawing upon their own traditions. Time effaced the traces, while individual carriers of the national memory and participants in the nation's history were dying out. Those activists of KOR sympathetic to the tradition of the Polish Socialist party were surprised to discover that even the memory of the PPS had died out in old bastions of Polish socialism such as Łódź, Radom, or Sosnowiec. The same thing applied to all other currents of social life during the interwar period. Without the reconstruction of intergenerational communication in human consciousness, the reconstruction of an authentic social life would be very difficult indeed.

Despite the fact that it was not certain until the end whether it would prove possible, the inaugural lecture by the Rev. Dr. Bronisław Dembowski (rector of the Church of St. Martin) on the subject of the social encyclicals of Popes Leo XIII and Pius XI was held on November 13, 1978, in the convent of the Franciscan Sisters. Unfortunately this was the last lecture to be held there, to the regret not only of TKN but also of the Franciscan Sisters and of Dembowski.

The attack on TKN began in January 1979, although the tactic of sending in "discussants" who were to "resist the enemy" had begun earlier. Although they were aggressive, not entirely polite, and had a tendency to digress from the topic of the lecture, these persons were nevertheless discussants. Jerzy Jedlicki, for example, whose lecture was often visited in this manner, was even pleased with this fact, since the young people, some of whom had some knowledge about the subject, introduced a polemical element. But this idyll did not last for long.

On January 9 twelve unknown persons tried to prevent Jacek Kuroń from lecturing on social pedagogy in his own apartment. After screams and insults, it was possible to throw them out, and the lecture did take place. The situation was similar during the lecture of Tomasz Burek, except that the discussants who had been asked to leave then made a disturbance on the staircase. Something more happened on January 24: approximately 120 (!) individuals invaded Kuroń's apartment and, filling all the available space, they screamed and brawled for three hours. They were predicting "TKN's funeral." On January 26, Kuroń's lecture was called off. In spite of this, four unknown people appeared in his apartment and proposed a discussion. Several minutes later, a group of over fifty individuals began a siege of his apartment. They kicked in the door, and when Kuroń tried to close it he was bitten on the hand. This situation lasted for approximately two hours, until the four discussants quieted down the attackers as they were leaving the apartment. On March 7, Kuroń's apartment was again under siege; students Mieczysław Książczak and Jarema Dubiel were beaten up; and Kuroń was thrown down the stairs. The electricity in his apartment was cut off for several hours. On March 14, Adam Michnik, who was to be the lecturer, was beaten up, together with Konrad Bieliński and a student, Jan Cywiński—4,000 zlotys were stolen from Bieliński's bag.

The most serious attack occurred on March 21. The lecture scheduled to take place in Kuroń's apartment had been called off because of the serious illness of Kuroń's father, who was suffering from a heart attack. A note to this effect was posted on the door. Despite this fact, goons pounded on the door, but it was not opened. The intruders caught Henryk Wujec, who was on his way to Kuroń's apartment. They beat his head against the door until he lost consciousness.[13] A doctor's examination, conducted later, established that the loss of consciousness was caused by a concussion. When Jacek Kuroń opened the door to help his friend, the goon squad entered his apartment.

The attackers seemed to be professional. They knew how to fight and knew exactly what effects to expect from each blow. Those designated to do the dirty work were clearly recognizable by their black leather gloves. They hit on order and stopped on command. Grażyna Kuroń was repeatedly hit with karate blows on both arms twisted behind her back. She was then lifted up by her neck. At this moment, one of the individuals directing the action intervened. Maciej, the son of Jacek and Grażyna Kuroń, a high school senior, was also beaten; the result was a concussion.

The beatings of Konrad Bieliński, Seweryn Blumsztajn, Wojciech Malicki, and Adam Michnik had somewhat less dangerous effects on their life and health. The leaders of the attack did not, however, let their subordinates touch Jacek Kuroń. They only blocked his way whenever he tried to help anyone. Perhaps they were waiting for him to start hitting back. Grażyna Kuroń appealed to two women accompanying the intruders to leave her apartment, if only because of her sick father-in-law. She heard in answer, "I did not come here to talk."

Throughout this entire time, Jacek Kuroń was appealing to the goons to get out of the apartment, since his father was suffering a heart attack, and they also might one day have someone close to them who might be sick. For the first time, friends saw this hard man almost breaking down— he could not even call an ambulance, since the intruders did not allow him to use his phone. Only after a long while did they allow him to call the emergency number.

During this entire time, the house was surrounded by police cars. The policemen were not reacting to interventions by the neighbors, who asked that the attack be stopped. The district police precinct answered telephone calls with claims that they already knew and that they had already tried to intervene. There are strong indications that the ambulance was also detained by the police, so that it arrived several hours after the last goons had left the apartment. But there is no proof of this. Finally, Henryk Kuroń, Jacek's father, was taken to the hospital in an ambulance.

Who were the attackers? Witnesses of successive attacks recognized known security functionaries among them, but they did not constitute the main body of these goon squads. Several persons had been identified by name even before the attack of March 21. These were activists of the Socialist Union of Polish Students. But only after the attack on Kuroń's apartment was there an attempt to gather more precise information about the members of the goon squads. Students of the Academy of Physical Education (AWF) were the biggest help in identifying the attackers, since it turned out that the members of the squad—especially of the group that invaded Kuroń's apartment on March 21—were members of the Socialist Union of Polish Students specializing in karate, wrestling, weight lifting, and boxing. The first to be recognized were Jerzy Folcik and Tadeusz Kulmacz, who were also the ones who hit the hardest.

It seems worthwhile to fix in public memory the names of the identified attackers: Jacek Balaun (AWF, boxer); Stanisław Bienia (AWF, weight lifter); Zdzisław Brzowski (Brzozowski? AWF, wrestler, goalie in Relaks); Leszek Drewniak (AWF, instructor in karate); Zbigniew Fiks (AWF, goalie in Relaks); Jerzy Folcik (AWF, chairman of the Socialist Union of Polish

Students at AWF); Andrzej Guziała (alumnus of the Main School of Planning and Statistics, and secretary of the Warsaw Council of the Federation of Socialist Unions of Polish Youth); Andrzej Kowalczyk (Warsaw University, economist, secretary of the Warsaw Council of the Socialist Union of Polish Students); Tadeusz Kulmacz (AWF, weight lifter, goalie in Relaks); Andrzej Łapiński (AWF, weight lifter); Andrzej Parzęcki (AWF, karate); Czesław Pisarkiewicz (Warsaw University); Marek Rudziński (Warsaw University, economy); Tomasz Sadowski (Warsaw University, economy, vice-chairman for ideology and education of the University Council of the Socialist Union of Polish Students); Jerzy Szczepaczyński (graduate in sociology); Ireneusz Tondera (Warsaw University, history); Wiesław Witrony (either Main School of Planning and Statistics or Warsaw University, economy). This is obviously a small percentage of the participants in the goon squads.[14]

The squads were organized by the Provincial Council of the Socialist Union of Polish Students, with the knowledge, or at the order of, Dr. Krzysztof Kruszewski, a secretary of the Warsaw Committee of PUWP. In April 1979, Aniela Steinsbergowa, a member of KOR's Helsinki Commission, together with a record keeper, Krystyna Iwaszkiewicz, took the depositions of eight witnesses to these events. The documentation concerning the activities of the goon squads was published in the *Madrid Report* of 1980.

Kuroń's observations about the ideology represented by the activists of these "socialist youth" (which were published under the title "Who Came to My House?" in *Information Bulletin* No. 2/28, pp. 33–34) are interesting in this context:

> So what is this world-view? Above all—it is Polish, because "we are Poles," "we love Poland," "we feel Polish." The words "Poland," "Polish," "Poles" occurred so often during the hours of screaming and shouting that when at one point I began to count while several patriots were shouting something at the same time, I could not keep up. What was to follow from this "Polishness," apart from the attacks on my apartment? If one were to consider the number of statements, what follows is hatred above all. "I hate Germans," one of the more active discussants would shout, "after what they did to us. . . . Hatred for Germans in general . . . was declared in a variety of ways and very often. Of course, this was mentioned above all in the context of hatred of me as a traitor to the motherland. . . . "My grandfather, during the war," one of them confessed, "shot seven traitors like you, Mr. Kuroń. I would shoot you too, but it is not allowed. . . . " One plump girl sitting on top of my table would shout once in a while, "I could tear him to pieces"—referring

to me, of course. Aggression was expressed by shouts, screams, insults, forcible intrusions into the apartment, kicking in the door, banging on the windows, and destruction of the stairwell. . . .

The subject of Jews was not missing either. Once in a while this topic would be alluded to, for example, either by referring to me as Isaac Kuroń, or picked up directly, for example by explaining my bad character by my "Jewish blood" (literally). Each time, the experts on the subject would straighten things out: "from this point of view, Mr. Kuroń is pure" (literally). Now I understand that a "true Pole" is racially pure, and feels and loves Poland; that is, he hates the Germans, the Jews, and traitors to the motherland, that is, people who have something in common with Germans or Jews.

How did the authorities respond to this attack? We have already mentioned the immediate attitude of the police to the case. Perhaps even more telling is the response of the Regional Prosecutor's Office in Warsaw-Żoliborz to a complaint about the crime filed on April 10, 1979, by the attorney Siła-Nowicki. On July 12, 1980, that is, one year and three months after the attack, deputy prosecutor Dariusz Czamarski sent a note to Siła-Nowicki and to the four wronged parties: Wujec, Kuroń, Folcik (!), and Fiks (!) informing them that the investigation had been dropped. This was a peculiar document, testifying both to lawlessness and to arrogance. In it the prosecutor stated that as some persons were entering Kuroń's apartment, others also wanted to enter, resulting in mutual pushing and elbowing. As a consequence, Wujec suffered "small swelling and blackening of his right eye and abrasion of the skin on his face and head, as well as a scratch on his right hand." In reality Wujec had suffered a concussion, after which the doctor gave him a twelve-day sick leave, recommending complete bed rest. The prosecutor's letter said that it was not possible to asscertain who had hit him, since Folcik and Kulmacz, whom he accused, denied the charges. Although Maciej Kuroń had stated in his deposition that while engaged in a tussle he struck random blows, it was impossible to establish whether Wujec had suffered his injuries because of this (!). Since Jacek Kuroń and his friends were acting against the law, and since Kuroń allowed some people to enter his apartment and prevented others from doing so, he was morally responsible for the incident. In light of this document one should be grateful to the prosecutor that he did not accuse Maciej Kuroń of causing Wujec's concussion, and vice versa.

The party authorities directly admitted organizing the goon squads. Their patron, Kruszewski, stated on May 4 during a meeting with party activists on the faculties of Warsaw institutions of higher learning that on the advice of its member Stefan Amsterdamski, TKN had decided to provoke a fight in order to let itself be beaten. During the meeting, Kruszewski complained that the explanatory work in colleges was not functioning properly: "I am personally displeased with the comrades from the colleges for acquiescing in the aura of disapproval created around those who risked their own skin for the party." The *Information Bulletin of the Warsaw University Committee of PUWP* also admitted that the goon squads organized in order to prevent the lectures of the Flying University were formed by the Warsaw Council of the Federation of the Socialist Union of Polish Youth.

The Warsaw University Council concocted its own version of the events in Kuroń's apartment, answering in this manner a leaflet of the SKS. According to the council, Kuroń and his friends had dragged the activists who had come to hear the lecture into the apartment and then beaten them up, with the result that others who had come with them could not restrain themselves. A similar version of events was presented by *Relacjonista,* published by the Information and Propaganda Commission of the School Council of the Socialist Union of Polish Students and the Main School of Planning and Statistics. It emphasized Wujec, in his role as the person most active in beating up the karate experts who had come to hear the lecture on social pedagogy.

An extremely original version of these events was presented in a letter addressed to the chairman of the Polish Academy of Sciences, Professor Witold Nowacki, by Jerzy Bolesławski, the chairman of the Warsaw Council of the Federation of Socialist Unions of Youth, and by the vice-chairman and secretary of this council. According to this letter, the lecturers Kuroń and Michnik began provoking brawls at their successive lectures, first verbally and then also physically. A goon squad headed by Wujec, who was not interested in the lecture or in the discussion, was disturbing and insulting members of the Socialist Union of Polish Students and beating them up. The authors of the letter asked the chairman of PAN for help in defending the good name of colleagues, the purity of whose actions and intentions could not prevent a carefully and effectively prepared campaign of lies and "a brutal and physical assault on them."

On April 28, 1979, during a festive celebration of May Day that was broadcast on television, Edward Gierek awarded a party card to Jerzy Folcik. Folcik was also delegated to thank the First Secretary in the name of AWF students who had been admitted to the party. It is difficult to judge whether Gierek was fully aware of the symbolic importance of this gesture, or whether he knew to whom he was presenting the party card—but it is certain that someone overdid it somewhere.

In the June 1979 *Information Bulletin* (No. 4/30, p. 46) appears the following notice:

> On May 18 and 19, 1979, in Jachranka on Zalew Zegrzyński, there was a meeting of activists of the Socialist Union of Polish Students (about 100 people), mostly students from Warsaw who had participated in the actions of goon squads against TKN. The prorectors for student affairs from Warsaw institutions of higher learning, together with Professor Jarema Maciszewski, the director of the Science Department of the Central Committee of PUWP, participated in the meeting, which ended with a libation.

Various groups of academics reacted to the goon squad action of March 21. For example, seventy-nine students of the History Department at Warsaw University signed a statement condemning the attackers from SZSP (two people from the department had participated in the squads). The activity of the squads was condemned by the Faculty Councils of the History Department and the Biology Department at Warsaw University, by a plenary meeting of the Institute Council of the Socialist Union of Polish Students, and by a plenary meeting of the Club of Catholic Intelligentsia and the Council of the Polish Philosophical Association.

On May 2, that is, after Gierek had presented Folcik with a party card, the Council of the Socialist Union of Polish Students in the Sociology Department posted a notice on the bulletin board citing a statement by the chairman of the University Council of SZSP, Szamałko, that ended with the words: "Provoking such events was in the interest neither of the University Council nor of the students." This notice also asserted that because "radical tendencies were growing among the group of activists from Warsaw youth . . . who participated in the discussions during the lectures of TKN . . . the board of the University Council had ceased late in February to direct university activists of the SZSP to these lectures. . . . Those members of the SZSP at the university who were present at the lecture [!] of March 21 were there without the approval, but also without the censure of the University Council."

As late as May 21, an SZSP goon squad prevented Prof. Adam Kersten from lecturing on "The Image of History in Polish Textbooks." After this lecture had been interrupted, Andrzej Celiński (a secretary of TKN and a member of KSS "KOR") was attacked, and his fingers were twisted in order to take away a cassette on which the brawl was recorded.

The action of the goon squads seriously disturbed TKN's activities. Some members of the society associated with KSS "KOR" suggested that the public lectures be continued, and offered their own apartments for this purpose. The idea was to break the terrorist action by stubbornness. There was also an expectation that the world publicity surrounding the events of March 21 would prevent a repetition of such brutality. The TKN authorities chose a different solution: it was decided that for the following academic year, TKN would adopt a method of closed seminar groups for which individuals would have to sign up. The locations and dates of these lectures would no longer be made public.

On April 3, Jacek Kuroń and Adam Michnik informed the Program Commission of TKN that in accordance with the suggestion of the society, they had decided to suspend their lectures.

During the period of the first attacks against TKN, Sten Johansson, a professor of sociology at the University of Stockholm and a chief theoretician and idealogue of the Social Democratic Party in Sweden, had come to Poland at the invitation of TKN. Needless to say, no goon squad interrupted his lecture about the program of the Swedish Labor Fund.

While the activists of the Socialist Union of Polish Students were beginning their attacks on TKN, NOWa published the first book in its series of the Scholarly Papers of TKN, *The Language of Propaganda*. TKN decided to organize systematically a variety of colloquia of specialists on socially important topics in the humanities and social sciences, and then to publish them. From then on, the publishing activity of TKN began to fill in the gaps in scholarly publications.

The Student Movement and the Struggle for the Autonomy of the Universities

The student movement continued to be an important factor in the growing national resistance, even though it did not assume mass dimensions, as its founders had hoped. The barriers of fear and inertia turned out to be just as difficult to overcome in this social group as in the others. Perhaps this dilemma was aggravated by the fact that the initiators and leaders of the student movement were not able to put in the forefront of their activities specific issues of immediate concern to students, and were unable to assume a role similar to that of a labor union. Nonetheless, the Student Solidarity Committees had quite a numerous and dynamic group of activists, who were visible in academic life. It seems that during this period, the Cracow and Wrocław Student Solidarity committees were the truly active ones, but since the only documents available at this moment are ephemeral publications, both hard to find and sought after by the police, all statements on this subject must be regarded as provisional.

The *Information Bulletin* of October and November 1978 (No. 25) carries information about the detention of some dozen people and of six house searches among the Poznań SKS activists in connection with the beginning of the official Sixth Festival of Student Culture in the Polish People's Republic. During the festival, the SKS distributed leaflets informing the participants that the organizers had not allowed a performance by Małgorzata Bratek, a student singer, and about reprisals against the Poznań students. Is it possible the Poznań SKS did nothing else for many months? Probably not. It must have had its everyday existence, but the author finds it difficult to reconstruct when its documents are missing.

The Cracow SKS began the 1978/79 academic year with several informational leaflet actions. In the course of the year it also published seven issues of a periodical called *Sygnał*. The Wrocław SKS began the academic year with a protest against the expulsion of two activists, Marek Adamkiewicz and Marek Rospond.

In January, a falsified bulletin of the Wrocław SKS, ridiculing and insulting one of its activists, Leszek Budrewicz, was distributed at Wrocław University. Among the distributors were not only "unknown perpetrators" but also Dr. Marek Cetwiński. The students whose names appeared as signatories on the falsified bulletin (Wiktor Grotowicz, Jacek Malec, Renata Otolińska, and Mariusz Wilk) issued a statement in which they (falsely, as it turned out), accused another faculty member of distributing the falsified bulletin. Despite their public apology for this mistake, disciplinary proceedings were initiated against them; and on the order of K. Fiedor, the prorector for educational affairs, their rights as students were suspended illegally even before the Disciplinary Commission had made its decision, making it impossible for them to take their fall semester exams. The Disciplinary Commission, composed of Dr. Z. Kegel, Dr. Świda-Łapieszka, and J. Zalewski, a fourth-year student in the Department of Political Science, decided to suspend them for half a year. The accused were not allowed to be represented. During the proceedings it was not only confirmed that Dr. Cetwiński had distributed the falsified bulletin but what is more, it turned out that the bulletin was also distributed by prorector Fiedor.

On June 3, thirteen students from Wrocław colleges questioned the honesty of the Disciplinary Commission in a public statement. On June 18, all university students from this group had their student rights suspended. In the meantime, a new forgery appeared at Wrocław University. Professor Lipiński defended the students in a letter to the rector of Wrocław University, and on July 5, TKN issued a statement in which it accused the authorities of Wrocław University of participating in a planned provocation. The five activists were allowed to return to the university in October 1979.

Finally, we must mention the statement of KSS "KOR" concerning the announced plan to change the statutes of Warsaw University. After citing the crucial formulations in the project, KSS "KOR" asserted:

> The planned extension of the powers of the minister and rector [elsewhere in the Statement it had been pointed out that the rector was to be nominated by the minister without the advice of the University Senate] signifies the liquidation of the remnants of autonomy and self-government at the University. The faculty and students will be subject to the legalized, arbitrary, and totally uncontrolled omnipotence of PUWP and of the rector nominated by the party. . . . The quality of higher education in Poland has always depended on tolerance and pluralism, which were the pride of Polish science and culture. The periods when these values faded out were the black pages in the history of Polish institutions of higher learning. This was always caused either by external enemies or by the pressures of antidemocratic movements.

The statement recalled the protest action of Polish professors against the proposed law on higher education of 1933:

> Today the threat to Polish science is incomparably greater. The passivity of scholarly groups toward the introduction of the proposed changes in the statutes of Warsaw University would constitute unacceptable behavior harmful to the whole of society.

Here one should also mention a fact that sheds a grim light on the postulate of the autonomy of science in Poland. This concerns the statements made by two members of KOR, Edward Lipiński and Jan Kielanowski, who were also members of PAN, during a session of the General Meeting of the Polish Academy of Sciences concerning a resolution to eliminate preventive censorship. *Information Bulletin* No. 4 (30) of May/June 1979 published two reports of this meeting written by these professors. In his report, Kielanowski presented the course of the meeting in a subtly ironic manner.

A week before the session, Lipiński and Kielanowski had discussed with each other what they wanted to say in the course of the meeting, and divided up their tasks. Since Kielanowski was to present a draft resolution against censorship to the assembled PAN members, he read a sketch of his speech to Lipiński. Reversing the agreed upon order of appearance Lipiński came first to the rostrum. He spoke about devastating effects of social sciences resulting from lack of honesty, presented the issue of the SZSP goon squads and the attacks against TKN, and protested against the police functions taken over by the Academy (preventing persecuted scholars from delivering lectures). He did not allow his speech to be interrupted, despite attempts by the chairman of PAN, Prof. Witold Nowacki.

After Lipiński's speech, Nowacki came to the podium. To everyone's surprise he read a response from a piece of paper which he took from his pocket, although there had been no time to write such a response. What was worse, his reply referred not to the statement of Lipiński, but to Kielanowski's speech (!). The situation was clear enough: the chairman of the Polish Academy of Sciences was either acquainted with Kielanowski's text in advance (who did the bugging? who read the contents of the discussion between Lipiński and Kielanowski to Nowacki?), or he had received "his" text to read from others (from where? the Central Committee? the Security Service?). *Ambo meliores.*

The polemics were pitiful. It is simply astonishing to what extent such situations and the desire to "refute" paralyzes otherwise intelligent people. Prof. Jan Szczepański stated that a modern state could not do without preventive censorship, as if he did not know that modern countries, if they are not totalitarian, manage quite well without such an institution, or as if he believed that the censorship itself was an indication of modernity.[15] At the same time, Prof. Szczepan Pieniążek came out with the call that "Dirty laundry should be washed at home!" and used this argument against TKN members who published critical articles about Polish matters in foreign journals. Kielanowski commented on this speech:

> [Pieniążek] advocates even the most brutal discussion at home, but without raising such issues abroad. There was no occasion to point out to him that with this statement—perhaps against his will—Professor Pieniążek was expressing his support for the idea of TKN and advocating the elimination of censorship.

But perhaps the saddest thing about this day was the fact that the resolution to eliminate preventive censorship was supported by only five scientists, among them the two members of KSS "KOR." Many others (but still a clear minority) abstained from voting. These were probably scholars who could not decide whether their dirty laundry should be washed at all.

The Sixtieth Anniversary of Independence

The sixtieth anniversary of Poland's regaining of independence after World War I was celebrated on November 11, 1978. KSS "KOR" decided to honor this occasion by publishing a special statement that made more precise the position of KOR on such fundamental questions as those of independence, and how to evaluate the period of independence of the Polish Commonwealth. A commission composed of Ficowski, Lipski, and Michnik was delegated to prepare a draft of this statement, which would be important for KOR's history. This draft was then discussed by the entire committee. It seems that no other statement of KOR was a creation of the entire committee to the same extent. Many amendments were introduced.

The text of the statement was distributed before and after a special Mass celebrated in St. John's Cathedral in Warsaw, and in other cities. Two thousand copies were distributed in Warsaw on this day. Before the Mass, those senior members of KOR who were healthy enough to do so participated in handing out the statement (Cohn, Kielanowski, Lipiński, Pajdak, Steinsbergowa, and Szczypiorski). This was the single such occasion in the history of KOR.

On November 10 a tablet honoring the memory of Józef Piłsudski was unveiled in St. Alexander's Church in Warsaw; and on November 11 a tablet honoring the memory of the commanders of the Home Army, Stefan Rowecki ("Grot") and Leopold Okulicki ("Niedźwiadek"), was unveiled in St. Jacek's Church. On the evening of November 11 a Holy Mass was celebrated in the cathedral by Bishop Bronisław Dąbrowski. A huge crowd filled the cathedral, the neighboring church of the Jesuit Order, and all of Świętojańska Street, as well as the neighborhood of Castle Square all the way to the market in the Old Town. Broadcast by megaphone, the Mass was heard throughout the entire area.

On the initiative of ROPCiO, after the Mass the crowds proceeded in the direction of the Tomb of the Unknown Soldier, where the first patriotic demonstration in many years took place. Thousands of people participated. National songs were performed and slogans chanted (among others, a cheer in honor of KOR was initiated by Andrzej Czuma, a leader of ROPCiO). As a committee, KSS "KOR" did not help to organize or participate in the demonstration at the Tomb of the Unknown Soldier, though KOR members and associates were present there. KOR always feared taking people to the streets in a situation in which the possibility of having a sufficiently large number of order guards was minimal. But the police did not intervene, and a beautiful and solemn celebration remained in the memory of the citizens of Warsaw.

Special Masses ordered collectively or individually were held in many places in Poland on November 10 and 11. In Gdańsk, the Security Service and the police detained persons posting leaflets containing information about special church services. Several house searches were conducted, and on November 11 a police trap was set in the apartment of Mariusz Muskat, which prevented a fairly large number of activists from participating in the Mass. Only Borusewicz managed to escape.[16]

Patriotic ceremonies constituted a special and distinct area of oppositional activity, particularly for ROPCiO. They took place in a solemn atmosphere, part religious and part patriotic, and in a conjunction typical of Polish culture they provided an opportunity for the expression of feelings that were usually stifled. KOR participated only in the most important of these ceremonies (this refers to KOR as an organization, not to its individual activists).

I think that these ceremonies must be seen in a positive light, although they awakened justified fears because of their tendency to strengthen a certain psychosocial model: the participants in such demonstrations often felt that by making an appearance they had fulfilled their patriotic and social duty, and had done all they were expected to do. In fact, however, the demonstrations almost automatically gave vent to their emotions and stereotypical experiences, which rarely resulted in action. In spite of this fact, the ceremonies played a positive role.

For Your Freedom and Ours

The topic of friendship with other nations and social groups fighting for human and civil rights throughout the Soviet empire was present during the entire history of KOR. The period in question was particularly lively in this respect. Never, neither before nor later, did these issues play such a significant role. An awareness of a common fate shared with other nations of the empire was one aspect of the political sensitivity of KOR activists, especially of those activists for whom links with dissident groups in other East European countries and in Russia stirred an impulse to action.

The term *sovietization,* which had a long career in the vocabulary of the opposition, does not refer to the threat that the national identity of one nation will be lost in favor of another. Sovietization threatens the loss of Russian identity as well, despite the fact that in the USSR in particular, Russification is one of the aspects of sovietization (one "soviet nation" led by one party would no doubt be more united if all citizens were to have Russian as their mother tongue). Nationalistic attitudes were rare among the activists of KOR, and where they did occur they were rather moderate. Thus, anti-Russian feelings were rarer than elsewhere. A Russian dissident was more than an ally for a member of KOR; to a large degree he was almost one of us.

Andrei Sakharov is a symbol of the struggle of the best representatives of the Russian nation for human rights. His committee was one of the sources of inspiration for KOR.

KSS "KOR" Communiqué No. 26/27 of January 1979 begins with a concise statement:

> On January 20 and 21, 1979, a representative of KSS "KOR," Zbigniew Romaszewski, met in Moscow with Professor Andrei Sakharov and his associates from the Committee in Defense of Human Rights. During the meeting, information was exchanged about the respect and defense of human and civil rights in Poland and the USSR. Principles of cooperation were agreed on.

Information Bulletin No. 2/28 of February/March 1979 published a long report by Romaszewski entitled "My Trip to Moscow."

By the end of 1978, all KOR members were as a rule deprived of the right to cross the borders of "our bloc," as the expression goes. A citizen who wanted, for example, to travel to East Germany would have his identification papers stamped, enabling him to travel within the bloc without restriction. This stamp was generally easy to obtain, but by this time a significant number of committee members had been deprived of theirs. Thus, when Romaszewski discovered that he had not yet been summoned anywhere to have his permission to cross borders taken away, he decided to go to Moscow, since he knew both the language and the city well (he had spent more than a year there while studying). Not without complicaitons, he managed to complete all the formalities through the state travel bureau "Orbis." Romaszewski managed to get to Moscow despite the denunciation of a chance fellow traveler who pointed him out to the Soviet functionaries of the border guard as a dissident and member of KOR, which made no impression on them whatsoever. Once in Moscow, Romaszewski visited Sakharov's apartment. Among the specific issues discussed was the participation of the defenders of human rights in the Soviet Union in the Polish dissident periodical *Krytyka*. On the following day, Romaszewski met with a group of Sakharov's associates. His return took place without trouble.

Contact with Sakharov's committee turned out to be easier and less bothersome than was expected. Romaszewski could not explain how this was possible. He wrote:

> During my entire stay, I did not notice any KGB activity around my person. To visit Sakharov three times and not to be asked for identity papers or followed was something I could not even imagine. This would have been impossible under Warsaw conditions. Apparently, greater respect for the role of law requires greater police activity. Perhaps the KGB believes that in case of need, anyone can in any case be locked up for dozens of years, so why would one want to waste time and effort in a senseless running around?

For a time it proved possible to establish channels of communication. Thanks to this, KSS "KOR" was able in its *Communiqué* No. 28 of March 1979 to publish the *Appeal* of December 8, 1978 (transmitted by telephone) of the Moscow Cooperation Group for the Fulfillment of the Responsibilities of the Helsinki Conference for European Security, together with an expression of support from KSS "KOR" dated February 14 and containing the sentence: "Remembering those who have paid for their uncompromising attitude with years of prison or with indefinite terms of confinement in psychiatric hospitals, we wish to expr ss our admiration and respect for the determination of all defenders of human rights in the USSR." The *Appeal* lists those articles of the Universal Declaration of Human Rights that are violated in the USSR, provides information about the movement in defense of human rights in the USSR, and mentions twelve basic demands of this movement. By the middle of January 1979, nearly 400 citizens of the USSR had signed this *Appeal*.

The relations with Czechs and to some extent also with the Slovaks were more lively. The KOR milieu always had a distinct sympathy for Czechs.[17] It seems that even before KOR was created, some of the activists had friends in Czechoslovakia. The first official sign of these ideological links was a telegram of condolences dated May 13, 1977 (published in *KOR Communiqué* No. 8) from the committee to the signers of Charter

77, which was sent to Jiři Hajek after the death of the great Czech philosopher, Jan Patočka, one of the creators of the charter. Patočka, an old and sick man, had died of heart failure after one of a series of strenuous interrogations. The telegram was answered by Jiři Hajek. The first illustrated issue of the *Information Bulletin* appeared after Patočka's death. It contained a photograph of Patočka which was laboriously glued into several thousand copies of the periodical.

On October 17, 1977, KSS "KOR" addressed to the participants in the Belgrade Conference on Security and Cooperation in Europe an appeal in defense of Vaclav Havel, Jiři Lederer, František Pavlicek, and Ota Ornest, all signatories of Charter 77 in Czechoslovakia whose trial was to begin that same day.

On October 31, KSS "KOR" made public a "Letter to Czech and Slovak Friends," to "the spokesmen of social protest," expressing solidarity and condemning the sentences handed down in this trial. The letter also contained the following remark:

> with regret and bitterness we recall that the Polish army also participated in the invasion of your country. We urgently wish that you not hold this against us, that you believe that this happened because of foreign constraint and against our will.

The answer was signed by spokesmen of Charter 77 Jiři Hajek, Marta Kubis, and Ladislav Hejdanek. It contained thanks for the expressions of solidarity and for all the actions of KSS "KOR" in defense of the imprisoned Czechs. In their letter the spokesmen of Charter 77 also wrote: "We never associated the participation of Polish troops in the crushing of the social reforms we undertook in 1968, which you mentioned, with the Polish nation."

In August 1978 representatives of KSS "KOR" and of Charter 77 met on the Polish-Czechoslovakian border, informed one another about their activities, discussed forms of cooperation, and issued a joint statement on the anniversary of the invasion of Warsaw Pact troops into Czechoslovakia, in which they stated:

> In these days of the tenth anniversary of the events of 1968, united in the defense of truth, human and civil rights, democracy, social justice, and national independence, we declare our common will to maintain these ideals and to act in their spirit. That inalienable human dignity which, as a value, gives meaning to the lives of individuals and of nations is the source of all our desires and actions.

Of course, on the tenth anniversary of the invasion of Czechoslovakia, almost all the uncensored press in Poland, and especially KOR's press, was filled with materials on this subject. The *Information Bulletin* from August/September 1978 carried a beautiful song about the second occupation in Hradec Kralove written by students in 1969.

On September 20, 1978, a second meeting took place in order to continue the talks. It was decided that permanent working groups should be created in order to provide for the rapid exchange of information; there were plans to organize a joint seminar, which unfortunately never took place; and a joint statement, or rather a communiqué, was issued with information about the meeting. A joint letter of greetings was also sent to the defenders of human rights in Armenia, Belorussia, Bulgaria, Georgia, Lithuania, East Germany, Russia, Rumania, the Ukraine, and Hungary.

Thanks to this meeting, KOR was able at the request of Charter 77 to publish and distribute a statement of September 2 signed by Charter spokesmen Marta Kubis and Ladislav Hejdanek concerning the convictions of three signatories of the charter, Ivan Manasek, Michał Kobal, and Jan Sims. *Communiqué* No. 22 also published a special note entitled "Charter 77 in the Summer of 1978," written in Prague especially for KOR. The *Information Bulletin* and *Głos* also published an interview conducted during this meeting by Jan Lityński and Antoni Macierewicz with Marta Kubis, Vaclav Havel, Ladislav Hejdanek, Pavel Landovsky, Peter Uhl, and "Jiři" (no last name mentioned) from Bratislava.

The third meeting was scheduled to take place on October 1. The Poles—and for understandable reasons, the Czechs even more than the Poles—wondered later whether this was not an extremely reckless move. Both security services were infuriated by the fact that they were unable to prevent the earlier meetings, and they had increased their state of alertness. There was also no real practical need for this meeting: all the most important things had already been discussed.

It is a fact that the last—prevented—meeting was more the fruit of friendly cooperation than the result of an urgent working need. We knew ahead of time that the Czechoslovak Security Service was conducting wide-scale preventive sweeps in the mountains near the border, and that the Polish Security Service probably even had some specific information. What is more, the Czechoslovak participants in the meeting, all of them, failed to obey the precautions previously agreed upon. Evaluating this meeting from the point of view of the principles of conspiracy, the meeting was a dangerous bit of nonsense. Except that, judging the matter from this point of view, Charter 77 would also have to be seen as nonsensical—what conspiracy makes the names of its participants public and scrupulously informs the authorities about the results of its work? So I emphasize that our actions—and this includes also contacts with KSS "KOR"—were and are legal.

This was written by Vaclav Benda.

The meeting was to take place on the so-called Road of Polish-Czechoslovak Friendship in Karkonosze. Three members of KSS "KOR" were detained on this occasion for forty-eight hours: Jan Lityński, Adam Michnik, and Piotr Naimski. Three representatives of Charter 77 were also detained: Jiři Nemec, Tomaš Petřive (also for forty-eight hours), and Jaroslav Šabata.[18] By order of the prosecutor, Šabata was placed under arrest on charges of assaulting a police functionary.

After detention, Šabata was beaten. When he was again roughed up and shouted at, he slapped a policeman in the face. During his court trial, without demeaning himself or equivocating, Šabata said, "I assert that I am not pleased with what I did," citing at the same time the circumstances and psychological motives of his action. On January 11, 1979, he was sentenced to nine months of imprisonment (for insulting an officer, not for assault), and on May 20 his sentence was extended for a year and a half on the basis of a previous conviction. For unknown reasons, Šabata's trial took place behind closed doors. Only his family and Zdena Tominova, one trusted observer, were admitted.

Even before the trial, on November 15, 1978, KSS "KOR" and Charter 77 sent an open letter to the Czechoslovak Parliament and to the Polish Diet demanding intervention on behalf of Šabata. On January 16, 1979, after the sentence was handed down, KSS "KOR" sent a telegram for Šabata to the spokesmen of Charter 77 containing expressions of solidarity and fraternity, including the traditional slogan from nineteenth-century flags of Polish national uprisings: "For our freedom and yours." *Information Bulletin* No. 1/27 of January 1979 published information from Prague about Šabata's trial, together with the text of his final speech. On June 6, KSS "KOR" made public a communiqué of the Czechoslovak Committee in Defense of the Unjustly Persecuted (VONS) of March 30, 1979, concerning Šabata's situation, with information about the removal of Šabata's attorney, Josef Doniš, from the bar by its "self-government" on June 30.

In the meantime, on May 29, the Czechoslovak democratic movement suffered a new blow: fifteen house searches took place in the apartments of all the members of the Committee in Defense of the Unjustly Persecuted, and ten of them were arrested. On June 6, the Polish Press Agency announced that "a court trial of ten Czechoslovak citizens accused of activity directed against the interests of the CSSR" had begun in Prague. The accused were: Otka Bednařova, Jarmila Bělikova, Vaclav Benda, Jiři Dienstbier, Vaclav Havel, Ladislav Lis, Vaclav Maly, Dana Nemcova, Jiři Nemec, and Peter Uhl. All were also activists of Charter 77. Among the arrested were the spokesmen of the charter, Jiři Dienstbier and Vaclav Benda; a third spokesperson, Zdena Tominova, was beaten by unknown perpetrators in such a manner that she found herself in a hospital. The function of spokesmen was taken over by Jiři Hajek and Ladislav Hejdanek.

On June 6, KSS "KOR" called on "all people of good will in Poland and throughout the world to demand the immediate release of Charter 77 spokesman Dr. Jaroslav Šabata and all the members of the Committee in Defense of the Unjustly Persecuted."

In July, signatures were gathered in Gdańsk, Cracow, Lublin, Warsaw, and Wrocław on a letter to the Czech and Moravian Episcopal Conference, to be sent to Cardinal Tomašek, appealing for the defense of the activists of VONS and the signatories of Charter 77, and for the protection of their families. The letter read in part:

> These people, admired and respected by all, have acted from deep humanitarian impulses consonant with the spirit of the teachings of the Church, which during the Second Vatican Council called on "those who have a talent for political activity or may be qualified for it . . . to act against the repression of individuals, against the usurpation of power, and against the intolerance of a political party" (*Gaudium et Spes* No. 75).

This letter was written on the initiative of Catholic activists of the opposition ("We join you in prayer") and cannot be attributed to any one group. KOR activists also played a part in it.

One pleasant gesture of friendship on the part of the Czechs, made at a very difficult time for KOR, was the publication in Prague in March 1979 of the first issue of a periodical (though unfortunately it seems that no further issues appeared) entitled *Poland and Us*. It included Michnik's essay on John Paul II (from *Information Bulletin* No. 24), a description of *Robotnik*, and an interview with Vaclav Benda, one of the spokesmen of Charter 77, about the relations between the charter and KOR. A portion of this interview has been cited above. There were also photographs of the meetings between the activists of Charter 77 and of KSS "KOR."

The relations between KOR Band Charter 77 did not end, but they were never again to be as lively and fruitful as during this period. The methods of communicating established during these meetings remained useful for a long time, but they were gradually cut off by the cooperating security services. Among other methods, in June, during the trial of VONS, every night between 12:00 and 2:00 a telephone would ring in the apartment of one of the members of KOR and a girl's voice would hurriedly transmit information. This occurred three times, and the telephone never rang again, which did not bode anything good. To this day, it is not known in Poland who was making the calls, or what happened to this woman.[19] The similarity between the two languages in matters requiring precision is more of a hindrance than a help: the feeling that one understands often turns out to be an illusion, and even leads to funny misunderstandings. Thus, conversations were conducted in "Slavic Esperanto," as it is sometimes called, or in German.

KSS "KOR" also joined the appeals in defense of Rudolf Bahro and other persons persecuted in the GDR. Its support was expressed, for example, in a cable to the participants in a seminar "For the Freedom of Rudolf Bahro" held on October 14, 1978.

The presence of the Hungarian writer Miklos Haraszti on the editorial board of a new periodical published by members of the KOR milieu, the quarterly *Krytyka* (which had a social-democratic tendency), was also a manifestation of communality. It reflected plans for broader cooperation between the Polish and Hungarian socialists.

Apart from all these actions, contacts, and statements indicating that KOR recognized that the struggle for freedom in every country of the Soviet empire was also our concern, the highly important, systematic work of informing the public continued to be carried out by the entire KOR press. A permanent column appearing in successive issues of the *Information Bulletin,* entitled "In Our Bloc," contained information in the form of short journalistic notes directly or indirectly describing freedom movements in the USSR and other "people's republics." Sometimes extensive informational materials were also included: for example, an article on "The Moscow Trials" was published in *Information Bulletin* No. 21/22 of June/July 1978 which contained detailed data about the trials of Yuri Orlov, Anatol Shcharansky, Alexander Ginzburg, and Viktor Petkus.

The Intervention Bureau—
New Attempts to Abuse Psychiatry

Polish problems obviously constituted the main focus of interest for the committee, and apart from the press, these were mostly issues dealt with by the Intervention Bureau. As usual, the bureau pursued at the same time a large number of different cases of various degrees of significance. It seems that during this period, the interventions connected with attempts to include psychiatric hospitals within the system of political repression were especially important. This method of repression had already appeared earlier, for example in connection with Stanisław Karpik, the peasant activist living near Siedlce.

I have already mentioned Jan Kozłowski (forty-nine years old), one of the most active members of the Temporary Committee of the Independent Trade Union of Farmers. Kozłowski was a private farmer in Chwałowice, near Stalowa Wola in southern Poland. Even before he began his oppositional activity, his biography was hardly banal. He was a peasant with a high school education. In the early seventies he played a role in the unmasking of the so-called Sandomierz Gang. At that time he was not working in agriculture, but was employed in the construction industry and had discovered abuses committed during the renovation of the historical buildings in the center of Sandomierz, which were falling down from neglect. The so-called Sandomierz affair became one of the most famous criminal affairs in the history of the PRL. Kozłowski narrowly escaped paying with his life for his social conscience, which did not allow him to keep silent: he was beaten up by "unknown perpetrators," who also attempted to drown him. He managed to defend himself, but by a "strange coincidence," it was Kozłowski himself who was arrested some time after this incident.

In March 1978, Kozłowski again made himself known as a person protesting against abuses. In a long document he wrote about thefts and embezzlements, he mentioned, among others, one of the favorites of the local party establishment. He was sued for libel. However, after learning of the social activities of the accused, the court ordered a psychiatric examination. The court experts, Drs. B. Żugaj and B. Kozłowska (from the same province, which is not irrelevant, because Kozłowski was in conflict precisely with the local authorities), presented an opinion that contained only a biography of the accused (no evaluation of his mental state, intelligence, coherence of thought, no reference to symptoms) and a recommendation that he be placed for observation in a psychiatric hospital (without setting a specified limit to the time required to conduct the tests).

Kozłowski went to two different psychiatrists in Warsaw, whose opinions left no doubt that he was normal (as one of them wrote: "the examined person is aware, coherent, factual, his mood is appropriate"). Kozłowski's attorney filed a complaint in an appeals court, unfortunately still in the same province. The court did not call new experts, and ordered that Kozłowski be placed in a psychiatric hospital. In a letter of February 2, 1979, KOR informed both the Polish Psychiatric Association and the International Psychiatric Association about Kozłowski's case, treating it as an attempt to abuse psychiatry as a means of political repression. All attempts to intervene proved futile. Kozłowski was placed in a psychiatric hospital in Jarosław, where he was tested between January 6 and 19, 1979. It was ascertained that Kozłowski was psychologically completely normal, with higher than average intelligence. The long arms of the Provincial Committee of PUWP in Tarnobrzeg did not reach as far as Jarosław.

The Workers' Defense Committee sent documentation in this matter to 960 Polish doctors of psychiatry; and acting in the name of KOR, Prof. Jan Kielanowski wrote a letter on March 15, 1979, to the general secretary of the World Psychiatric Association, Prof. Peter Borner, stating that the understanding which the position of KOR was receiving among Polish psychiatrists, "together with the course and results of psychiatrists' tests, have confirmed our strong faith in the professional honesty of Polish psychiatrists. We believe that the behavior of the court experts can be regarded as a completely exceptional occurrence." Unfortunately, the persecution of Kozłowski did not end with this episode (as we will learn in the following chapter), and the opinion of Kielanowski, which was roughly correct, shortly turned out to be too optimistic.

In May 1979, Mirosław Kimmes, who was detained by the police in connection with the gathering of signatures on an appeal for a televised broadcast of the pilgrimage of Pope John Paul II to Poland, was immediately—with no prior medical examination and without the knowledge of his family—transported to the mental hospital in Kochanówek, near Łódź. The chief doctor of the hospital ward, Barbara Wolczak, told KSS "KOR" member Józef Śreniowski, who was intervening on behalf of Kimmes, that "If someone occupies himself with gathering signatures on a petition rather than with his wife, child, and home, then it is his own fault if he finds himself here in the hospital." Luckily, it was possible to get Kimmes out despite the fact that a competent doctor had ascertained that he had a mental illness that manifested itself exclusively by his gathering signatures on a petition. As late as the spring of 1980 KOR noted further attempts to abuse psychiatry in this manner.

Other Cases of the Intervention Bureau

The trial of Witold Rozwens, who was accused of the unintentional murder of a child, was the most notorious of the cases investigated by the Intervention Bureau. During the time of KOR's existence, Colonel Rozwens served first as chief administrator of the Office of the Prosecutor General, and then as a director of the Department of Prophylactics in the same administration. He was known to the wider public from an appearance on television in the spring of 1977, when he made a statement concerning the arrest of the members and associates of KOR. The public could learn from Rozwens that Stanisław Pyjas was a drunkard and that KOR had connections with foreign intelligence.

On August 11, 1978, Rozwens, who was himself drunk, hid himself in the courtyard of a gamekeeper's lodge near Biała Podlaska in an attempt to ambush the dogs of a neighboring peasant which, during the previous night, had torn the skin of a goat hunted by Rozwens. A three-and-a-half-year-old boy, Mariusz Chacewicz, was the victim of this dog hunt. Around 8:40 P.M., Rozwens twice fired buckshot at the dog. The distance was sixteen meters at most, and supposedly Rozwens did not see the child. The boy was hit with 14 shot, which means that both of the two shots were "well aimed." The dog was unharmed.

A blood test, conducted at a time when it seemed that the whole case would be covered up, did not serve Rozwens very well. It was ascertained that he had no alcohol in his blood, while as the investigation discovered later, Rozwens, together with his hunting companion, had indeed drunk a large quantity of Stock and brandy.

Attorney Witold Lis-Olszewski, an associate of the Intervention Bureau of KOR, represented the prosecution in the name of the child's parents during the trial against Rozwens. Shortly after this case, he was forced into early retirement, but that is another story. Rozwens was sentenced to three years imprisonment; though on appeal it was suspended. He was fined 30,000 zlotys.

An unintentional murder caused by shooting while drunk does happen occasionally. What was different about Rozwens's case was the manner of behavior exhibited during the trial, which also permeated the atmosphere during the events and explained much about the behavior of the accused—the actions of a feudal lord, a co-owner of the PRL. Jan Walc captured it in his reports from the trial. The publication of these reports in the *Information Bulletin* caused a major controversy within KSS "KOR." Seweryn Blumsztajn, the editor of the *Bulletin,* had doubts as to whether anything more than an absolute minimum of information should be printed in the *Bulletin,* but he let himself be persuaded otherwise. After the publication of the first three of Walc's reports, the *Information Bulletin* published a polemic entitled "Rozwens Not by Sight," which was signed "MM." Without judging who was right, Walc or the reader who wrote the polemic, the very fact of a disagreement about the boundaries of the moral responsibilities of journalists who use strong words in this type of case speaks well about the sensitivity of the KOR milieu.

The December 1978 *Information Bulletin* carried a typical note about a case which the Intervention Bureau could not take up. On Mokotów Fields in Warsaw, three plainclothes police functionaries and one uniformed policeman beat up two fifteen-year-old boys who were walking their dogs. The boys were also stunned with gas. Then they were handcuffed and transported to the police precinct in Warsaw-Ochota, where, as a result of beatings, Marek Żelazny suffered a concussion, a broken nose, and numerous face, neck, chest, back, and hand injuries. Late in the evening, the boys were transported to the Children's House of the Police. The attention they received there was helpful and even cordial, and the police personnel in the Children's House helped to elucidate the truth about the crime. The hospital of the Ministry of Internal Affairs also issued a truthful medical report. The father of the badly beaten child was a professor at the Warsaw Polytechnic, who refused, however, to cooperate with the Intervention Bureau. The bureau was not familiar with the further course of events, but in any case, there were no signs that the Warsaw courts ever tried the police functionaries who had beaten up Mark Żelazny.

This incident illustrates the problem the Intervention Bureau often faced: the unwillingness of the persecuted (in this case the father) to demand justice publicly. Various motives were involved. Fear was the most common, but not the only one. This situation made the struggle against this type of crime much more difficult.

The *Information Bulletin* described this case, which was famous at the time in Warsaw, or more precisely, among the Warsaw intelligentsia.

Without doubt, the authorities of the police must have been uncomfortable about the event: to beat up the child of a professor in Poland constitutes a much more serious problem than to beat up the child of some worker. So, probably, the parents of the beaten child received some assurances from the police that the case would be settled outside the courts. In the *Information Bulletin* only the initials of the victim's name were used, but the author believes that after three years, such discretion would be an exaggeration, since the details of the case were known to a very large number of people.

Yet another case conducted by the Intervention Bureau is worth describing. The reader may recall the case of Jerzy Grzebieluch described in the preceding chapter. He was struck in a pedestrian crossing by a car driven by policemen who then beat him up, which resulted in permanent disability. Grzebieluch, who had no intention of forgoing his rights or giving up his claims, became from then on subject to police repression. As a result of delays in the Provincial Court in Katowice, the suit he brought to obtain compensation for his suffering and loss of health was still unresolved in 1978, when Grzebieluch was again subjected to new repressions.

Earlier, his strawberry field had been plowed under (!); he was accused of stealing his own wood (the accusation was later withdrawn, but he never got his wood back); permission to build a pigsty was withdrawn after it had already been partially built; and he was detained several times. During one of these detentions, "unknown perpetrators" broke into Grzebieluch's farm buildings in order to destroy his beehives, ruin some of his machinery, and spray a dog from a gas revolver (which is used in Poland only by the police, is unavailable for sale, and must be registered as a firearm, so that its possession requires a police permit). Piotr Szewczyk, the provincial deputy prosecutor, refused to launch an investigation into the burglary.

Grzebieluch was deprived of his means of livelihood, even though he was the owner of a farm and had the qualifications appropriate to run it (a higher agricultural education). Thus he began trying to find work. The employment office, however, did not answer his petitions. In May 1978 the Regional Court sentenced Grzebieluch to one year of limitation of liberty, accompanied by forced labor, since he was late in paying his alimony (200 zlotys a month); work was supposed to be assigned by the Town and Commune Office in Łazy (where Grzebieluch lived). The head of this office, W. Bogał, told Grzebieluch, however, that "For enemies there is only the cleaning of toilets and garbage dumps."

On November 13, 1978, Grzebieluch was asked to pay court costs of 5,500 zlotys or spend a year in prison (although the law in Poland does not allow for imprisonment for failure to pay court debts).

On November 29, 1978, a bailiff, accompanied by the police, entered Grzebieluch's house in order to confiscate his refrigerator under the pretext of an unpaid water bill. When Grzebieluch's elderly mother showed a stub for the payment, an attempt was made to snatch it away from her, which Grzebieluch tried to prevent. A brawl ensued, and Grzebieluch locked up the bailiff in one of the rooms. On December 18, 1978, Grzebieluch was charged with use of force and threats, and with depriving a state official of his freedom!

On January 8, 1979, Grzebieluch found work as a mason in the Mysłowice Enterprises of Industrial Construction. On January 25 there were telephone calls to this enterprise from various people claiming to be a judge in a Regional Court, a functionary at the city police headquarters, a functionary of the Security Service, and a curator of a Regional Court, all of whom demanded that Grzebieluch be fired immediately from his work, since his employment was "interfering with the court case against him." On January 27, Grzebieluch was fired, and immediately afterward the Regional Court (Judge Janina Grudzińska) ordered him to serve one year in prison because the accused had not found employment.

And all this began when Grzebieluch was hit by a police car in a pedestrian crosswalk, then beaten by the police (ten weeks of hospitalization) and made permanently disabled—and all that the victim had asked was that his rights be respected. Both Grzebieluch and KOR were impotent. The only possible thing was to sound an alarm. On February 5, 1979, KSS "KOR" issued a statement in this matter, describing the state of affairs in great detail.

The detail with which Grzebieluch's case has been described here is not accidental. No general explanation or description of the fate of those who find themselves in conflict with the police in Poland and fail to surrender immediately is adequate, since any such explanation would sound incredible. Only a detailed presentation of an individual case, one of many, makes one aware of the problem. The facts cited above were, as was customary for KOR, pedantically investigated in the awareness that every mistake could result in a trial for libel or slander.

There were many discussions in KOR as to whether such cases should be made known generally. If they were, citizens might become frightened and their desire to resist might be paralyzed from the very beginning.

The result might be acquiescence or even cooperation in terror, but it might also be public mobilization in the struggle against evil. As a rule, KOR chose to protest loudly and to publish all the available data. Those who drew the conclusion that it was better not to make waves when dealing with the police certainly lost nothing by it, whereas those who were ready to take up the struggle against injustice in full consciousness (often even if they themselves were not involved) were the true addresses of KOR's statements. KOR appealed above all to them.

Another important and interesting case was that of Zygmunt Kaleta from the Lenin Steel Mills in Nowa Huta. The Intervention Bureau helped him in his struggle to obtain justice. Kaleta was an interesting mixture, a good professional (a mason of industrial furnaces in a converter-oxygen steel mill), a religious activist (the initiator of a petition to reestablish in Cracow the traditional route for the Corpus Christi procession), and a defender of workers' interests in a situation where the existing trade unions represented the interests of the employer. He came out against infringements of work safety and health regulations, and in February and March 1978, when masons in converter furnaces who had gone on strike were punished with a cut in bonuses, Kaleta began to collect signatures in order to initiate a group legal action. The management retreated, and the rules governing the distribution of bonuses introduced at that time were beneficial to the workers. But Kaleta heard that he would no longer be tolerated in his department of the steel mill. The conflict erupted a short while later. Kaleta refused to work with a ladle that, according to him, was overdue for renovation and in its present condition endangered human life. He was fined and transferred to another department. Kaleta quit his job, and he could not find any other work because of an administrative prohibition against hiring workers who had left the Lenin Steel Mills. In bureaucratic jargon, this was done in order to prevent "the excessive rotation of personnel"; in effect, it made the worker into a slave attached to the steel mills. Kaleta decided to return to the steel mill, but he wanted to work at what he knew best, that is, in converter furnaces.

On December 11, 1978, and January 17, 1979, the Labor Court in Cracow considered Kaleta's case. Despite the hundreds of cases before Regional Appeals commissions and labor courts which KOR had registered previously, it knew of no case that had been so thoroughly investigated. It was discovered, for example, that the signatures on a letter from workers with whom Kaleta had worked before, in which he was portrayed as an argumentative man with whom they did not want to work, were extorted by threats of repressions at work (the collection of signatures was organized by the director of the Furnace Conservation Department, engineer Stefan Dziedzic). The nature of Kaleta's conflicts with the management was examined, and it was demonstrated that conflicts had occurred whenever, in accordance with safety regulations, Kaleta demanded the interruption of work if it was dangerous to life. (The director, Szkutnik, arguing with Kaleta in court, invoked the necessity of sacrifices on the part of the workers.) The court also discovered that witnesses called to the trial had been coached by the management how to testify.

The Labor Court ordered that Kaleta be reinstated at work and be paid compensation. The court costs were to be paid by the Lenin Steel Mills.

Obviously the Intervention Bureau of KOR dealt with a large number of cases. Here we have mentioned only those that were particularly notorious and which illustrate general problems.

The Report on the State of Hospital Care and the Pharmaceutical Crisis

Hospital care has always been one of the sore spots of life in the PRL. The inclusion of all employed citizens in a general, free health care system was accomplished in postwar communist Poland more radically than during the interwar period, when social insurance was left in an unsatisfactory state, though it was not scandalous for a poor country. Nevertheless, the communist authorities in postwar Poland were never able to fulfill their social obligations in this area, and the situation always became worse in periods of numerous crises. Investment in health services regularly received the lowest priority. Since there was a permanent lack of Western currency, imports of medical equipment were always inadequate. For decades Poland has suffered a shortage of building materials; hospitals, both the new ones and the ones needing renovation, have suffered the most. During the period of rapidly deepening crisis in the latter half of the seventies under the rule of Gierek, the situation became tragic, especially since the state took upon itself new obligations it could not avoid in the face of the growing dissatisfaction of the peasants: health insurance was extended so as to also include the farmers.

KSS "KOR" decided that one of the tasks of social self-defense was to see that a proper share of the allocation of limited means should be directed to health services, since the existing conditions were already threatening the biological bases of national life. More and more often, one could hear alarming news that women were giving birth in the corridors of obstetric hospitals; that the state of hygiene was worsening so rapidly that infections regularly accompanied all surgical procedures, that the waiting period for places in hospitals was becoming so long that the sick were being admitted in advanced stages of their diseases, and so on.

In May 1979 a group of doctors close to KOR prepared a concise report about the general state of hospital care. Since KOR never received permission to make public the names of these doctors, we will have to revert here to a formula known from newspapers: "name and address known to the editor." The report was not only published but also widely distributed to those people and institutions that could have had an influence or at least could have exerted pressure in this area. Along with other materials published in the KOR press, the report emphasized that in addition to such causes as the general crisis and the policy of short-changing medical care in comparison with other areas of social life (especially in comparison with allocations for the Security Service and the police), the increasingly evident social stratification based on a system of various privileges for the power elite played a significant role in this area as well.

One drastic example of this state of affairs was the construction of the government clinic in Anin, near Warsaw (sometimes in publications one also finds the name of nearby Międzylesie). This luxurious government clinic was built in record time whereas the construction of a hospital in the Bródno district in Warsaw had already taken ten years, and its completion was still nowhere in sight. By the end of 1977 the entire Health Care Fund, which was supported by a supposedly voluntary tax imposed on the working people, had collected only 3,244,000,000 zlotys, while the cost of building the government clinic exceeded 1,500,000,000 zlotys. The price of one hospital bed (that is, the cost of the entire investment divided by the number of places) in this clinic for the privileged was 13,000,000 zlotys, whereas the cost of a hospital bed for a common citizen of the PRL was estimated at 1,200,000 zlotys.

The area of private rooms in the Anin clinic was 16m^2, while the Polish norm is 6m^2 for a sick person. In Warsaw it is only 4.2m^2. Moreover, the clinic was furnished with the most modern diagnostic, therapeutic, and other equipment; it had a large swimming pool, gymnasia, and automatic laundries and ironing rooms, imported from Denmark, the United States, and West Germany. Four hundred persons were employed to serve 120 patients.

In addition to Anin and other government-party hospitals, clinics, and sanatoria, Poland also has a system of separate health and hospital care (hospitals of the Ministry of Internal Affairs, army hospitals, etc.) in which standards are higher than those available in generally accessible medical services. There is hardly another area of social life in Poland which offers such a striking illustration of the thesis of the "new class" composed of the party and government bureaucracy and of the apparatus of coercion.

The pharmaceutical crisis was a second issue in this general area which KOR addressed, or rather tried to address. Supposedly, at one time the Polish pharmaceutical industry developed in the postwar period was adequate. Eventually, investment in this area was neglected, and when there were great difficulties with Western currency during the second half of Gierek's reign, pharmaceutical imports were cut drastically. Sporadic and occasionally quite serious difficulties with the purchase of medications in pharmacies had been occurring for a long time, but by the last quarter of 1978 the situation became catastrophic. More and more often it was impossible to find basic drugs in pharmacies, and the number of medications lacking grew ever greater. These shortages ranged from a lack of cotton wool to a lack of drugs necessary for saving lives. Alarms were sounded in all regions of Poland. More and more often, doctors asked patients to have their families search for medications on their own. There was a shortage of diffusion fluid, surgical gloves, disposable hypodermic needles—in a word, there was a shortage of everything.

On December 4, 1978, KOR addressed an open letter to Marian Śliwiński, the minister of Health and Social Services, concerning the lack of medications. The writing and publication of this letter was preceded by long and difficult preparations that involved gathering information throughout Poland by KOR associates in accordance with the instructions of professionals. The text of the letter was written in consultation with doctors and pharmacists. The letter contained a concise description of the state of supplies in the pharmacies and a list of deficiencies in the Polish pharmaceutical industry, and it emphasized the discriminatory neglect of these needs in foreign trade. The letter concluded with the following statement:

> In this situation—if radical changes are not possible—KSS "KOR" announces its readiness to appeal to the Polish ethnic community living abroad, asking them to organize an action to supply the sick people in Poland with the most urgently needed medications unavailable on the Polish market. The

constant help offered to our society in past years by the Polish community is well known and very important. We believe that today, just as always, the Polish ethnic community would respond with compassion to an appeal prompted by the biological danger facing our society.

At the same time, we are appealing to you today, Mr. Minister, to agree that the institutions under your control should act as intermediaries between the sick and the donors, to whom those institutions you designate would transmit the names and addresses of patients, together with the names of their medications, on the basis of written medical prescriptions. The patients or their families would receive these medications at their own addresses, which would prevent possible abuses.

The Social Self-Defense Committee "KOR" will await a positive response from you, Mr. Minister, for four weeks. A longer silence must be regarded as a negative answer. In this case, the Committee will appeal to citizens to undertake the action of organizing social committees to act as intermediaries between the ill and the Polish ethnic community abroad. Otherwise, the health situation in our country is going to deteriorate from month to month, and the perspective of an irreversible disaster will become a reality.

In fact, KOR did not expect that the minister of health would be concerned about the health of citizens to such an extent as to undertake cooperation with KOR or to search for a solution similar to the suggestion offered by the committee. As usual for KOR, the letter was sent at a time when the plan of action was basically ready and when the initial steps had already been undertaken.

Above all, no one in KOR believed that the committee would be able to deal with this task alone. No one doubted that the action could be successful only with the support of the Church. What was needed was both its moral support—important both inside Poland and abroad—and its organizational help, even if only in the form of premises which the police and the Security Service would hesitate to enter, and which could serve as locations where prescriptions could be filled once they had met specific conditions and been verified by specialists, doctors, and pharmacists as well as by public controllers. Since KOR wanted the initiative to be nationwide, only the Church, through its parishes, could ensure both that general information be passed and that proper communications be maintained between the ill or their doctors, and the centers managing the action.

This center would be run by a citizens' committee composed both of citizen-activists and of competent specialists. According to KOR's plans, the composition of this committee should be such as to facilitate as much as possible its cooperation with the Church, that is, the committee would be composed basically of faithful and practicing Catholics. KOR saw no need to ensure any sort of representation for itself on the committee.

After some initial talks, KOR succeeded in assembling a group of people willing to begin the necessary work, and the composition of this group gave hope that large social reserves could be mobilized to perform the daily functions connected with such an action. At the same time, a parallel emigré Polish committee would be created in the West to organize the collection of funds, the purchase and mailing of medications, and so forth.

KOR activists living abroad investigated the possibility of obtaining donations from, among others, pharmaceutical companies, which could take the form of opening accounts for a given amount to be donated as a free supply of medications produced by the given firm. These projects and the state of the preparations were presented to the secretary of the Polish Episcopate, Bishop Bronisław Dąbrowski. Aleksandra Korewa and KSS "KOR" member Jan Józef Lipski participated in the talks (the latter's participation was to end when the appeal announced in the letter to Minister Śliwiński was made public, and when the citizens' commission was formed and its existence made public).

KOR and the activists of the future committee saw two possibilities: the more desirable was that shortly after the announcement of the action, the government, for reasons of prestige, would find the action unsatisfactory and would find the means necessary to take over the initiative itself; the less desirable would involve a lack of reaction on the part of the authorities, and after several months, the avalanche of increased needs would necessitate greater institutionalization of the entire undertaking. Still, the first variant seemed more likely, especially in view of the fact that the very publication of the letter caused a partial, and as it quickly turned out, a brief improvement in the situation.

On January 25, 1978, KSS "KOR" issued a statement based on detailed surveys showing an improvement in the supply of drugs, even though such an improvement was not universally observed, for example, in Lower Silesia. The March *Communiqué* of KSS "KOR" carried a letter signed by the director of a pharmacy (name and address known to the committee) dated February 24, 1979. This was the only instance in which KOR published such authorial material, but it was done because of the importance of the matter and the factual tone of the letter. This letter was critical of the January 25 statement of KOR ("wishful thinking by the group"), and presented the existing situation in a very competent manner. As an evaluation, it was congruent with the constantly conducted updated surveys of KOR.

It is necessary to add that the distribution apparatus had invented a method designed to upset any study of the supply of medications to pharmacies. Whereas in 1978 a given drug would either be available in a pharmacy for a long time or could not be found there at all (either regionally or throughout all of Poland), from the inception of the study, the drug would appear in minimal quantities from time to time, and only in a single pharmacy. Very often, the persons conducting the surveys for KOR were unable to give an unequivocal report, such as, for example, "Thyreodium is lacking" or "is available." It was possible only to note that "it is available sometimes very rarely in locations that are difficult to predict."

Unfortunately, the talks with the secretariat of the Episcopate (usually with Rev. Franciszek Gościński, the director of the secretariat's office) proceeded slowly. Finally, Bishop Dąbrowski asked for a detailed memorandum containing: (a) an evaluation of the current situation in pharmaceutical supplies; (b) the organizational plan of the action; and (c) a precise formulation of what help was expected from the Church. Since the surveys were being conducted continuously (parenthetically, to the irritation of KOR associates) and the entire plan of action was thought out in detail, the memorandum was presented five days later. To the surprise of those who delivered the memorandum, this was two days after a session of the Main Council of the Episcopate. The next session of the Main Council was to be of a ceremonial rather than a working nature, since it was connected with the pilgrimage of Pope John Paul II, and the following meeting was scheduled only for the beginning of September.

At the same time, it did not appear likely that the situation in regard to pharmaceutical supplies would improve, and without the participation of the Church the action was bound to fail. There was nothing left to do but to wait until September, despite the fact that there was no more urgent issue. After the meeting of the Main Council of the Episcopate early in September 1979, the Secretariat of the Episcopate announced that the Church authorities were not interested in this issue. The decision was not made by the Main Council itself, since the issue was not on the agenda of the council's meeting.

This may well have been the biggest failure of KOR during the five years of its existence. It concerned an issue of special importance from the point of view of social self-defense and humanitarian principles. The attempt to neutralize one of the causes of the worsening state of health of the nation was unsuccessful; the suffering of hundreds of thousands of people was not alleviated; and it was even difficult to estimate the number of lives that could have been saved. Obviously, the authority of KOR also suffered, although in this case, this aspect of the matter did not seem very important to the members of the committee.

The pharmaceutical situation continued to be very bad. This sentence must be treated, however, as a statement based not on documentation but only on sporadic observation, since the systematic studies of supplies were abandoned. Data about the biological dangers facing society were presented in a paper on "Problems of Social Policy" presented by Jan Malanowski during the first and only official meeting of the Seminar "Experience and Future" (DiP) held on November 14.[20] The paper was published (with minor abridgments) without the permission or knowledge of the author in *Information Bulletin* No. 2/28 of February/March 1979:

1. The mortality rate has increased (in 1972 there were 8 deaths per 1,000 citizens; in 1977 there were 9).

2. The mortality rate for infants has increased, though only slightly (in 1976 there were 24 deaths for every 1,000 births; in 1977, 24.5 deaths).

3. There has been a disquieting rise in the number of persons suffering from tuberculosis, which has not been included in the Statistical Yearbook, but was noted by the Diet Health Commission.

4. There has been an alarming increase in the number of suicides.

Among the European countries of Comecon we occupy next to last place in the number of hospital beds per 10,000 citizens. There are 74 beds for every 1,000 people in Poland, while the USSR has 119, the GDR 108, and Hungary 81. The number of hospital beds per 10,000 citizens has not changed in Poland since 1970. . . . It should be remembered that over one million patients were admitted by hospitals with unimproved accommodations. Let us add to this that the number of beds in psychiatric hospitals decreased during the period in question, and that it also fell significantly in anti-tubercular hospitals and sanatoria, despite disquieting information about the increase in the number of tubercular patients. . . .

The shortages of drugs affect some 607 items among the 2,159 which can be found in the Polish list of medications. . . .

Part of the cause for the increased mortality in Poland is undoubtedly connected with the limitations on the production of medications and with the shortage of hospital beds. . . .

Unfortunately, it must be said that KSS "KOR" accomplished next to nothing in this area, apart from alarming public opinion.

The Press and Uncensored Publications

The Intervention Bureau always received the highest priority in KOR, but the press and other publications were also important areas of activity for the committee and its milieu. In order to present a sketch of KOR activity in this regard we must begin with a quick overview of the events and issues that occupied the uncensored press during this period.

One of the basic types of information carried in the uncensored press concerned Church issues, often involving the publication of Church documents mutilated by the censorship.

Among other things (we mention only those events discussed in detail and including quotes), the KOR press provided information about:

- a strong statement by the 162d Plenary Conference of the Polish Episcopate against censorship;

- the lecture of Primate Wyszyński on May 29, 1978, in the Catholic Theological Academy in Warsaw on the fifteenth anniversary of the encyclical of John XXIII, *Pacem in terris;*

- the letter of Primate Wyszyński to Minister Kąkol of June 1978;

- the Letter of the Polish Episcopate to the Diocesan and Monastic Clergy concerning membership in the Catholic association Caritas and concerning the Retirement Fund for the Clergy (June 15, 1978);

- the sermon of Cardinal Wojtyła to teachers, delivered at Jasna Góra on July 2, 1978;

- the August 1978 lecture to the clergy by Bishop Jan Tokarczuk of Przemyśl, given in the Catholic University in Lublin and concerning the perspectives of development for the Church in Poland;

- the pastoral appeal of the bishops for an annual day of social mass media (September 17, 1978);

- the September letter from Rev. Franciszek Blachnicki to the Provincial Prosecutor's Office in Nowy Sącz, concerning repressions against the Recollection Oases;

- the 165th and 166th Plenary Conferences of the Polish Episcopate (October 5 and November 28 and 29, 1978);

- a memorandum from forty-two deans of the Przemyśl Diocese to the Przemyśl Voivode dated October 13, 1978, concerning discrimination against the theological seminary in Przemyśl;

- a letter from Reverend Pylak, the bishop of Lublin, to Minister Kąkol, of November 24, 1978, concerning discrimination against religious pilgrimages on the part of tourist and transport enterprises, and about attempts to prevent the construction or renovation of churches;

- a memorandum from the Plenary Conference of the Polish Episcopate to the government of the PRL, concerning the situation of the family in Poland (February 8, 1979);

- the Week of Christian Culture held in April 1979 in more than twenty Warsaw churches.

The uncensored press carried extensive information about the convention of the Polish Writers' Union held on April 7 and 8, 1978, in Katowice, and about the general meetings of chapters, especially of the Warsaw chapter, preceding the convention. During the Warsaw meeting, the board of the chapter was attacked for preelection machinations, and above all for discrimination against certain members (the politically motivated elimination of some poets from the list of participants in the *Poetic Autumn*). The *Information Bulletin* published a speech by Andrzej Braun taped at the meeting, and *Zapis* published most of the important speeches from the Katowice convention.

The session devoted to problems of education, organized by the Polish Sociological Association, was also an important event. The session was preceded by a scandal: Prof. Władysław Markiewicz demanded that the organizers withdraw the paper of Dr. Bolesław Gleichgewicht from Wrocław (a mathematician and member of TKN) because of its subject—the earnings of teachers, and the paper of Ireneusz Gugulski because of the author.[21] Markiewicz demanded that in place of these two papers, two others be put on the program: one written by him and another by Dr. Frycie. This demand was accompanied by the threat that otherwise the Polish Sociological Association would be put under the tutelage of the Internal Affairs Department of the District Office. The organizers accepted these conditions. Despite this, the session played a positive role and took place in an atmosphere of open and sharp discussion.

The twentieth anniversary of *Więź*, a Catholic monthly that made enormous contributions to cultural, social, and intellectual life, and played a large role in the rapprochement and mutual understanding between the Catholic and secular milieus, received sympathetic and exhaustive comment in the uncensored press. The press also provided information about a Toronto Congress on "Polonia 78—Polonia of Tomorrow," which had been passed over in silence by the official media.

Much attention to PAX and related matters was provoked by the death of Bolesław Piasecki, the leader of the group that described itself as Catholic and which for years had collaborated with the communists. This group played a particularly diversionary role against the Church and society during the Stalinist period, and in 1956 and 1968.

One event that echoed widely was a speech by Stefan Bratkowski, the founder of the Seminar "Experience and Future" and the future president of the Association of Polish Journalists, delivered at a meeting of the party cell of the association. Copies of the text of this speech were being circulated before it was published in its entirety in *Information Bulletin* No. 29.

Obviously the election of Cardinal Karol Wojtyła to the papacy provoked an enormous wave of commentaries and informational materials. The person of John Paul II has been present constantly, from the moment of his election, in public life in Poland, and the press is continuously writing and giving information about him.

The uncensored press, both that of KOR and others, contains in addition a great deal of information and articles (sometimes in the form of serious research papers) on social, political, economic, cultural, ideological, or historical (especially modern) topics; it has carried interviews and documents, and all of this cannot be discussed or even listed here. These materials, in addition to their effect on readers who read it when it was current, will also be of great importance for future students of the times.

During the period under discussion, the periodicals of the KOR milieu, such as the *Information Bulletin*, *Głos*, and *Robotnik*, continued to appear, as did the periodicals of groups associated with KOR, such as *Zapis*, *Puls*, *Indeks* (SKS), and *Sygnał* (Cracow SKS). ROPCiO continued to publish *Opinia* and *Bratniak*. We should also mention other periodicals not connected at all with either of these groups, such as the Lublin *Spotkania* or *Postęp*. New periodicals also began to appear.

The first issue of *Krytyka* appeared in the summer of 1978. It was a quarterly connected with the KOR milieu, close to the social-democratic traditions of the PPS (as emphasized by its title, which referred to a periodical published around the turn of the century in Cracow and edited by Wilhelm Feldman). The editorial board of the first issue was composed of Stanisław Barańczak, Konrad Bieliński, Mikloš Haraszti (Hungary), Vaclav Havel (Czechoslovakia), Jacek Kuroń, Jan Lityński, Adam Michnik, Stefan Starczewski (editor-in-chief), Jan Walc, and Roman Wojciechowski. The interest taken by the members of the editorial board of *Krytyka* in events occurring in other countries of the bloc is expressed by the fact that in the second issue of the periodical, published in the fall of 1978, an extensive selection of papers written by Slovak and Czech writers and documents of Charter 77 were published; *Krytyka* No. 9 of 1981 carried a selection of articles by members of the Hungarian intellectual opposition.

The first issue of *Placówka*, a periodical for the countryside, which was edited, among others, by peasant activists and publicists close to KOR, appeared early in 1979, as already mentioned in connection with discussion of the peasant movement.

The first issue of *Robotnik Wybrzeża (The Coastal Worker)*, the organ of the Initiating Committee of Free Trade Unions on the Coast, was published in August 1978. The second issue included, among other things, a photographic record of the ceremonies held on the eighth anniversary of the December 1970 events.

The first issue of *Biuletyn Dolnośląski* (the *Bulletin of Lower Silesia*), the organ of the Club of Social Self-Defense in Wrocław, appeared in June of that year.

In January 1979 in Cracow, the first issue of a student magazine entitled *Merkuriusz Krakowski i Światowy* was published by a group of people associated with KOR.

Early in 1979 appeared the first issue of the quarterly *Res Publica*, which did not make public the composition of its editorial board, although it was generally known that it was edited by an informal group of young intellectuals of neo-conservative orientation. This periodical was devoted to theoretical political, cultural, philosophical, and historical problematics, and distinguished itself by a very high level of argument. The articles it published were usually anonymous, or signed only with initials (usually easy to decipher). Stefan Kisielewski (Kisiel) often published in *Res Publica* under his own name. Since this book is a history of KOR, it is not irrelevant to mention that this group, neutral as far as quarrels within the opposition were concerned, always enjoyed the best of relations with KOR.

The first issue of ROPCiO's periodical for the villages, *Gospodarz*, was published in December 1979. It was edited by Bogusław Studziński and Piotr Typiak. This periodical also was appreciated among KOR sympathizers.

In June 1978 and early in 1979, two periodicals connected with Moczulski's group were published for the first time: *Droga (The Road)* and *Gazeta Polska (The Polish Gazette)*; they distinguished themselves by a distinct, though often veiled aggressiveness toward KOR (without mentioning the name of the target).

In February 1979 there appeared the first issue of _Rzeczpospolita (Commonwealth)_, an irregular periodical of the Committee for National Self-Determination, edited by Marian Piłka, Ryszard Pyżyński, and Wojciech Ziembiński. This committee was created as a result of dissension within ROPCiO. _Rzeczpospolita_ was chiefly concerned with the problem of possible participation in the elections to the Diet; it paid great attention to patriotic anniversaries and emphasized the cult of Józef Piłsudski.

The quarterly _Aspekt_ was also connected with ROPCiO groups, and later with the Movement of Free Democrats. It was edited by Andrzej Mazur and Andrzej Ostoja-Owsiany, and devoted to social and humanistic problematics, broadly understood. It seems that only two issues of _Aspekt_ ever appeared, although both were of high quality.

Of course, throughout this period other publications appeared and disappeared. They might be listed at some future time in some bibliography. Here I will cite only one example: _KSS "KOR" Communiqué_ No. 28 notes, under the rubric of "Repressions": "In Poznań on January 31, [1979] there was a house search of the apartment of Edmund Chruściński [a driver in the ARDOM Enterprises and the editor of an unofficial bulletin in the Enterprises]. The pretext was a search for articles stolen from a store. Documents of KSS "KOR," materials for the next issue of the bulletin, and photographic equipment were found and confiscated."

To the extent of its ability, KOR tried to aid various press initiatives, often even those of a very ephemeral character. This policy was based on the principle that a new independent group would form around an independent paper. In order to avoid technical problems, specialists from NOWa published their own widely distributed instructional materials on how to construct the simplest printing device, the so-called frame.

The Independent Publishing House NOWa still had no competition as far as the publication of books was concerned. During the period in question, it had already published well over fifty volumes. But new publishing houses also appeared: the _Głos_ Library launched its activities with the publication of Bohdan Cywiński's _Poisoned Humanities_, and _Spotkania_ also began to publish its own series. The Cracow Student Publishing House (KOS) also began its activity, mostly in the literary field. Of all the uncensored publishing houses, KOS was especially concerned with the graphic quality of its publications. There was also the Third of May Constitution Publishing House, which was connected initially with

ROPCiO but later became completely independent and also cooperated with KOR. Somewhat later, the publishing house Showcase of Literature was organized in Poznań; it specialized in poetry. The number of these publishing houses was increasing with time, offering readers an ever greater number of books and periodicals.

The press and publishing movement was truly powerful by the end of the period under discussion. Every month there appeared close to 100,000 copies of periodicals, brochures, and books. *Robotnik* was the largest of all the uncensored periodicals: it was a biweekly published in editions of 20,000 copies by means of an offset technique.

Repressions Against KSS "KOR" and Associated Groups

Repressions against the dissident groups did not cease throughout this period. Nor did the authorities alter their repertoire: numerous detentions, house searches, dismissals from work, beatings (both by the police and by "unknown perpetrators"), and so on; the long series of these events was pedantically noted by the successive *KSS "KOR" Communiqués* on several densely printed pages every month. It is impossible of course to reprint them here; and in any event, they would not add much to our knowledge of KOR.

Starting with *Communiqué* No. 24 of November 24, 1978, the editors began the custom of summarizing typical police repressions. In order to appraise the extent of these phenomena, we might cite data from three *Communiqués:*

Communiqué No. 24 (from October 16 to November 24, 1978): "Altogether there were forty-eight detentions . . . [including] three accompanied by beatings . . . and thirty-three house searches; there was also one police trap set up in an apartment."

Communiqué No. 25 (from November 25 to December 17, 1978): "Altogether there were fifty-seven detentions . . . and forty-three house searches; three police traps."

Communiqué No. 26/27 (from the end of December 1978 to the end of January 1979): "Altogether there were fifty detentions . . . and forty house searches, and six cases of beatings by functionaries of the Security Service and the police."

Obviously, not all the cases noted in the *Communiqués* concerned activities of KOR.

With two exceptions, we shall not mention here detentions and searches, methods that were employed quite generally. The first was used, as a rule, out of pure malice, though occasionally it did have a practical aim, for example, to prevent someone from attending a trial or a meeting; the second sometimes did involve a search for an actual reason, but it seems that it was also used just as often simply as a means of annoyance.

On November 21, 1978, the Security Service conducted three house searches and detained thirteen people from the group (that is, practically the entire group, if one excludes friends and sympathizers) of *Spotkania*, a periodical of young Lublin Catholics respected by KOR and connected with it by ties of camaraderie. For the first time—if one excludes the case of Second Lieutenant Jagiełło—the dissidents searched and detained were dealt with by the Army Prosecutor's Office, which caused understandable worry. The investigation concerned the connections between the *Spotkania* group and Piotr Jegliński and Kazimierz Charzewski.

Piotr Jegliński, a former student at the Catholic University in Lublin, had lived and studied in Paris since 1974. There, he organized help among émigré groups for the democratic opposition in Poland, and especially for his friends at *Spotkania*.

Kazimierz Charzewski, as a student in Dresden, had cooperated with the democratic opposition in Poland since 1976, helping transport émigré publications into Poland. In October 1977 he was arrested by the Security Service, and as a result of the complicated and difficult circumstances of his life, he agreed to collaborate with them. Some of the searches in Lublin were a result of this collaboration. Charzewski, who by that time had finished his studies in Berlin, was sent to Paris in order to establish closer contact with Jegliński (there was a plan to entice Jegliński to East Berlin and to arrest him there), and also with Polish Catholic groups in Paris, and then to infiltrate Radio Free Europe. In circumstances difficult to explain fully, Charzewski was unmasked and arrested by the French police. After his arrest, Charzewski revealed the circumstances of his collaboration with the Security Service in a letter to the editors of *Spotkania*. Charzewski's arrest became a pretext for the Main Army Prosecutor's Office to bring charges of espionage against Jegliński (who was still in Paris).

On November 24, *Spotkania* issued a statement about this case, which was quoted in its entirety by KSS "KOR" in its *Communiqué* of December 6, which also noted:

> Any attempt to link the intellectual and editorial effort of the *Spotkania* group with espionage activity is utter nonsense. . . . Polish society has not

forgotten the era of Stalinism, when any dissatisfaction with the policy of the party, any attempt to think and act independently, was treated as cooperation with foreign intelligence.

The episode had no further consequences.

The second case—this time of mass searches and police detentions—was connected with an attempt to destroy a monument to Lenin in Nowa Huta by means of explosives, which took place on the night of April 17. The explosion caused minor damage to the monument, but it broke windows in neighboring houses. Following this, the Security Service and the police conducted searches, detentions, and interrogations (the list of names published in *KSS "KOR" Communiqué* No. 29 lists 203 persons from some thirty locations; not all the people agreed to have their names published). In its statement of April 20, 1979, KSS "KOR" declared:

> Given conditions in Poland . . . this could only have been a provocation or an irresponsible escapade, which is now being used for political repressions.

and:

> The investigative forces are well aware that none of these people caused the explosion, and that the searches and detentions were not necessary to the investigation. It is widely known that from the time of its creation in 1976, the opposition has never engaged in acts of violence, and that on many occasions it has advocated the necessity of striving peacefully for democratic changes.

The explosion in Nowa Huta was more a provocation than an irresponsible escapade. For several months before this, lecturers at party meetings had stubbornly repeated that "the opposition was preparing its armed forces and intended to change its tactics to terrorist attacks." The perpetrators of the explosion were never found. But the problem of the explosion that destroyed Lenin's shoe disappeared as quickly as it had appeared. It turned out to be a noisy dud, just as the firecracker in the censorship building on Mysia Street in 1968 was an argument kept in reserve for the most drastic variant of events on the eve of the suppression of writers, students, and "Zionists."

KOR still had to deal with the case of Tomasz Michalak. Michalak, a photographer and an associate of KSS "KOR" and of NOWa, was detained on April 18. During a search of his apartment, his photographic equipment was confiscated, as well as the furnishings of a print shop and photographs of banknotes that were to serve as a graphic motif for a book jacket he was working on. He was absurdly accused of owning the equipment for the purpose of counterfeiting money. The prosecutor issued a three-month detention. In addition, Michalak was a very sick man. His stay in jail threatened to jeopardize his health.

Communiqué No. 29, which carried information about Michalak's arrest, also included a statement from KSS "KOR" dated April 27. *Information Bulletin* No. 29 (which included *Communiqué* No. 29) published a statement from NOWa supported by the *Information Bulletin* itself. On May 21, KSS "KOR" sent a letter to Amnesty International asking it to intervene on Michalak's behalf, and including the statement by NOWa mentioned above. The editorial boards of *Głos*, *Placówka*, *Puls*, and *Zapis* also issued statements in Michalak's defense. In July, the editorial board of *Robotnik*, together with KSS "KOR," issued an appeal for the defense of Michalak that was sent to a large number of trade unions around the world, together with an introductory letter from KOR and *Robotnik*. Approximately 10,000 copies of the appeal were widely distributed in June and July. During the period of Michalak's stay in prison, every copy of NOWa publications included a glued-in text of the statement by the publishing house in Michalak's defense. On July 17, Michalak was released from jail. The investigation against him continued all the same, and as often happened, it was not known how it ended or even whether it had ended.

One of the routine methods of repression in Poland—and not only of repression, since sometimes it is difficult to understand what is at issue and why—is the refusal of a passport. KOR, which theoretically understood the importance of the problem and the contradiction between this practice and international obligations, was nevertheless not very eager to deal with this problem. People were being beaten up, arrested, imprisoned, dismissed from work—and by comparison, the refusal of a passport (except in certain special circumstances) could not be regarded with a great deal of indignation. Thus, such cases were noted rather irregularly. Nevertheless, in one instance, such a refusal was met with a sharp and effective reaction by KOR. KSS "KOR" member Jan Lityński had a very sick child (Down's syndrome). It turned out that a treatment in a special hospital in West Germany had shown positive results. But the treatment had to be repeated periodically. The passport authorities refused to issue a passport to the child's grandmother, Regina Lityńska. After two published letters from KSS "KOR" to the International Red Cross (of October 7 and 27, 1978), Regina Lityńska finally received permission to travel abroad together with her granddaughter.

KOR also intervened on behalf of persons who were improperly not allowed into Poland, but these interventions were unsuccessful. For several years there has been an agreement between Poland and Sweden that visas are not necessary to travel from one country to the other. Yet Polish authorities repeatedly turned back from ports or airports Swedish citizens who had emigrated from Poland in 1968/69. In general, former Polish citizens who had become citizens of other countries after their emigration were admitted to Poland. In the cases under discussion, one could not resist the obvious conclusion that these refusals were dictated by anti-Semitism. In its statement of October 9, 1978, KOR wrote:

> Let us remember the great harm inflicted on our society and on the good name of Poland by the anti-Semitic policy of the authorities in 1968. The closing of our border to people because of their Jewish descent is a continuation of this policy.

Among the lesser forms of repression were fines imposed on various occasions against the owners or tenants of apartments made available for TKN lectures; or against distributors of leaflets (not, God forbid, for the leaflets but for littering the streets, even when the leaflets were handed out from hand to hand); or for shouting slogans (a detained KOR activist never shouted any political slogans, but said loudly to chance passersby: "My name is such and so, please let people know about my detention by calling 39-39-64." This was Kuroń's telephone number. Sometimes the person's own telephone number was also given; such appeals were successful in about half the cases); or for hindering identification by the police; or sometimes for participating in an "illegal meeting" (for example, one Wrocław meeting on March 5, 1978, cost 38,000 zlotys); or for anything else and for God knows what.

Apart from the imposition of fines, which maintained at least formally the appearance of a legal procedure, the confiscation of money found in apartments or on the person being searched was a general practice. A typical and by no means isolated case is the one mentioned in *Communiqué* No. 28 of March 1979: "On February 23, there was a search in the apartment in which Roman Wojciechowski was staying; he was detained afterward for forty-eight hours. The police confiscated 6,874 zlotys, $5, a radio, approximately forty incomplete copies of *Krytyka*, and an English book on the history of the KGB, along with a manuscript of the first chapter of Wojciechowski's book on prisons." We can see that even the change carried in one's pocket might be confiscated. The Security Service was obviously not interested in what the robbed person would live on.

Dismissals from work also continued. The most sensational case in this area occurred in March 1978 in the Enterprises of Electronic Computing Technology (ZETO) in Wrocław, and concerned Jerzy Trybulski, the general director and founder of the enterprises and one of the pioneers of Polish computer science. Trybulski, who was not at all connected with the opposition, was dismissed for "failure to maintain political security in the enterprises." This referred to the fact that in the fall of 1977, many employees of ZETO, among them Piotr Starzyński, one of the most active associates of KSS "KOR," had signed an appeal from Amnesty International for a political amnesty throughout all the countries of the world. This led to a cycle of interrogations conducted among the employees and management of ZETO which lasted several months. The party organization in ZETO protested against the firing of Trybulski, but this resulted only in the dissolution of the party executive body in ZETO. However, it was clearly associates of KOR or persons connected with other dissident groups who were dismissed from work more often than directors who were simply slow to resort to repression.

On March 20, 1978, KSS "KOR" associate Mieczysław Grudziński was dismissed from the Institute of the Organization of the Machine Industry. The members of the Employees Council of the local trade union, who had initially protested against his dismissal, gave up their protest after being threatened during individual talks. Three other employees of this institute, who in the summer of 1977 had defended the imprisoned KOR activists during an open party meeting, were also forced to change their place of employment or were fired. The names of these persons were never made public, since the interested parties did not grant permission to do so.

On April 20, 1978, the Warsaw SKS issued a special statement "On Personnel Policy in Institutions of Higher Learning," which was prompted by the dismissal from Warsaw University of a young historian, Marek Barański, who was an associate of KOR and an activist in TKN. This happened three weeks after he had defended his doctoral dissertation, which was very highly regarded by such authorities in Polish medieval studies as Aleksander Gieysztor and Gerard Labuda. The Science Council of the Institute of History at the University adopted a resolution demanding a retraction of this dismissal. A letter of protest signed by 28 assistant professors and graduate students and by 257 students of the institute was sent to the rector of the university, Zygmunt Rybicki.[22] All this was to no avail.

The SKS statement contains names of many faculty members dismissed from Warsaw University or transferred to other work during the two preceding years: Konrad Bieliński, Andrzej Celiński, Czesław Czapow, Kazimierz Friske, Katarzyna Górska, Mirosława Grabowska, Włodzimierz Grudziński, Wanda Kaczyńska, Andrzej Kajder, Ewa Ligocka, Maria Łoś, Antoni Macierewicz, Wojciech Ostrowski, Adam Podgórecki, Paweł Śpiewak, Tadeusz Szawiel, and Marek Tabin. On the basis of an analysis of twenty-one personnel decisions made during the previous two years at Warsaw University, the statement asserted that the school authorities used only political, and not scholarly, criteria in the selection of faculty members.

On April 30, KSS "KOR" member Henryk Wujec was summarily dismissed from the TEWA enterprises.

On October 5, KSS "KOR" associate Paweł Bąkowski was dismissed from the Institute of Meteorology and Water Management, but the Regional Appeals Commission annulled this decision several weeks later.

On October 12, one of the most distinguished European specialists in the area of surface metrology was dismissed after twenty-five years of work in the Institute of Precision Mechanics. This dismissal was connected with his participation in the reproduction of the "Survey of the Foreign Press" for the *Information Bulletin*.

On November 5, KOR associate Jerzy Nowacki was fired from work in the Cultural House of the Housing Cooperative Grunwald.

On November 29, mechanic Lech Wałęsa, an activist of the Initiating Committee of Free Trade Unions, was dismissed once and for all from ZREMB, whose employees had already prevented his dismissal once before. At about the same time, ROPCiO participant Jacek Bartyzel was dismissed from his work in the housing cooperative in Łódź.

Toward the end of December, ROPCiO activist Andrzej Woźnicki was dismissed from work at the Medical Equipment Repair Shop in Łódź.

On February 1, 1979, an associate of KOR was fired from a temporary appointment in the Television Film Studio POLTEL.

In March of that year, Mieczysław Macierzyński, a member of the Peasant Self-Defense Committee of the Grójec region, was dismissed from work in a dairy. Peasants collected signatures on an appeal in his defense.

On May 24, Joanna Duda-Gwiazda, a founding member of the Initiating Committee of Free Trade Unions on the Coast, received her notice from the Center of Ship Technology.

On August 23, Bogusław Śliwa, a prosecutor in the Regional Prosecutor's Office in Kalisz, was disciplinarily dismissed from his job. He was guilty of unwillingness to cover up a murder committed with the participation of a policeman. His letter concerning this case, addressed to the Council of State on March 3, 1978, was known to KOR and had been published in the *Documents of Lawlessness*.

The Qualifying Commission's rejection of the candidacy of Jacek Bierezin for membership in the Writers' Union (ZLP) was somewhat different, and caused quite a stir. Bierezin was an associate of KOR from the beginning; he was also the editor-in-chief of the independent, uncensored Łódź periodical *Puls*. A resolution of the PUWP cell in ZLP dated October 23, 1978, against publication in Polish émigré presses was cited as the basis for this treatment (one of the collections of Bierezin's poetry had been published by the Literary Institute in Paris). In Poland the refusal of membership in the so-called creative unions, of which ZLP is one, has greater significance than in the case of other associations. The creative unions give their members the same social benefits as those enjoyed by people who are permanently employed. The results of such a rejection are therefore comparable to those when one is refused employment.

But this kind of repression was not used on a mass scale. It is difficult to say why. Perhaps the circumstance that a dismissal from work was often accompanied by a widening of the conflict played a role in this decision: the colleagues of those who had been fired often protested, and sometimes effective resistance was put up by the management of institutions and factories. As we have seen, occasionally there were even timid protests from the trade unions. All of this might have discouraged the authorities from dismissing people too often.

Beatings were more common than dismissals. The list of those who were beaten, whom I do not wish to forget, is perhaps monotonous, but it is also symptomatic. The following list does not include the beatings connected with the attacks of goon squads on TKN or the assault against the actors from the "Theatre of the Eighth Day."

On April 19, in Wrocław, a student from the Wrocław SKS, Roman Kołakowski, was beaten by unknown perpetrators; this was meant just as a warning, so he was not beaten very badly.

On April 28, Kołakowski was again beaten, and more severely.

On May 12, the police beat Marek Adamkiewicz, another activist of the Wrocław SKS. He was beaten four times during the night.

In the spring of the same year (the exact date is difficult to establish, since the event was not noted in the *Communiqué* because on this occasion the beating really appeared to be accidental), unknown perpetrators beat up KOR associate Roman Wojciechowski in a coffee shop; he suffered broken ribs and a broken hip as a result.

On December 29, 1978, Wojciechowski was interrogated in Warsaw police headquarters. During the interrogation, the security functionary showed Wojciechowski a handwritten slip acknowledging the receipt of money for information given to the police. It was signed "Grochowski," but was written in the very cleverly forged handwriting of Wojciechowski. Then the functionary told Wojciechowski what would happen if several criminals were to be presented with a probable version of events, according to which it was Wojciechowski who had helped the police to capture them, and then if they would be offered an opportunity to eliminate him. One important aspect of this "project" was a realistic description of a slow throat-cutting by the perpetrators of this revenge. The circumstances would be arranged in such a manner that everyone would believe that this was just a settling of accounts among criminals hired by KOR. The functionary interrogating Wojciechowski also stated that he knew the assailant who had beaten him in the spring, but that Wojciechowski, as a harmful individual, was not under the protection of the forces of order.

The following excerpt is a quotation from the complaint lodged by Wojciechowski in the prosecutor's office:

> At one moment, the employee of the Security Service asked me whether I loved my seven-year-old daughter. I did not answer. He then began telling me about the perversion of the Gołaszewski brothers, who after murdering me would probably want to "play" with my seven-year-old daughter. He asked me whether my awareness of the fact that my little daughter might well become a victim of degenerates would not convince me to cooperate with the Security Service, which would assure security to me and to my family.

The prosecutor's office did not react to Wojciechowski's complaint.

On May 28, 1978, Krzysztof Wyszkowski was beaten by the police in Gdańsk.

On August 3, in Giżycko, KOR associate Sławomir Karolik was beaten in the face (he had participated in a leaflet action in defense of Błażej Wyszkowski).

On August 5, the police beat Zenon Pałka from Wrocław after he was detained in Warsaw. On August 7, after he had been convicted for supposedly disturbing the peace and sentenced to two weeks in jail, he went on a hunger strike. On August 14, after seven days of fasting, he was beaten again, since he resisted being force-fed.

On August 17, a functionary of the Security Service beat a detained member of KSS "KOR," Henryk Wujec.

On September 1 in Radom, during an interrogation the police beat an associate of *Robotnik*, Jacek Filipowski.

On September 9, in the City Headquarters of the police in Sopot, the police beat KSS "KOR" member Bogdan Borusewicz.

On September 17, Janusz Rożek, an activist of the Peasant Self-Defense Committee of the Lublin Region, was beaten in the Police Headquarters in Milejów. On September 20, Rożek, accompanied by approximately 100 peasants, filed a complaint in the prosecutor's office in Lublin.

The severe beating of Kazimierz Świtoń, which had serious consequences, took place on October 14. He was arrested, and the action in his defense followed.

On September 15, Jan Zapolnik, an activist of the Initiating Committee of Free Trade Unions on the Coast, was beaten in Gdańsk.

On November 12, Wojciech Jeśmian, an associate of KSS "KOR" from Łódź, was beaten in Białystok.

On December 20, the old and very sick Edmund Borucki (the father of Grażyna Kuroń) was not beaten, but tortured and abused. During a house search, functionaries of the Ministry of Internal Affairs put spectacles on his nose and with threats and shouts forced him to read aloud from the *Information Bulletin*. The effort worsened the condition of the sick man, and his sore throat became more painful. After his daughter and son-in-law, the Brukwickis, returned from work, it turned out that 100 West German marks had disappeared from a drawer.

The damage done to automobiles by unknown perpetrators, which was often inflicted on cars belonging to KOR activists, could have had consequences no less dangerous than the beatings. On November 12, 1978, it was discovered that bolts had been removed from the wheels of Barbara Toruńczyk's car. Luckily, this was noticed in time.

On December 11 or 12, the clutch line in the car of Maciej Rayzacher was filed down. Fortunately, it broke while the car was moving slowly and in a situation that was not threatening. A file was left behind under the hood as a "memento."

On January 21, 1979, Jan Tomasz Lipski and two other participants in the leaflet action in defense of Świtoń were beaten with clubs in the city headquarters of the police in Katowice.

On January 25, KOR associate Józef Baran was beaten during a detention in the street by plainclothes functionaries of the Security Service. His arm was broken.

On February 13, in Myszków, unknown perpetrators beat an associate of *Robotnik*, Jan Łaszko. An appeal to release Świtoń bearing twenty-one signatures was taken away from him.

On March 2, Jan Kozłowski, a peasant activist who was traveling to Zbrosza Duża in order to participate in the lectures of the Peasant University, was beaten in the police headquarters in Grójec.

On May 24, Janusz Rożek was beaten in the police headquarters in Milejów.

On May 25, KSS "KOR" associate Jacek Pilchowski was choked during an interrogation in Wałbrzych.

On May 26, Tadeusz Wolf from Kalisz was beaten in the police headquarters in Poznań.

From time to time, imprisonment longer than forty-eight hours was used as a method of repression, but this required at least a conviction by a sentencing board of misdemeanors.

On March 7, Bogusława Blajfer was sentenced to seven days in prison in connection with her participation in a discussion meeting in Wrocław on March 5. On the same day and for the same reason, Jolanta Bujwind and Janina Stasiaczyk were sentenced to three months of forced labor (with a 25 percent deduction in salary for the state treasury).

On May 19, Elżbieta Lewińska and Wojciech Jeśmian were caught in front of the WIFAMA factory in Łódź while distributing *Robotnik* (these were occasional actions undertaken to present *Robotnik* to workers in factories in which there was as yet no distribution cell; it facilitated later contacts). They were sentenced to three months imprisonment. Since the court (which serves as an appeals court when the sentencing board orders arrest) upheld the sentence, KOR, because of the severity of the punishment, sent telegrams to Amnesty International on August 23 and September 7.

On October 3, Roman Kściuczek, a member of the Initiating Committee of Free Trade Unions in Katowice, was sentenced to three months imprisonment for disobeying regulations concerning public order.

On December 6, Philippe Riés, a French journalist from *Informations Ouvrières*, was arrested in Świnoujście while traveling from Poland to Sweden. He was charged under Article 270 § 1 of the Criminal Code;[23] and also under Article 271 and Article 273 § 2 in connection with the previous charge.[24] Following his arrest, there were searches in the apartments of those KSS "KOR" members and associates with whom Riés had met in Poland. KOR protested against this imprisonment in its statements of December 12 and 18. Many French social and professional organizations, among them the Union of French Journalists and individual sections of the CGT trade unions, defended Riés. The embassy of the PRL in France received 15,000 protest telegrams. On December 10, the Congress of the Force Ouvrière appealed to the International Federation of Journalists to join in the protests. Several thousand people demonstrated in front of the Polish embassy in Paris on December 14. The demonstrators demanded the release of Riés and Świtoń. Riés was released.

On December 18, Second Lieutenant Henryk Jagiełło was sentenced to one year in prison by a Navy court-martial for possession of a single copy of *Opinia* and a single copy of *Bratniak*. On appeal, the Supreme Court suspended the sentence for three years.

KOR associate Sławomir Karolik was detained on March 1 and sentenced on March 2 to a fine of 4,800 zlotys or ninety days in prison for misdemeanors in Giżycho. The invented pretext was disturbing the peace and the breaking of two safety helmets on a barge. Since his family was never informed about his detention or about the possibility of buying him out, he was transported to the prison in Olsztyn, which he left only on April 10.

One could go on listing the varieties of repressions, both banal and inventive, but this is probably sufficient.

The Financial Report of the Social Self-Defense Fund for the Period September 1977–September 1978

The details of where the money collected by KSS "KOR" was allocated has been described in the preceding chapter. Someone was thrown out of work and persecuted for his activities, or sometimes for the mere expression of his views, and he had to be helped (unless he declared that he did not need help). A sentencing board would impose fines, and usually the loss in the private income of the convicted person had to be compensated for. The investigative activity of the Intervention Bureau cost money. Ever greater sums were consumed by printing and publishing activities (a large part of the money spent in this area, for example for the leaflet actions, was either directly or indirectly connected with help for those in prison). More and more often, KOR had to donate or lend money for initiatives that were independent from KOR.

The periodization of this history of KOR that has been adopted here obviously does not correspond with the periods covered by the financial reports. Thus, the summary of the financial report cited below, following

Communiqué No. 23, covers a period which ended not even halfway into the time we have been discussing in this chapter. This report covers the period from September 20, 1977 to September 20, 1978.

STATEMENT OF ACCOUNTS OF THE
SOCIAL SELF-DEFENSE FUNDS COUNCIL OF KSS "KOR"
FOR THE PERIOD 9.20.1977–9.20.1978

During the past year, that is, from the time of the transformation of the Workers' Defense Committee into the Social Self-Defense Committee "KOR," the Social Self-Defense Funds Council made decisions about the expenditure of the following sums of money:

- for financial and legal aid provided by the Intervention Bureau of KSS "KOR" to the victims of lawlessness: 1,000,000 zlotys.

- for the support of the educational activities of the Society for Scientific Courses and for aid to people repressed because of their participation in this activity: 125,700 zlotys.

- for financial support to the Independent Public Library: 47,000 zlotys.

- for help in organizing a Sociological Library to collect the results of scientific research in this field that are unavailable to the public: 2,000 zlotys.

- for financial aid to the Student Solidarity Committees: 30,850 zlotys.

- for technical means necessary for the publications of the independent press and books: 345,159 zlotys.

- for the publication of the *Information Bulletin* and of the *KSS "KOR" Communiqué:* 150,600 zlotys.

- for the publication of the sociopolitical monthly *Głos:* 167,434 zlotys.

- for help in financing the literary quarterly *Puls:* 30,000 zlotys.

- for help in financing the periodical *Robotnik:* 19,000 zlotys.

- for help in financing the periodical of young Catholics, *Spotkania:* 35,000 zlotys.

- for telephone calls, telegrams, travel, and other organizational costs: 35,560 zlotys.

TOTAL SPENT: 2,006,303 zlotys.

In addition, loans in the amount of 400,000 zlotys were extended to support publishing activities. They are to be paid off by December 31, 1978 (this includes 250,000 zlotys borrowed by the Independent Publishing House; to this date NOWa has paid back 203,290 zlotys).

OF THE TOTAL EXPENDITURES:

49.2% was designated for aid to the persecuted (the Intervention Bureau);
38.2% was designated for the financing of independent publications;
6.2% for the Society for Scientific Courses;
2.4% for libraries;
1.8% for telephone calls, telegrams, travel, etc.;
<u>1.5%</u> for Student Solidarity Committees.

100.0% TOTAL.

The Social Self-Defense Committee "KOR" wishes to thank all donors in Poland and abroad for their financial support.

This financial report requires several comments. How did one arrive at the round sum of 1,000,000 zlotys spent by the Intervention Bureau? The bureau received money in lump sums, to be accounted for *ex post facto*, depending on the need (the total amount and the approximate frequency of payments were defined only for orientation purposes). One million meant that, for example, the last lump sum of 80,000 zlotys had already been paid to the Intervention Bureau, but not yet accounted for, and what is more, not fully spent.

As far as credits were concerned: some independent institutions that made use of KOR loans preferred that their borrowing money from KOR and the size of their loans not be made public (obviously this did not affect the presentation of their cases by the Funds Council during meetings of KOR in order to obtain remission of their debts). The Funds Council and KOR honored such requests, if without enthusiasm. They created a somewhat equivocal situation in which, while KOR was treated as an institution with which one might have relations, one did not admit to these relations in polite society.

Finally, the item "telephone calls, telegrams, travel, and other organizational costs" was in fact greater than cited. The expenses of the Intervention Bureau are presented as a grand total, while it was precisely the bureau which spent large sums of money on these items.

It is necessary to add that from a certain point of view, these accounts do not reflect the financial aspects of KOR very precisely. They describe the expenses that passed through the Social Self-Defense Funds Council, which had only cash under its control. Typographic and binding equipment, and occasionally also other tools (for example, electric typewriters, tape recorders, etc.) were bought in the West by KOR associates living abroad (the major roles here were played by the brothers Aleksander and Eugeniusz Smolar, and by Jakub Święcicki in Sweden, but also by a relatively large group of KOR sympathizers in various countries). The money spent in this manner came from the Citizen's Committee directed by Edward Raczyński and from the Appeal for Polish Workers, and was accounted for in the West, while Poland received the equipment. The word *Poland* is used here on purpose, since the principal recipient of this equipment was not KOR but NOWa, which served as the typographic base for KOR. NOWa also distributed the equipment to other centers and provincial editorial boards, in this way participating in the technical organization of all publishing enterprises, which as a result controlled their own equipment, even if they maintained only loose contact with KOR.

The amount designated for *Robotnik* is strikingly small. This was a result of the fact that all donations from workers, if they did not come with specific instructions that they were for aid to the persecuted, were retained by *Robotnik,* while a large part of the money which came in as a result of the distribution of other periodicals, especially of the *Information Bulletin,* went into the coffers of KSS "KOR."

The accounts do not show any money disbursed to the Initiating Committees of Free Trade Unions. The explanation is simple: if *Robotnik Wybrzeża* or *Biuletyn Dolnośląski* needed typographic equipment, this would not be reflected in the accounts of KOR, as we have already seen. If people were subjected to repressions, the Intervention Bureau came in to help; if it was necessary to print tens of thousands of leaflets in defense of Błażej Wyszkowski or Świtoń, this was reflected above all in the financial accounts between KOR and NOWa (this was the principal means by which NOWa paid its debts).

It is understandable that because of the status of KOR, which from the point of view of the legal statutes of the PRL was not very precise, and because of a number of other complications, the form in which financial accounts were made available to the public had to remain as it was.

Changes in the Membership of KSS "KOR"

According to an announcement in *Communiqué* No. 20 of May 30, 1978, KSS "KOR" gained a new member in the person of *Jerzy Ficowski,* a poet and prose writer, an essayist, and a student of the works of Bruno Szulc and the editor of his correspondence; Ficowski is also a student of Gypsy folklore and a translator of Gypsy, Jewish, and Spanish poetry, as well as a writer of popular song lyrics. He was a soldier in the Home Army, and took part in the Warsaw Uprising in the "Baszta" Regiment on Mokotów; he was decorated with the Cross of Valor. He is also a coeditor of *Zapis*.

On July 28, 1978, KSS "KOR" and Funds Council member *Wacław Zawadzki* died at the age of seventy-eight. He was extremely popular among literary and intellectual groups in Warsaw. The basic biographical information about him can be found in chapter 3. Here I will only cite a portion of the memorial statement by KSS "KOR" on the day of Wacław Zawadzki's death, since I am convinced that it portrays the essential character of the man truly and exactly.

> Above all, he was a man of extreme kindness and disinterested helpfulness, which can be found only rarely; in him it was pure and uncompromising. What to the eyes of many looked like acts of sacrifice, what was generally regarded as a contribution deserving of recognition or even admiration, he saw simply as the quiet and modest fulfillment of his responsibilities, as something completely natural and normal. The undisturbed internal cheer which he exuded was not only a characteristic of his personality but also a form of courage. This sunny disposition never left him, despite the hard experiences and the dangers which fate did not spare him, and despite the illnesses that plagued him. He brightened more than one grim moment with his patient smile. In his ideals and in his actions which reflected them, he was so dependable and true that even his jokes—an antidote for pathos, which he hated—seemed to imply the stretching out of a helpful hand. Once, less than two years ago, after he had refused to admit a group of Security Service functionaries masquerading as workers into his apartment, and had received a letter threatening that a time would come when he would feel a "hard worker's fist" on his head, when a certain well-wisher expressed his concern that Mr. Wacław did not have sufficient physical strength and that he was living alone, Zawadzki reassured him with a smile and said, "And what should I fear? I can no longer die young." Those who did not know him better were sometimes astonished to discover the great stature of this physically small and unprepossessing, seemingly shy man.

His friend Józef Rybicki delivered a graveside tribute to Wacław Zawadzki in the name of KSS "KOR."

Communiqué No. 23 of October 16, 1978, carried information about two new members of the committee:

Wiesław Piotr Kęcik graduated from the faculty of the Jesuit Fathers in Cracow in 1968 after having studied philosophy, but he did not choose the ecclesiastical path, although he remained a faithful and practicing Catholic. He was connected with the secret organization "Ruch" (whose leader was Andrzej Czuma), and was arrested and sentenced to three-and-a-half years of imprisonment. He served his entire sentence between 1970 and 1973. In 1974 he began studying classical philology at Wrocław University, graduating during the period of KOR's existence. He was an associate of KOR from the time of its formation, occupying himself primarily with peasant issues. He participated in the work connected with the organization of the Peasant Self-Defense Committee of the Lublin Region. He was the editor-in-chief of *Placówka,* and a member of the Center for Peasant Thought. His wife Marzena, a Polish philologist and ethnographer who, while still single, was also imprisoned in connection with "Ruch," participated in all the activities of her husband. During the time of KOR she took an important part in the organization of the Peasant University in Zbrosza Duża.

Jerzy Nowacki is a Polish philologist and alumnus of Poznań University, a beginning writer and a student cultural activist connected also with the "Theatre of the Eighth Day." He was also a founding member of the Student Solidarity Committee in Poznań. He was associated with KOR from the beginning of its existence.

The composition of the Funds Council also changed. Shortly after the co-optation of Piotr Naimski as deputy treasurer (and cashier) had been approved by the committee, the death of Wacław Zawadski meant the loss of one of the members of the Funds Council. Moreover, *Communiqué* No. 23 of October 16 noted that for reasons of health, Józef Rybicki would have to give up part of his responsibilities. He remained on the editorial board, but resigned from the Funds Council, where he was replaced by Henryk Wujec. After this, the composition of the Funds Council remained unchanged until the dissolution of KOR, and even longer, since the council had to work on the liquidation of the committee's assets.

The Movement in Defense of Civil and Human Rights

Although it is not a part of our subject, that is, of the history of the Workers' Defense Committee, the histories of two very different groups—ROPCiO and the Seminar "Experience and Future," which emphasized its nonparticipation in the opposition—must be discussed briefly in order to acquaint the reader with the general situation during the period in question. As mentioned earlier, ROPCiO went through a series of splits which weakened it as a movement. Briefly, the chronology of events was as follows.

The Third National Meeting of ROPCiO took place on June 10, 1978. During this meeting the position of spokesman was eliminated (until then, it had been held by two people: Andrzej Czuma and Leszek Moczulski). Shortly afterward, in addition to *Opinia*, a new periodical called *Droga* began to appear, edited by Leszek Moczulski. The two periodicals printed inconsistent reports of the meeting. It quickly became common knowledge that there was deep dissension within ROPCiO, and that during this Third Meeting the most serious accusations had been leveled.

The Fourth National Meeting of ROPCiO participants was called for November 18–19; a number of people connected with the periodical *Opinia* (that is, Czuma's group) did not participate. "The Meeting decided that the mandates of the Financial Council and the Press Office, established during the previous meeting in June 1978, have expired" (these institutions were temporarily connected with *Opinia*). The Council of ROPCiO Spokesmen was formed (with Moczulski and Głogowski, signatories of the Founding Declaration of ROPCiO).

On November 21, twenty-seven persons, including eight signatories of the Founding Declaration of ROPCiO (among them Andrzej Czuma, Marian Gołębiewski, Kazimierz Janusz, Stefan Kaczorowski, Marian Piłka, Leszek Skonka, Edward Staniewski, Bogusław Studziński, Piotr Typiak, and Wojciech Ziembiński), signed a statement which concluded:

> We regret to state that . . . two signers of the Founding Declaration of the Movement in Defense of Human and Civil Rights, Leszek Moczulski and Karol Głogowski . . . , have, in the October 19 issue of a periodical edited by the Council of ZINO [the Group of Social Initiatives] for the purpose of registering [initiatives], included the totalitarian PUWP within the democratic movement in Poland. We declare that Leszek Moczulski and Karol Głogowski have by their own behavior excluded themselves from the Movement in Defense of Human and Civil Rights in Poland, and that we can no longer cooperate with them.

On December 9 and 10, "thirty-eight persons with the right to vote" participated in the Fourth National Meeting of ROPCiO which took place in Warsaw. The communiqué from this meeting, signed by Czuma, Gołębiewski, Janusz, Studziński, and Ziembiński, "on the authorization of the Council of Signatories of the Movement in Defense of Human and Civil Rights," states that "the programmatically open character of ROPCiO allowed for the destructive activity of certain persons and groups who undermined the spirit of our ideological assumptions." Thus it was decided that the form of the movement's activity should be changed by formalizing membership in ROPCiO. In addition, a Social Fund of ROPCiO was created, and procedural principles were adopted for the Financial Council.

At the same time, on December 10 in Warsaw, the Fifth National Meeting of ROPCiO was taking place. Forty-seven representatives from thirteen provincial groups were present. This meeting asserted that "the Movement of Defense is not an association, and has neither members nor statutory authorities." The Fund for Human Rights was established, and its Council nominated. On December 14, 1978, three participants in this meeting, ROPCiO spokesmen Andrzej Mazur, Leszek Moczulski, and Marek Marian Skuza, issued a statement in which they asserted that the group from the Consultative Group of *Opinia* "does not have the right to speak in the name of the Movement in Defense of Human and Civil Rights in Poland."

The disintegration of one of the oppositional groups cannot be considered a positive phenomenon. Still, the results were positive as well as negative. If one is to believe that cooperation between oppositional groups, and thus also between ROPCiO and KOR, is a desirable phenomenon, then it turned out that this cooperation was easier after the breakup. It seems that the paradoxical result (unfortunately still not to the fullest extent desirable) was such that the degree of integration within the opposition increased rather than decreased, even though various biases and inhibitions were still present.

I am unable to fix the date of an unpublished KOR resolution (it seems that it was connected with the cooperation of KOR and ROPCiO groups in Gdańsk, so perhaps it must be dated as early as December 1977), which constituted a kind of instruction for local groups associated with the committee, and which approved of joint actions with similar ROPCiO groups.

This attitude of KOR did have certain effects, some temporary and others more permanent and institutional. The immediate effects included the joint celebrations of the Gdańsk anniversaries and the Szczecin leaflet on the occasion of May Day signed by "the participants in RO[PCiO] and sympathizers of KSS 'KOR.'" The more permanent effects included above all the Club of Social Self-Defense founded on June 29, 1979, in the Wielkopolska and Kujawy Regions, where, despite some tension, the cooperation between KOR and ROPCiO activists was not bad. Very important in this respect was the Kalisz group, whose activists, such as, for example, Antoni Pietkiewicz, were never aggressive toward KOR, and participated in the already mentioned preparations for creating a new political formation to continue the traditions of the Polish Socialist party. The Club of Social Self-Defense in Lower Silesia, which was created in May 1979, was on the whole closer to KOR. In Łódź as well, the Independent Discussion Club was another place where the cooperation between the oppositional groups was not bad. In Warsaw, a meeting between KOR members and ROPCiO participants took place only once, and during a later period, in the apartment of Kazimierz Janusz (one of the activists with whom KOR maintained good relations, just as it did with Jerzy Brykczyński or Bogusław Studziński). Though unfortunately not repeated, this meeting was very useful, since it contributed to mutual understanding and allowed for a new arrangement in the cooperation of ROPCiO activists with the Intervention Bureau of KOR.

Unfortunately, information about the activities of the Clubs of Social Self-Defense and other similar initiatives is difficult to come by, since the Wielkopolska group, for example, did not publish its own periodical, and the regional press (including the widely distributed *Bulletin of Lower Silesia*) is difficult to find even today.

The Seminar "Experience and Future"

The Seminar "Experience and Future" (DiP) never wanted to be included in the opposition. At the time of its formation it included numerous intellectuals and activists, both party members and others who believed not only in the need for reform but also in cooperation with PUWP toward the realization of the goals of the reform movement. This was the fundamental difference between DiP and KOR (not to mention some other oppositional groups). KOR's short-term goals were also directed toward reform, but the reforms were to be a result of organized social pressure instead of cooperation with the authorities.

Stefan Bratkowski, a member of PUWP and a well-known and enterprising journalist, was the principal initiator of DiP. Its original membership included at one and the same time members of the Central Committee (Mieczysław Rakowski and Andrzej Wasilewski!), advisers of the Gierek team, and activists from both TKN and KiK, and even some associates of KOR (such as Jerzy Zieleński, a publicist; and we could mention quite a few other members of DiP who helped KOR on various occasions). DiP began its activity in connection with the Association of the Free Polish University. On November 14, 1978, the first—and also the last—meeting of the seminar took place, during which a party professor, Jan Malanowski, read a paper on social policy in Poland. The paper prompted a lively discussion.

The authorities then demanded that DiP meet several conditions, the fulfillment of which would have made the next seminar devoid of any sense and it did not take place. Among other things, the authorities demanded the dissolution of the "service team" chosen during the November meeting, which was to serve both as a secretariat and as an editorial board (Stefan Bratkowski, Kazimierz Dziewanowski, Bohdan Gotowski, Jan Górski, Andrzej Krasiński, Jan Malanowski, Klemens Szaniawski, Andrzej Wielowieyski, Andrzej Zakrzewski, and Witold Zalewski). DiP did not agree to these conditions. The service team then began to work on diagnostic-programmatic materials, conducting a survey among its members (as one could easily expect, the party dignitaries immediately withdrew from DiP). The results of this work turned out to be both serious and valuable; it was of a high intellectual quality and a credit to the group. In some oppositional groups it was viewed very critically; nevertheless, the team was regarded as a very positive phenomenon in a critical social and economic situation requiring a search for solutions.

There was yet another reason why DiP gained the approval of at least some KOR activists, those who, from the beginning of the committee's activities, had expected the formation of a group to mediate between the opposition and the party-government forces, which could play an important role in indicating possible reforms to the authorities and would have a greater chance of being listened to than the opposition. The fact that for such a long time a mediating group was not formed between the authorities and the opposition led one to suspect that the persons able to fulfill such a task did not feel responsible for the fate of Poland.

The General Situation in Poland in the Spring of 1979 and KOR's Search for a Program

In the spring of 1979, everyone was aware that an unavoidable catastrophe was approaching. Its approach was unnoticed only by those who did not want to see it, because that was more convenient for them. Those who failed to sound the alarm at this point, or made no attempt to help save the country, despite official self-satisfaction, are in one way or another compromised and bear part of the guilt.

In November 1978, Andrzej Burda, a professor of criminal law at Marie Curie Skłodowska University in Lublin, returned his party card. He explained his decision in a long letter to the party organization.

In February 1979, Janusz Beksiak of the Institute of Political Economy in the Main School of Planning and Statistics, a party member for thirty years, returned his party card and resigned from Gierek's team of economic advisors. He did so in protest against the authorities' disregard for professional expertise.

On March 16, Stefan Bratkowski made a dramatic speech at the party meeting of the Association of Polish Journalists. He argued that soon it would be too late for effective reforms, and that an honest national debate on the state of the Commonwealth was a precondition for any reform that could restore a minimum of public trust in the government.

It was clear that despite voluminous writings by the opposition, and in spite of such demonstrative warnings on the part of the wisest or the most honest activists of PUWP who were horrified by the situation, nothing at all would ever move the ruling team and the party. The catastrophe was approaching. Predictions of such a catastrophe can be found not only in such desperate demonstrations as the return of party cards by Burda and Beksiak, not only in the speech of Bratkowski, which was later circulated throughout Poland and certainly all over Warsaw, but also (and primarily) in the KOR press.

An article by Jacek Kuroń printed in *Information Bulletin* No. 3 (29) of April 1979 begins as follows:

> The basic premise of these thoughts is the fear that we are threatened by an explosion of social anger on a scale greater than those of June 1956, March 1968, December 1970, and June 1976, taken together. Such an explosion can very easily become a national tragedy (the probability of Soviet military intervention). . . . I do not doubt that all of us consider riots as an evil which we should try to prevent. Regardless of the threat of Soviet intervention, the Polish authorities—as was proven in December 1970—will not recoil from homicide, and they will surely still find the strength for that. The entire democratic opposition wants to realize its striving for parliamentary democracy and national sovereignty by peaceful means. I consider attempts to overthrow the system now—unless we are forced to do so—as irresponsible. The great costs of such an undertaking are certain; the national tragedy very probable; and any success doubtful.

Thus expressing his fear that an outburst would occur before social self-organization would be sufficiently advanced to prevent an explosion, while at the same time constituting a sufficient means of pressure on the authorities (he saw an inseparable connection between the prevention of an explosion and success through pressure), Kuroń recommended the initiation of a movement of social pressure (revindication) active also within official structures (for example, by appealing to the lower rungs of the trade unions). Moreover, he demonstrated the possibility of combining this process with the alternative variant: that is, with the presentation of a minimum opposition program.

> In the event the suggested minimum program of the opposition would become the program of a revindication movement, this movement would have greater control over the faction that would like to gain its support, and greater chances of becoming independent.

Reading these texts, one must remember that both Kuroń and Bratkowski believed that the explosion could come at any moment—probably by the summer of 1979. We know today that the events that led to the creation of Solidarity took place a year later and took a different course, probably because there was one more year during which independent social structures and their activities had a chance to develop.

It is not my task to wonder what would have happened if . . . It is a fact, however, that Kuroń's article accelerated the polarization within KSS "KOR." The *Głos* group, headed by Macierewicz, was especially firm in arguing for the continuation of KOR's existing program of creating independent parallel structures, and thus somewhat changed emphasis in the tactics suggested by Kuroń. Shortly afterward, in *Information Bulletin* No. 7 (33), there was a separate "gloss on the discussion" (as it was described by the authors) that was in part a polemic on Kuroń's article: "Notes About the Opposition and the Situation of the Country," written by Jan Józef Lipski and Adam Michnik.

These authors wrote:

> Kuroń bases his reflections on the possibility of a violent explosion of social anger. We fully share his concern about the possible consequences, but we believe that the problem of the functioning of a democratic opposition in society is broader than, and partially independent of, the vision of an approaching explosion. An explosion might result from the blockage of normal means of putting social pressure on the authorities, but the organization of

this pressure through official structures is a constant means of defending
society against totalitarianism; it has constituted a part of this defense for
very many years, also during those periods when the situation was not so
tense as at present. Thus the contrast between the opposition and the so-
called revindication movement might appear misleading.

And further, more bluntly:

> Should one work by creating independent institutions unrecognized by the
> authorities, or struggle for renewal within official institutions? This question
> is reminiscent of the classical problem of whether one should wash arms or
> legs? The answer is: both.

The article also pointed out—no longer as a polemic against Kuroń—
that "independent institutions . . . could not function at all if there were
no broad intermediate sphere between open opposition and the apparatus of coercion, . . . this is the sphere in which the majority of our
society lives and functions." Forgetting this fact could lead to the isolation
of the opposition.

According to the authors of the article, "independent institutions [that
is, according to Kuroń, the political opposition] are fragments of a broad
movement for the revindication of civil rights, of a movement whose
goal is the democratization and enfranchisement of our society." Lipski
and Michnik also regarded as premature Kuroń's remarks "about the
relationship between the movement of revindication and political opposition, and the various groupings, factions, and coteries within the
power apparatus," simply because nothing was known about the actual
programmatic conflicts within the party, so that the problem was purely
theoretical and currently irrelevant. The Polish October and the Prague
Spring suggested the conclusion that "the opposition must guard its
independence and distinctiveness as a fundamental value." Obviously it
would be absurd to maintain that the opposition could remain neutral
in a situation in which the authorities, or some of their members, were
to attempt to appeal to society.

Something else was also important (several paragraphs earlier, the
authors had pointed out the necessity of considering the "complicated
geopolitical situation of Poland"):

> Trade unions, here and now—regardless of whether these will be unions
> created alongside the official ones, or official unions controlled by the em-

ployees from below—provide a means for coexistence with the authorities as they are, and for at least a temporary partnership, by means of which the totalitarian authorities could be forced gradually to make concessions. A trade union activist who says that he will not dirty himself by talking with the authorities . . . had better turn to other activities.

The article ends with the following paragraph:

We must always remember not to indulge in the naive hope that the power of the PUWP, based ultimately on the military might of the USSR, will disappear any month now, or from one day to the next. The prospects for us are ultimately optimistic, but they involve a long period of coexistence alongside the rule of a single totalitarian party. What ideas this party will adopt about defending its monopoly of power, and what conditions or reforms this party will be forced to accept under the pressure of society, are not matters of indifference. The scale of possibilities is enormous. In every situation, the opposition will have to protect its identity, but one cannot assume that there are no conditions under which the opposition would ever engage in a dialogue on a specific topic at a time when there would be a chance to broaden civil liberty in Poland.

In practice everything went on as before, except for one thing: many issues and actions were undertaken under the pressure of this vision of a threatening explosion and the need to channel the accumulated energy in the direction of rational change. *Robotnik* especially began to make serious preparations, which involved the promulgation of the principle that strikes should take place in the factories and not in the streets (after a time this was expressed in Kuroń's bon mot: "Instead of burning the committees, form your own!") and in establishing channels of communication in the event of a wave of strikes.

The statement of KSS "KOR" of May 1979 "On the Dramatic Economic, Social, and Moral Situation in Poland," published in *Communiqué* No. 30 of May/June 1979, was clearly a compromise among the strategic tendencies sketched out above.

We are convinced that at present, social self-defense must express itself by overcoming moods of passivity, by organizing society in defense of its own aspirations into independent institutions (Peasant Self-Defense Committees, Free Trade Unions, Workers' Commissions, Student Solidarity Committees), and in the struggle to achieve an authentic self-government for unions, associations, cooperatives, etc.

In addition, the statement raised two immediate tactical issues: the struggle for inflation compensation for workers, and the struggle to find the forms and means of providing aid to family farming among the peasants.

The document ends with a dramatic appeal:

> Anxiety for the fate of the Motherland should lead to a general debate on the basic and immediate problems of contemporary life in Poland. Given our present situation, this is a matter of fundamental importance for our future; the solution of these problems cannot be achieved simply by changes in personnel. . . . The refusal to tell lies at work and in social activity, and the acceptance of truth as a civic virtue, should become one method of renewal.
>
> With a sense of responsibility, we assert that our country is in a dramatic situation. Faithful to our program of social self-defense, we turn to all Poles with an appeal for solidary action in the name of overriding national and social interests. What is at stake are goals, values, and desires common to all Poles, regardless of differences in political convictions, ideological self-definitions, or organizational associations. Historical experience shows that in times of danger we are capable of courage and of sacrifice for the public good.
>
> No one can absolve us of our responsibility for Poland.

Many conditions had to be fulfilled for the situation to change in the desired direction: above all, social determination in striving for change had to increase, along with discipline to push back the danger of a wild explosion. The organizational and educational activities of KOR constituted an important element, since they were thought out and consciously directed. But they were not sufficient. The pilgrimage of John Paul II to Poland was, so it seems, the factor that determined the fulfillment of these two conditions.

9

From the Visit of Pope John Paul II to the Signing of the Gdańsk Agreements
(June 1979–August 1980)

The Polish Pilgrimage of John Paul II

All the dramatic appeals, the struggles in search of solutions, the quarrels and polemics, and even the conflicts over the program, the strategy, and the tactics of the movement were taking place at a time marked by the constant presence of John Paul II, who was elected pope on October 16, 1978. His words, reaching Poland from Rome and from other places throughout the world, constituted one of the fundamental elements influencing the social situation in Poland, and his pilgrimage to Poland in June left its mark on the consciousness of the entire nation, above all on the young. This is such a vast subject that not only is it impossible to exhaust but its ramifications cannot even be indicated here. One thing can be said: spiritually, Poland before June 1979 and Poland after June 1979 seemed to be two different countries. Who knows whether the breakthrough that occurred then was not deeper and more essential than the one that took place in August 1980? In any event, the pope's visit was a condition, or rather an inspiration, for the Gdańsk Agreements.

In the history of KOR this visit coincided with an intensification of the consciousness of an impending catastrophe which influenced the entire period to be discussed in this chapter. In addition, a short time later, after prolonged preparatory work, the *Charter of Workers' Rights* was announced, a document that set forth the direction of the demands to be posed by the growing workers' movement in the immediate future, and which was also an important factor linking the creation of *Robotnik* and the formation of the Initiating Committees of Free Trade Unions with the strike in the summer of 1980 and with Solidarity. Nevertheless, these important facts from the history not only of KOR—as I would venture to claim—but also of contemporary Poland, were of a range and significance different from those of the pilgrimage of John Paul II, if only because they reached groups that were already active and not a mass audience, and because they could influence only one area of life. Pope John Paul II spoke to the entire nation, and he was regarded by an overwhelming majority as the highest authority, regardless of religious or even ideological differences.

After October 16, 1978, all of Poland lived, as it were, in a state of intoxication and expectancy. Joy over the election of a Polish pope merged with hopes more difficult to specify. This mood was accompanied not only by an intensification of religious life but also by ever more daring public manifestations of unofficial, genuine patriotism, in its noble rather than obscurantist version; by the growth of the spirit of social resistance in defense of human dignity and truth in public life; by a recognition of the duty to bear responsibility for all national and social life; and by increased courage, for which John Paul II appealed.

At the same time, the public was aware that the choice of the new pope was determined above all by two factors: the first and the most important was the personality of Cardinal Karol Wojtyła; but the second, also an important factor, was the authority of the Polish Church, which was able to find a victorious path and assure itself total independence in difficult situations, thereby gaining the admiration of the whole world. It must be said that the election of John Paul II also increased the already great authority of the primate of Poland, Stefan Cardinal Wyszyński. Everyone knew to what extent the Church in Poland and the entire nation were indebted to the primate for the unusual situation that existed in the country during the latter half of the twentieth century, a situation that would appear incredible to anyone familiar with the Bolshevik system, with its consistency and ruthlessness, and even its efficiency whenever the destruction of values and interpersonal ties are at stake.

All this created a specific atmosphere for the pilgrimage of John Paul II and for his reception in Poland, an atmosphere that was both populist and intellectual in a common acceptance of the values proposed to everyone, to the entire nation, by the Polish pope. This was the case—and it must be emphasized strongly once again—not only for Catholics but also for those of other faiths and nonbelievers as well.

KSS "KOR" published two documents before the pope's arrival. A letter addressed to the pope on May 19 reads in part:

Holy Father . . . in Your Holiness we find a spokesman for the best values of Polish culture, a culture that is free from narrow nationalism, a culture that is based on tolerance and pluralism, a culture that is associated with the Christian world of values. We find this sense in your sermons and messages, and especially in the encyclical *Redemptor hominis*, which is so important to us.

The letter cites the following portions of the encyclical as those that were of special importance to the KOR milieu:

And if the rights of man are violated under conditions of peace, then this becomes an especially painful, and, from the standpoint of progress, an incomprehensible manifestation of a struggle against man. . . . The Church has clearly formulated its attitude toward those political systems which have limited the rights of citizens, and robbed them of their inalienable human rights, and done so supposedly for the highest good, which is the good of the state—while history has shown that this is only for the good of a specific party that identifies itself with the state. . . . The very fundamental sense of the existence of the state as a political community lies in the fact that the entire society which forms it . . . thereby becomes, as it were, the master and ruler of its own fate. This sense is not realized whenever, instead of authority exercised with the moral participation of the society or the nation, we witness the imposition of authority by a specific group over all the other members of society.

In the second document, KSS "KOR" proposed that the Polish pilgrimage of John Paul II be honored with a general amnesty.

Such a law, based on humanitarian assumptions, should above all: a) free the invalids, the elderly, and mothers of small children; b) release those who have spent 15 years or more in prison without interruption; and c) it should lead to the reduction of long-term sentences. As long as the present prison rules remain in effect, all prisoners should be allowed to serve out their sentences under a more lenient prison regime.

The statement also contained a brief factual description that criticized the state of the Polish prison system and penitentiary policy.

KSS "KOR" was aware of the fact that the visit of Pope John Paul II, an honored moral authority, constituted something more than an occasion to raise this very important and overdue social issue. Nevertheless, there was some concern within KOR about the reaction of public opinion to the statement. The issues of an amnesty and of a humanitarian prison policy were not popular in Polish society. What finally prevailed was the great moral stature of Jan Zieja, who argued that the document should be made public because John Paul II, who had expressed his interest in the fate of prisoners on many occasions, would surely understand the intentions of KOR and react to them positively. Moreover, KOR had an obligation to present this important social problem to the citizens frankly and courageously, in accordance with its conscience and in the hope that in this manner KOR could contribute to the rectification of mistakes and to the adoption of humanitarian attitudes.

The party was also preparing in its own way for the arrival of the pope. It was training activists and issuing instructions in a manner that was astonishing even to those accustomed to this kind of nonsense: the activists and apparatchiks were fed a diet of hatred and bunk. *Information Bulletin* No. 4/30 of May/June 1979 published two such party instructions. In a stenograph of instructions dated March 10, intended for PUWP secretaries in the province of Zielona Góra, the following revelations may be found:

> It is known, for example, that the visit of Pope John Paul II to Poland is not dictated only by his love for his country or by the desire to visit his relatives. He did not leave the country such a long time ago, and it is known that he does not love his socialist motherland—he is even famous for this.

Similarly, during a training course, Warsaw teachers who were also party members were told in March that:

> The pope is our enemy, since he said a Mass for Pyjas. Because he is unusually talented and has a great sense of humor, he is dangerous, since he can charm everybody.

Indeed.

But in addition to these preparations, other strange things were also happening in Poland prior to the arrival of the pope.

On April 23 in Tychy, the local authorities attempted to move a cross that had been standing in the center of the city for 180 years. The attempt to remove the cross was made so brutally and barbarously that the residents of the city demonstrated against it. The cross remained in place.

KOR found out that during the day and in the night of May 2, attempts were made to set fire to two churches in the province of Kalisz. In Tłokinia, near Kalisz, the wooden door of a church was doused with a flammable liquid and set on fire. In Władysławów, a similar liquid was poured over a side altar and a fire was started. Luckily, in both cases the fire was discovered in time, before it could spread. During interrogations conducted later (on various pretexts) among a group of people from Kalisz who had links with the opposition, the police authorities were clearly interested only in a single issue: how had KOR received information about the fires?

More dangerous and symptomatic was the setting on fire—also in May—of the convent of the Franciscan Sisters Servants of the Cross on Piwna Street in Warsaw (which is already familiar to the reader; the convent is connected with the Church of St. Martin, where two years earlier the famous fast had been held in defense of the imprisoned KOR activists and participants in the 1976 workers' demonstrations). The fire spread dangerously, but was put out before it could cause greater damage. On this occasion it seemed that the circumstances surrounding this affair might be clarified somewhat, since the perpetrator had been caught; but the investigation got stuck halfway through. The question of whether there were more such incidents can be answered only by the Church authorities.

The *Information Bulletin* also published information prepared by the Main Headquarters of the Police for the Central Committee of PUWP and the Ministry of Internal Affairs. The most interesting part of this text is a chapter on "Directions for Actions by the Administration and the PUWP Apparatus," which amounted to a program of anti-Catholic actions using provocations and infiltration.

Setting churches on fire with the help of "unknown perpetrators" during the period preceding the pope's visit was basically a symbolic act, though certain more specific goals might also have been envisaged. However, the struggle by the Church and the faithful to be allowed to build churches also grew to symbolic proportions. This was becoming a pattern and a model for an independent and autonomous social ingenuity that ignored prohibitions. It offered hope both to the faithful and to non-believers that if some small village in the middle of nowhere could manage, despite the prohibitions of party committees, the Security Service, and the police, to build a church with its own hands simply because people wanted to build a church and needed one, then all the people together could build a free Poland—a Poland in which everyone would be able to pray according to the dictates of his faith, in which everyone would be able to teach others what his consciousness and knowledge had taught him, and to undertake together with others all collective actions as long as they were not against the public good. The great work of building the churches despite prohibitions and persecutions, inspired and promoted above all by a seminary colleague of John Paul II, Bishop Ignacy Tokarczuk from Przemyśl, was also a training ground in the struggle for a future Poland, one in which KOR found an inspiration and a model to emulate.

One of the subjects of negotiation between the Church and the authorities was the issue of including the Marian sanctuary in Piekary among the locations which the pope would visit during his pilgrimage to Poland. Archbishop Wojtyła had participated for many years in the religious ceremonies in Piekary. The communists, however, knew only too well the role of Piekary in religious life in Silesia to be willing to agree to this. They did not want to see John Paul II in Piekary.

From May 17 to 27, Kazimierz Świtoń fasted in the Basilica of Our Lady in Piekary in anticipation of the pope's visit there. On May 21 he was joined by Zdzisław Bradel, a member of the editorial board of the Lublin *Spotkania.* They broke their fast at the request of the bishop of Katowice, Herbert Bednorz, who feared that the fast could be used as a provocation to incite public disorders and disturb the pope's visit.

Nine beautiful days lay ahead for Poland.

The Polish pilgrimage of Pope John Paul II has been described in a variety of ways: in chronicles, journalistic reports, essays, and so on. The pope's homilies and statements are well known. This is not the place to discuss his visit in detail. Perhaps it is necessary only to recall that although virtually the whole nation participated in the ceremonies and demonstrations to honor the guest, the visit was a great occasion especially for the young, who were won over completely by the pope. He was able to establish a direct and live contact with young people better than anyone else.

All the ceremonies took place in a religious, patriotic, and social spirit. Until then, no one in the Church had been able to unify all these factors into such a coherent and consistent whole. Thus, John Paul's homily about the virtue of courage was understood by everyone, and especially by the young people, as a challenge. The visit was also a lesson in open patriotism, as distinct from nationalism, which the pope taught in many places, but especially in Auschwitz, where he made a special point, stopping at the tablet commemorating the martyrdom of the Jews. For other reasons, the statement about the Russians delivered by John Paul II in Auschwitz was of great educational significance for the millions who listened intently to every sentence he spoke.

In connection with John Paul's visit, there occurred a brawl over a banner displayed by students from the Warsaw Polytechnic, which KOR described in detail. The residents of the student dormitory Mikrus, which was visible from the route traveled by the pope, decided to hang out a banner with the quotation: "You are the hope of the world, the hope of the Church, and my hope." The matter had not been cleared with the administration of the dormitory, nor with the school or the pseudo self-management council of residents, because of the example of the neighboring dormitory Riviera, the residents of which were not allowed to display a banner reading: "Don't fear, open the door to Christ" (the prohibition was issued by the District PUWP Committee). Although Riviera hung out its banner anyway, it was torn down by the adminstration. The banner for Mikrus was prepared by the students of the Department of Technical Physics and Applied Mathematics, who also hung it on the building late in the evening. Three hours before the arrival of John Paul II, a group composed of members of the residents' council and administration employees, directed by M. Jasiński, deputy adminstrative director of the Warsaw-Polytechnic attempted to tear down the "Mikrus" banner. They tried to break into the rooms and cut the ribbons holding it up. The students barricaded themselves in their rooms and managed to defend themselves, and the banner was saved.

Shortly after the battle over the banner, the Polytechnic authorities decided to move the students residing in Mikrus to a location in a distant Warsaw suburb (Mikrus is located only some ten minutes by foot from the buildings of the Polytechnic). On June 25 students issued a statement protesting the decision to relocate them as a form of punishment, especially as it was also made during the examination period. In their statement they thanked the Polytechnic Council of SZSP for its support. The Faculty Council agreed to regard the students' statement as their own. In July the rector, S. Pażymkiewicz, rescinded the decision and ordered that the matter be reexamined. From then on, the Security Service took a particular interest in the students of Mikrus.

It is impossible not to mention yet another phenomenon that accompanied the pope's pilgrimage: the visit liberated and revealed enormous social resources invisible in everyday existence, which had been, or so it seemed, long destroyed by communist education. A great spontaneity and freedom combined naturally with a rare degree of self-discipline and respect for order, which the guards who were to maintain order had only symbolically to enforce. These guards, for their part, showed how easy it was to introduce the elements of organization, if only this is accompanied by general acceptance and consent. People acted different: kinder to one another, disciplined yet free and relaxed, as they enjoyed these few days of internal, shared freedom. It seemed as if people had been transformed. The nation showed its other face. These were truly unusual and extraordinary days.

During this time, KOR (and the entire opposition) discreetly stepped aside, so as not to complicate the situation in a period when the authorities had to accept everything that was going on around them, or even in spite of them. They tried to put a good face on a bad business, which incidentally was quite pathetic and sometimes even grotesque. But the situation was also tempered by John Paul II's beneficence, since he clearly did not want anyone to feel excluded or ill treated.

Perhaps this explains why KOR was somewhat bitter about what seemed to be the only dissonance during these lofty days. John Paul II met with a relatively broad group of Catholic activists and representatives of Catholic intellectual and artistic milieus one evening in the primate's residence on Miodowa Street. Present were the deputies to the Diet who in 1968 had not considered it appropriate to join the protest of the Znak group, when one representative of this group, Jerzy Zawieyski, had expressed publicly the only possible honest point of view; there were those who in 1976 had looked on indifferently as Stanisław Stomma, the one just man, had protested against the introduction of shameful amendments to the Constitution; there were those who, along with others, had approved of the 1976 price increases, only to retract them a day later with equal servility; and there were those who had remained indifferent to the torture of the Radom and Ursus workers, despite the fact that thousands of citizens later persecuted for their courage were demanding that this issue be raised in the Diet.

It was known that the guest list had been compiled in the secretariat of the Episcopate. No one expected that representatives of KOR or ROPCiO would be invited. But there was bitterness that no one thought to invite Halina Mikołajska, the actress who, over the past several months, had acquainted people with John Paul II's poetry by reciting it in churches around the country, and who had been persecuted with a vehemence meted out to few others. Her presence would have been a symbol and a compensation for all those who had been beaten and imprisoned because they had tried to extend a Samaritan hand to the persecuted. Unfortunately, her absence was equally symbolic.

Among those invited to Miodowa Street was Józef Rybicki, a distinguished activist of the anti-alcoholism campaign and a member of the Anti-Alcoholism Committee of the Episcopate. He told me that when he saw those with whom he had been invited, and saw who was missing, he hesitated, wondering whether he ought not to leave the meeting, though he knew of course that he ought not to do it because of the Honored Guest.

This was of course only one episode, which could not change the image of these unusual days.

The Charter of Workers' Rights

Robotnik No. 35 of December 1, 1979, published the *Charter of Workers' Rights,* a document that can be regarded as yet another step toward Solidarity. It was signed by more than a hundred activists from all over Poland, most of them connected with KOR and *Robotnik,* several associated with ROPCiO, and a few persons not involved with either of these groups. The *Charter* dealt with issues of specific interest to the workers: a minimum living wage, free Saturdays and Sundays for miners, a forty-hour work week, issues of work safety and health, the independence of promotions from political and other kinds of beliefs, and the like. The signatories—107 persons from various industrial centers in Poland—believed that it was time to demand a solution to these problems. Later, the fight for the same workers' demands was taken up by Solidarity. Two sentences from the *Charter* aptly characterize its contents:

> We want to begin with problems whose solutions—even if only partially— appear possible even now. . . .
>
> Only independent trade unions supported by the workers they represent have any chance of resisting the authorities; only such trade unions can constitute a force with which the authorities will have to reckon, and with which they will negotiate on a basis of equality.

Among the signatories of the *Charter,* both workers and intellectuals, one can find names which less than a year later, during the crisis of the strike in the Gdańsk Shipyards, would become familiar to the whole world: Lech Wałęsa, Anna Walentynowicz, Andrzej and Joanna Gwiazda, and Andrzej Kołodziej, together with other activists of the Initiating Committee of Free Trade Unions, the editorial board of *Robotnik,* and many others.

The *Charter of Workers' Rights* was distributed in successive printings of over 100,000 copies to almost all the industrial centers in Poland. The importance of this document was not limited to its programmatic contents and suggestions of specific methods and goals of action but it also played an important organizing role. After its appearance, organized workers' groups which saw the necessity of forming workers' commissions—at first in secret—to initiate collective actions, began to approach *Robotnik* and the individual signatories of the *Charter*. It was really only after the publication of the *Charter* that one could speak of a network of workers' groups, some of which had existed earlier as distribution groups for *Robotnik,* while others were only now getting organized under the influence of the *Charter,* which played an important role in the strike movement of July and August 1980.

The Initiating Committees of Free Trade Unions and the Workers' Commissions

On October 11, 1979, the two Initiating Committees of Free Trade Unions already in existence (one on the coast, that is, in the Gdańsk-Gdynia-Sopot tri-city area, and another in Katowice, whose members included activists from Katowice, Gliwice, Bielsko-Biała, and Wodzisław Śląski) were joined by a third such committee on the western coast. It was founded by eight activists from Szczecin and Gryfino who were associated with KOR and *Robotnik* (Danuta Grajek, Tadeusz Kocielowicz, Stefan Kozłowski, Bronisław Modrzejewski, Jan Paprocki, Stanisław Podolski, Jan Witkowski, and Mirosław Witkowski). The new committee referred to the *Charter of Workers' Rights* in its declaration.

The first issue of a KZ WZZ monthly for the western coast, entitled *Robotnik Szczeciński* (*The Szczecin Worker*), appeared in May 1980, edited by the initiating group and Andrzej Kamrowski. It contained both regional information from Szczecin factories and articles dealing with more general problems. The periodical was to have appeared as early as the previous November, but the Security Service had prevented this. KOR gave financial and technical assistance to *Robotnik Szczeciński.*

On January 23, 1980, the workers from the Gdańsk Elektromontaż founded a Workers' Commission in their workplace. The idea of workers' commissions had been discussed on several occasions in *Robotnik,* and was based on Spanish experiences dating from the final period of General Franco's rule. In Spain, workers' commissions were operating illegally, and even in secret, moving only gradually into the area of overt actions (in order to fulfill their goals they naturally had to come out into the open). Such commissions, linked to specific workplaces, could not have a strictly representative character, since they were not elected but self-nominated. Their goal, however, was to express the needs and desires of specific teams of workers, so that the commissions had to take upon themselves, as far as possible, the functions of trade unions. This very fact compelled them to strive for the highest degree of representativeness possible under the circumstances. Obviously, the Workers' Commission in Elektromontaż was connected with the coastal KZ WZZ. This was a result not only of direct contacts and cooperation but also of a personal connection: the commission was headed by Lech Wałęsa, who found work in Elektromontaż after being fired from ZREMB. Other members of the commission included Sylwester Niezgoda (a driver), Teofil Koszałka (a car technician), Zbigniew Dąbrowski (a locksmith), and Edward Słapa (a welder).

The commission was formed in the aftermath of the firing of twenty-five workers (further dismissals were also announced). These dismissals were of a political nature: a large number of workers from Elektromontaż had participated earlier in the Gdańsk ceremonies commemorating the events of 1970, and many of them were connected with the coastal KZ WZZ. Good workers who could not be accused of any misdeeds were fired. Often they were the only breadwinners in their families (even the factory council of the official trade unions expressed objections to some of these dismissals). The statement announcing the formation of the Workers' Commission was signed by 168 people (out of approximately 500 employees of Elektromontaż).

On January 30, KSS "KOR" issued a statement expressing its solidarity with the Workers' Commission at Elektromontaż in Gdańsk, and appealing to trade unions throughout the world to defend trade union activists in Poland.

On January 31, the commission called for a rally in the cafeteria of Elektromontaż. The directors of the plant personally blocked the doors to the cafeteria, but several dozen workers managed to get inside anyway. The workers demanded that the dismissals be rescinded, that proposed future dismissals be approved by the Workers' Commission, and that the workers be given an inflation supplement adjusted every quarter. The management promised to rescind the disciplinary firing of Wałęsa.

Tadeusz Szczepański, a driver and associate of the coastal KZ WZZ who had participated in the demonstration near Shipyard Gate No. 2 on the anniversary of the Gdańsk massacre, was also among those fired from Elektromontaż on January 15. On January 16 he disappeared without a trace. All attempts to locate him were unsuccessful. On February 9 his disappearance was reported on a local radio station in Gdańsk. On February 13 KSS "KOR" issued a communiqué about his disappearance, giving his personal data, a description of his appearance and clothing, and asking that information be transmitted to Borusewicz, Gwiazda, or Wałęsa.

Some time after May 20—the exact date was not established—Szczepański's body was found in the Motława River; his head was injured and his feet had been cut off. It was never possible to explain the causes and circumstances of his death, or to examine the files of the investigation that must have been conducted in this matter. The police did not allow persons carrying wreaths from the coastal KZ WZZ and from KSS "KOR" to attend Szczepański's funeral. Lech Wałęsa, Sylwester Niezgoda, and Maryla Płońska were detained for forty-eight hours (Płońska was dragged into a police car by her hair). The site of the funeral was surrounded by the police and Security Service. During the night, "unknown perpetrators" beat up Piotr Karczewski, who had attended the funeral, taking with them his identity card and the keys to his apartment, but leaving his money behind.

The investigation of this matter undertaken by the coastal KZ WZZ and by the Intervention Bureau of KOR did not provide any new information. In spite of all the circumstances presented here, which led to the suspicion of a terrorist police murder, neither the KZ WZZ nor KOR were ever able to make any specific charges, because the materials at their disposition were insufficient.

Strikes Between June 1979 and June 1980

The year separating the Polish pilgrimage of John Paul II and the large wave of strikes that began on July 1, 1980, was without doubt a period of increasing social tension and growing awareness that the authorities would make concessions only when faced with strikes, regardless of whether these concessions were to involve changes in the system of bonuses or work norms, or deeper changes in the social life of the country. Even so, strikes were resorted to only in moderation, as if the workers were gathering their forces, waiting for a big battle, and were therefore unwilling to engage in immediate, specific skirmishes. Of course there were a number of short-lived, limited strikes resulting from specific demands concerning wages or work norms; but regarding this period it is impossible not to accede to the official terminology, which avoided the taboo word "strike" and spoke instead of "work-stoppages."

Something else, however, should have alarmed the authorities. More and more often the strikes, which were still weak and timid, had non-economic causes: workers were protesting repressions used against their colleagues, as was the case in the Gdańsk Elektromontaż. Solidarity with the persecuted is always dangerous for the persecutor, and it threatens the very essence of a totalitarian system.

On December 16, 1979, Departments W-2 and W-4 of the Gdańsk Shipyard reacted with a short warning strike to the detention of their colleagues in connection with the ceremonies on the anniversary of the December 1970 events. On December 31, eighty workers from Department W-2 again began a warning strike demanding that the management abandon its plan to punish Anna Walentynowicz by transferring her to a different department.

Robotnik considered strikes in defense of colleagues as "an important stage in the development of an independent workers' movement in Poland," since "solidarity, and the defense of one's colleagues and leaders, are necessary conditions for the existence of a workers' movment."

Jan Karandziej, a welder from Department K-2 in the shipyard and an associate of the coastal KZ WZZ, was also defended by his colleagues when he was dismissed in January 1980, though not with a strike but with a letter to the management signed by twenty-eight workers. Disciplinary reprisals followed.[1] The employees of Elmor reacted in a similar manner in May 1980, when coastal KZ WZZ member Alina Pieńkowska was transferred from the factory health center. Since it was not easy to dismiss her (she was the only breadwinner in her family, and had an occupational illness that afforded her special protection), she was falsely accused of having left work on many occasions and of having mistreated patients. Her transfer was protested by 311 workers in a special letter, as well as the factory council of the official trade union.

It must be said, however, that such protests in defense of colleagues were taking place at that time only on the Gdańsk coast and only within the sphere of the direct influence of the KZ WZZ. There was nothing surprising about this. The tri-city area was already saturated with uncensored publications, not only those of KOR but also from local groups, and the activists from the area were dynamic individuals. Still, new groups distributing uncensored publications and self-educational groups were being created all over Poland. Many of these groups were small, but wherever they were formed, rapid changes in the workers' attitudes soon followed. Not only were people becoming generally aware about their own situation (about those issues they experienced directly) but they also began to realize that nothing would change unless they joined in collective, organized action. We were amazed and overjoyed when we discovered the receptivity of the workers, especially the young workers, and their willingness to learn about society. This willingness was accompanied by a concern about national issues, not only about the symptoms of the economic crisis that was affecting everyone but also about national culture. The activists of KOR never encountered any lack of understanding or disrespect for the tasks of NOWa or TKN; on the contrary, the possibility of contributing to these institutions or benefiting from them was a source of pride.

The list of strikes noted by KOR during this period was not very long. It is certain that most of the smaller conflicts escaped registration, and we might suspect that a full list, such as is probably kept in the Ministry of Internal Affairs, would be much longer.

On June 26, 1979, there was a strike in the furniture factory in Mszawa Dolna to protest cuts in premiums. This was a punishment for the participation of a large part of the work force in the pontifical mass in Nowy Targ.

On July 10 there was a strike in the Cotton Textiles Factory in Moszczenica, near Piotrków, in protest against meat shortages and wage issues.

On October 11 there was a strike in Department K-2 of the Northern Shipyard in Gdańsk, where workers were demanding changes in the system of calculating wages; the strike was unsuccessful.

On December 15 a strike began in the Polkowice mine (of the Lublin Copper Mines). This was the biggest strike in Poland since June 1976. The night shift in one section of the mine did not emerge from underground after the shift was over. The workers demanded an increase in the number of days off, a raise in wages so that they would match the wages paid in coal mines, and an improvement in the supply of foodstuffs to the stores. On December 16 miners in the eastern field of the Polkowice mine joined the strike; on December 17, miners from the western field joined as well. The strike was won. While the strike was still in progress, the Security Service made itself at home in the offices of the mine, rummaging through personnel files. The workers threatened that they would answer any reprisals against them by striking again. All the same, after the conclusion of the strike, the mine council of the official trade unions was suspended because of the support it had given the miners.

Workers in the Radom Telephone Plant struck toward the end of January 1980. This strike was precipitated by wage demands.

On March 20 and 21, there was a strike by employees of the Gdańsk Building Enterprises at the construction sites of Gdańsk-Zaspa and Tczew—along with the equipment storage and maintenance crew—altogether some 70 percent of the workforce. The strike resulted from a reduction in the so-called thirteenth-month salary. The wage demands were not completely satisfied, but workers chose new plant and departmental councils to the official trade unions.

A short warning strike also took place in Department 6200 of the Kasprzak Enterprises (radio and tape recording equipment) in Warsaw, as the result of a drastic reduction in earnings. A license to produce Grundig radios and tape recorders had been purchased "thriftily," that is, without instrumentation or detailed technology. The license was to be paid for with exports. It turned out that under these conditions, only 10 percent of production met the strict technological requirements. The workers saw no reason why their salaries should suffer because of nonsensical decisions made without their participation. On May 8 at 4:00 P.M., during the second shift, an actual strike began on the export production line of Grundig, and Department 6100 also joined the strike. At 6:00 P.M. police surrounded the plant. An agreement with the management was reached nevertheless (the earning losses in February and March were to be compensated). On May 13 and 14, the workers struck again in order to force the mangement to live up to these promises, at least in part. On May 15, a strike erupted in three departments of a locomotive factory in Lublin, over the issue of bonuses for the workers. The strike was a success, but later the management failed to make good all its promises.[2]

Patriotic and Religious Demonstrations

During the period between the pope's visit and the wave of strikes of 1980, a number of patriotic demonstrations took place in Poland, especially in Gdańsk and Warsaw. KSS "KOR" took no part in the organization of these demonstrations, and in every instance tried to remain on the sidelines. It neither interfered with nor participated in the organizational work. This policy reflected a deeply held conviction that if even one such demonstration led to a confrontation with the police (and if the police authorities had decided to have a confrontation, it would have taken place), the result would have been to slow down the work of the opposition, which was developing in ever broader spheres of social life. Nevertheless, the results of these demonstrations, organized above all by ROPCiO, were regarded highly by KOR. They played an important and generally positive role in the molding of social attitudes. The word "generally" has not been used here accidentally, and reflects a number of reservations:

1. There was fear that the demonstrations would not only awaken desirable patriotic attitudes, and above all the desire for sovereignty, but would also awaken illusions that these desires could be realized easily and quickly, and this could even prove dangerous.

2. There was concern about the tendency to replace work on the foundations of the future and the ever more rapidly approaching break-through with simply finding an emotional outlet in the antique shop of Polish patriotic phraseology, beloved by almost all Poles; a fear, that is, of being more attuned to verbal acts than to the organization of an independent social life.

3. There was a fear that, given the great frequency of patriotic cel-ebrations, all reasonable proportions would be completely distorted be-tween actions directed toward one anniversary or another and away from true social work, or even educational work designed to reconstruct a knowledge of Polish history.

4. There was fear of a new dislocation of the historical consciousness of the nation, which was coming into its own for the first time in years. Here we can cite two examples, to make clear what was at stake: the patriotic demonstrations were clearly revealing an enormous increase in the uncritical adulation of Józef Piłsudski (which had been significant even before the demonstrations). Piłsudski's existence had until then not only been passed over in silence by the official media but much had been done to root out his memory completely. The cult of Piłsudski has its *raison d'être*, a symbol of aspirations to national independence, but—to put it euphemistically—he was not a good patron of democratic ideals. And the second example: while in its educational work TKN reminded students about Katyń, the Molotov-Ribbentrop pact, and similar histor-ical events, this was accompanied by lectures and publications that at-tempted to present other noble and valuable currents of Russian culture as well—the resistance of people in the USSR whose thought differed from that of the ruling party and who had the courage to tell the truth also about Katyń. When awareness of these issues is generated mainly

in the course of various demonstrations, there arise simplifications and deformations that can easily become a breeding ground for hatred and nationalism. However, we must admit that the organizers of the patriotic demonstrations, or at least the wiser ones among them, who were genuinely guided by the standards of Christian ethics, were well aware of this danger. It was precisely Andrzej Czuma, a leader of ROPCiO, who, while leading a demonstration and presiding over ceremonies at the Tomb of the Unknown Soldier, reacted sharply to the slogan, "We will avenge Katyń," by arguing that we do not want revenge, only truth and justice.

The fears and reservations presented above characterized the opinions of most KOR members and associates, but they were not shared by the group gathered around the periodical *Głos*, two outstanding members of which, Macierewicz and Naimski, were not only members of the committee from the very beginning but were among its creators. Both Macierewicz and Naimski stated clearly that they would not forgo their participation in the organization of patriotic demonstrations. KOR saw no reason, nor did it feel able to forbid its members to do anything that did not go against the principles of the committee, or did not involve activity directed against the committee, or usurp the right to represent it. And so it was simply acknowledged that the *Głos* group would cooperate with ROPCiO (the Czuma group) in the organization of patriotic demonstrations. Obviously, it is one thing to organize an action, and thus to take upon oneself the responsibility for the results, and something else to participate individually. Many members and associates of KOR, especially among the young or middle-aged, took part in the demonstrations.

The first demonstration during the period in question took place on the anniversary of the Warsaw Uprising on July 31. After a Mass in the cathedral (which for many years had been requested traditionally by the veterans of the Home Army), several thousand people marched to the Tomb of the Unknown Soldier and demanded the return of "tablets ignominiously removed, which commemorated the struggles of Polish soldiers during World War I and during the Polish-Soviet War of 1920." An excerpt was also read from the final order of General "Niedźwiadek" Okulicki, the last commander-in-chief of the Home Army, who was murdered in the USSR.

The second demonstration took place on the fortieth anniversary of the beginning of World War II. After services in the cathedral, about 1,000 people carrying wreaths, flags, and torches marched to the Tomb of the Unknown Soldier to lay their wreaths. Józef Janowski, a ROPCiO activist, spoke about the tragedy of the Polish nation trapped between two enormous totalitarian states. Patriotic hymns were sung, including the national anthem.

The Confederation of Independent Poland (KPN), founded the previous day, made its first appearance during this manifestation (I will discuss it in greater detail later).

On September 17, Masses were celebrated on the anniversary of the 1939 invasion of the Soviet army into Poland. On that day KOR issued a long statement asserting that the authorities of the USSR were guilty of genocide against their own peoples, and mentioning the following crimes committed against Poland: (a) The Ribbentrop-Molotov pact; (b) the violation of the Polish frontier on September 17, 1939 (and thus a violation of the nonaggression pact); the (unsuccessful) incitement of Polish soldiers to murder their officers (in leaflets signed by General Timoshenko); the arrest of approximately 230,000 prisoners of war, of which barely 82,000 survived (it is impossible to say today what percentage died from illness and hunger, and what percentage from other causes); (c) the imprisonment or deportation to Asia in 1939–1941 of from 1,600,000 to 1,800,000 Polish citizens, of which approximately 600,000 died of hunger, poverty, exhaustion, and disease. In 1944, after the Germans were expelled from the eastern regions of the Second (interwar) Commonwealth, further deportations took place. These included the deportation of over 30,000 soldiers of the Home Army, whose fate remains generally unknown. In 1945 sixteen members of the highest authorities of the Underground Polish State were deceitfully kidnapped after having been invited to talks, and then tried and sentenced in Moscow (one of them, and one of the few ever to return from the USSR, was Antoni Pajdak, a founding member of KOR and an activist of the Polish Socialist party and trade unions); (d) the murder, in the spring of 1940 in Katyń Forest, near the village of Gniezdovo near Smolensk, of 4,500 Polish officers from a camp in Kozielsk. During the same period, some 10,000 prisoners of war from similar camps in Ostaszków and Starobielsk also disappeared without a trace.

KSS "KOR" stated:

> The Social Self-Defense Committee "KOR" proclaims that to this day the government of the USSR has not acknowledged that the Stalinist regime of the USSR was guilty of the crimes of genocide listed above, and has not tried to prosecute those who were responsible. Similarly, the government of the

PRL has not attempted to clarify the issue of Katyń and other Soviet crimes. On the contrary, it has used all the means at its disposal to prevent the truth from becoming public. The directive issued by the Main Office for Control of the Press, Publications, and Performances which prohibits any mention of the Katyń murders in the press and in other publications can serve as one example of this. In this manner, according to the criminal law binding in the PRL, the Polish government bears a share of the responsibility for the crime of concealing and preventing attempts to gather evidence and to bring to justice those responsible for genocide.

(It is incomprehensible why, after Khrushchev's speech and after the acknowledgment of so many Stalinist crimes, this particular issue has remained taboo, even though this policy has brought more harm than good.)

The next anniversary, that of November 11 (the restoration of independence to Poland in 1918), was celebrated above all by the Security Service, which on this day conducted fifty searches, including two police traps, detained eighty-four people, seventy-five of whom were detained for forty-eight hours or longer, used tear gas on two occasions, and beat eleven people.

By now it was almost a tradition that patriotic demonstrations would be preceded by a Mass in the cathedral, after which people would march to the Tomb of the Unknown Soldier. On this occasion there was a provocation that took place near the cathedral when the head of the demonstration (led efficiently for the entire time by Andrzej Czuma, who had a megaphone) reached Palace Square (Plac Zamkowy) from Świętojańska Street. The demonstrators were suddenly attacked by a large group of civilians, who, however, were armed with no weapons (not even clubs), apart from a tear gas pistol. The tussle was brief and the attack was repulsed. Nevertheless, one banner was lost and several wreaths and torches were destroyed. The demonstrators resisted passively; the thugs were not permitted to get through and were chased away, but they were not beaten (nor did they resort to beating). It is difficult to say what purpose this attack served. It was too mild to constitute an attempt to provoke a riot. Once the thugs had been pushed back, they made no further attempts to disrupt the demonstration. The police did not intervene. On the contrary, on the corner of Krakowskie Przedmieście and Miodowa Street, two busy thoroughfares, they were efficiently directing traffic.

At the Tomb of the Unknown Soldier, a crowd of approximately 2,000 was addressed by Wojciech Ziembiński, Bronisław Komorowski,

Andrzej Czuma, and Józef Janowski. Although Andrzej Czuma called attention to the fact that the demonstration was organized by ROPCiO and KSS "KOR," Nina Milewska also spoke on behalf of the Confederation of Independent Poland (Leszek Moczulski and others had been detained). After the demonstration, several people, including Czuma, were detained by the police.

The sequel to these events occurred on December 10 in the District Office of Warsaw-Center before a sentencing board for misdemeanors, where Włodzimierz Barel sentenced Czuma and Ziembiński to three months in prison, and Janowski and Komorowski to one month, for organizing a demonstration without permission, disturbing traffic, and displaying "demonstrative disrespect for the Polish Nation, as manifested in the fact that at a place held sacred by Poles, the Tomb of the Unknown Soldier, the symbol of all those who fell in the struggle for independence, the accused made statements that demonstrated their lack of respect and contempt for the Polish Nation which was accused, among other things, of lacking independence; these actions of the accused constitute an unacceptable transgression." After the sentences were handed down, several dozen associates of ROPCiO and KOR sang the national anthem. While the activists were leaving the building, the Security Service hurled anti-Semitic insults at them.

On the following day, KSS "KOR" protested against the sentences in a special statement, the conclusion of which read:

> We declare that these sentences constitute a public demonstration of slanderous disrespect for the Polish nation, which, deprived of its fundamental rights, has been using various methods in its struggle for freedom and independence, which has been taking place in various fields for over forty years.

The statement was also signed by the Club of Social Self-Defense of Lower Silesia and by the Club of Social Self-Defense of the Kujawy and Wielkopolska Regions.

In connection with the ceremonies of Cracow commemorating the anniversary of independence, a group of activists was not only detained but also beaten, when, following a Mass celebrated in Wawel Cathedral, they went to lay wreaths at the Tomb of the Unknown Soldier (Anna Mietkowska, Adam Jastrzębski, Marcin Mońkowski, and Wojciech Sikora from the SKS; Wojciech Oracz from the editorial board of *Spotkania;* Karol Domagalski from ROPCiO; and Krzysztof Bzdyl from KPN).

On February 26, when the Regional Court fixed the date on which those who had been sentenced were to begin serving their sentences,

KSS "KOR" and ROPCiO issued two identically worded statements. These statements also addressed the cases of Jan Kozłowski, Józef Kolano, Edmund Zadrożyński, Bogdan Grzesiak, and Zygmunt Urban; and, more generally, it also protested against actions of the police and the Security Service directed against the democratic opposition. Despite the important differences in their tactics of conducting their struggle toward common goals, the fact that ROPCiO and KOR issued identical statements on such an important issue testified to a rapprochement between the two groups on basic issues.

If this was the case, however, then why was the statement not issued jointly? After all, such a joint statement would have constituted an even more significant demonstration of unity. In fact, a joint text was being prepared, when Edward Staniewski, who directed the press office of ROPCiO, publicly launched a slanderous attack against KOR. His action resulted in a crisis of confidence, since the leaders of ROPCiO did not dissociate themselves clearly and publicly from this statement. Only the common sense of several persons from both groups managed to save the situation, so that something approximating a joint statement could be agreed on. In order not to exacerbate ill feelings, KOR and its press passed over this incident in silence. Shortly afterward, Staniewski ceased to work as the director of ROPCiO's press bureau and became more closely associated with Ziembiński's Committee for National Self-Determination, and less with Czuma's group, which continued to use the name ROPCiO.

The anniversary of the Katyń massacre is in April. In its statement of April 11, KOR called on "Polish citizens and émigrés to commemorate the anniversary of Katyń not in a spirit of revenge, but in a spirit of truth and fraternity among all people of good will of all nations." The statement contained words of thanks directed to the fighters for human and civil rights in the USSR, who have also demanded publicly that the truth about Katyń be made known.

Masses in honor of the murdered officers were celebrated in Katowice, Cracow, Łódź, Poznań, Szczecin, Tarnów, Toruń, and Warsaw. They were accompanied by police detentions, but on a relatively minor scale. The Katyń commemoration in Tarnów was especially impressive. On April 20, a memorial Mass celebrated there was attended by barely 500 persons (it had not been announced publicly ahead of time); however, on April 27, after a Mass had been announced in the independent *Wiadomości Tarnowskie* (1,500 copies) and on posters (400 copies), the services were attended by 7,000 people who filled the Church of the Philippian Fathers and overflowed into the street. Patriotic and religious songs were performed by a choir from the Jesus' Heart Parish in Rzędziny. In Łódź, in the Jesuit church, Reverend Miecznikowski read a letter on the anniversary of the Katyń murders from the Pastoral Emigré Center, signed by Cardinal Rubin and Bishop Wesoły. Two thousand obituaries were distributed in Poznań, where a Mass was celebrated by Bishop Aleksander Hauke-Ligowski and six other priests. In his homily, Bishop Hauke said, among other things: "Let us pray for the henchmen who are still alive, that they confess and show contrition, and for those who have died, that God be merciful."

The Katyń anniversary ceremonies in Warsaw were accompanied by a disgusting anti-Semitic episode. On May 12, as a memorial Mass was being celebrated on the anniversary of the death of Marshal Piłsudski, leaflets containing a picture of an open grave in Katyń Forest were distributed inside and outside the cathedral, with the following caption:

> One of the open mass graves. Artificially made hills were noticed because of trees which had been newly planted on them. This initiated the search. During the first investigations, bodies in Polish uniforms were discovered. The Polish officers who were captured by the Soviets became victims of the Jewish thirst for blood. Their twisted bodies lie in a grave face down.

The leaflet was being distributed by very young people, so there was concern that regardless of where the inspiration came from, this incident might have been perpetrated by someone other than hired agents. KOR member Józef Rybicki identified the source of the photograph and the caption: they were from a brochure entitled *Katyń* written by an Andrzej Ciesielski (probably a pseudonym), published by Hitler's propagandists and first distributed in Warsaw in 1943. KOR reacted to this incident in a statement of June 6 that described the incident and concluded:

> Anti-Semitism is a traditional weapon, used once by the Tsarist police, and then by the totalitarian system. KSS "KOR" warns against submission to anti-Semitic propaganda, no matter who is using it. We should remember that in 1968 the apparatus of power, including the Security Service, attempted to use anti-Semitism to fight against the democratic movement of students and intellectuals. Similar attempts were often undertaken in the struggle against the democratic opposition during the last four years of its activities. We warn the young distributors of anti-Semitic leaflets, whose ignorance and gullibility have been exploited, that they have become tools of the same forces that want to destroy the democratic and independence movement and to disgrace the name of Poland throughout the world.

Regardless of the other aspects of this case, it was a profanation of the memory of those who had been murdered and who were now being used for despicable purposes, and an insult to the memory of Piłsudski, who was far removed from anti-Semitism.

On April 27, 1980, in Nowa Huta, on the tenth anniversary of the events connected with the erection of a cross in that city, there was a demonstration of a religious character, although it was not organized by the Church, but by one of the recently created oppositional groups— the Christian Community of Working People—which emerged from the periodical *Krzyż Nowohucki* (*The Cross of Nowa Huta*); the organization was founded by engineer Franciszek Grabczyk, a member of the editorial board of *Robotnik* and an associate of the Intervention Bureau of KSS "KOR." The name of the periodical referred to a cross constructed in Nowa Huta by the faithful in 1970, which irritated the authorities, whose attempts to remove it caused stormy demonstrations on several previous occasions. Approximately 1,500 people took part in the demonstration. Even before it took place, engineer Grabczyk and Jerzy Budyń, another member of the Nowa Huta Christian Community, were detained for forty-eight hours. During the demonstration, agents of the Security Service attempted to pull from the crowd several persons who had organized the demonstration (KOR associate Józef Baran, KPN member Adam Macedoński, and Łukasz Świerz), but the other participants did not allow this to happen. I am unable to provide an exact date for the creation of the Christian Community of Working People, but the group existed under this name by January 1980.

On the national holiday commemorating the anniversary of the adoption of the Constitution of May 3, 1791, the most elaborate ceremonies took place in Gdańsk. They were organized by the Young Poland Movement. Approximately 20,000 leaflets were distributed. A Mass in the Marian church attracted some 15,000 people. After the Mass, about half of this group walked to the monument of King John III, where speeches were delivered by Dariusz Kobzdej, Tadeusz Szczudłowski, and Nina Milewska. Flowers were placed at the monument, torches were lit, and the national anthem was sung. After the demonstrators had dispersed, functionaries of the Security Service brutally beat several participants: Tadeusz Szczudłowski from ROPCiO; Magdalena Modzelewska, Maciej Grzywaczewski, Mirosław Rybicki, Piotr Bystrzanowski, Janusz Karolik, Dariusz Kobzdej, and Piotr Szczudłowski, all from the Young Poland Movement; and Nina Milewska from KPN. The functionaries also pulled the hair of Milewska's eight-year-old son Michał. The adults were beaten and kicked even while they were lying down, and then were beaten again as they were being transported in police vans. While unconscious, Bystrzanowski was thrown out of a car outside the city. Szczudłowski and Kobzdej were kept under arrest and sentenced to three months in prison (the sentencing board was composed of Jerzy Dąbrowski, Eugenia Dobrzyńska, and Antoni Radziwiłko). The board held its session in police headquarters. A statement from the Young Poland Movement named the following functionaries of the police and Security Service as responsible: Col. Władysław Jaworski, the chief of the Security Service in Gdańsk; Lt. Col. Raniewicz and Lt. Col. Jan Czechowicz also from the Security Service and Lt. Col. Zenon Ring from the police.

On May 15, KSS "KOR" sent a letter to Amnesty International containing the names of twenty-two people who had been beaten by the police and the Security Service since the end of February, and appealing for intervention. The list included the names of those beaten on May 3 in Gdańsk. A letter containing the names of those who were beaten was sent at the same time to thirty-one professors who also served as deputies to the Diet. This letter was signed on behalf of KSS "KOR" by Jan Kielanowski. Not a single one of the addressees ever answered KOR or Kielanowski. It was also not known that any of them ever took any steps in this matter.

Demonstrations on the Anniversary of the Events of December 1970

As mentioned previously, since 1977 the workers' protest and the massacre of 1970 had been commemorated by demonstrations, especially in the tri-city area. One might say that this anniversary had become an annual holiday of the opposition. From the time the Initiating Committee of Free Trade Unions was founded on the coast, the KZ WZZ became the organizer and host of the ceremonies. KSS "KOR," together with other dissident groups, called for a celebration throughout the entire country, above all through participation in anniversary memorial Masses. KOR published the times and places where these services were to be held, together with information about demonstrations in several cities (Gdańsk and Warsaw, among others).

The Security Service attempted to paralyze the ceremonies. A large wave of searches and detentions was organized. Approximately 200 persons were detained for forty-eight hours (many of them twice or even three times). Fifteen persons were put under arrest on the basis of prosecutor's sanctions. They were accused of membership in an association that planned to commit a crime.[3] The group was composed of activists from both KOR and ROPCiO: Bogdan Borusewicz, Mirosław Chojecki, Andrzej Czuma, Józef Janowski, Bronisław Komorowski, Sergiusz Kowalski, Dariusz Kupiecki, Jan Lityński, Antoni Macierewicz, Piotr Naimski, Marian Piłka, Edward Staniewski, Tadeusz Stański, Adam Wojciechowski, and Henryk Wujec. They were released on December 19.

The arrest of such a large number of people did not deter the opposition. *Robotnik* wrote truthfully: "People who had been actively engaged in oppositional work felt that their ranks had grown many times over. Both familiar and unknown people were coming to them and asking how they could help, or suggesting what could be done." The walls were becoming covered with signs: "KOR-RO" (the Movement in Defense of Human and Civil Rights had begun using the acronym "RO" somewhat earlier, since it was shorter and sounded better than ROPCiO). The signs were the result of an agreement reached between the two groups. Both groups intended to cover walls and fences with these initials. If this did not happen, it was only because the authorities came to their senses and released those who had been arrested.

In Gdańsk, shortly before the anniversary, posters and leaflets from the coastal KZ WZZ and the Young Poland Movement called people to take part in a wreath-laying ceremony in front of Gate No. 2 of the shipyard, to be held on December 18 at 2:20 P.M. On the day of the anniversary, the shipyard was idle. An official free day was announced "to save energy."[4] After the preliminary wave of searches and detentions, force was not used during the demonstration itself. The Security Service and the police were not active. Between 5,000 and 7,000 people gathered in front of Gate No. 2. Torches were lit, and hundreds of bouquets of flowers were placed at the gate. There was a wreath from the editorial board of *Robotnik*. The crowd sang the national anthem and "God Save Poland." Those assembled heard speeches by Dariusz Kobzdej from the Young Poland Movement, Rev. Bronisław Sroka, Maryla Płońska from the KZ WZZ, and Lech Wałęsa. Since there were fears that the Security Service would not allow Wałęsa to attend the demonstration, he had gone into hiding before the ceremonies in order to avoid being detained along with others who were prevented from laying wreaths; he was then transported to the gate hidden in a container. Following *Robotnik*, I shall cite here only the beginning of Wałęsa's speech:

> My name is Lech Wałęsa. I am one of those who formulated and bear responsibility for the slogan "We will help." I was a member of the First and Second Strike Committees in December 1970. Today I am in the same situation as all of us who have gathered here. We do not have the monument which Gierek promised us in the shipyard. We must hide and force our way in order to be allowed to honor our colleagues who fell here.

He also asked (unfortunately the oppositional press did not cite this portion of his speech) whether talks always had to be conducted in such dramatic circumstances, while committee buildings were burning, and why the authorities did not want to talk peacefully, right there and then.

It looked as if the authorities planned to prevent a repetition of these yearly demonstrations in front of Gate No. 2 of the shipyard. Late in June 1980 there was a meeting of Gdańsk architectural planners called by the vice-voivode of the province of Gdańsk, Langer. At the meeting it was decided that a supermarket would be built in front of Gate No. 2, and that the fence of the shipyard and the entrance would be moved somewhere else. The square would have been eliminated in this manner. The situation changed only two months later, and shortly afterward, three crosses now well known in Poland and throughout the world were erected in the square.

Memorial Masses were also celebrated in Kalisz, Cracow (approximately 1,000 participants), Legnica, Poznań, Warsaw (5,000), and Wrocław (2,000). In Szczecin, flowers were placed on the graves of the victims of December 1970. One incident reflecting the deepening disagreements and conflicts within KOR occurred in connection with a Mass celebrated in Warsaw in the Capuchin church on Miodowa Street.

Basic disagreements about street demonstrations had occurred in KOR even before the demonstration of November 11. Obviously, nothing had changed in this respect by December. The differences of opinion and the divisions remained the same. At the same time, however, there was a tendency within KOR toward increased cooperation with ROPCiO (Czuma's group) and the Young Poland Movement, since the goals of their struggles were the same, and in the existing situation, their differences concerned tactics, the style of action, and emphases on fundamental ideological principles. The last of these differences is worth stressing, and the ideology of the Young Poland Movement might serve as a good example. The Young Poland Movement had basically a neo-nationalist ideology, though the *neo* is very important. While emphasizing its Catholic character, this group significantly modified the traditional contents of Polish nationalism in the spirit of tendencies expressed in the Church after the Second Ecumenical Council. The problem of sub-ordinating the individual to the state was already far removed from the form tending toward totalitarian solutions,[5] which it had assumed during the interwar period, and was now formulated, let us say, more in the spirit of Cardinal Wyszyński than in the spirit of ideologists of Polish nationalism such as Roman Dmowski and Zygmunt Balicki. Significantly, while the editors of *Bratniak*, the organ of the Young Poland Movement, liked to quote Dmowski, they avoided citing his fascist and chauvinistic remarks. Also, the Young Poland Movement was not an anti-Semitic organization. Despite the fact that social-democratic and PPS tendencies were strong in KOR, its cooperation with this kind of right-wing group was still possible. At some point during the formation of a free Poland, their paths would have to part, but at this point the cooperation could be quite close.

Under these circumstances, KSS "KOR" (and not just the *Głos* group) participated in the organization of the December ceremonies together with activists from ROPCiO. The KOR member who ordered the Mass in the Capuchin church on Miodowa Street committed the first blunder by not giving the Church authorities sufficiently precise information about the purpose of the Mass. What was worse, only on the very day of the ceremonies did KOR learn that the program had been expanded: ROPCiO, together with the *Głos* group, had decided that a march would form after the Mass, and that it would proceed to the nearby monument to Jan Kiliński (a much shorter route than was usually the case, when people marched to the Tomb of the Unknown Soldier), where a state-ment would be read and speeches made.

The majority of KOR members believed that it was not acceptable to call people to participate in a Mass and then to offer them in addition a street demonstration that could end in any number of ways. People have the right to be told exactly what they are going to be involved in, and the leaflets that contained the appeal of the committee and other such publications, such as obituaries in churches, had mentioned only a Mass. Moreover, by calling for participation in a Mass which in addition to its religious aspect was also in the nature of a demonstration, KOR had taken upon itself the moral responsibility for whatever might hap-pen. Thus it was possible that the police might beat those leaving the church, and KOR would be held responsible in the eyes of the victims

and of public opinion. Thus, there was a grievance against Antoni Macierewicz and Piotr Naimski—a grievance they did not want to acknowledge—that by concealing their designs from KOR they had been disloyal.

Several hours before the Mass it became clear that this time a provocation could not be avoided. Police cars were concentrated near the
intended demonstration, and groups of easily recognizable civilians
could be observed in the courtyards of nearby houses and on street
corners. This situation prompted a hectic search for the organizers of
the street demonstration. It was not easy to find them; some had been
preventively detained, while others were deeply hidden and would attempt to reach the church only at the last moment. Luckily, it seems that
two of the organizers were located at the last moment. Their inspection
assured them that KOR activists who had demanded that the street
demonstration be called off were warning them for good reason. Shortly
before the beginning of the Mass, the decision was made to cancel the
march to Kiliński's monument.

The church authorities, who were also worried about the situation
(for the same reasons as some KOR members), even attempted to cancel
the Mass, but it was too late. The organizers, however, did not want to
forgo their opportunity to read the text of their statement to those
gathered in the church. The statement was signed by six ROPCiO participants and four persons from the editorial board of *Głos* (Ludwik
Dorn, Urszula Doroszewska, Antoni Macierewicz, and Piotr Naimski).
This event caused additional displeasure among the other members of
KOR. It was known that the Church did not approve of political pronouncements being delivered on their premises, and that was their right.
It was also known that there were at least some persons in the secretariat
of the Episcopate who did not have much sympathy for KOR. KOR
simply did not want to be burdened with decisions which it not only did
not make but to which it would never have agreed.[6]

A statement of KSS "KOR" about this incident was issued on December 31. It expressed regret that the superiors of the Capuchin church
were not properly informed about the purpose and the character of the
Mass, and that "a document with political content which was unfamiliar
to the Social Self-Defense Committee 'KOR' and which was signed by
ten persons" had been read over a megaphone in the church. The general position was formulated as follows:

In the conditions of Polish national life, places of religious worship have
on many occasions in the past and to this day served as locations where

intentions and attitudes toward national and social aspirations could be expressed. We understand, however, that the Church, as the only host of such places, must not only be informed about the content and the form of activities which anyone intends to undertake in places of religious worship but also has the right to set acceptable limits to these activities on the basis of its own religious and moral mission.

This issue became a subject of many disagreements and conflicts among KOR activists and in the KOR press, and it deepened the dissonance that had existed earlier.

Disagreements in KOR over Its Communiqué and Relations with the Second Internationale

It is impossible to disregard this most absurd chapter in the history of KOR, although I would gladly resort to any pretext to be able to pass over this particular episode in silence. The reader must be well aware by now that disagreements had arisen much earlier among those KOR members who were most active politically. It is difficult to say just when these disagreements began, although they manifested themselves very clearly when, after the basically consensual (though hotly debated) formulation of the Declaration of the Democratic Movement and the funding of its organ *Głos*, there was a serious clash over the publication in *Głos* of an article by Michnik. As a result of this disagreement, Kuroń, Michnik, and several others left the editorial board of *Głos*. It must be added, however, that in spite of this a total break did not occur, and that not only did KOR not fall apart for this reason but what is more, these antagonisms were not so serious as to result in a situation in which the publication of an article in the *Information Bulletin* or *Głos* under one's own name would immediately be interpreted as a declaration of membership in a faction.

In this manner the KOR milieu acquired two parallel periodicals, which were sometimes distributed by the same people. Nevertheless, the polarization was increasing, even if it was not defined "ideologically" at the time. Today, with the benefit of hindsight, these divergences appear more distinct than they seemed at the time; and the polemics that followed the publication of Kuroń's article in 1979 (already discussed) are one indication of this. After the initial conflicts over Michnik's article in *Głos* and Kuroń's paper came conflicts over the demonstration which resulted in a rapprochement between the *Głos* group and ROPCiO. The situation grew more complex when yet another conflict came to the fore, this time over contacts with the Second Internationale.

Somewhat earlier than the events discussed here, probably even before the spring of 1979, KOR had received information that the possibility existed that it might be accorded observer status at the Second Internationale. Certain preparatory steps were required such as for example the nomination of someone who would be authorized to have contact with the Second Internationale on behalf of KOR. The idea was suggested by several distinguished activists from the Swedish Social-Democratic party, who wanted to introduce KOR into the Second Internationale on the same observer principles as those by which Jiři Pelikan represented Charter 77. On the Polish side, this was the result of the work of Maria Borowska and Jakub Święcicki.

Even among the part of KOR with social-democratic tendencies, the issue caused some discomfort. Despite the fact that at least half of the members of KOR could describe themselves as social democrats, KOR did not have a social-democratic character as a whole. But what was at stake was not membership but observer status, which was connected with KOR's defense of workers' rights. At the same time, Ludwik Cohn, who had the greatest experience with international socialist activity (dating primarily from the interwar period but reinforced by later interests and studies), was skeptical about the project, claiming that the Second Internationale would be in no hurry to establish official contact with the East European opposition. In spite of these considerations, the social-democratic group within KOR approved the project, mainly because of a desire not to antagonize the Swedish social-democrats who had made the suggestion.

Most KOR members viewed the project in a negative light, treating its eventual realization as a sign of a social-democratic declaration and because it would create involvement on the part of the committee. A significant number of KOR members opposed the project not for political reasons but because they wanted to maintain the relatively apolitical character of KOR, which meant that the committee should not go beyond its general goals of democracy and independence by further specifying its political program. For this reason the idea was rejected unequivocally by Rev. Jan Zieja, Halina Mikołajska, Professor Kielanowski, Maria Wosiek, and others.

The *Głos* group protested against the project more sharply, opposing the domination of KOR by social-democratic tendencies, and their opposition transformed the conflict into a distinctly political issue. Finally, a compromise was reached: if KOR would also have an opportunity for international involvement in areas other than the Second Internationale, then the suggestion of the Swedes could be accepted. As a result, KOR sent off two letters on September 16, 1979.

The first was an answer to the invitation extended to KOR by the Liberal Internationale to participate in its congress. The letter was signed on behalf of the committee by Jan Józef Lipski, and stated that Jan Gross and Tadeusz Walendowski were to represent KOR at the congress, and that Jakub Święcicki would also be authorized to represent KOR in further contacts with the liberals. The important part of the letter was contained in two sentences: "We believe in the unity of the nations of Europe and of the world, based on their sovereignty. Such unity is impossible without the participation of the societies of Central and Eastern Europe."[7]

The second letter, signed by Ludwik Cohn, was addressed to the Socialist Internationale, using the Swedish Social Democratic Workers' party as an intermediary. In this letter KOR authorized Leszek Kołakowski and Aleksander Smolar to represent the committee in its contacts with the Internationale. The letter stressed that "KSS 'KOR' is composed of persons of various ideological and political orientations."

Nothing came of these letters (as Cohn had predicted), perhaps because of the interference of certain Polish socialist activists in the West, such as Stanisław Wąsik, who was in contact with the Second Internationale and considered KOR's step to be a disloyal maneuver designed to undermine his own group. The relations with friends in the Swedish Social-Democratic party remained as good as they had been before. These two letters concerned mostly the internal history of KOR.

Finally, there was a long and tiresome disagreement over the manner in which the *KOR Communiqué* should be published; for some time it had been appearing as a part of the *Information Bulletin*. This conflict consumed an enormous amount of time and frayed many nerves.

Since there was competition between the *Information Bulletin* and *Głos*, the *Głos* group presented the issue in the following manner: the joint publication of the *Bulletin* and the *Communiqué* (which was the only organ of KOR for which KOR was entirely responsible) conveyed the impression that the *Bulletin* expressed the views of the entire committee and not just of the *Bulletin*'s editorial board and its authors. This was misleading and improper, and simply intolerable to the *Głos* group, since they saw the *Bulletin* as an expression of a political tendency they did not share. The situation could be remedied by publishing the *Communiqué* separately. There was the problem of what this would mean in practice. No one could forbid the *Bulletin* from reprinting the *Communiqué* in its entirety, nor would this even be desirable. Nonetheless, the *Communiqué* was on the order of an official publication; it contained KOR documents (statements, appeals, letters, resolutions, financial statements, lists of reprisals that KOR guaranteed had actually occurred, etc.). Although these documents were generally interesting, they were not very attractive journalistically. Thus, the *Bulletin* would have been happy to use this material more freely: to summarize certain parts of the *Communiqué*, or skip altogether material that was less important or less interesting. This arrangement was not satisfactory for KOR.

The question of why *Głos* did not want to reprint the *Communiqué* itself was quite sensibly answered with the argument that a significant number of copies of both periodicals were going to the same people, so that it did not seem worthwhile to waste valuable paper and effort on duplication. The opponents of these changes cited technical arguments that were probably more illusory than real. Macierewicz and Naimski offered to print the *Communiqué* on the machines of *Głos*, but with money from the Social Self-Defense Fund. The conflict was becoming deeper, while various people made exceedingly ridiculous statements and nasty remarks. At the same time, both sides offered some rational arguments. In the midst of the dispute, Macierewicz and Naimski resigned from the Editorial Board of KOR.

This was a serious split. Given the growing internal polarization in KOR, it was increasingly important for the Editorial Board to represent not only the sum of the individual authors, but also the variety of attitudes among KOR members. A situation in which certain statements of KOR, made in the name of the committee by the Editorial Board, might be questioned or not accepted by other members and activists of the committee was difficult to accept, since it threatened the further work of the committee. Thus, attempts at mediation were undertaken mainly by Józef Rybicki, and independently by Jan Józef Lipski (whose name continued to appear in the list of "permanent associates" of *Głos* despite the fact that he rarely published anything there). An agreement was reached and a text was adopted on December 7. It stated basically that the title page of the *Bulletin* would no longer carry the title of *KSS "KOR" Communiqué;* the *Communiqué* would appear separately and be paid for by the Social Self-Defense Fund, though printed on the machines of *Głos*, while the *Bulletin* would continue to reprint the *Communiqué* in its entirety, preceding its text with the statement: "We are reprinting the *KSS "KOR" Communiqué* transmitted for publication by the committee." Moreover, the *Communiqué* itself would from now on contain the following sentence printed immediately below the title: "The position and opinions of KSS 'KOR' are expressed only in the *KSS 'KOR' Communiqué.*"

The text of this agreement, published in *Information Bulletin* No. 3 (34) of November/December 1979, was longer and formulated more pedantically. It was printed as information for the readers, who were very surprised by this half-page of print. Most of them had no doubt but that someone in the committee, or the committee as a whole, had gone mad.

The agreement had one more proviso, which was not published: Macierewicz and Naimski agreed to serve as candidates in elections to the new Editorial Board. However, during the KOR meeting that took place on December 7, after the unanimous adoption of the text concerning the new arrangement for the publication of the *Communiqué*, elections were held to the Editorial Board, and Macierewicz and Naimski refused to join the board. It is easy to see that these developments did not have a positive influence on future cooperation.

Changes in the Membership of KSS "KOR" and Its Commissions

During the period in question, the committee co-opted one new member: the journalist Ewa Milewicz. She had been active in the committee from very early on, and was an associate of NOWa and of the *Information Bulletin*. Her membership was dictated by the need to confer a proper status to Milewicz so that her statements would be regarded as authoritative. She was one of the most efficient and enterprising KOR associates.

On August 3, 1979, Prof. Adam Szczypiorski, a founding member of KSS "KOR" (born on October 10, 1895), died in Kruk near Gostyń, where he was spending his vacation together with his family.

KSS "KOR" Communiqué No. 43 of September 1, 1980, stated that "At his own request, for personal, family, and professional reasons, Jerzy Nowacki from Poznań ceased to be a member of KSS 'KOR' as of July 1980."

The Editorial Board of KSS "KOR" also changed during the period in question. As we know, the reason for the new elections held on December 7, 1979, was the departure of Macierewicz and Naimski as a result of the disputes over the mode of publication of the *Communiqué*.

Since the names of the members of the Editorial Board were not made public (for reasons explained earlier), I have some difficulty establishing the exact composition of the board, and I fear that I may make a mistake. No minutes were kept at KOR meetings, and the memories of the participants are not infallible, especially since other members of the committee (Lipski, for example), regularly availed themselves of their formal right to participate in meetings of the Editorial Board. The most probable list of board members elected at the meeting of December 7 were: Ludwik Cohn, Jerzy Ficowski (who, however, withdrew from participation in the work of the board a short time later), Jan Kielanowski, Anka Kowalska, Jacek Kuroń, Edward Lipiński, Adam Michnik, and Aniela Steinsbergowa.

On January 17, KOR organized another commission: the Helsinki Commission in Poland, whose members included Ludwik Cohn, Edward Lipiński, Zbigniew Romaszewski, and Aniela Steinsbergowa, which was to evaluate the compliance of the Polish authorities with the Final Act of the Conference on Security and Cooperation in Europe. The commission was given two tasks: (1) to maintain contacts with similar organizations in other countries, and (2) to prepare a report for presentation to the Madrid Conference. The commission prepared the *Madrid Report*, which was compiled mainly by Romaszewski, while Aniela Steinsbergowa oversaw its legal aspects (the state of Cohn's health did not allow him to participate intensively in the work of the commission). But the *Madrid Report* belongs to the next chapter of KOR's existence: the period of Solidarity.

Zofia and Zbigniew Romaszewski continued to direct the work of the Intervention Bureau.

The membership of the Social Self-Defense Funds Council also remained unchanged.

Repressions Against KOR and the Opposition

Police and parapolice repressions constitute an important chapter in the history of KOR and of the opposition, if only because widely used police methods necessarily influenced the activity and the attitudes of the opposition. Dissident groups often reacted with an offensive to especially outrageous actions by the police, such as imprisonment on false pretenses or dismissals from work. As one example we might cite the large leaflet action in Upper Silesia organized in defense of Świtoń. At that time, in addition to materials directly related to Świtoń, KOR also distributed other materials in the hope of extending the influence of the opposition. Pyjas's death initiated a student movement that represented a significant portion of the democratic opposition. Dismissal from work in the Gdańsk Elektromontaż led to the creation of the Workers' Commission in that plant, and so on.

What was the extent of the repressions during this period? (In previous sections of this chapter we have discussed some repressions that will not be mentioned here, except by referring the reader to previous sections.) A summary from the *KSS "KOR" Communiqué* should provide an answer to this question. The summary for January 1980, an ordinary month, reads as follows:

> In January twenty searches were conducted, including one police trap; two searches were conducted while the owners of the apartments were absent (in one case, this involved breaking in). Thirty-seven persons were detained for forty-eight hours, two for over twenty-four hours, thirteen for approximately twenty-four hours, and thirty-nine persons for shorter periods. On three occasions, interventions by the police and the Security Service prevented the holding of meetings and of a poetry reading in private apartments. In one instance, a private car was searched. Four people were threatened during their interrogations. Three persons were dismissed from their jobs, or the decision to dismiss them was finalized. The Regional Court upheld sentences handed down by the sentencing board in the cases of four people. On several occasions, activists of the democratic opposition were not allowed to leave the cities in which they live, or they were forced to return to their homes by being put on a return train. One of those detained was kidnapped from a bus stop.

Obviously, because of the celebrations of the anniversary of the 1970 events, December looked quite different. In addition to the "normal course" of repressions ("in December 1979, in addition to the special mass action . . . there were sixteen house searches . . . and thirty-nine detentions. One person was threatened with a beating, and two were escorted to a train to return them home. Two persons were detained in order to prevent them from giving a lecture or a reading. During one search, the police deliberately destroyed beehives and haystacks. Twelve persons were punished with fines or arrest"), there was also a "special action" that lasted several days ("in many places in Poland the police conducted mass arrests and searches. . . . The mass character of these police actions precludes the possibility of a precise listing of the names of all those who were subject to repressions. In several cases it was impossible to establish precise times of detention and release. It is known that the number of detentions exceeded 200, that there were many cases in which people were held . . . for longer than forty-eight hours, and that at least twenty persons were detained twice or even three times, or for as long as some seventy or even a hundred hours without a prosecutor's sanction being issued. Fifteen persons received prosecutor's sanctions").

Detention for sixty or one hundred hours without a prosecutor's sanction is, formally speaking, a serious crime, but when a person can be badly beaten or even killed in police headquarters, such a detention in itself amounts only to a nasty trick or a minor distress. The lists of those who were detained sometimes give the impression that the police bore a special grudge against certain people. Thus, if we read in the *Communiqué* that "on December 17, Danuta Stołecka's apartment was searched for the fourth time while she remained under arrest" (the dates of the previous searches were: December 11, plus forty-eight hours, or to use the jargon of the arrested, a "four eight"; December 15; December 16, plus "four eight"), then we know that the indubitable fact of the particular energy and intensity of Stołecka's activity does not fully explain such a concentration of house searches and detentions. She must have incurred someone's particular wrath, or else—as was once done with Mikołajska—the police were attempting to drive her to a nervous breakdown.

And, since we are on the subject of Mikołajska: on January 15, the police again entered Stołecka's apartment in Wrocław (on December 8, the police managed to detain Stołecka again for several hours, this time taking her from the university), but this time not the hostess, but her guest, Halina Mikołajska, was detained and sent back to Warsaw on the next train. This was not without reason, since Mikołajska was preparing a very dangerous, almost a terrorist act: she was scheduled to recite the poetry of Andrzej Jawień (the pen name of Karol Wojtyła)!

Luckily, one usually did not remain a police favorite forever, though some names constantly reappear in the *Communiqués*. Thus, for example, Zenon Pałka was repeatedly subjected to beatings, and in March 1980 alone he was detained five times. There was also a long period in which Michnik was fashionable, so that when on one occasion his and Kuroń's documents were checked in the street, and Kuroń was taken while Michnik was left behind, this caused some astonishment: after all, they were supposed to be detaining Michnik too. But the fashion for Kuroń never waned. His antagonist Macierewicz also could not complain of being forgotten by the Security Service.

Searches were often accompanied by destruction. There is some question of whether the damage was simply a result of vandalism or a by-product of the search. In any case, essential materials for production were often destroyed in peasants' farms. It is enough to cite *Information Bulletin* No. 2 (36):

> On February 21, in Osina Wielka, near Ziębice (Wałbrzych Province), there was a search of the house, the farm, and the courtyard of Maria Szczygielska, an editor of *Placówka* . . . ; bales of hay were scattered, and composition boards in the attic were ripped apart, as was the insulation in all the buildings; the soil in the greenhouse was also dug through.

> Górna Wieś near Błonie. On March 15 there was a search in the house and on the farm of Edward Koleja, an associate of *Placówka*, while he was away from home. His beehives were dismantled, which led to the destruction of the apiary. A dog house in the courtyard was also destroyed. Several issues of *Placówka* were found and confiscated.

> On the night of March 19 in the Górne colony near Milejów, unknown perpetrators broke the windows in three greenhouses belonging to Janusz Rożek (of the Peasant Self-Defense Committee). Because the temperature was − 11° Centigrade, his vegetables froze.

Such happenings were less common in the cities. But when the police really wanted to harass someone, they did not lack inventive ideas:

> November 15: there was a search and a trap set up in the apartment of Kazimierz Świtoń—from 10:30 P.M. to 1:40 A.M. Floors were torn up and cabinets taken apart.

Or, as was elegantly formulated in *Communiqué* No. 38 of March 31, 1980: in Henryk Wujec's apartment during a search on March 1, 1980, "Captain Celewski . . . did not show what objects he was taking away."

There were large-scale detentions in connection with the case of Jan Kozłowski, which will be discussed in a separate section.

One of the most scandalous cases was the treatment of KOR associate Jerzy Geresz. In January 1980, during the detention that followed his visit to Świtoń, the Katowice Security Service had already threatened Geresz with severe punishment if he ever tried to visit Świtoń again. On May 23, the police stopped Geresz in Katowice and detained him for forty-four hours in Sosnowiec. After this, he was taken in handcuffs all the way to Tarnów province and left in a forest, with the threat that if he returned to Katowice, "he would regret it to the end of his days." On July 17, Geresz was stopped again after he left Świtoń's apartment, and beaten in police headquarters. It should be added that Geresz is 65 percent disabled as a result of having been hit by a car. On July 18, he was to be judged by a sentencing board for misdemeanors (chairman: H. Piwowarczyk; members: Ł. Fechner and W. Bartos; prosecutor: senior ensign Rudzki of the police) under the pretext of having refused to show his identification papers to the police. Geresz asserted that no one had asked him for his papers, and that instead he had been beaten. This claim was not put into the court record because it bore no relation to the case! He was sentenced to a fine of 3,000 zlotys or 60 days of imprisonment. He did not have the money, so he was transported to a prison in Mysłowice. He was not allowed to file an appeal, and in violation of the Code of Criminal Procedure, no one was informed of his arrest or whereabouts. His friends and his elderly father, a peasant from Podlasie, searched for Geresz for a month. In jail, Geresz, who had felt ill (he had earlier undergone a stomach operation), was not allowed to see a doctor. On July 23, when prison authorities refused him a Bible that he had had with him at the time of his arrest, he began a hunger strike and was immediately beaten again. After three days, however, he was given his Bible. After a month, because there was no answer to the letters he had sent (among others, to the mayor of the city and to the chairman of the Council of State), Geresz again began a hunger strike. During the first three days, he was repeatedly mistreated in his cell by privileged criminal prisoners with whom he was being kept. The warden of this section of the jail encouraged these sadists to torment Geresz. On August 24, he was released: the attempt to locate him was successful, and Świtoń paid the outstanding fine. With his wrists handcuffed behind him, Geresz was put in a police car and driven to a forest, where he was let out. This was after almost eight days of a hunger strike and after multiple severe beatings in his cell. Since this took place in Katowice province, Geresz again went to see Świtoń.

On September 17, the sentencing board for misdemeanors in Warsaw-Center sentenced Adam Wojciechowski (ROPCiO) to two months of unconditional imprisonment for disturbing the peace.

On December 11, 1979, a Swedish citizen, Björn Laqvist, was stopped in Świnoujście as he was crossing the Polish border with a duplicating machine. He was placed under arrest. Fearing a worsening of his situation, the Swedish consulate in Warsaw asked KOR to delay issuing a statement on the grounds that Laqvist would be released. When their hopes failed, KOR issued a public statement on January 4, 1980. It read in part:

> On many occasions KSS "KOR" and the entire democratic opposition in Poland have appealed to their friends around the world to bring duplicating machines to Poland. We are still asking them to do so. In our country it is impossible to purchase a duplicating machine. Independent publishing, for which the duplicating machines are necessary, is indispensable to the development of our national culture. Because of the state printing monopoly and because of preventive censorship, these duplicating machines are used to publish works by outstanding authors banned by the censorship, such as the works of Witold Gombrowicz, Jerzy Andrzejewski, or Günter Grass. The arrest of Björn Laqvist is yet another violation of the International Covenant on Civil and Political Rights, which constitutes a legal norm in Poland. We demand that our friend be released immediately.

This statement, translated into English, was sent to many representatives of public opinion, especially in Sweden. It was accompanied by explanatory letters from Edward Lipiński, Jacek Kuroń, or Jan Józef Lipski. On January 29, Laqvist was released and expelled from Poland after he paid a customs fine imposed by the authorities.

Before the commemorations of the anniversary of the December massacre of workers on the coast, fifteen activists of KOR and ROPCiO were arrested in Warsaw and received prosecutor's sanctions (see the section on "Demonstrations on the Anniversary of the Events of December 1970").

On December 17 in Legnica, Zygmunt Urban, a member of KPN, was arrested for having allegedly assaulted a functionary of the police. Despite fifteen years of experience at his job, Urban, a librarian, was dismissed on August 31 for participating in papal ceremonies in June at Jasna Góra (he had used a day off from work in order to attend them). On December 17, Urban was being interrogated by the police. When he started feeling ill (he suffered from a disease of the nervous system), the police refused to interrupt the interrogation. He wanted to leave the room, and for this, he received a one-month prosecutor's sanction on the basis of an article that provides for a punishment of up to eight years imprisonment for "whoever commits an active assault on a functionary of the police." On January 17, the investigation (!) was extended for another month.

In March, Anatol Lawina (an associate of KOR and of NOWa) was sentenced to three months in prison for distributing leaflets calling for a boycott of the elections to the Diet. On the same grounds, Adam

Wojciechowski (ROPCiO) was sentenced to two months imprisonment (on appeal, the sentences were reduced by one month each). This was part of a preventive action of repression conducted before the elections. KSS "KOR" appealed in a letter of April 5 to Amnesty International to intervene in these cases. There was also no shortage of dismissals from work.

On June 25, Robert Kaczmarek, an activist of the Academic Ministry and an associate of the SKS, was dismissed from the Institute of Energy Systems Control in the Mining and Metallurgical Academy in Cracow. He was denounced for selling *Merkuriusz Krakowski i Światowy* (a student periodical).

On August 7, Piotr Starzyński, a computer programmer and an associate of KOR and member of the Social Self-Defense Committee of Lower Silesia, was fired from MERA-ELWRO in Wrocław. He could only find work as an unqualified orderly in a hospital.

On September 10, the Regional Labor Court in Łódź dismissed the claims of an electrician from Pabianice, Marek Chwalewski, who was suing the Łódź Chemical Plant Organika. On the basis of an earlier decision by the same court, the plant was required to respect the work contract with Chwalewski and rehire him. They did so, only to dismiss him two hours later (!). On the second occasion, the composition of the court was different. Chwalewski was unemployed for two years.[8]

On October 9, two signatories of the *Charter of Workers' Rights*, Mirosław Witkowski and Stanisław Podolski, were dismissed from work in Gryfino (Szczecin province).

On November 22, coastal KZ WZZ member Andrzej Bulc was not allowed to enter the grounds of ELMOR, where he worked, despite a decision by the Regional Appeals Commission ordering that he be reinstated to his job.

On November 27, KOR associate Stanisław Siekanowicz was given notice by the state archives in Gorzów, where he was employed. After this, on three successive occasions, the workplaces to which he was directed by the Employment Bureau failed to hire him after a trial period.

In December, twenty-five workers from the Gdańsk Elektromontaż were fired for having participated in the demonstration on the anniversary of the massacre of 1970 (see the section on "Initiating Committees of Free Trade Unions and Workers' Commissions").

In January, coastal KZ WZZ member Andrzej Kołodziej was dismissed from his job at the Gdańsk Shipyard.

On February 9, 1980, the Ministry of Science, Higher Education, and Technology issued a final approval of the dismissal of Dr. Michał Siciński from his work in the Mining and Metallurgical Academy. He had been detained on two occasions for his contacts with the SKS and TKN.

On April 1, Mieczysław Klamrowski was fired from the Gdańsk Shipyard in connection with the October strike in Department W-2.

On April 30, Piotr Franielczyk, a lathe worker, was fired from the Lower Silesian Factory of Electrical Machines (DOLMEL) in Wrocław. He had refused to sign a declaration that he would discontinue his oppositional activity.

Beatings were even more common.

On August 16, an associate of the Young Poland Movement, Jacek Kominek, was beaten in Koscierzyn.

On September 3, a member of the KZ WZZ for the western coast, Stanisłas Podolski, was beaten in the police headquarters in Szczecin.

On September 27, two associates of *Robotnik* from Rzeszów, Jan Nowak and Janusz Szkutnik, were beaten in the police headquarters in Warsaw.

In the section on Polish-Czechoslovak relations the case of the beating of students detained near the Center of Czechoslovak Culture will be discussed.

On October 27, a uniformed police officer beat coastal KZ WZZ member Andrzej Kołodziej on the face after printing equipment was found in Kołodziej's possession during a search in the workers' hotel.

On November 9, Bogdan Borusewicz was beaten during his detention in Warsaw (following a police interruption of a meeting of the Editorial Board of *Robotnik*).

I have already mentioned the beatings that occurred in connection with the ceremonies on the anniversary of the restoration of independence on November 11.

On November 12, "unknown perpetrators" beat Bronisław Modrzejewski, a member of the KZ WZZ for the western coast, as he was going to work on a night shift (on October 31 he had been assaulted in the street, and there had been an attempt to drag him into a car, but he had managed to defend himself and his attackers escaped). His left hand was paralyzed as a result of injuries. During the beating, the attackers shouted that this was his punishment for free trade unions.

On November 15, Tomasz Mróz from Bytom was beaten after having been detained in Świtoń's apartment.

On November 23, KOR associate Wojciech Ostrowski was beaten as he was being released from the police headquarters.

On February 4, Ryszard Świtoń, the son of Kazimierz and an activist of the KZ WZZ in Katowice, was beaten on the street by some not entirely "unknown" perpetrators—the victim recognized among them some of the agents who had conducted surveillance of his father. Passersby rescued Świtoń from the hands of the thugs, who escaped.

On February 21, Zbigniew Staruch from Tarnów was beaten about the face in the police headquarters in Bochnia.

On February 23, an associate of the KZ WZZ in Katowice, Jan Świtoń (another son of Kazimierz) was detained in Zawiercie. At the police headquarters his face was burned with a cigarette.

On February 25, Wiktor Karpiński and Krzysztof Lachowski, two students in the Department of Technical Physics and Applied Mathematics at Warsaw Polytechnic and residents of the dormitory Mikrus, were beaten. On the previous day the police had found printing equipment and some uncensored publications in the room occupied by the two students. Lachowski was tortured with particular cruelty and beaten every time he referred to Article 166 of the Code of Criminal Procedure (the right to refuse to give evidence if the person being interrogated fears that the answer may expose him to criminal sanctions). He was doused with hot (not boiling) water, and a match was stuck in his ear and the threat made that his ear drum would be punctured. He was also threatened with being locked up in a cell with homosexuals who would know they had permission to rape him. On February 29, the Polytechnic Council of SZSP published a leaflet with the Security Service version of this case.

On February 14, Czesław Chomicki was detained in Radom.[9] The agents accused him of hitting a man who tried to take a taxi without waiting for his turn at the taxi stand. After being detained, Chomicki was taken to a drunk tank, probably to make the case look more spectacular. After this, his wife Danuta was beaten up when she arrived at the drunk tank, trying to find out what was going on. On February 15, the court in Radom in summary proceedings tried Chomicki for hooliganism. Witnesses to the event, including the alleged victim, denied the police version. The defense attorney, Władysław Siła-Nowicki, demanded a medical examination because of the visible signs of beating on Chomicki's face. The notorious Judge Elżbieta Dobrowolska (known from the Radom trials of 1976) denied the request. The defense attorney announced that because of the signs of beating visible on Chomicki's face, he would have to call the judges, the prosecutor, and the reporters, as well as all those present in the room, as witnesses. The case was postponed. Before this took place, Judge Dobrowolska removed an observer from KOR, Ewa Soból, from the courtroom.

On March 7, KOR member Henryk Wujec was struck while he was being detained in Warsaw.

On March 14, "unknown perpetrators" beat Marek Kozłowski, an associate of KOR in Słupsk.

On March 17, Janusz Jarosz (Cracow SKS) was beaten in a police car.

On March 18, Marek Rospond was badly beaten in the police headquarters in Cracow. His beard and mustache were burned.

On March 18, SKS associate Janusz Gwózdziewski was beaten and strangled in the police headquarters in Cracow. He was forced to sign a statement promising to cooperate with the Security Service. After his release, Gwózdziewski informed SKS and KOR that he had been forced to do this.

On March 18, an associate of KSS "KOR" and NOWa, Tomasz Michalak, who was blind in one eye and had very poor sight in the other, was kicked downstairs in the police headquarters.

On March 20, Michalak, who had been released in the morning after a forty-eight-hour detention, was again detained by the police and beaten.

On March 23, an associate of KSS "KOR" in Wabrzeżno (Toruń province) and of the KZ WZZ, Bolesław Niklaszewski, was detained for the third time that month. He was beaten by a cellmate "for fighting against the system in the PRL."

Also in March, KSS "KOR" associate Sergiusz Kowalski was beaten in the face in police headquarters.

On April 22, Anna Walentynowicz was kicked in the legs while being detained. After she had suffered two days of arrest, a doctor excused her from work for five days.

On April 22, Bogdan Borusewicz was detained for two days and beaten.

On April 22, Zenon Pałka, a KOR associate who refused to submit to a test designed to discover traces of chalk and ink on his skin, was kicked and beaten in the police headquarters in Wrocław.

In the section on patriotic demonstrations, I have already mentioned the beatings that took place on May 3 in connection with the anniversary of the 1791 Constitution.

On May 6, Jerzy Godek (SKS) was beaten in the police headquarters in Cracow.

On May 23, Tadeusz Zachara (ROPCiO) was beaten after having been detained in the province of Tarnobrzeg.

On June 8, in Lębork (Słupsk province), Ludwik Prądzyński, a worker from Gdańsk detained in connection with the leaflet action in defense of Marek Kozłowski from Słupsk, was beaten by a police officer in the police headquarters.

This list, probably monotonous to the reader but important to those beaten, is almost certainly not complete.

The cases of Mirosław Chojecki, Bogdan Grzesiak, Jan Kozłowski, Marek Kozłowski, and Edmund Zadrozyński deserve special attention in this account of repressions.

The Cases of Mirosław Chojecki and Bogdan Grzesiak

On March 25, 1980, Mirosław Chojecki, the head of the Independent Publishing House NOWa and a member of KSS "KOR," was arrested. Bogdan Grzesiak was rearrested on April 15; he had been in jail from February 6 to February 29, in connection with the same case.

In January 1980, employees of the Polish Trade Agency who had collaborated with NOWa on the publication of the excellent memoir by Jan Nowak, *Courier from Warsaw,* offered NOWa a duplicator that was to be scrapped. Two days after the equipment was transported to Joanna Górecka's apartment, a search was made and the duplicator was confiscated.

After the arrest of Grzesiak, KOR issued a joint statement with NOWa on February 15 describing the events and concluding with the sentence: "We declare that Bogdan Grzesiak is a political prisoner, and that we will use all available means to secure his release."

On April 5, KOR appealed to Amnesty International to intervene in the case of Chojecki. The letter contained a biography of Chojecki together with a description of his contributions and of the circumstances of the case, as well as of the more general context in which it occurred.

On April 9, KSS "KOR" together with NOWa issued a new statement in defense of Chojecki; and on April 30 a telegram was sent to Amnesty International in connection with Chojecki's hunger strike.[10] On April 15, Grzesiak was rearrested; both Chojecki and Grzesiak were accused of the theft of a duplicator.

On May 10, after many interventions and both Polish and foreign protests, Chojecki was released. He was defended by the Polish Sociological Association, among others; and approximately 150 members of the Polish Writers' Union protested. There was also a protest from the Printers' Union and the Publishers' Union in the United States. Günter Grass published a letter in defense of his Polish publisher. A fast that was held in the parish church in Podkowa Leśna in May 1980 had the defense of Chojecki and Grzesiak as one of its goals. NOWa also conducted a leaflet action in their defense. The agency Interpress told foreign correspondents that Chojecki was released because of the personal intervention of Gierek, and that the investigation against him had been stopped. This latter statement was a lie, as KOR soon discovered. Grzesiak remained in prison, and the preparations for his trial were proceeding. The entire maneuver of releasing one of the accused, while detaining the second, and at the same time giving out false information through Interpress, was probably designed to break down Grzesiak, who refused to implicate Chojecki. But these calculated maneuvers did not succeed.

On May 11, KOR again wrote to Amnesty International to appeal for help in defending Grzesiak. Earlier, when the case of the duplicating machine had just begun, Chojecki wrote an open letter to the Diet which is worth summarizing here, if only because it contains a factual and detailed account of the repressions used by the Security Service and, as a result, constitutes perhaps the best possible illustration of the life of an activist of the democratic opposition in Poland.

Chojecki states that from the time of his first detention (on September 30, 1976), he had spent approximately five months in jail, which amounts on average to one day per week. His apartment was searched fifteen times, and a personal search was conducted roughly eighty times. Only in three instances did these searches take place on orders of the prosecutor, but the prosecutor's office always authorized the actions of the police *ex post facto*. Chojecki cited a long list of the Articles of the Criminal Code used as pretexts for the searches (including suspicion of burglary). During the searches the following objects were confiscated: three packages of canned meat, printer's ink, a typewriter, a jar of curry, a roll of adhesive tape, clippings from the current official press, tapes with recordings of jazz music, approximately 6,000 zlotys, computer programming handbooks (Fortran), a bag, a pair of scissors, sheets of clean paper, and the contents of one garbage can—altogether some 500 items are mentioned in the reports. In the case of the canned meat, the prosecutor, J. Chłopek, expressed his suspicion that it might have been in Chojecki's possession as a result of some criminal activity, while the sentencing boards, both in the original decision and on appeal, authorized its confiscation. During one of the searches, the confiscation of books taken from Chojecki was approved by the director of the Customs Office at the airport, Jan Kaliniak.

In December 1976, a bailiff issued a decision ordering the confiscation of all monetary sums sent to Chojecki. The order was never rescinded.

On many occasions Chojecki was threatened with death, and he was beaten several times. The prosecutor's office never answered any of his complaints, despite the fact that it was legally obliged to do so. Chojecki cites the numbers of some fifteen cases that were brought against him by various prosecutor's offices. Over the course of three and a half years, the sentencing boards imposed fines on Chojecki which amounted to some 19,500 zlotys. In October 1976, on orders from the Security Service, he was dismissed from his job at the Institute of Nuclear Research.

We must add that Chojecki had activists in his family as well. The *Information Bulletin* referred to them when it published a letter from Jan Walc to the courier "Kama." Maria Stypułkowska-Chojecka, Chojecki's mother, who as a soldier of the Home Army and member of the Kedyw had participated in the assassination of the chief of the Warsaw Gestapo, Kutschera.

Thirty years old, Bogdan Grzesiak is a professional printer, who, as he declared in his concluding speech during his later court trial, participated in the work of KOR and NOWa for ideological reasons, in order to serve Polish culture, which was being destroyed by censorship.

The trial of Mirosław Chojecki, Bogdan Grzesiak, and two printers from the Polish Trade Agency, Jerzy Ciechomski and Wiesław Kunikowski, took place on June 12. It was observed by official representatives of the Polish PEN Club and the Polish Writers' Union. The expert who served as a witness asserted that the duplicating machine in question was thirteen years old and beyond repair, since the spare parts needed for this purpose could only be bought with foreign currency, which the Polish Trade Agency did not have at its disposal. The day after the duplicating machine was taken from the Polish Trade Agency, there was a meeting of the Inventory Commission, which was supposed to write the duplicating machine off as scrap. The trial also concerned the printing of Jan Nowak's *Courier from Warsaw* on the printing equipment of the Polish Trade Agency.

Prosecutor Detko voiced the opinion that it should be a matter of indifference to the court whether what was printed by the accused was *Courier from Warsaw* or *Alice in Wonderland;* while the defense demanded that the court records include the expert opinions of Professors Aleksander Gieysztor, Stefan Kieniewicz, and Maria Turlejska, who confirmed the value of Nowak's book for historical studies. The court (chairman Aleksandrow, jurors Siciński and Kinus) sentenced Ciechomski and Kunikowski to one year of imprisonment (suspended) and fines of 10,000 zlotys, and Chojecki and Grzesiak to one and a half years of imprisonment (suspended) and fines of 15,000 zlotys.

The Case of Jan Kozłowski

The reader is already acquainted with Jan Kozłowski, a peasant activist and publicist, a member of the editorial board of *Placówka* and of the Center for Peasant Thought, and of the group advocating the formation of a trade union for private farmers. He was persecuted and beaten on many occasions by unknown perpetrators, and an attempt was made to place him in a psychiatric hospital, and even to drown him.

On October 7, 1979, as Kozłowski's family was sitting down to dinner, an unknown perpetrator broke a window in Kozłowski's house (in the village of Popowice, near Stalow Wola). The family ran out of the house and saw a man escaping. Kozłowski's neighbor, Tadeusz Kolano, identified the man as twenty-two-year-old Marek Pyrkosz, a local hooligan and good-for-nothing who was suspected of collaborating with the Security Service. After the man's escape, Kozłowski, together with his fourteen-year-old daughter, went to Radomyśl to notify the police about the assault. Kozłowski's statement to the police in Radomyśl was lost under unexplained circumstances.

In the meantime, Pyrkosz accused Kozłowski and Kolano of beating him. All the witnesses, except for Pyrkosz's mother and wife, who upheld his version of the events, were of the opinion that the accused could not have beaten Pyrkosz. Over a hundred villagers signed a statement presenting Kozłowski and Kolano in the best possible light. Moreover, the witnesses complained to the court that the report contained evidence that they had not given. According to Pyrkosz, Kozłowski and Kolano had assaulted him on a road and beaten him with a wooden fence-post or a stick. They managed to catch him despite the fact that he was running away (Pyrkosz was twenty-two-years-old, Kozłowski forty-nine, and Kolano fifty-two).[11] Afterward, Pyrkosz returned home (according to this version he would by that time already have suffered a fractured skull), got on a bicycle, and rode three kilometers to Chwałowice, where the postmaster dressed his wound, since (according to Pyrkosz's testimony) his wife and mother did not consider it proper to do so and instead allowed him to go out into the night and ride the bicycle, although he was badly injured. Neither the postmaster nor Pyrkosz's wife and mother heard from Pyrkosz at that time that the reason for his sorry state was a beating he had suffered.

There is no doubt that Pyrkosz did suffer an accident, and that it was serious, since he had to spend thirteen days in the hospital. The doctor called to testify as an expert could make no definitive statement about the cause of these injuries, but he did not exclude the possibility that they may have resulted from a bicycle accident.

The last word belonged to the court: "There has been no pressure on this Court. It is true that the authorities and institutions have called us many times, but we consider this to be an expression of their healthy interest in the case. . . . The Court did not submit to any pressure. . . . The only directives which we tried to obey were the instructions from our superiors, the Provincial Court in Sandomierz, which ordered us to fulfill all the requirements of the procedures of the Polish criminal process. . . ."[12] The Court has treated this case as it deserved to be treated, that is, as a criminal trial in which we have investigated the course of events without any bias. . . . The Court has remained impartial."

The sentences handed down on February 1, 1980, called for two years of imprisonment for Jan Kozłowski, one and a half years of imprisonment for Tadeusz Kolano, and heavy fines. KOR had no doubt about what scenario was being "played." This was not the first attempt to render Kozłowski harmless as an activist. The role of Kolano was also clear: this was not the first time KOR had encountered a situation in which a witness was eliminated by being accused himself (for example, the case of Brożyna). This time, there was further corroborating evidence in the fact that during his initial testimony, Pyrkosz had claimed that he was beaten by Kozłowski; Kolano appeared in his testimony only after it turned out that he would be a difficult witness and would help the defense.

It might be added that the villagers had no doubt about the character of Pyrkosz, just as they had no doubt that Kozłowski and Kolano, respected men and no longer young, could not have been guilty of the crimes with which they were charged. A statement characterizing the contributions of Kozłowski, and his personal biography, was issued jointly by Prof. Andrzej Burda of the Marie Curie-Skłodowska University, who was also a former prosecutor general of the PRL (during the early Gomułka period); by the Reverend Edward Frankowski, a parish priest from Stalowa Wola; by Colonel Franciszek Kamiński, the former commander of the Peasant Battalions fighting against the Germans during the Occupation; by Tadeusz Nawrocki, a senior activist of the peasant movement and a pedagogue; and by Piotr Typiak, a distinguished activist of the peasant movement and an editor of *Gospodarz*. They were joined by Jakub Antoniuk, another senior activist of the peasant movement and a former commander of the Peasant Battalions in the Białystok district; by Władysław Bartoszewski, a historian and writer, the general secretary of the Polish PEN Club, and an officer of the Home Army and member of the Jewish Aid Council during the Occupation; by Kornel Filipowicz, a writer and member of TKN; by Professor Jan Kielanowski, a member of PAN, TKN, and KSS "KOR"; by Dominican Father Jan Andrzej Kłoczowski; by Professor Edward Lipiński, a co-founder of KOR and member of KSS "KOR"; and by Jan Józef Szczepański, a writer and member of the editorial board of the Catholic *Tygodnik Powszechny* and of TKN.

A Committee in Defense of Jan Kozłowski was created in Lublin. Its members included Janusz Bazdyło from the editorial board of the *Catholic Encyclopedia*, who was also a co-editor of *Spotkania*, Professor Andrzej Burda, Dominican Father Ludwik Wiśniewski, from the Academic Ministry, and five students from four institutions of higher learning in Lublin. KSS "KOR" wrote about the case and presented its position in a statement dated February 3, 1980.

The case of Kozłowski was heard on appeal in the Provincial Court in Sandomierz on May 26, 1980. Kozłowski remained under investigative arrest from February 1 to May 26, despite the fact that the investigative procedures had been completed, and also that the sentence against him was not yet legally valid, so there could be no reason to fear any machinations. It was also improbable that a farmer more than fifty years old would try to escape from the justice system, abandoning his family and farm. Even in the PRL, there is no custom of resorting to such methods when a sentence is of comparable severity (Kolano was released during this time).

The day before the appeals case was to be heard, Masses were held in support of the release of Kozłowski and Kolano in Sandomierz and Stalowa Wola. Informational leaflets were handed out in both cities, beginning on May 23. Representatives of various dissident groups came to observe the trial. They included observers from KOR, a number of senior activists of the peasant movement, priests, students of Lublin colleges (mostly from the Catholic University of Lublin), and the villagers of Popowice. A speech by Władysław Siła-Nowicki, Kozłowski's attorney, made a great impression. He showed that the court had conducted itself in exemplary fashion during the introduction of evidence, and in this manner had demonstrated the innocence of the accused, so that it was shocking to everyone that the evidence it had so carefully introduced was then completely disregarded. This was exactly what had happened. On May 29, the Provincial Court upheld the sentence of the lower court.

After the trial, the Security Service (or rather "unknown perpetrators" who did not show their identification) tried to kidnap from the street those who had observed the trial as spectators. During one such attempt, friends of the person who was being abducted began defending him. One of the kidnappers escaped, but the other was taken to the police precinct by a large group of participants in the trial. Father Wiśniewski, entered the police building to demand that the kidnapper be identified. But he did not return. The group was surrounded by police cars and ordered to disperse; in answer it sang "God Save Poland." Police action began. Approximately fifty people were detained. Together with those arrested earlier for distributing leaflets, or merely for attempting to attend Kozłowski's trial, this meant that over seventy people were detained. Apart from several persons who were released a few hours later, all those detained spent forty-eight hours under arrest in Sandomierz and in several nearby towns. Among those detained were two of Kozłowski's daughters: Jolanta (she was twice held for forty-eight hours, during which time she refused to eat and drink, and was taken to a hospital), and Lucyna (forty-eight hours). Twenty people were sentenced to fines for hooliganism ranging from 1,600 to 4,800 zlotys. One of these "hooligans" was seventy-two-year-old Tadeusz Nawrocki, an activist of the peasant movement, a distinguished pedagogue, and a former scouting activist and deputy to the Diet for two terms. Another "hooligan" was the artist Zofia Baniecka, who had been a courier for the General Staff of the Peasant Battalions during the war. Janusz Obłęka, Wojciech Onyszkiewicz, Wojciech Somoliński, and Tadeusz Zachara suffered beatings while under arrest. Jan Józef Lipski was kicked and suffered a leg injury as a result (the prosecutor's office, answering his complaint accompanied by a doctor's certificate, stated that he probably had injured himself).

In accordance with KOR's custom, the defense of Jan Kozłowski and Tadeusz Kolano also involved an extensive leaflet action conducted both in the cities where the trials were held and in other towns in the province of Tarnobrzeg. Three thousand copies of *Placówka* devoted to the case were distributed in Sandomierz, together with thousands of leaflets, a special KOR publication entitled *The White Book of Jan Kozłowski*, and other independent publications. KOR sent a cable to Amnesty International asking it to intervene on behalf of Kozłowski and Kolano.

Only the general strike on the coast in August 1980 brought freedom to Kozłowski (Kolano was released earlier). Kozłowski was on the list of political prisoners whose release was demanded by the striking workers.

The Case of Marek Kozłowski

The case of Marek Kozłowski was somewhat different.[13] Jan Kozłowski's case demonstrated how the police can expend a great deal of energy in order to strike down a man with a particular social temperament and an inner need to fight against corruption (after all, Kozłowski had begun by unmasking the Sandomierz gang), who, thanks to his stubbornness and his talent, was becoming a peasant leader. Something else was important in the case of Marek Kozłowski: this case revealed the operation of the police-penitentiary system in Poland; it displayed the mechanisms as a result of which social reeducation is made impossible in this system, and how the police act to the detriment of public order.

As a seventeen-year-old boy Kozłowski participated in a burglary. As a result, he was imprisoned. This sentence was justified, and no one questioned it: the sentence and its justification describe what actually happened.

On the second occasion, however, Kozłowski found himself in jail for a different reason. KOR (and all who had something to do with these matters or were interested in them) knew very well that the police habitually used a procedure of extracting incriminating evidence from those who have been punished once on some previous occasion. Often these people incriminate themselves, unable to endure the beatings. In this manner the police improves its statistics concerning the detection of criminals; such statistics play an important role in the evaluation of police work (in terms both of the institution as a whole and of individual functionaries). When the accused has already been found guilty in the past, the courts do not, generally speaking, examine the evidence carefully. In this manner the possibility of becoming an honest person again is closed to many citizens of Poland. Sooner or later they must go back to jail. At most, they might be able to benefit from an offer to serve as an informer. KOR carefully investigated the second accusation and trial of Kozłowski, and had no doubt that Kozłowski was correct in claiming he was innocent.

At that time he was sentenced to five years in prison for an alleged theft of razor blades, a sink, and a sweater. He spent the entire five years in jail without being paroled. An amnesty, which pardoned the functionaries of the prison in Czarne who broke his jaw, did not extend to him. Kozłowski heard about KOR while still in jail. After his release he came to the Intervention Bureau in June 1979, and described prison conditions in the PRL to the bureau (the bureau was collecting such descriptions). He also offered his cooperation. It is easy to understand that KOR had to be cautious and inquisitive in such cases. After Kozłowski's trustworthiness was confirmed, he became one of the many associates of KSS "KOR." He began work as an orderly in an emergency room, since he believed that in this manner he would increase his chances of encountering cases that would be of interest to him. That is, he decided to devote himself to the investigation of police beatings. By July 1979 he had discovered and presented the Information Bureau with documentation concerning the beating of Tomasz Kościewicz.

On July 13, 1979, the police in Słupsk detained a young electrician named Kościewicz as a witness to a theft (about which Kościewicz knew absolutely nothing). Afterward, he was interrogated about other crimes, about which he also had no information. When he refused to clean the toilet in the prison, he was beaten up. This resulted in a fractured skull with a hemorrhage of cerebrospinal fluid, a broken jaw, an open fracture of the nose, and an open wound on his arm. After three weeks in a hospital, Kościewicz was allowed to go home. Sixty-seven days later (still on medical leave), Kościewicz described what had happened to him. Altogether, Kościewicz was on leave for 120 days, and then had to receive a disability pension.

Kościewicz's account of what happened to him ends as follows:

> From my own experience, I know that the prosecutors do not react to complaints of this kind, but on the contrary, react in the opposite direction, together with the police and the "independent" courts. As a result, the victim is usually convicted and the perpetrators go unpunished. I can cite the example of my friend Karpiński, who was shot together with Pęski by a functionary of the police, one of them in the head, which could have been fatal, and the other in the arm. As far as I know, the perpetrator of this act got off scot free because he was a policeman. Besides, my case is not unique, and I did not seek justice by appealing to the legal system, since I believe that this could only lead to failure. Apart from my health, which I have already lost, I could lose money which I do not have, or what is worse, my freedom, since the police often accuses such persons of acts they did not commit, while the prosecutor's office and the court take the side of the police. For the above reasons I am forced to present my case, above all, to the Self-Defense Committee KSS "KOR."

Afterward, Kościewicz was convinced by KOR (that is, by Kozłowski acting on behalf of the Intervention Bureau) to initiate the necessary legal steps. A trial of the policeman who had beaten up Kościewicz began in the Regional Court in Słupsk on March 3, 1980. The policemen were sentenced to two and a half and two years of imprisonment. But working for the Intervention Bureau was not enough for Kozłowski. He also distributed approximately 10,000 leaflets in Słupsk (mainly in defense of Mirek Chojecki), using a method worked out in Warsaw during the elections to the Diet.[14] He also posted obituaries on the anniversary of Katyń.

On April 28 of that year, Marek Kozłowski was again arrested. This time he was accused of two crimes: one of them was threatening a local prostitute with a knife. Bożena N. suddenly remembered this fact, after being in prison for over half a year (her case is immaterial), and felt the need to lodge a complaint. The second crime was violent assault of a functionary of the police. This charge was perhaps closer to the truth: when some policemen brutally abused a drunk in a restaurant, Kozłowski told them that they should not do this. As a result he was detained, but he was not beaten. The police prosecutor demanded that the sentencing board sentence him to three months of imprisonment, but the board decided that a fine of 2,000 zlotys would be sufficient. Now the police returned to this case, which had already been tried once, because it turned out that perhaps Kozłowski had grabbed one of the policemen by his belt. Kozłowski wrote to his mother from prison: "It was all up to me; I could have avoided jail, but I chose honor instead."

The strike on the coast brought him his freedom as well.

The Case of Edmund Zadrożyński

The case of Edmund Zadrożyński constitutes an important chapter in the history of KOR, since much energy was put into the defense of this early associate of KOR who had been active almost from the beginning of the committee's existence, and in certain respects this case was more complicated than the others.

Zadrożyński appeared at KOR together with a group of over forty workers who had been fired from their jobs in the Pomeranian Foundry and Enamel Shop in Grudziądz following a strike on June 25, 1976. This group, as noted earlier, caused a sensation in KOR and was the subject of great admiration. This was basically the only case in which the workers had organized themselves on such a large scale. They took their grievances to regional appeals commissions and to the labor courts, and they created a mutual aid organization. Their delegation that came to Warsaw presented excellent detailed documentation of their cases. Later, the KOR worker activists in Grudziądz initiated a variety of actions, all very specific and one might say "positivistic"; these activists became a pressure and opinion group concerned with issues that were usually dealt with by communal self-managements.

Zadrożyński was among the most active members of this group, and sooner or later something had to happen. It did. But KOR did not notice immediately what actually happened. On July 1, 1979, Zadrożyński was arrested and accused of having participated in breakins. On July 9, KOR, together with the editorial board of *Robotnik,* issued a statement describing the social role of this associate and member of the editorial board of *Robotnik,* and protesting against the charges brought by the prosecutor's office. As it turned out shortly, the pretext used to arrest Zadrożyński had been provided by his two sons (who did not participate in the social work of their father), who had indeed committed criminal acts. One of them, Mirosław, was convinced by the Security Service to accuse his father of participation in burglaries, and what is more, of directing a gang of thieves. Mirosław Zadrożyński explained this change in a twenty-page memorandum, which he retracted in the courtroom, only to retract his retraction, which violated the principles of criminal procedure. Retracting his retraction, Mirosław Zadrożyński stated that he had previously changed his testimony because his attorney, Jan Olszewski, had threatened him that Michnik and Kuroń would spill his blood if he should testify against his father! His codefendant, Zdzisław Wojnowski, also retracted, and then retracted the retraction of his testimony. Articles in *Życie Warszawy* and *Prawo i Życie* were already claiming a great victory when everything went to pieces. It appeared that the police had resorted to a provocation and that Mirosław Zadrożyński had been forced to give testimony by being beaten. The evidence did not make any sense, and it turned out that only the son who was promised freedom was accusing his father. In order to generate some additional ammunition, the prosecution also reached back to an old court sentence from some twenty years earlier, which dealt with long-forgotten conflicts in the family. This also violated the law. The Regional Court in Grudziądz sentenced Zadrożyński on March 13, 1980, to three years in prison.

The defense of Zadrożyński was conducted through extensive action on the part of the citizens of Grudziądz; 870 of them sent letters to the Episcopate, the Marshal of the Diet, the Office of the Prosecutor General, and KSS "KOR."

A leaflet action was also a part of Zadrożyński's defense. On October 21, 1979, 5,000 sets were distributed in Grudziądz consisting of a leaflet containing the statement about Zadrożyński by KOR and *Robotnik*, the *Appeal to Society* of KSS "KOR," and the *Charter of Workers' Rights*. Leaflets were also distributed in Toruń and Iława.[15] Again, *KOR Communiqués* printed lists of those who had been caught while distributing leaflets. But not all of the distributors were caught. On February 29, 1980, 3,000 such sets (KOR's and *Robotnik*'s leaflet in defense of Zadrożyński, the *Charter of Workers' Rights*, and a copy of *Robotnik*) were distributed in front of the thirteen largest factories in Warsaw.

Zadrożyński was also released thanks to the strikes in August 1980.

For Your Freedom and Ours

One of the continuing tasks of KSS "KOR" was to follow the fate of oppositional movements in other countries of the Soviet bloc, to inform the Polish public about their activities, and to express solidarity with them.[16] In July there was a successful attempt to organize a joint statement from KOR and dissident groups in Moscow in defense of the Czechs and Slovaks imprisoned for activity in connection with Charter 77. The statement was signed by all the members of KOR and by the following Russians (in order as in the document): Viktor Nekipelov, Tatiana Osipova, Malva Landa, Helena Bonner, Yuri Yarym-Ageev, Naum Meiman, and Sofia Kallistratova from the Moscow Helsinki Watch Group; Irina Zholkovskaya-Ginzburg from the Political Prisoners' Aid Fund; Yuri Kiselev from the Initiating Group to Defend the Rights of the Handicapped; and Leonard Ternovsky and Vyacheslav Bakhunin from the Working Commission on Psychiatry; as well as Andrei Sakharov, Tatiana Velikova, Grigori Vladimov, Aleksander Lavet, Ivan Kovalov, Nina Komarova, Vladimir Malinkovich, Maria Petrenko, Irina Grivnina, and Igor Khochluvkin. The members of KOR were deeply convinced that the words of this statement were not just empty phrases:

> We believe that the ideals for which Jarmila Bělikova, Vaclav Benda, Otka Bednařova, Jiři Dienstbier, Vaclav Havel, Ladislav Lis, Jiři and Dana Nemec, Peter Uhl, Jaroslav Šabata, and the other defenders of human rights in the CSSR, Russia, and Poland are being persecuted today, will always win out in the hearts and minds of Czechs, Slovaks, Poles, and Russians, and that they will bring our nations closer despite the policies of their governments.

Apart from the defense of the imprisoned, this was work for the future.

On August 22, 1979, KSS "KOR" received an "Appeal to World Public Opinion" issued on August 15 by Karel Careli Soukup, a singer and a signatory of Charter 77, who stated that on August 20 he would begin a fast in defense of political prisoners in Czechoslovakia. KOR expressed its solidarity with the appeal and carried information about preparations for a collective fast to be held in Poland. The text of the statement, together with a list of sixty political prisoners in Czechoslovakia, was to be transmitted to the Czechoslovak embassy in Warsaw by a KOR delegation composed of Aniela Steinsbergowa, Ludwik Cohn, and Jan Kielanowski. Since the embassy refused to accept the statement, it was sent by mail. On the morning of August 20, Karel Careli Soukup, David Nemec, and Tomaš Liška were detained in Warsaw. They were transferred to the Czechoslovak police on August 22. On August 25, Soukup and Nemec were released, while Liška was taken to a psychiatric hospital.

The fast announced by KOR in August did not take place as planned because of the arrest of the Czechs, who were supposed to participate in it. It began on October 3. The KOR press carried extensive information about the trial held in Prague on October 22 and 23. The report printed in the *Information Bulletin* begins:

> We cannot be indifferent, as the pope said to those gathered in St. Peter's Square, we cannot be indifferent to the trial taking place in Prague, Czechoslovakia, a country that is dear to us, just as we cannot be indifferent to the problem of the Vietnamese boat people, or the starving people in Cambodia, or toward the fate of those who have disappeared in Afghanistan or in Chile.

As far as possible, the *Information Bulletin* tried to include also the *Information of Charter 77*.

On October 22, the day on which the Prague trial began, agents of the Security Service attacked a group of students who planned to conduct a protest demonstration in front of the Center of CSSR Culture in Warsaw. The assault was brutal, and passersby attempted to help the students. Uniformed policemen were brought in to back up the Security Service, and they used tear gas. Among those detained were activists of the Cracow SKS (Bogusław Bek, Iwona Galińska Wildstein, Anna Krajewska, Marek Kucia, Grzegorz Małkiewicz, Andrzej Mietkowski, Marian Piątek, Wojciech Sikora, Bronisław Wildstein, Paweł Witkowski, Jarosław Zadencki, and Ewa Zalewska); of the Warsaw SKS (Jakub Bułat, Jan Cywiński, and Jerzy Szczepański); and an associate of *Robotnik* from Radom,

Ewa Soból. All the detained were released after forty-eight hours. More than seven months later (!), Andrzej Mietkowski was convicted by a sentencing board to a "warning, with a note to the college." In Cracow, approximately 1,000 leaflets were distributed in connection with the detention of the students in Warsaw, leading to new reprisals.

Information Bulletin No. 3/37 published in their entirety two documents sent from Slovakia: "A Letter from Slovak Catholics to Agostino Casaroli" and "A Brief Description of the State of the Catholic Church in Slovakia in 1979." It also summarized two other documents: "The Religious Situation in Slovakia" and "News from the Life of the Church in Slovakia."

The Ukrainian subject was represented in the KOR press during this period mainly by a letter from Jan Kielanowski to Valentin Moroz, published in June 1979 (in *Information Bulletin* No. 31/32, pp. 77–78). I shall cite only the most important part of it:

> History shows that the quarrel between Poland and the Ukraine has led to the enslavement of both countries. Let this dispute be forgotten now and forever, and let our path be a common one. Can either of our nations be truly free when the other is enslaved? Let us stop dwelling on the painful wrongs which we have inflicted on one another; let us forget the hostility that was inflamed by others; let us renew our old traditions of cooperation and friendship.

There was also a long article entitled "Fraternity," which dealt with the situation of the Church in the Ukraine. It was signed "(ap)."

The exile of Sakharov caused great concern in Warsaw. KOR reacted to it in a statement of January 24, 1980, expressing solidarity with Sakharov, and the KOR press published several articles, including "The Exile of Andrei Sakharov," written by Jan Kielanowski and published in *Information Bulletin* No. 35.

The Fast in the Church of the Holy Cross in Warsaw

This was the second protest fast in the history of KOR. Preparations for it had been under way, as we already know, since August. Unfortunately, the planned participation of the Czechs turned out to be impossible.

Perhaps the word "protest," which was used to describe this fast, is not the best; it might be better to call it a "solidarity" fast. The participants in the first fast in the Church of St. Martin in May 1977 and their spokesmen stressed the moral nature of their act, and as I noted in the appropriate place in this text, it is true that the sense of this first fast, which was also expressed outside of it, was provided by the atmosphere of fraternity, of a common bond in a renunciation dedicated to those whom the participants wanted to help. For this reason the designation "solidarity" fast is more correct, giving as it does a positive accent to the community of those taking part in the fast with those fighters for human rights who have been deprived of their freedom in Czechoslovakia and Poland, and an even broader unity with all people of good will.

One lucky idea was to broaden participation in the fast beyond a single oppositional group. Colleagues from ROPCiO who expressed a clear desire to participate were invited to do so. In a sense, then, this was a KOR-ROPCiO fast, but only "in a sense." Simply speaking, fifteen people fasted. A fast is not a situation in which one represents someone else (or a group). Thus we will list only the names of the participants, all already well known to the reader.

On October 3 the fast was begun by Jacek Bierezin, Andrzej Czuma, Kazimierz Janusz, Anka Kowalska, Jacek Kuroń, Jan Lityński, Rev. Stanisław Małkowski, Jerzy Markuszewski, Adam Michnik, Halina Mikołajska, and Mariusz Wilk. On October 4 they were joined by Konrad Bieliński; on October 5 by Antoni Macierewicz and Kazimierz Wóycicki; and on October 6 by Joanna Duda-Gwiazda. The fast ended on October 10.

At the request of those who were fasting, Jan Kielanowski and Jan Józef Lipski served as spokesmen for the group. Piotr Krasucki served as the main medical doctor, though when necessary he was joined by Marek Edelman and Wojciech Celiński. The priest of the parish of the Holy Cross was informed about the plan to hold a fast of some dozen people by Rev. Jan Zieja. The participants were given a room in a building adjoining the church, where the church offices and classrooms were located, over the apartments of the missionary priests who had been connected with the church for several centuries. Because of the crowded conditions, it was difficult to isolate the participants in the fast, as had been done in the Church of St. Martin: some of those fasting could be met in the relatively large corridor, linking the first floor rooms, which was furnished with benches, or in the courtyard. Here the guests arrived, usually unknown persons who came following the afternoon mass. People brought flowers to the participants, which they placed at the altar; those fasting (or their spokesmen) were also offered monetary donations for KOR, ROPCiO, and the free press. Guests were not allowed into the main room.

Visits were a distraction, but they also had an advantage: they created a link with people who supported their act of solidarity. The guests asked questions, and a dialogue was initiated. But one event, which occurred on the seventh day of the fast, would have been impossible in the Church of St. Martin. A Swedish television crew came to report on the fast. They were let into the courtyard only, where some of those fasting had come out, encouraged by the weather. The crew was accompanied by a journalist from *Polityka,* Marta Wesołowska, who right at the start (perhaps correctly from the point of view of the journalistic trade) made a pointed remark. Others present protested against the aggressive style of her entrée, and her lack of tact. This was not an appropriate time to antagonize people who had not eaten for seven days. A quarrel erupted, and the situation became very unpleasant. The spokeman for those fasting, Jan Józef Lipski, waited too long to intervene and suggest to Marta Wesołowska that she should talk to him, since this was the reason for his presence. The episode left a bad taste. It is a pity it took place at all.

An atmosphere of moral seriousness was assured mainly by the daily Masses. The participants, people of various beliefs, decided unanimously to stay together also during the Masses. This was an obvious consequence of their sense of community, which united them throughout the week. To me, a nonbeliever, this decision seemed very proper and correct, and having spent as much time as I could with those taking part in the fast, I was left with the memory of an authentic and uncommon experience. This was possible also because the Masses were celebrated and the homilies offered by our friends: Rev. Jan Zieja, Rev. Stanisław Małkowski (a participant in the fast), Rev. Bronisław Dembowski, and Dominican Father Jacek Salij. They were able to find a common language with all the participants without compromising the religious character of their homilies. Their attitude and friendship made up for all the bitterness caused by the unpleasant episodes.

I cannot resist the desire to cite a kind of document that is perhaps unusual for a book of this type: a prayer offered by the faithful during the Mass celebrated at the end of the fast. The author is not cited. He asked for acceptance of the text he had written on the grounds that those taking part in the fast were the most interested and competent parties in this matter.[17] The prayer of the faithful, as an integral part of the liturgy of the Holy Mass, cannot be treated as a normal authorial text:

Jesus Christ, you who suffered your wounds for us, let your Church with our pope, our bishops, our priests, and all people serve you faithfully, humbly, and without fear: you who were persecuted, be with the persecuted; you who were imprisoned, be with the imprisoned; you who were condemned, be with the condemned. We implore you . . .

Jesus Christ, you who were unjustly convicted by Pontius Pilate, open the gates of the prisons; let our sisters and brothers go free [here there was a list of names of the imprisoned Czechs and Slovaks]. We implore you . . .

Jesus Christ, you who in the hour of your mortal suffering said "Father, forgive them," teach us the forgiveness we need in order to forgive and the love we need in order to love those who pursue and denounce us, and persecute and slander us and our brothers. Let evil or hatred never enter into their hearts or ours. We implore you . . .

Jesus Christ, you who were resurrected in glory, let our sisters and brothers enter into your glory. Remember all those who in all places and from the beginning of time have perished as victims of war, oppression, and trials; as victims of wrath, vengeance, and crime; those who have died in dungeons and prisons, in streets and in stairwells, or in camps; those who suffered sudden or slow deaths, or were beaten or hunted down, or died from exhaustion, cold, and hunger. We implore you . . .

Jesus Christ, Holy Lord, Mighty and Eternal, help us to hope, strengthen our love; let us preserve among us the unity of our hearts, just as today while we stand before your altar, and for all the days to come, so that our fasting, our renunciation, our sacrifice, and our prayers shall not be in vain. Forgive us our trespasses as we forgive those who trespass against us. We sinners implore you to hear us, O Lord.

An appeal signed by those who began the fast on October 3 was distributed in Warsaw during the fast in the form of leaflets entitled "In the Defense of Our Czech Brothers." The distribution was particularly intensive on Sunday, October 7. On that day two KOR members, Zbigniew Romaszewski and Henryk Wujec, were detained for forty-eight hours for handing out leaflets. The participants in the fast concluded it by issuing another statement in which they once again recalled the purpose of the fast, thanked the Church for providing shelter, and thanked as well the known and unknown friends who had offered their help and solidarity.

The fast was the cause of yet another difficulty, one more serious than the conflict with Marta Wesołowska. In connection with a conference, or perhaps in connection with the fast itself, Bishop Bronisław Dąbrowski, the secretary of the Episcopate, visited the Church of the Holy Cross. He spoke there with representatives of those who were fasting (Andrzej Czuma and Halina Mikołajska), and during this exchange he made references to an intrusion and a disturbance of the work of religious instruction, adding however that there was no question in this case of seeking help from outside. Andrzej Czuma took upon himself the brunt of the conversation, or actually of the polemic.

The Church of the Holy Cross was surrounded not only by hordes of secret police agents but also by journalists. The press noticed the bishop and surrounded him, asking that he make a statement about the fast. They were invited to a press conference at the Episcopate, which took place several hours later in the secretariat of the Episcopate. Press conferences are generally not in the style of the Episcopate, and occur very rarely when particularly important events are taking place. Bishop Dąbrowski repeated to the journalists more or less the same things he had said earlier to Andrzej Czuma and Halina Mikołajska.

This event became the subject of many commentaries in Warsaw, and not only in Warsaw. Those who were unsympathetic to the democratic opposition often cited it as proof of the negative attitude of the Church toward the opposition. In time, people began to forget who had taken part in the fast (or pretended that they did not remember), and in various later versions and interpretations, the incident with Bishop Dąbrowski was interpreted as having an anti-KOR character. As a consolation for the participants in the fast, Primate Wyszyński extended an invitation to Czuma's wife while the fast was still in progress (the primate had been a friend of Czuma's parents even before the war). He asked questions about the fast kindly, and did not voice any objections.

The full solidarity of the colleagues from ROPCiO was also a consolation to the KOR participants. The people from ROPCiO showed no sign of thinking that everything could be blamed on KOR, which was in a more difficult situation since there were also nonbelievers among the KOR participants. I am aware of the fact that Czuma and Janusz might even feel insulted that something so obvious is being mentioned here, but all sorts of things happen in life, and this book is a first attempt to describe events and people involved in matters that today are already a part of history.

As a result of this episode, KOR tried to arrange an audience with the primate. The idea was not to raise the issue of the fast—this was impossible unless the primate wished to raise this issue himself—but to present to him KOR issues as KOR saw them. In KOR there was no division between believers and nonbelievers,[18] but on this occasion it was decided that the delegation to the head of the Catholic Church in Poland would be composed of Catholics: Mikołajska, Kielanowski, and Wujec. The primate received the delegation. I have difficulty establishing the exact date of the audience, since there was no official communiqué from the meeting (not that KOR wanted to hide anything, but a communiqué would have required agreements on the wording, and this would have stripped the audience of its proper character and would have involved introducing an element of negotiations between the two parties into the meeting, which was out of the question as far as KOR was concerned). The audience did not produce any surprises. In their report to KOR the delegates agreed that the primate was sympathetic. One proof of this was that he authorized Kielanowski and Mikołajska to turn to Reverend Piasecki, the chaplain and secretary to the primate, whenever they decided that something important should be transmitted from KOR to the primate, and that Piasecki would immediately pass the information on to the primate himself. The audience convinced KOR that one should not succumb to hysteria and panic whenever something worrisome happens which is not, basically, of primary importance.

On October 5, two peasants involved in the Peasant Self-Defense Committee of the Grójec region, Jan Grób from Wola Sułkowska and Janusz Lorenc from Model, joined the fast but they fasted in the church in Zbrosza Duża. On October 7, Eužn Brikcius, David Nemec, Marketa Nemcova, Josef Resler, Pawel Šmida, and Petruška Šustrova began a solidarity fast for the same purpose in Prague. At the same time, VONS (the Committee in Defense of the Unjustly Persecuted) sent a telegram thanking those who were fasting in Warsaw in the Church of the Holy Cross.

The Elections to the Diet

Since neither a true Diet nor true elections exist in Poland, it seemed that when the authorities decided to hold the ritual they refer to as "elections to the Diet," nothing important would follow for KOR. Perhaps KOR would issue a statement asserting that it would be a good thing if at some time elections really did take place in Poland, and perhaps add that at one time, though long ago (only the very elderly could remember those days), there were indeed genuine elections in Poland. It was also surely necessary to remind the citizens who for several decades now have participated in this ritual that if, every four years, one participates in a collective lie, this participation cannot be viewed as a matter of indifference as far as human dignity and morality are concerned.

Such at least was the opinion that I shared with some of my friends. But on this occasion, everything turned out differently. We underestimated the young people's lively reaction to official slogans. On this occasion the young members of the opposition, who had duplicating machines and paper at their disposal, had no intention of letting the party get away with its elections. There was nothing that could be done but to accept the situation, since the intentions of these young people were noble and did not run counter to the ideals of KOR. This was the origin of the preelection campaign of KOR, which was also a campaign of the entire opposition (groups connected with ROPCiO attached rather great importance to the "elections," and had no doubt that involvement was worthwhile).

The effects of the action were beneficial: it demonstrated clearly the presence of the opposition in public life, and showed that its possibilities were already quite large. The problem that remained was: under what slogan should this campaign be conducted? The attitude that prevailed in KOR was not to call for a boycott of the elections but only to inform people that voting was not a morally or politically indifferent act, and to state clearly that "we will not vote." The KSS "KOR" statement of February 24, 1980 (that is, one month before the elections, which were scheduled to take place on March 23) explained the issue in the following words (I cite only excerpts):

> Voting for a single list of candidates, which is in fact the list of the party-state authorities, cannot be called elections. The Diet, which is formally chosen through such putative elections, but is really nominated by the PUWP, has nothing in common with a real Diet except for the overused name. It is not a parliamentary institution; it does not represent Polish society even to the smallest degree; it is not and cannot be a sovereign organ of the will of the people. . . .
>
> The members of KSS "KOR" declare that under these conditions they will not go to the ballot boxes, since they believe that participation in this painful farce insults the civil and human dignity of every member of our society.

This was the opinion of most KOR members, and it was discussed extensively in an article in the *Information Bulletin*. But the *Głos* group, for example, was of the opinion that we should call for a boycott of the elections.

Why were the majority of KOR members not eager to call for such a boycott? There were two reasons. It was known that the election results were rigged even when the citizens dutifully participated in them. It was thus even more likely that the elections would be falsified now, and KOR would be able to unmask this only here and there. But even the actual state of affairs did not look hopeful to everyone. Inertia and fear, which for years have played a part in the habit of participating in these "elections," could lead to election statistics that would be very different from those the opposition would have preferred, even if KOR were to involve itself intensively in the boycott.[19] Why should one undertake a struggle, only to have to explain later the reasons why one lost? Moreover, such an explanation would not be very convincing abroad, even if it were convincing in Poland.

Hundreds of thousands of leaflets were dropped over Polish cities. They usually fell from the roofs, "catapulted" according to Western journalists, but in fact a different technique was used (already described in the chapter on Marek Kozłowski). Some of these leaflets contained the statement of KOR, while others were appeals from various oppositional groups for a boycott. One must admit that the scale of this action was impressive. In Warsaw alone, KOR scattered over 200,000 leaflets (on March 20, 21, and 22, 100,000 leaflets were distributed in central parts of the city during the hours of the heaviest traffic); 30,000 in Cracow; 30,000 in Gdańsk; and 30,000 in Wrocław. The numbers were smaller in other cities, but in any event KOR groups alone distributed well over 300,000 leaflets. There were posters as well. Sometimes even small groups that had their own printing facilties (for example, the Third of May Publishing House) were able to organize leaflet actions on the scale of a large organization. It is reasonable to estimate that the number of leaflets scattered around the country was not less than half a million.

Police action intensified again during the preelection period. A KOR statement of March 16 (that is, one week before the election) mentioned 50 searches and over 50 detentions. In the course of the following week there were another 80 searches and over 120 detentions. During this period a number of people were detained twice, or three, four, or even five times (Zenon Pałka). Many of the beatings we have already noted took place precisely during this period.

The data KOR was able to collect about the elections are fragmentary, as one might have expected. One of the election precincts in Warsaw-Wola had 62 percent attendance; in Warsaw-Saska-Kępa—80 percent, of which 15 percent went into the booth; in the election precinct on

Tyniecka Street (Warsaw-Mokotów)—83 percent attendance (after their report, the Election Commission was informed by a higher level commission that the district did not include 2,450 persons, but only 2,050, which wonderfully improved the attendance to 99 percent). Generally speaking, the attendance in Warsaw was between 70 and 80 percent.

Information Bulletin No. 36 published five anonymous reports by members of election commissions. The method used most often to falsify the results was simply to inform election commissions that the number of people entitled to vote was smaller than that on the list of citizens. The commission would then calculate the attendance in terms of the smaller number. Only between 25 and 50 percent of students from Warsaw dormitories voted. KOR published a statement condemning the falsifications in the computation of attendance.

KSS "KOR" Communiqué No. 39 included a statement by Antoni Macierewicz and Piotr Naimski concerning the contradiction they perceived between the declaration that "KSS 'KOR' did not call for a boycott of the elections" (from the committee's statement of March 28) and the above-cited statement of February 24, which declared that members of the committee would not themselves participate in the elections. In addition, both Macierewicz and Naimski expressed the opinion that the Editorial Board had exceeded its authority when it issued this statement, since it was only authorized to issue statements that had the character of an intervention.

This was yet another symptom of the conflict between the *Głos* group and the rest of KOR.

The Press and Publications

Periodicals of KOR or of groups close to KOR continued to appear during this period, and there were also new periodicals.

The first issue of the literary-social periodical *Tematy* (*Topics*) appeared in Wrocław in October 1979. The periodical was edited by a group of young writers and publicists connected with KOR and with the Lower Silesian Social Self-Defense Club, as well as with the Wrocław SKS (as the reader has probably noticed, these three groups overlapped significantly): Leszek Budrewicz, Wiktor Grotowicz, Janusz Paśkiewicz, Krzysztof Turkowski, and Mariusz Wilk. *Tematy* published literary works, including a great deal of poetry, as well as articles devoted especially to the problems and events of the student movement.

Alternatywy, published by the Literary Publishing House (headed by Janusz Korwin-Mikke) was an original periodical that represented a truly pure liberal laissez-faire orientation. It was edited with flair and had a tendency toward fulminations verging on paradox (for example, it launched a sharp attack against all forms of social insurance).

The first issue of *Kurier Akademicki,* a periodical of students from the Catholic Theological Academy connected with the KOR and SKS movements in Warsaw, began publication in the spring of 1980.

Also in the spring of 1980, a new student periodical, *Po prostu bis,* began appearing in Cracow.

In the section on the KZ WZZ we have already referred to the publication of *Robotnik Szczeciński.*

The first issue of an ephemeral satirical periodical, entitled *Czerwony Kapturek* (*Red Riding Hood*), connected with the student milieu and edited by Jakub Bułat, also began appearing in the spring. I am unable to ascertain how many issues were published, probably two or three.

Tarnowskie Wiadomości (*Tarnow News*), edited by Zbigniew Staruch, was also connected with the KOR milieu.

Kronika Lubelska, a periodical of participants in ROPCiO, began publication in 1980 as well.

Unfortunately, because of the splits within ROPCiO, and because of a sharp conflict between the Third of May Publishing House, which until then had been publishing *Opinia,* and some members of *Opinia*'s editorial board, *Opinia* was again published only as a typescript. Because the reading public had become accustomed to other forms of publication, the influence of *Opinia* declined.

The press sensation of this period was caused without doubt by the third, special issue of *Przegląd Prasy Zagranicznej* (*Review of the Foreign Press*), a periodical published by the Third of May Publishing House, whose general orientation was similar to that of the *Information Bulletin.* This special issue was devoted to the pilgrimage of Pope John Paul II to Poland, and contained the texts of his homilies and foreign press opinions concerning his visit. The cover, with a portrait of the pope in color, and both color and black-and-white photographs inside, attracted attention. This was a demonstration of the abilities of the uncensored press. The publication of the issue was possible only thanks to significant financial help (a loan) offered by the Social Self-Defense Fund.

NOWa still dominated the publishing houses. It increased its prestige even more through its participation in the thirty-first International Book Fair in Frankfurt am Main. Among some 5,000 publishers, NOWa attracted great interest and attention, despite the modest graphic appearance of its publications. The booth with independent Polish publications was organized by Andrzej J. Chilecki, and exhibited issues of the periodicals *Zapis, Puls, Krytyka, Biuletyn Informacynjy, Głos, Robotnik, Opinia, Bratniak,* and others. Unfortunately, the Polish edition of Günter Grass's *The Tin Drum* got lost somewhere along the way and never arrived.

Other publishing houses were working alongside NOWa: "Klin"; the Library of *Głos;* the Library of *Spotkania;* the Peasant's Library; the Poznań Showcase of Writers and Critics; the Notebooks of the Poznań SKS; and the Cracow Student Publishing House, which published its books with the care of bibliophiles and, given this level of editorial care, in surprisingly large editions. One publishing house connected with TKN, with NOWa's permission, used NOWa's trademark—a small letter "n" (though actually quite large)—with the number "2" printed inside it. There were also ephemeral publishing efforts (for example, *The Hungarian Diaries of Wiktor Woroszylski* bore the label of the Samizdat publishing house), which occasionally was simply a pseudonym for already well-known publishing houses. All of this constitutes an extremely interesting subject for a bibliographer or bibliologue, but despite the fact that I might even possess the necessary qualifications to try my abilities in this area, the task will have to be undertaken elsewhere and by someone else. One thing can be said with certainty: the publishing movement between 1976 and 1980 constitutes a large chapter not only in the history of the oppositional movements but also in the history of Polish culture.

The press also supported various activities of the KZ WZZ and of the Intervention Bureau: *Robotnik,* the *Information Bulletin,* and other periodicals called on the authorities to respect the labor law (there were also constant demands for changes in the Labor Code, even if these changes would signify only a return to its original form, before the "reform" that made it significantly more oppressive). The periodicals raised such issues as working and wage conditions, bonuses, contract work, work safety and hygiene, and the like.

For example, *Information Bulletin* No. 34 of November/December 1979 published a long article entitled "Linking Education with Production," which described violations of the Labor Code in the "Pollena-Uroda" plant in Warsaw, which "socially" (?) employed school children in jobs that contributed nothing to their education and were harmful to their health (they were inhaling freon in the aerosol department, or enamel vapors in the tube department). The practice concealed pure exploitation.

Information Bulletin No. 37 of May 1980 also published excerpts from a document prepared by the Department of Work Safety and Hygiene and of Social Issues in the Ministry of Mining (including a list of mining accidents in April 1980 that had not been mentioned in the official press). The commentary stated that the documents testified "to gross negligence concerning the most basic rules of work safety, to noncompliance with the formal requirements of safety in particularly dangerous kinds of work, . . . to improper organization of work, which meant that conservation and repair work had to take place during the actual operation of the machinery, and to negligence in the control and conservation of the machinery."

Simultaneously, *Robotnik* and *Information Bulletin* No. 38 of June 1980 published an article by Józef Śreniowski, "The Textile Workers," which supplemented an article printed in *Polityka* by citing additional data and facts without which any picture of working conditions in the Łódź textile factories would have to be considered incomplete. In the same issue of the *Information Bulletin*, Joanna Duda-Gwiazda from the coastal KZ WZZ described an accident in the Northern Shipyard—on June 18, 1980, there was a gas explosion in the power station of unit B 406—caused by requiring work at excessive speed, which induced the workers to use methods that turned out to be simply suicidal. Approximately 100 persons were present in the area where the explosion occurred. Eight people were killed instantly, and several more died in hospitals. The author of the article had difficulty establishing the actual state of affairs; because of an information blockade in the hospitals, she was only partially able to ascertain the number of victims.

The *Information Bulletin* also provided news about such events as the banning of the performance of a symphony composed by Stefan Kisielewski, and it paid attention to developments within the Polish Writers' Union.

Generally speaking, the KOR press constitutes a rich mine of information about the social, economic, and cultural situation in Poland.

The Church and Social Movements of Polish Catholics as Presented in the KOR Press

One of the tasks of particular importance for the entire oppositional press, including that of KOR, was to provide information about Church matters.

As far as possible, the KOR press attempted to publish either in their entirety or in excerpts such Church documents as the Communiqués of the Plenary Conferences of the Episcopate and pastoral letters. It also published information about the struggle to construct new churches. For example, the trial of Rev. Adam Michalski and Tadeusz Radochański for the illegal building of a church in the Kmiecie district of Przemyśl was described in detail in *Communiqué* No. 33 of October 16, 1979. The verdict in this trial was particularly scandalous from a legal point of view. The trial was supposed to take place in the Regional Court in Przemyśl on October 12. Several hundred parishioners had gathered in the court-room on that day. The court ordered a recess in the proceedings, and the statement that "the accused did not show up" was entered into the records. On October 15, *Nowiny Rzeszowskie* (*Rzeszow News*) announced a verdict reached without having heard the defendants or witnesses for the defense. Michalski was sentenced to one year imprisonment, sus-pended for five years, to 230,000 zlotys in fines, and to 40,000 zlotys in court costs; Tadeusz Radochański had to pay a fine of 80,000 zlotys plus 15,000 zlotys in court costs.

The KOR press devoted much attention to attempts by the authorities to rebuild the neighborhood of Jasna Góra in such a way as to make pilgrimages and mass religious ceremonies more difficult. KOR issued a statement on this matter on January 28, 1980.

Occasionally, attempts to present the readers of the oppositional press with Church documents met with difficulties. The Press Office of the Secretariat of the Polish Episcopate did not provide access to some public documents, sometimes even to those that were received without difficulty by foreign journalists. For example, the press statement by Rev. F. Goś-ciński, the director of the Secretariat of the Polish Episcopate, denying claims made by the deputy director of the Office for Religious Affairs, Merker, in *Die Welt,* was made available only to foreign correspondents and was published in *Le Figaro.* As a result, *Information Bulletin* No. 35 of January/February 1980 had to present the contents of this document by translating it from the French. As the editorial board declared, not without some surprise, "Such a 'polemic' between the Church and the state taking place exclusively in the foreign press is an event without precedent in the history of the PRL."

The Student Movement

The more the oppositional movement grew, the more dif-ficult it became to distinguish the student movement as a separate entity. Following the period of the Student Solidarity Committees, various forms of oppositional activity began to overlap, perhaps even at the expense of specific problems of the students and of institutions of higher learning. In any case, students could be found in all the activities of the opposition and in all its institutions, and they did not form separate groups.

Some events of importance to the dissident student movement have already been discussed in other contexts: for example, the conflict of students from the dormitory Mikrus with the administration during the pilgrimage of John Paul II, which was followed by searches and interrogations among the students living in this dormitory. We have also mentioned the participation of young people from the Academic Ministry in Lublin in the Sandomierz trial, of Jan Kozłowski, and the demonstration of Cracow and Warsaw students, who protested against the imprisonment of Czech and Slovak dissidents.

The students of Mikrus in Warsaw (mainly from the Department of Technical Physics and Applied Mathematics, but also from the Departments of Mechanical Engineering, Energy, and Aviation at Warsaw Polytechnic) were closely associated with KOR. The cultural commission of the residents' council of the Mikrus dormitory became the center of these students' activity. This commission organized a series of meetings entitled "Polish Biographies and Generational Experiences." The cycle was inaugurated by Krzysztof Wolicki, who spoke about October 1956, despite a prohibition issued by the board of the residents' council against holding the meeting. It seemed that it would be impossible to arrange a meeting with Stefan Bratkowski, but finally he was able to speak at the club Amplitron, in the Department of Electronics. A meeting with Stefan Kisielewski, "a representative of the radical right wing" who "systematically slanders Poland in the Paris *Kultura*," could not be held at all (these descriptions of Kisielewski are quoted from the statement justifying the prohibition).

A chronicle of the activities of the cultural commission was presented in a wall newspaper entitled *A Hundred Times Your Head Against the Wall*, which had a known editorial board and was displayed in Mikrus and in the main building of Warsaw Polytechnic. It was regularly torn down by functionaries of the Polytechnic Council of SZSP and the Polytechnic administration, but it was posted again with equal regularity, with the addition of the names of those who had been observed tearing it down.

On May 7, the student court of the Riviera and Mikrus dormitories approved the suspension of Waldemar Maj, the chairman of the cultural commission, by the board of residents of the dormitory. This action was possible only because both the residents' council and the student court had a membership dictated by SZSP and PUWP. In the fall of 1979, as new elections to the self-government were taking place, Malicki, the electoral commissar from SZSP in the Polytechnic (not to be confused with KOR associate Wojciech Malicki) simply deleted Maj's name from the list of candidates. A boycott of the elections in the Department of Technical Physics and Applied Mathematics did not help. The students of Mikrus protested in a collective letter demanding that the elections be repeated and that the list of candidates also be open to persons who were not nominated by SZSP. The elections were repeated, but the list of candidates remained unchanged. Again protests and boycotts were the response.

A short time later, the names of Waldemar Maj and Krzysztof Gajewski were deleted from the list of students designated to receive prizes automatically awarded for academic excellence. This decision by Dean W. Leksiński was motivated by the participation of Maj and Gajewski in the editorial board of *A Hundred Times Your Head Against the Wall*. Similarly, increases in the scholarships of Wiktor Karpiński and Krzysztof Lachowski, which had been approved in a vote by the students, were not honored. As a demonstration, their colleagues compensated the losses of the punished students by giving them a part of their own prizes.

On February 24, about a dozen functionaries of the Security Service entered Mikrus. They conducted a number of searches, confiscated some printing materials, uncensored publications, private correspondence, and personal belongings (for example, stamp collections), and did not always enter all the confiscated materials in their reports. On the following day, Wiktor Karpiński and Krzysztof Lachowicz, called to give evidence as witnesses, were beaten in the Warsaw headquarters of the police (see the section on repressions), while the school authorities began disciplinary proceedings against the beaten students and their colleagues. At the same time, the departmental authorities and SZSP began an "informational action" by presenting the version of events supplied by the Security Service during meetings with departmental employees. Dr. Z. Żekanowski, the first secretary of the Basic Party Organization of PUWP, was particularly active in this smear campaign, together with the assistant dean, Dr. Leksiński.

The disciplinary spokesperson, Dr. Lidia Bialoń, demanded that four students be suspended for one year (Karpiński, Klincewicz, Lachowski, and Łopacki). She justified her motion on the grounds that the confiscated objects (books, paper, and printer's ink) were flammable and had "nothing to do with the subject of their studies." A disciplinary commission chaired by Dr. E. Pluciński found Łopacki not guilty, and punished the remaining three students with reprimands and warnings for "keeping materials and equipment in their rooms which had nothing to do with the subject of their studies," and for "failing to obey the directives of the university authorities, and thus injuring with their behavior the good name of the school and the dignity of students." On the basis of a decision made by Assistant Dean Leksiński, these students were expelled from the dormitory, regardless of their financial situation.

On May 20, four Warsaw students who were active in the KOR movement (Jacek Czaputowicz from the Higher School of Planning and Statistics, Anna Iwanowska from Warsaw University, Wojciech Frąckiewicz from the Catholic Theological Academy, and Teodor Klincewicz from Warsaw Polytechnic) founded an Academic Intervention Bureau designed to defend student rights against threats and against lawlessness and abuses of the law directed against students. The first issue that the Academic Intervention Bureau took up involved the expulsion, in violation of the regulations governing students, of Janusz Majewski, a fourth-year student of philosophy at Warsaw University. Majewski was an activist of the independent student movement and a member of the Young Poland Movement. He appealed to the rector the decision of the directors of the Philosophical Institute at the University. He was supported by the Institute's Council of SZSP and by numerous students and faculty members. The assistant dean for student affairs, Prof. Stanisław Orłowski, confirmed the expulsion on June 3. Luckily, the day was already drawing near when those who had been expelled from the universities because of their views would return to school. KSS "KOR" issued a statement in defense of Janusz Majewski.

An initiative of a more general character originated among students in Cracow. On December 9, 1979, during the Fifth Reporting and Elections Conference of SZSP at the Jagiellonian University, Małgorzata Bator, a student, made a motion to dissolve the union. A short time later, a group of SZSP activists close to the Cracow SKS began to gather signatures on a petition calling for an Extraordinary Congress of SZSP, for the purpose of giving formal consideration to the issue of dissolving the organization and creating a new student organization that would have the character of an independent student trade union. The organizers of this action formulated "A Report on the State of the Socialist Union of Polish Students," published in the SKS periodical *Indeks*, which for some time had been appearing in Cracow rather than Warsaw.

This student initiative was supported by a group of Cracow intellectuals: Izydora Dąbska, a professor of philosophy; Stanisław Foryś, a doctor of economy; Hanna Malewska, a writer and former editor-in-chief of the Catholic monthly *Znak;* Krzysztof Penderecki, the rector of the State Academy of Music; Stefan Smoliński, a professor of chemistry; Andrzej Staruszkiewicz, a doctor of physics; Rev. Józef Tischner, a doctor of philosophy; Henryk Wereszycki, a professor of history; Jacek Woź-niakowski, a doctor of the history of art; Andrzej Wroński, a doctor of logic; and Stanisław Zapiór, a professor of chemistry.

On April 29, a student legalizing committee composed of fifteen students, in accordance with the "law on associations," requested the president of Cracow to issue a permit for the activity of a student organization entitled the Academy of the Renewal Movement (ARO). In June, ARO brought out the first issue of its periodical, *Po prostu bis,* the title of which referred to the weekly of students and young intellectuals published in the fifties under the title *Po prostu.*

By April 17, the demand to dissolve SZSP had been signed by 1,715 Cracow students, and the campaign moved on to other academic centers. A short time afterward came the great strike movement of the summer of 1980. On September 2, 1980, the first Initiating Committee of the Independent Union of Students was formed in Gdańsk. An explanation of the subsequent fate of the Cracow initiative and its links with the later Independent Union of Students will be left to future historians of the student movement.

The student community in Cracow was the most active during this period. The Wrocław movement, following its successful campaigns against expulsions in October 1979, had lost its momentum. Its activists were working as members of the Social Self-Defense Club of Lower Silesia and in KSS "KOR," or in such publishing initiatives as *Tematy* and *Biuletyn Dolnośląski.* The Warsaw SKS had been swallowed up by KOR, which was operating out of Warsaw, so that even the stubborn battles of the students from Mikrus had little to do with the SKS. In January 1980 the Poznań SKS published a text describing the situation existing in institutions of higher learning and suggesting ways in which the existing state of affairs could be changed.

The Peasant Movement and the Problem of the Villages

During the period in question, the peasant movement also lost much of its momentum. In a struggle to survive, it acted mostly in self-defense. This was especially apparent in the first peasant committee, that of Milejów parish, where Janusz Rożek obviously had no intention of giving up, but since he was harassed with constant searches and detentions and his farm was being ruined (in part by unknown perpetrators), he was unable to do as much as he had done before. Breakups in ROPCiO were reflected here as well: for example, some of the activists of this committee, especially Niessen, attached themselves to the Confederation of Independent Poland.

Zbrosza Duża, the center of the Peasant Self-Defense Committee of the Grójec Region, was the most active area. It was precisely here that an unusual comedy performance was arranged by the police: on the night of January 31, a crying woman began banging on the door of Rev. Czesław Sadłowski, begging him to come to her sick father. When the priest opened his door, some dozen attackers forced their way in, grabbed the priest by the throat, and slapped him in the face. After a two-hour search of the church buildings, with no witnesses (the priest was held under guard in the sacristy), a duplicating machine, fifty-one reams of paper, and uncensored publications were confiscated. In the morning, Sadłowski was taken to Radom. He was alternately threatened and encouraged to cooperate. After being fingerprinted and photographed, he was finally released.

The Peasant Self-Defense Committee of the Grójec Region issued a communiqué in this matter dated February 3. It decided: (1) to send a delegation to the Radom voivode demanding a written apology to the priest and the return of the duplicating machine and paper; (2) to organize a warning strike by not delivering milk on February 11; (3) not to take part in the elections, and to call on others to boycott them, reminding everyone that it is immoral to lie; (4) to install new locks and a burglar alarm system in the church, which would alert the village about any further attacks; (5) to try to get a new duplicating machine without waiting for the answer of the voivode; (6) to increase the edition of the *Bulletin* of the committee; and (7) to thank Reverend Sadłowski for his work in defense of the rights of peasants and believers. KSS "KOR" described the attack on Sadłowski and on the church in Zbrosza Duża in a statement of February 3, 1980.

One issue that exemplified the policies of the state toward peasants was the integration of land in Przywory Duże, a village in the parish of Wiśniew, and the persecution of Jan Dołęgowski, into whose defense KOR invested a great deal of energy. KOR was aware of the practice of conducting land integration in a manner calculated to maximize the losses of individual private farmers. Ever since the collectivization campaign, the power apparatus had treated the farmers as enemy number one, and it did so with a persistence and consistency that surely were worthy of a better cause. The Peasant Self-Defense Committee in the Rzeszów Region was created in order to defend the farmers against such practices. The policy of the authorities was complicated by two additional factors. First, the integration of land could become an ideal method to introduce conflict into a village, which was significant if one were relying on the *divide et impera* method of control. Second, land integration opened up great possibilities for corruption. When a village was divided into those who gained from the integration of land and those who lost from it because of biased methods of integration, the peasants who tried to defend themselves were threatened with revenge by organized local gangs.

This was the case in Przywory Duże in the province of Siedlce. The integration was conducted in a seemingly surrealistic manner. One farmer whose land had been divided into sixteen pieces still owned fifteen pieces after the integration. In several cases, property that had been in one piece before integration was divided into several pieces afterward. Behind all this there was corruption. The prosecutor's office refused to investigate the matter despite a written complaint by one of the peasants, from whom a surveyor had accepted a bribe. Other local and even central agencies did not react to the complaints either. On the contrary, the police, the prosecutor's office, and the courts, for reasons known only to them, gave special protection to the accused surveyor. KOR issued a statement concerning this problem on July 9, 1979, citing several examples that proved that it was of great social and economic importance.

Jan Dołęgowski was one of the peasants who had sustained a loss because of land integration in Przywory Duże. He organized a protest of others in similar circumstances. In October 1978, Dołęgowski was beaten up in the presence of the Provincial Integrating Commission. In November 1978 two of his bullocks were poisoned. He intended to take their carcasses to be examined on the following day, but before he could do so, the police appeared and took him to Siedlce, where a sentencing board levied a fine against him for failing to remove the carcasses. Two of his teeth were knocked out during an overt assault in February 1979. In March 1979 five more cattle belonging to Dołęgowski were poisoned. In June 1979 a large firecracker was thrown into his house. It destroyed his furnace and some furniture. At the same time, a sign reading "End Integration" was scrawled on his wall. On July 15, 1979, Dołęgowski was again beaten up. The neighbor who beat him warned that on the next occasion he would throw not a firecracker but a grenade.

The prosecutor's office did not react to his complaints. The State Insurance Office refused to insure his cattle.

On October 2, 1979, at 1:15 A.M., fires were set simultaneously in Dołęgowski's barn, in a cow shed located near his house, and in another cow shed belonging to him located in a field a mile away. His entire harvest, five cattle, thirteen pigs, twenty-five chickens, and his farming equipment went up in flames.

Around the same time, the deputy director of the Provincial Geodesic Bureau offered some of the peasants who had been hurt by the integration of land certificates for a car or a tractor, an apartment in Warsaw, and so on, in exchange for the withdrawal of their complaints. The director of the Department of Agriculture, Food Economy, and Forestry in the Provincial Office in Siedlce made an offer for the state to buy Dołęgowski's land for a reasonable price. Dołęgowski was not paid an insurance premium for the property lost in the fire. He was also refused allocations of building materials and fertilizer.

On April 15, 1980, Dołęgowski was beaten up by the village administrator. On April 16 he was arrested by the Security Service in Siedlce, and the regional prosecutor accused him of beating people who in reality had beaten him.

In April, KOR sent an open letter in this matter to the Diet Judicial Commission and to the Club of Deputies of the United Peasant party. Unfortunately, apart from publicizing once again how the justice system operates in the PRL, KOR was unable to accomplish anything else in defense of Dołęgowski. The strikes of the workers in August brought him his freedom.

The Society for Scientific Courses

The third year of the activities of TKN was formally inaugurated on November 2, 1979, with a lecture by Władysław Bartoszewski on "The Polish Undergound State during the Nazi Occupation." In fact, the lectures had already begun in October, and in October the practice of detaining lecturers had once again been put into effect. On November 16, the Security Service and the police invaded Bartoszewski's lecture on "Polish-Jewish Relations since 1918." A search was conducted in the apartment in which the lecture was taking place, so that it could not continue. Both the owner of the apartment (Piotr Naimski) and the lecturer were tried before a sentencing board. The proceedings were observed by a large audience. This was something new: until then, only the owners of apartments where lectures were held were forced to pay fines. For the first time, the lecturer was fined as well.

The list of repressions and persecutions used against TKN is a long one. Goon squads were not employed again, which does not mean that assaults ended. On November 23, TKN member and KOR associate Wojciech Ostrowski was beaten with clubs. In practical terms, the actions of the police paralyzed the open series of historical lectures, while the seminar groups functioned almost without disturbance.

Toward the end of 1979 an International Committee to Aid the Society of Scientific Courses in Poland was formed in the West. Its members included nearly seventy distinguished intellectuals from the West, including several Nobel Prize laureates.

The relations between KOR and TKN became even closer. TKN organized a Fund to Aid Scholars designed to offer scholarships to graduates of colleges, or, in exceptional cases, to students before graduation, who possessed the qualifications to continue research work, but who had been expelled from schools for ideological reasons. Professor Władysław Kunicki-Goldfinger, a member of the Polish Academy of Sciences, became chairman of the Council of the Fund to Aid Scholars, which was to decide who would receive the scholarships. Its administration was entrusted to the Social Self-Defense Fund, which meant that the treasurer of KOR, Jan Józef Lipski, also participated in the work of the Fund to Aid Scholars. In December 1979 the Social Self-Defense Funds Council appealed for financial contributions to support the Fund to Aid Scholars.

More and more often, TKN directed its efforts toward large-scale publishing activities, which were to include the publication of textbooks. However, most of these plans were still in their early stages. TKN planned to inaugurate the new academic year 1980–1981 with a document to which it attached great importance: a long "Letter to Teachers and Educators" (a full six pages almost without margins or spaces between lines), which was a programmatic statement of great ideological significance. The document was signed on behalf of TKN by Władysław Bartoszewski, Władysław Bieńkowski, Marian Brandys, Stanisław Hartman, Władysław Kunicki-Goldfinger, Marian Małowist, Tadeusz Mazowiecki, Jan Józef Szczepański, and Jacek Wóźniakowski. It was published in the KOR press in June 1980.

Self-Declared Catholic Movements and Groups

Much attention has been devoted here to issues and phenomena that did not strictly belong to the history of KOR but, like the Student Solidarity Committees, were so closely intertwined with the history of the committee that they had to be noted. The same consideration applies even more to ROPCiO, which for a time constituted a second and parallel oppositional current, and which could have grown, under more propitious circumstances, into a competitor of the committee. The history of ROPCiO constantly crossed the history of KOR, and involved many areas of cooperation. There were other groups that never cooperated with KOR, such as KPN, which simply hated the committee, or the Committee in Defense of Life, Family, and the Nation, which KOR somehow did not trust. And there were also movements and groups toward which KOR was sympathetic and which were respected by the committee, but which nevertheless remained distant, if only because there were few personal contacts between these movements and KOR, and so there was no cooperation.

This was the case with the Catholic youth movement called Light-Life, which brought minors together. On principle, KOR did not work in high schools and did not try to organize young people who had not yet begun college or work nor did it view favorably attempts to organize such young people (for example, by KPN), so there was no opportunity for KOR to exercise its influence. Obviously, KOR associates knew some of the priests involved in the Light-Life Movement, and some older activists of that movement as well. Among them, for example, was an old friend of mine, with whom I shared a common language; but this had no consequences for institutional connections, which were simply lacking. Nevertheless, KOR was electrified when at Jasna Góra, on March 2, 1980, 460 participants in the Fifth National Congregation of Representatives of the Light-Life Movement signed a wonderful declaration.

People who were fighting for their rights and needs, especially the most important of them—the right to the free expression of one's faith or beliefs—were always regarded by KOR as allies, although sometimes as allies sui generis, since not all of them knew—or even wanted to know—that they were allies, and perhaps would never go beyond the range of those issues that were most important to them, even if other problems should have been no less important from the point of view of their own interests.

In short, the Light-Life Movement, known also as the Oases, could remain primarily a devotional movement. For KOR, both for believers and nonbelievers within the committee, the minimum without which one could not speak about more or less generally accepted Christian ethics was based on the model of a Samaritan who hastens to help a person who has been beaten, even if he sees that the thugs are coming back, and that now they will also be able to beat up the rescuer. At the same time, both believers and nonbelievers in KOR felt distaste for the modern Pharisee who would first ask: "Were you not, by any chance, beaten by the police?" and upon receiving a positive answer, would depart with the words: "Manage as best you can, my good man, I will not involve myself in politics, I only serve God and the Greatest Good." And here, suddenly, a mass movement of Catholic youth had declared very clearly and without "diplomatic" ambiguities that it wanted to stand on principles that KOR could only applaud. A new quality of social life in Poland was being born before our eyes.

The declaration was a very important document, because it clearly formulated the responsibility of involving Catholic youth in public life. Although this document does not belong to the history of KOR or even of the opposition, except insofar as it was published by the oppositional press, it deserves some attention here since it was a symptom of an entirely new situation. This was of crucial importance for the committee as well, since it defined the context in which the committee was to be active; and although everything proceeded differently from what was expected in March 1980, this act on the part of Catholic youth was also very important for future events.

The first chapter of the declaration was entitled "The Seriousness of the Situation and the Temptation to Escape." After concluding that the situation was critical in almost all areas of national life, the declaration went on to say:

> . . . above all, one must face critically the problem of a human being entangled in multiple systems of dependence, who has been denied his freedom and whose dignity as a man has been degraded.

The declaration counts alcoholism among the greatest tragedies of national life. Alcoholism

> is not just a symptom of a tragic national situation. . . . Faced with the surrounding reality, communities of the Light-Life Movement might wish to

succumb to the temptation to escape from reality by creating, on the margins of it, groups whose existence would be based on God's words and evangelical love, but which, because of their atmosphere, would become places of contrast, oases where people feel good and forget about the problems and sufferings of their brothers . . . one must, however, demand that precisely these people who have discovered such "oases" become fully involved in and responsible for all the problems and sufferings of their brothers, among whom they are living.

The second chapter of the declaration contained an "Explanation of the Concept of Political Involvement." It stated that the crisis we were living through had a clear cause: "We know that it is our internal and external situation." All attempts to change this situation were to be regarded as political activities.

> The principles which Catholics should adopt toward political life were clearly defined in the documents of the ecumenical council, especially in the fourth chapter of the Pastoral Constitution about the Church in contemporary life. Basically, political activity is understood as activity for the general good, and it is evaluated positively, so that to an extent it is even a responsibility of believers.

"Political involvement" under totalitarian conditions has negative connotations; but the problem arises again "whenever there are democratic movements striving to defend fundamental human rights and human freedom, and which accept the risks of persecution, of the loss of freedom, or even life itself."

The third chapter is entitled "A Testimony to the Truth as a Liberating Involvement." It is based on a quotation from the encyclical *Redemptor hominis,* which also cited the words of Christ: "The truth shall make you free." It is necessary to bear witness to the truth regardless of the consequences; "no one can deprive us of our freedom except ourselves." One needs only to get rid of fear.

> If all the people, or at least a large part of our society, were to testify to the truth courageously, concretely, and simply, without regard to the consequences . . . a real liberation force would be introduced into national life, and its influence would be marked in all areas of life, including the political sphere.

The fourth chapter dealt with practical applications. First, the declaration took a stand with regard to the elections, describing them not so much as a political act but as a matter of conscience.

Whoever believes that he can honestly, in accordance with his convictions, express trust in the entire governing system, its program, goals, and methods, should confirm this by the public act of participating in the elections. But whoever cannot do so according to his conscience should bear witness to the truth by the only possible means, by not participating in the elections.

Concerning the party membership of Catholics, the declaration cited the words of Christ: "But let your communication be, yea, yea, nay, nay: for whatsoever is more than these comes of evil."

The declaration also takes a clear stand with regard to the dissident movements:[20]

> We declare that the courageous act of bearing witness to the truth, and the defense of the proper rights of man, in which some of our brothers are involved, often at the risk of their own lives, deserves deep respect, and all moral and other kinds of support dictated by our evangelical love and circumspection.

In its conclusion, the declaration asserted that the existing situation created an opportunity to bear witness to Christ and to the truth, and that this opportunity should be exploited:

> It would be a great loss for the future of the Church in Poland if we did not answer the holy call for a multiplicity of ways of bearing testimony to the truth. . . .
>
> At a time of such enormous threats, we want to undertake our deaconship of national liberation according to the principles stated above, in the spirit of Christian love for all our brothers, especially those who remain enslaved by false doctrines and those who, despite being aware of the truth, cannot summon the courage to respect it, so that Christian truth should bring true liberation to everyone.

The declaration of the Light-Life Movement has been summarized here in some detail in spite of the fact that it does not belong to the history of KOR. One must remember, however, that this was a mass movement. In a nation in which the overwhelming majority is faithfully Catholic, the young people were perhaps not more religious, but more fervent, more likely to look for ways in which their faith could be integrated and made to accord with their lives. More than any other document, this declaration explained and laid the foundations for an understanding of the processes that were to take place in Poland. The declaration was perhaps not surprising if one considers the pilgrimage of John Paul II to Poland and the effect it had on young people. But I think that KOR was also needed in order for this declaration to be written, and its existence allowed one to hope that the work of KOR was not in vain, regardless of what the future might bring. But the converse is also true: I believe that KOR would not have become a historical reality were it not for the fact that the attitude expressed in the declaration existed already *in potentia* in Polish social life in 1976.

Getting back to earth, it is necessary to add that this beautiful declaration might have borne fruit had it been written earlier. It turned out, however, that some time had to elapse between such a clear expression of principles and their practical consequences: after all, a new mode of life was being suggested not to several dozen young people, but to thousands. During the spring and summer of 1980, not much of this could be translated into the language of social practice. Looking back at the summer of 1980, both a social activist and a security agent, and in the future probably also a historian, would be more likely to notice the small Young Poland Movement than the morally and numerically powerful Light-Life Movement.

Committees of believers were being created on the borders between the democratic opposition and the Church. After the creation of the first such Committee for the Self-Defense of Believers in Opole Stare, which took place some time earlier, a Committee for the Self-Defense of Believers was created in Przemyśl in association with the newly constructed church in the Kmiecie district of the city (it was thanks to this committee that KOR had information about the struggle for religious freedom in the Przemyśl region); then came the Committee for the Self-Defense of Believers in Cisowe, formed by 293 persons.

The period in question also witnessed a broad campaign to gather signatures on a petition requesting that Masses be broadcast on radio and television. A significant number of the younger associates of KOR participated in this action, but older KOR activists were also among its organizers (such as Grzegorz Liese). KOR provided partial financing for this action, though not much money was required. However, it was necessary to print leaflets and banners, and to pay for the quickly disappearing pens of the organizers, since the distracted signatories often simply put them in their pockets by reflex.

The Seminar "Experience and Future"

It is impossible to ignore the subsequent works of DiP, since they played a significant role in the formation of attitudes among the intelligentsia. In any case, the *Report on the State of the Commonwealth and on Roads Leading to Its Repair* was an important and valuable work. It is not surprising that it was immediately discussed in detail in the *Information Bulletin,* and then immediately duplicated by NOWa. Almost on the eve of the strikes in the summer of 1980, the second document from DiP was published. This was entitled "How Do We Get Out of This?" and was completed on April 30. It was based on a survey conducted among members of the intelligentsia, to which there were 141 replies. Over one third of these responses were made by party members. This work did not have the social resonance of the first work; one felt that it was simply too late.

The Fast in Podkowa Leśna

It is difficult to introduce order (such as could be reflected in a logical sequence of sections) into the mass of seemingly minor and major issues that constituted the contents of every chapter of the history of KOR. The fast in the church in Podkowa Leśna is among those pieces of the history of KOR that are difficult to place. From my subjective point of view, examining the history of KOR from a short-term perspective, the fast was already an introduction to the social storm of July and August 1980. This was so not because it played a particularly important role in preparing the events that followed a very short time later (though the fast was not without its significance), but, because as we already noted above, one could feel the approaching storm in the air.

The third fast in the history of KOR began on May 7, 1980, in the parish church of St. Christopher in Podkowa Leśna, that is, in the church of Rev. Leon Kantorski, a tried and true friend of KOR who, immediately upon learning about the formation of the committee, had ordered a collection in the church intended for aid to the workers from nearby Ursus. Kantorski was also among the priests connected with the Light-Life Movement. The fast was again held for the purpose of appealing for the release of prisoners, and as an expression of solidarity with Mirosław Chojecki and Dariusz Kobzdej, who were fasting to protest their jailing. In the statement initiating the fast, the participants also named others who were being held at the time: Andrzej Czuma, Jan Dołęgowski, Bogdan Grzesiak, Tadeusz Kolano, Jan Kozłowski, Marek Kozłowski, Roman Kściuczek, Anatol Lawina, Bolesław Niklaszewski, Tadeusz Szczudłowski, and Edmund Zadrożyński, as well as unnamed Bielorussians, Czechs, Lithuanians, Russians, Germans, Slovaks, Ukrainians, and representatives of other nations who were imprisoned for truth and justice and who were fighting for goals common to all of us.[21]

The fast was to last for ten days (from May 7 to 17), but not all the participants were able to take part for the entire period. Various responsibilities and circumstances did not allow some persons to take a leave for such a long time. Thus, the following list of names of the participants also includes the dates of their participation: Seweryn Blumsztajn (7–14), Jarosław Broda (7–17), Jerzy Brykczyński (7–11), Leszek Budrewicz (7–17), Tomasz Burek (10–17), Jerzy Godek (7–17), Marian Gołębiewski (7–12), Aleksander Hall (7–17), Krystyna Iwaszkiewicz (7–17), Jan Karandziej (10–17), Wiesław Kęcik (7–14), Sergiusz Kowalski (7–14), Ryszard Krynicki (7–17), Jacek Kuroń (7–17), Ryszard Łagodziński (13–17), Mieczysław Majdzik (11–17), Lesław Maleszka (9–17), Renata Otolińska (7–17), Tibor Pakh (13–17), Wiesław Parchimowicz (8–17), Janusz Przewłocki (13–17), Aleksandra Sarata (9–17), Rev. Tadeusz Stokowski (11–17), Kazimierz Świtoń (7–17), Bronisław Wildstein (10–17), Mariusz Wilk (7–17), Róża Wózniakowska (7–17), and Tadeusz Zachara (7–12).

While describing the previous fast, I already expressed my opinion that one participates in a fast as an individual, and not as a representative of some organization. Therefore, the names listed here were not accompanied by organizational affiliations. However, it is worth mentioning the fact (and a careful reader will be able to figure this out from the list) that on this occasion the participants again came from KOR as well as ROPCiO and the Young Poland Movement; that among them were intellectuals as well as workers; and that students were accompanied by persons closer in age to their parents. The list was geographically diverse as well: Budapest, Gdańsk, Katowice, Cracow, Warsaw, Wrocław. Piotr Krasucki served as a physician; Kazimierz Janusz from ROPCiO and Jan Józef Lipski from KOR served as the spokesmen.

The location of the fast was excellent. The church in Podkowa Leśna had, for a long time already, thanks to its priest, been an influential center of social and religious life. Reverend Kantorski felt deep unity with the intentions of the fast, cared for its participants, and convinced his parishioners of the need for solidarity with those who were fasting. His homilies were responsible to a large extent for the atmosphere that prevailed during the fast.

Never before was there such a close contact with people visiting the church in order to pray with those fasting, on weekdays as well as on Sundays. This was the result of a certain superiority of parishes in small towns over those in large cities: there was greater social integration among the parishioners who knew each other well and who constituted a community to a much greater extent than urban parishioners. But the location was also ideal: the parish hall, including a large room for the exclusive use of those who were fasting, allowed for quite comfortable sleeping arrangements, as well as for holding conversations and discussions that would not disturb others who were trying to rest. The rooms were connected internally with the church, which was surrounded by an area where not only a breath of fresh air but even walks were possible.

The contacts established in Podkowa Leśna, and the conversations held there, turned out to be of priceless value for the future. There was time for the joint consideration of issues that were usually pushed into the background by current events. Ideas concerning the project of a Workers' Commission in Ursus were born precisely in Podkowa Leśna, during talks with Zbigniew Bujak and Zbyszek Janas.

The fast was supported by the solidarity of the local population and visitors from other cities throughout its entire duration. This was expressed, for example, in a letter signed by 952 people, and in a letter from young people and children of the parish, who decided that during the period of the fast they would not avail themselves of such pleasures as movies, television, ice cream, or cookies, and would donate the money saved in this manner for "the free word." At Masses celebrated during the fast, over 80,000 zlotys were collected for freedom of speech.

After the fast, a commission was formed whose task was to decide what to do with the money. The members of the commission were the spokesmen of the fast, Janusz and Lipski, and (at the suggestion of Lipski) Aleksander Hall. It was decided that the money should be used for the educational publications of the Society for Scientific Courses.

Mirosław Chojecki, Jan Dołęgowski, Stanisław Karpik, and Tadeusz Kolano were released during the fast. Chojecki came to the church, and with the permission of the priest, during the Mass he thanked everyone for their support.

On May 9, those fasting issued a statement in which they expressed their solidarity with the faithful in Podkowa Leśna who had fought for the preservation of a chapel in Otrębusy.

On May 14, the participants addressed a letter to the chairman of the Council of State asking for clemency for the brothers Ryszard and Jerzy Kowalczyk, who had already spent ten years in prison. They had been sentenced to fifteen-year terms for causing an explosion in the hall of the Higher School of Education in Opole, in protest against the use of this room for ceremonies in connection with the anniversary of the formation of the Security Service.[22] Also on May 14, several days after

Chojecki's release, participants in the fast appealed to everyone to defend Grzesiak.

The conclusion of the fast, after the last common Mass, was accompanied by a large demonstration in which several thousand people participated. The fast in Podkowa Leśna enriched the moral accomplishments of the opposition by a new act of resistance to the use of force.

THE REPORT OF THE EXPENDITURES
OF THE SOCIAL SELF-DEFENSE FUND
20 SEPTEMBER 1978–20 SEPTEMBER 1979

1.	The Intervention Bureau	1 570 600
2.	Telephone calls, telegrams, etc.	91 789
3.	Society for Scientific Courses	82 150
4.	Peasant University–Peasant Movement	36 150
5.	Student Solidarity Committee	9 236
6.	Free Trade Unions, Katowice	7 000
7.	*Information Bulletin* and *Communiqué*	339 258
8.	*Robotnik*	199 000
9.	*Placówka*	173 000
10.	*Głos*	162 767
11.	*Puls*	39 500
12.	Peasant Library	35 000
13.	*Krytyka*	30 000
14.	*Indeks*	10 000
15.	*Przegląd Zagraniczny*	5 000
16.	Publishing activity	192 660
	Total	2 983 110

Creditors of the Social Self-Defense Fund

1.	Expenditures of NOWa	175 700
2.	Third of May Publishing House	154 000
3.	*Spotkania*	140 000
4.	Free Trade Unions, Katowice	19 200
	Total	489 300

Total expenditures for the period 9.20.78–9.16.79

	2 983 110
	489 300
Total	3 472 410

Creditors from the previous accounting year

1. *Opinia*   56 400
2. Student Solidarity Committee, Cracow   35 000

This document differs by only one word from the one published in *Communiqué* No. 35: "Flying University" was corrected to "Peasant University" (in Zbrosza Duża). This was a proofreader's error. Basically, Item 2 in Expenditures should be supplemented by "travel," since it includes all reimbursements for travel that, like the telephone calls, cost quite a lot of money.

The Period of the July and August Strikes in 1980

The great wave of strikes in July and August did not surprise KOR, which had been expecting an explosion of workers' dissatisfaction for a year. The strikes did, however, exceed all expectations, and the result, the Gdańsk Agreements, could not have been anticipated with certainty even as late as several days before they were signed.

On July 1 a strike began in Ursus, or rather in several of its departments. There were also short strikes on the same day in the Sanok Bus Factory, Autosan, and in the Factory of Specialized Machine Tools, Ponar, in Tarnów. From this day on, for over two months there was not a single day in Poland without a strike.

On July 3, on the third day of the strike in the Repair and Energy Department in Ursus, a Workers' Commission was formed. Its demands included an increase in the allowance for work under conditions hazardous to health. The group headed by Bujak and Janas was thus making its existence known. By that time there was already information that strikes were occurring in the Warszawa Steel Mill (a partial strike), in the Automobile Spare Parts Factory Polmo in Tczew, in the Communications Equipment Manufacturing Plant in Mielec, and in the Rzeszów Construction Enterprises.

More and more often, the striking workers demanded guarantees of safety for the strikers. Among the demands made by the strikers, there were some that went beyond matters of wages and social conditions particular to the plant. On July 9 the striking work force of the Żyrardow Technical Textiles Factory demanded that their inventories and accounts be audited by the Highest Office of Control. Also on July 9 a demand that was to enjoy great popularity and was to recur in various workplaces was formulated in the Communications Equipment Manufacturing Firm in Świdnik, near Lublin: family allowances should be the same as those received by the police. A strike committee was chosen in that factory.

On July 10 two departments of the truck factory in Lublin went on strike. A strike committee was formed the following day. From then on, the strike in Lublin grew every day; and on July 14 a general strike was announced throughout the entire city. On July 15 the locomotive works of the Polish State Railways went on strike, and on July 16 all the railroad workers in Lublin joined in, creating a joint strike committee. Here the demands had a new emphasis: there was talk of dissolving the plant council of the trade unions, which was servile to the employer, and there was also discussion of calling new elections. On July 16 the Cooperative of the Visually Impaired in Lublin, which was also on strike, created a Workers' Commission. The size of the strikes in Lublin was such that it is no exaggeration to claim that there was a general strike throughout the entire city. This was true especially following an unsuccessful attempt to bring in scabs from outside Lublin, who refused to work once they learned of the appeal of the strike committee. On July 18 all public transportation in the city stood still. This was something more than strikes in individual factories. At the same time, news that the strikes were spreading was coming in constantly from different areas.

On July 19 the local authorities in Lublin assured the strike committee of the Lublin railroad junction that *Sztandar Ludu,* the organ of the Provincial Committee of PUWP, would issue an apology to the strikers for the insulting comments it had made in that day's issue of the newspaper. An agreement was signed in which the authorities acceded to all demands of the strikers, although two demands concerning changes in the retirement age and the introduction of an inflation allowance for all railroad workers throughout the entire country were passed on to the central authorities for a decision. The agreement was signed by the strike committee, a director, the president of the city, and the voivode. The Cooperative of the Visually Impaired, which continued to strike, demanded that its Workers' Commission be permanently recognized as the representative of the trade union in the factory. The cooperative ended its strike on July 23, but the Workers' Commission was not dissolved.

On July 19 Lublin's *Sztandar Ludu*—and this newspaper only—published a "Communiqué from the meeting of the Politburo of the Central Committee of PUWP held on July 18, 1980, concerning the situation in Lublin." From the communiqué one could learn that "the Politburo has approved the decisions of the government concerning the realization of the demands of the factories, and the creation of a commission to be headed by Mieczysław Jagielski, who is a member of the Politburo and the vice-premier of the Council of Ministers, as well as a deputy from the Lublin region. After the workplaces have returned to normal work, this commission will carefully consider the demands that have been made and will present them to the government of the PRL."

All the factories in Ostrów Wielkopolski went on strike on July 24.

A strike of the City Public Transportation Enterprises began in Warsaw on August 11, and gradually all bus and streetcar lines joined the strike.

At that time the management of the Gdańsk Shipyard had a brilliant idea: they gave notice of dismissal to Anna Walentynowicz, a member of the coastal KZ WZZ. Several thousand leaflets in her defense appeared in the city on August 14, and at 6:00 A.M., Departments K-1 and K-3 of the Lenin Shipyard in Gdańsk interrupted production. Other departments joined in. A rally began at 9:00 A.M., and a strike was proclaimed. A strike committee was formed. Its primary demands were the rehiring of Anna Walentynowicz and Lech Wałęsa, the erection of a monument to the memory of the victims of December 1970, guarantees that there would be no reprisals for the strike, a raise of 2,000 zlotys a month, and family allowances matching those in the police. Wałęsa became the head of the strike committee. A workers' guard was formed, whose task was to prevent anyone who did not have a pass from the strike committee from entering the shipyard. A prohibition against alcohol was observed in the shipyard.

On August 15 the strike spread to the Paris Commune Shipyard in Gdynia (Andrzej Kołodziej, a member of the coastal KZ WZZ, became the head of the strike committee in Gdynia; he had begun working in that shipyard only two days earlier, after being dismissed from the Gdańsk Shipyard). On August 15 the shipyards, the ports, and all public transport and industrial enterprises associated with the shipyard were all on strike. At noon, the communication lines linking Gdańsk, Gdynia, and Sopot with the rest of the country were cut. The Polish Press Agency announced for the first time that there were "work stoppages." Gierek returned from his vacation in the Crimea.

On August 16, around 3:00 P.M., after the management had given a verbal promise to accede to the wage demands, the majority of the members on the strike committee of the Lenin Shipyards (the composition of which was rather accidental; in some less decisive departments, the management had succeeded in introducing its own people into the committee) voted to end the strike, and Wałęsa announced that the strike was over. It was a dramatic moment; some of the workers demanded that the strike continue as an expression of solidarity with other enterprises on the coast where no one was talking to the strikers. Wałęsa called off the strike, but some of the shipyard broadcasting system was turned off, while the management was calling for the evacuation of the plant through other megaphones. But approximately a thousand workers remained. In the night, delegations from twenty-one striking enterprises came to the shipyard, and the Inter-Factory Strike Committee (MKS) was formed. It issued its first communiqué, which was distributed in the form of a leaflet. This very important document must be cited:

> As a result of an agreement among the work forces of the enterprises and factories on the coast, an Inter-Factory Strike Committee located in the Gdańsk Shipyard has been created on August 16. The goal of the MKS is to coordinate the demands and the strike actions of these enterprises and factories. A text has been formulated listing the demands and postulates which have been jointly adopted by the strike committees. It has been decided that the strike will continue until these demands and postulates of the workers have been met. The MKS is authorized to conduct talks with the central authorities. The decision to end the strike will be made by the MKS. After the strike ends, the MKS will not be dissolved: it will oversee the implementation of the demands and organize free trade unions.

Workers were gradually returning to the Lenin Shipyards in order to rejoin the strike. New plants were joining the MKS. By August 18 there were already 156 such plants.

The board of the MKS, headed by Lech Wałęsa, was composed of Joanna Duda-Gwiazda, Andrzej Gwiazda, Stefan Izdebski, Lech Jendruszewski, Jerzy Kmiecik, Zdzisław Kobyliński, Andrzej Kołodziej, Henryka Krzywonos, Stefan Lewandowski, Bogdan Lis, Józef Przybylski, Lech Sobieszek, Tadeusz Stanny, Jerzy Sikorski, Anna Walentynowicz, and Florian Wiśniewski. Several days later, Dr. Wojciech Gruszewski from the Gdańsk Polytechnic and writer Lech Bądkowski were also made members of the board.

The delegation from the MKS transmitted to the Gdańsk voivode the famous list of Twenty-One Demands which has been cited in many publications.

On August 18 an Inter-Factory Strike Committee was created in Szczecin.

The Security Service and the police began a sharp attack against KOR.

On August 19 the MKS in Gdańsk issued a formal demand, addressed to Premier Babiuch, that the central authorities begin negotiating. A government commission arrived in Gdańsk, whose chairman, Tadeusz Pyka, immediately began talks with certain strike committees behind the back of the MKS.

On August 19 the Lublin locomotive works elected a Free Plant Council, headed by Czesław Niezgoda.

On August 20, the MKS in Gdańsk issued a statement in which the first of the twenty-one demands was singled out: "Without independent trade unions, all the other concessions might be taken away in the future." The MKS also decided that the strike committees that joined the MKS could not conduct separate talks with the authorities. As a result of pressure from the workers, all negotiations of this kind had been broken off. Pyka was recalled to Warsaw at night. By that time, the MKS in Gdańsk already represented 304 strike committees. The MKS in Szczecin represented 30. The local press announced that one initial condition that must be met before talks would be undertaken with the strikers was their rejection of KOR and the Young Poland Movement.[23]

Also on August 20, sixty-four distinguished intellectuals issued an *Appeal* calling on the government to recognize the MKS and to begin negotiations, and calling on both parties to act reasonably and with moderation. Within a matter of days, 200 other intellectuals had joined the *Appeal*. Two days later, 55 intellectuals from Poznań expressed their support for the demands of the striking workers on the coast.

Support for the demands of the striking workers was also expressed by the Peasant Self-Defense Committees in the Grójec and Rzeszów regions, the Independent Trade Union of Farmers, and the editorial boards of independent periodicals of the peasant movement. On August 21, a government delegation headed by vice-premier Jagielski came to Gdańsk and made new attempts to avoid talking with the MKS. Because of attacks by the mass media against "antisocialist forces," Lech Wałęsa declared: "Nobody is instigating us, but I am familiar with the activities of KOR"; and he then proceeded to describe the history of KOR to the MKS.

At 10:00 A.M., a government delegation headed by vice-premier Kazimierz Barcikowski came to the Warski Shipyard in Szczecin in order to begin talks with the Szczecin MKS, which on that day represented 82 strike committees. By the following day, it represented 100 such committees.

In the Mechanical Plant in Ursus, near Warsaw, a Workers' Committee of Solidarity with the striking workers on the coast was created.

On August 23, Lech Wałęsa called on the authorities to cease their repressions against persons aiding the strike. At 8:00 P.M., a government delegation headed by Jagielski arrived at the Lenin Shipyard in Gdańsk in order to conduct talks with the MKS. On the same day, the Free Gdańsk Print Shop in the Lenin Shipyard published the first issue of the Strike Information Bulletin *Solidarity*, edited by Konrad Bieliński and Mariusz Wilk. Late in the evening, a delegation from the MKS in Szczecin arrived at the Gdańsk shipyard. Both Inter-Factory Strike Committees agreed that the issue of free trade unions would constitute their basic demand.

On August 24 a group of signatories of the August 20 *Appeal* by sixty-four intellectuals came to the MKS in Gdańsk. They formed the Experts' Commission of the MKS (Tadeusz Mazowiecki, chairman; Bohdan Cywiński; Bronisław Geremek; Tadeusz Kowalik; Waldemar Kuczyński; Jadwiga Staniszkis; and Andrzej Wielowieyski). On the same day, during the Fourth Plenary Meeting of the Central Committee of PUWP, Gierek announced a new law governing trade unions and new elections to plant councils. The first secretary of the Provincial Committee in Gdańsk, Tadeusz Fiszbach, stated that the MKS in Gdańsk had the mandate of both striking and nonstriking workers on the coast to conduct negotiations, and that the strike was not a result of the activities of antisocialist groups.

On August 25 the Szczecin MKS represented a total of 142 workplaces. The disconnected telephone lines stood in the way of the talks in Gdańsk, and the MKS demanded that telephone connections be restored as a precondition for talks.

On August 26 two working commissions began negotiations in Gdańsk. The MKS commission was headed by Andrzej Gwiazda, and the government commission by the Gdańsk voivode, Jerzy Kołodziejski. By this time the MKS represented almost 500 workplaces. The Thorez mine began a strike which quickly spread through the Wałbrzych Mining District.

By August 27 the Inter-Factory Strike Committee in Wałbrzych represented thirty-six workplaces. On the same day, a solidarity strike began in Ursus.

On August 28 the mines in the copper mining district began a strike in solidarity with the coast.

An Inter-Factory Strike Committee was created in Wrocław; on August 28 it represented seventy workplaces.

On August 29 a Commission of Experts of the MKS was created in Szczecin. It was composed of Andrzej Kijowski, Andrzej Tymowski, and Janina Walukowa; 300 enterprises had joined the MKS. Another MKS was created in Krosno. This was the day that finally tilted the balance:

a dozen or so coal mines in the Katowice and Rybnik mining districts went out on strike, as did the steel mills Katowice and Baildon.

By August 30 the negotiations in Gdańsk had already reached an advanced stage. Wałęsa raised the issue of the arrested KOR activists in Warsaw.[24] An agreement between the MKS and the government delegation was signed in Szczecin.

On August 31 in Gdańsk the two parties signed the successive points of the agreement. The MKS added a list of names to the fourth point (the release of political prisoners). Vice-premier Jagielski did not want to offer any written guarantees. Finally, faced with the resolute attitude of the MKS, Jagielski declared that before noon on September 1, all the prisoners named on the list would be released.

At 5:00 P.M. an agreement was signed between the government commission and the Gdańsk Inter-Factory Strike Committee, which by then represented approximately 700 enterprises (the official signing of the final protocol took place several hours later). Lech Wałęsa announced that the strike was over.

On September 3, following three days of negotiations, an agreement was signed between the government commission and the MKS in Jastrzębie. Strikes began also in Bytom, Zabrze, Gliwice, and Katowice (eleven mines). The miners demanded written guarantees that the agreement signed in Jastrzębie would apply to them as well.

A strike began in the Nowotko Mechanical Enterprises in Warsaw in response to a statement published in *Głos Pracy* by the chairman of one of its departmental councils, who had stated that there were no calls among the workers for the creation of free trade unions. Local strikes, often similar to those in Nowotko Enterprises, erupted here and there throughout the month of September; but after the main demands had been won, the strike movement began to die out.

This has not been a calendar of strikes, since altogether several thousand strikes took place. It is significant, however, that by the end of September the principal and often the only reason for the strikes was solidarity with the coast.

KOR in July and August 1980

Sometimes one meets with the opinion that KOR organized the strikes. This is not true. If it were so, I would surely emphasize this fact, both because of my respect for historical truth and out of pride that KOR was able to do so much. But the truth lies elsewhere.

The Workers' Defense Committee taught that society had to demand the rights it deserved. It familiarized workers with the idea of a strike as a means of achieving goals that were otherwise impossible to achieve; it indicated the possibility of strike demands that would go beyond economic issues: free trade unions, the elimination of censorship. KOR also suggested specific tactics for striking, which involved the maximum internal organization of a strike and thus lessened the possibility of a provocation—remaining locked up in the factories instead of taking to the streets, and negotiating with the authorities through elected representatives. The committee prepared its associates in the factories to become strike activists in case of need. It brought to their attention the importance of maintaining communication with KOR, and of providing information at such moments. But not a single strike was ever organized by KOR.

Obviously it was no accident that no one knew better than the Gdańsk activists what to do when large-scale strikes would occur. Their training has been described by Anna Walentynowicz in the film *Workers 80*, and by Jan Lityński, the editor-in-chief of *Robotnik*, in an interview he gave to *Res Publica*. On the Gdańsk coast, between 100 to 200 people had gone through social self-education circles created by the systematic, ant-like work of such people as KOR member Bogdan Borusewicz, the Gwiazdas, and the entire Initiating Committee of Free Trade Unions: people such as Anna Walentynowicz and Lech Wałęsa, the brothers Krzysztof and Błażej Wyszkowski, Alina Pieńkowska, Maryla Płońska, Andrzej Kołodziej, and Andrzej Bulc. It was also not without significance that relations among the various oppositional groups were nowhere else as good as in Gdańsk. Their differences did not prevent unity when something needed to be done together in order to bring them nearer to their common goals.

KOR played a double role in the July and August strikes. First, KOR was involved in the preparation of the workers' consciousness for the strikes. This was mainly the achievement of *Robotnik*. Second, KOR tried to assure the strikers that there was an information service available. This was probably the greatest indisputable success of KOR. Bluffs and myths had to go: KOR was present, it performed its function, and it turned out that it was able to do something no one else was able to do, despite the fact that KOR never boasted of its strength the way others did. And, after all, what sort of strength was it? It was only sufficient to do what was done. A KOR team directed by Konrad Bieliński organized a print shop in the Gdańsk shipyard and edited the strike daily, *Solidarity*.

Ewa Milewicz, who was also in the shipyard, organized and maintained communications between the shipyard and the rest of the coast.

How did this information service work? Usually the pattern was the same: a strike would begin in some plant in the morning. If there was anyone present connected with KOR, of if there was a group of distributors of *Robotnik*, or simply someone who had copied some telephone number from the *Communiqué*, that person went to the telephone. KOR had to know about it. Thus, by the early afternoon, KOR not only had the necessary information but also was quickly trying to confirm it. A little later, it would already be possible to provide journalists from the press agencies accredited in Warsaw and the foreign associates of KOR[25] with a full information service: who was striking? was it a whole plant or only part of the work force? what were the demands? had a strike committee been formed? who was heading it? what was the attitude of the management to the strike? In the evening, radio stations throughout the whole world read the news; it was also read in Polish. This was important: in 1976 the workers from Ursus, fearing that their strike would not be noticed and would therefore be less successful, had gone out onto the railroad tracks to paralyze national and international rail traffic.

Jacek Kuroń's telephone always functioned as the information center in KOR. Anyone who learned anything considered it his or her responsibility to call Jacek. Much information came in over other telephones, in calls to Jan Lityński, Zofia and Zbyszek Romaszewski, Aniela Steinsbergowa, Anka Kowalska, or Jan Józef Lipski; but finally it all went to Kuroń. Usually the phone was answered by Jacek, his wife Grażyna, their son Maciej, or Grażyna's father Jacek Borucki, or often by guests or even "an orderly." When the phone began ringing nonstop, Ewa Kulik (an activist of the Cracow SKS who was living temporarily in Warsaw) moved into Kuroń's apartment. She spent twenty-four hours a day near the telephone, ate, slept, and studied while attending to it. Since she knew English well, she managed wonderfully: people throughout the world called to find out what was happening. Kuroń's house—which throughout the entire existence of KOR served as a club, a hotel, a press office, and a coordination center—began to resemble a madhouse. But everything worked.

When the strike movement began to spread, shifting from place to place throughout the entire country, there was a need to form regional centers that would gather information and transmit it to the "central office." For example, KOR member Wojciech Onyszkiewicz worked in

Lublin, together with Jerzy Zieleński, an experienced journalist, a member of DiP, and an associate of KOR. It was there that contact was established between KOR and KPN: a local group affiliated with KPN offered cooperation to Onyszkiewicz, because they wanted to do something during this exciting period. This appears to have been the only instance of a more formal contact between KOR and KPN in the entire history of the opposition. The Security Service learned about the arrival in town of this small KOR team. Despite repeated attempts, Onyszkiewicz and Zieleński were not arrested, thanks to help from workers and intellectuals. Obviously, searches and detentions continued throughout the whole period; a more serious offensive against KOR was mounted on August 18.

Above all, telephones began going dead one after another. The blockade was so extensive that the communication and information system of KOR was almost entirely paralyzed. However, the blockade was broken once in a while by using telephones made available by associates or sympathizers of KOR who were less familiar to the Security Service. KOR also attempted to maintain contact with the country through couriers equipped with the telephone numbers of as yet unidentified telephones.

Four issues of *Robotnik* appeared during the strikes, and the number of copies was increased to 40,000.

When KOR learned of the strike in Ursus, it became clear that something very important was beginning, and it was by no means obvious that KOR would be able to make its views known several days later. We exaggerated a little, since the authorities, who were completely unfamiliar with the social atmosphere and were living in a world of illusions, failed to notice for a long time that these strikes, deceptively similar to earlier ones, were in fact entirely different and were leading to something completely new. In order to be aware of this, one had to possess a social sensitivity similar to that of KOR.

KOR met on July 2 and issued a statement providing information about the strike in Ursus and in the POLMO Enterprises in Tczew, and confirming information about other strikes. KOR expressed its solidarity with the strikers, and demanded that full official information about price increases for certain kinds of meat and cold cuts be made available and that the actual supply of food be made public. At the same time, KOR warned the government against provoking the public, and called for negotiations with the workers' representatives. The statement included an appeal to the workers:

We appeal to all work crews throughout Poland, warning them against protests which the authorities might exploit in order to provoke riots.

The method which can be used most effectively—and with the greatest safety for the entire nation—by workers demanding recognition of their interests and of the interests of the whole society, involves self-organization in the workplaces and democratic elections of independent workers' representatives who will present demands in the name of the workers, conduct negotiations with the authorities, and lead the actions of the workers in a responsible but decisive manner. The workers must be aware that only solidary action can bring positive results. Above all, the authorities must not be permitted to initiate any manner of reprisals against the participants in the strikes, or against persons who were either really, or in the imagination of the authorities, serving as leaders of the workers' protest.

We appeal to the entire society to support the workers' demands with expressions of solidarity.

KOR's statement of July 11 presented the complicated situation with regard to changes in prices, which had become the spark that ignited the strikes; it provided information about fourteen strikes that were then in progress, and about the creation of three departmental workers' commissions in Ursus. It also repeated the most important parts of the statement of July 2, which is cited above. The July 11 statement also contained a concise diagnosis of the economic inefficiency of the system and a five-point program of immediate actions necessary to save the country from a catastrophe:

1. The initial work on changes in the economic system and in the methods of decision making, which is necessary in the nearest future, must be preceded by a general public discussion. The governmental program of reform must be clearly formulated and must include a timetable for its implementation—"otherwise, the immediate activities of the government will be answered by immediate actions on the part of individual social groups."

2. The policy of destroying individual farming has to be changed. "Private ownership of land and the freedom to buy and sell it must be guaranteed." Private family farming must be accorded the same rights as the state and cooperative agricultural enterprises.[26]

3. For as long as changes in agricultural policy will not produce results, and if the state authorities are unable to assure an adequate supply of meat, a system of rationing must be introduced temporarily.

4. It is necessary to publish data about the current state of the economy.

5. "The authorities must understand that they will not be able to avoid

negotiations with society, though to a large extent, whether these negotiations will take place in an atmosphere of peace or in an atmosphere
of sharpening conflict depends on the authorities."

> The Social Self-Defense Committee "KOR," in accordance with its goals,
> wishes to emphasize with particular force the necessity of restoring basic civil
> rights. . . . Observance of these rights on the part of the government will
> create the possibility of achieving an understanding concerning the most
> urgent economic, political, and social reforms.
> Employees must be allowed to meet and nominate workers' commissions,
> employees' commissions, independent trade unions, and other representative
> bodies able to defend the workers' interests. . . .
> The law on associations and assemblies must be changed.
> Changes must be introduced into the Labor Code, especially Art. 52 § 1,
> which allows for dismissal from work for having participated in a strike. The
> right to strike must be legally guaranteed. . . .
> In addition to purely economic factors, one of the basic causes of the present
> economic situation is the muzzling of society through censorship and the
> monopoly over the mass media . . . prohibiting not only the expression of
> true opinions which circulate among the public but also of statements by
> experts whenever they are considered inconvenient. . . .
> Preventive censorship should be eliminated in the national interest, and
> the press law changed. . . .
> Reprisals against people involved in independent social and political activ-
> ities must cease. The rights of the police and the Security Service should be
> limited.
> The courts should be made independent again. All political prisoners must
> be released immediately.

This was already a broad and realistic program for a social movement
that was to be born any moment.

On August 8, KOR issued a statement that contained an attempt to
evaluate the strike movement up to that point in time, and which stressed
three important factors:

> 1. The strikers are often well organized; they do not leave their workplaces,
> and they make their demands peacefully.
> 2. Strikes are occurring throughout the whole country—the power of one
> strike is magnified by all the other strikes.
> 3. Information about strikes, and about demands, and the conditions under
> which agreements are being reached, are being collected and distributed.

KOR regarded the creation by workers of authentic representative bodies that would not dissolve after the strike was over as one of the most significant achievements of the strike movement. The statement also mentioned cases of beatings: KOR associate Stanisław Śmigło and Konrad Turzyński, a member of the Young Poland Movement, were beaten in Toruń. In Warsaw the police beat a courier who operated between the Stalowa Wola factory and KOR (whose name is not recorded because he did not want it to be mentioned). Bożena Kędzierska, a KOR associate in Stalowa Wola, had her hair pulled and was threatened with death. The statement also listed cases of arrests and threats for helping provide KOR with information about the events.

On August 13, KOR published a statement concerning a strike in the City Public Transportation Enterprises, and an incident that took place at the intersection of the two busiest streets in Warsaw in the center of the city. The statement noted the completely peaceful and orderly nature of the strike, and stated at the same time:

> Regardless of whether the brawl on the corner of Aleja Jerozolimskie and Marszałkowska was instigated by the proponents of reprisals against the workers or by irresponsible individuals, the effects of such behavior can be used to combat the emerging workers' movement. We emphasize strongly: the power of this movement lies in its solidarity, discipline, peace and rationality. Anyone who provokes brawls is acting in the interest of the political police and for repressions against society.

On August 18, KOR, together with the editorial board of *Robotnik*, issued a statement announcing the formation of the Inter-Factory Strike Committee in Gdańsk, which in the future, after the strike, was to transform itself into the Provincial Council of Free Trade Unions. The basic task for the present was the creation of free trade unions. The authorities had to recognize them if any understanding were to be possible. Written assurances of safety for all the strikers were also necessary. Further, the statement listed the most important issues that needed to be settled immediately through negotiations between the strikers and the government: an inflation supplement indexed according to changes in the rate of inflation (which should, above all, compensate those who earned the least); full information, not constrained by censorship, to be provided by the government about the economic situation and the creation of conditions for a discussion of the program of reforms; the participation of free trade unions, peasant representatives, intellectuals, local self-government groups, and cultural and scientific associations in social life and in social control; guarantees of the inviolability of private land ownership and the accordance of equal rights to family farming; and an end to police discrimination against strikers, their families, and persons gathering information about the strikes.

> Whenever . . . the political police intervene, whether in an overt or a covert manner, these negotiations should be broken off. . . . The fulfillment of the demands of the striking workers on the coast, the release of all political prisoners, and the cessation of Security Service interventions into the activities of the independent workers' movement throughout all of Poland constitute the most elementary conditions for a return to social peace.

A statement from KOR of August 21 carried information about the attack of the Security Service against KOR and the demand that those who had been detained be released, as well as an appeal to supply KOR with information concerning reprisals against strikers and about the activities of the independent groups representing the workers.

On August 23 the committee issued information about further police actions against KOR, and protested against the practice of extending the already overused method of detention without prosecutor's sanctions for more than forty-eight hours. Also on August 23 the committee issued a statement in which it protested against the government's attempts to stall the negotiations with the Inter-Factory Strike Committees, which had been undertaken with excessive delay, and were now increasing economic losses. KOR appealed for public expressions of solidarity with the strikers through statements and resolutions, and by collecting money for the strikers.

On August 29, KOR announced that Lech Wałęsa, speaking in front of the gate of the Gdańsk Shipyard, had stated that the authorities had not allowed him to address the workers on radio and television in order to appeal for workers' solidarity with the demands of the MKS in Gdańsk without further widening of the strike action. KOR stated that it supported Wałęsa's appeal.

On August 30, in its next statement, KOR announced that the prosecutor's office had charged the following members and associates of KOR with membership in an association having a criminal intent, and placed them under investigative arrest: Jan Ajzner, Seweryn Blumsztajn, Mirosław Chojecki, Ludwik Dorn, Aleksander Gleichgewicht, Mieczysław

Grudziński, Stefan Kawalec, Wiesław Kęcik, Jacek Kuroń, Jan Lityński, Adam Michnik, Zbigniew Romaszewski, and Andrzej Zozula. Leszek Moczulski from KPN also received a prosecutor's sanction.

The majority of these people had been arrested earlier, in a manner that can only be considered a mockery of the law. Since detentions can last only forty-eight hours, the arrested person was taken from one police precinct to another, which was called a new detention. At first, a formal "release" was followed immediately by a new detention, right in front of the door of the police headquarters. But when one of the detainees, Henryk Wujec, managed to escape during such a release, even this formality was abrogated. As we know from a secret instruction from Prosecutor General Lucjan Czubiński published later during the times of Solidarity, this method was used with the knowledge and even on the orders of the institution whose mission was to protect the legal order it represented.

On September 1 all the detained and arrested persons and those political prisoners who had been convicted for alleged criminal activity were released.[27]

The signing of the formal agreements with independent representatives of the workers—the first in the history of the PRL—initiated a new chapter in the history of Poland, and the last chapter in the history of KOR.

10

From the Gdańsk Agreements to the Dissolution of KOR
(September 1980–September 1981)

KOR and Solidarity

The creation of the independent trade union that after several days adopted the name "Solidarity" (the same name as that of the daily strike bulletin of the Inter-Factory Strike Committee in Gdańsk) radically changed the situation of KOR. The goals that KOR had set before society could and should now be taken over by a great mass social movement, of which Solidarity was the most important element. Moreover, the new and gigantic trade union was able to make certain that the social demands that had previously been expressed by KOR would be acted upon in an incomparably more effective manner than could have been achieved by the committee. However, until Solidarity organized itself and settled down to this work, it was clear that KOR still had reason to exist.

On September 11, KOR issued a statement in which it thanked and expressed "deep gratitude to the MKS of the tri-city area" for making the release of the arrested members of the democratic opposition a condition that had to be met before the end of the strike. The members of KOR once again stressed in their statement that only a dialogue between the government and democratically elected representatives of the workers could lead to effective solutions. They also stated that the goals and tasks of KSS "KOR"—the struggle against repressions for political, ideological, religious, or racial reasons, and the defense of those who had been wronged or persecuted—had not changed. These goals were shared with the newly created independent trade union.

Thus, in the most natural manner, all the activists of KOR, a numerous and socially experienced group, joined Solidarity. In their places of employment, KOR members and associates were the originators of the first attempts to form the initiating committees of the new trade unions. Quite often, because they were trusted within their particular milieus, they were elected to posts within Solidarity on various levels, including the highest. Jacek Kuroń became an expert adviser to the then-emerging National Coordinating Commission (KKP) in Gdańsk, while Andrzej Celiński became its secretary. Jan Lityński helped in the formation of the union in Wałbrzych, where *Robotnik* had a number of associates; others, like Henryk Wujec, became members of regional Solidarity authorities. Antoni Macierewicz, together with a group of his friends from *Głos,* organized a consultation and information center that played an important role while Solidarity in Warsaw and the surrounding region was still in its first organizational stages.

Many editors, authors, and technical associates of KOR periodicals began organizing a Solidarity press. Printers from the many independent publishing houses had both experience and necessary equipment to contribute to the creation of printing facilities in the new union. In September, the most important institution within KOR, the Intervention Bureau, prepared a report on its activities signed by Zbigniew and Zofia Romaszewski, and it then became the Intervention Bureau of the Mazowsze (Warsaw) Region of Solidarity; the new bureau kept the most active associates from the time of its activities in KOR, and its work was still directed by the Romaszewskis, who also had an important part in organizing intervention bureaus in other regions. In March 1981, after several earlier national congresses, all these bureaus jointly created the National Intervention Bureau of the Independent Self-Governing Trade Union (NSZZ) Solidarity.

With the exception of Gdańsk and Szczecin, Solidarity did not have as yet, during its organizational stages, a sufficient amount of money at its disposal. At the same time, there was a need for an enormous number of brochures, informational leaflets, instructions, and projects, which would be destined not for a relatively small group but for almost every workplace where employees expressed the desire to form an independent trade union. The entire printing plant of KOR and of publishing houses close to KOR worked mainly to meet these needs, and drew money from the Social Self-Defense Fund, which spent almost 400,000 zlotys for this purpose. Similarly, the Intervention Bureau, though it was already working in Solidarity, was also paid by the fund. During the earliest period the fund covered 100 percent of the bureau's costs; but even later, significant sums continued to be drawn from the fund, since not all the cases of the bureau could be considered purely union matters.

In December the National Coordinating Commission nominated a Defense Committee for Prisoners of Conscience. Its members included many activists of Solidarity, including Lech Wałęsa, together with members of TKN and members and associates of KOR.[1] Under these new conditions, as almost all the members and associates of KOR began working for Solidarity, the work of the committee itself ended almost immediately. The frequency of the periodicals published by groups close to KOR also declined. Nevertheless, the committee was not silent, especially since the official press, which praised the agreements and bowed down to the striking workers, at the same time intensified its attacks against KOR. Thus, as early as September 19, a KOR statement cited the words of the Inter-Factory Organizing Committee of the Independent Self-Governing Trade Unions on the coast concerning the attacks of the mass media against the democratic opposition:

> Attacks are multiplying in the local and central press throughout the entire country against people described by the government as "antisocialist forces," who are allegedly trying to infiltrate the independent trade unions. This campaign began back during the strike. It was asserted then that antisocialist forces were inciting the workers to strike, and making them demand independent trade unions. Before the Agreements, those who demanded independent trade unions were described as opponents of socialism. Now the same thing is being repeated during various closed meetings. The press, on the other hand, no longer attacks independent trade unions, but only those individuals who supposedly try to push their way into the unions. The MKZ declares that it knows nothing about any antisocialist forces which have ever attempted to take over the independent trade union movement.

Since the attacks of the mass media against the democratic opposition did not cease, and since, in spite of the Gdańsk Agreements, the investigations against some members of KOR had not been officially dropped, on October 31 all members of the committee addressed a joint letter to the Provincial Prosecutor's Office in Warsaw asking that the investigations against KOR members be discontinued. The members of the committee who were arrested in August were charged on the basis of Article 276 § 1 (see chapter 9). The signatories of the letter stated that since the accusation had been formulated as "participation in an association using the name Social Self-Defense Committee 'KOR,' whose goal it was to engage in criminal activity, among other things, the dissemination of publications which do not have the right of circulation," then, in the first place, the Prosecutor's Office, acting on the basis of the Code of Criminal

Procedure, had no right to charge only certain members of the group rather than charging all of them; and second, the lack of the right to circulate publications applies to the transport of forbidden publications across national frontiers, and does not concern publishing houses that are located and operated inside Poland. In addition, the Gdańsk Agreements contain a paragraph in which the government undertook to limit such censorship.

The letter had no effect, but the press twice published communiqués from the Polish Press Agency concerning the continuing investigations against members of KSS "KOR." And yet, during all this time, despite the fact that the composition of the committee was public and well known, no one ever presented any member of KOR with specific accusations that were being investigated. But under the circumstances prevailing at the time, these events were of marginal importance. What was important from KOR's point of view was to conclude its work on the *Madrid Report*.

The Helsinki Commission (see chapter 9) was named in January 1980 and given the task of preparing a document about violations of human and civil rights in Poland. The commission was composed of four members of KOR: Ludwik Cohn, Edward Lipiński, Zbigniew Romaszewski, and Aniela Steinsbergowa. The title page of the *Madrid Report* also listed the names of twenty-four associates of the Intervention Bureau and of six lawyers who had helped the Intervention Bureau.[2] The *Report* was edited by Zbigniew Romaszewski. Because NOWa was intensively involved in work on behalf of Solidarity, the *Madrid Report* was published by the Third of May Publishing House.

The *Madrid Report* reached the West in the middle of October.[3] Thanks to the efforts of a group of people from the Polish Studies Center in London, a shortened version was translated into English and published within a month, and was then delivered to every participating delegation at the Madrid Conference on the day it began. The full Polish version was sent to the secretariat of the conference along with a request that it become an official document of the Conference on Security and Co-operation in Europe. Later the *Madrid Report* was published in English in its entirety by the Polish Studies Center in London and the U.S. Helsinki Watch Committee, with the assistance of the Appeal for Polish Workers.

The *Report* is composed of systematic descriptions of the various problems involved in the implementation of basic human and civil rights as they are defined by the International Covenant on Civil and Political Rights. It also contains various documents, such as verdicts in trials, medical certificates, court records, testimonies by witnesses to various events, and the like. The discussions include issues such as: basic human rights and their legal protection in the light of the Constitution of the PRL; the political and social inequality of citizens; the right to freedom of association; the right to freedom of speech; passport and visa issues; labor law; abuses of the investigative organs and of the justice system (by the police, the Security Service, the prosecutor's offices, the courts, the sentencing boards for misdemeanors, and the prison system—data on these subjects is based on the *Documents of Lawlessness* and on the case of Pyjas); and finally, there is a summary of the repressions against activists of the democratic opposition. In other words, the *Madrid Report* is an invaluable and extensive monograph based on material evidence dealing with the problems of lawlessness. It represents the sum of four years of the committee's work.

On November 17, KSS "KOR" issued a statement on the occasion of the start of the Madrid Conference, which concluded:

> Human and Civil Rights cannot be regarded as an internal problem of any individual country; these rights belong to all humanity. The Helsinki Commission in Poland, created by KSS "KOR," presented the Madrid Conference with materials concerning the degree of compliance with human and civil rights in Poland. On our behalf, Mr. Zbigniew Romaszewski was to report on these issues to the conference. Unfortunately, to this day he has not received a passport.

Attacks in the mass media led to an increased public interest and to questions concerning the democratic opposition. The entire issue of *Robotnik* No. 63/64 of October 10, 1980, was devoted to the subject of KSS "KOR" and its initiatives prior to August. For its part, *Tygodnik Solidarność* (*Solidarity Weekly*) conducted a long interview with the members of the editorial board of *Robotnik*. In addition, many other union periodicals explained what KOR was, what the Initiating Committees of Free Trade Unions were, how the Intervention Bureau functioned, what NOWa and other institutions associated with the democratic opposition had done, and so on.

Basically, cooperation with KOR was accepted in the new union with respect and sympathy. KOR activists, its members and associates, generally met with no difficulty if they wanted to volunteer as candidates to Solidarity offices, whether on the level of an enterprise, a region, or in the National Commission, or later as delegates to the First Congress of Solidarity in Gdańsk. During the electoral campaign, those who could claim participation in KOR were generally assured of success.

At the same time, one could observe a significant minority that regarded KOR with suspicion, or often even with undisguised hatred. This is often the case in public life, but I could never understand why, after KOR members had spent four long years of hard work, leading abnormal lives that threatened our health, our income, and often our professional position, after suffering many searches, forty-eight-hour detentions, and sometimes arrests of two months or more—there were still some in Solidarity, and not just in the government, who saw us as enemies. This is a separate topic on which I shall not dwell here.

In any case, KSS "KOR" had no intention of functioning as a mentor to Solidarity, and did not make statements concerning union matters or positions adopted by its democratically elected authorities. Since most of the specified current issues were taken over by Solidarity, the committee issued public statements more and more rarely. Nevertheless, KOR was often believed to have played a decisive role in many Solidarity decisions, both on the regional and the national level. This, however, was a misunderstanding. Those activists and experts of the union who were connected with KOR represented only themselves or their electors in Solidarity, and not the committee, where nothing was said, either generally or in detail, about the directions KOR activists should take within Solidarity, what they should aim for, or what they should fight against. There was only one directive: the Workers' Defense Committee supports Solidarity.

The description, "a KOR person," was becoming historical. It was becoming a fragment of one's biography to be respected by an overwhelming majority of the members of Solidarity. It was known, however, that KOR had never been politically homogeneous—and especially not during its last two years. This state of affairs was becoming more pronounced.

In this respect, it is necessary to understand the role of the Solidarity advisers who came from KOR. A group of Warsaw intellectuals who went to the shipyard in August 1980 stayed on in the union in the role of advisers. However, these were not people from KOR, but founders and lecturers from the Society for Scientific Courses, which was always close to the committee, but could not be regarded as an agency of KOR. During the period of Solidarity, as these people became engaged in practical activity, the distance between them and KOR increased even more. The same must be said about the lawyers who since 1976 handled the burden of defending KOR clients and KOR activists. They were associated with the committee, but on a different basis from the others: their cooperation involved work in their profession on cases which their colleagues were not eager to undertake. During Solidarity, the distance increased between KOR and these attorneys and advisers of Solidarity.

Although KOR activists could be found as regional Solidarity authorities or even in individual enterprises (e.g., Michnik in Nowa Huta), when people refer to KOR members who were Solidarity advisers, they usually mean Jacek Kuroń. Thus, I take full responsibility for asserting that it was precisely Jacek Kuroń, along with other Solidarity advisers from KOR, who were forces of moderation. For example, Kuroń was among those activists of Solidarity who were often, because of their authority and popularity, asked to put down strikes which the National Commission saw as factors that inflamed the situation and at the same time interfered with the possibility of pursuing issues that had greater priority. Kuroń performed this function quite often, although he was probably aware that it would not make him popular. He believed, however, that one had to act first of all in accordance with one's conscience and in the interest of Solidarity, regardless of whatever side effects this might have. Perhaps he even believed that his popularity would not suffer. Others, however, who like to accuse him of all seven cardinal sins, showed no eagerness to perform these functions themselves.

Despite the differences among the members and associates of KOR, concerning various problems discussed within the union, KOR was sometimes charged with playing a role which it did not play. These anti-KOR attitudes and moods were by no means general, as is sometimes suggested, but they were voiced often and loudly. For example, leaflets written by some unidentified persons were distributed demanding: "Release Leszek Moczulski, call the KSS 'KOR' heirs of Stalin to account!"[4] Publications also appeared making personal attacks on certain members of KOR (for example, Edward Lipiński and Ludwik Cohn). The Socialist Publishing House published three previously unpublished versions of Cohn's memoirs, which had been taken from him by the Security Service during a series of house searches. KOR protested against this abuse, especially since the works of this publishing house were distributed primarily among Poles living abroad.[5]

As one can see, the atmosphere of antipathy toward KOR was systematically nourished by the Security Service. Sometimes it was simply a reflection of personal conflicts between people associated with KOR and other oppositional groups. For example, this was the case in Łódź, where KOR member Józef Śreniowski was active. The conflicts that developed between him and the Łódź Inter-Factory Initiating Committee (MKZ) were further inflamed by its advisers, members of ROPCiO whose attitude was very strongly anti-KOR.

Under these conditions, the board of the MKZ in Łódź was negatively inclined toward KOR. Both Andrzej Słowik, the chairman of the Łódź MKZ, and Jerzy Kropiwnicki, the deputy chairman, exhibited this attitude, despite the fact that in all matters concerning Solidarity, both of these activists occupied positions in the National Commission which were similar to those of the activists and advisers who had come from KOR, and their differences were minor compared with what they shared. Nevertheless, even after the MKZ in Łódź got rid of its advisers from ROPCiO, no rapprochement between KOR and Słowik and Kropiwnicki ever took place. Only in the Mokotów prison cell that I shared with Kropiwnicki after December 13, 1981, did we manage to explain all this to each other and become close friends.

Similar problems, though caused by other issues, existed in Wałbrzych. Jacek Pilchowski, a Wałbrzych activist from the old KOR cadre and a member of the editorial board of *Robotnik*, invited Jan Lityński to Wałbrzych to work as an adviser together with a group of activists from Wrocław. In the meantime, Jerzy Sienkiewicz,[6] the chairman of the Initiating Committee in Jastrzębie, who was affiliated with PAX and who played a generally ambiguous role during this period of the activity of Solidarity, was conducting a policy of extraterritorial expansion for Jastrzębie, and through clever maneuvers he brought about a sharp conflict between the mine committees in the Wałbrzych Mining District and the rest of the local Solidarity. As a result, the entire Wrocław group of the associates of the MKZ in Wałbrzych were eliminated, and Lityński's role was severely limited. This was possible only because the authority of the Jastrzębie committee was very strong, and people said in one breath: the Gdańsk, Szczecin, and Jastrzębie Agreements. These conflicts mellowed when Jerzy Sienkiewicz, who lost the trust he had enjoyed in Jastrzębie and in the National Commission, was removed from his post (which he answered by attacks on Solidarity in the official press, conclusively separating him from Solidarity).

The Secret Instructions of the Prosecutor General

At the very time when the authorities were affirming their desire to cooperate with NSZZ Solidarity and to fulfill the Gdańsk Agreements, Prosecutor General Lucjan Czubiński wrote an instruction manual for his subordinates entitled: "Notes on Hitherto Employed Methods for

Prosecuting Participants in Illegal Anti-Socialist Activity." This document was transmitted to the authorities of Solidarity in the Mazowsze Region by a printer, Solidarity member Piotr Sapeło. On November 20 a search was conducted in the regional offices of Solidarity, and Jan Narożniak, a mathematician and KOR associate who was duplicating this document, was arrested. Narożniak and Sapeło were charged with divulging state secrets (the document was marked "secret").

The board of the MKZ in the Mazowsze Region declared on November 25 that a union delegation had tried unsuccessfully to discuss this matter with the authorities, and that the authorities refused to release the imprisoned. As a result, November 27 was to be a day of strike readiness. Justifying its decision, the board stated:

> The document was marked "secret." But not everything marked "secret" should be secret. Thefts and wastefulness were secret, incompetence and stupidity were secret, anything that the authorities wanted to hide from the people from fear of compromising themselves and incurring their righteous wrath was secret; the crimes of the police and the Security Service on the Coast in 1970 and in Ursus and Radom in 1976 were secret. The uncovered prosecutor's document was also secret, because if it had been public, people could have learned that it amounted to a threat to the activity of the Independent Trade Unions. It was also necessary to hide the fact that the prosecutor's office was advising the police and the Security Service to continue breaking the law.

Both KSS "KOR" and NOWa, where Narożniak worked as a printer, also protested against his arrest.

What was in this document that suddenly led to such a crisis in the relations between the authorities and Solidarity (the most severe crisis that fall, with the possible exception of the conflict over the registration of the union)? Above all, the document contained a short history of the struggles of the prosecutor's office with the opposition since 1964. In this description, the prosecutor general expressed his concern that already in 1964, "alongside many revisionist proposals to change the power system in the PRL, there were demands to create independent trade unions in Poland and to grant the working class the right to strike." These demands, as we can learn from the document, had been made at that time by Karol Modzelewski (a press spokesman for the National Coordinating Commission of NSZZ Solidarity) and Jacek Kuroń (an adviser to this commission)[7] in their *Open Letter*. Czubiński then went on to state that the dissemination of information about reprisals "could cause further disturbance of public peace." The prosecutor acknowledged that he did not possess sufficient material evidence to warrant arresting the dissidents, and therefore he recommended that evidence be collected diligently by, among other things, coercing people into giving testimony.

A letter KSS "KOR" addressed to the Diet in connection with this document stated, among other things, that the recommendation to gather material evidence, which would enable the Office of the Prosecutor General to charge the opposition with preparing an armed overthrow of the government of the PRL, constituted a mockery of the law. There are no regulations in Poland that would allow the prosecutor general to use repression as a means of preventing criminal activities. In other words, the document contained instructions on how to use illegal methods in order to combat "antisocialists" forces, or—given the new circumstances—the inconvenient activists of Solidarity.

Meanwhile, the atmosphere was becoming more inflammatory. Since the authorities were unrelenting, and more people had learned about the contents of the "Instructions" of the prosecutor general, new demands were added to the insistence that those arrested be released. There were demands that those responsible for the document be punished, and calls for an investigation of the state of the rule of law by a special Diet commission in cooperation with Solidarity; demands, as well, to establish who was responsible for the crimes committed against the workers in 1970 and 1976; and to limit the budget and control the expenditures of the Ministry of Internal Affairs and the prosecutor's office.

A strike began on November 27. The Inter-Factory Initiating Committee was transformed into an Inter-Factory Strike Committee and moved to the Ursus enterprises. After midnight, Sapeło and Narożniak were released. The regional union representatives decided to call off the strike, but then it turned out that the Warszawa Steel Mill intended to strike until the other demands were also met, which obviously could not be accomplished immediately. On the following day, the Polish Press Agency issued a communiqué that announced future talks between the authorities and Solidarity, but did not specify their subject. Lech Wałęsa, together with representatives of the regional board of Solidarity in Mazowsze, went to the Warszawa Steel Mills and attempted to convince the Solidarity branch in the plant to end the strike. The workers refused. Ony Jacek Kuroń, dragged out of bed in the middle of the night, managed to convince the workers that the demand that all the requirements be fulfilled immediately was unrealistic, and that it was necessary to return to work.

The strike ended.[8] Many of Kuroń's friends were not pleased with his intervention, on the grounds that a compromise that provided no guarantee the authorities would act in accordance with the law was unsatisfactory. There are also reasons to suspect that some of the activists of Solidarity begrudged Kuroń his personal success with the workers in the Warszawa Steel Mills.

In January 1981, Lech Wałęsa again asked Kuroń to intervene with the striking workers in Bielsko-Biała, who were demanding that a voivode notorious for exploiting his position for personal gain be removed. During a rally, Kuroń explained the role of the "nomenclature." He told the assembled that the demand to fire this or that corrupt apparatchik struck at the very heart of the methods of co-optation used by the authorities, without however changing the principles according to which the system functioned. Thus, it was necessary to attempt to subject the decisions of the power apparatus to social control by the trade unions, self-governments, creative associations, and others. This was precisely what Solidarity was doing. In February, Jacek Kuroń "put down" a student strike in Poznań. As a result, a group of activists from the Independent Student Union sang to him on his birthday a parody of a popular interwar song, "Love will forgive you anything," which they changed to "Kuroń will forbid you anything." Several other incidents of this kind could be cited.

On many occasions, I heard complaints that right after his release from jail, Kuroń had gone straight to the Inter-Factory Initiating Committee of the Independent Self-Governing Trade Union, and that in this manner he had emphasized the role of KOR and in a way confirmed the attacks against the strike movement, according to which strikes were instigated by KOR. Regardless of the actual role of the members and associates of KOR in the Gdańsk strike, I must say that I was neither surprised by what Kuroń and other associates of KOR did, nor could I myself adopt an attitude different from theirs on this subject. The very idea that, at a time when the entire society was regaining its right to act as a subject, we alone were to be excluded for tactical reasons and obliged to observe how right they had been, who for four difficult years had never "compromised" themselves by being active, or at least did not compromise themselves to the same extent as KOR—psychologically, this was simply unacceptable.

On November 30, KOR issued a programmatic statement that asserted in part:

3. The independent social organization cannot and should not undertake activities aiming at the overthrow of the government. The external threat delineates the boundries of possible change. . . . 11. The Social Self-Defense Committee "KOR" warned the public on many occasions against the catastrophic effects of government policies during the last several years, while it also warned the public against rash actions and desperate behavior.

In December, during a lecture to the Workers' University of Solidarity in the Rosa Luxemburg Enterprises in Warsaw, Jacek Kuroń, explaining "What is Solidarity?" warned the workers:

It is obvious that the union has to recognize the possibilities and the conditions of the economy before making its demands. At the same time, this recognition of possibilities cannot be expressed only by the activists and leaders of the union. It must be the attitude of all unionists.

In an article entitled "Are We Threatened by an Intervention?" published in the November *Robotnik,* Kuroń stated:

we cannot cross one boundary, which is the overthrow of the communist authorities. We will avoid crossing it only when we establish institutional forms of negotiation. Without this, each successive, and, given the present conditions, unavoidable conflict threatens an explosion, and by the same token, creates a risk of an unintended overthrow of the government.

In an interview for the periodical of the Independent Student Union at the Main School of Agriculture in Warsaw, Kuroń said in part:

we have to continue a dialogue and negotiations with the authorities. The government is an important partner in everything that is going to take place without ending in a tragedy. . . . This is why each government team must be welcomed with hope and . . . I maintain that even those in power, the power élite, nominate this government [of Jaruzelski] with the same hope and for the same purpose.

At about the same time, Adam Michnik ended his article "Hope and Danger," published in the *Information Bulletin,* with the following words:

It is true that I am not postulating here either a struggle for independence or a striving for parliamentary democracy, though I always declared how dear these values are to me, and I am not recanting these declarations today. I claim, however, that whoever believes today that these demands are realistic is basically taking a step away from common sense and a sense of national responsibility.

I postulate a compromise with the authorities, with authorities I do not like, authorities whose principles I do not approve, but who function for us today in the same way as a plaster cast for someone who is sick: it is burdensome, but necessary. Our changed situation demands a thorough revision of everyone's thinking, both the authorities' and our own. We were allowed to think differently when we were risking only our own heads, our own freedom, but now, when the national "to be or not to be" is at stake, we must change our thinking. One may not like the authorities, but one must regard them as partners in negotiations.

The proponents of the tough line for Solidarity constantly accused Kuroń of a willingness to conciliate, or even to capitulate, on the basis of a supposed plan of an alliance with some mythical faction in PUWP. Yet, because of the official press and the constantly whispered party-police propaganda, many continued to view Kuroń and KOR as terrible extremists with knives in their teeth.

In this regard, a statement made by Rev. Alojzy Orszulik, the director of the press office of the Episcopate, to a foreign journalist caused a great deal of bitterness. Orszulik said on this occasion that a sentence in a statement by the Episcopate concerning the necessity of behaving reasonably in the present situation referred both to the activities of the Confederation of Independent Poland, and to KSS "KOR" and Jacek Kuroń. This line was immediately picked up by the *Trybuna Ludu* and other official papers. Protests were heard from activists of the Catholic intelligentsia, a number of whom were also KOR activists. A Vatican spokesman announced that Orszulik was speaking exclusively in his own name and had not stated the position of the Episcopate. On January 5, Primate Cardinal Wyszyński accepted a delegation from the regional office of Solidarity in Mazowsze, which also included two members of KOR, Henryk Wujec and Adam Michnik. In this manner, the uncertainty was eliminated concerning the attitude of the Church toward the role of the members of KSS "KOR" in Solidarity. But the attacks against KSS "KOR" continued. It seems that the authorities had decided to find a scapegoat for their signing of the Gdańsk Agreements.

In *Biuletyn Aktualności* (*News Bulletin*) No. 10 of the Provincial Committee of PUWP in Warsaw, Albin Siwak stated:

Among the million party members who are also members of Solidarity, there are a significant number of those who will fulfill any demand made by the party. . . . The party members who are in Solidarity should be instructed that it is their responsibility to make sure that the movement of which they form a part should not become a counterrevolutionary movement directed by KOR. Members of the party must choose whether they will listen to KOR or to the resolutions of the Central Committee.

It seems that this was an undeserved compliment for KOR. To compare the executive power of a governing party with a thirty-one-person body of people of various views, both political and ideological, seems to be a symptom of a persecution mania.

On January 7, the National Coordinating Commission issued a statement that asserted:

There have been attempts, using distorted or overtly mendacious information, to slander some activists and advisers of Solidarity in the mass media. This concerns above all Jan Rulewski, the chairman of the Bydgoszcz MKZ, and Jacek Kuroń, an adviser to the National Coordinating Commission of the Union. We consider this repeated attempt to divide Solidarity into "good" and "bad" as an action which strives to break up our union and to destroy its independence.

On February 9, the Polish Press Agency again reported on the investigations of KSS "KOR." It seems that this announcement constituted a response to the committee's letter of October 31, 1980, in which KOR had asked that the investigations be discontinued. In answer to the communiqué of the press agency, the committee issued a statement in which it once again questioned the propriety of continued investigations in the light of Polish law, restating the goals and methods of the activities of the committee and noting the fact that Solidarity was now fulfilling the same goals and that members and associates of KSS "KOR" were now involved in the work of the independent trade union. Voices from various groups were raised in defense of KOR. Filmmakers protested against the campaign of slander and expressed their fear that this kind of accusation might constitute an attempt to burden Solidarity with responsibility for the "truly antisocialist forces responsible for the present crisis."

A very sharply worded resolution was adopted by the MKZ in Małopolska:

Aware of the invaluable role which this committee has played in the process of integrating the working classes during the period preceding the explosion of social protest in August 1980, and appreciating the contributions made by KOR members and associates in preparing the first programmatic guidelines of the emerging trade union movement, as well as their lively and creative presence in the work of advisory and initiating groups of our union, we consider the attacks and threats directed against these people to be directed against all of us. . . . We will not permit an unending storm of false accusations to be directed against people who are highly respected by us and indispensable to the union.

Similarly, the MKZ of Mazowsze stated that Solidarity would protect its members. Students also made their views heard. The seminar "Experience and Future," in its third report entitled "Society in the Face of a Crisis," described the achievements of KOR in breaking down the barrier of fear and defending the workers in a chapter on "Independent Groups." The work mentions the respect the committee had earned among the workers because of this defense, and added:

> the contributions of KOR, and the contributions of many other independent groups, must be acknowledged now by the political opponents of KOR as well, when the leaders of the party and the state are themselves making comments and demands for which, only a short while ago, independent activists were being slandered and persecuted.

Repressions

Despite the optimistic statement from DiP that "only a short while ago, independent activists were being slandered and persecuted," their persecution continued. Members of the democratic opposition were detained and often beaten, whether they were now activists of Solidarity, or Rural Solidarity, or the Independent Student Union. In January the MKZ of Mazowsze issued a sharp protest against the brutal beating of Jerzy Geresz, whose name will be familiar to the reader from previous chapters. Students from Cracow and former members of the SKS spoke about the beatings and searches, which were far from being over, during a meeting with a representative of the Security Service held at the Jagiellonian University. A member of the MKZ in Gdańsk was held in isolation for five days and interrogated about Anna Walentynowicz (from the KZ WZZ) and KOR member Bogdan Borusewicz. The record of these reprisals against members of Solidarity was now being kept by the union periodicals.

Among those still in prison were Krzysztof Bzdyl, Zygmunt Goławski, Tadeusz Jandziszak, Leszek Moczulski, Tadeusz Stański, Jerzy Sychut, Romuald Szermietiew, and Wojciech Ziembiński.

In March, KSS "KOR" issued a statement in which it again declared that imprisoning people for their political views was contrary to the Gdańsk Agreements. It also stressed that the imprisoned were being defended by the Committee for the Defense of Prisoners of Conscience, by peasants from the Rzeszow region, and by students. Professor Kielanowski and Reverend Zieja vouched for Wojciech Ziembiński in the prosecutor's office; the strike committee of the City Transportation Enterprises (MPK), the MKZ, and scientists and artists from Wrocław vouched for Tadeusz Jandziszak.

A February 9 communiqué of the Polish Press Agency announced a new charge against Jacek Kuroń and Adam Michnik in addition to violations of the same article of the Criminal Code on the basis of which the investigations against KOR had been conducted during the last three years. On March 5, Kuroń was detained, and provincial deputy prosecutor Jackowska presented the additional charge against him from Article 270 § 1 of the Criminal Code, stating that from November 1980 to the present time, Kuroń had degraded and ridiculed the system and the leading organs of the PRL at various public meetings in Warsaw and other cities. Kuroń was ordered to report twice a week to the police precinct in Warsaw-Żoliborz. Michnik was also ordered to report to the police precinct.

On March 10, unknown perpetrators beat eighty-six-year-old KOR member Antoni Pajdak. Tear gas was sprayed into his eyes as well. Unknown authors distributed anti-Semitic leaflets attacking members and associates of KSS "KOR."

The Press and Other Independent Initiatives

The KOR press was appearing more and more rarely, and some periodicals suspended publication altogether. The last issue of the *Information Bulletin* (vol. 5, no. 7) was dated October/November 1980; but in its statement of February 11, 1981, KSS "KOR" stated in part:

> In the meantime, we will preserve close contacts with the Independent Publishing House NOWa and with the independent press which grew out of our group. The editorial boards of periodicals appearing outside of the censorship, including the *Information Bulletin*, *Głos*, *Krytyka*, *Puls*, and *Robotnik*, have assured us that they will not cease publication for as long as the voice of public opinion will be constrained in any manner.

Robotnik, which was appearing regularly throughout this entire period (the last issue is dated December 3, 1981), was then—as the headline indicated—an organ cooperating with NSZZ Solidarity in the Mazowsze, Małopolska, Świętokrzyskie, Jelenia Góra, and Toruń regions. Since each of these regions published its own editions of this periodical, the number of copies was enormous indeed.

In addition to the periodical listed in the statement, *Zapis* also continued its publication during the entire period. There were numerous new publishing initiatives in addition to NOWa, for example, Krąg, whose associates came from the KOR movement. NOWa participated in the Frankfurt Book Fair for the second time, which was held in the fall of 1981, where its books again caused a sensation.

The Society for Scientific Courses announced in November that it was going to continue its activities; and in January 1981, TKN issued a statement on "The Tasks of TKN Given the Current Situation in the Country," in which it asserted that the independent trade union was a new area of activity and cooperation for TKN:

> This [cooperation] began when the appeal of the Polish intellectuals taken to the Gdańsk Shipyard . . . gained the confidence of the strike leaders, thanks to which the commission of experts, composed mainly of active members of our society, was created at the Gdańsk MKS, later at the MKZ, and finally at the National Coordinating Commission of NSZZ Solidarity.

Toward the conclusion of its statement, TKN declared:

> For as long as we do not see the possibility of unconstrained activity in the "official" institutional framework, and of publishing our lectures and *Notebooks* in normal publishing houses, we will not apply for a change in our status. We will be pleased when the appropriate moment for this will arrive.

The published list of TKN lecturers continued to contain, in addition to some new names, those of Edward Lipiński and Adam Michnik.

The Events in Otwock

The events in Otwock were described by Jan Walc in *Tygodnik Solidarność*.[9]

The police had detained—not without cause, it seems—two people, but while detaining them, they had also beaten them brutally; one of them had to be taken to a hospital in Warsaw, though it turned out that despite appearances and symptoms, his condition was not serious, and he was sent back to jail. By that time, the railroad station precinct of the police was surrounded by a growing crowd. Local activists of Solidarity alerted the Mazowsze regional authorities of the union. The director of the Intervention Bureau sent an experienced associate of the bureau, Jan Walc (a talented journalist, as well as a literary critic and historian). Thanks to the authority conferred by his official Solidarity pin, Walc managed to restrain the mob somewhat. Romaszewski arrived a short time later. The crowd wanted to lynch a corporal of the police who was one of those who had beaten up the detainees, and to set fire to the police precinct, which was located in a small wooden building.

The reason for this explosion was not accidental. To activists of the Intervention Bureau, Otwock was known as a place where the police often resorted to beatings, and beat people severely and with delight. The Intervention Bureau was constantly being alerted to this fact. The police in Otwock did not have an easy job: the suburban commuting trains and larger stations on their routes were traditional places for almost daily brawls of hooligans. But the bestiality of the local police was also notorious. Now the residents of Otwock wanted to avenge themselves.

The only way in which the lives of the policemen could be saved was to negotiate with the mob. The two KOR activists knew that they could not allow a lynching. It was often discussed in KOR that a day might come when it would be necessary to risk one's life in order to save the lives of persons who were hated, who had beaten and abused others. In addition to the policemen, a prosecutor and a commander of the local police were also in the precinct house, all in a state of shock, unable to lift a finger. Romaszewski and Walc entered the police precinct building convinced that they might be burned together with the besieged policemen, but that they had to defend them to the end. They appealed to the mob to be reasonable until they both lost their voices. To no avail. Twice, those on the inside managed to put out fires.

Nearby detachments of ZOMO were waiting, ready for action, but bringing them in meant death to the besieged. The ZOMO commander, Lieutenant Rusinowicz, persistently stated on the telephone that he was ready to launch an attack. Romaszewski, Walc, and the prosecutor begged him not to do so. The KOR activists asked that the detainees be released in order to pacify the crowd. The authorities refused. As Walc later wrote:

> Counting the minutes was like during a take-off. The command did not want to release Cugała, since this would diminish the authority of the police.

Is this authority more important than the head of the red-haired corporal? Not to me . . .[10]

Only when the building had been doused with gasoline from canisters did the headquarters of the police release Cugała. Even the authority of the Solidarity activists would have been for nothing. They would all have burned together. The arrival of the second beaten detainee, Mariański, was also delayed until the last moment. It was falsely claimed that he had been in a drunk tank, but he was actually in jail. The president of Warsaw, Jerzy Majewski, wanted to use the ZOMO. Negotiations were taking place at the rank of deputy minister Rakowski, who was located in Warsaw by Michnik. Mariański had to be carried in. Michnik immediately took charge of the crowd: "My name is Adam Michnik. I am an antisocialist force." This caustic statement from *Trybuna Ludu,* which was used to describe KOR activists, was well taken and applauded. But when Michnik said that those who were guilty would be punished, the crowd asked for guarantees. Michnik was treated like one of them. Whoever did not know it earlier learned that Michnik had also sometimes been beaten by the police. But there were no guarantees. They must be forced, through our solidarity, to stop the beatings. Bujak also spoke. The crowd dispersed; it was now morning. The captain of the police extended his hand to Michnik: "I am sorry, perhaps you will not want to accept it, but I want to thank you." Michnik shook the captain's hand; the captain stood at attention and saluted.

The red-haired corporal was still alive. The friends of Romaszewski and Walc from KOR were glad that they had escaped with their lives, and that they passed the most difficult test of the moral attitude they had voiced for years. But only a few days later, the press alluded to the fact that actually KOR, and especially Solidarity, was guilty of inciting the riot.

This was essentially the last action of KOR. Perhaps the red-haired corporal is again beating people, but we were proud of Romaszewski and Walc, of their attitude and their courage, and of Michnik, that he was able to defuse the situation for good with just a few sentences, and of the men from the local Solidarity, who throughout this entire time bravely helped to restrain the crowd.

But not everything in Otwock quieted down immediately. At dawn on that day, after the crowd had dispersed, the building was set on fire, which was not difficult to manage, since several canisters of gasoline had been poured over it only a few hours earlier. Luckily, there was no one inside. On the third day after the building fire, a train car was set on fire in the station under very dubious circumstances, and windows were broken in shopping pavilions. In the evening, the local Solidarity formed street patrols wearing union armbands. The police disappeared from the streets of the town, which finally quieted Otwock down.

In its statement of May 10, KSS "KOR" did not devote much attention to information about these events, but it briefly recalled the long struggle of the committee for the rule of law in Poland, stating that the fundamental reasons for the lack of confidence in the police, and for such explosions of anger against them, were the crimes of 1970, 1976, and 1978, which have never been prosecuted. Under these conditions, the immediate cause of events of what took place in Otwock could turn out to be something out of all proportion to its possible consequences.

> The Social Self-Defense Committee believes that the police should be an institution combatting crime, and that it should fulfill its responsibilities in compliance with the law. Such an institution is needed by society. We know well that among the functionaries of the police there are honest people who want to fulfill their social responsibilities in accordance with the law. The correction of the present state of affairs and the purging of the criminal element from the police, the punishment of those guilty of abuses of power, beatings, tortures, and common crimes—all this is needed not only by the entire society, but also by the honest functionaries of the police, and by the police as an institution.

The defense of the policemen and the prosecutor besieged in the police precinct station in Otwock was an act on the part of KOR members, but also of activists of Solidarity, who in 1976, five years earlier, had begun to act to save the workers from reprisals from police and prosecutors.

Several days after this statement, KOR issued what appears to have been its last letter before its dissolution. Upon learning of the assassination attempt against the pope, KOR wrote:

Warsaw, May 14, 1981

Holy Father,

> Together with the Polish nation and all people of good will throughout the world, for whom you are the highest authority in the aspiration to goodness and justice, we send you heartfelt get well wishes.

Social Self-Defense Committee "KOR"

The Dissolution of KOR

In the spring and early summer of 1980, the KOR milieu was involved in a discussion concerning an issue of great importance to the activists: should KOR be dissolved or not? The arguments in favor of dissolution were based on a recognition of the existing state of affairs, and were supported by the feeling shared by some activists of the committee that a radical change of circumstances demanded drastic decisions. KOR's activity was indeed subsiding, although this did not mean that its members and associates were no longer active but only that now they were active in Solidarity. However, it was difficult to consider the KOR activity. It is true that membership in the committee or association with it served as a good identity card within Solidarity (the reader already knows that this was not the case with everyone, but it was sufficiently true to assure entrance into the union's structures on the basis of such prior trust), but again this was another matter. The links that had bound people together for four important years also remained, though the conflicts that divided them remained as well. In any case, whatever one's opinion about old "veteran" ties among people living in a new social reality, such links are a human phenomenon, one that is unavoidable and sometimes even positive when accompanied by feelings of unity and strength.

Jacek Kuroń was the principal proponent of the dissolution of KOR. He emphasized that any KOR activity could be interpreted as external interference in Solidarity affairs, and as such, would not be well received inside the union. This was not a healthy situation. On this occasion, the activists of *Głos* agreed with Kuroń. The link with KOR had been uncomfortable to them for a long time, and they were searching for other alliances and reference points. The older members of KOR resisted the dissolution most strongly. They argued that their accumulated capital of social trust might still play an important role, and might prove invaluable in uncertain situations. But even they finally agreed to the dissolution, since they were aware that this authority itself, if it were no longer supported by real activity, would not last for long.

Moreover, the disintegration within KOR itself was also deepening. The conflict between the group from *Głos* and the milieu of the *Information Bulletin*, *Robotnik*, and *Krytyka* was becoming sharper. Józef Rybicki, who participated in the work of KOR until the very end, also stressed that he was losing his interest in KOR activities, since he was becoming involved in activities connected with circles of veterans of the Home Army, who intended to form their own special association. Andrzej Celiński, one of the main founders of TKN and at this time one of the most influential activists of Solidarity (as secretary of the National Coordinating Commission, he was close to Wałęsa), was becoming less and less happy with a situation in which on the one hand he cooperated closely with Kuroń within KOR, and on the other, during arguments among the advisers of Solidarity, he felt closer to, for example, Bronisław Geremek.

Unfortunately, no minutes were kept at KOR meetings during this time, and historians both now and in the future will have difficulty describing what went on inside them, or even when they took place (although for at least two years, KOR had met usually, though not invariably, on the first Friday of every month).

In any case, the decision to dissolve KOR was made, and the author believes that it was made sometime during the first days of July. At the same time, both the press campaign and the whispered gossip led everyone to fear that the First Congress of Solidarity, for which the union was preparing full steam, might not take place. Therefore it was decided that the resolution to dissolve KOR, adopted during its plenary meeting, would become binding only after it had been announced from the rostrum during the Congress of Solidarity. The task of reading the document announcing the dissolution of KOR (together with a speech to be made in his own right) was entrusted to the nestor of the committee, Prof. Edward Lipiński.

Given the impossibility of finalizing all the financial matters from one day to the next, the decisions made in connection with the dissolution of KOR provided for the continued activity of the Social Self-Defense Funds Council, which would remain active until all the existing funds were liquidated in a gradual and rational manner or, alternatively, transferred to other institutions, until appropriate instructions were issued to persons who were collecting money for KOR abroad, and until a final audit statement of the funds' accounts was made public.[11] The conclusion of the work of the Social Self-Defense Funds Council was rendered impossible by the declaration of the state of war.

The announcement of the dissolution of KSS "KOR" took place during the second session of the National Congress of Delegates of NSZZ Solidarity. On September 28, 1981, Lipiński read the statement of KSS "KOR" concerning its decision to dissolve itself. It concluded:

We believe that everyone who ever shared the goals of the Workers' Defense Committee, and later of the Social Self-Defense Committee, should today support Solidarity to the best of his ability and talent, and be active in its ranks or in its behalf. . . .

On this fifth anniversary of the creation of the Workers' Defense Committee, we regard our activity as concluded. No one can claim that this decision has been dictated by fear of dishonest attacks from the official Polish or foreign propaganda. In making this decision we remain fully faithful to the values we tried always to serve: honesty and truth.

There were among us people of various generations, traditions, and ideological orientations. We were united by our concern for all those who were beaten and wronged. We wanted to bear witness to this, regardless of personal danger or political tactics, and regardless of who was being persecuted. We were guided by our belief that "without an independent Poland on the map, there can be no just Europe."

We have served the cause of Polish freedom, and the freedom of Poles in Poland, to the best of our ability, as our consciences and a civic understanding of the situation dictated. We were guided by an ideal of a Poland which could once be proud of its tolerance and freedom, of a Poland which could be a common fatherland for Poles, Belorussians, Lithuanians, Ukrainians, and Jews, a fatherland for all its citizens, regardless of their language, religion, or national origin.

It is not for us to judge our own work. We wanted only for it to be a contribution to the great national task: the creation of an independent, just, and democratic Poland.

After he had finished reading the document, Lipiński asked the audience to honor with a minute of silence two deceased members of the committee, Prof. Adam Szczypiorski and Dr. Wacław Zawadzki.

Even after this final act, another small chapter in the history of KOR occurred. In itself it was rather minor, but it was widely noticed and variously interpreted, and affected both nerves and health.

On the day of Lipiński's speech, the delegation from the Radom Region of NSZZ Solidarity introduced a motion to the effect that the congress should pass a resolution thanking KOR. The chairman of the Radom region explained why it was this particular region that was introducing the motion, which—given the events of 1976 and the enormous work which KOR had accomplished in Radom—was rather obvious. Late in the evening, after the conclusion of the plenary meetings, the delegates from the Mazowsze region met in a hotel. During this meeting, Paweł Niezgodzki suggested that the delegation of Mazowsze should introduce a countermotion. This was a long and affected statement, containing a number of formulations from the preface to the project of the program of Solidarity, as well as many other statements, such as that Poland has been Christian for a thousand years, that the Church and the pope have played an enormous role in creating the situation that made this congress possible, and so on. The motion also contained a single sentence—positive—about the democratic opposition, without any specific mention of KOR (though it was not the democratic opposition, but KOR that was dissolving).

This motion was supported by a minority of the Mazowsze delegation (and board), a group that for some time prior to this had been assiduously combatting KOR—the chairman of the region, Zbigniew Bujak, and those members of the board and presidium who were close to Bujak. During the first session of the congress, this group had organized a semisecret meeting to which it did not invite a number of delegates from various regions. Since one of the participants in this meeting was reported to have said that only "true Poles" were to be admitted, the name immediately stuck to the group as a whole. This event caused sharp conflict within Mazowsze, and eventually led to a new election of the presidium of the board in the region, and to the strengthening within it of Bujak and the advocates of the line he represented. But this is a different story.

During the night meeting of the Mazowsze delegation, there was a very sharp exchange of views, as a result of which Jan Józef Lipski said that KOR was not, after all, active in order to collect gratitude; and he announced that he would ask the Radom delegation to withdraw its motion, since an inevitable discussion as to whether KOR had contributed to Solidarity a lot, a little, or nothing at all would be humiliating to the members and associates of KOR.

On the following day, Halina Mikołajska and Jan Józef Lipski asked Andrzej Sobieraj to withdraw his motion. After some resistance, Sobieraj agreed, saying that after all, KOR members had the final say in the matter. The motion was withdrawn. Shortly afterward, however, the first reading of another motion that concerned the same issue took place. It was introduced by the chairman of the Małopolska region, Bogusław Sonik. In answer to this, Niezgodzki presented his countermotion, and a storm erupted in the hall. While waiting for his turn to speak, Jan Józef Lipski suffered cardiac disturbances and had to be taken to a hospital.

It must be said that the Radom motion was preferable to the Małopolska text, because it presented the issue of KOR's contribution in a clear and morally satisfactory manner, without being just a tribute. A vote was taken, and the Radom motion was passed by an overwhelming majority. But a bad taste and a somewhat bitter feeling remained. Those who had opposed the idea of thanking KOR did gain a certain victory after all: the impression was left that the matter had led to a sharp struggle, and that the evaluation of KOR within Solidarity was less unequivocal than was really the case. If the members of KOR had had thicker skins and simply insisted on a vote, very few people would have remembered this incident. It was these members of KOR, or rather two of them, who introduced all the confusion and made the situation more dramatic than it deserved to be.

And is this silly episode to serve as a conclusion to the history of KOR? It must, since the Social Self-Defense Committee "KOR" no longer existed. Much was left behind, and much will survive for a long time to come: in the people who participated in its work, or those who benefited from it, in Solidarity, in several important years of Polish history, in the effects that will last for many years, and also in the books and periodicals that constitute a material proof that all this was not just a dream.

Postscript

Tomorrow I return from London to Warsaw.

The junta of General Jaruzelski has announced a trial of KOR. I want to have the honor of sitting in the defendants' dock together with my friends, whom I accompanied in the struggle for a better Poland during those several years. I want to participate in the last chapter of the history of KOR, just as I participated in all the other chapters in succession, from the beginning.

This will be a battle for truth, for the memory of KOR. I do not believe that this memory can be hurt by a trial ordered by the heirs of those who once murdered without trials, or handed down draconian verdicts against the soldiers of the Home Army and the Peasant Battalions, and against the civilian authorities of the Underground Polish State of World War II, the heroes of the struggle of the Polish nation for independence on all fronts and in all areas of life. Later, during a long series of political trials, those who had fought for the same thing as their predecessors, though no longer in an atmosphere of mortal terror, were judged and made to pay a not insignificant price for the service they rendered to Poland and to its culture.

I want, together with my friends, to bear witness to the truth during this trial.

What did we fight for? First, we fought simply so that the workers who were beaten, imprisoned, and dismissed from their jobs would not be abandoned and alone, and so that they and their families would be able to live a little more easily through the period of fury directed against them by the apparatus of violence. Later, we broadened our goals, singling out two at the very end of the road: democracy and independence. We tried not to delude anyone that these would be easy to realize. So, from day to day, we spoke and wrote mainly about more immediate matters and—above all—we worked hard to achieve them. Only rarely on our lips—to paraphrase the words of the poet Cyprian Norwid, to whose work I devoted many years of my life—could one find the word

457

"fatherland." In our daily activities we dealt with other things: here someone was beaten, there someone was thrown out of work, people lacked medications (we lost this issue, but it was not really our fault), the censorship had again confiscated the works of a poet, in the mines people were working beyond their strength, peasants were being deprived of their land, a chapel was destroyed where people wanted to pray, and so on and on, from day to day, until sometimes our arms dropped from weariness. We fought against the bestiality of the police, and against the stupidity of the rulers, or rather what seemed stupidity but was finally based on their interests, against lies in the schools, in the press, on television, and finally also against the inertia and fear of our fellow citizens. We published the books of the greatest Polish writers of the twentieth century, and also of newcomers who perhaps will not all enter the history books concerned with our national literature, but whose road had to be cleared so that the national culture could live a fuller and richer life. We taught and helped teach students, and we prepared workers for their future roles as union activists and fully enfranchised citizens. And all of this was a drop in the ocean of needs, despite the fact that it was beyond the strength of those who did all this.

And we were hated. Sometimes we found this feeling where we least expected it. This was the most difficult thing. But we also had moments of joy, and even triumphs, the two most important of which came when the last workers left their prisons after the events of 1976, and again when Solidarity was created.

With pride and a full sense of responsibility, I assert that we were necessary to the creation of Solidarity. More than ever, KOR was a voice in the wilderness preparing for its arrival. Thus, when Solidarity was dealt a blow—I am sure it was not the final blow, as we can see even today—we had, sooner or later, to face the court, or rather become objects of revenge.

When this last chapter of the history of KOR comes to an end, a great chapter in the biographies of each of us will also come to a close. KOR is already history, although it is living history, which contributes to the formation of the present and the future. But Solidarity, for which we began working in the corridors of the courtroom during the first Ursus trial on July 17, 1976, is not just the past, not just history. I believe that Solidarity is not only a present reality but also a future fact. Perhaps this will not be exactly the future for which we worked in KOR, not independence and democracy right away, but in any case, some new piece of the road leading toward these final goals.

I would like to add one more word here—socialism, and I would not be alone among the KOR activists in this. This is why, just before the Jaruzelski war, we organized Clubs for a Self-Governing Commonwealth: Freedom-Justice-Independence, in order to realize this goal as well. But this was no longer the history of the committee. We in KOR often emphasized that it brought together people of various orientations and ideologies. On the eve of difficult trials, let me also enter this word into my own personal confession of faith.

London, September 14/15, 1982

Postscript to the American Edition

Two years have passed since the day in London when, having finished the last sentence of the postscript to this book, I boarded a plane to Warsaw several hours later. Much has happened during this period—to Poland, to the people of KOR, and to me.

Let us begin with what is less important. Just as I expected, I was arrested immediately upon my return to Poland, and—for the fourth time in my life—I found myself under investigative arrest in the Mokotowska Street prison in Warsaw. Again it was only for a short time. Before the Christmas holidays, when I was already undergoing treatment in a cardiological clinic, my arrest was suspended and the guards were removed from the door of my hospital room. However, the threat of a political trial still hung over me.

When I left the hospital a month later, I was as free as a citizen of the Polish People's Republic is ever free in his own country, which is to say, to a minimal degree—although of course this is still quite different from being kept in jail.

In July 1983 I benefited from an amnesty for the first time. I had no choice, since the law made no provision for an opportunity to reject the amnesty. At that time the charges against me, concerning the organization and direction of a strike in the Ursus tractor factory following the imposition of martial law, were conditionally dropped. There remained the prosecutor's charge, which was not covered by the amnesty, according to which my friends from KOR and I had sought to overthrow the government by force. The next amnesty, of July 1984, conditionally dropped this charge as well, again without providing us with the possibility of rejecting the amnesty and demanding a trial.

To be honest, not many people in Poland believed that the trial of KOR would ever take place. It would have been very inconvenient for the government to speak publicly or semipublicly (in the courtroom) about what KOR was really doing. The indictment contained no specific allegations, and aroused ridicule rather than fear, even though it indeed threatened several years of imprisonment. But no one in Poland believed that the charge of attempting to overthrow the government by force could be proven. KOR members were too realistic and intelligent for such an approach; they viewed the use of force as inadmissible, if only because, in the improbable case of a victory, the use of force invites dictatorship and terror.

From the very beginning, the prisoners from the leadership of Solidarity and from KOR were treated by the government simply as hostages. Their imprisonment, or rather their transfer from internment camp to investigative arrest in Mokotów prison, took place neither because some legal procedures had been finalized nor because some new facts had been discovered. Instead, this transfer was an act of revenge for the years 1976–1981 when KOR had to be tolerated. Moreover, this was also an angry response of the government to the mass demonstrations of August 31, 1982. Later, whenever the government feared new demonstrations, it threatened that the situation of the prisoners would get even worse.

Kuroń, Michnik, and Wujec were put in the internment camp right at the beginning of Jaruzelski's war. Romaszewski was imprisoned later; he was a member of the underground leadership of the Mazowsze (Warsaw) region of NSZZ Solidarity, and before the authorities managed to arrest him he had time enough to organize the underground radio *Solidarity*. Lityński, whose arrest warrant expired without the prison administration's notice while he was out of jail on a temporary pass, did not return to jail but instead went underground. The remaining KOR members were reading the legal records in their cases and preparing for trial. Michnik wrote quite a lot during this period, and smuggled his articles out of jail despite the fact that the Mokotów prison, and especially the investigative section of the Ministry of Internal Affairs, is a strict isolation institution. This obviously infuriated the authorities.[1] And so the time dragged on—almost two years in Mokotów prison, and before that the internment camp, which for these people scarcely differed from jail—altogether over two and a half years.

In Poland and around the world, the question was asked: how long could this go on? It is true that during the years of Stalinist terror, and even today in many different countries of the world, such a question could be regarded as nonsensical. Nevertheless, everyone knows that the military régime in Warsaw tries (with varying consistency and success) to make a good impression. There was talk of forced exile. Semi-officially, there were offers of temporary voluntary emigration. Finally, during the winter and spring of 1983–84, negotiations were conducted between the government and the Church concerning conditions for releasing the "eleven," that is, the four KOR members plus the seven members of the top leadership of Solidarity, whose situation was identical with that of the KOR members except that they had not been indicted. (Here an aside: the distinction made between the four KOR members and the rest of the "eleven" was rather artificial, since both Romaszewski and Wujec are members of the highest executive body of Solidarity—its National Commission—while Kuroń and Michnik serve as advisers to the Solidarity leadership.

The price the authorities claimed to be willing to pay for even the temporary departure of this group of leading opposition activists in Poland was the release of *all* political prisoners. One could see clearly that the situation had nothing to do with law or legality, and that it involved simply the treatment of prisoners as hostages useful for trading in the international forum. It was also a form of moral blackmail against these prisoners, and finally a bluff, since it turned out that the price the government was willing to pay would be paid anyway several months later, by the government alone, in the form of an amnesty for political prisoners.

It is, however, also important to note that the authorities requested the mediation of the secretary general of the United Nations, who, in a prison courtyard, discussed with the eleven prisoners the conditions under which they would be ready to leave Poland, supposedly only temporarily. From today's perspective, it is clear that the communist authorities were willing to compromise their judicial system in order not to allow the political trials to take place, which were based on false, absurd accusations which they themselves had concocted.

All those imprisoned—both those from KOR and those from the leadership of Solidarity—declared unanimously: we do not consider ourselves guilty of any crime; either release us *unconditionally* or prove our alleged guilt in front of a court! Jacek Kuroń strengthened this demand by announcing a protest fast.

And suddenly, on July 9, 1984, after months of stalling, and with a scant few days of warning, the date of the trial was set for July 13. Immediately, those of us who were free began preparations for a solidarity fast.

It is difficult to understand why the trial was scheduled to take place immediately before the amnesty was announced. In fact, the trial lasted scarcely a single day and did not proceed beyond the stage of the initial formalities. One might suspect that the plan from the very beginning was to interrupt the trial before it entered the stage of introducing evidence, since this evidence could only have concerned help for persecuted workers and the defense of human and civil rights.

Through all these difficulties, the members of KOR and the seven Solidarity activists not only managed to preserve their honor but also emerged with greater moral authority as people of tough character, steadfast and principled, who were ready to choose the solution most painful to themselves when they were convinced that the good of the cause demanded this.

Today all of them are free, together with many other political prisoners, whose release was to have been made dependent on their declaration of at least temporary loyalty and the voluntary relinquishing of their civil rights, as the government had been demanding.

For how long will they remain out of jail?

At this time, some members of KOR are out of prison (some after a long period of imprisonment), while others remain underground (for example, the members of the underground regional leaderships of Solidarity who are in hiding: Bogdan Borusewicz in Gdańsk, Konrad Bieliński and Jan Lityński in Warsaw, Józef Śreniowski in Łódź), and still others are abroad, where they found themselves when the state of war was declared (Stanisław Barańczak, Seweryn Blumsztajn,[2] Mirosław Chojecki). Many associates of KOR remain active in the Solidarity underground, or involved in publishing activities outside the reach of the censorship. It seems that only a few have given up and gone back to private life.

And what about Poland?

The state of war crushed the numerically impressive but still rather loosely organized open structures of Solidarity. It paralyzed all free social life in the country. The authors of the December coup were unable, however, to destroy the underground. Hundreds of printed underground periodicals, many editions of books, and often effective economic strikes, and so on—all constitute a spectacular indication of the strength and the extent of resistance. The new government trade unions still represent a minority, and even they are not loyal beyond question. But the period of demonstrations and massive strikes is over. New demonstrations still occur often, but they are not as large or impressive as before. The masses, loyal to Solidarity in the majority, are not ready today for great actions, and do not believe in their effectiveness. For them, it is a time of waiting, and a time of persistent underground work for particularly determined groups. One might say that as things stand now it looks as if KOR—and the democratic opposition in general—had multiplied thousandfold. But no one today can come up with a distinct perspective and a program of action. The state of suspension between "yesterday" and "tomorrow" continues. "Today" is still an elusive state of affairs, sometimes felt to be more than temporary, a kind of pseudo-existence.

In the long term this is a dangerous state of affairs, felt less by those who continue to be active through underground struggle than by the rest of society.

Today in Poland only the Church lives an authentically free life under the tolerance of the authorities. December 1981 further strengthened the influence and authority of the Church, along with its real potential for focusing social energies. The Church is looking for a solution to the present situation, though so far it has not found one. The highest Church dignitaries sometimes shock by their "risky" statements; but at the same time, the Church unites, integrates, and offers the possibility of an authentic and open social life to many people. The Church often donates its organizational, housing, and other facilities for social, educational, and cultural work.

The government—supported now more by the police apparatus and the army than by the Communist party—is, however, looking for ways to pacify the country: to disintegrate, terrorize, and stupefy society. Sometimes it succeeds, but its failures are still more numerous, and made even more painful by the fact that as long as there are underground structures of Solidarity which, even if they are weakened, still constitute a genuine force, the government cannot easily launch a frontal attack against the Church, in order to push it out of social life and limit it to definite religious functions defined as narrowly as possible. This leads to frustrations of a different order from those suffered by the citizens, and is the source of such government ideas as those consisting of a law instituting exile as a form of punishment, and of a law to allow for convictions *without* court trial for "obvious" (?) crimes. Poland is a country in which the law of *neminem captivabimus nisi iure victum* has been in force since 1425, yet it now faces the possibility of an even deeper descent into barbarism. This is not always noticed by public opinion in the West which easily accepts at face value various empty declarations or descriptions of states of affairs that depart from reality, together with propaganda that is sometimes primitive and sometimes crafty and sophisticated.

Just as the ideas of Solidarity are still alive in Poland, so also the real effects of the impulse that gave birth to KOR eight years ago are luckily still with us, and they have been strengthened despite the December catastrophe. Those who were fully active in the movement in defense of human and civil rights and in the fight for free trade unions numbered only a few hundred people, yet today there are tens of thousands, and behind these, millions more. This can be a source of cautious optimism.

The goal of this book, however, was not to promote optimism or pessimism, but to give an account of events which are now part of history, of an immediate and living history, such that without knowledge of these events it is difficult to understand Poland today.

Warsaw, September 1984

Appendixes

The Workers' Defense Committee was formed on September 23, 1976. The Diet of the Polish People's Republic was informed of this in an open letter by Jerzy Andrzejewski, which was sent to the Marshal of the Diet. At the same time, the Workers' Defense Committee addressed the following appeal to society and to the authorities of the PRL:

Warsaw, September 23, 1976

APPEAL TO SOCIETY AND TO THE AUTHORITIES OF THE PRL

The workers' protests against the excessive price increases, which was an expression of the opinion of virtually the entire society, were followed by brutal persecutions. In Ursus, Radom, and in other cities, demonstrators have been beaten, kicked, and arrested en masse. Dismissals from work have been the most widespread form of reprisal; along with arrests, they struck with particular severity at the families of the persecuted.

As a rule, these reprisals have involved violations of the law on the part of government organs. The courts have issued verdicts without material evidence; and dismissals from work have violated the regulations of the Labor Code. Testimony has been extorted by means of force. Unfortunately, such procedures are not new in our country. It is enough to recall the illegal repressions used against the signatories of letters protesting against changes in the Constitution, when people were thrown out of work, expelled from schools, illegally interrogated, or blackmailed. But it has been a long while since the repressions have been as massive and as brutal as in recent times. For the first time in many years, arrests and interrogations are now accompanied by physical terror.

The victims of the current repressions cannot count on any help or defense from those institutions whose mission it is to help and defend them, such as the trade unions, whose role has been pathetic. Social welfare agencies also refuse their help. Given this situation, this function must be assumed by the society in the interest of which those who are now being persecuted were protesting against the price increases. Society has no other means of defense against lawlessness than solidarity and mutual aid.

For this reason, the signatories of this Appeal are forming a Workers' Defense Committee which will initiate various forms of defense and help. Legal, financial, and medical aid is needed. Equally important is full information about the persecutions. We are convinced that only public presentations of the actions of the authorities can constitute an effective defense. This is why we are asking anyone who has been persecuted, or who knows about persecutions, to transmit this information to the members of the Committee.

According to information in the possession of the members of the Committee, 160,000 zlotys have thus far been collected and used for purposes of aid. But the needs are much greater. Only a broad social initiative will be able to meet these needs. Wherever the repressed live, throughout the country, it is the responsibility of society to organize itself in order to defend them. In every social group, in every work-place, courageous people should be initiating collective relief actions.

The repressions used against the workers constitute violations of fundamental human rights recognized both by international law and by Polish law: the right to work, the right to strike, the right to express one's opinions freely, and the right to participate in meetings and demonstrations. This is why the Committee is demanding amnesty for those arrested and convicted, and that all the persecuted be returned to their jobs. In making these demands, the Committee wishes to express its solidarity with the Resolution of the Conference of the Episcopate of September 9, 1976.

The Committee calls on society to support these demands.

We are deeply convinced that by creating the Workers' Defense Committee and initiating its activities, we are fulfilling a human and a patriotic responsibility and serving well the Fatherland, the Nation, and Mankind.

In its regularly published *Communiqués*, KOR repeats its appeals for further financial, legal, and medical aid for the repressed, and reminds the readers of its goals.

KOR is demanding:

- the employment of all those dismissed from work in jobs that accord with their qualifications; they should also regain their continuity of work and any former professional and social rights which they may have lost;

- an unconditional amnesty for all those arrested and convicted for participating in the demonstrations;

- the disclosure of the full extent of the repressions that have been used, and of all circumstances connected with the workers' protests of June 25, 1976; and

- the identification and punishment of those who are guilty of violating the law, torturing and beating the workers.

When these demands have been fulfilled, the Workers' Defense Committee will have no reason for continuing its existence.

Workers' Defense Committee

Warsaw, September 29, 1977

DECLARATION

The Workers' Defense Committee was created on September 23, 1976, in order to bring legal, financial, and medical aid to those subjected to repressions following the June strikes and demonstrations; in order to return all those who had been dismissed to work consonant with their qualifications; in order to make sure they would retain their seniority at work and all other social and professional rights; in order to disclose the full extent of the repressions and all other circumstances connected with the workers' protest of June 25, 1976; in order to identify and punish those guilty of violating the law or resorting to the use of torture; and in order to demand the creation of a Special Diet Commission to investigate impartially these problems of public concern. Should these demands be fulfilled, KOR would have no reason to continue its existence.

All of those arrested for taking part in the events of June 25, 1976, are now free. Most of those who were dismissed from work have been rehired, although, with few exceptions, in worse conditions and without retaining their continuity of work. Demands for official disclosure of the extent of the repressions, and of the names of those responsible for tortures and for other forms of violation of the rule of law, have not been met. The Diet of the PRL has remained deaf to the voices of public opinion demanding the formation of a Special Diet Commission for an impartial investigation of all the circumstances surrounding the June events.

The primary goal of KOR has been to bring financial, legal, and medical aid to the victims of the post-June repressions. For the most part, this action has been completed, although help is still necessary in a certain number of cases. At the same time, however, during the period of KOR's existence many people who have been persecuted for political reasons not connected with the June events have also come to the Committee in search of help in their struggle to obtain their rights. KOR has learned of many problems connected with illegal actions by the Security Service, the police, the justice system, the prison system, etc. KOR could not evade these important social tasks; this was reflected, among other things, in the creation of the Intervention Bureau, and in the announcement that a Social Self-Defense Fund would be created. Under these circumstances we, the signatories, consider it necessary to broaden the tasks and the activities of the Committee. We hereby agree to transform KOR into the Social Self-Defense Committee.

The Social Self-Defense Committee "KOR" will demand the fulfillment of those demands of the Workers' Defense Committee that have not yet been fulfilled, and will continue to offer aid to those victims of the repressions following the June events who still need such help.

It will be the task of the Social Self-Defense Committee "KOR" to:

1. Fight against repressions used for political, ideological, religious, or racist reasons, and provide aid to the people persecuted for such reasons.
2. Fight against violations of the rule of law, and provide aid to the victims.
3. Fight for institutionalized guarantees of civil rights and freedoms.
4. Support and defend all social initiatives intended to realize human and civil rights.

The first year of activity by the Workers' Defense Committee has documented the tragic state of the rule of law in Poland. This concerns above all abuses of power by the investigative agencies, the prison system, and the courts and sentencing boards. We will continue our activity because we are convinced that the most effective weapon against the use of coercion by those in power is the active solidarity of the citizens. This is so because the main source of the illegal willfulness of the authorities is the defenselessness of a society that is deprived of institutions independent from the state and capable of protecting the rights of individuals and groups according to their interests.

The Social Self-Defense Fund

The Social Self-Defense Fund was formed on October 11, 1977. At that time it also defined its area of activity. The members of the Fund signed the following statement:

The Social Self-Defense Funds Council is subject to election and recall by a simple majority vote in a plenary meeting of the Social Self-Defense Committee "KOR." The Council will administer the Social Self-Defense Fund according to its internal regulations.

The Social Self-Defense Fund is to serve the goals specified in the resolution of September 29, 1977, which transformed the Workers' Defense Committee into the Social Self-Defense Committee "KOR," along with such other goals as may be specified in the future during plenary meetings of the Social Self-Defense Committee "KOR."

The Social Self-Defense Fund is to be composed of:

(a) financial assets transferred from the Workers' Defense Committee, and

(b) individual or collective donations.

The activities of the Social Self-Defense Fund are to be controlled by the Social Self-Defense Committee "KOR."

Rev. Jan Zieja—chairman, Halina Mikołajska—secretary, Jan Józef Lipski—treasurer, Jan Kielanowski, Edward Lipiński, Piotr Naimski, Józef Rybicki, Wacław Zawadzki.

The Social Self-Defense Committee "KOR" wishes to thank all contributors in Poland and abroad for their financial support.

Social Self-Defense Committee "KOR"

APPEAL FROM THE
SOCIAL SELF-DEFENSE COMMITTEE "KOR"

Wherever we find people persecuted in our country, it is the responsibility of society to organize in order to defend them. In every milieu, in every workplace courageous people should be willing to initiate collective forms of aid. We appeal to the repressed to use all the legal means to which they are entitled in order to defend themselves. The Social Self-Defense Committee "KOR" is willing to assist them in this to the best of its ability.

The Social Self-Defense Funds Council created by the Social Self-Defense Committee "KOR" appeals to all people of good will to make individual and collective donations to support the goals of the Fund.

The Social Self-Defense Fund distributes funds according to the goals of the Social Self-Defense Committee "KOR," and in particular, it:

• gives financial aid to those persecuted for political or ideological reasons, and to the victims of lawlessness or abuses of power; and

• supports social initiatives designed to realize human and civil rights.

The initiatives receiving support include, among other things, independent publications, scholarly lectures, and cultural events.

Should a donor wish to donate money for a specific purpose, his wishes will be respected.

The expenditure of the collected funds is directed by the Social Self-Defense Funds Council according to needs.

We ask that donations be handed only to members of the Funds Council or to other trustworthy people.

The Funds Council is composed of: Jan Kielanowski, Edward Lipiński, Jan Józef Lipski, Halina Mikołajska, Józef Rybicki, Piotr Naimski, and Rev. Jan Zieja (chairman).

We appeal to everyone to transmit reliable information necessary for the work of the Social Self-Defense Committee and its Intervention Bureau to Jacek Kuroń, Jan Józef Lipski, or Aniela Steinsbergowa.

We appeal to everyone to inform us of any violations of civil rights and freedom.

On June 18, 1978, the Initiating Committees of Free Trade Unions on the coast and in Katowice, together with activists of the workers' movement, issued the following appeal:

To: All Working People in Poland and Trade Unions Throughout the World

A new period of struggle in defense of material and human rights began two years ago for working people in Poland. These rights are guaranteed by the Constitution of the Polish People's Republic, the International Covenant on Civil and Political Rights, and the Convention of the International Labor Organization regarding Trade Unions.

The events of June 1976, during which mass protests by workers forced the authorities to annul their drastic food price increases, proved once again that the working people in our country are deprived of any possibility of support from the official Trade Unions. These unions, directed by the single governing party, not only failed to oppose erroneous decisions on the part of the authorities, but also participated actively in the persecutions directed against the protesting workers.

As a result of the awareness of this state of affairs, cooperation was established between workers and members of the intelligentsia. This constitutes an important achievement for Polish society. This cooperation has exercised a decisive influence on the formation of the democratic opposition, the development of which has supported the independent trade union and workers' movement. The founding of the biweekly periodical *Robotnik* in September 1977 accelerated the process of promoting cooperation between groups of workers and members of the intelligentsia in Silesia, in Radom, Gdańsk, Grudziądz, Cracow, and Łódź, and in Warsaw.

Initiating Committees of Free Trade Unions were established in Katowice on February 23, 1978, and in Gdańsk on April 29, 1978. These worker activists are today among the most persecuted people in Poland: they have been arrested on many occasions; they are threatened with dismissal from their jobs; they are subjected to administrative fines; they are kept under surveillance and often searched; they are virtually deprived of the right to travel inside their own country; etc. As we have announced in our statements, there have been cases of beatings that endangered life and health.

At present, two activists of the Initiating Committees of Free Trade Unions, Kazimierz Świtoń from Silesia and Błażej Wyszkowski from the Coast, are now in prison as a result of verdicts handed down by sentencing boards acting at the discretion of the state administration and in violation of the rule of law. Błażej Wyszkowski is on a hunger strike in prison, and artificial feeding is being used to keep him alive. His health and perhaps even his life are in danger.

The Initiating Committees of Free Trade Unions on the Coast and in Silesia, together with activists of the independent workers' movement, declare in solidarity their protest against these persecutions, and announce that they will continue their activities and will not let themselves be broken or frightened by repressions. We call on all working people in Poland to express their active solidarity with our struggle for freedom of association in Independent Trade Unions. We call on all working people in Poland to organize themselves in order to defend the persecuted wherever they may be. We call on Trade Unions around the world to support the independent working people's movement in Poland, and above all to defend our imprisoned friends energetically. We also ask Amnesty International to defend the imprisoned.

The Committee of Free Trade Unions in Katowice
Bolesław Cygan, Wodzisław Śląski, ul. Marchlewicka 1/9
Roman Kściuczek, Mysłowice, ul. W. Kubicy 15
Zdzisław Mnich, Bielsko-Biała, ul. Milusińskich 2/24
Jan Świtoń, Katowice, ul. Mikołowska 30/7
Władysław Sulecki, Gliwice, ul. Królewskiej Tamy 13/1

On behalf of the Initiating Committee
of Free Trade Unions on the Coast
Andrzej Gwiazda, Gdańsk, ul. Wejchera 30 m. 118
Edwin Myszk, Sopot
Krzysztof Wyszkowski, Gdańsk, ul. Pomorska 14 m. 1

Activists of the Independent Workers' Movement
Leopold Gierek, Radom, ul. Sportowa 29 m. 10
Józef Śreniowski, Łódź, ul. Laurowa 2
Edmund Zadrożyński, Grudziądz, ul. Świerczewskiego 17/5

Warsaw, October 10, 1978

APPEAL TO SOCIETY

The workers' protest in June 1976 revealed a deep crisis in the economic and social life of our country. The two years that have elapsed since that time have been sufficiently long to warrant the expectation that the authorities would at least have sketched our directions for resolving the crisis. Unfortunately, during these two years the causes of the explosion have not been removed, and various new sources of tension have been introduced. Growing disorganization and chaos have ravaged the economic, social, and cultural life of the country. In this serious situation, we consider it our responsibility to present to Polish society an evaluation of the situation, together with an attempt to indicate what possible remedies are available to society. We would also like our statement to serve as a warning to the authorities against continuing their policy of deliberate disregard for genuine social problems, and against their evasion of the responsibility for solving these problems. The results of such policies have on many occasions proven tragic for society, and the entire responsibility for this rests with the authorities.

I

1. The increase in prices for foodstuffs that was rejected by the public in 1976 has been replaced by hidden price increases. There exists a widespread practice of introducing more expensive goods labelled with new names onto the market, while eliminating cheaper goods. This tactic has been used with a number of industrial goods and with most foodstuffs, even including bread. The increase of prices in the state trade is also reflected in private trade, causing a severalfold increase in the prices of fruits and vegetables. The scale of this phenomenon is difficult to determine, but there is no doubt that together with the official price changes, inflation is actually much higher than one would conclude on the basis of official data.

Difficulties with supplies are constantly increasing, both in the area of industrial goods and of foodstuffs. It is impossible to purchase many items in the stores without standing in lines, an enormous waste of time, or engaging in bribery or nepotism.

The problem of supplying the population with meat has not been solved. It is difficult to consider the extensive network of commercial stores as a solution, since in these stores the price of a kilogram of sausage equals the daily wages of an average worker (150–200 zlotys per kilogram). Meat rationing has been introduced recently in several dozen industrial enterprises (e.g., the "Warszawa" Steel Mills and the Róża Luxemburg Enterprises). We do not know whether a system of meat rationing is necessary at this time. Until the state authorities publish full data on the availability of meat (production, export, and consumption), it will be impossible to adopt a position on this matter. It is certain, however, that any proposed rationing system should encompass the whole of society and be ratified by it. The hidden price increases and the supply difficulties have caused dramatic rises in the cost of living, and hit the poorest social strata particularly hard.

2. The state of health services is alarming. Chronic underinvestment over a period of years has recently been reflected in a decrease in the number of hospital beds (in psychiatry and obstetrics: *The Statistical Yearbook 1977*). The overcrowding and the technical conditions in a great many hospitals, which have never been renovated since the prewar period, create sanitary conditions that endanger the health of patients.

Insufficient nutrition and the lack of medications available in the hospitals and on the market are also obstacles to treatment.

The construction of a special modern government hospital for dignitaries in Międzylesie, and the special transport of medications, can be regarded in this context only as an expression of the full awareness on the part of the authorities insofar as the state of health services for the population as a whole is concerned; while the collection of contributions from the public for the Social Health Fund constitutes a cynical abuse.

3. The past several years have also brought about no improvement in the dramatic situation in housing. The number of people waiting for apartments grows larger every year, while the waiting period grows longer. This is coupled with a systematic increase in the cost of housing, which significantly burdens family budgets (monthly rent together with credit payments in housing cooperatives can run as high as 3000 zlotys).

4. The authorities are attempting to make up for the disorganization of the economy through an increased exploitation of the workers. The average working day of many occupational groups has often been lengthened. Drivers, miners, construction workers, many other occupational groups now work ten to twelve hours a day.

The fact that miners were deprived of free days to compensate them for free Saturdays, that work is required on Sundays, and that a single day's absence even for the most valid of reasons (such as death in the family, or illness) leads to a loss of approximately twenty percent of a monthly salary— all this can be compared only with early capitalist exploitation.

5. A comparison of the daily earnings of a worker with prices in a commercial store reveals yet another worrisome fact: a growing social inequality. Earnings are overly differentiated (without much regard for qualifications). There are enormous differences in retirement benefits. We have now in Poland families who are struggling under extremely difficult living conditions, and a small number of families who have no financial worries whatsoever.

Another factor deepening social inequalities is the extensive system of privileges for groups associated with the authorities: privileged supplies, special health services, allocation of housing and building lots, foreign currency, and special recreational areas. These are only a few of the facilities available to small leadership groups. As a result, we are witnessing the growing social alienation of groups associated with the authorities, and their inability to notice the real social problems. When we learn that funds designated for the development of agriculture are being used to build a government center in Bieszczady, and that in connection with this, local residents are being dislodged from the village of Wołosate, we are forced to view this fact as a proof that the authorities have lost all touch with reality.

More and more often, one can observe children inheriting the privileged position of their parents. The principle of equal opportunity for all young people is becoming illusory.

In a situation where the economic crisis threatens all of society, and especially the underprivileged groups, the assurance of special privileges to the governing groups provokes righteous anger and moral indignation.

6. The deepening crisis in agriculture is a fundamental factor in the economic, political, and social situation in the country. The consequences of a policy of discrimination and destruction of family farming, which has been conducted for thirty years, are now becoming visible. In spite of this, the production from one hectare of arable land in private hands is still higher than the production from one hectare of arable land in state agriculture. Still, gigantic investments are directed to the State Agricultural Farms and to production cooperatives despite the fact that the costs of maintaining State Agricultural Farms exceeds the value of their production.

Over the past several years, difficulties connected with the general state of the economy have been particularly evident: lack of coal, fertilizers, cattle feed, farming machinery, and building materials. This limits to a great extent the investment possibilities of peasant farms, and leads to the exodus of young people to the cities.

Disorganization and corruption in the purchasing centers cause wastage of already produced farm goods.

At present, following the introduction of dues for retirement insurance for farmers, the financial responsibilities of the peasant farm to the state often exceed half of its income. The refusal by over 250,000 farmers throughout the country to pay retirement dues best illustrates the attitude of the peasants toward state agricultural policy.

7. The violations of the rule of law exhibited during the June events turned out to be a commonly used policy. Beatings of detainees by organs of the police are not isolated cases, but constitute a form of police mob rule which is sanctioned by the higher authorities.

The materials gathered by the Intervention Bureau of the Social Self-Defense Committee "KOR" which have been published in the *Documents of Lawlessness* demonstrate the full impunity of the police and the Security Service. Even the most dramatic cases of murders of persons who were being detained does not result in any punishment of those functionaries guilty of such crimes. In the case of the murder of Jan Brożyna, the desire to protect the real murderers went so far that the investigation was entirely fabricated, as was the court trial. All this ended in the death in prison of a major witness, and in long prison sentences for two other people whose guilt was never proven.

The activities of the sentencing boards for misdemeanors, which have been greatly extended at the expense of the court system, do not respect even the appearances of legality. The Office of the Prosecutor General, in disregard of the law, does not react to complaints that are filed; while the Council of State, the Diet, and the Ministry of Justice remain deaf to all information about the degeneration and anarchy that prevails in the investigative agencies and the justice system.

8. The usurpation by the party of the exclusive and totally arbitrary right to issue and impose judgments and decisions in all areas of life without exception has created a particular threat to Polish science and culture. Drastic limitations of the extent and freedom of scientific research and the publication of its results, especially in the humanities and social sciences such as philosophy, economy, sociology, and history; the stiff demands of the imposed doctrine, which has lost all the characteristics of an ideology and been transformed into a system of dogmas and unrestricted commands dictated by the authorities; the staffing of scientific positions with incompetent people who simply comply with the directives of the rulers—all of this brings harm to Polish culture, and not only hinders its development but also the preservation and cultivation of its former achievements. Literature, theater, and film— those branches of culture dominated by language—are especially vulnerable to the arbitrary throttling of the freedom of thought and to the annihilation of creative activities. Under these conditions, culture is being deadened, while literature, an enormously important element in the spiritual life of the nation, though unmensurable in its effectiveness, is either reduced to the role of an executor of the orders of the authorities or forced to divorce itself completely from expressing the truth about the surrounding reality, or else is simply tolerated as a harmless "flower on the sheepskin."

The preservation of culture has been reflected for several years now in initiatives in support of publications beyond the reach of state control and a science independent of official and distorting falsehoods.

The system of preventive censorship harms not only culture and science, but the entire social and economic life of the country. Censorship stifles not only all signs of criticism, but also all authentic information that could equip society with self-knowledge about its actual situation, which could prove undesirable for the authorities. *The Book of Prohibitions and Directives of the Main Office for Control of the Press, Publications, and Performances* published by KSS "KOR" demonstrates the extent of the censor's interference in all areas of life. Ever greater regions of silence, made infertile by the discrimination against living contemporary culture, are invaded by monstrously inflated and omnipresent ersatz products privileged by cultural policy: multifaceted entertainments and numerous pop song festivals are shabby substitutes for culture. This constitutes in fact the main object of such popularization, and fulfills its role by blocking the deeper cultural aspirations of society and by systematically debasing its spiritual needs.

The most distinguished representatives of science and culture are subject to prohibitions against publication. The more ambitious films are not allowed to be shown. Entire periods of contemporary history are passed over in silence or falsified. The Polish Episcopate, the highest moral authority in the land, has warned against this phenomenon, seeing in it a threat to the national and cultural identity of society. The threat to culture and art posed by the censorship has been discussed at Congresses of the Polish Writers' Union and the Polish Sociological Association, and is the subject of a pronouncement by the Polish PEN-Club.

The system of disinformation constitutes a vicious circle that does not spare even the authorities who created it. According to *Życie Warszawy*, 65% of the data supplied by statistical units reporting to the Main Office of Statistics is falsified, and this estimate must be regarded as optimistic. It is impossible to make correct decisions on the basis of false information. Under these circumstances, paralysis must overwhelm the entire life of the country.

The authorities fear society, and are therefore unable to provide it with the truth about the current situation. The so-called "economic maneuver" propounded as a solution to the crisis turned out to be only a set of immediate, arbitrary, and uncoordinated interferences into the economic life of the country. The result of this policy is only an increasing disorganization of the economy:

- the freezing of investments has led to billions in losses because construction that had already started was never completed;

- drastic limitations in imports have led to weeks of idleness in factories across Poland;

- the plunderous export of foodstuffs has increased shortages on the domestic market;

- the dissolution of the planning system, together with the simultaneous denial of the market economy and the retention of an anachronistic system of directing enterprises by order and commands, has eliminated all regulatory mechanisms from the economy.

The system based on arbitrary and irrevocable decisions by state and party authorities who see themselves as infallible has caused immeasurable damage to the social consciousness of the nation. The persecution of independent views, together with the use of coercion to extort an unconditional compliance with all directives coming from above, has formed attitudes that lack all ideals, and has fostered duplicity; the spread of conformism, servility, and careerism has been encouraged throughout society. These characteristics serve as recommendations in the staffing of leadership positions. Competent, enlightened, and independently minded people are deprived of the possibility of advancement, and often even of a job.

The total lack of consideration for public opinion means that an overwhelming majority of the citizens have ceased to identify themselves with the state, and feel no responsibility for it.

Radical economic reform is necessary. But even the most thoroughly developed and most consistent reforms will not be able to change anything if they run up against a barrier of public indifference and despair.

The economy will not be revived by Conferences of Workers' Self-Governments which blindly obey the PUWP. Committees of Social Control selected from among the authorities, and at their service, will not reach down to the sources of inefficiency, corruption, and illegality. The only result of such actions will be to increase the disorganization of life throughout the country.

II

Polish society possesses tremendous reserves of initiative, activity, and energy which are capable of overcoming the present crisis. The one condition which is necessary to free them is to allow for the creation of true representation for all social groups. It is also necessary to publish accurate data concerning the economic and social situation. Only when these conditions are met (in cooperation between the authorities and society) can a detailed program be formulated for the repair of the economic system and the social situation. Such a program could be worked out in the course of a broad public discussion involving the participation of independent experts. Without the realization of these conditions, all attempts to establish contact with society will only be transformed into a dialogue between the authorities and themselves.

1. The experiences of December 1970 and June 1976 have demonstrated that it is possible to force the authorities to make concessions by means of social pressure. Nevertheless, the effects of these activities turned out to be short-lived. The authorities were very quickly able to deprive a disintegrated

society of the gains it had achieved. Only constant, general, and organized pressure can prevent this from happening again.

Toward the end of 1975, there was a discussion of projected amendments to the Constitution that were proposed by the authorities. The proposals formulated in the letters and petitions of citizens during the course of this discussion can be considered new formulations of the goals of social activity. These goals included guarantees of freedom of belief, freedom of speech and information, freedom of association and assembly, freedom of the press, and that the state authorities should acknowledge their responsibility to society. Activities striving toward these goals should serve to restore social links that are being destroyed by the system of monopolistic and centralized power. These activities should be undertaken independently of the existing official organizational structures.

Not powerless despair, but a decisive, determined, and dignified demand for the respect of its rights, put forward by society, can lead to the restoration of these rights and can build a road toward the repair of the Commonwealth. One expression of this conviction was the proposal for a social program entitled the *Declaration of the Democratic Movement,* which was developed in the milieu of the Workers' Defense Committee and was signed by over 100 people (*Głos* No. 1). Its program of social self-organization constitutes an alternative to the growing danger of an elemental social explosion which could drive the country to a national catastrophe.

The correctness of this sketch of a program has been confirmed already through the creation of a number of independent social initiatives:

- The defense of the workers' interests has been undertaken by the biweekly *Robotnik;*

- Because of the discredited character of the official trade unions, initiating groups of Free Trade Unions have been created in Silesia and in Gdańsk;

- Late in June 1978, the Temporary Peasant Self-Defense Committee of the Lublin Region was created, followed early in September by the Peasant Self-Defense Committee of the Grójec Region. These Committees constitute independent representations of sixteen villages in the province of Lublin and twenty villages in the province of Radom. The biweekly *Gospodarz* is devoted to the problems of peasants;

- The Intervention Bureau of the Social Self-Defense Committee "KOR" was created in order to expose violations of the rule of law and provide aid to the persecuted;

- Student Solidarity Committees have been created in many institutions of higher learning across the country in order to break the monopoly of the SZSP and to form an independent movement to defend the rights of students and universities;

- The Society for Scientific Courses was created in response to the enslavement and falsification of science. Groups of several dozen distinguished scholars from the Society have, during the past academic year, organized a series of semester-long lecture courses in which several hundred students could learn and study in an atmosphere of truth and seriousness that was not marred by political phraseology;

- The state publishing monopoly is being broken by the development of an independent press. Sociopolitical periodicals and the Independent Publishing House (NOWa), which publishes the works of authors condemned to silence by the authorities, constitute expressions of the revival of cultural life.

III

The independent social activity reemerging in the course of the past several years is based above all on the organization of authentic public opinion, on the defense against reprisals, on the formulation of genuine social demands, and on the interruption of the state monopoly over the dissemination of information. Participation in these activities is open to everyone.

1. There is a need for the broadest possible discussion of the social and economic situation in the country. The authorities will not initiate anything; however:

(a) every citizen can and should participate in public meetings, and present the facts known to him about the social and economic situation in the country, and demand true information from the authorities, and he should pose demands and try to get them passed as resolutions during these meetings. In this manner it was possible in many enterprises in the summer of this year to achieve the payment of average wages for work stoppages caused by the management. In this manner in 1956, Polish society participated in a national discussion and forced the state authorities to make far-reaching concessions.

(b) every citizen can and should initiate within his own circle a discussion on the subject of living and working conditions, and about the economic and social situation in the country. Such discussions should lead to the formulation of authentic demands for changes in one's own occupational group, and initiate work on a program for restoring the Commonwealth. These discussions should serve as the seeds of action both within official institutions and outside of them.

(c) every citizen can and should participate in the breaking down of the state monopoly on information. This can be done, for example, by distributing independent press materials and by informing independent institutions about the problems within one's own environment, about social demands and postulates.

2 It is necessary to organize to defend one's rights. Only the organized can elect their own genuine representatives. All Polish citizens who are members of trade unions or corresponding farmers' organizations have the possibility of electing authentic representatives to all trade union posts and of formulating a program for defending the interests of the employees. For example, miners who are waiting to no avail for the elimination of required work on Sundays and of the twelve-hour working day could make these problems into a union election issue, voting only for those candidates who promise to undertake to implement their demands. Citizens who are denied the possibility of action through generally discredited official organizations have the option of organizing new associations, like the peasants from the Lublin and Grójec regions, who have formed Peasant Self-Defense Committees in order to defend their interests. The same method can be used in all social groups.

3. It is always easier to fight in an organized manner. Every strike, every collective action on the part of factory workers or villagers can achieve its goal if it will act in solidarity and in a disciplined manner. This is especially important when coercion on the part of the authorities leads to indignation, anger, and despair. The participants in the struggle have to be defended with even more decisiveness than the demands that have been made. Without organization and solidarity we can achieve nothing.

4. The International Covenant on Civil and Political Rights states:

ARTICLE 19: "1. Everyone shall have the right to hold opinions without interference. 2. Everyone shall have the right to freedom of expression; this right shall include freedom to seek, receive and impart information and ideas of all kinds, regardless of frontiers, either orally, in writing or in print, in the form of art, or through any other media of his choice."

ARTICLE 22: "1. Everyone shall have the right to freedom of association with others, including the right to form and join trade unions for the protection of his interests."

This Covenant was ratified by the Council of State in March 1977 and constitutes a legal norm applying to everyone in Poland.

When Polish society will be able to organize itself to defend its rights, this very fact will mark the beginning of the process of overcoming the social, economic, and political crisis. The deepest cause of the crisis in our country is the expropriation of rights from citizens and of sovereignty from the state.

Social Self-Defense Committee "KOR"

On the dramatic economic and moral situation in the PRL:

May 1979

To the Public

Over the past several months we have witnessed an accumulation of dangerous phenomena in the area of economic life, in the mood of public opinion, and in the activities of the police and repressive organs.

The momentum of economic growth has been drastically reduced because of the catastrophic state of energy supply and transport, and because of a radical reduction in imports. For all practical purposes, the system of planning and coordination no longer exists. For this reason alone, one third of our productive forces are standing idle. The debt has grown to such proportions (15 billion dollars in 1979) that there are no adequate means to meet current payments. Four billion, one hundred million dollars—that is, roughly one half of all Polish exports to the dollar market—must be designated to service the debt (that is, payments and interest). Increases in the debt are being prevented by shutting down all production that involves the import of materials and machinery. At the same time, coal, the basis of all our exports, is often sold for barely half the going price, since the foreign ships delayed in our ports cost us about half of the price of the coal. The so-called "modernization effect," which was anticipated as a result of enormous investments made between 1971 and 1975, which were based mostly on credits, has been entirely lost. Unfortunately, most of these investments were in heavy industry, while the infrastructure (transport, energy, services, etc.) and light industry were neglected. Credits received from the West were also lost because of ill-conceived investments.

The policy of privileges for socialized agriculture worsens the conditions of individual farming, which bears the main burden of feeding the country. This year we can again expect a decline in the production of food. Real wages are decreasing, and even now, in many low-income families with many children, one can find poverty. If the lack of medications, vitamins, and infant formula is added to this, it will be no exaggeration to claim that certain social groups are facing a biological threat.

All of this results in feelings of bitterness, irritation, and dread.

At the end of thirty-five years of existence of the PRL, an abyss separates the authorities from the nation. The explosion in the PKO Rotunda in Warsaw gave rise to the circulation of contradictory statements and rumors, which grew out of the suspicion with which all official announcements are received. In the suspicions that emerged at that time, one could observe the alienation of the authorities, whose secret and incomprehensible actions are perceived by the public as a threat. It is difficult to ignore the dangerous consequences of this phenomenon in a situation in which there is a lack of institutions capable of facilitating communication between the authorities and the public, and when social conflicts cannot be expressed in an organized manner, but gravitate instead toward violent and desperate confrontations.

In an atmosphere that threatens public peace, one would expect that the authorities would behave responsibly and reasonably. But the contrary is occurring. On many occasions the authorities have engaged in actions that incite tension and worry; they seem to be provoking explosive conflicts which may have incalculable consequences. In the village of Wola Żarnowska, as a result of land integration, some farmers were dispossessed of portions of their land, while deliberately intoxicated tractor drivers from the local SKR, supported with peasant money, were plowing already planted fields under. On April 23 in Tychy an attempt to move a cross that had stood in the city center for 180 years was conducted so barbarously that there was a spontaneous demonstration by the townspeople. Goon squads organized by the Socialist Union of Polish Youth not only make lectures of the Society for Scientific Courses impossible, but use brutal physical force. They invade private apartments and beat up everyone present. Recently this resulted in two concussions and the severe beating of a woman. After the independent press revealed the name of one of the leaders of the goon squads, who was an active participant, and a complaint was filed against him in the prosecutor's office, the same man, a common criminal who is also a student of the Academy of Physical Education and the chairman of the Academy's Council of SZSP, and whose name is Jerzy Folcik, publicly received a party card from the hands of Edward Gierek in a ceremony broadcast on television. During the same ceremony, Jerzy Folcik also made a speech on behalf of all the students who were awarded party cards (*Trybuna Ludu* of April 30, 1979).

The attempt of an unknown perpetrator to destroy the monument to Lenin in Nowa Huta was exploited by the authorities for the purpose of conducting a broad action of searches, interrogations, and detentions in the milieu of the democratic opposition.

We have often expressed our conviction that the origins of the phenomena sketched above must be located in the manner in which the authorities function, in the relations between the rulers and the ruled.

We do not and cannot agree to a situation in which

- our nation is deprived of independence;
- human and civil rights are violated despite the recognition of these rights in the law of the PRL;
- the principles of political democracy, which serve as the basis for life in civilized societies, and which constitute an achievement of our national development, are not being realized;
- the laws of the PRL are simply empty words; all forms of defense of citizens' rights are only illusions; all representative institutions are a fic-

tion; the independence of the courts has been forgotten; the justice system is depraved; and the values of human dignity and personal freedom have been erased;

- fundamental guarantees of the freedom of conscience, religion, and opinion are not respected. State interference into Church matters is repressive; access to mass media is a state monopoly; culture and science are dependent on the political authorities and subject to the arbitrary control of the power apparatus;

- the moral state of society is being constantly degraded; all responsible positions in the administration, economy, education, justice system, etc. are staffed with people whose only qualification is their compliance with the directives of the PUWP, which causes the spread of cynical attitudes, careerism, and cunning; there exist high crime rates, and a large group of socially marginal people; alcoholism is devastating society, both as a consequence of social demoralization and a crisis of collective values, and as a result of the organization of the market, in which alcohol is the most easily available product: profits from the sale of alcohol bring in 10 percent of the state's revenue;

- the inefficiency of the national economy is deepening; the attack on individual farming continues; inertia and bureaucratic parasitism are replacing economic policy, while corruption is becoming more and more dangerously widespread, especially in relations between peasants and local authorities;

- the material situation of significant strata in society is worsening, social services are being painfully reduced, and the inefficiency of the health services and day care for children casts deep shadows over the lives of families. In contrast to this, one can observe the sumptuous life of certain groups, which is especially revolting when it concerns members of the power apparatus.

The explosions of bitterness and despair in Poland (June 1956, December 1970, and June 1976) were paid for with the blood of Polish workers. Avoiding the next explosion depends above all on the actions of the authorities, but also on the civil behavior of all of us.

The deepest national interest dictates that we should engage in such civil actions. We are convinced that at the present moment, social self-defense must be expressed by overcoming passivity through the organization of society in defense of its goals into institutions independent of the authorities (Peasant Self-Defense Committees, Free Trade Unions, Workers' Commissions, Student Solidarity Committees), and in the struggle to achieve authentic independence for self-governments, associations, cooperatives, etc.

All of us, or almost all of us, belong to various official organizations: most of us because of the necessities of life, because the state has a virtual monopoly on work and organizations; often however, we belong to these organizations of our own free will—this applies, among others, to all members of PUWP. We participate in meetings of these organizations, and our silence about whether we want this situation or not expresses support for the authorities and sanctions the present state of affairs. It is futile to look for personal responsibility. It is rather necessary to think about what each of us can do for the common good.

In our *Appeal to Society* in the fall of 1978 we wrote: "Every citizen can and should participate in public meetings, and present the facts known to him about the social and economic situation in the country, and demand true information from the authorities, and he should pose demands and try to get them passed as resolutions during these meetings. In this manner it was possible in many enterprises in the summer of 1978 to achieve the payment of average wages for work stoppages caused by the management. In this manner in 1956, Polish society participated in a national discussion and forced the state authorities to make far-reaching concessions."

It is high time to realize that this kind of participation has become a civic responsibility.

We must force the state and party authorities to publish a full account of the economic, social and political situation. It is also necessary to initiate a national discussion of this account and the ways in which the crisis can be overcome; and it is necessary to elaborate a program of reforms that could be implemented with everyone's help. The first step to be taken toward such a debate is to conduct public negotiations with management concerning an inflation compensation that would rise together with the cost of living. We also note the urgent need to define forms and means of providing aid to family farming, without which we cannot overcome the food crisis. It is necessary to improve the nutritional state of numerous social groups which are living on the borderline of poverty—above, all, multi-children families and retired persons.

We believe that a sense of civic responsibility for the fate of the country should direct the economic, social, educational, and political experts to present programs for the renewal of the Commonwealth both to the authorities and to public opinion in all possible forms. The independent publications are open to future-oriented political programs and to specific, factual expertise and suggestions for change, but we also appeal for the use of all available public communications media.

Concern over the future of the Fatherland should lead to a general debate on the basic and immediate problems of Polish reality. At present, issues of fundamental importance for our future are at stake; no personnel changes can bring about a solution. In the serious national dialogue to be undertaken about the problems of the country, the awakening of civic initiative is our common responsibility. No one can be excluded from this debate.

An honest attitude on the part of each of us can add up and lead to the improvement of the general moral and social situation. A refusal to tell lies at work and in social actions, and the acknowledgement that truth is a civic virtue, should become means of renewal.

With a full sense of responsibility, we assert that the situation in our country is drastic. Faithful to our program of social self-defense, we turn to all Poles with an appeal for solidary actions in the name of a higher national and social interest. What is at stake are goals, values, and desires common to all Poles regardless of their political convictions, ideological self-definitions, or organizational affiliations. Our historical experience has shown that in moments of threat we are able to exhibit courage and make sacrifices for the public good.

No one can relieve us of our responsibility for Poland.

Social Self-Defense Committee "KOR"

May 19, 1979

STATEMENT

On the eve of a great event for the Polish nation—the visit of the Holy Father—we wish to bring the public's attention to the tragic fate of tens of thousands of people in prisons and labor camps. During the first seven months of his pontificate, John Paul II twice expressed his interest in the fate of prisoners (on Christmas and during his visit to Mexico).

In our country, in connection with the preparations for the pope's visit, decisions about early paroles for prisoners have been held up. This fact is characteristic of the penal and penitentiary policy in the PRL.

Poland is a country with one of the most severe penal systems. The average length of prison terms is constantly increasing: in 1966 it was 13.9 months; by 1976 it had increased to 25.1 months. The number of sentences longer than two years grew from 8.3 percent in 1965 to 26.3% in 1976. In 1976, fifty-six persons per 100,000 adults were sentenced to unconditional imprisonment for a period longer than two years, and eight persons for a period longer than five years. For Czechoslovakia, the comparable figures are thirty-nine and three; for Hungary, twenty-five and three; for Italy, eighteen and three; and for England, ten and one.

Approximately 200,000 persons pass through penal institutions in Poland in any given year. In 1970, there were 2,400,000 people living in our country who had been convicted at least once during the period 1965–1970 as a result of state prosecution by the courts. If we consider the fact that the majority of these people were men, it appears that nearly one adult man in every five has been stigmatized as a criminal. This is not even a full account, and its updating in 1979 will increase the number to 2,900,000. This does not include those who were not sentenced after investigative arrest, as well as a sizeable number of prisoners from the Stalinist period who after 1956 did not again become entangled with the justice system.

The situation among adolescents and minors is no better. Twelve to fourteen percent of all men are punished by imprisonment or reform school before they reach the age of twenty-one.

Are such severe penalties effective?

No. Recidivism after the second conviction is approximately 50 percent. Eighty percent of all boys who have spent time in reform schools are later punished again.

These facts demonstrate that penal and penitentiary policy is not fulfilling its role. Making penalties more severe or multiplying the number of criminals is not going to eliminate the real causes of criminal behavior.

One of these causes is alcoholism, which is rampant in our country and leads to the dissolution of families and causes young people to turn to crime.

Attitudes of moral indifference are encouraged within the society whenever the educational tasks of schools are replaced with propaganda and ideological functions, while traditional moral models are deliberately destroyed. The fact that the public does not identify itself with the state, and that social and economic life is becoming more and more disorganized, resulting in enormous wastefulness, leads to the disappearance of all sense of responsibility and a disrespectful attitude toward the law. In the flood of multiplying orders and prohibitions, we are all becoming criminals. Draconian sentences will not halt the plague of corruption. To conquer this it is necessary to reinstate self-government and authentic social control, which are being destroyed systematically by the state. In many of our statements we have described the demoralization within the investigating agencies and in the justice system. The severe sentences being handed down are often based on false testimony by the functionaries of the investigating agencies, or on admissions of guilt extorted by physical coercion. This leads to the withering away of a sense of justice and the dissolution of any connection between crime and punishment in the consciousness of society.

The prisons are overcrowded. The work of prisoners is included in the National Economic Plan. Prisoners are forced to perform hard physical labor in a state of constant undernourishment (the daily allowance of food is 9.85 zlotys). The greatest part of their earnings are withheld for the state budget. Certain kinds of work, especially the so-called social actions (which includes work for the private benefit of individual members of the authorities) are not paid at all. A refusal to work or the inability to work leads to a reduction of the food allowance by half (five zlotys) and a prohibition against any additional purchases.

The treatment of prisoners as an unpaid labor force, and their employment in the simplest manual labor, excludes the possibility of training them in occupations which might be useful once they are released.

At the same time, the liquidation of high schools in prisons eliminated the importance of learning as a resocializing factor which enabled a convict to find his place in society following his release.

A prisoner has no possibility of participating in religious observances.

The limitation on correspondence (strict regime: one letter every two months; normal regime: two letters per month), and the limitation on the number of visits (strict regime: once every two months, thirty minutes through a wire mesh; normal regime: once a month without direct contact) help to break family ties.

Since 1974, the right to receive one two-kilogram package is a prize that is awarded by the warden not more frequently than four times a year. The contents of the package are strictly limited.

The rules enforced in prisons give the warden an opportunity to decide many issues on his own, arbitrarily. In connection with the low qualifications and primitive educational level of prison personnel, this room for arbitrariness makes the situation of the convict even more tragic. Beatings and more refined methods of physical terror are common. The immobilization of the prisoner by tying him with special belts to a table (for up to forty-eight hours) can lead to permanent paralysis of his limbs, and often even to death, which is then reported by the prison personnel as a heart attack. This is one example of how an exceptional preventive means, which was only to be used under special circumstances, is being used as a method of thoughtless sadism and cruelty. Sadism and cruelty are constantly present in our jails, and make it impossible to see these institutions as concerned with rational resocializing activities, but rather as a system for breaking down human dignity. It should be no surprise that in this situation, suicides, self-mutilations, and hunger strikes are common among prisoners. Operations after acts of self-mutilation (including opening the stomach cavity) are performed without anesthesia, which increases the mortality rate due to operational shock. *Data on this subject is never made public by the Central Office of Penal Institutions.*

Given this state of affairs, we believe that an immediate and radical change in penal and penitentiary policy is indispensable. It should include:

1. A significant reduction of the average length of sentences;
2. The creation in penal institutions of conditions for resocialization by:

- eliminating tortures and beatings,
- assuring the prisoners of a possibility of learning a trade and educating themselves, including higher education,
- allowing them the possibility of frequent, unconstrained contacts with family members and friends,

- assuring them of pastoral care,

- improving their living conditions significantly, and eliminating hunger, cold, and forced labor as a means of repression, and

- excluding all other forms of breaking down the human dignity of prisoners.

3. Possibilities must be opened for social aid to prisoners and their families by reviving such institutions as "Patronat," which would allow for a minimum of social control by permitting access to prisons.

It is also necessary to restore to the Church the charitable organization "Caritas," which was illegally taken away.

The historical event of the Holy Father's visit to Poland should serve as an occasion to initiate the first steps toward remedying the existing conditions.

We appeal to the highest authorities in the Polish People's Republic to take this opportunity to announce a general amnesty. As against other amnesties in past years, it should apply to all prisoners without exception. This law, based on humanitarian principles, should above all

- free invalids, the elderly, and mothers of small children,

- free those who have spent 15 years in prisons without interruption, and

- lead to the reduction of long prison terms.

It should also insure that all prisoners be transferred to milder conditions in which to serve out the remainder of their sentences, for as long as the present regulations remain in effect.

Social Self-Defense Committee "KOR"

In connection with the pilgrimage of John Paul II to Poland

July 1, 1979

STATEMENT

Between June 2 and June 10 we have witnessed and participated in events of exceptional importance which deeply affect the whole of society: John Paul II, the Polish pope, visited his Fatherland.

Before we even managed to compose ourselves after the first emotions, it was obvious that the experience we had lived through was already exercising a tremendous influence, and that this influence would continue to grow. This was not only because the pope's pilgrimage to Poland was a holiday for the whole nation and the occasion for an unprecedented general manifestation of joy and affection. The more important reason was that many millions of Poles had participated directly or indirectly in meetings with the Holy Father and had heard from him a message of extraordinary importance for the entire nation and for each of us individually.

The visit of the pope was above all a religious pilgrimage. For John Paul II, the Christian religion is identical with the idea of the freedom and autonomy of man, with justice and love as a principle of coexistence among people and nations in the most profound sense: "It is necessary to work for peace and understanding among the people and the nations of the whole world. It is necessary to seek rapprochement. It is necessary to open the borders" (from his homily in the Cracow Błonie). This is why "the great issue of man" naturally became the main subject of the homilies and speeches of the Holy Father. The pope appealed for a "just fulfillment" of needs, rights, and tasks on the part of every member of the nation (from his homily in Jasna Góra, June 5); he spoke out against all forms of degradation of the human individual. In his moving homily in Auschwitz he condemned the various forms of totalitarian coercion that deprive a person of his most fundamental rights. In the homily spoken in Mogila-Nowa Huta, he stressed the especially important role of the "dignity of work" understood as "the measure of human dignity": "Christ would never agree for a man to be seen, or to see himself, as a mere tool of production, or that he be judged and evaluated only according to this standard." At the same time, the Pope showed that the problem of national rights was an integral part of the problem of human rights. In his speech in Belweder he stated: "Peace and understanding among nations can be built only on principles of respect for the objective rights of every nation, such as the right to exist, to be free, to respect social and political subjectivity, and to create its own culture and civilization." In the spirit of consistent universalism, the pope spoke about nations which have "lived with us and among us," which have suffered together with us (homily in Victory Square, and the Auschwitz homily); and he called for a "lasting reconciliation of the nations of Europe and of the world" (homily in Jasna Góra). In his last, farewell speech, the pope said, "Our time demands from us that we not shut ourselves in behind inflexible boundaries when the good of mankind is at stake. Everywhere man must have an awareness and assurance of his authentic citizenship; that is, I would say, the consciousness of his priority in any configuration of relations and forces."

Millions of Poles, regardless of their world view, listened to the pope's words with understanding, enthusiasm, and warm emotion. In every place visited by the pope one was struck by the great discipline and order that prevailed, the excellent organization of the gatherings, and the inner concentration of the listeners. The demonstration of such enormous maturity on the part of society is one of the most valuable experiences occasioned by the pope's pilgrimage. At the same time, the constant applause that accompanied the statements of the Holy Father certified to what an extent his words had been awaited, how appropriate his message about the "primacy of man" was, and how it met the deepest emotional needs of society, which cannot accept a lack of respect for the rights of the individual and the rights of the nation. Certainly, for many people in Poland as well as those beyond its borders, the words of the pope summoned up the moral responsibility to undertake or intensify the struggle in defense of these rights.

This is also our responsibility.

Social Self-Defense Committee "KOR"

CHARTER OF WORKERS' RIGHTS

(*Robotnik,* special issue No. 35 of December 1, 1979)

Whereas:

- citizens are deprived of the right to participate in decisions that concern them;
- the basic rights of the working people are limited, such as the right to safe and sensible work, to respectable wages, and to rest;
- there is a deepening of social inequality and injustice;
- there is a lack of institutions to defend the working people—this is certainly not being done by the official trade unions;
- the workers are deprived of their basic right to defend themselves, that is, the right to strike;
- the costs of all the mistakes committed by the authorities and the costs of the current crisis are being placed on society, we have undertaken actions the long-term goal of which is to create a system of self-defense for the working people, and above all to create independent trade unions.

We want to begin with problems whose solutions—even if only partially— appear possible even now.

(1) Wages

- wages should rise a least at the same rate as the cost of living; it is necessary to introduce an *inflation compensation;*
- everyone must be guaranteed a *minimum standard of living;* groups of experts should calculate this minimum and correct it according to increases in prices; families earning less than the minimum should be compensated with special allocations;

- there is a need to eliminate glaring and unjustified wage differentials;

- work stoppages, changes in work norms, etc., cannot lead to a reduction in wages;

- workers performing the same type of work under the same conditions should be paid according to uniform wage scales, regardless of the industry in which they are employed.

(2) Working Time

- it is unacceptable to force people to work overtime, to work additionally or "socially"; miners must have Sundays and holidays off;

- everyone must be guaranteed the same number of free Saturdays presently available;

- we must aim to introduce a *40-hour work week* without reduction of wages.

(3) Work Safety

- safety regulations and norms must be *unconditionally observed;* special commissions should be established with broad rights, including the right to shut down a plant; commissions responsible for work safety and hygiene, accident investigating commissions, and workplace doctors must be *institutionally independent* of the management of the workplace;

- no one who has lost his health as a result of harmful conditions in his workplace should be deprived of the benefits and the pension to which he is entitled;

- verification of the current list of occupational diseases is necessary;

- *night work for women* must be eliminated; women must not be forced to perform hard physical labor.

(4) Privileges

- the evaluation of employees and promotions cannot be based on party membership, political convictions, or views about the world;

- goods, such as bonuses, apartments, or vacations, must be distributed overtly; the principles according to which these goods are distributed should be made public, together with the names of the persons receiving them;

- it is necessary to eliminate the privileges of groups connected with the authorities (police, party apparatus): special allocations of scarce goods such as apartments, land, building materials, cars, separate medical care, luxurious vacation houses, special pension rights, etc.

(5) Coercion to Act Contrary to One's Conscience

- no one should be forced to perform immoral acts: to inform on others to superiors in the PUWP, the Security Service, etc., or to participate in witchhunts against inconvenient people:
- no one should be forced to produce junk, to work under conditions that are hazardous to oneself or to others, or to falsify the results of one's work, to report lies, etc.

(6) The Labor Code

The Labor Code in force since 1975 must be thoroughly amended. Regulations deleterious to employees have been introduced into it. Its articles are ambiguous, and as a result they can be and often are interpreted according to the interests of the employers.

In particular:

- article 52, used as an anti-strike law, must be changed (it was used as grounds for dismissals from work after June 1976); the right to strike must be *guaranteed by law;*
- the management of a workplace must explain in writing to anyone who is being fired the grounds for his dismissal; the employee should continue working until his case has been tried in all the courts to which he has the right to appeal; during court proceedings the person should have the right to be represented by counsel;
- union activists chosen by the employees should be legally protected from being fired, also for a period of time after their term of office has expired.

We believe that the realization of these demands depends in part also on our own attitude. The fact that workers can win concessions from the authorities and management has been confirmed both by the great workers' demonstrations—in 1956, 1970, and 1976—and by numerous strikes.

For many months now we have been feeling the effects of the crisis on our own skins: supply is constantly worsening, commuting is more difficult, wages are going down and prices are rising, work time is being extended in many plants, free Saturdays are being taken away, and stoppages are multiplying. If we do not begin to defend our interests today, our situation will only become even worse.

In order to win, however, we must shake off the sense of impotence, we must cease to accept passively the limitation of our rights and the worsening of our standard of living. We must seek out the most effective forms of action.

There are many possibilities:

1. Strikes, even small ones, are without doubt an effective method of action. Generally, however, they are effective only in the short run. In order not to

squander the achievements of a strike, its participants must choose representatives who will oversee the implementation of their demands. If the workers are able to act with solidarity and are not afraid, they can force the management to make concessions with the threat of a strike alone: by presenting a petition, or by sending their representatives to the management.

2. Much can be achieved by the mere dissemination of information. It is necessary to speak loudly and to protest when we witness an injustice, or when someone is being abused; it is necessary to publicize the existence of cliques and privileges, negligence and wastefulness, violations of rules of work safety and hygiene, and attempts to conceal accidents. It is necessary to discuss such issues with one's colleagues and raise them at meetings, to demand that the authorities take a position, and to inform independent social institutions and the editorial boards of independent periodicals.

3. There are many problems within plants that can be solved by the official trade unions. It would certainly be better for us if they were not as inert as they are today. One must demand that the plant councils of the unions defend the interests of the employees, use union meetings for discussions, and elect people to the plant councils who will implement such demands.

4. The constant activity of workers' groups is a necessary condition if our actions are not to be accidental and deal only with immediate problems. Such groups, initially even in secret, can formulate programs of action, organize activities, mold public opinion, and eventually reveal their existence as independent workers' committees.

5. Wherever there are strong organized groups of workers able to defend their representatives should they be dismissed from work or arrested, committees of free trade unions should be formed. The experiences of working people in Western democracies have proven that this is the most effective way in which the interests of employees can be defended.

Only independent trade unions supported by the workers they represent have any chance of resisting the authorities; only they can constitute a force with which the authorities will have to reckon and with which they will negotiate on a basis of equality.

We, the signatories of this document, commit ourselves to work for the realization of the postulates contained in the Charter of Workers' Rights.

We are also establishing a relief fund, and declare that we will contribute to it regularly. We designate the money accumulated in the fund for the purpose of providing aid to people dismissed from work as a result of independent trade union activity.

APPENDIX

Our activity is legal.

By ratifying the International Covenants and the Convention of the International Labor Organization, the authorities of the PRL recognized:

I. THE RIGHT OF EMPLOYEES TO UNIONIZE

Article 2 of Convention No. 87 of the International Labor Organization (*Dziennik Ustaw* No. 29/1958, item 25).

All employees and employers without exception have the right, without receiving any prior permission, to form organizations according to their own wishes, with the only condition being that they obey their own statutes.

Article 8, section 1a of the International Covenant on Economic, Social, and Cultural Rights (appendix to *Dziennik Ustaw* No. 38/1977, item 169).

The states parties to this Covenant undertake to assure everyone of the right to form and join trade unions of their own choosing, in order to support and defend their social and economic interests, under the sole condition of adherence to the statutory regulations of their given organizations. The use of this law cannot be subject to any limitations other than those provided for in a democratic society in order to defend national security interests or public order, or to protect the rights or freedom of other persons.

II. THE RIGHT TO STRIKE

Article 8, section 1d of the International Covenant on Economic, Social, and Cultural Rights.

The states parties to the Covenant undertake to assure the right to strike on the condition that it be used in accordance with the laws of a given country.

BIELSKO-BIAŁA

Zdzisław Mnich, ul. Milusińskich 2 m. 34.

GDAŃSK

Bogdan Borusewicz, Sopot, 23 Marca 96 m. 24, historian and editor of *Robotnik*.
Andrzej Bulc, Zamenhoffa 18m. 16, electronic technician, Initiating Committee of Free Trade Unions on the coast.
Joanna Duda-Gwiazda, Wejhera 30 m. 118, engineer, Coastal KZ WZZ.
Andrzej Gwiazda, Wejhere 30 m. 118, engineer, Coastal KZ WZZ.
Andrzej Kołodziej, fitter, W-3 Gdańsk Shipyard.
Zenon Moskal, Klonowicza 1E, metalworker, R-3 Gdańsk Shipyard.
Alina Pieńkowska, Fitelberga 8 m. 3, nurse.
Andrzej Skowron, Klonowicza 1E, fitter, K-2 Gdańsk Shipyard.
Bernard Wachowicz, Podkarpacka 5a m. 8, fitter, K-2 Gdańsk Shipyard.
Anna Walentynowicz, Grunwaldzka 49 m. 9, crane operator, Gdańsk Shipyard.
Lech Wałęsa, Wrzosy 26c m. 5, automobile mechanic.
Błażej Wyszkowski, Danusi 5 m. 24, engineer.
Krzysztof Wyszkowski, carpenter.
Jan Zapolnik, Kościuszki 18m. 2, tel. 41-53-79.

GIŻYCKO

Leszek Bartezal, Mickiewicza 14 m. 9, electrician.
Henryk Jurgo, Sikorskiego 4 m. 5, electrician-mechanic.
Sławomir Karolik, 30-lecia PRL "A" bl. 5 m. 77, musician.
Bożena Luczys, Kamionki near Giżycko.
Leszek Łachowicz, Kętrzyńskiego 9 m. 1, electrical technician.
Mieczysław Malitka, Olsztynek-Ameryka, driver-mechanic.
Zbigniew Oledno, Mickiewicza 16 m. 7, electronics engineer.
Mirosław Ternozek, Sikorskiego 9 m. 1.
Andrzej Żagań, Dąbrowskiego 11 m. 1.

GLIWICE

Ryszard Gorczewski, Pszczyńska 107 m. 11, miner, "Gliwice" mine.
Andrzej Spyra, Pszczyńska 118b m. 25, tel. 32-30-50, technician, editor of
  Robotnik.

GRUDZIĄDZ

Maksymilian Mozdziński, Puławskiego 17 m. 7.
Edmund Zadrożyński, Świerczewskiego 17 m. 5, tel. 270-97, editor of *Robotnik*.

KATOWICE

Kazimierz Świtoń, Mikołowska 30 m. 7, tel. 514-919, radio technician, KZ
  WZZ in Katowice.
Jan Świtoń, Mikołowska 30 m. 7, mechanic, KZ WZZ in Katowice.

CRACOW

Tadeusz Basięga, Lenin Steel Mills.
Ryszard Bogacz, Lenin Steel Mills.
Anatol Borucki, Lenin Steel Mills.
Alojzy Bożyszczko, Lenin Steel Mills.
Roman Buda, Lenin Steel Mills.
Eugeniusz Budzyński, Lenin Steel Mills.
Antoni Goliński, Lenin Steel Mills.
Franciszek Grabczyk, Nowa Huta, Os. 1000-lecia 30 m. 40, engineer, editor
  of *Robotnik*.
Władysław Gruszka, Lenin Steel Mills.
Stefan Guspiel, Lenin Steel Mills.
Zygmunt Kaleta, Nowa Huta, Os. Dąbrowszczaków 14 m. 1, senior mason of
  industrial furnaces.
Bronisław Ligenza, Lenin Steel Mills.
Józef Mordyła, Lenin Steel Mills.

Lucjan Motyka, Lenin Steel Mills.
Elżbieta Mrozowska, Lenin Steel Mills.
Franciszek Skrzypiński, Lenin Steel Mills.
Romuald Tolski, Lenin Steel Mills.
Jerzy Wojtal, Lenin Steel Mills.
Stanisław Żaczkiewicz, Lenin Steel Mills.

LUBLIN

Kazimierz Dziewa, Leonarda 11 m. 54, Cooperative of the Visually
   Handicapped.
Ryszard Dziewa, Leonarda 11 m. 54, Cooperative of the Visually Handicapped.
Stefania Jakus, Hutnicza 4 m. 44, Cooperative of the Visually Handicapped.
Kazimiera Lis, Junoszy 47 m. 24, Cooperative of the Visually Handicapped.
Ryszard Lis, Junoszy 47 m. 24, Cooperative of the Visually Handicapped.
Edward Nurzyński, Wajdeloty, Cooperative of the Visually Handicapped.
Stanisław Witer, Leonarda 11 m. 2, Inter-Provincial Trade Cooperative of the
   Handicapped.
Wiesława Wróblewska, Junoszy 47 m. 41, Cooperative of the Visually
   Handicapped.

ŁAZY

Jerzy Grzebieluch, Kościuszki 25, engineer.

ŁÓDŹ

Jadwiga Szczęsna, Zawiszy Czarnego 7 m. 8, office worker.
Stanisław Szwarocki, Franciszkańska 38 m. 17, weaver.
Józef Śreniowski, Laurowa 2, tel. 734-70, sociologist, editor of *Robotnik*.
Leszek Witkowski, Dzierżyńskiego 8 m. 50, electrical mechanic.

MYSZKÓW

Jan Łaszek, M. Curie-Skłodowskiej 10a m. 3, tel. 314-25, mechanic.
Ireneusz Maligłówka, 1-go Maja 115, driver.
Edward Pytlarz, Ślęzany near Lelów, mechanic.

NOWA RUDA

Stefan Kowalczyk, Zielona 4, miner.

PABIANICE

Marek Chwalewski, Konopna 8 m. 10, electrician.

POZNAŃ

Edmund Chruściński, Działki ul. Wolności 13.

PRZEMYŚL

Stanisław Frydlewicz, Wernyhory 1, mechanic.

RADOM

Wiesław Kobyłko, automobile mechanic.
Hanna Ostrowska, Koszarowa 15.
Ewa Soból, Malczewskiego 9 m. 12, worker.

RUDA ŚIĄSKA

Maksymilian Kubiczek, Miodowa 16, miner in Halemba II mine.

SKAWINA

Mieczysław Majdzik, Spokojna 4, welder.

SZCZECIN

Kazimierz Dobosz, Trzebierz Szczecińska ul. Brzozowa 7.
Danuta Grajek, Gryfino, B. Chrobrego 18 m. 11, office worker, KZ WZZ of the Western Coast.
Andrzej Jakubcewicz, Noakowskiego 30 m. 2.
Andrzej Kamrowski, surveyor, KZ WZZ of the Western Coast.
Tadeusz Kociełowicz, Mazowiecka 17 m. 6, tel. 424-14, KZ WZZ of the Western Coast.
Stefan Kozłowski, Aleja Jedności Narodowej 47 m. 2, lathe worker, editor of *Robotnik*, KZ WZZ of the Western Coast.
Bronisław Modrzejewski, Gierczaka 43 m. 1, KZ WZZ of the Western Coast.
Zdzisław Podolski, Gryfino, ul. Kościelna 10 m. 1, technical mechanic, KZ WZZ of the Western Coast.
Marian Stańczyk, Gryfino, ul. Wodna 13.
Jan Witkowski, Gryfino, Słowiańska 5 m. 1, radiotechnician, KZ WZZ of the Western Coast.
Mirosław Witkowski, Gryfino, Zielona 6 m. 1, worker, KZ WZZ of the Western Coast.

TARNÓW

Wacław Mojek, Kościuszki 16, artist.
Zbigniew Staruch, Zawadzkiego 12 m. 5, driver.

Toruń

Mirosława Sędzikowska, Chełmża, Świerczewskiego 12 m. 36, tel. 827-01,
   Polish philologist.
Stanisław Śmigiel, Mickiewicza 91 m. 8, electronics engineer.

Wałbrzych

Jacek Pilchowski, Dunikowskiego 70 m. 7, technician, editor of *Robotnik.*

Warsaw

Henryk Bąk, engineer.
Teodor Klincewicz, student of Technical Physics and Applied Mathematics at
   Warsaw Polytechnic.
Mieczysław Książczak, student of Polish philology at Warsaw University.
Dariusz Kupiecki, Grabowa 4 m. 3, tel. 433-133, mathematician, editor of
   Robotnik.
Jan Lityński, Al. Wyzwolenia 9 m. 125, tel. 287-104, mathematician, editor
   of *Robotnik.*
Witold Łuczywo, Korczyńska 11 m. 18, tel. 428-736, engineer, editor of *Robotnik.*
Wiktor Nagórski, Gagarina 11 m. 49, tel. 412-315, computer scientist.
Wojciech Onyszkiewicz, historian, editor of *Robotnik.*
Zbigniew Romaszewski, Kopińska 36a m. 57, tel. 222-925, Intervention Bu-
   reau of KSS "KOR."
Henryk Wujec, Neseberska 3 m. 48, tel. 426-338, physicist, editor of *Robotnik.*

Wodzisław Śląski

Bolesław Cygan, Marchlowicka 1 m. 9, worker.

Wrocław

Jerzy Filak, physicist, Pl. Gotwalda 17 m. 3.
Krzysztof Grzelczyk, Wieczorka 118 m. 19, Social Self-Defense Club.
Jacek Malec, student, Student Solidarity Committee.
Ludwik Werle, Brzeska 27 m. 25, tel. 441-715, automobile mechanic.

Zabrze

Józef Wiewiórski, Damrota 68a m. 10, miner in the Zabrze mine.

August 18, 1980

APPEAL

We appeal to all working people in Poland. We are facing great changes whose form depends on all of us—the striking workers and the whole of society—but also on the authorities.

An Inter-Factory Strike Committee (MKS) representing Strike Committees from 21 workplaces in the Tri-city area was formed there on the night of August 16. This Committee is the only representative of the strikers authorized to make the decision to end the strike. The MKS is to be transformed into a Provincial Council of Free Trade Unions. This success is a result of the solidarity of the entire workforce.

KSS "KOR" and the editorial board of *Robotnik* wish to express their complete solidarity with the striking workers and the MKS, and their admiration for the workers' attitude.

1. The search for solutions to the present economic situation must begin with the formation of authentic representatives for the strikers: free trade unions. We must bring about a situation in which strikes will cease to be the only means of defending the interests of workers, and we must insure that growing conflicts be solved by regular negotiations. The workers should dissolve their existing plant councils and elect free representatives in free elections.

The authorities could express their good will—without which any understanding is impossible—by recognizing the Strike Committees, Workers' Commissions, and Plant Councils that are now being created, and which are independent of the Central Board of Trade Unions (CRZZ), as the only permanent representatives of the workers, and through legislative recognition of their status. This would mean that the authorities would in no way interfere with the dissolution of the compromised plant councils which must resign. It would also mean that the authorities forego their previous methods of destroying independent social representations. Written guarantees of safety for all the strikers and the freedom of action for Strike Committees must also be guaranteed in writing. Representatives of the workforce should consult with one another in order to reach agreement on joint demands, and in order to act with solidarity for their realization, just as happened in the Tri-city area.

2. The first issue that must be negotiated between the workers' representatives and representatives of the authorities should be the introduction of a permanent inflation compensation to maintain the standard of living. This accords with the demands of the strikers who justified their insistence on wage increases in terms of the growing inflation. Toward the end of the year, representatives would again negotiate for an inflation compensation for 1981.

The inflation compensation cannot favor those who earn the most. It should compensate the cost of living above all for those who earn the least. This is why it should be the same for everyone and allocated to every family member.

3. Everyone is aware that an increase in wages alone—without an increase in the supply of goods to the market—must lead to overt or concealed price increases, to the disappearance of goods from the stores, and to speculation. Wage increases have only an immediate effect and significance. The authorities agree to wage concessions, and in this manner avoid solving serious political and social problems. It is necessary to take immediate steps intended to improve the situation and to halt any further decline in the standard of living.

The authorities must above all present full information about the present state of the economy, and create the conditions for a free and open discussion of the program of changes and reforms, which should be unconstrained by the censorship. Premier E. Babiuch has called for a discussion; but his statement was a glaring example of how this discussion should not be conducted: it did not contain a single important bit of information or a single proposal.

The economic policy conducted until now, which has been completely exempt from all social and professional control, has brought about an unmitigated disaster. One condition that must be met in order for the country to overcome the economic crisis is the organization of institutions in Polish public life that are independent of the authorities. Such institutions would represent the interests of individual social and occupational groups, and would include free trade unions, representatives of the peasants and the intelligentsia, local self-governments, and scientific and cultural associations. This is why we place such high hopes in the creation of authentic workers' representative bodies that would be able to exert permanent influence on the policies of the authorities.

4. The lack of meat and of basic foodstuffs is above all the result of a policy that has been aimed primarily at the socialization of agriculture. The authorities must therefore guarantee the inviolability of private ownership of land, together with the freedom to buy and sell. Privileges must end for socialized and cooperative agriculture. Individual farmers must have equal rights in the areas of purchasing and selling goods, prices, taxation, credits, and legal protection. They must also be enabled to purchase the necessary production materials: machines, animal feed, coal, etc., which until now have been allocated above all to inefficient and expensive state and cooperative farms.

5. All the strikes are taking place in a serious and peaceful atmosphere. The workers have demonstrated their responsibility for the fate of the country. Nevertheless, some of the strikers and members of Strike Commissions are being discriminated against by functionaries of the Security Service. Their families are being blackmailed, and their apartments searched; they are fol-

lowed and sometimes even detained; threats and provocations are being used against them. To a much greater extent this applies to people gathering information about strikes. Information is being blocked, telephone connections have been interrupted, and millions are being spent for equipment and personnel used for surveillance, espionage, and interrogation. Once again the authorities are attempting to use police methods to squelch the truth and destroy independent civic initiatives. This is evidence that they feel no responsibility for the fate of the country. Wherever the authorities still attempt to tell lies, and wherever the political police enter either secretly or overtly— *negotiations should be broken off.*

It is the responsibility of every Pole to express his solidarity with the striking workers and to oppose police coercion. The fulfillment of the demands of the striking workers—the release of all political prisoners, and an end of interventions by the SB into the independent workers' movement sweeping the entire country—are the most elementary conditions for the return of social peace to Poland.

Social Self-Defense Committee "KOR"
and the Editorial Board of Robotnik

Warsaw, September 11, 1980

STATEMENT

Our country has found itself in a situation which allows one to hope that the long-standing economic and political crises will be overcome. We are indebted for this to the attitude of the Polish workers who, supported by an overwhelming majority of other citizens, have developed and fought a victorious struggle for the idea of a genuine compromise between society and the authorities.

During the past few weeks, Polish society has demonstrated its desire to recover its human and civil rights, together with its vitality and determination in the struggle to democratize public life. This has been proven by the solidarity among all the strata of the Polish nation, including workers throughout Poland, peasant groups, intellectuals, and the Church. One important aspect of this solidarity was exhibited in the creation of the Commission of Experts to the Gdańsk MKS, which played an important and positive role during the negotiations. KSS "KOR" declares its full solidarity with the strikers, and expresses its admiration for the courage and wisdom of the striking workers on the Coast. We thank all people of goodwill who took part in the gathering and transmitting of information about the strikes. We are deeply grateful to the MKS in the Tri-city area, who insisted that the release of imprisoned activists of the democratic opposition be one of the conditions for ending the strike. The victory of the workers on the Coast is a common victory for all of us.

From the moment of its creation, KSS "KOR" has warned the public against the disastrous consequence of the policy of the state authorities, and against decisions which were made without social participation, against concealing the truth about the situation in the country, and against corruption and violations of the rule of law. We have stressed on numerous occasions that only a dialogue between the authorities and democratically elected representatives of the work force can lead to effective political solutions.

We would like to declare emphatically that KSS "KOR" is and will remain a social and not a political institution. KSS "KOR" is a group of people of various political and philosophical orientations whose tasks and goals were formulated unequivocally at the time KSS "KOR" was created, and which remain unchanged.

These tasks and goals are:

- to struggle against repressions for ideological, religious, or racial reasons, and to aid those who are being persecuted;
- to struggle against violations of the rule of law, and to aid those who have been wronged;
- to struggle for institutional guarantees of civil rights and freedoms; and
- to support and defend all social initiatives aiming to implement human and civil rights.

The goals formulated in this manner unequivocally characterized our attitude toward the newly created Independent Self-Governing Trade Unions that are striving to protect the basic rights of working people, as guaranteed by the United Nations Charter of Civil and Political Rights and by the Final Act of the Helsinki Accords.

The trade union movement which is developing across the country, and which even today unites hundreds of thousands of people, is of critical importance for the future of our country.

Aware of our small capabilities compared with the general character of social desires, we wish to offer all the help we can provide.

This concerns the exchange of information and the making available of our experience in the conduct and organization of independent social activity. At the same time, until the union movement forms its own cells and settles down, we will continue, to the best of our ability and strength, to engage in interventional activities in order to protect the activists of the newly formed movement from repressions.

The fear of repressions is not unfounded. The ban against all information about the trade union movement in the mass media, and attempts to intimidate workforces and prevent them from joining the NSZZ constitute violations of the agreements made with the Inter-Factory Strike Committees, and undermine trust in the intentions of the authorities.

By entering into negotiations and signing the agreements with the Inter-Factory Strike Committees, the authorities have abandoned the methods of terror which they always used previously to quash workers' demands. One way in which the authorities could demonstrate the permanence of these changes, and their good will, would involve the publication of all information about the circumstances in which the massacre on the Coast in 1970 occurred, and those in which the persecutions of the workers from Radom and Ursus took place in 1976. No personnel changes can provide a guarantee that agreements will be implemented. Only the complete consistency and solidarity of society in demanding the implementation of their realistic demands can bring about conditions for social peace.

We believe that the agreements between the authorities and the Inter-Factory Strike Committees, which have been negotiated so laboriously, unequivocally define the field of dialogue between society and the authorities. All attempts to avoid this dialogue would lead only to an increase in social tension and to a loss of the equilibrium which the stated has recovered with such great difficulty.

Social Self-Defense Committee "KOR"

On the socio-political situation in Poland following the Gdańsk Agreements

November 30, 1980

Statement

I. The great spontaneous movement of protest—the July and August strikes—has led to authentic negotiations and to an understanding between the authorities and the striking workers. This understanding has been described as a social contract, and it contains an agreement involving the genuine participation of society in the formulation and adoption of decisions which concern it.

The multi-million strong independent and self-governing trade union "Solidarity" constitutes the most important achievement of Polish society, a model of self-organization for everyone and a radical breakthrough in relations between the authorities and society. Centralized dictatorship over the whole of social life is no longer possible.

II. NSZZ "Solidarity" is a guarantee for the formation of self-government movements in all areas of collective life: among peasants, intellectuals, and young people. By the very fact of their existence, independent social insititutions—trade unions, self-governing peasant movements, artistic, scientific, and cultural associations, and student organizations—favor the overcoming of the deep crisis which resulted from the dissolution of social bonds. Their task is to strive for the democratization of public life, to make an organized society into a true partner in negotiations with the authorities, and later to share in the joint implementation of the goals agreed on.

III. Independent social organizations cannot and should not undertake actions leading to changes in the system, or to the overthrow of the government. The external threat defines the boundaries of possible change.

IV. The formulation of a program of economic and political change is the first condition which must be met; we must also formulate methods and deadlines for the implementation of such a program. This is the first order of the day. Otherwise our country will drown in a chaos of sharp conflicts.

At present the party and state leadership is unable to formulate such a program without broad social cooperation. It is necessary for all conscious elements of Polish public opinion to take part. The discussion about reforms conducted before now has been riddled with limitations by the censorship and failed to meet general expectations. No one should be muzzled or disqualified. We appeal to all milieus to begin work immediately on a program of reforms. KSS "KOR" announces its readiness to participate in these projects and discussions.

V. Radical but only short-term changes in industrial investment policy have already been announced. In the past, mistakes in this area have played a major role in the emergence of the present economic crisis. The perspectives of a long-term balanced policy in this area are still open, however, and they should be subject to a national discussion, as should the role and rights of central and regional economic authorities, the degree of independence of plants, the extent of production in the private and artisan sectors, production cooperatives, the activities and rights of employee self-management, and other issues. "Solidarity" must play an important part in the decision-making process on all these issues.

VI. The restoration of healthy relations in the villages is of central importance. The owners of individual family farms must recover the possibility of efficient and profitable work, on which the feeding of the nation depends. These farms should be allowed to grow, for example, through the breaking up of those deficit state farms and pseudo-cooperatives which do not promise quick improvement. The hereditary ownership of land and the right to its sale and purchase should be guaranteed. The allocation of tools, animal feed, fuel, fertilizers, and building materials should be directed above all to privately owned farms, which is justified by their productivity and the efficiency of their output. Organized and independent individual farmers should be given the opportunity to protect and develop the great traditions of the Polish peasantry, as well as to defend their own interests.

VII. The state of education and the fate of teachers deserve particular care. The current curricula do not reflect our needs and are not congruent with the principles of modern pedagogy. Teachers are subjected to political pressure and discrimination, are overworked, and are burdened with too much administrative responsibility. All of this leads to their discouragement and does not promote improvement in their qualifications. Until recently all of this was aggravated by exceptionally low salaries and insufficient supplies in the schools. As the result of a decisive protest, which culminated in an occupational strike of teachers who were members of NSZZ "Solidarity," a decision was reached to increase the expenditures for education in the budget. Thus, we might expect a certain gradual improvement in this area, but we must remember that this is just a first step on the road to rescue education.

VIII. The neglect of the health care system is extremely painful. Funds from public collections in Poland and abroad are used for showy investments such as the Child Health Center, while the general state of hospitals, especially pediatric and psychiatric hospitals, is constantly worsening, and plans to increase the number of hospital beds were never implemented. Thoughtless and harmful decisions to liquidate certain institutions led last year to a hunger strike by patients in one of the Warsaw hospitals. The availability of medicines was never worse. The salaries of health care employees has been alarmingly low; this applies to orderlies and nurses as well as to young doctors and experienced specialists. In this situation it is no exaggeration to claim that outpatient and hospital care in Poland is being largely supported by the conscious dedication of health service employees. Just as in the case of education, certain specific steps to improve the state of health care were taken only as a result of a decisive protest supported by an occupational strike.

IX. Recently a whole series of abuses committed by functionaries of the organs of authority have been revealed. The popularity of this phenomenon testifies to the fact that it could not have remained unknown to the prosecutor's office. No beneficial changes in the general situation are possible without fundamental changes in the justice system and the investigative organs. The rule of law is an indispensable condition for stabilization. It is necessary to expose those responsible for the concealment of abuses, for the beatings of students in March 1968, for the massacre of workers on the Coast in 1970, for the tortures committed against workers in Ursus and Radom in 1976. It is necessary to guarantee the independence of courts, and to subject the activities of the Security Service and the Prosecutor's office to social control.

X. These are the basic proposals for current action—and not all of them.

If these issues are not addressed, our existence as a nation may be endangered. Programs of reforms should be published in the press and in other mass media. Public opinion has a right to judge specific suggestions originating from the authorities, from specialists, and from society at large. It is necessary to develop methods that will lead to a continuing dialogue between the authorities and society.

XI. KSS "KOR" has on many occasions warned public opinion against the catastrophic effects of the policies of the authorities over the past several years, while also warning society against reckless demonstrations and acts of desperation. We wish to express our admiration for the wisdom of the workers who have fought in a responsible and effective manner for their own rights and for the rights of the entire nation. We speak out today in full consciousness of our civic responsibility and full awareness of the dramatic situation.

KSS "KOR" is composed of people of various ideologies. We are united by our common concern for the independent existence of the nation, a striving for democracy and the rule of law in Poland, a struggle against lawlessness, and by the defense of human and civil rights. We speak out and we shall continue to speak out on political matters when they are relevant to the goals mentioned above, which govern KSS "KOR." We are not speaking out against a system that would be based on social justice and real social control of the industrial means of production.

We appeal for a continuation of the process of democratization which began with the signing of social contracts. There is no other path for us.

Social Self-Defense Committee "KOR"

Warsaw, September 23, 1981

STATEMENT

In the summer of 1978, an action began to help workers persecuted for their participation in the June strikes. On September 23, 1976, we formed the Workers' Defense Committee, which was to work for this purpose. We constituted a group of people holding various political opinions and representing a variety of ideologies. We were united by the conviction that the most proper way to stop the lawlessness was by means of solidary social action and the creation of independent social institutions to express the will of social groups and effectively defend their civil rights. Our action was based on the conviction that civil and human rights are inalienable, and our awareness of the fact that every society must defend itself against coercion. During the next year we organized financial, medical, and legal aid for thousands of workers who had been dismissed from their jobs, beaten in MO headquarters, and arrested.

In September 1977, after all the workers from Radom and Ursus had been released, the Workers' Defense Committee decided that it was necessary to extend its goals and tasks in such a manner as to encompass all people from all social strata and groups who were being deprived of their rights and left unprotected. At that time the Workers' Defense Committee adopted the name of Social Self-Defense Committee "KOR," and formulated four basic goals for its activity:

1. To struggle against repressions used for reasons of conscience, politics, religion, or race, and to give aid to those persecuted for these reasons.
2. To struggle against violations of the rule of law, and to help those who have been wronged.
3. To fight for the institutional protection of civil rights and freedoms.
4. To support and defend all social initiatives aiming to realize human and civil rights.

The strength of our movement lay in human solidarity. Generous help on the part of defenders of human and civil rights in Poland and abroad, especially of Poles living abroad, provided material support for our activity, ranging from aid to those who were illegally deprived of their jobs to the support of many serious initiatives. However, our activity would not have been possible were it not for the democratic movement which grew and developed around us into hundreds and thousands of associates and activists. Paying no heed to persecutions and various police repressions, searches, arrests, and frequent beatings, they printed and distributed our documents and statements, collected and transmitted information, founded and directed independent periodicals such as the *Information Bulletin, Biuletyn Dolnośląski, Głos, Krytyka, Puls, Robotnik,* and finally the distinguished publishing center NOWa. They distributed hundreds of thousands of leaflets informing society about the need for self-defense as a reaction to the illegal behavior of the police, the Security Service, and the justice system. They established numerous contacts with workers, peasants, students, and members of the intelligentsia, contacts which in many cases grew into permanent ties. They stood before courts and sentencing boards for misdemeanors accused not of their real activity but of hooliganism or brawling.

It was thanks to them that we were able to establish the Intervention Bureau which provided aid to persecuted people who appealed to it from all across Poland. Thanks to them, we were able to organize the information bank that helped to break down the barrier of silence and falsehood surrounding all violations of the law perpetrated by the authorities of a state which signed the Covenant on Civil and Political Rights. In a word, it was thanks to these people that we were able for years to fulfill the role in the service of which we called ourselves the Social Self-Defense Committee.

We were not subjected to the toughest trials: we could act above all because of social support. We owe much to the late Cardinal Stefan Wyszynski, the Primate of Poland, who often defended us against persecutions; and we also owe much to the other moral authorities from the world of science and culture in Poland and abroad. We were deeply convinced that only an open challenge to lawlessness could bring about the defeat of this lawlessness, and that a final end to this lawlessness could be accomplished only by an *entire* society which stands in solidarity against coercion used against any group of citizens or any individual citizen.

Today, the truly powerful tools of social self-defense are the independent social institutions, and above all NSZZ "Solidarity," which is an authentic representative of society. When we first engaged in our open and unequal struggle, we did not expect such a rapid fulfillment of our vision of a society which would generally demand independence, self-government, justice, control over the economy and over decisions by the authorities, democracy and openness in social life, a fundamental widening of freedom of thought and of speech, access to the mass media, and an end to reprisals against people whose views are not shared by the authorities. If the government will live up to its social agreement, all decisions shaping the lives of Polish citizens will not be discussed on the highest levels with delegates of the many million strong "Solidarity."

NSZZ "Solidarity" has created and is forming many agencies and commissions designed to take up issues with which the Social Self-Defense Committee "KOR" has been dealing for the past several years to the best of its ability and strength. Many members and associates of the Committee are today members of "Solidarity," often working for "Solidarity" either as experts or simply as people with many years of experience.

We believe that everyone who ever shared the goals of the Workers' Defense Committee and later of the Social Self-Defence Committee should today support "Solidarity" to the extent of his ability and talent, and be active in its ranks or on its behalf. We believe that today society is ready to promote changes in our country, which has been devastated by totalitarianism, corruption, and the lawlessness of the authorities. We believe that today, during the First Congress and the first democratic elections to positions of authority in "Solidarity," the struggle for the renewal of the Polish Commonwealth should be entrusted to its forces and intentions.

On this fifth anniversary of the creation of the Workers' Defense Committee, we regard our activity as concluded. No one can claim that this decision has been dictated by fear of dishonest attacks from the official Polish or foreign propaganda. In making this decision we remain fully faithful to the values we tried always to serve: honesty and truth.

There were among us people of various generations, traditions, and ideological orientations. We were united by our concern for all those who were beaten and wronged. We wanted to bear witness to this, regardless of personal danger or political tactics, and regardless of who was being persecuted. We were guided by our belief that "without an independent Poland on the map, there can be no just Europe."

We have served the cause of Polish freedom, and the freedom of Poles in Poland, to the best of our ability, as our consciences and a civic understanding of the situation dictated. We were guided by an ideal of a Poland which could once be proud of its tolerance and freedom, of a Poland which could be a common fatherland for Poles, Belorussians, Lithuanians, Ukrainians, and Jews, a fatherland for all its citizens, regardless of their language, religion, or national origin. It is not for us to judge our own work. We wanted only for it to be a contribution to the great national task: the creation of an independent, just, and democratic Poland.

Social Self-Defense Committee "KOR"

Jerzy Andrzejewski, Stanisław Barańczak, Konrad Bieliński, Seweryn Blumsztajn, Bogdan Borusewicz, Andrzej Celiński, Mirosław Chojecki, Ludwik Cohn, Jerzy Ficowski, Rev. Zbigniew Kamiński, Wiesław Piotr Kęcik, Jan Kielanowski, Leszek Kołakowski, Anka Kowalska, Jacek Kuroń, Edward Lipiński, Jan Józef Lipski, Jan Lityński, Antoni Macierewicz, Adam Michnik, Halina Mikołajska, Ewa Milewicz, Piotr Naimski, Wojciech Onyszkiewicz, Antoni Pajdak, Zbigniew Romaszewski, Józef Rybicki, Aniela Steinsbergowa, Józef Śreniowski, Maria Wosiek, Henryk Wujec, Rev. Jan Zieja.

Notes

Introduction

1. Should anyone object to the placing of *Robotnik* right next to the Initiating Committees of Free Trade Unions, let me only recall what Lech Wałęsa, who was generally reticent toward KOR, said during the "Solidarity" Convention in the fall of 1980: "I also grew out of the KOR movement"; not to mention the various remarks of Anna Walentynowicz and others.

1: Prehistory of KOR

1. See chap. 1 n. 5.

2. Prof. Lipiński was the last person to get rid of his party card—and he did so during the period of KOR's existence. Lipiński was the only person in KOR who remained a communist in any sense, for he sympathized with its Eurocommunist variant.

3. As a co-organizer of the "Letter of 34," Jan Józef Lipski was detained for forty-eight hours, a practice which at that time was rarely used against intellectuals.

4. After a time, the club moved to the House of Culture in the Old Town in Warsaw, the same place in which the Club of the Crooked Circle had been active before its dissolution.

5. After the war, Manturzewski and Lipski organized a youth club called the "Neo-Pickwickians," and in 1953, during the dark Stalinist days, they participated in the activities of an illegal club of a dozen or so young scholars who attempted to conduct group studies in the social sciences, and who formulated (even before Djilas, in 1953) the concept of the "new class." The club was broken up by the Security Service; its founder, Czesław Czapow, was arrested, although luckily this happened during a period of slight improvement and slow liberalization of the general situation after the death of Stalin. The members of this club formed the core of the group active in *Po prostu* early in 1957, which finally took over the leadership of the Club of the Crooked Circle.

6. The justification of the sentence in Blajfer's trial contained an unusual curiosity: immediately after citing a leaflet entitled "Fascism will not pass, there is no return to Stalinism," there occurred the following sentence: "This kind of information has all the characteristics of false information in the sense of Art. 23, Para. 1 of the Small Criminal Code."

7. One should mention that Rejtan was a significant precursor, an eighteenth-century deputy to the Diet who resorted to a hopeless demonstration—lying down in the doorway of the Diet chamber—in an attempt to prevent the ratification of the partition of Poland.

8. Wujec was connected with the work of the committee from the very beginning; together with the Band of Vagabonds, he organized aid for the workers of Ursus.

9. The text of this letter was published in *Aneks*, no. 12 (1976), 45–59.

2: *"June Events" of 1976*

1. In later trials the accusation of theft was common, but KOR was never able to find any trace of the group that had broken the store windows.

2. The same method of beating had been used in 1970 after the December demonstrations in Gdańsk. The "path of health" is a gruesome joke, since it also refers to the jogging courses used for health or in training. This punishment has its own tradition: it is the same as the "punishment of clubs" used in the Russian army in the nineteenth century, which often ended in death or permanent injury. Poles forced to serve in the Russian army were often victims of this punishment.

3. This is an organ of the administration, not a court, although it does have the powers of a court in passing sentences of up to three months imprisonment and levying fines of up to 5,000 zlotys. These boards are staffed not by professional judges but by nominated persons, most often retired functionaries of the police and Security Service. A police officer acts as prosecutor; defense is not always allowed.

3: *Founding of the Workers' Defense Committee*

1. This is a paradox: Poland was at that time (in the 1930s) ruled by a dictatorship, even if a relatively mild and nontotalitarian dictatorship; it was a dictatorship nevertheless, directed against the communists, among others.

2. Both this and other documents mentioned below were published in *Aneks*, No. 12 (1976), 35–45.

3. See *Aneks*, no. 12 (1976), 37.

4. Adam Michnik was excluded from all activities very early on. An attempt to obtain from Jean-Paul Sartre an invitation for Michnik to visit France was successful, and there were strong indications that he would receive a passport, which was indeed the case. In this situation it was clear that the propaganda and organizational possibilities Michnik would have in the West would be of greater value to the KOR milieu than his work in the relief action, where it was possible to replace him. Thus it was decided that he should not become conspicuous to the Security Service before he left Poland. After his departure Michnik did a lot of good for KOR in the West, demonstrating tremendous energy and intelligence, and a grasp of the situation. He formally became a member of the committee just prior to his return to Poland in May 1977.

5. The intensification of surveillance in September indicated that the committee, which was still in the process of formation, had only a minimal chance of holding another meeting. As a result, a different technique was adopted: each proposal was presented to all interested parties by couriers (usually other members of KOR), and opinions and suggested amendments to the text were collected in this manner, so that later, after re-editing, the next "circulation" could take place. During the first months of KOR's existence, all the documents of the committee, including the initial ones, were composed in this arduous manner.

6. This action was initiated by Władysław Winawer, the defender of Kazimierz Moczarski.

7. Obviously this was true for only as long as the police did not move against the committee as a whole. The general opinion was that a young member of KOR, as a less anonymous person, would be safer than an informal associate.

8. The chairman of each meeting was nominated during KOR gatherings. This role was played by a number of people, most often by Ludwik Cohn.

9. In Prof. Lipiński's apartment, which became the meeting place for the entire committee, there was barely enough room for the actual number of KOR members, and then only because there were always a few absences even at the more populous meetings.

4: Ethos of the Workers' Defense Committee

1. It must be said that, as is usually the case in such situations, it will not be possible to present the role of the wives of the KOR members exhaustively and exactly; they bore the principal consequences of their husbands' and their own involvement, despite the fact that they were more rarely detained and that the prosecutors did not present them with warrants for their arrest. Anyone who had had some experience in these matters knows that it is better to be the one who is arrested than the one who is left at home to carry on the responsibility for the family, and often for the social work left by the husband as well. (*Editor's note:* Grażyna Borucka-Kuroń, who was freed from an internment camp for reasons of health, died in November 1982.)

5: From the Founding of KOR to the Death of Pyjas

1. Zofia and Zbigniew Romaszewski had gradually taken over matters connected with organizing help for the prisoners; they were formally put in charge of this area of activity when the Intervention Bureau of KOR was created.

2. The authorities visibly tried to cut off the defendants from attorneys that had not been provided by the court.

3. The speeches of the defense attorneys, published among others in the KOR publication *In the Name of the Polish People's Republic*, belong today among the basic documents of this period.

4. In Poland, the positions of chairmen of public service associations are in practice staffed by nomination.

5. An unemployed person in the Polish People's Republic becomes a second-class citizen; a person punitively dismissed from work immediately loses the right to use socialized medical services; if he is fired for any other reason, he loses these rights after a few months. If the person is waiting for a cooperative apartment, for which he has already paid a significant sum of money, he can forget all hope of ever receiving what he deserves. An unemployed person may register at the state employment agency, but this will not result in the payment of unemployment compensation. This issue has never been taken care of, despite the fact that in many occupations unemployment has existed for years. A policeman who checks the identity papers of an unemployed person (on the identity card there is a stamp from the place of work) immediately becomes more severe and ruthless than on the average, and this is a general practice.

6. Such a blow, well known to criminals and to specially trained commandoes, usually causes a concussion.

7. This sentence should not be understood as a moral apology for a Supreme Court that appears impotent but well intentioned and full of a sense of justice. On the contrary, this court, with the rare exception of cases too shocking in their absurdity, has upheld the decisions of the lower court. The speeches of attorneys for the defense in the Radom and Ursus cases heard in the Supreme Court can serve not only as indictments against the police and the Security Service but also indirectly against the Supreme Court itself. Nonetheless, among the many members of the Supreme Court there must have been only a few trusted judges who followed orders, since in the trials the same names occurred over and over again: Polony, Pustelniak, Młynkiewicz, Matysiak. These people are just as responsible for the fate of the Radom and Ursus workers as those who beat them with clubs in the "paths of health." Morally they are perhaps even more repulsive. Even in the lower courts, only selected judges are allowed to try such cases. Thus, the same judges would constantly reappear. In Radom, Judge Elżbieta Dobrowolska was in the forefront: a still young, energetic, and even aggressive woman whose appearance harmonized well with the term used by the Radom workers to describe her, though this referred to her morality rather than her looks.

8. *Information Bulletin* no. 8 (February 1977), a special edition entitled *Radom: June 1976.*

9. KOR came across him more than once. He was an expert in particularly improbable, but important cases, who always established that the impossible was possible and certified it with the authority of his medical degree. Prof. Zdzisław Marek also made himself known in connection with the death of Stanisław Pyjas and with the death of a man killed in police headquarters (the Tarnów trial).

10. The first case—of Stanisław Pietraszko—will be discussed further in connection with the death of Stanisław Pyjas.

11. See *Aneks* no. 13/14 (1977), 93–94.

12. The *Madrid Report* appeared in English under the title *Prologue to Gdansk,* published by the Institute of Polish Affairs in Great Britain and the U.S. Helsinki Watch Committee, an American citizens' committee on Helsinki among whose members are many distinguished American intellectuals. Earlier, the Institute of Polish Affairs had prepared at great speed a selection of materials several dozens of pages long, which was delivered to all the delegations participating in

the Conference on Security and Cooperation in Europe taking place in Madrid in November 1980.

13. This diocese, led by Bishop Ignacy Tokarczuk (a seminary classmate of the future Pope John Paul II), distinguished itself by the building of dozens of "illegal" churches without receiving permission from the authorities and despite obstacles imposed by the administration and the Security Service.

14. [*Editor's note:* This pamphlet was published in the West by *Aneks* (London, 1977).]

15. The signatories were: Daniel Bell, Włodzimierz Brus, Mary McCarthy, Robert Conquest, Pierre Emmanuel, Gustaw Herling-Grudziński, Leszek Kołakowski, Edward Lipiński (the only signatory from Poland), Golo Mann, Czesław Miłosz, Iris Murdoch, Denis de Rougemont, Laurent Schwartz, Ignazio Silone, Piotr Słonimski, and Alfred Tarski.

16. Rybicki, who was very pained by the anti-Semitic campaign of 1968, was not aware at the time of the role Moczulski had played in *Stolica*.

17. But without anti-Semitism, with a moderate nationalist ideology, without a trace of fascist ideas, without Russophile tendencies. One might ask in this situation why the Young Poland Movement has been described as "neo-endecja" (National Democratic party in Poland before World War II)? This results primarily from their acceptance of the rest of this ideology, as manifested itself externally in their appeal to the ideas of Roman Dmowski.

18. This was KOR's name for various false leaflets and letters and other such mystifications which usually originated from the Security Service or circles related to it.

19. This is the same high school from which came the student scouts of the Black Troop No. 1 who played an enormous role in the history of KOR.

20. This commission, nominated by the government, approves academic degrees as a compliant political agency. The nature of the decisions made by this agency is well characterized by a conversation between Ryszard Bender, a deputy to the Diet and at the same time a professor at the Catholic University in Lublin, and Kazimierz Kąkol, the minister for religious affairs. Kąkol stated directly that the authorities could not approve the habilitation of Łukasz Czuma since he had signed a political letter, specifically the letter from students and employees of the Catholic University and associates of the Academic Ministry concerning the creation of a special Diet commission.

21. After August 1980 the Polish Scouting Union did not try to raise the issue of their rehabilitation and return to the organization.

22. Anticipating events a little, we might mention already that a short time later KOR activists were indeed accused of common crimes.

23. There, one does not say "in the cell."

24. Such books were seized during a search in the apartment of Władysław Bartoszewski, who was working, among other things, on a history of the Jews under the Nazi occupation, and in the apartment of the Naimskis: Małgorzata Naimska is a Hebrew scholar.

25. [London: Puls Publications, 1981—*Editor's note.*]

26. Those who did not like the committee often referred to KOR members as "korniki" (borers), which was taken more as a joke than as an insult.

27. How this was done is illustrated by an anecdote: "Tadzio, tell me, how do you spell 'Zionist'?" "I don't know, but before the war it was spelled with Ż" (in Polish the word for "Jew" is "Żyd").

6: *The Death of Pyjas to the Transformation of KOR*

1. It is true that the links between this newspaper and the Security Service were never so intimate as between 1968 and 1980.

2. The picture of Mirek Chojecki and KOR associate Pawel Bakowski carrying black flags at the head of the demonstration was seen around the world.

3. A kind of house arrest in which gradually everyone who comes to a given apartment is arrested.

4. The numbers in parentheses refer to the relevant articles of the Criminal Code:

Art. 11 § 1. Whoever intends to commit a prohibited act and behaves in a manner leading directly to the commission of this act is responsible for the attempt, even if the act does not take place.

§ 2. Attempt occurs also when the perpetrator is unaware that the commission of this act is impossible because of the lack of a subject against whom the crime could be committed, or because of the use of means which are unsuitable for the planned act.

Art. 58. In the event of conviction for a continuous crime, the court can impose a penalty up to the highest provided for by the regulations increased by one half, but without exceeding the maximum limits for a given type of penalty.

Art. 132. A polish citizen who enters into an understanding with a person acting on behalf of a foreign organization in order to harm the political interests of the Polish People's Republic is subject to imprisonment for a period of not less than six months nor more than five years.

Art. 271 § 1. Whomever disseminates false information which might seriously harm the interests of the Polish People's Republic is subject to imprisonment for up to three years.

§ 2. If the perpetrator commits the crime described in § 1 while abroad, or transmits information described in § 1 to a foreign center conducting activities against the political interests of the Polish People's Republic, he is subject to imprisonment for a period of not less than six months nor more than five years.

Art. 273 § 1. Whoever commits an act described in Articles 270–272 using printing or other mass media means is subject to imprisonment for a period of not less than one year nor more than ten years.

§ 2. Whoever prepares, stores, transports, carries, or mails a manuscript, printed matter, or other object containing contents described in Articles 270–272, in order to disseminate them, is subject to imprisonment for a period of not less than six months nor more than five years.

§ 3. In the case of a conviction for a crime described in § 1 or § 2, the court may decide the case on the basis of tools or other objects which were not the property of the perpetrator but were used in the commission of the crime.

5. Jacek Bocheński, Kazimierz Brandys, Marian Brandys, Witold Dąbrowski, Andrzej Drawicz, Jerzy Ficowski, Andrzej Grzegorczyk, Anna Kamieńska, Andrzej Kijowski, Tadeusz Kowalik, Bohdan Kosiński, Seweryn Pollak, Julian Stryjkowski, Anna Trojanowska, Wanda Wiłkomirska, Wiktor Woroszylski, Maria Zagórska.

6. This letter was signed by Rev. Dr. Tadeusz Styczeń, Dr. Jerzy Gałkowski, Rev. Tadeusz Szostak, and Sister Teresa Wojtarowicz.

7. Because of the future role which the signatories of this letter were to play in Solidarity, their names are perhaps worth citing: Maria Dziewicka, Bronisław Geremek, Helena Hagemejer, Tadeusz Kowalik, Karol Modzelewski, and Jan Strzelecki.

8. In the light of the information provided at the time by Bishop Dąbrowski, it seems unjustified to attribute a special role to the intervention of Iwaszkiewicz in Lipski's release, especially since this intervention took place on the day of Lipski's release and could not have brought about such immediate results.

9. Obviously, Szechter's letter was published not by *Trybuna Ludu* but by the uncensored press.

10. The burden of reprisals was shifted to wage discrimination and the extraction of court costs regardless of the material situation of the convict.

11. *Information Bulletin* No. 10 of May 1977 and No. 11 of the same month, as well as No. 12 of June and a large part of No. 13/14 which was dated July/August.

12. In January 1978, Jan Józef Lipski had to undergo heart surgery.

13. When the Funds Council was nominated, Prof. Jan Kielanowski was not yet a member of KOR.

14. For example, Bogusław Sonik, the chairman of the Małopolska region delegation to the First Congress of Solidarity in Gdańsk.

15. Marek Tarniewski was the pen name of Jakub Karpiński. The work published by NOWa was the first chapter of a book known in Poland as *The New Regime and the Revolution*, which was published in Paris as *Evolution or Revolution* (Literary Institute, 1975).

16. *Information Bulletin* No. 38 of June 1980.

17. Here praise is due to the weekly *Polityka*, which described Niedźwiedzki's case and thus prevented a repetition of this kind of lawless behavior.

18. The letter from Tadeusz Mitak sent to KOR on September 26, 1977, can serve as an example: "I work in the Radom Automobile Repair Enterprises, in the PS Department. I am a transport employee. On September 22, 1977, the foreman directed me to take two engines to the bases in the brake department. I finished this work at approximately 6:30 P.M. At approximately 8:00 P.M. I entered the brake department to return the repair key. The brake department was empty, but I noticed torn warranty cards of engines, scattered tools, and broken bottles. One of the workers' lockers was open. All this was witnessed by Jarosław Wolak, who entered the brake department together with me. I informed the foreman, Głowacki, about this matter. At 11:00 A.M. on the following morning, a functionary of the police, Lieutenant Korczak, came to my house together with the commander of the Industrial Guard. They took me to the shop, where

I was interrogated together with the workers on the second shift. During the interrogation, Lieutenant Korczak, despite my explanations that I had nothing to do with the damage, threatened me with a sentence for sabotage if I would not admit to being guilty. Then I was handcuffed, as were three other workers, and driven to the City Headquarters of the police in Radom. At the headquarters I was beaten and kicked. There were demands that I plead guilty to actions I did not commit. A man detained in some other case, whose name was Sobol, was beaten in my presence until he was unconscious. I was released after forty-eight hours. During my absence my apartment was searched. During the search, a functionary of the police insulted my parents' lodger by calling her a prostitute. I believe that the illegal treatment to which I was subjected is to a great extent connected with the sentence I received for participating in the events of June 1976. I am asking the Workers' Defense Committee for protection. On many occasions I was stopped by functionaries of the police and treated very aggressively. Since my six-year sentence has been suspended for five years, I am afraid that the police are striving to imprison me again."

19. Władysław Bieńkowski was a prewar communist. During the war he was an outstanding participant in the communist resistance movement. As a friend of Gomułka, he twice played an important political role: once immediately after the war, and again after October 1956, as minister of education. He parted with Gomułka as a result of their divergent conceptions of policy towards the Church (on many issues Bieńkowski represented the most liberal position in the country). Bieńkowski is the author of several political books (published abroad), in which he sharply criticized the social, political, and economic aspects of the system. Andrzej Kijowski is one of the most distinguished literary critics in Poland; an outstanding essayist and prose writer, he was, during this period, publishing his works mainly in the Catholic *Tygodnik Powszechny*. Stefan Kisielewski is one of the most popular figures in Polish intellectual life: a writer, an excellent feuilletonist in *Tygodnik Powszechny*, a composer, and an adherent of liberal ideas.

7: *Transformation of KOR to the Initiating Committees*

1. We must add—and the careful reader will have noticed proof of this—that the labor courts did occasionally hand down verdicts against the state employer. It seems that the judges in the sector of the justice system were less carefully selected from the point of view of compliance with orders and degree of opportunism.

2. Yet another title with reference to tradition, except this time it is not entirely clear what tradition; the weekly *Głos* published around the turn of the century was in the nineteenth century an organ of a group that slowly worked out a nationalist program, while in the twentieth century it was taken over by a very different group of radical left-wing intelligentsia. This ambivalence and lack of clarity proved to be a dangerous inheritance.

3. In other libraries, for example the Warsaw University Library, the designation for this was "cim," which stood for "cimelia."

4. Andrzej Celiński, at that time not yet thirty, was jokingly called "Rector" or "His Magnificence."

5. As was usually the case with the groups described in this book, this time also the name was drawn from tradition. The Society for Scientific Courses was an institution that continued the Flying University openly and legally during the period of the 1905 revolution under the Russian partition; it began to conduct academic studies, though as yet without state certification or the title of a university.

6. An organ of this association.

7. The Intervention Bureau was especially pedantic in investigating cases involving placement in a psychiatric hospital, both because of the practice of abusing psychiatry by the Security Services in the USSR and because similar attempts had been observed in Poland. Luckily, they were sporadic and unsuccessful, largely thanks to the efforts of the Polish Psychiatric Association.

8. The *Documents of Lawlessness* testify to the fact that this was not the only incident of this kind. The *Documents* describe a case involving four streetcar passengers beaten by the police and then accused of a hooligan assault on a functionary of the police. The incident and the beating occurred because the wife of a minor police officer traveling with her husband tripped over the prosthesis of one of the passengers. Two women were among those beaten. But the case of the "Theatre of the Eighth Day" had a different character because it was not so accidental, and began because the accused were being followed.

8: *Initiating Committee to Pilgrimage of Pope John Paul II*

1. In West Germany, Sulecki became an activist of the émigré Polish Socialist party. He testified as a witness on Polish violations of the Helsinki Agreements before a congressional commission of the United States. He made a good impression with his factual and authentic answers.

2. Anna Walentynowicz spoke about this a little in the film, *Workers 80*.

3. It has to be admitted that he indeed gave a slap (on the behind, with a badminton racket) to a child hitting a small tree with the racket. Even if one agrees with the fact that he had no right to apply physical punishment to someone else's child, the sentence seems to be an exaggeration.

4. In the PRL such "firearms" also require permits.

5. Since there were sometimes fears that KOR could be exposed to the risk of transmitting information that was not true (police beatings were treated by the young associates almost like a medal), the victim was required to submit to a medical examination in order to receive a medical certificate; and in any case, independently of the doctor's examination, the victim should lodge a complaint in the prosecutor's office concerning the commission of a crime, despite the fact that the prosecutor's office either would not react or would do so only perfunctorily, without attempting even to interrogate the plaintiff.

6. Councillor Siła-Nowicki was an officer of the Kedyw, the Diversionary Command in the Home Army.

7. The peasants clearly associated this with the system of granting retirement

privileges to those of them who were giving their land to the government. Since 1956, when Gomułka not only slowed down the collectivization of agriculture but also made possible the dissolution of those collective farms which the peasants did not want to preserve, the countryside has lived and continues to live in fear of a return to the policies of collectivization, reacting very nervously to any signs suggesting this possibility.

8. KOR was represented by Ludwik Dorn, Wiesław Kęcik (who was to become a member of the Committee a short while later and who dealt with peasant issues), Jan Józef Lipski, and Andrzej Zozula (a son of one of the elder activists of the peasant movement, and a cosigner of the memorandum on the pension law for individual farmers).

9. Anna Godzalanka-Bojarowa was an activist of Wici, before the war; after the war was a member of the Peasant party, a deputy to the Diet, and deputy minister of education, as well as voivode of Lublin.

10. Zdzisław Ostatek was the future chairman of the Temporary Initiating Committee of Rural Solidarity.

11. This day, the Green Holiday, is the traditional holiday of the peasant political movement.

12. Alumni of the Main School of Rural Economy had to wage a hard battle, which ended in a compromise, in order to preserve the traditional name of the school.

13. The archives contain an announcement to the effect that the lecture had been called off. It is smeared with blood.

14. The recurring word "goalie" attracts attention here. In today's slang this is the name for a bouncer, an employee of a restaurant or night club who is responsible for removing troublesome or impolite customers. A more detailed explanation of the function of a "goalie" is contained in the weekly *Kultura* of September 2, 1979, in an article by Grzegorz Nawrocki entitled "Goalies," which describes the criminal practices of this milieu: extorting ransom, or "penalties" confiscated into one's pocket, for things such as breaking a glass, and above all, beatings, including some which resulted in an 8 cm. fracture of the skull and paralysis of one side of the face.

15. It is perhaps worth noting that Prof. Szczepański made his appearance in the *Information Bulletin* as the protagonist of a note, "Prof. Szczepański Denounces . . . "; during a meeting of the Diet Commission on Culture, Prof. Szczepański made a speech against uncensored publications because . . . they used up paper, which was in short supply.

16. Borusewicz, Chojecki, Macierewicz, and Narożniak were especially famous in KOR for their ability to escape the police.

17. This is by no means common in Poland (especially in the older generation). Poles frequently accuse the Czechs of taking over a part of Zaolzie after World War I, while Poland was engaged in war with Soviet Russia, despite the fact that a plebiscite was supposed to decide which country this area should belong to. Later, in 1938, Poland took this area away from the Czechs—unfortunately, at a time of mortal danger to the Czechoslovak state from Nazi Germany. In addition to these complaints, there is the more recent memory of Poland playing the role of an occupier alongside other armies of the Warsaw Pact in

1968, and stifling the desire of the Czech and Slovak nations for democracy. On the other hand, Poles often stress with antipathy the reluctance of the Czechs to fight for their independence in an armed struggle. Luckily, so far we have not yet gotten into an armed uprising against the Soviet authorities.

18. Dr. Jaroslav Šabata (fifty years old) is a psychologist, a former member of the Communist party, and was even a secretary of the Czechoslovak Communist party in the important region of Brno, and one of the leaders of the Prague Spring. In 1972 he was sentenced to six and a half years in prison. He was released early, after serving five years. He was in Sudety as one of the spokesmen of Chapter 77.

19. In 1982 the author accidentally met in London a young Czech woman who turned out to have been this unknown telephone caller.

20. We will return to this initiative later.

21. A teacher of Polish punitively transferred from the Rejtan High School for signing a petition to form a Diet commission to investigate the events of June 1976.

22. Rector Rybicki became famous in 1968 by introducing police detachments into the university grounds, and then by large-scale repressions against students and faculty members.

23. Article 270 § 1 of the Criminal Code states: "Whoever slanders, maligns, or degrades the Polish Nation, the Polish People's Republic, its system, or its leading institutions, is subject to imprisonment for a period of not less than six months nor more than eight years."

24. See chap. 6 n. 4.

9: From Pope John Paul II to Signing of Gdańsk Agreements

1. For example, a worker seen by a supervisor who was not dressed in his work clothes five minutes before starting work would be given a tardy slip.

2. As July of that year demonstrated, the locomotive shop played a key role in the general strike in Lublin.

3. Article 276 § 1. Whoever participates in an association for the purpose of committing a crime is subject to imprisonment for a period of not less than six months nor more than five years.

§ 2. If the association involves the use of arms, the perpetrator can be sentenced to imprisonment for a period of not less than one year nor more than eight years.

§ 3. Whoever organizes or leads an association as described in § 1 or § 2 is subject to imprisonment for a period of not less than two years nor more than ten years.

4. This was a period of particular difficulty as far as the supply of electrical power was concerned; nevertheless, the idea this time was to prevent the workers on the first shift, who end their workday in the shipyard at 2:00 P.M., from attending the celebrations.

5. This was demonstrated to some extent in the polemic between Kuroń and Hall.

6. For example, KOR teams handing out leaflets on various occasions, often in front of churches, were instructed not to distribute them on the church grounds, not only not during a Mass, but simply never, even though this increased the danger to the distributors.

7. The text published in the *Information Bulletin, Communiqué* No. 33, makes reference to "the society . . . of central and eastern Europe," but this is a typographical error; KOR did not believe that such a society existed, nor did it wish for one to exist. But it is no accident that the document refers to "central and eastern Europe": people in Poland do not like for Poland to be regarded as a part of Eastern Europe, despite the fact that today this is a political reality.

8. Chwalewski was the author of an appeal to the Diet to hold a referendum concerning changes in the Polish Constitution, and was also a signatory of the *Charter of Workers' Rights.*

9. A worker convicted in 1976 to one of the longest prison terms (nine years).

10. The cable contains an error regarding the date on which the fast began: April 15. Only after Chojecki left the prison was it known that he had begun his hunger strike on April 8. He had been force-fed.

11. Various ages were cited for these people in various documents. Here the data is taken from a KOR statement, since the information officially cited by the committee was generally checked carefully.

12. There was no explanation of why the subordinates of the court in Stalowa Wola suspected that usually the court there acted otherwise.

13. These two activists are not related; the similarity between their names is accidental.

14. The leaflets would fall from a roof after the nylon string holding them together was burned through by an attached Marlboro cigarette.

15. This city was not included in the plan of action, but one of the teams distributing leaflets ended up there after escaping from agents of the Security Service, and decided that there would be no harm if the residents of Iława were to gain a little from this as well.

16. In spite of the weakening of contacts with the Czechs, as a result of the increased state of alert among the security apparatuses of both countries, it was still possible to maintain some links.

17. Those who took part in the fast or were connected with it in some other capacity know well the name of this person.

18. Zieja was very much opposed to the use of such terms when KOR matters were being discussed, but sometimes this could not be helped.

19. The number of people who did not participate in previous elections was certainly much higher than the figure quoted officially; nevertheless, this was a minority, which does not mean that those who did vote were truly "for" the candidates.

20. Without using this term, it speaks of "those who take great risks and very courageously use a variety of methods—though without resorting to force or coercion—to fight for justice, human dignity, and basic human rights in the new society."

21. The naming of these nations was a result of the fact that there was specific information about individuals under arrest there.

22. The case of the Kowalczyk brothers kept returning to the agenda of social life in Poland, at meetings of the Polish PEN Club and the Polish Writers' Union, among others, as well as in the statements of KOR and its press. No one was surprised that the planting of explosives should be punished with prison terms, and the defense of the Kowalczyks did not signify approval of their act. This was always emphasized. Nevertheless, the act was committed in a manner that precluded any injury or loss of life; while a sentence of twenty-five years meant the complete ruin of the lives of these young men, one of whom had a child.

23. The Security Service conducted searches and detained over twenty KOR members (Chojecki, Kuroń, Lityński, Michnik, Romaszewski, Śreniowski, and Wujec) and associates of KSS "KOR" (Dariusz Kupiecki, Marek Beylin, Wojciech Celiński, Jan Cywiński, Krystyna Iwaszkiewicz, Witold Łuczywo, Zenobia Łukasiewicz, Wojciech Ostrowski, Wacław Pikulski, Małgorzata Pawlicka, Jan Sęk, Maciej Strój, and Wojciech Frąckiewicz).

24. The members and associates of KOR received prosecutor's sanctions based on Article 276 § 1 of the Criminal Code (see chap 9 n. 3).

25. Above all, these were: Eugeniusz Smolar in London, his brother Aleksander in Paris, and, more rarely, Jakub Świecicki in Sweden.

26. Here an author's note: the limitations of the self-government of agricultural cooperatives were such that the differences between them and State Agricultural Farms were only formal.

27. With the exception of the Kowalczyk brothers, a promise was made that actions leading to amnesty would be undertaken; but, as usual with promises made by the party and the government, it was not kept.

10: *Gdańsk Agreements to Dissolution of KOR*

1. Earlier, in September, as a result of the efforts of a group of people devoted to this issue, the "Patronat" Association for Aiding the Imprisoned and their Families (which was ordered dissolved in the forties) was reactivated. Among its members were several KOR members and many associates, including a number of lawyers who had previously cooperated with the Intervention Bureau.

2. Jerzy Geresz, Krzysztof Hagemejer, Aleksander Horodyński, Krystyna Iwaszkiewicz, Joanna Jankowska, Jarosław Kaczyński, Janusz Klekowski, Jan Kelus, Ewa Korulska, Zofia Kowalczkowa, Anka Kowalska, Marek Kozłowski, Mieczysław Książczak, Jacek Kuroń, Jan Józef Lipski, Jan Lityński, Grzegorz Lise, Zenobia Łukasiewicz, Mirosław Michalik, Jacek Pilchowski, Maciej Rayzcher, Zofia Romaszewska, Jan Walc, and Bogdan Zalega.

Attorneys: Andrzej Grabinski, Witold Lis-Olszewski, Jan Olszewski, Władysław Siła-Nowicki, Stanisław Szczuka, and Jacek Taylor.

3. *KSS "KOR" Communiqué* No. 45 contains the following note under the rubric of "Repressions": "On October 29, there was a search of the apartment

of KSS 'KOR' member Zbigniew Romaszewski. The *Report on the State of the Observance of Civil and Human Rights in the PRL*, prepared by the Helsinki Commission in Poland, was confiscated."

4. Leszek Moczulski was arrested on September 23. On September 25, KSS "KOR" issued a statement protesting against this imprisonment, and on November 15, in a statement connected with the imprisonment of Wojciech Ziembiński and Zygmunt Goławski, it once again appealed for the release of Moczulski.

5. This case involved a bluff naively accepted by one of the activists of the PPS abroad, who, in spite of warnings, believed a supposed emissary and leader of an allegedly widespread social-democratic organization popular in the PRL especially among the workers, which somehow was never noticed either during the 1980 strike movement or later. In Poland, this individual was also believed by Michał Jagło, a co-founder of the Center for Peasant Thought, who reached an agreement with a group that was supposedly called the Center for Socialist Thought; this provoked a crisis and the break-up of the Center for Peasant Thought.

6. He should not be confused with the later chairman of the mining commission in Solidarity, Henryk Sienkiewicz; these activists had nothing in common apart from their name.

7. The number of factual errors in Czubiński's "Information" provides food for thought. According to this document, Kuroń and Modzelewski were convicted in 1965 of "attempting to overthrow the system in the PRL by force"; while in reality neither Kuroń nor Modzelewski was ever charged with this, but were sentenced instead for "distributing false information that could harm the vital interests of the Polish state." It also seems that the prosecutor general should know the name of Halina Mikołajska, the name of Macierewicz, and the full name of KSS "KOR" (the document claims that in September, KOR transformed itself into "a Social Solidarity Committee 'KOR'").

8. We must add that Solidarity later neglected this issue, and only in Radom did Solidarity try for many months to talk to local authorities about compensation for the workers who were victims of reprisals following the June events, and for a public acknowledgment of who was responsible for these repressions. These talks produced no results.

9. No. 7 of May 15, under *"Otwock, May 7"*—this was the formula commonly used as an introduction to information about beatings or detentions by the police that was published in *KOR Communiqués*.

10. One of those who were beaten.

11. As we have already noted, after the formation of Solidarity, the union, which was in the process of getting organized, received financial help to develop its typographic and printing capabilities in the amount of 400,000 zlotys. The Intervention Bureau, which began working under the auspices of Solidarity as early as September, also drew on the Social Self-Defense Fund because of the nature of some of the cases conducted by the Bureau. When KSS "KOR" was dissolving, it issued the following communiqué: "At the meeting held on September 23, 1981, KSS 'KOR' authorized the Social Self-Defense Funds Council, composed of Jan Kielanowski, Edward Lipiński, Jan Józef Lipski, Halina Mi-

kołajska, Piotr Naimski, Józef Rybicki, Aniela Steinsbergowa, Henryk Wujec, and Jan Zieja, to continue the activities of the Fund in accordance with the intentions of the contributors."

Postscript

1. A selection of essays and political articles by Adam Michnik is being prepared by the University of California Press, and is scheduled for publication in 1985.

2. Seweryn Blumsztajn attempted to return from Paris to Poland in February 1985, but was turned away by the Polish authorities who stamped his passport "invalid" and sent him back to Paris on the same Air France plane that brought him to Warsaw.

Index

Abortion, 20
Abramowski, Edward, 11, 203
Academic Intervention Bureau, 402
Academic ministries, 19–20, 23, 79, 400
Academy of Physical Education (AWF), 70, 268, 271
Academy of the Renewal Movement (ARO), 403
Adamkiewicz, Marek, 208, 274, 312
Adamowicz, Antoni, 91
Adamski, Stanisław, 35
Adamski, Wiesław, 215
Agricultural policies, 256–257, 261–262, 427, 476, 484
Ajzner, Jan, 167, 203, 430
Albee, Edward, 160
Alcoholism, 338, 409–410, 488
Alternatywy, 396
Amnesty, 169, 170–171, 186–188, 235, 333, 460, 462
Amnesty International, 56, 159–160, 245, 310; appeals to, 235, 251, 308, 315, 354, 370, 374, 380
Amsterdamski, Piotr, 153
Amsterdamski, Stefan, 11, 211, 271
Andrzejewski, Jerzy, 11, 17, 27, 45, 46, 52, 138, 179, 180, 467
Aneks, 61, 213
Aneks, 114
Anin, 294, 295
Anti-Semitism, 16, 17, 20; against KOR, 139–140, 155, 239, 309, 447; KOR on, 352; in ROPCiO, 121; in Security Service, 85, 350
Antoniuk, Jakub, 378
Appeal, 421, 422

Appeal for Polish Workers, 113, 114, 319, 435
"Appeal to Society and to the Authorities of PRL," 51, 52, 252, 253, 254–255, 280, 385, 467–468, 474–482, 486
Arkuszewski, Wojciech, 19, 154, 157
Arrow, Kenneth J., 160
Aspekt, 304
Association of Polish Journalists, 301, 326
Association of Polish Lawyers, 127
Association of Polish Theatre and Cinema Artists, 237
Association of the Free Polish University, 325
Attorney's Council, 236
Auschwitz, 336
Awejde, Gustaw, 8

Babicz, Ryszard, 126
Babiuch, Edward, 27, 420, 502
Baden-Powell, Robert, 14, 18
Bądkowski, Lech, 420
Bafia, Lech, 183, 224
Bahro, Rudolf, 285
Baildon, 423
Bąk, Henryk, 261
Bakhunin, Vyacheslav, 385
Bąkowski, Paweł, 311
Bal, Jan, 240
Balaun, Jacek, 268
Balcerak, Andrzej, 143–144
Balicki, Zygmunt, 357
Band of Vagabonds, 17–18, 48, 54, 58
Baniecka, Zofia, 380

DATE DUE

DEC 18 1990		
NOV 2 6 1990		
DEC 1 5 1990		
JAN 1 5 1991		
45230		Printed in USA